American Higher Edu

Higher education in the United States is a complex, diverse, and important enterprise. The latest book in the *Core Concepts in Higher Education* series brings to life issues of governance, organization, teaching and learning, student life, faculty, finances, college sports, public policy, fundraising, and innovations in higher education today. Written by renowned author John R. Thelin, each chapter bridges research, theory, and practice and discusses a range of institutions – including the often overlooked for-profits, community colleges, and minority serving institutions. A blend of stories and analysis, this exciting new book challenges present and future higher education practitioners to be informed and active participants, capable of improving their institutions.

John R. Thelin is Professor of Higher Education and Public Policy at the University of Kentucky, USA.

Core Concepts in Higher Education

Series Editors: Edward P. St. John and Marybeth Gasman

The History of U.S. Higher Education: Methods for Understanding the Past
Edited by Marybeth Gasman

Understanding Community Colleges
Edited by John S. Levin and Susan T. Kater

Public Policy and Higher Education: Reframing Strategies for Preparation, Access, and College Success
Edited by Edward P. St. John, Nathan Daun-Barnett, and Karen M. Moronski-Chapman

Organizational Theory in Higher Education
Kathleen Manning

Diversity and Inclusion: Supporting Racially and Ethnically Underrepresented Students in Higher Education
Rachelle Winkle-Wagner and Angela M. Locks

Fundraising and Institutional Advancement: Theory, Practice, and New Paradigms
Noah D. Drezner and Frances Huehls

Student Development Theory in Higher Education: A Social Psychological Approach
Terrell L. Strayhorn

Law and Social Justice in Higher Education
Crystal Renee Chambers

Qualitative Inquiry in Higher Education Organization and Policy Research
Penny Pasque and Vicente Lechuga

American Higher Education

Issues and Institutions

John R. Thelin

Routledge
Taylor & Francis Group

NEW YORK AND LONDON

First published 2017
by Routledge
711 Third Avenue, New York, NY 10017

and by Routledge
2 Park Square, Milton Park, Abingdon, Oxon, OX14 4RN

Routledge is an imprint of the Taylor & Francis Group, an informa business

Library of Congress Cataloging in Publication Data
Names: Thelin, John R., 1947– author.
Title: American higher education : an introduction to issues and institutions / by John R. Thelin.
Description: New York : Routledge, 2017. |
Series: Core concepts in higher education | Includes bibliographical references and index.
Identifiers: LCCN 2016042131| ISBN 9781138888135 (hardback) | ISBN 9781138888142 (pbk.) | ISBN 9781315713649 (master ebook) | ISBN 9781317498605 (mobipocket/kindle)
Subjects: LCSH: Education, Higher–United States.
Classification: LCC LA227.4.T53 2017 | DDC 378.00973–dc23
LC record available at https://lccn.loc.gov/2016042131

ISBN: 978-1-138-88813-5 (hbk)
ISBN: 978-1-138-88814-2 (pbk)
ISBN: 978-1-315-71364-9 (ebk)

Typeset in Minion
by Wearset Ltd, Boldon, Tyne and Wear

Printed and bound in Great Britain by
TJ International Ltd, Padstow, Cornwall

For Our Students – Past, Present, and Future

CONTENTS

Series Editor's Introduction   ix

Preface   x

Acknowledgments   xii

Chapter 1   Introduction: Higher Education Inside and Out   1

Chapter 2   Bricks and Mortar: Creating the American Campus   17

Chapter 3   Teaching and Learning   45

Chapter 4   Students and Student Life   73

Chapter 5   Faculty and the Academic Profession   95

Chapter 6   Governance and Organization: Structures and Cultures   122

Chapter 7   Fiscal Fitness: Budgets and Finances   150

Chapter 8   Intercollegiate Athletics: Higher Education's Peculiar Institution   175

Chapter 9   Public Policies: The Campus and Federal, State, and Local
             Governments   200

Chapter 10   Fund-raising and Philanthropy: The Nonprofit Sector   225

Chapter 11   Research and Development: The Enterprising Campus   250

Chapter 12   Colleges and Consumerism: Cost and Price of Higher Education   276

Chapter 13   Innovations and Internationalization in American Higher
             Education   301

Chapter 14   Conclusion: Beyond Business as Usual   327

Index   352

SERIES EDITOR'S INTRODUCTION

As co-editor for Routledge's *Core Concepts in Higher Education* series (along with Edward St. John), I am pleased to introduce John Thelin's new book *American Higher Education: Issues and Institutions*. I've been waiting for a book that speaks to higher education in a broad way, written by a scholar who understands the many facets of higher education better than anyone I know, and from a rich historical perspective.

For those who know John Thelin and have read his work, you know that he is a beautiful writer, he is funny and lively, and he is a great storyteller. You also know that he can bring research within the realm of higher education to life. He has the ability to lift stories off the page and to engage those who often do not care about context or history.

In *American Higher Education: Issues and Institutions*, Thelin confronts all of the issues we face operating in higher education from the enterprise of universities to college rankings to leadership to the changing student population to faculty roles to money and its role. Students and scholars reading Thelin's work will have an immediate and vast foundation for understanding American higher education unlike anything we have provided to date.

Perhaps what I enjoy most about Thelin's writing is that he is extremely well read, a characteristic that is rare in our field. As a result, he weaves current events, literature, history, media, and mainstream commentators throughout the chapters, providing the reader with a sense of how connected higher education is to the rest of the issues we face as a nation. Thelin understands that higher education does not operate in a vacuum.

When it comes to John Thelin, I am biased. John has been my mentor for nearly 22 years. He is the reason that I decided to become a professor and to pursue historical research. During my doctoral program and since I graduated with my Ph.D., he has been a steadfast advocate and champion for me. It is a pleasure to include him in the *Core Concepts in Higher Education* series not only because his work is the very finest we have to offer in the field of higher education, but because he is my friend and someone I admire greatly.

Marybeth Gasman
University of Pennsylvania
Series Co-Editor
Core Concepts in Higher Education *Series*

PREFACE

WHAT CAN YOU EXPECT IN THIS BOOK?

American higher education is fascinating and perplexing – both as an enterprise and as a field of study. In this book you can expect to find a blend of stories and analyses that provide insights, information, and inspiration about the *issues* and *institutions* that define and animate higher education. As part of the *Core Concepts in Higher Education* series, this book takes seriously the charge of dealing with significant matters and trying to promote informed and authentic leadership for colleges and universities. The aim of this book is to provide a TripTik of sorts on this fantastic voyage that helps identify significant issues and their essential principles. This can be invaluable because higher education is at the heart of decisions and discussions about what we are – and want to be – as a nation.

WHO IS THIS BOOK FOR?

This book is written to gain the attention and respect of several constituencies associated with higher education. First are those who are new to the field, whether as professionals and/or as graduate students. As such, this audience has substantial overlap with the membership of the Association for the Study of Higher Education (ASHE) and such professional groups as NASPA, the group for student affairs professionals in higher education. Second are faculty, staff, trustees, and those in academic leadership roles such as presidents, provosts, and deans. Top administrators, no matter how busy with daily demands, can gain from good reading about the institutions in which they work and lead. Third, this book is intended to be useful to those outside colleges and universities – such as policy analysts, state and federal government officials, congressional staff, legislators, foundation leaders, and members of the business community. Fourth, this book is meant to provide a readable introduction for those whose professional work is in higher education outside the United States. American colleges and universities are distinctive – but they also are peculiar. Our policies, programs, and practices are not always self-evident in their logic and design.

WHAT ARE THE BOOK'S SPECIAL FEATURES?

This book discusses significant issues associated with the following chapter themes and topics:

- Bricks and Mortar: Creating the American Campus
- Teaching and Learning
- Students and Student Life
- Faculty and the Academic Profession
- Governance and Organization: Structures and Cultures
- Fiscal Fitness: Budgets and Finances
- Intercollegiate Athletics: Higher Education's Peculiar Institution
- Public Policies: The Campus and Federal, State, and Local Governments
- Fund-raising and Philanthropy: The Nonprofit Sector
- Research and Development: The Enterprising Campus
- Colleges and Consumerism: Cost and Price of Higher Education
- Innovations and Internationalization in American Higher Education.

The format for this book is that each chapter will start with a section called *Setting and Overview* that introduces the chapter title and topic, followed by sections on, respectively, *Issues*; second, *Characters and Constituents*; and, third, a discussion of *Complexities and Conflicts*, with implications for decision-making. These in turn will lead to sections called *Connections and Questions*; followed by a distinct section dealing with *Diversity and Social Justice*. Then, a section designated as *Conclusion* will present a concise summary and interpretation of the various components covered throughout the entire chapter. In addition to the *Notes* providing citations of sources, each chapter will conclude with a concise, selected bibliography of *Additional Readings*.

Each chapter is self-contained. The design and scope of the book are such that one can read about one's own field of expertise to gain a grounding. And, since each chapter is fluid in prose style and concise in length, this book provides a reasonable way to learn about the significant issues and concepts in a variety of fields and topics outside one's own area of specialization.

ACKNOWLEDGMENTS

I am grateful to Professors Marybeth Gasman and Edward St. John for having invited me to write this book for their series on *Core Concepts in Higher Education*. For many years I've relied on their own scholarly articles and books – and their insights. So, it's an honor to contribute to this distinctive series for which they serve as Co-Editors.

Colleagues, conversations, correspondence, and coffee have been crucial to my work. And it's the colleagues who bring higher education to life as a topic and as our genuine calling. My thanks to Michael A. Olivas, Greg Britton, Stan Katz, Bruce Leslie, Jim Axtell, Ronald Ehrenberg, Maresi Nerad, Bennett Boggs, Amy Wells Dolan, Neal Hutchens, Margaret Clements, Katherine Chaddock, Linda Eisenmann, Gerald St. Armand, Christian Anderson, Richard K. Lieberman, Clifford Adelman, Luther Spoehr, Dorothy Finnegan, Charles Clotfelter, Eric Snyder, Tod Massa, Ralph Crystal, and many other colleagues for their insights and sound priorities. Richard W. Trollinger, my colleague and co-author on several articles and a book, has fostered my knowledge and appreciation of philanthropy in American higher education. I am indebted to three distinguished professors who reviewed the manuscript: Ann E. Austin of Michigan State University, William G. Tierney of the University of Southern California, and Catherine Epstein, Dean of Amherst College.

Journal editors who have been supportive of my work include Scott Thomas and Leonard Baird (Emeritus) of the *Journal of Higher Education*, Jonathan Imber of *Society*, and Nancy Beadie of the *History of Education Quarterly*. I think the editors and writers of *Inside Higher Ed* and the *Chronicle of Higher Education* are crucial to excellent discussion and analyses about issues facing colleges and universities. I appreciate having had a chance to listen to, write for, and work with Doug Lederman, Sarah Bray, Goldie Blumenstyk, and Scott Jaschik.

Over three decades I've had the honor of being a guest speaker and visiting scholar at the University of Georgia's Institute of Higher Education, including being invited to present their annual McBee Lecture in 2012. I am indebted to colleagues James Hearn and the late Thomas G. Dyer, Jr. for having provided a forum to meet and talk with their graduate students. My affiliation with Claremont Graduate University's Higher

Education Program's faculty and students since 1978 includes having been a visiting professor and guest speaker. For this I thank Jack Schuster, Scott Thomas, Daryl Smith, and their graduate students and alumni.

The Association for the Study of Higher Education – well known as "ASHE" – has been my primary scholarly and professional affiliation since its founding in the mid-1970s. Executive Director Kim Nehls orchestrates a superb conference and brings together a mix of scholars to which I look forward every year for presentations and papers. I'm beholden to the History of Education Society for having provided a stimulating forum of excellent writing and research on higher education's past. A happy convergence has been HASHE – an informal, lively group of historians of higher education.

Since 2006 I have been a charter member of the American Enterprise Institute's working group on higher education. Our periodic meetings in Washington, D.C. bring together disparate representatives and presentations of innovative organizations and institutes along with members from the higher education groups and associations, congressional staffers, and representatives of foundations and federal research agencies. It's exhilarating and challenging – and has added to my perspectives on innovation in the higher education enterprise.

In more than 40 years of university teaching I have been fortunate to have thoughtful, appreciative students at the University of Kentucky, Indiana University, and the College of William & Mary. In fact, the appreciation goes from me to them. I am impressed by and proud of their own contributions to higher education as leaders and scholars.

The University of Kentucky has been a good place for me to teach, write, and talk about higher education. It's also been a great place to be part of a campus community where I have an opportunity to observe the prospects and problems of the contemporary American university. I owe special thanks to Dean Mary John O'Hair of the College of Education and to my colleagues in the Educational Policy Studies department for their support. This has included providing funding for some parts of editing the book. Doctoral candidate David M. Brown, who has co-authored essay reviews with me, took time from his own Ph.D. studies in our department to assist me with researching and editing this book.

The University of California, Berkeley – my graduate school alma mater – provided me an opportunity to learn from some of the most outstanding higher education scholars ever. I owe thanks to my Ph.D. advisor Geraldine Jonçich Clifford and to several mentors now deceased – Martin Trow, Earl Cheit, Henry F. May, Harold L. Hodgkinson, Clark Kerr, Carlo Cipolla, and Lawrence Levine. My commitment to fusing past and present in studying higher education, combined with respect for principles over balance sheets, are legacies of one of my mentors, the late Howard F. Bowen of Claremont Graduate University.

Anna Sharon Thelin-Blackburn has read and listened patiently and edited sections of this book – as has been the case for my manuscripts and publications over many years. She always encourages me to read widely in many genres and to look for the truly memorable things within a pile of documents and sources. As an editor she has a keen eye to see and then correct weak transitions and a deft hand to delete extraneous prose.

The opportunity to write a book published by Routledge of the Taylor & Francis Group is memorable. I am indebted to Editor Heather Jarrow for her excellent comments and support at all stages of the project, ranging from the prospectus to book publication.

Her publication team of Editorial Assistant Rebecca Collazo, Production Editor Hannah Slater, and Copy-Editor Georgina Boyle have been outstanding in their expertise and most helpful to me as an author.

I hope this book appropriately conveys my thanks to these colleagues and mentors by serving well those who study and care about higher education.

1

INTRODUCTION

Higher Education Inside and Out

SETTING AND OVERVIEW

Higher education in the United States is a successful, prestigious enterprise that simultaneously elicits international praise along with intense critical debate at home. It is newsworthy, commanding attention on the front page and the sports page, along with being the focus of press conferences of governors and even central to State of the Union addresses by Presidents of the United States. This abundance of daily images and information calls for a primer to guide present and future leaders through the labyrinth of colleges and universities, both inside and outside the campus. The aim of this book is to provide a TripTik of sorts on this fantastic voyage that helps identify significant issues and their essential principles.

This can be invaluable because higher education is at the heart of decisions and discussions about what we are – and want to be – as a nation. "Going to college" surfaces as a topic at the dinner tables of American families. It spreads to employers, corporate executives, chambers of commerce, alumni, donors, sports fans, congressional subcommittees, state houses, and even to the White House. It is one of the foremost bonding experiences in American life, cutting across social, political, racial, and religious lines. Higher education is serious business. And, it's not just about money. Higher education time and time again gravitates back to consideration of values and principles. It means that the study of higher education as a field is timely and significant. This book is intended to make your commitment to this topic worthwhile.

Years ago the monthly magazine *Popular Mechanics* featured ads for a book titled *Mysteries of the Universe Explained*. The sensational advertising was attractive to curious adolescents (and often their parents). So, the temptation today is to pitch a book about higher education as something equally amazing, such as *Mysteries of the Universities Explained*. Unfortunately, that's a hard promise to keep. A sane, modest proposal is that this book will provide curious readers with *The Mysteries of the University Explored*. Most significant questions about higher education can hardly be answered once and for all. What we need is a spirit of informed inquiry about enduring issues associated with our colleges and universities.

1

A profile of higher education in the United States suggests its formidable size and presence. Each year more than 20 million students enroll at 4,599 degree-granting institutions. Yet this snapshot does not suffice to convey the complexities and textures of higher education. A crucial social fact is that we are a nation of *college builders*. Both in the 21st century and the 17th century – and all the centuries in between – colleges have been coveted and prestigious. Every new community wants the benefits and stature of a college or university. It's comparable to landing a professional sports team for your metropolitan area. A university, just like a major league baseball franchise, makes a community – whether a city or a state – complete. As one governor and a state university president proclaimed together at a press conference in 1947, "You can't have a great state without a great state university!"

An article in the *Washington Post* on January 23, 2015 reinforced this American attitude toward higher education by using CIS data to provide a link to an interactive map site that charted over time the founding date and locale of each new college. Readers could "watch colleges spread across the country like confetti with this map that traces U.S. History and Higher Education."[1] Starting with Harvard in 1636 and continuing over five centuries, one can see how building colleges has accompanied demographic changes of settlement and migration. When, for example, one moves the pointer along the calendar axis and stops at 1865 one sees a bucketful of confetti sprinkling over the national landscape – to signal the founding of numerous land grant institutions by state governments – testimony to the 1862 Morrill Act.

The mapping patterns are fascinating because they show graphically regional movement such as East to West – and also the in-fill *within* each region and state, from rural to urban. Even these highlights of cartography understate the college building story. In addition to the year-by-year growth in the *number* of institutions, there is the continual update on enrollment growth *within* an institution that might have been founded long ago. Consider that the American university with the highest enrollment in 1909 was Columbia University, with 6,000 students.[2] Today, Columbia reports an enrollment of 29,000. Other universities have even more dramatic tales to tell about internal expansion. In 1940 Indiana University had an enrollment of 5,000 students. By 2015 this will have increased sevenfold, to 35,000.

Another source of institutional founding that gets overlooked sometimes is the community college. For example, the *Washington Post* article and its map dealt only with four-year degree-granting colleges – a restriction that left out one of the great American innovations – over 1,700 public community colleges, most of which did not exist before 1970. Ironically, this is precisely the institutional category that received attention from the President of the United States in January 2015. Community colleges now enroll more than half of all college freshmen each year – and about one-third of all undergraduate enrollments nationwide.

A good insight to draw from this map is to think of colleges as having grown from a cottage industry and blossomed in the past century as a major enterprise in American life. This is what the late Clark Kerr had in mind in 1960 when his theme for the prestigious Godkin Lectures at Harvard was that higher education in the United States was emerging as a mature "Knowledge Industry."[3] According to Kerr, what steel and railroads had done for the American economy of the 19th century, so would colleges and universities do for the late 20th century. He spoke as president of the prestigious University of California – a multi-campus system in which Berkeley and UCLA were known as key parts of the "Knowledge Factory." Metaphors and analogies comparing the campus with business corporations were compelling to the American public, to governors, and, obviously, to business executives – all of whom applauded the prosperity of American business in the decade following World War II. But that was then. What are the images that come to mind for the American campus in the 21st century?

A fresh perspective comes from Janet Napolitano in a talk she gave on September 30, 2014 after having completed her first year as president of the University of California – the same institution where Clark Kerr had served as president and the source of inspiration for his postwar description of the "Knowledge Factory." Here are some excerpts from the new president's views as insider and outsider in what she called "My Freshman Year":

> To linger for too long on the vastness and complexity of the University of California is to risk a form of intellectual paralysis. With its 10 distinct campuses, each a major university in its own right, five medical centers, three national laboratories, and an agricultural and natural resources division with representatives in every corner of California; with its $24 billion budget, its more than 230,000 students, and its 190,000 employees – nuclear scientists, literature professors, doctors and nurses, staff members of all types (some union, some not), you name it – the University of California is one of the largest, most complicated organizations in the world.[4]

Napolitano, as a university president, learned that symbols of campus loyalty and college sports were important. She learned a lesson and admitted:

> I no longer wear red. Once was enough for the Old Blues of Berkeley, as Cal alumni are called, and for the Bruins of Los Angeles, not to mention the Banana Slugs of Santa Cruz or the Anteaters of Irvine. Message received. Blue and gold will define my sartorial palette ever more.

Since she had earlier served as Governor of Arizona and as U.S. Secretary of Homeland Security, Janet Napolitano was no stranger to bureaucracy. Nonetheless, serving as a university president provided new lessons about how campus governance works. She characterized her first-year experiences as one of being humbled at every turn, noting:

> My very first night on a campus as president of the University of California was at UC Merced – and I do mean "night." Merced is our newest campus and does not yet have a lot of classroom space, so classes start early and run late, six days a week. This biology class started after 9 p.m. There were two dozen undergraduates, most of whom I was told were first-generation college students, peering into their microscopes, hours after the sun went down. Talk about a passion for learning!

A campus transmits an ethos of learning. She continued:

> This passion is infectious. These students don't come to UC to mess around. They come to learn, and along the way, to be transformed. Thousands upon thousands of UC alumni were first-generation immigrants and the first in their families to attend college. Today, that tradition continues, as reflected in the unparalleled number of students we enroll who are low-income, hail from underrepresented

minority groups, or are first-generation college students. But all, it must be said, are academically qualified. They earn their way in.

She also noted that she had been "humbled by professors, the research they do, and their dedication to students":

> In the first few months of my time here in California, I made an effort to visit every campus and as many related UC outposts as possible. Along the way, I learned some of the key distinctions that exist on the academic side of public research universities. One is the distinction between basic research and applied research.... The blend of teaching and research is its own phenomenon. It's the magic mix that leads both to creating new knowledge and to educating students, not just instructing them. And finally, I learned that beyond research, and beyond teaching, faculty members have a seat at the table of leadership. Shared governance is one of UC's key values.

The President concluded her recollection with the observation:

> As I traveled throughout California, one thing I absorbed was just how much the mission of UC extends beyond the borders of our campuses, and out into the world. I knew that the reach of the university was long, but I did not understand that it was also deep – farm advisers in every county, counselors in hundreds of high schools, research exported around the globe.

Humbling. Complex. Inspiring. All of the above characterized initiation into the role of university president. No doubt there's some presidential pride in Napolitano's observations – and, no doubt, it is justified. Another lesson is that the modern campus can be bewildering, both to a new president and an entering freshman student – as well as to a returning adult student or a governor. The modern American university elicits emotions from A to Z – but for starters, just within the letter A, it goes from "Awesome!" to "Awful!" Critics are pervasive parts of college and university affairs. Whatever importance one places on higher education as an industry, an undeniable fact of institutional life is that in the United States, the appeal and survival of colleges and universities are based largely on their ability to inspire enduring belief and loyalty among constituents inside and outside the campus.

ISSUES

The significant issues facing higher education in the United States cut across past, present, and future. This seamless web persists because the really important questions and problems seldom are resolved once and for all. It is useful, for example, to know how and why the prototypical American campus acquired its present form – and why the bricks and mortar of campus construction provide the setting for issues associated with teaching and learning and with how such groups as students, faculty, and administration have staked out their spaces and concerns within the institution. The issues associated with the internal workings of a college or university, however, ultimately extend to the broad arenas of public policies. This means that higher education really is not isolated from popular culture or from legislation and other external relations. And, it has become a truism that both the American economy and its higher education institutions exist in a global setting. The implication for colleges and universities is that there is an undeniable creative tension in awareness of and interaction with higher education in other nations. A theme that pervades these considerations tends to involve issues of equity and access – an emphasis that signals both our American ideal of increased, optimal equity combined with the reality that we still fall short on this goal.

CHARACTERS AND CONSTITUENTS

The University of California, profiled earlier, is an important institution – but it is hardly typical. For comparison, let's move to look at three different institutions in terms of their respective geography, history, mission, and support: Liberty University in the mountains of Virginia; LaGuardia Community College in Queens, New York; and, third, the Universities at Shady Grove campus of the University of Maryland.

Appearances can be deceptive. Liberty University, founded in 1971, appears to be a traditional institution. It enrolls 13,800 undergraduates and 5,800 graduate students on its residential campus characterized by historical revival red brick and white column buildings in Lynchburg, Virginia. Its affiliation with the Southern Baptist Conservatives of Virginia shapes its heritage, mission statement, and campus ambience. What is not readily evident is that Liberty University has been innovative in starting a flourishing Internet program. It enrolls over 100,000 students per year in its online courses – a new source of tuition revenues and connection with students and alumni. The *New York Times* was sufficiently impressed by the institution's aspirations to send a reporter to visit the campus and write about the prospects for intercollegiate sports. Liberty University has the resources to go along with its passion to be a nationally powerful Baptist football program, tantamount to being the "Notre Dame of Baptists."[5]

Another profile of diversity comes from LaGuardia Community College in Queens, New York. Founded in 1968 and opened for classes in 1971, this two-year public institution is part of the City University of New York. Its campus and constituencies represent diversity and change in American higher education. Instead of the traditional bucolic green space of liberal arts colleges, it is housed in the former Ford Instrument Company building and the historic Sunshine Biscuits Building in urban Long Island City in the Borough of Queens. Its enrollment is just under 49,000 students – with about 54 percent going full time. Its students represent people from 160 different countries who speak 127 native languages. The student body is 53 percent Hispanic, 18 percent Asian, 18 percent Black, 9 percent White, and 2 percent Other. Although many students concentrate in associate degree programs in business, nursing and health sciences, education, and technology, LaGuardia Community College has gained national recognition for the value and appeal of its courses and major in philosophy.[6] Outside the classroom, LaGuardia Community College has acquired its own sense of community. A retired campus gardener took initiative to create green spaces and flower gardens in the small spaces between buildings – a project that attracts volunteers among students, staff, faculty, and alumni.

LaGuardia Community College is a "no frills" campus. It exudes a "no nonsense" aura as its student lounge area is filled around the clock with informal study groups of students helping one another, relying on laptops for data and strollers for childcare. Discussions are intense yet quietly respectful so as not to disturb fellow students at other tables. Since most students come from modest income families, an announcement that subway fares are going to be increased threatens the ability of many students to pay their college bills.

And, finally, the Universities at Shady Grove (USG), founded in 2000, introduced a new concept: a collaboration of nine public degree-granting institutions that brings some of the top programs from across the state to one convenient facility in Montgomery County near Washington, D.C. Whereas many two-year public institutions such as LaGuardia Community College enroll students for the first two years of undergraduate studies, the Universities at Shady Grove offer a markedly different option: all their students are transfer students from affiliated universities. USG provides courses and programs for the final two years of bachelor's degree studies – with students receiving their degree from the college where they started their program. Its enrollment of 4,000 students per year is divided between 2,600 undergraduates and 1,400 graduate students. The daily schedule is committed to providing a college education that is affordable and accessible. Program options are for full time, part time, day, evening, and weekend basis so as to promote flexibility and degree completion. Coordination among the state's community colleges tends to make transfer to USG manageable. Small classes combined with a "one stop" shop of student and academic services exemplify a new model of effectiveness and efficiency. One often thinks of the typical college student as a recent high school graduate, between the ages of 18 and 21. At USG the non-traditional student is the new tradition. The average age of undergraduates is 29, and for graduate students it is 33. Most are first-generation college enrollees.

The brief inside-out views of the University of California and Liberty University along with LaGuardia Community College and USG foster appreciation for the diversity of American higher education. It is complex and comprehensive, competitive, and fueled by consumerism. And, as critics note, it also can be complacent and contradictory. One may protest that there is no profile of *my* college or university. A resolution is for readers to observe and then write a profile of their own home institution. Sociologist Gareth Morgan's *Images of Organizations* presents a good exercise for translating a bulk of statistical data into meaningful units. The task is to attribute images to a college or university.[7] Drawing from the animal realm, a university that is stuck by being pulled simultaneously in different directions might qualify as the personification of Dr. Doolittle's mythical beast, the "Push Me Pull You." A college in denial about information might be likened to an ostrich, with its head buried in the sand. A university system with eight campuses could be compared to an octopus. Amidst this menagerie, a helpful way to bundle these complexities is to consider that the campus is a *chameleon*. It can change its characteristics and stripes in the blink of an eye, depending on the setting and lighting – and the audiences.[8]

One way to organize images comes from the Carnegie Classification. It originated in 1973 and now is under the stewardship of the Center for Postsecondary Research at Indiana University. It includes 2,870 four-year degree and 1,729 two-year degree institutions:

- Doctorate-granting Universities (290 institutions)
- Master's Colleges and Universities (727 institutions)
- Baccalaureate Colleges and Universities (809)
- Associates Colleges (i.e., community colleges) (1,729 institutions)
- Special Purpose Colleges
- Tribal Colleges.

Each category warrants its own calling card about its respective missions. Even though locating a particular institution within this framework provides some orientation, it still reinforces the reminder that American higher education is complicated and diverse – and no taxonomy can by itself present a categorization that is not superficial. For example, although public four-year universities enroll the largest portion of students among all institutions, they are not the largest number of institutions. That is because these campuses tend to have high enrollments.

The list of this book's chapter titles are interesting topics, yet relatively neutral. All this changes when one adds to the mix a focus on debates dealing with higher education. It is a creative tension prompted by new books and studies about the issues. And when those issues include critical analyses of colleges and inequalities, the pace quickens and the temperature rises. This was the case in 2014 with release of *Ivory Tower*, a documentary film shown in movie theaters and on campuses. Here was a 90-minute, high-budget, fast-paced collage of images and commentaries that received a special award from the Sundance Film Festival. Its promotional poster illustrates how higher education becomes dramatic "news":

> As tuition rates spiral beyond reach and student loan debt passes $1 trillion (more than credit card debt), *Ivory Tower* asks: "Is college worth the cost?" From the halls of Harvard, to public colleges in financial crisis, to Silicon Valley, filmmaker Andrew Rossi assembles an urgent portrait of a great American institution at the breaking point.

Through profiles at Arizona State, Cooper Union, and San Jose State – among several others – *Ivory Tower* reveals how colleges in the United States, long regarded as leaders in higher education, came to embrace a business model that often promotes expansion over quality learning. But along the way we also find unique programs, from Stanford to the free desert school Deep Springs to the historically black all-women's college Spelman, where the potential for life-changing college experiences endure. Ultimately, *Ivory Tower* asks, "What price will society pay if higher education cannot revolutionize college as we know it and evolve a sustainable economic model?"

Throughout the *Ivory Tower* documentary, the filmmaker focuses on Prof. Andrew Delbanco of Columbia University, both to follow him through a typical day of teaching, advising, and research – all in the midst of undergraduates who have created their own campus subcultures – and also for his insights on what college was, what it is, and what it should be.[9] At the same time that *Ivory Tower* was released, Goldie Blumenstyk, senior writer for the *Chronicle of Higher Education*, wrote a timely book with the provocative and challenging title, *American Higher Education in Crisis?*[10] Her findings are emphatic and puzzling. She deliberately leaves readers with the question, "Are these crises exaggerated? Are they solvable or perennial?"

COMPLEXITIES AND CONFLICTS: IMPLICATIONS FOR DECISION-MAKING

Higher education as a field of study and practice gains heat and light when one takes the descriptive Carnegie Classifications and links them to other factors and characteristics. Yet the Carnegie Classification does not completely fill the bill. It is a first cut and provides a skeletal structure, and is a taxonomy that is intended to be neutral and descriptive, not normative in character. In fleshing out details, it's useful to consider higher education as a *drama* played out within the structures of a campus – and across lines. It is a mix of vertical and horizontal institutions, with a large cast.

Ratings and Rankings

Since 1984 such popular magazine surveys as *U.S. News and World Report* propelled higher education into the ratings and rankings mode that characterizes restaurants, sports teams, and other pursuits in American life. This preoccupation raises complex questions of validity – namely, do surveys truly measure what they purport to measure? Are the categories *significant* and *pertinent*? Meaningful differences and accurate data – all the questions of logic one encounters in an introductory statistics class – surface here in the high-stakes ratings and consumerism competition among colleges and universities. Alexander McCormick, Professor at Indiana University and director of the Carnegie Classification project, has written with humor and insight about the uses and abuses of the Carnegie Classification – along with other attempts to compile institutional evaluations and rankings.[11]

A recurrent question and challenge is whether higher education can respond to national and public demands. The conventional wisdom is that colleges and universities are resistant to change. Is this so? What if one were to modify the depiction and say that higher education changes slowly – but in a substantive way? It is conservative but not impervious or indifferent to change and innovation. A case in point is the criticism that today in the United States there is a surplus of under-employed or unemployable Ph.D.s. Perhaps so. And this is problematic. However, the matter becomes murky when one recalls that in an earlier era, the "crisis" presented to higher education was a national problem – namely, a shortage of Ph.D.s. Between 1948 and 1968 universities rallied and tooled up to create graduate programs that were demanding and effective; Ph.D. programs offered by universities in the United States became respected worldwide. Dorothy Finnegan's research on graduate students who completed Ph.D.s at American universities c.1963–1966 indicated that, on average, each received between three and five firm offers of tenure track faculty appointments.[12] High respect was coupled with high demand and relatively low supply. This was illustrated in an anecdote of a provost at a new satellite campus of a flagship state university who expressed in frustration in May 1968, "How do the governor and Board expect me to find and hire fifty tenured professors by September?"

Problems! What was a provost to do? More pertinent, how many provosts today would relish that work order? The reminder is that crises are a constant in American higher education – but the crisis of one decade may well be reversed later. Preoccupation with immediate problems often obscures the memory that, over the long haul, American colleges and universities have responded sincerely and often effectively to demands levied upon them by external constituencies, including corporate employers, federal agencies, the military, and state legislatures. The nature of colleges and universities is to make commitments that are enduring.

Fluctuations in external demands from year to year are evident when one focuses on a datum, followed by projections – in this case, enrollments. Consider the following press release:

> Enrollment in U.S. colleges and universities declined in 2013 for the second straight year as registrations in two-year colleges tumbled. College enrollment

dropped 2.3 percent to 19.5 million, a decline of 463,000, according to a U.S. Census Bureau report released today. Enrollment in two-year colleges fell 9.6 percent to 5.27 million students, while four-year college enrollment rose 1.2 percent.... A cumulative decline of 930,000 for 2012 and 2013 follows a period of steady increase in higher education sign-ups from 2006 through 2011, when college enrollment rose by 3.2 million.[13]

What is not clear here is the issue that follows from this news. Is the presumption that enrollment growth is good, therefore it should be extended year-by-year, ad infinitum? But that would be an absurd goal. A dubious administrative response at the campus level would be for many colleges to devote more resources to competing for enrollments among a shrinking, already familiar pool of potential students. Growth may be good, but unlimited growth is not. Nor does the press release provide much resolution or reassurance on the problem of affordability. College access and enrollment are only partial gains if one finds that completing a bachelor's degree while incurring a high amount of student loan debt does little to help someone become part of the American middle class.

Another source of conflict comes from the stature of higher education in the United States as a model and magnet worldwide. Along with the prestige that American colleges and universities holds for students, professors, administrators, and government leaders internationally, there is dissent. In 2015 China's Education Minister sounded alarms about the threat of foreign ideas, especially from universities in the United States: "Young teachers and students are key targets of infiltration by enemy forces," noting that "some countries, fearful of China's rise, have stepped up infiltration in more discreet and diverse ways." Minister Yuan Guiren sees Chinese schools as the "ideological front line" in a battle against concepts like rule of law, civil society, and human rights. And, any "wrong talk" in social science and philosophy forums was to be silenced.[14]

Education Minister Yuan's concerns puzzled many scholars in China who noted that more than 274,000 Chinese students per year study abroad at colleges and universities in the United States. Furthermore, there was a strong rebuttal to the Ministry of Education's rhetoric, noting that Chinese students – and China – had gained immensely from this academic interaction. Furthermore, the central principles of China's government – communism and socialism – were ideas pioneered in the West, not in the East. This sudden, unexpected shift in policies and priorities indicates the potholes and fluctuations even in such swift currents as the globalization of higher education – and the worldwide search for talent.

In sorting through crises in higher education, probably the one certainty is that each generation of higher education leaders will claim that the problems they face in their own time are greater and more urgent than those of either the past or future. To leaven our preoccupation with our higher education problems today, consider that the 1969 volume of *Current Issues in Higher Education* was titled "Agony and Promise" – an equally suitable theme in 2016. Another way to "share the pain" across decades and generations is to recall that one of the most influential books for institutional planning 35 years ago was Lewis Mayhew's *Surviving the Eighties* – a perceptive work published at a time when analysts projected that between one-fourth and one-third of colleges and universities in the United States would close their doors due to insoluble financial problems. This perspective from the past offered little consolation in March 2015, when all of American higher education was saddened and traumatized to learn that Sweet Briar

College in Virginia was opting to close due to its sustained precarious financial condition.[15] Even though this decision later was rescinded, it still does provide a sobering reminder of the mixture of fragility and endurance that characterizes American higher education.

CONNECTIONS AND QUESTIONS

This preponderance of information, ranging from categories and on to ratings and rankings, leaves a clear, essential, yet problematic question: namely, "What do we wish our colleges to be? How and for what purposes do we wish our colleges to educate and to serve?" Probing these significant questions need not be a lonely pursuit. Over the past 40 years, higher education as a field of study and systematic inquiry has blossomed in graduate degree programs and as a topic for researchers, writers, and publishers. Today there are more than 200 master's degree programs in higher education and such related fields as student affairs, with more than 100 doctoral degree programs. Higher education flourishes as a subject attractive to specialized periodicals and publications as well as books published each year by academic and university presses, along with commercial and trade publishers. In sum, it is a lively field. In an era when many professional and commercial fields have highly polemical, superficial "trade papers," higher education has the benefit of outstanding reporting and journalism that continually prompts, prods, and probes. Foremost are the *Chronicle of Higher Education* and *Insider Higher Ed.* As befits the digital age, each provides daily online versions whose coverage ranges from headlines to reflective analyses. Furthermore, the *Chronicle of Higher Education* publishes each year a *Gazette* issue that is a useful reference source on major categories of data.

Those who wish to track data and decisions about colleges and universities also are fortunate to have numerous sources from government agencies and various higher education associations. The United States Department of Education collects and presents systematic databases on such postsecondary education issues as enrollments, degrees conferred, income and spending, retention rates, and even on how student-athletes compare and contrast with the total student bodies at the institutional and national levels of analysis. The foremost federal database goes by the acronym IPEDS – "Integrated Postsecondary Education Data Systems." IPEDS was preceded by HEGIS – "Higher Education General Information Survey."

Scholarly and professional groups, including the Association for the Study of Higher Education (ASHE), the Council for Advancement and Support of Education (CASE), and numerous other national groups provide outstanding reports and monographs. The *Journal of Higher Education* has provided scholarly analyses and critical essays for over 80 years. In Washington, D.C., established associations, including the American Council on Education (ACE) and the Association of American Universities (AAU), coexist with an exciting proliferation of new, nimble higher education think tanks and advocacy groups such as the Institute for Higher Education Policy (IHEP). Universities are host to research institutes, such as the University of Pennsylvania's Center for Minority Serving Institutions. All this signals that higher education has come of age as an important field with diverse viewpoints and excellent analyses.

CONNECTIONS WITH DIVERSITY AND SOCIAL JUSTICE

The higher education issues introduced thus far ultimately converge on significant questions about diversity and social justice in American life. What greater testimonial to the importance of going to college than this? If higher education were divorced from equity and opportunities, it would be a dull topic. But it is not. To the contrary, it is center stage. Since the massive federal legislation from 1964 to 1972 – including the Civil Rights Act, the Higher Education Act, and Title IX – the most egregious legal forms of exclusion based on such non-merit factors as race, gender, ethnicity, and religion have been made contrary to the law of the land. Passing laws and legislation, of course, is not the entire story. The sequel is that in practice and policy, implementing these laws and achieving their goals of non-discrimination have been persistent, albeit incomplete and unfinished. Furthermore, we need to reconsider whether some national policies and reports, such as *A Nation at Risk* and, more recently, *No Child Left Behind*, have been counter-productive in genuinely promoting educational access and opportunities.

As research on social justice and equity in higher education gets better and better, the findings seem to be worse and worse. In other words, the *diversity* in American higher education has accelerated in the past 30 years to overlap with *inequalities*. Colleges that are prestigious and expensive have tended to attract – and enroll – a student body that is increasingly privileged and prosperous. Conversely, colleges and universities with scant resources have become the college home of a large concentration of students who come from modest income families. These trends reinforce what social scientists call the "opportunity gap."

Making sense out of enrollment trends, the composition of a student body, and problems of paying for college are perplexing. For example, returning to President Janet Napolitano's comments about the University of California, one encounters complex data and mixed signals about whether affordability and access are increasing (or decreasing) for underserved modest income groups. Between 2008 and 2012 the university's proportion of students in the lower income categories increased noticeably. In 2012–2013, 42 percent of all undergraduates at the University of California qualified for Pell Grants. On the face of it, this is a very high number and percentage – as Pell Grant eligibility is one of the best proxies to identify a student with substantial financial need. So, in terms of expanding access, it is heartening.

What appears to be an extension of opportunity may be muted by the added information that the severe economic recession meant that many University of California students whose families had been relatively affluent had, unfortunately, suffered losses of job and income – thus driving incumbent students down the ranks. This is a different dynamic than a university succeeding in drawing more applicants and enrollees from heretofore underserved modest income populations. Most likely one has a combination of the two processes.

All the data and talk about budgets and finance of higher education and related funding models shrink in importance when one introduces questions of how as a nation we make college admissions and graduation reasonable and realistic to our entire national constituency and its characteristic diversity of a population of about 319 million individuals. That is not exclusively a higher education issue – it is central to the larger issue of what the United States is about as a nation. The Statute of Liberty is one point of entry. In addition to its real and symbolic importance is entry into each and all of our colleges and universities. Who goes? Who is excluded? Who succeeds? Who fails? And why? Far from being trite or obvious, these questions go to the heart of what higher education in the United States is about.

Just about every family with children who are seniors in high school in the United States gets anxious in the spring. Why? Because that is when colleges send out their letters of acceptance, rejection, and "wait list." No matter whether you are a banker on Wall Street or a greeter at Wal-Mart, you will be concerned about the letters your daughter or son receives from colleges. No amount of wealth or privilege completely shields you from uncertainty or rejection. Conversely, even if the odds are long, no amount of poverty or exclusion completely prohibits you from hoping for good news for your daughter or son who has applied to college. At best it is testimony to the high stakes and great opportunities of going to college. At worst, it calls for our informed examination and exhumation of what went right – and what went wrong. So, in a strange way, going to college provides a shared experience that cuts across our differences. Is this perhaps the ultimate shared American experience?

This optimism ultimately breaks down. A troubling finding is that although American higher education is strong overall, it is characterized by tracking that tends to increase differences according to one's advantages (or disadvantages) in race, income, and early educational opportunities. Political scientist Suzanne Mettler analyzed this in her 2014 book, *Degrees of Inequality*, concluding that the politics of federal programs intended to enhance access have "sabotaged the American Dream."[16] Consistent with Mettler's study, a 2015 report by the Pell Institute analyzed data over 45 years and observed that although the college-going gap between students from rich and poor families has narrowed since 1970, it is accompanied by the troubling finding that the gap in bachelor's degree completion by family income has doubled. In 2013, students from the wealthiest income quartile had about a 77 percent chance of completing their degree, whereas only 9 percent of students from the lowest quartile of family income did so.[17]

CONCLUSION

Among all the issues and topics that are central to the forthcoming chapters, there are some issues and episodes dealing with the most defining characteristics of higher education in the United States that resurface time and time again.[18] Marbled within the chapters of this book one finds that discussions involve the following:

The Paper Chase of Charters and Degrees

Charters and degrees are the formal signs that a college or university is legitimate in its right to operate and in certifying that students have completed a systematic course of study. When a government or ecclesiastic body granted formal charters to universities at Bologna, Italy, Paris, France, and Oxford, England, this meant that higher learning had the requisite protections and responsibilities that would allow it to endure without harassment or arbitrary actions. And, central to this formal status was the power to grant academic degrees – a good sign that education was significant, formalized, and serious. Numerous colleges and universities in the United States have ritualized celebrations of these seminal documents on "Charter Day." Typically, an academic procession is followed by having the president or provost read from the historic charter, with acknowledgment to the governor or other representatives of state government along with the board of trustees. From time to time, charters are transformed into volatile news items. Or, more accurately, *meddling* with charters and mission statements becomes a serious matter. Such was the case in February 2015 when the Governor of Wisconsin took it upon himself to alter the University of Wisconsin's statutory charter by deleting language about "The Wisconsin Idea" and "search for truth" in favor of language about "job creation and work force development."[19] The spirited response from university constituents quickly led the Governor's Office to retract the charter changes as a "drafting error." In fact, these were deliberate components of proposals for budget changes. The episode demonstrated that in higher education, the rhetoric and rituals of the past are still pertinent for present deliberations about institutional mission.

Academic Credit and Credibility

Another concern that surfaces in conjunction with academic charters is that of *legitimacy*. This pertains to public and professional acknowledgment that degrees granted by a particular institution are bona fide. This is a modern version inherited from the medieval guilds (including universities – along with barbers, surgeons, apothecaries, and other learned professions). How does society guard individuals and the public against academic fraud? On May 20, 2015, an editorial in the *New York Times* focused on "A Rising Tide of Bogus Degrees."[20] The concern was Axact, a software company based in Pakistan whose degrees (and degree holders) presented their academic credentials worldwide. Websites broadcast videos from the United States, with spokespersons who promised students as paying customers the opportunity to enroll in programs from "Columbiana" and "Barkley." In fact, uncertainties about academic degrees extend further than these flagrant abuses originating from a software company in Karachi.[21] At the same time Corinthian Colleges, a nationwide for-profit, degree-granting institution in the United States, declared bankruptcy. Its campuses were shut down and the federal government assumed responsibility for more than 100,000 students who had taken out federal student loans in order to enroll at Corinthian.[22]

Regional and professional accreditation agencies in the United States have foremost responsibility for monitoring institutional credibility, but this is no easy task. At heart the concerns resurrect some essential questions usually raised in college courses in statistics and in logic: namely, "How does one know whether the degree passes tests of validity and reliability? What does a particular degree measure or connote?" The questions are basic and familiar. They are deceptive because although the questions are clear they are not simplistic. They go to the heart of essential questions about the purposes and effectiveness of the education and experiences of colleges and universities. Sound answers are persistently difficult and elusive to provide, leaving the higher education establishment with unresolved issues.

Access, Affordability, and Choice

Changes to admissions requirements combined with new student financial aid programs have gradually extended access to higher education, to decrease exclusion on the basis of non-merit factors including gender, religion, race, ethnicity, and income. Affordability has been promoted by scholarships from private foundations and numerous federal programs. Resources include Pell Grants, as part of the 1972 reauthorization of the Higher Education Act. Yet, starting around 1978, with a drift and then an abrupt shift to emphasis on student loans as the heart of federal student aid, the effectiveness and goals of the original programs changed. Beyond student financial aid, the Title IX legislation in 1972 formalized equal opportunity and increased awareness of barriers to participation in educational programs. By 2015 the troubling finding was that enrollment in prestigious academic institutions – both public and private – had skewed toward a shrinking percentage of American families who are able to provide their children with educational benefits and affluence. This is analyzed in a companion book in the *Core Concepts in Higher Education* series – namely, Edward St. John, Nathan Daun-Barnett, and Karen Moronski-Chapman's influential work, *Public Policy and Higher Education: Reframing Strategies for Preparation, Access, and Success* (2012).

Intercollegiate Athletics

College sports has been a defining and controversial feature of colleges and universities in the United States since the late 19th century. This sounds superficial, until you recognize that the large presence of intercollegiate athletics is unique – and a source of curiosity to those outside American higher education. This became evident to me in hosting a group of visiting students and faculty from European universities at a football game played by student-athletes from rival college teams before a crowd of 70,000 spectators. It left our international guests thrilled by this extracurricular activity that really was center stage. It also is problematic because most colleges and universities have yet to reconcile college sports with their educational mission, let alone their budget. At some universities with big-time college sports programs, a president is most likely to be fired due to problems related to intercollegiate athletics.

Boards of Trustees and Shared Governance

American colleges and universities are distinctive worldwide in their arrangement to vest ultimate power in external boards. This usually is connected to a strong presidential office. It contrasts with conferring authority to an internal group such as faculty or students. In many nations a central ministry of education controls universities. The structure of trustees works well in some cases and solves some problems related to decision-making. At the same time, it is problematic because it places great authority in a group – the board – that is not necessarily informed about or responsible for the educational mission of the institution it is empowered to oversee. An example that attracted nationwide attention was the University of Virginia in 2012, when the Board of Visitors abruptly fired the president – but soon thereafter retracted their decision due to opposition from faculty, staff, students, alumni, and even a former president of the university.[23]

Criticism of Boards of Trustees elicits a counter-argument – namely, that problems in campus decision-making are not really due to dysfunctions of the board, but rather, attributable to another constituency. As suggested by William Bowen and Eugene Tobin's 2015 book, *Locus of Authority: The Evolution of Faculty Roles in the Governance of Higher Education*, reform ought to include rethinking the power given to faculty.[24] Such is the legacy of shared campus governance where, according to Clark Kerr, the only shared item is central heating.

To write about higher education in 2016 indicates that our colleges and universities are at the end of an era that stretches back about 30 years. Starting in 1985 American higher education had survived and was started to recover from more than a decade of double-digit inflation, budget cuts, and declining enrollments. The period 1985 to 2015 was hardly trouble-free. It was, however, an era in which many institutions were ambitious and affluent – characteristics that prompted boards of trustees to embrace a distinctive style of consumerism. It was predicated on pursuit of donors, student applicants, and construction projects to raise academic prestige and keep pace with rival institutions. Cornell University economist Ronald Ehrenberg's 2000 book, *Tuition Rising*, documented how this preoccupation made reducing expenses or tapering tuition charges unlikely.[25] A sequel in 2015 was Kevin Carey's case study of the transformation of George Washington University from an affordable urban commuter campus into a showcase of "luxury packaging and prestige pricing." The president and board emphasized fundraising and high tuition to allow spending on constructing new buildings and recruiting talent. It was "the perfect representation of what, for good and for ill, American higher education has become."[26]

Carey's observation is sobering. If by 2015 an era of academic abundance and aspiration was winding down, the challenge now is to look forward – as a participant in making thoughtful changes in higher education. Whether one looks at the past or present, our colleges and universities in the United States are a work in progress, with an interesting mix of noble aspirations and incomplete achievements, not to mention disappointments and dysfunctions.

NOTES

1. Susan Svrluga, "Grade Point: Watch Colleges Spread Across the Country Like Confetti with This Map That Traces U.S. History," *Washington Post* (January 23, 2015).
2. Edwin E. Slosson, *Great American Universities* (New York: Macmillan, 1909).
3. Clark Kerr, *The Uses of the University* (Cambridge, MA: Harvard University Press, 1963).
4. Janet Napolitano, "My Freshman Year," speech of September 30, 2014, as reprinted in *Inside Higher Ed* (November 30, 2014).
5. Bill Pennington, "In Virginia's Hills, a Football Crusade," *New York Times* (November 10, 2012) p. A1.
6. Margot Adler, "Philosophy Valued at One Community College," *National Public Radio* (January 4, 2011).
7. Gareth Morgan, *Images of Organizations* (Beverly Hills, CA: Sage Publishers, 1986).
8. John R. Thelin, "The Campus as Chameleon: Rethinking Organizational Behavior and Public Policy," in John C. Smart, Editor, *Higher Education: Handbook of Theory and Research*, vol. 2 (New York: Agathon Press, 1986).
9. Andrew Delbanco, *College: What It Was, Is, and Should Be* (Princeton, NJ: Princeton University Press, 2012).
10. Goldie Blumenstyk, *American Higher Education in Crisis?: What Everyone Needs to Know* (Oxford and New York: Oxford University Press, 2014).
11. Alexander C. McCormick, "Hidden in Plain View," *Inside Higher Ed* (May 10, 2007).
12. Dorothy E. Finnegan, "Segmentation in the Academic Labor Market: Hiring Cohorts in Comprehensive Universities," *Journal of Higher Education* (November–December 1993) vol. 64, no. 6, pp. 621–656.
13. John Lauerman, "Enrollment in U.S. Colleges Declines for a Second Year," *Bloomberg* (September 24, 2014).
14. Dan Levin, "China Tells Schools to Suppress Western Ideas, with an Exception," *New York Times* (February 10, 2015) p. A7.
15. Scott Jaschik, "Sweet Briar Will Close," *Inside Higher Ed* (March 1, 2015); Scott Carlson, "Sweet Briar's Demise Is a Cautionary Tale for Other Colleges," *Chronicle of Higher Education* (March 13, 2015) pp. A1, A6, A8.
16. Suzanne Mettler, *Degrees of Inequality: How the Politics of Higher Education Sabotaged the American Dream* (New York: Basic Books, 2014).
17. Margaret Cahalan and Laura Perna, *Indicators of Higher Education Equity in the United States: 45 Year Trend Report* (Philadelphia: University of Pennsylvania Alliance for Higher Education & Democracy and The Pell Institute for the Study of Opportunity in Higher Education, 2015). See also, Richard D. Kahlenberg, "The Widening Income Gap in Higher Education – and What to Do About It," *Chronicle of Higher Education* (February 3, 2015) in "The Conversation: Opinion and Ideas" section.

18. John R. Thelin, "Five Important Changes in Higher Education from the Past Five Hundred Years," *EvoLLLution* (March 4, 2013).
19. Ry Rivard, "The Power of the Wisconsin Idea," *Inside Higher Ed* (February 5, 2015).
20. "A Rising Tide of Bogus Degrees," *New York Times* (May 20, 2015) p. A19.
21. Declan Walsh, "Fake Diplomas, Real Cash: Pakistani Company Axact Reaps Millions," *New York Times* (May 17, 2015) p. A1.
22. Paul Fain, "Corinthian's Cloudy Future," *Inside Higher Ed* (June 20, 2014). See also, Stephanie Gleason, "Corinthian Colleges File for Chapter 11 Bankruptcy: For Profit Recently Closed Its Remaining Campuses," *Wall Street Journal* (May 4, 2015).
23. Richard Perez-Pena, "Ousted Head of University is Reinstated in Virginia," *New York Times* (June 26, 2012) p. A1.
24. William G. Bowen and Eugene M. Tobin, *Locus of Authority: The Evolution of Faculty Roles in the Governance of Higher Education* (Princeton, NJ: Princeton University Press, 2015). See also, Colleen Flaherty, "New Book Argues for More Effective, Collaborative Methods of Shared Government," *Inside Higher Ed* (January 5, 2015).
25. Ronald Ehrenberg, *Tuition Rising: Why College Costs So Much* (Cambridge, MA: Harvard University Press, 2000).
26. Kevin Carey, "The Absolut Rolex Plan: How Luxury Packaging and Prestige Pricing Can Transform a Humble Commuter School," *New York Times Education Life Magazine* (February 8, 2015) pp. 16–17.

Additional Readings

Goldie Blumenstyk, *American Higher Education in Crisis?: What Everyone Needs to Know* (Oxford and New York: Oxford University Press, 2014).

Derek Bok, *Higher Education* (Princeton, NJ: Princeton University Press, 2014).

William G. Bowen and Eugene M. Tobin, *Locus of Authority: The Evolution of Faculty Roles in the Governance of Higher Education* (Princeton, NJ: Princeton University Press, 2015).

Andrew Delbanco, *College: What It Was, Is, and Should Be* (Princeton, NJ: Princeton University Press, 2012).

Christopher Jencks and David Riesman, *The Academic Revolution* (Garden City, NY: Doubleday Anchor, 1968).

John Lombardi, *How Universities Work* (Baltimore, MD: Johns Hopkins University Press, 2013).

Suzanne Mettler, *Degrees of Inequality: How the Politics of Higher Education Sabotaged the American Dream* (New York: Basic Books, 2014).

Edward P. St. John, Nathan Daun-Barnett, and Karen M. Moronski-Chapman, *Public Policy and Higher Education: Reframing Strategies for Preparation, Access, and Success* (New York: Routledge, 2012) (Core Concepts in Higher Education Series).

Mark Schneider and K.C. Deane, Editors, *The University Next Door: What Is a Comprehensive University, Who Does It Educate, and Can It Survive?* (New York: Columbia University Teachers College Press, 2014).

2

BRICKS AND MORTAR

Creating the American Campus

SETTING AND OVERVIEW

College presidents often use commencement speeches to remind the audience that the campus is "more than bricks and mortar." That may be true, but bricks and mortar – and architectural legacy and monuments – are memorable and influential. This chapter provides a guide to understanding the physical plant and architecture of the various kinds of colleges and universities and shows how various groups are stewards and stakeholders who create – and play out – the higher education drama within the architectural setting.

Consider a picture postcard that presents a panoramic aerial view of a flagship state university campus in 1955 – about 60 years ago. It's a graphic reminder of *both* change and continuity. The landscape is familiar. The landmarks are less so because over time almost all buildings on a campus are changing exhibits. Look closely to see what has been added, what has been torn down. Can you find your own building there? Even the statue of the founding president may have been moved. Walking the campus to make sense of this real estate is no trifle, as the state university shares in the trend with Johns Hopkins, Brown, Harvard, and many other colleges and universities of being its city's largest employer and among its largest landowners.

New construction for a university is always a major topic. Think how different the flagship state campus will look if the state's General Assembly were to approve the $200 million proposals a state university has requested for the coming two years.[1] These biennial projects accumulate to create a huge coagulation of new building and spending. In 2016 many major universities had between $1 billion and $2 billion worth of construction in progress. Just in the matter of bricks and mortar, the American campus is a work in progress and under construction. A good case study analysis of construction and costs characterized by monumental and stark new designs of glass and steel is provided by Nikil Saval's profile and photographs by Ofer Wolberger of the University of Cincinnati in September 2015:

- Stadium Expansion for $86 million
- Center for Design and Art for $35 million

- Center for Molecular Studies for $46 million
- Campus Recreation Center for $111 million
- Engineering Research Center for $37 million
- Lindner Campus Center for $116 million.

These cumulative construction projects cost $431 million. According to Saval's article and photographic essay in the *New York Times Magazine*, the University of Cincinnati now has $1.1 billion in debts – "largely because of its construction boom." The spending is predicated "on the idea that new buildings can help turn provincial universities into outré, worldly 'academical villages'." The comprehensive strategy has been for a university to leverage the appeal of magnificent architecture to increase enrollment by about 30 percent, with emphasis on attracting students from out of state and also from other nations. These are relatively new constituencies that will pay a substantially higher tuition rate than the traditional base of commuters and "in-state" students. It is the culmination of a "decades-long bid to turn a quiet commuter school into one with a global reputation." Author Saval concluded that the financial gamble is coupled with the risk that the "university will turn into a luxury brand, its image unmoored from its educational mission – a campus that could be anywhere and nowhere."[2]

Contemporary emphasis on glass and steel towers brings to mind corporate hotels in the booming Peachtree business district of Atlanta from 1970, with dazzling designs by famous architects. In fact, the University of Cincinnati's predilection for expensive designs has been called "starchitecture." The American campus also can be, as Thomas Gaines has written, a "work of art."[3] It includes the essential contributions of such great pioneering landscape architects as Beatrix Farrand, whose design principles about foliage, trees, lawns, and benches transformed American colleges into more than a haphazard collection of buildings.[4] Or, as a group of architects observed, university planning and its architecture is "the search for perfection":

> The environment of a university – what we term a campus – has long been the setting for some of history's most exciting experiments in the design of the built environment. Christopher Wren at Cambridge, Thomas Jefferson at Virginia, Le Corbusier at Harvard, Louis Kahn at Yale and Norman Foster in Berlin: the caliber of practitioners that have worked for universities is astounding.[5]

Invoking such noble visions associated with famous cases set a high standard for the educational mission as well as the architecture of what we are, and what we want to be. The postcard aerial view is quaint – but it needs to be brought to life at ground level. For example, when Duke University opened its new Gothic Revival campus in 1931, professors were delighted with the magnificent building spires – but dismayed to find out that the architect had failed to provide offices for some faculty. In one department, three professors shared what had been intended to be a broom closet.[6] So, the grand visions also need to be reconciled with the round of life of all campus constituents – ranging from the president, donors, and board to the faculty, students, staff, and custodians. Otherwise a beautiful campus is just an empty stage set.

Those of us who study higher education and work with and at colleges and universities should avoid the temptation to take the campus for granted or to be indifferent to its influence. Worth keeping in mind is the recollection by a prominent novelist who observed:

For me, there are four things that all college campuses have in common: mystery, tradition, hope and a sense of limitless possibility. I felt that when I first set foot on the Radcliffe campus as a 16-year-old freshman, and I still feel that way now, more than a quarter of a century later…. Part of the mystery was the hugeness of the new place, and my instinctive understanding that I would discover things there that would change my life. I went to college to have my life changed – I think in various ways we all did.[7]

One way to understand the campus is to think of the board game, *Monopoly*. Instead of a city's fictional streets such as "Ventnor Avenue," "Park Place," "Marvin Gardens," and "Park Place," the archetypal American campus has an historic administration building, probably with a name such as "Old Main." That's no exaggeration, as it fits exactly with hundreds of colleges and universities – so much so that it was the inspiration for and title of a book.[8] Another unit on almost every campus will be a "Department of Buildings and Grounds" or "Physical Plant." Once in a while one finds an exception – such as the University of California, Berkeley, which for decades claimed the distinction of having a "Department of Grounds and Buildings."

In addition to tracking down "Old Main" or "Founders Hall," another way to bring history to life on the American campus is to seek out what each institution has come to regard as its distinctive "sacred ground." At the University of Illinois it is the Morrow Plots – the oldest continuous working research farm that has provided information on crop yield and soil composition for almost 150 years, the birthplace of "scientific agriculture." The Plots were sufficiently important that they were to be protected from side effects of new construction. In the early 1970s plans for an eight-story undergraduate library had to be changed to a subterranean design because the proposed tall building's shade would have intruded on the sunlight and growing patterns of the Plots.

The saga of "sacred ground" pervades American campuses. At the University of North Carolina in Chapel Hill, it's the old well. The University of Virginia community respects and reveres "The Lawn." At the University of California, Berkeley a space adjacent to Sather Gate was an historic sanctuary for student groups to set up informational tables. It gained fame in the 1960s as the contested ground for the legendary "Free Speech Movement." For entering freshmen at the University of Georgia, the "sacred ground" is the entry way between the city of Athens and the university. Widespread recognition of this architectural motif as a symbol of the university was expressed in a novel way as part of the 1985 university bicentennial: The Arch became the graphic motif on state of Georgia license plates. In addition to being an icon of alumni pride, the historic Arch serves a didactic purpose to socialize new students into the academic culture of the University of Georgia. During orientation week a dean told freshmen in no uncertain terms, "This is The Arch. If you are serious about your education, enter here. If you want Arches, go to McDonald's."

The dean's serious point was well made – and well intended. Ironically, to malign McDonald's "Arches" actually overlooked the prestige and influence that colleges and universities have exerted on our nation, even on corporate life. Instead of the conventional remark, "Why can't a college be run like a business?" McDonald's reversed the flow. They dared to ask, "Why can't a business look like a college?" And the answer was that company executives constructed an impressive national training center in suburban Chicago, a campus – named "Hamburger University" – that became the "sacred ground" of a "corporate campus."

Elsewhere, at UCLA when the campus opened in 1929 located on a bleak bean field, local donors and supporters decided that no self-respecting campus could be complete without a "Founders' Rock." The pragmatic solution was to import a huge boulder, which became a source of "instant history" and an enduring landmark.

These examples show how the modern American university campus connects past and present. Two symbols for the American campus over the past half-century are a construction crane and a bulldozer.[9] It's higher education's odd couple, since they are both complementary and contradictory. How they coexist – sometimes in cooperation, sometimes in conflict – is part of growth and change. A century ago the largest university enrolled 6,500 students. Today, many exceed 50,000. Most universities have stayed anchored on their historic grounds – while annexing new property. Urban universities such as Columbia and the University of Pennsylvania are landlocked. To start a new building, one has to tear an old one down to free up space.

Heroic and historic architecture has another lifeline to higher education. A famous building often is the inspiration for the institutional "branding." Official logos on letterheads, buildings, vehicles, billboards, and coffee mugs showcase the architectural heritage. The public appeal of the historic, monumental campus is magnetic. A resurgence of higher education in the South became a source of regional pride and heritage that led the editors of *Southern Living* magazine in 1983 to provide the following invitation – and guide – for campus visits:

> The South's varied college campuses speak individually of time and place and of generations who have walked the quadrangles. Fall is a fine time to read their storied facades.... When the South goes to campus in fall, to visit college students or attend special events, the camps itself is part of the draw. Whether a revered landmark, a quiet oak-lined quadrangle, or the historic disarray of fraternity row, the image evokes lives lived and years passed. We want them to remain and indeed, college campuses have been good repositories of memory. Southern campuses vary greatly in size, physical setting and period of development. They are expected to be beautiful and you will often hear people comparing one campus to another like paintings seen in a museum.[10]

Advocates of distance learning and MOOCs (massive open online courses) need to keep in mind that alumni and students seek and like association with the physical plant of the campus. And, even if a college relies on Internet courses, it still requires a major building from which to produce and broadcast web-based courses. The University of Phoenix and other for-profit institutions have heeded this message well, as their various classroom sites and centers are state of the art in design and facilities. The lure of distinctive campus architecture is sufficiently strong that even the clandestine fly-by-night Internet diploma mills in Pakistan discussed in the Introduction chapter take pains to make certain their websites include full-color photographs of impressive college buildings. And, they display a remarkable consistency in that both their campus scenes and prospectus for college degrees are equally imaginary.

Taking Stock of Campus Architecture and Institutional Heritage

The preceding vignettes suggest how higher education is a source of a rich legacy of architecture and environmental design. The campus and its various structures, whether old or new, are no less than the stage set in which the higher education drama, led by a cast of students, professors, staff, and administrators, takes place. To understand this requires us to consider the study of the American campus to be an active, thoughtful undertaking, not a passive spectator sport. To promote that approach, this section is to provide guidelines to analyze systematically a selected building on a college or university campus. Select a building on a particular campus and then analyze it according to the following criteria:

- Date of construction – and also, date(s) of renovation
- Description of size, floor plan, exterior, style
- Are there any distinctive symbols, icons, landmarks, markers, monuments, or murals? Have these been a source of loyalty and pride – or, perhaps, a source of divisiveness and conflict within the campus community?
- Functions: How has it been used? Has this changed over time? Are there informal uses that depart from official uses?
- Connection with Campus Plan: How is it integrated into total campus design?
- Legends and lore: Are there any legends or bits of campus lore associated with the building? How does it tie into the saga and history of the campus? Are there particular student memories associated with the building?
- Does the style and design of the building illustrate important characteristics in the history of American higher education?
- What sources or documents did you consult to find out about the building? Are there additional sources to which you would have liked to have had access?
- How does the institution "use" or depict history and heritage? Does it invoke one version while forgetting others? Does it, for example, reject the past and emphasize the future? Does this "useful past" embellish the historical record?
- How does your case study of a particular building and its host campus mesh with the context of secondary sources and other publications that define your usual readings about higher education?
- If you were a new member of the campus community (e.g., president, dean, faculty, staff, or student), what should you know about the campus architecture and saga that would assist you in your socialization and effective work within the campus?

In taking on this observational assignment, we understandably are attracted to the monumental famous buildings that define a particular college or university. It's also interesting to try to figure out what is the most *despised* building on campus. Are generations of alumni, for example, bonded by a shared contempt for a dining hall that served bad food? How about the bursar's office where one went to pay lab breakage fees or other penalties? Where did the "Mean Dean" hold court to mete out disciplinary penalties to students or to expel some renegade campus group? Was there a building regarded by faculty and staff and students with disdain? Was the least prestigious, most outmoded structure used as an outpost where a program or group was relocated – perhaps to punish some derelict department or office?

Sometimes, an institutional saga involves grabbing victory from the jaws of defeat. For example, bad campus architecture sometimes can kindle good spirits among campus constituencies. Evans Hall at the University of California, Berkeley, constructed in 1972, was so forbidding in its monolithic, reinforced concrete appearance that students immediately called it "Fort Evans." It has become a perverse source of cohesion on campus because no one has ever had anything good to say about it. Meanwhile, each year a campus group has sponsored a "coloring contest" to bring some life to the exterior of drab Evans Hall.

ISSUES

Mapping the Patterns and Routes of Campus Life

In addition to considering buildings, it also is useful to reconstruct patterns of usage by individuals within a campus environment. This can be done by a mapping exercise, either by field study observation or by use of an Internet app. For example, think back to your undergraduate education and reconstruct on a campus map the paths and patterns of where you went on a typical day. Contrast this with a comparable mapping of your routes and destinations as a campus employee today. Often what one finds is that an undergraduate who is a member of a residential campus community has difficulty recalling a single "typical day" map. Rather, there probably are two profiles – perhaps a "M–W–F" and a "T–TH–S" version. Rushing between classroom buildings, walking long distances to band rehearsal, doing volunteer service at the tutoring center, or reaching the gymnasium for a workout tend to produce a complex pattern of zig-zags indicating a full, busy schedule of curricular and extracurricular activities. For those familiar with – and comfortable in – their campus, the mapping exercise may seem obvious, even frivolous. Consider, however, the findings of anthropologist Michael Moffat in his 1989 study of freshmen at Rutgers University, *Coming of Age in New Jersey*: one of the most bewildering aspects of college life for freshmen, especially first-generation students, is acquiring the ability to navigate the complex, concentrated campus environment.[11]

In contrast, for some college and university employees, the paths, rounds, and routes of a typical day often are simple and clear: arrive at the parking facility, walk to one's campus office, and at 5 p.m. return to the parking facility. Yet in between the extremes of the linear employee schedule and the frenetic student routes, there are numerous variations. It would be fascinating to map a president's daily schedule to see how the demands of guest appearances at special events, fund-raising receptions, ribbon-cutting ceremonies, press conferences, board meetings, flights to alumni gatherings, and staff meetings all come together in a pattern.

Campus Construction over Time: In-Fill and Expansion

The typical "traditional" college or university has undergone simultaneously in-fill within its historic core and annexation of new properties on the perimeters of the campus. The changing configurations of buildings reflect these trends. Many colleges and universities display a pattern of development similar to changes in metropolitan communities that over the past half-century can be characterized by the shift from train stations to airports. Train stations usually are located in the hub of civic and commercial activity, whereas airports are far from downtown. University facilities must accommodate visitors, clients, or spectators and provide these external constituents with ample parking, and tend to follow the airport model. One such new addition at the outer rungs of a campus has been "the research park." In some cases this is on a land tract adjacent to campus – or, more frequently, a few miles away. Inspired by the success of North Carolina's "Research Triangle," universities have developed new sites. Perhaps the most conspicuous examples of new development outside the historic core are locations for new football stadiums and basketball arenas designed to accommodate large spectator audiences.

Changes in Intercollegiate Athletics Facilities

If one looks at the campus map from the 1950s often one finds that the major athletic facilities – a basketball arena and a football stadium – were located in the center of campus. The logic was that this was a focal point of student and alumni gathering. An event such as a "homecoming game" brought back alumni to the campus – and football brought cohesion to the campus. Hundreds of college football stadiums were built following World War I and were dedicated in honor of alumni, students, and citizens who served in the military and lost their lives during the war. And, typically, these architectural tributes bore the names of "Memorial Stadium," "Memorial Hall," or "Memorial Coliseum." These were monumental structures, generously funded by alumni and statewide donors. Typically the original seating capacity was about 40,000 to 50,000.

This general trend is demonstrated in the 1954 state university postcard mentioned at the start of the chapter, in which one sees in the center of campus a large basketball arena that seated 10,000 fans. Across the street, known as "The Avenue of Champions," was a football stadium with classical arches and motifs whose seating capacity was 35,000. The football stadium was razed in 1974, replaced by a new facility with more than twice the seating along with acres of parking spaces – but located about two miles south of the campus, far from the academic core. The basketball coliseum remains in use, but not for men's varsity basketball. In 1976 the men's varsity basketball team started playing in a civic arena located downtown – a mile north of the campus – with seating capacity of about 24,000. The ecology of campus life and public activities was substantially changed, having moved from the center to the perimeter.

One reason the campus is a stage is that how – and for whom – facilities are designed changes dramatically over time. Whereas the demand for spectator sports has increased at many universities, elsewhere it has declined. Hence, for markedly different reasons, the football stadium today often is no longer found in the center of campus. At the University of Chicago the football stadium was packed for every home game for over a quarter-century when the university team was a power in the Big Ten Conference. Its name was memorable in its fortuitous brevity in honoring a donor – it was "Marshall Field," named in honor of Marshall Field, the Chicago department store founder. Years later, the stadium was renamed Stagg Field, in honor of long-time Chicago football coach and athletics director, Amos Alonzo Stagg. But the stadium fell into neglect after the university dropped football in 1939, following a 61 to 0 loss to Harvard.

Even though weeds and plants grew in the deserted grandstands, beneath the surface the stadium was recycled to serve another purpose: during World War II its locker rooms were the secret laboratories of the Manhattan Project in which teams of physicists and chemists developed the hydrogen bomb. So, the University of Chicago's team may have lost the football game, but its scientific team helped, literally and substantively, to win the war. This led to no dedication of a shrine to that historic contribution. The stadium was razed and its space was used by one of the later university presidents as a corn plot for his genetics research. Eventually the valuable central campus real estate became the site for the Regenstein Library. All that remained was a plaque noting:

On December 2, 1941
Man Achieved Here
The First Self-Sustaining Chain Reaction
And Thereby Initiated the
Controlled Release of Nuclear Energy

Monumental Controversies over Monumental Buildings

Belief and loyalty are crucial to creating a strong college identity.[12] However, some landmark buildings that are inspiring today often faced opposition when they were first built. A good example in 1929 was the University of Pittsburgh's magnificent "Cathedral of Learning," praised as the ultimate example of "Girder Gothic." A full story of this building requires digging into the organizational culture. The autocratic chancellor, John Bowman, put the university at financial risk with his obsession to build the expensive iconic cathedral. His building project also created a long-lasting chasm between the administration and board pitted against students and faculty – tensions that festered and eventually cost Bowman his job.[13]

At about the same time a Yale undergraduate, William Harlan Hale, wrote in a campus magazine, *The Harkness Hoot*, deploring the expenditure on the Sterling Memorial Library for "a monument of lifelessness and decadence," concluding that "none can surpass it in extravagance."[14] Not all Gothic Revival projects in the 1920s and 1930s were as grim as the stories at the University of Pittsburgh and Yale's library. When Yale University housed its Sterling Memorial Gymnasium, which included two Olympic-size swimming pools, an indoor polo ground, along with basketball courts and locker rooms, students celebrated it as "The Temple of Sweat." In the same spirit, Gothic Revival design made the new Rockefeller Chapel at the University of Chicago impressive. Alas, form did not always harmonize with official functions, as students adapted buildings to their own priorities. The university president candidly told a group of distinguished visitors who entered the chapel's solemn interior, with a reference to undergraduate socializing and conduct, that "More souls have been conceived than saved within these walls."

Official Functions versus Actual Uses: The Real Life of Campus Buildings

Not only have generations of students imposed their own priorities and uses on buildings, they also have left a legacy of imaginative nicknames for these structures. At Brown University in 1964 when the John D. Rockefeller, Jr. Library opened, appreciative students affectionately called it "The Rock." Administrators thought this was flippant, and asked students to cease using the name. Students then complied, but displayed a streak of rebellion against authority by adopting a new nickname – "The John." Administrators immediately reconsidered and said it was fine with them if students called it "The Rock." And so it is called to this day, as the university celebrated the building's 50th anniversary in 2014.

At Miami University in Oxford, Ohio, the Georgian Revival complex known as Upham Hall was widely acknowledged as a beautiful and functional building for classrooms and offices. Since its construction in 1948 the building's arch has won the hearts of undergraduates as a place for proposals, engagements, wedding photographs, and vow renewals. Campus legend has it that a kiss under the arch means a couple will marry. So, on Valentine's Day each year at midnight, couples wait in line to kiss underneath the archway's lantern. Miami University has an extraordinarily high rate of alumni marriages (about 14 percent of the alumni base) and nearly 80 percent of undergraduates admit to having kissed under the arch. Miami students and alumni broke a Guinness World Record in 2009 when more than 1,000 couples renewed their wedding vows in the shadow of Upham Hall on a single day.[15]

Adversity has tended to strengthen affiliation with Alma Mater. Natural disasters and unexpected calamities such as campus fires and floods at one time or another have destroyed architecture, as well as artifacts and records of college and university life. Usually such crises lead to a surge of collective loss – and generous resolve to raise money to restore the historic structures. There also is another social dynamic operating in the aftermath of a campus fire: When the registrar's office burned down, years of transcripts were destroyed. This allowed generations of alumni to make indisputable claims to have been honor roll students. Such is the power of student memory!

However, in some cases, colleges and universities experience bouts of institutional amnesia when a board of trustees deliberately omits and then ignores the past. For example, in most university administration headquarters there will be a boardroom whose walls are adorned with the commissioned oil painting portraits of each of the college presidents. It's a motley crew of presidents – some who were beloved, others who were nondescript. For the most part, the institutional sentiment is that one who has served as president warrants a memorable portrait. It's the exceptions to this custom that are bewildering. At Pomona College in California, for example, the board has had a long tradition of commissioning portraits of its presidents since the college's founding – and displaying them chronologically in a campus gallery. The exhibit includes an interesting placard:

The Missing President

You may have noticed that there is an unexplained gap between the tenures of Presidents Baldwin and Gates. If you check a list of Pomona's presidents, you will find a gap occupied by President Franklin LaDu Ferguson (1897–1901). President Ferguson is the only one of Pomona's eight former presidents not represented by a portrait. His four-year term was noted for capital expansion, including the building of the President's House, but was marred by governance conflicts and controversy that ultimately led the Board of Trustees to request his resignation. Unlike his predecessor, Ferguson did not enjoy later recognition by the College.[16]

The details not provided by the placard were that President Ferguson evidently had used his office as a site from which to pursue numerous personal real estate investments using college funds. Not only were the real estate deals illegal, they were disastrous – resulting in a loss of money that put the college at risk. The president was soon fired and forgotten.

Questions about whom a college or university honors, whether with portraits or in naming buildings, provide clues to the standards and values of one era. These may change drastically later. At the College of William & Mary, one building constructed in the 1920s honored a favorite son of the college who was an alumnus and, later, was elected President of the United States. "Tyler Hall," named in honor of John Tyler, seemed to have been a logical and positive choice. Ultimately, however, the honor was transient. About 60 years later the College's Board of Visitors voted to change the name of the building in honor of donors – in this case a couple whose fortune was made in finance and reputation in philanthropy, Wendy and Emery Reves. Their generosity made possible refurbishing the building and providing funding for an International Center in 1996. And, a few decades later, the college's one-time favorite son, who had become an architectural orphan, gained a new lease on longevity, if not life. President Tyler's name was placed on another college building.

We look to colleges and universities as symbols of enduring values. The appeal of revivalism in architecture is one sign of this, as the American campus has been the site of Georgian, Colonial, and Gothic Revival. Although not very frequent, even Egyptian Revival found a home in the original building for the Medical College of Virginia. Yet the historicism of revival architecture contrasts with the rush to name buildings and centers. This is especially swift when a beloved alumnus is a generous donor and has gained political fame and respect. Such was the case at Wheaton College in Illinois, which honored alumnus Dennis Hastert, who had served in the U.S. Congress as Speaker of the House and who also was a generous donor to Alma Mater. The meteoric rise changed direction in 2015 when Hastert faced indictments on violation of federal banking laws along with allegations of sexual misconduct with a high school student years earlier. These revelations led the college to remove the name of a long-time alumnus, benefactor, and respected public figure who had fallen from grace. Such incidents are traumatic and troubling to all parties – and are not undertaken lightly or capriciously.[17] Comparable examples of dramatic rises and falls in the naming of campus buildings and monuments have included Joe Paterno, long-time football coach at Pennsylvania State University. It is doubtful that such decisive acts of removal resolve the problems or provide a satisfying catharsis. Rather, the shift from the "Hall of Fame" to the "Hall of Shame" endures as a scar and a drain on the institutional morale and its heritage.

Naming rights for buildings endure as a source of historic symbolism that often brings clashes of celebration with controversy. It is no less than a situation in which constituents of the institution decide and then project answers to the question, "Who is remembered with great honor?" In a later section in this chapter we consider some cases and trends involving the volatile politics of social justice and exclusion in which architecture and names play a central role.

No Longer on the Map: The Disappearance of the Faculty Club

One change over the past half-century has been the disappearance of the faculty club as a traditional campus site. It was replaced by or renamed as a "Center" for various administrative and alumni functions. Most likely its closure signals the diffusion of faculty across a large campus that makes lunchtime gatherings unlikely. For younger faculty, there would be more demand for a center that provided some combination of childcare and coffee breaks. Meanwhile, presidents, provosts, athletics directors, and vice presidents needed a watering hole and convention center at which to entertain lobbyists and host prospective donors, influential alumni, and legislators. Faculty had lost power and prestige and now were marginal to such events.

At Johns Hopkins University, there were ripples of a counter-revolution, as some senior faculty wanted

> to restore the club to a place of prominence in Johns Hopkins's intellectual life. They remember what it used to be like. During the club's golden age in the '50s and '60s, some 16 chairs – every one of them filled – would be crowded around

the big table. Departments would reserve tables in the main dining room, and come noontime, professors strolled over for lunch with their colleagues.

According to long-time members,

> Those were the days when Milton Eisenhower, president of Johns Hopkins and brother of Ike, held court at the club, bantering with colleagues over meat loaf and mashed potatoes. Junior faculty members debated the issues du jour with senior professors, and scholars mingled across departmental lines.[18]

By 2015 fewer than 70 colleges or universities nationwide belonged to the Association of College and University Clubs. The question for university officials was less "How do we save the faculty club?", and more a healthy and open-minded exploration of "What services and facilities do our faculty seek today?"

New Additions to the Campus

Whereas some buildings have disappeared from the campus of 1954, several new ones have sprouted. The campus security office often was manned by a handful of retired police whose main role was to patrol the grounds as a kindly nightwatchman. Today, in contrast, a university police department has its own building, a fleet of squad cars, bicycles for its officers to patrol the campus, and its officers are licensed to carry firearms and make arrests.

In addition to new administrative and service units, the expansion of campus structures is intertwined with changing curriculum, innovations in settings and technology for teaching, and the ascent of expensive research and development. The presence of what has been called "big science" has transformed the modern university campus. Investment in research, mainly through the pursuit of federal research grants and foundation grants, requires a comparable investment in new office space and support services for administering grants, tracking budgets, and probably creation of a separately incorporated research foundation. It also leads to the creation of centers and institutes. It is not unusual for a major research university to have more than 200 such research centers or institutes. Some may be accommodated in old houses in residential neighborhoods adjacent to the campus, but accommodating laboratories and computers often requires constructing new, state-of-the-art campus buildings.

Another new addition to the campus that now is ubiquitous is the computer center. The first one housed Univac – a large computer whose radio tubes made the entire building glow at night. When the facility was first opened in 1946, promotional materials proclaimed that the

> Computation Laboratory's calculator perform mathematical miracles. Constructed to house Harvard's Computation Laboratory, including the Automatic Sequence-Controlled Calculator. First of the large-scale digital calculators, this remarkable machine, accurate up to forty-six figures, performs statistical analyses and tabulates, integrates, and evaluates. It was built and presented to Harvard by International Business Machines Corporation.[19]

Today every college and university has a computer center, testimony to the pioneering role of Harvard's 1946 computation laboratory building. Yet the pacesetter of the post-World War II era now strikes us as unwieldy and obsolete. Microtechnology and software and hardware engineering have made the computer center both omnipresent and much smaller and more efficient. Carrying out calculations to 46 figures seems more elementary and arithmetic than being a mathematical miracle. There is another legacy from the 1946 building: a proliferation of data systems and buildings to house them on a campus, ranging from systems maintenance functions of internal budgets to high-powered original research involving "big data" and other databases. One also finds a statistics department – along with each academic college having its own statistics courses and instructors.

The Student Center: Is It a Home for Student Life and Activities?

Some of the grand student unions constructed a century ago, such as Indiana University Memorial Union, endure and thrive. But at most campuses, expansion of offices and services provided by the Vice President of Student Affairs created a need for new buildings and offices. In 2016 the professional vocabulary of student services refers to the student center as "the university's living room." It includes offices – and sometimes, separate buildings – for career planning and placement, academic counseling, student health services, a student psychological counseling center, new student activities and clubs, special interest groups, and a diversity center. Also, the proliferation of student organizations drives the demand for more meeting rooms and conference sites. Student activities, of course, include state-of-the-art recreational centers.

Is the Library the Heart of the Campus?

Libraries, often hailed as "the heart of the campus," have changed. Although the historic main library may have been continued, now one finds decentralized branch libraries and more dependence on Internet and online sources. Major additions and their expenses are invisible but invaluable. Atmospheric control for humidity and temperature are essential for preserving valuable manuscripts and documents. Wooden card catalogs have been replaced by banks of computer terminals. University archives, once associated with keeping rare documents, have had to add space and staff to tend to government and institutional requirements on keeping electronic records of university budgets and business. A large library poses a problem: given its large size, one might expect it to accommodate hundreds, perhaps thousands, of users on a given day. Yet the parking lot has only 50 spaces.

Colleges of medicine have become a conspicuous source of recent growth. Addition of a teaching hospital, and creation of new "bio" departments such as biochemistry and bioengineering, along with alliance of a college of nursing, a school of allied health, a college of pharmacy, and a college of dentistry, have created a model for a "health science campus" of its own. Sometimes this is adjacent to the historic campus. Harvard Medical School is in downtown Boston, across the river from the historic Harvard Yard. Elsewhere, such as the case with Cornell University, the "main" campus is in its historic location in Ithaca, while the Academic Medical Center is in New York City.

Campus Construction and the Quest for the Residential Campus

Among the more enduring quests of colleges and universities is that of becoming a truly "residential campus." Dormitories and, better yet, residential quadrangles represent an American version of Oxford and Cambridge. Another pragmatic benefit is that if students live on campus, they are more likely to be under the watchful eye of campus officials and deans of student life and residence life. In fact, building dormitories to accommodate all, or most, undergraduates is expensive and seldom completely fulfilled, except perhaps at liberal arts colleges that enroll fewer than 2,000 students.

Even the most historic, well-endowed institutions have to work at this. A good example was in 1965 when the new University of California at Santa Cruz opened and pledged to provide a campus that "made the university seem smaller as it grew larger." This architectural sleight of hand was to be carried out by building a honeycomb of new residential colleges with a limit of about 600 students per college. Each had some unifying, distinctive curricular or educational theme, along with apartments for designated resident professors and their families. One delay was that college construction was not completed in time for the first group of entering freshman to arrive. The solution was to proclaim in the view book to prospective students that they would be "academic pioneers" who lived in "covered wagons of the 20th century."[20] Decoding the college recruitment rhetoric, this meant in prosaic terms that students would be living in trailers.

A comparable situation on a smaller scale took place at Princeton in the mid-1990s. More admitted students accepted Princeton's admissions offers than the registrar and deans had anticipated. The result was an unexpected shortage of campus housing for freshmen. Trailer parks were the stop-gap solution – and, as an enticement, students who opted for these temporary residences were offered a discounted price. As often is the case, undergraduates create a world of their own that does not square completely with adult plans. It turned out that the trailers became the popular, fashionable place to live among students.[21]

Why is achieving a completely residential campus difficult? First, existing dormitories become obsolete after about 40 or 50 years. Second, there are good reasons for some students to live off campus. They may wish to live in fraternities and sororities. Numerous commercial developers provide amenities and lodgings that are more attractive than campus housing. Third, the kinds of educational benefits ascribed to a residential campus usually refer to institutions with small enrollments and selective academic admissions. Furthermore, at such institutions, superb residence hall facilities usually are integrated into the genuine curricular dimensions of teaching and learning – a feat far more complex than merely building new, comfortable dormitories.

CHARACTERS AND CONSTITUENTS

How does architecture connect to the various constituencies associated with academia? Who builds campus structures – and who uses them and for what purposes? Famous architects may design campus buildings and make presentations to Boards of Trustees about proposed plans, complete with renderings of how a campus is intended to look. Eventually, however, the way various characters and constituents use buildings is set and then changed by generations of members of the campus community. One good answer for understanding how buildings are brought to life is to rely on sociologist Burton Clark's study, *The Academic Life: Small Worlds, Different Worlds.*[22] Its conceptual framework combined with specific case studies provides a guide. A key is to draw from the mapping exercise of a student or campus employee outlined earlier in the chapter. The difference is that to understand the campus as a complex community one has to discern groups. Individual mapping patterns become useful when they are bundled to construct profiles of collective behavior, i.e., how do particular groups within a campus community organize their day and how do they stake out "turf" within a campus? The collective profiles and patterns are especially significant because they allow us to gain some approximations of life within a complex academic institution. These can be building blocks for the ethnography sociologist Burton Clark had in mind. One study of academic libraries showed that students loved the campus library – but reading, research, and study were far down on the list. Most important was that the library was a good place to socialize and meet friends.

Donors: Why Do They Give Large Gifts for Campus Construction? Renovation and Transformation

A customary lament by college and university presidents is that wealthy donors often seek landmark memorials as their legacy. As one president noted, "Every campus has a bell tower…" The good news is that major gifts by alumni often are more thoughtful, as they show appreciation for a campus that provided the architectural setting for a memorable undergraduate experience and stands out as a source of donor satisfaction that shapes future construction. Maintaining Johns Hopkins University's residential character and distinctive student extracurricular activities: Michael Bloomberg, former mayor of New York City who made a fortune in creating financial information systems, was an engineering major as an undergraduate at Johns Hopkins University in the early 1960s. Whatever influence his formal studies had on his later professional and business success, Bloomberg has focused much of his philanthropy to Alma Mater on architecture connected with his campus experience outside the classroom. His generosity has been intended to show his gratitude for the opportunities Johns Hopkins provided him to be a leader and participant in a range of activities, including having served as president of his senior class, his fraternity, and the campus-wide Greek fraternity council. In contrast to a boring and socially exclusive high school experience in suburban Boston, he found the Baltimore campus to be engaging and open, a great place to learn leadership and service. The student life complemented the intense academic work. When Bloomberg graduated in 1964 his first gift was a $5 donation – seemingly small, but hardly insignificant, as he established a custom of personal giving that persisted. By 2015 Bloomberg's total donations to his alma mater have surpassed $1.1 billion – much of it for the School of Public Health that now bears his name and, foremost, the renovation and restoration of the Homewood campus where he flourished in student life.[23]

COMPLEXITIES AND CONFLICTS: IMPLICATIONS FOR DECISION-MAKING

The various cases and episodes presented thus far are intended to be both interesting and illustrative. They suggest some recurrent, deep principles and complexities in decision-making that all colleges and universities will face in balancing decisions and resources among demands for construction and instruction.

Confronting the "Edifice Complex"

About a century ago, anthropologist Thorstein Veblen coined the term "conspicuous consumption" to explain the behavior of ostentatious spending whose intent was to convey a person's great wealth. The counterpart for American higher education might be called "conspicuous construction." It is a concept that overlaps with another higher education syndrome – the "Edifice Complex," which has been described as a preoccupation with large-scale architecture that connotes the legacy of a key figure, such as a president or donor.

Architecture as Appeasement

The foremost appeal of campus construction for a college or university president is that it is a visible, obvious way to show that one is "doing something substantial." It also provides the base for a strategy to pit one unit against another – building a new parking structure for the medical center one year, an addition to the football stadium the next, and then, to satisfy student affairs, new dormitories the following year. A problem is that the habit of spending for new buildings tends to trump, for example, devoting resources to faculty hiring. Such is the dilemma in state-sponsored matching fund programs. A good example is the Commonwealth of Kentucky's generous program known as "Bucks for Brains" for its research universities. Terms of the original deal for the "Research Challenge Trust Fund" was that for every dollar the state flagship university raised to recruit a nationally ranked professor, the state's fund would add a dollar. The program worked well, but after about five years, university officials pressed the state government to amend the aims and terms to include attracting donors for new campus construction. "Bucks for Brains," originally intended to attract faculty talent, was shifted to allow the funding to go toward "Bucks for Bricks."

Another reasonable concern about preoccupation with massive construction is whether it is effective in helping a university achieve its ultimate, self-professed goals. New medical center facilities usually are among the most expensive of projects. When a vice president for an academic medical center joins with the president of a university to proclaim at a ribbon-cutting ceremony for a new medical complex that it represents a "campaign for good health," a "war on the state's sickness and mortality trends," it's hard – and potentially mean-spirited – to question motives or means. Yet a taxpayer, alumnus, and donor made a fair point in writing,

> I appreciate the university president's ambition to "make death a beggar" in the state, and the state government's subsequent economic support of his plan for reducing the rates of cancer, heart disease, and stroke in the state. However, does it really require a new $265 million multidisciplinary research building on campus to figure out that our state citizens need to stop smoking, eat a healthier diet and get regular exercise? Wouldn't this money be better spent funding health and dietary education programs, improving the access to healthy food and constructing walkable communities throughout the state? I understand that those tasks aren't nearly as glamorous as a new research center, but working to prevent root causes of these maladies would seem to be the more ethical and economically beneficial solutions to these pervasive problems.[24]

This specific query connects to the larger issue of the relation of universities and their research and services – sometimes criticized as "building castles in the desert." The residual point is that a magnificent campus may – or, may not – accomplish goals and deliver services. One could have a great university that ultimately makes little impact on the problems it purports to solve – a highly ranked business school in a state whose economy flounders, a medical center in a region with low health rankings, a superb law school that, despite its towers and library, resides in a community marked by inequitable access to legal services.

An ambitious president whose board of trustees shares the goal of rising in the rankings probably can be persuaded that magnificent architecture is a good way to attract affluent students and donors.[25] Campus activities that have the charisma to attract donors can acquire a habit of spending on both construction and renovation. Consider the case of the University of Pittsburgh in 1974, where the university invested in lavish improvements of its athletic facilities. The winning football coach of the University of Pittsburgh told reporters that his championship season gave him leverage to demand locker room renovations. "Carpeting floors doesn't win ball games for you. But it sure makes things more comfortable."[26]

Setting Priorities on What to Build

The issue is not simply whether or not to build. Rather, it is how to build thoughtfully. An example of poor decision-making is the following university press release about "Ground Broken for University Golf Club":

> The weather could not have been better: clear skies dotted by broken clouds, temperatures about 68 degrees, and the air stirred by a gentle breeze. A perfect afternoon for golf. So it was appropriate that the university president, the athletics director and other university officials spent Thursday at the University Club golf facility, west of town, shovels in hand and tossing dirt to break ground for the new club. "Anyone who likes to be on a golf course can look around and see we will have something special," the president told about 40 people at the groundbreaking ceremony. The University entered a licensing agreement last year with University Clubs of America, a Columbia, South Carolina, firm that has established similar relationships with several other universities.... The president noted that the course is not limited to use by the varsity golf teams. The club also is open to university faculty, staff, alumni, and students who choose to join.

Furthermore,

> The University Club will provide a much-needed gathering spot for our faculty staff, students, alumni, and friends to enjoy fellowship and recreational opportunities. The University Club agreement established a $5,000 initiation fee plus $150 monthly dues for faculty and staff.

For some this was good news. However, one doubts that many assistant professors or lab assistants will be rushing to join, given the $5,000 initiation fee and $150 per month dues. What is puzzling to reconcile is that this is the same university that bemoans a lack of support from its state government. It also claims it is sympathetic to faculty and student requests for laboratory space, research support, as well as roof repairs for classroom buildings.

Setting Priorities on What to Tear Down

An increasing dilemma for colleges and universities is to acknowledge that many of the "new" buildings constructed in the late 1960s and early 1970s have become old – or, at least, middle aged. Their liability is increased by their era – built in a time of inexpensive fuel for heating and air conditioning, they tended to be hermetically sealed. Many were built quickly, using poured concrete, resembling a Pentagon-style building. One architectural historian observed that these buildings represented a change in campus planning – from "classical dreams to concrete realities."[27] They were functional and accommodated a burst of new departments, expanded faculty hiring, and an increased number of students. Now, many are tired – and maintenance and repair costs are high. In sum, they have become expendable, as they drain both the spirit and budgets of colleges in the 21st century.

A "best-case scenario" for renovation and revival comes from Yale University, where an alumnus, Richard Gilder of the Class of 1954, donated $20 million to restore, clean, modernize, and reimagine the historic library entrance hall, known as the nave.[28] This building, which, as noted earlier, was ridiculed for its faux historicism when constructed in 1930, has grown to be part of the academic culture of the university. The renovation changed the function of the original section from serving as a passage way to becoming established as a destination for students and faculty to gather, talk, and study. Even though the wooden library card catalogs are obsolete, they were maintained for a sense of historical continuity. Architects noted that the most difficult part of the project was installing modern air conditioning and electrical systems because the library's cathedral spire was constructed from limestone and had little allowance for hollow spaces to install new duct work and other infrastructure components.

Who and What to Honor in Naming Buildings?

At times there is a perfect match of a building's mission, architecture, and its monuments. For example, Hilgard Hall, the historic College of Agriculture Building at the University of California, Berkeley, has chiseled in marble the prominent inscription:

TO PRESERVE FOR HUMAN SOCIETY THE VALUES OF RURAL LIFE

Classical revival architecture was combined with bas-relief sculpture of heroic heads of cattle, shocks of wheat, bunches of grapes, and other symbols of agriculture. Yet even this faces changes, as the College of Agriculture changed its name to the College of Natural Resources. Furthermore, these noble populist expressions of a land grant university became increasingly difficult to reconcile with the renamed college's highly commercialized research relations with corporations such as Novartis.

Many colleges and universities take a path of least resistance and honor major donors. This is understandable. It also is neither inspiring nor thoughtful. Former presidents are another predictable but disappointing category for candidates. Having deliberations and discussions across numerous campus constituencies about priorities in the kinds of contribution and kinds of character a campus ought to honor can be both challenging and enjoyable. In contrast to the generic, vague language of mission statements, agreeing on criteria for the naming of buildings and monuments could truly help a campus community clarify its values for past, present, and future.

Deferred Maintenance

According to architectural historian Richard P. Dober, "The facilities and campus grounds of many colleges and universities are beginning to show their age." Dobler's observation is strongly reinforced by facilities managers at numerous colleges. Scott Carlson's 2008 study for the *Chronicle of Higher Education* led to the conclusion that "As campuses crumble, budgets are crunched." New construction has more magnetism and funding than maintenance. One estimate was that a state university such as the University of Maryland's flagship campus at College Park had a backlog of $620 million for building repairs.[29] This figure has increased over the last several years for two reasons: first, inflation means that deferred maintenance goes up; second, yet more buildings and facilities join the ranks of those in disrepair.

Deferred maintenance leads to what is called in the facilities industry the "run-to-failure mode" – more commonly known as "running buildings into the ground." Repairs are convenient to ignore because they often are out of sight – plumbing, heating, and cooling systems are underground or within walls; and, second, they lack glamour to attract donors. But they are ultimately inescapable. A leaking roof might be a nuisance repair of $50,000 – but failure to tend to it could lead to water damage of valuable research materials and equipment. For the physical plant director, this leads to hard choices. "Digging up a water line and clamping or temporarily patching it might cost $10,000, but replacing the line would cost $900,000." The problem with opting for the short-run solution is that a corroded section of pipe might fail five or six times in a single year.

Some university decisions about institutional priorities and mission have an unexpected but indelible impact on construction. A serious commitment to become a "research university" that seeks federal research grants is a good example. For a president, provost, and academic dean, deliberations over whether to try to create a "steeple of excellence" in one of the physical sciences have relatively little concern with such expenses as faculty salaries. They may be expensive, but they are predictable – and they are a small part of the investment when analyzed as part of a long-term academic enterprise. Rather, the way the consideration is framed is whether a particular professor has the potential to bring in research grants that will pay for the costs of laboratory space and equipment. The prospect of indirect cost revenues and grant dollars can be intoxicating. Often overlooked is that federal research agencies seldom provide funding for laboratories and other research facilities. Research grant dollars usually cannot be used for capital improvements. Whatever gains or benefits a university acquires from staking out a serious research enterprise, it will entail a new set of large expenses for research buildings. Typically these facilities have a relatively short life, as obsolescence of laboratory design, air conditioning systems, and heavy equipment will require yet more investment in construction. Academic construction costs will most likely be borne by the state government. At one state university medical center, the state government approved a 120-bed expansion at the university hospital, noting that it was just the latest step in a $1 billion construction project. The Executive Vice President for Health Affairs commented that for the university health care unit, "Construction is likely to be a constant … for the foreseeable future."

One dimension of the over-investment crisis that burdens university budgets is that new construction usually trumps restoration or maintenance of existing buildings. One solution for presidents and the development office is to require donors for capital projects to earmark a certain percentage of their gift for long-term maintenance and repairs. This is unspectacular but necessary – and acts as a hedge against a monumental building leeching resources from other parts of the campus for years to come.[30]

Elevators and Parking Lots

It's fortunate that the expansion of higher education enrollments since about 1910 has been accompanied by some technological changes, including elevators in classroom and administrative buildings. How else could you reach your class on the 34th floor of the academic tower? And, since we are a nation dependent on cars, think of how different our campuses would be – both for better and for worse – if there were no parking lots for them? However, in a classic trade-off of economics as the art and science of choices, many colleges and universities often have to face the fact that new construction for the performing arts center, the animal husbandry clinic, or the living and learning residence hall means that students and staff will lose parking spaces. One consequence of the growth in the number of students and staff – and their parked cars – is that the typical campus today is very inhospitable to visitors who seek a place to park and who may not be familiar with the campus terrain.

Meanwhile, in a predictable spirit of student consumerism, undergraduates, joined by their parents, will picket and protest to find out why each and all of them cannot have a reserved parking space – both at their dormitory and at their classroom building. Only in America – and in American higher education – can one bring together such generous goals and conflicting interests in the competition for space and resources. Clark Kerr noted in 1960 in *The Uses of the University* that parking was one of three intractable problems facing a university president. When UCLA opened in 1929 the campus was known as "the university on wheels." It had a shortage of parking for students on its very first day of classes. This problem has persisted into the 21st century.

UCLA may have been distinctive in 1929, but overcrowding is universal. At some campuses, paying for a parking pass is compared to having obtained a "hunting license." One has the right to search and seek, but no guarantee of landing the coveted parking spot. An interesting exercise is to read the website for a university's parking service. It is not unusual to have about 50 different parking pass designations. One trend over the past 30 years has been to do away with "faculty" as a preferred parking status. It usually is replaced by a more generic "employee" pass. As one "walks the campus," it is useful to observe who qualifies for reserved spaces and how, especially in central campus parking lots.

How should a modern university resolve the parking dilemma? I have no complete solution. One university – the University of California, Berkeley – has used this chronic problem as an asset: as a way to shows its rewards and priorities, it has reserved parking for each Nobel Prize-winning professor. The coveted parking spaces proclaim:

UC Berkeley
Reserved for
NOBEL LAUREATE
Nobel Laureate Reserved Space
Parking Permit Required at All Times

New Considerations and Challenges for Spectator Sports

Intercollegiate athletics are often praised as the "front porch" of the university. And usually this has been a signal for investment in growth. For about three decades following World War II, growing popular interest in attending big-time college football games led many universities to expand seating up to about 70,000 to 80,000. Around 1990 yet another round of stadium expansion took place in what resembled an arms race to claim bragging rights for having the largest stadium in the conference or, perhaps, in the nation. Hence, such football stadiums as "The Big House" at the University of Michigan and the stadium at the University of Tennessee in Knoxville had capacities, respectively, of 109,900 and 106,000. Tennessee's Neyland Stadium peaked with seating for 104,071 in 2004, but its capacity was deliberately reduced to 102,455 in 2010. Looking beyond the crowds for the University of Tennessee home stadium, nationwide the single game high attendance was 109,061 in 2004 at the University of Michigan. On balance, attendance in the high-powered conferences had risen persistently in the early 21st century, but it was not certain that the rate of increase would continue indefinitely due to a combination of structural and technological limits on seating capacity combined with changing demands of spectators.

A decade later priorities even at the super power conferences have changed. Today the renovation of stadiums and arenas faces a new set of considerations. For decades the conventional practice was to add more seats so as to increase attendance and ticket revenues. Some universities are taking a different approach. Princeton renovated its historic Palmer Stadium, reducing the number of seats from 50,000 to 35,000. The rationale was that Princeton students no longer attended games because they were busy playing other sports or participating in other campus activities. The Princeton team now had to compete with numerous National Football League teams and nearby college teams for public spectators. Even in the Southeastern Conference, where football is powerful and pervasive, student attendance has dropped. In college basketball, new arenas tend toward having fewer seats – with emphasis on larger, more spacious luxury boxes. A new fact of life is that television revenues have replaced ticket sales as the major source of athletic department revenues, especially for about 75 universities with big-time programs that are members of powerful conferences. Stadium design in the 21st century is starting to reflect this new intercollegiate sports model. Major expenditures will tend to focus on refinements, such as providing state-of-the-art scoreboards, super-sized television screens, and enhancing Wi-Fi and other technological connections. As noted earlier, building new stadiums far from campus is necessary to provide adjacent land for parking, as tail-gating and other social activities lasting for several days by alumni and other fans have made the game in the stadium only one of many featured activities.

An irony of financing intercollegiate athletic stadiums and arenas is that these facilities gain great benefits when college sports are legally classified as educational activities. It means a stadium for large crowds can, perhaps, be designated as an educational facility – not unlike a classroom building or laboratory or library. Donors receive charitable deductions on their individual income tax returns and universities can claim property tax deductions. Yet the facilities really have little justification as sites of *educational* activities. The games are under the auspices of the athletics department, which usually is an auxiliary enterprise or even a private corporation, with no accountability or connection to the provost or to academic deans. Furthermore, stadiums are notoriously cost-inefficient. They may be used for a small number of events: for example, home football games. But usually they are not accessible for use by student groups or other campus organizations. Sometimes there are scattered external events – such as hosting the state high school band tournament. But fear of damage to turf and other concerns tend to restrict usage and access. Given that most college football programs even at the NCAA Division I level are not financially solvent or self-supporting, institutional investment in spectator sports facilities warrants careful review and reconsideration.

A good illustration of this last point comes from Temple University in Philadelphia. For many years its NCAA Division I football program had not been very successful in winning games or in attracting large crowds. By 2015, however, the fortunes and character of the football team had changed substantially. A victory over in-state rival Pennsylvania State University – a perennial championship squad – suggested that the Temple Owls had truly moved up several notches in reputation and reality. In the same season, contending for the conference championship and then receiving a bid to a post-season football bowl game reinforced a new winning character. It also meant that Temple's athletics director, president, and board of trustees inherited a new, high-stakes question: should Temple invest in building its own new football stadium – or should it continue to "rent" from the local NFL team, the Philadelphia Eagles, for Saturday use of the Eagles' stadium? Nearby, the University of Pennsylvania had its own historic large stadium, Franklin Field. The Philadelphia Eagles most likely would raise Temple's Saturday rental rates substantially, given the program's success and added ticket sale appeal. Was a championship NCAA Division I football program going to endure? If so, did this projection warrant the university to consider seriously investing in their own new, large state-of-the-art football field?

Moving a Campus

Even though most colleges and universities project a character of "being built to last," there are instances where the trustees of an institution decide to move from the historic campus and relocate to a new one. Today Pepperdine University elicits awe and envy with its modernistic campus located on the cliffs above Malibu Beach outside Los Angeles. Often overlooked, however, is that until moving to this new site in 1972, Pepperdine was located on what was called the "Vermont Avenue campus" in South Central Los Angeles – primarily a commuter school preparing undergraduates for entry-level professions and jobs, under the auspices of the Church of Christ.

New Campus without Historic Buildings

Many colleges and universities today that are stately, established, and even historic were once brand new and unadorned. What has been a serious problem at every new campus is how to create a sense of heritage – of "instant history." At the new UCLA campus, opened in 1929, acres of bean fields and vacant tracts did not evoke collegiate nostalgia. Something was missing from the academic landscape. A 1932 guidebook for the city of Los Angeles advised tourists:

> The buildings, erected in 1929, stand on grounds thickly bordered with ice plant, but lack the ivy and shade trees of older institutions of learning; the groupings of these buildings has the efficiency and orderliness possible only when a full-grown institution is transplanted to a new site.[31]

Efficiency and orderliness – admirable characteristics for a factory, a government agency, or a hospital – failed to provide the monuments and nostalgia that endeared a campus to its alumni and surrounding community. Along with construction of new buildings inspired by the Italian Renaissance and medieval Bologna University, UCLA eventually projected its own distinctive connection of past and present.

Virginia Commonwealth University, known as VCU, was created in the late 1960s through some interesting combinations. It brought together disparate free-standing professional schools that had been known loosely as Richmond Professional Institutes and then was joined with the Medical College of Virginia. It was a modern university in a medieval configuration. For all the celebration of gothic towers on the American campus, cathedrals were not universities. The authentic medieval university was diffused throughout its host city, without a campus or greenspace. In this sense, then, Virginia Commonwealth University resurrected the medieval university design. It did so unapologetically, as its "view book" for prospective undergraduates stated, "If you're looking for tradition, bring your own ivy...." The elaboration was that

> VCU is Virginia's contemporary university in an urban setting. As such, our version of a rolling green campus is often a cobblestone street with a traffic light and our university lake is a puddle from last night's rain. Therefore, we only have room for a few sprigs of ivy. Unlike ivy, we can't be contained. Like Carrie Nation, we're a break with tradition. We're different and we're proud of it.

Since 1970 the founding of hundreds of community colleges and new comprehensive colleges, combined with the growth of "non-traditional students" – commuters, lifelong learners, adults who return to college – have changed the higher education landscape. These institutions and their students become a substantial part of higher education enrollments, and colleges have started to embrace rather than ignore them. Tisa Ann Mason's study, *The Commuters' Alma Mater*, looked at the profiles of the college student experience at commuter institutions and found that planning for a student center and student services now called for a substantial reorientation. Instead of billiards rooms and big-screen television sets, varsity sports, and fraternity and sorority houses, non-traditional students, including commuter students, wanted safe, well-lit parking lots, library hours extended into the evening, and readily available day-care centers for their children. Having student service offices open in late afternoon and evening, as well as readily accessible computer terminals, are unspectacular yet undeniably important requests that ought to shape campus planning discussions.[32]

CONNECTIONS AND QUESTIONS
Funding and Financing

A traditional means for funding campus construction is reliance on private donations. All colleges and universities pursue this – but, with varied prospects. Well-endowed, prestigious institutions with successful alumni, obviously, are best positioned to raise substantial money for renovation and new construction. State or public universities usually are allowed to rely on loans in the form of state-issued bonds. In some cases, a private or independent college may qualify for eligibility – but in most cases this is the dominant purview of public colleges and universities. Even though one may know how much money a university has received for construction in terms of private gifts and bond authorizations, this does not tell how much a college or university is spending in a given year on construction.

Even a summary profile that announces an institution has $1 billion construction projects in progress is incomplete because it represents an overlay of several projects, each with its own starting and finishing date – and, again, is silent on the matter of how much a college is spending on construction in its annual operating budget. One place to get information on the yearly expenditure is in the budget – or, better yet, the end of fiscal year "operating statement." Typically this is entered under the category for "debt servicing."

Also helpful is to look for ways in which internal constituencies, such as students, may be taxed as a source of construction revenue. This can be under mandatory student fees or, perhaps, some other particular categorical definition. It is a way in which a present generation of students pays forward for facilities that may be used by future generations of students. Of course, the reverse is true – a current group of students most likely are using student activities facilities or a gymnasium that were paid by student fees from a preceding student generation.

State colleges and universities in the 21st century also have ventured into private financing arrangements, especially for dormitories.[33] State university presidents and boards endorse the strategy, especially in an era where state monies through appropriations or bonding authorizations are deemed inadequate to meet the construction needs and demands of a campus. They do so by contracts with a Real Estate Investment Trust (also known as a "REIT") – companies such as Education Realty Trust, Inc., Provident Resources Group, Inc., American Campus Communities, Inc., and Campus Crest Communities, Inc. One proposal is for the REIT to spend as much as $500 million on construction, renovations, management, and also demolition of campus housing. The REIT would receive student housing payments.

But the lingering issue ultimately is control and care of the campus. It is a matter of stewardship as well as ownership. Furthermore, there may be state-by-state differences – or, case-by-case considerations – on whether the private firm building on the state university grounds is eligible for state and local tax exemption. Often overlooked in public–private construction contracts is the question of who owns the land? At a state university, it is not always clear whether it is the state government, the state university, or a private corporation. Furthermore, there is no certainty that any "savings" by the university will be passed on to reduced prices or "savings" to students as residents.

Prior to the recent interest in having private developers pay for and build state university dormitories, public–private arrangements have been complicated. Many state universities have affiliations with private corporations, in the form of a "university foundation," a "university research foundation," an alumni association, a university medical foundation, or an incorporated "university athletics association." Each has its own board of trustees, and although each has some affiliation with the university, they are legally distinct from the university and its board of trustees.

Private foundations with some university affiliation also have their own endowments. The upshot is that it is not clear who has ultimate control and ultimate possession or financial responsibility for the property and for the buildings. The creation of private dorms at a public college represents an additional move by colleges and universities into privatization by means of "outsourcing." Its costs–benefits in terms of educational experience and institutional mission, whether in dining halls, garbage collection, student housing, or other campus services, remain uncertain and even problematic.[34] Nor do such contractual arrangements speak to the really important educational issue about how faculty, courses, and instruction are integrated into the new campus housing – the dimensions that are most crucial to harnessing campus housing to the educational experience and outcomes.

Even though a handful of large-scale, conspicuous cases have attracted attention, equally impressive is how few state universities have ventured into the private dormitory financing scheme. One liability of it is that the university's contract with the private financier may hold for as much as a century. Given that most campus dormitories become obsolete or dilapidated in less than 50 years, this leaves the state university in a precarious, long-term obligation. This latter question becomes a substantive issue when one reads that state university officials tell reporters that they "want the university to get out of campus housing." Unfortunately, they cannot do so even with the private REIT arrangements. If they really wished to do so, they would not offer housing on campus at all and leave student housing and choices to off-campus private developers. What the private dormitory financing deals really do is free the state university to spend yet more on construction by forgoing state bonds on the dormitories.

CONNECTIONS WITH DIVERSITY AND SOCIAL JUSTICE

Perhaps the most conspicuous and volatile connection of campus architecture to diversity and social justice is that of institutional heritage and names of buildings. What had been a long-simmering question turned volatile on June 17, 2015, as news spread about the Charleston, South Carolina church shootings.[35] Questions about symbols such as the Confederate flag were followed by reconsideration of statues of such historic figures as Jefferson Davis, President of the Confederate States of America. In the case of Transylvania University, quite by chance its demolition of two decaying dormitories built in 1964 – named for Jefferson Davis (an alumnus) and Henry Clay (a supporter and some-time law professor) on June 10, 2015 – allowed the university to be spared some hard choices.[36] But the reprieve was temporary, especially since Henry Clay endures as a state and regional icon even though alumnus Jefferson Davis has fallen out of public favor. One question that calls for consideration is whether colleges and universities have established monuments and memorials that honor leaders and pioneers who ended racial exclusion and discrimination.

Preoccupation with the monuments and memorials, however, may deflect attention away from other issues that link the campus to issues of social injustice and lack of civility – whether for race or gender. Foremost is acknowledging that even if monuments and icons are purged, it means little if the culture of a campus has not changed.[37] Analysis of a campus includes usage patterns of access and exclusion. Far north of the campuses with statutes of Confederate leaders, there is a less conspicuous yet equally deep legacy: segregation within the campus. Whether de facto or de jure, where and how do students of color and other under-represented groups find a place for extracurricular and curricular activities on a campus? If, indeed, "history matters," it's important to keep in mind that Jesse Owens, who was a national hero for winning four gold medals at the 1936 Olympic Games in Berlin, also had been a student at Ohio State University. Whatever national fame he had gained for his athletic achievements, he and all other African American students were prohibited from eating in the dining halls or living in the dormitories on campus.

The widespread media coverage of debates over Confederate monuments on campuses in the South during the summer of 2015 tended to gloss over some equally important considerations. First, such monuments and memorials were hardly an exclusive part of higher education in the South. Yale University, for example, renewed its campus deliberations on the legacy of having one of its residential colleges being named after alumnus John C. Calhoun.[38] Second, long before the controversies and news articles of 2015, some institutions had thoughtfully reconsidered campus heritage and ties with slavery and segregation. A foremost example of this was Brown University. In 2003, Brown University's newly inaugurated President Ruth Simmons appointed a Steering Committee on Slavery and Justice. The committee, which included faculty members, undergraduate and graduate students, and administrators, was charged to investigate and to prepare a report about the university's historical relationship to slavery and the transatlantic slave trade. It was also asked to organize public programs that might help the campus and the nation reflect on the meaning of this history in the present, on the complex historical, political, legal, and moral questions posed by any present-day confrontation with past injustice. The committee presented its final report to President Simmons in October 2006. On February 24, 2007, the Brown Corporation endorsed a set of initiatives in response to the committee's report.[39]

An interesting tribute to opportunities lost and the price of omission can be found at the University of Maryland's Baltimore campus. The Frances Carey School of Law includes the Thurgood Marshall Law Library. It is not named for an alumnus or a donor. Rather, it honors a remarkable son of Baltimore whose professional achievements as a lawyer and, later, as a Supreme Court Justice led by example in advancing civil rights. As the university's public relations information notes, Thurgood Marshall was never denied admission to the Carey School of Law. After all, as a young student he never applied because he knew that the campus was racially exclusive and he would not be eligible for admission. So, the University of Maryland honors a distinguished jurist who was an alumnus of Howard University's School of Law. Such are the ironies and nuances of historical memory in campus bricks and mortar.

If the thoughtful naming of campus buildings is perhaps one way to redress earlier legacies of exclusion and discrimination, it also can be abused as a convenient way to reduce consciousness of past policies. Consider Morgan Hall at the University of California, Berkeley, constructed in 1952 as the offices and laboratories for the Department of Home Economics, whose long-time chair was the distinguished chemist Agnes Fay Morgan. Over four decades she had personified the plight of the talented female scientist whose national research recognition did not receive comparable resources or rewards at her home campus. Morgan retired as department chair in 1954. A year later, without consultation, the university dissolved the department at Berkeley and then transferred it to the Davis campus. When the building was renamed "Morgan Hall" in 1964, it was a bittersweet, hollow honor for Professor Morgan.[40] A residual consideration is that the pyrrhic victory of a monument to a valued member of the academic community after her death or retirement might have included fair treatment and funding during her scholarly years of active teaching and research.

CONCLUSION

One of the hearty perennials of American higher education has been the ritualized, obligatory photographs of groundbreaking ceremonies for new campus buildings. Along with football and basketball games, such events bring together college and university trustees, donors, presidents, and alumni – and even, perhaps, students and faculty – in the happy labor marked by shovels and construction worker hard hats. No one seems to notice or mind that the dignitaries shoveling the dirt probably have not done manual labor in decades – if ever. The symbolic association brings together dollars and dreams with bricks and mortar and educational visions. One is hard pressed to find a greater concentration of energy and aspiration than the building and repeated renewal of the American campus. It sets the stage for the remarkable prospects and problems that define the round of academic life.

One good turn deserves another. Nowadays the groundbreaking ceremony is just the first in a series of campus construction media events. Taking a cue from Scandinavian builders centuries ago, university public relations officials and deans invite the press to a "topping off ceremony," in which a small tree is placed atop the last beam installed at the height of the project. But since this usually takes place before completion of the interior refinements, it leaves room for a future event: the official dedication ceremony.

Campus celebrations of construction usually elicit self-congratulations. University officials, for example, are quick to explain that the magnificent new buildings have helped attract a record-setting cohort of new students that is unprecedented in both quantity and quality, setting new records for enrollment totals and academic honors at entrance. The buildings are hailed for their impact on student retention and graduation rates – although this is a puzzling claim since the buildings are new and the attracted students have not been on campus long enough to know one way or the other whether their academic performance and graduation rates will signal an improvement over earlier generations of students. University presidents also point out that demolition of an old student union building was a sorely needed move because "consumer savvy" high school graduates expect and demand the grandeur of a brand new $177 million steel and glass student center. The confidence and certainty of these claims are hard to resist at the campus ceremonies that herald the new academic year and the new architecture. In fact, however, we do not really, or at least completely, know how campus construction and academic architecture alter the college experience, especially as a factor in undergraduates' academic work and degree completion. Beyond the press releases and website video clips, however, the bold announcements represent wishful thinking and expensive investment rather than conclusive findings. Perhaps those who lead, plan, and fund American higher education have rediscovered the inspiration of Kevin Costner's 1989 Hollywood movie about creating a baseball stadium, as the "field of dreams" is realized as the "campus of dreams." Both share the belief, whether for students or spectators, "If you build it, they will come!"[41] And this is the enthusiastic optimism and energy that make the American campus both endearing and enduring.

In this chapter a great deal of the discussion of campus architecture has been associated with the importance of heritage and historical themes. An emphasis on the real and symbolic importance of monuments and memorials, however, should not be mistaken for casting the American campus as a mausoleum or museum. Looking at an existing building or a proposed new one, it's important to consider its importance – is it functional? Is it monumental? Is it beloved by users and participants? In other words, either its construction or maintenance ought not to be by default "business as usual." It should fulfill some explicit, justifiable purpose.

NOTES

1. Linda Blackford, "UK Seeking More than $200 Million from Lawmakers for Building Projects," *Lexington Herald-Leader* (January 8, 2014) p. A1.
2. Nikil Saval, with photographs by Ofer Wolberger, "If You Build It…," *New York Times Magazine* (September 13, 2015) pp. 48–55.

3. Thomas A. Gaines, *The Campus as a Work of Art* (New York: Praeger, 1991).
4. Diana Balmori, "Campus Works and Public Landscapes," in Diana Balmori, Diane K. McGuire, and Eleanor M. Peck, Editors, *Beatrix Farrand's American Landscapes: Her Gardens and Campuses* (Sagaponack, NY: Sagapress, Inc., 1985) pp. 127–196.
5. Jonathan Coulson, Paul Roberts, and Isabelle Taylor, *University Planning and Architecture: The Search for Perfection* (New York: Routledge, 2011).
6. Robert F. Durden, *The Launching of Duke University, 1924–1949* (Durham, NC and London: Duke University Press, 1993). See also, book review by John R. Thelin in *The Journal of Southern History* (February 1995) pp. 176–178.
7. Rona Jaffe, "College Towns, U.S.A.: The Dream Revisited," *Travel and Leisure* (1981) vol. 11, pp. 34–50.
8. Samuel Schuman, *Old Main: Small Colleges in Twenty-First Century America* (Baltimore, MD: Johns Hopkins University Press, 2005).
9. S. Williams, "The Architecture of the Academy," *Change: The Magazine of Higher Education* (March–April 1985) pp. 14–30, 50–55.
10. Philip Morris, "Walk Through History on Campus," *Southern Living* (September 1981) pp. 82–87.
11. Michael Moffat, *Coming of Age in New Jersey College and American Culture* (New Brunswick, NJ: Rutgers University Press, 1989).
12. Burton R. Clark, "Belief and Loyalty in College Affiliation," *Journal of Higher Education* (June 1971) vol. 42, no. 6, pp. 499–515.
13. Christian K. Anderson, "Building an Icon: The Rise and Fall of John G. Bowman, Chancellor of the University of Pittsburgh, 1921–1945," in Roger L. Geiger, Editor, *Iconic Leaders in Higher Education: Perspectives on the History of Higher Education* (New Brunswick, NJ: Transaction Publishers, 2011) vol. 28, pp. 137–160.
14. David Dunlap, "Yale University Library Revives Entrance Hall," *New York Times* (December 27, 2014) p. A15.
15. Andrea Edin, "Upham Hall, Miami University," unpublished manuscript (September 30, 2014). Quoted with permission of the author.
16. "The Missing President: Pomona's Presidential Portrait Gallery," *Pomona College Magazine* (Fall 2004) vol. 41, no. 1.
17. Sarah Pulliam Bailey, "After Indictment, Wheaton College Removes Dennis Hastert from Center Named after Him," *Washington Post* (May 31, 2015) "Acts of Faith" section.
18. Alison Schneider, "Empty Tables at the Faculty Club Worry Some Academics," *Chronicle of Higher Education* (June 13, 1997) p. A12.
19. President and Fellows of Harvard College, *Education, Bricks and Mortar: Harvard Buildings and Their Contribution to the Advancement of Learning* (Cambridge, MA: Harvard University, 1949) p. 59.
20. John R. Thelin, "California and the Colleges," *California Historical Quarterly* (Summer 1977) vol. 56, no. 2, pp. 140–163; see esp. pp. 159–162.
21. Annette John-Hall, "Students Are Housed in Trailers, and They Think It's Fantastic," *Philadelphia Inquirer* (March 8, 1996).
22. Burton R. Clark, *The Academic Life: Small Worlds, Different Worlds* (Princeton, NJ: Princeton University Press, 1987) (Special Report for the Carnegie Foundation for the Advancement of Teaching).
23. Michael Barbaro, "Bloomberg to Johns Hopkins: Thanks a Billion (Well, $1.1 Billion)," *New York Times* (January 27, 2013) pp. 1, 16.
24. Robert Kelly, "Letter to the Editor," *Lexington Herald-Leader* (April 14, 2015) p. A9.
25. Kevin Carey, "The Absolut Rolex Plan: How Luxury Packaging and Prestige Pricing Can Transform a Humble Commuter School," *New York Times Education Life Magazine* (February 8, 2015) pp. 16–17.
26. "A Majors Success," *Time* (December 2, 1974) p. 84.
27. Gay Brechin, "Classical Dreams and Concrete Realities," *California Alumni Monthly* (March 1978) pp. 12–15.
28. David Dunlap, "Yale University Library Revives Entrance Hall," *New York Times* (December 27, 2014) p. A15.
29. Scott Carlson, "As Campuses Crumble, Budgets Are Crunched," *Chronicle of Higher Education* (May 23, 2008) p. A1.
30. Bruce C. Vladek, "Buildings and Budgets: The Overinvestment Crisis," *Change: The Magazine of Higher Education* (December 1978–January 1979) vol. 10, no. 11, pp. 36–40.
31. *Los Angeles: A Guide to the City and Its Environs* (American Guide Series compiled by the Works Progress Administration in Southern California) pp. 208–209.
32. Tisa Ann Mason, *The Commuters' Alma Mater: Profiles of College Student Experiences at a Commuter Institution* (Williamsburg, VA: The College of William & Mary Doctoral Dissertation, 1993).

33. Ronda Kaysen, "Public College, Private Dorm," *New York Times* (January 25, 2012) p. B1; Dawn Wotapka, "Kentucky Wants to Get out of Campus Housing," *Wall Street Journal* (December 13, 2011); Douglas Priest and Edward P. St. John, Editors, *Privatization and Public Universities* (Bloomington: Indiana University Press, 2006). See also, Gary C. Fethke and Andrew J. Policano, *Public No More: A New Path to Excellence for America's Public Universities* (Stanford, CA: Stanford Business Books of Stanford University Press, 2012).

34. Kellie Woodhouse, "As Institutions Outsource They Should Keep Their Mission – and the Vendor – Close," *Inside Higher Ed* (July 21, 2015).

35. Madeline Will, "Colleges Ponder Their Options When Racism Is Set in Stone," *Chronicle of Higher Education* (February 20, 2015) p. A15; David Brooks, "The Robert E. Lee Problem," *New York Times* (June 26, 2015) p. A23; Steve Thomma and Anita Kumar, "After the Confederate Flag, What Will Be Next?," *Lexington Herald-Leader* (June 25, 2015) p. A9 (McClatchy Washington Syndicated Column).

36. "Transy in Transition," *Lexington Herald-Leader* (June 10, 2015) p. A3.

37. Katherine Mangan, "Removing Symbols Is a Step, But Changing a Campus Culture Can Take Years," *Chronicle of Higher Education* (July 10, 2015) p. A14.

38. Noah Reminick, "Yale Grapples with Ties to Slavery in a Debate over a College's Name," *New York Times* (September 12, 2015) pp. A18–A19.

39. Brown University Steering Committee on Slavery and Justice: Full Commission Report on Memorials (2007).

40. Maresi Nerad, *The Academic Kitchen: A Social History of Gender Stratification at the University of California, Berkeley* (Albany: State University of New York Press, 1999).

41. Nikil Saval, with photographs by Ofer Wolberger, "If You Build It…," *New York Times Magazine* (September 13, 2015) pp. 48–55.

Additional Readings

Diana Balmori, "Campus Works and Public Landscapes," in Diana Balmori, Diane K. McGuire, and Eleanor M. Peck, Editors, *Beatrix Farrand's American Landscapes: Her Gardens and Campuses* (Sagaponack, NY: Sagapress, Inc., 1985) pp. 127–196.

Jonathan Coulson, Paul Roberts, and Isabelle Taylor, *University Planning and Architecture: The Search for Perfection* (New York: Routledge, 2011).

Peter Morris Dixon et al., Editors, *Robert A.M. Stern: On Campus – Architecture, Identity, and Community* (New York: Monacelli Press of Random House, 2011).

Richard P. Dober, *Campus Architecture: Building in the Groves of Academe* (New York: McGraw-Hill, 1996).

Thomas A. Gaines, *The Campus as a Work of Art* (New York: Praeger, 1991).

Daniel R. Kenney, Ricardo Dumont, and Ginner S. Kenney, *Mission and Place: Strengthening Learning and Community through Campus Design* (New York: American Council on Education/Praeger Series on Higher Education, 2005).

Samuel Schuman, *Old Main: Small Colleges in Twenty-First Century America* (Baltimore, MD: Johns Hopkins University Press, 2005).

Paul Venable Turner, *Campus: An American Planning Tradition* (Cambridge, MA: Massachusetts Institute of Technology Press, 1984).

3

TEACHING AND LEARNING

SETTING AND OVERVIEW

Today at American colleges and universities one finds thousands of courses and hundreds of undergraduate degree programs, ranging from Anthropology to Zoology – and probably with everything in between. This abundance brings to mind the pledge that entrepreneur turned philanthropist Ezra Cornell made in 1865: "I would found an institution where any person can find instruction in any study." And so he did! To the amazement of historic universities in Europe, Cornell's ambitious American dream came true – at his namesake university and also at colleges and universities nationwide.[1] A contemporary university may have as many as 20 academic colleges or schools, each with its own dean. Here is a roster from one university: Agriculture, Arts & Sciences, Engineering, Education, Business, Communications, Architecture, Fine Arts, Social Work, Public Policy, Pharmacy, Nursing, Allied Health, Medicine, Dentistry, Law, Public Health, Forestry, Library and Information Science, Graduate School, Continuing and Professional Studies, and Divinity. The names of these academic units vary from one campus to another. For example, the University of Virginia has *both* a School of Business and a School of Commerce. Given this curricular cornucopia, our nation's higher education motto ought to read, "Only in America!"

All these academic programs attest to the attractiveness of colleges and universities to Americans. And, they are attractive to international students as well. In fall 2013 total enrollment in all colleges and universities in the United States – including two-year community colleges along with four-year and graduate institutions – was just under 20 million students. In 2011–2012, colleges conferred about a million associate degrees, 1.8 million bachelor's degrees, 754,000 master's degrees, and 170,000 doctoral degrees.

How does one make sense of this sprawling achievement? The conventional wisdom is to rely on a college's official catalog for a guide to the courses of study. On close inspection, however, although this kind of document may provide a starting point, it is an incomplete and, perhaps, a misleading source to understand the varieties of teaching and learning that take place in higher education.[2] This chapter goes beyond the official catalog to try to analyze *who* teaches *what* and *how*. This ultimately connects the

45

curriculum to the fundamental philosophical question of "higher education for what purposes?"

These considerations are inseparable from what and how *students learn* both from the formal and *hidden* curricula in various kinds of institutions, and with distinctions between undergraduate education, professional schools, graduate programs, and other settings. This chapter emphasizes the interaction and negotiations between the teachers and taught – a relationship that creates a dynamic setting which is more animated and interesting than the course catalog. An understanding of teaching and learning eventually suggests that formal learning outcomes and mastery of information coexists with such informal yet powerful matters as the *socialization* and *certification* of college students into adult life as citizens and professionals.[3] In addition to how much (or, how little) a student learns in terms of information from formal instruction, colleges and universities are a powerful source of transmitting and reinforcing distinctive sets of values and attitudes to their students. We also know that peer influence among students is potent in shaping what information and values are extracted from the formal course of study and inculcated into undergraduates.

Risk-taking, conformity, creativity, exploration, confidence, timidity, working within forms, fear of failure, avoiding hard work, learning how to navigate bureaucracies, as well as acquiring facts merely hint at the variety and often conflicting array of potential messages the curriculum as part of the college experience conveys. It varies from college to college, and from one department to another. As a result, the college curriculum is a high-stakes arena in which the politics and polemics of interest groups continually vie to form – and re-form – the academic course of study.

ISSUES

Consideration of the college curriculum is parsed into four major questions: First, "Is the curriculum in American higher education heir to a 'legacy of lethargy'"? Second, "Has distance learning and online instruction in the past decade transformed the curriculum?" Third, "How have varied external and internal constituencies made the college curriculum both a forum and battleground for polemics and politics?" The fourth major question is, "What are the relationships between teaching and research?" These four issues hardly exhaust the possibilities for understanding academic courses of study, but they do provide systematic focus for starting the curricular exploration.

Is Higher Education Heir to a "Legacy of Lethargy"?

A primary issue that brings together numerous related concerns is that the curriculum in American higher education is heir to a "Legacy of Lethargy."[4] Consider the following framing of the issues from a July 2015 article in *The Atlantic*:

> For the most part, colleges and universities have changed very little since the University of Bologna gave the first college lectures in 1088. With the exception of Massive Open Online Courses, or MOOCS – free lectures and courses on the Internet – most university learning still requires students to put their butts in seats for a certain number of hours, complete a list of courses, and pass tests demonstrating that they learned from those courses (or were able to successfully cram for over the course of a few days). But a new model is upending the traditional

college experience, and has the potential to change the way universities – both new and old – think about learning. Called competency-based education, this new model looks at what students should know when they complete a degree, and allows them to acquire that knowledge by independently making their way through lessons. It also allows students who come into school with knowledge in a certain area to pass tests to prove it, rather than forcing them to take classes and pay credits on information they already know.[5]

This is a disconcerting historical snapshot because although "competency-based education" may be exciting, it is not new. After World War II numerous colleges gave returning military veterans opportunities to demonstrate what they had learned to allow them to waive redundant academic courses and receive advanced placement. The term "competency-based education" came into widespread use in the early 1970s and was part of the lexicon of higher education long before 2015. It can be found within course syllabi and also in academic departments' degree requirements and strategic plans. It frequently crops up in licensure and certification examinations. So, it may have an invigorated presence today at such institutions as Western Governors University – as featured in the 2015 *Atlantic* article – but it is hardly "new."

As for unrelenting reliance on lectures, the jump from Bologna to Berkeley between 1300 and today calls for some careful reconsideration about the accuracy of the claim. The lecture format fell from favor for several centuries, especially in American colleges from about 1636 to 1890. Its resurrection in the late 19th century signaled that a new generation of instructors was led by full-fledged professors whose scholarly expertise meant they had something important and informed to say to students. It also meant that college officials considered students sufficiently mature to listen and take notes – skills seldom on display in courses that used daily recitations. These historical details underscore the need to explain how colleges and universities have come to acquire the various features associated with the curriculum today.

If you like reading Gothic novels, you might find some fascination in the story of campus curriculum reform. Since at least the 19th century, when the course of study was said to rely too much on the "dead" languages of Latin and Ancient Greek, critics of academe have shared the horror writer's preoccupation with the morbid. "Changing the curriculum," according to an age-old truism, "is harder than moving a graveyard." Or, goes the corollary, the progress of an institution "will be directly proportional to the death rate of the faculty."[6]

Critics tend to portray curriculum change as a slow, painful death by boredom – drawn out over long meetings, finally expiring in the form of tabled motions or appointment of a task force. It's a "legacy of lethargy" that supposedly dates back to the infamous Yale of Report of 1828 (often maligned as the prototypical "Campus Committee Where Time Stood Still"). It was a document that led generations of academics to think of curricular content as "the furniture of the mind."[7] For decades thereafter, student memoirs complained of weary teaching and rote assignments, the same ones endured by their grandfathers. How does one explain this curious reputation for terrifying dullness? Why is the college curriculum said to be so resistant to change? Is there truth in the popular wisdom (often attributed to Henry Kissinger) that "academic politics are so vicious because the stakes are so low"? We will explore this question on page 134 in Chapter 6 dealing with Governance and Organization.

Are There Forgotten Sources of Change?

The effort to redesign an undergraduate curriculum often is slow. But this is an incomplete account because the curriculum ultimately is about teaching and learning. And, those activities bring into the spotlight teachers and students. These acts and characters are not a story of deadly tedium. The curriculum is characterized by energy, drama, innovation, and surprising – even unexpected – outcomes. In their moments of gloom and horror, critics and reformers would do well to recall some of the ways in which the course of study has changed, and may change again.

For all the stereotypes of a stagnant curriculum, sometimes the curriculum changes too quickly. In the 1540s when Henry VIII, King of England, invoked the Act of Supremacy, he also abolished canon law as a field of study at Oxford University. With one fell swoop (matching the one that dispatched his estranged wife), he lopped off the curriculum and sent the professors packing. Why? He had relied heavily on the canon law faculty to provide him with a carefully researched legal justification for annulment of his marriage – but the prestigious Oxford professors had failed to deliver. The royal edict was, "Class dismissed!"

Evidently this imperial model of "top-down" reform has surfaced from time to time, even in the modern United States. In the early 1950s, notes historian Rebecca Lowen, the provost at Stanford University threatened to eliminate the history and classics departments because these academic units had a bad record of attracting external research grants.[8] Or, consider the events that shook the State University of New York system in the late 1970s when the system headquarters responded to a budget crunch by compiling a "necrology list" of programs targeted to be eliminated. This was one "Dean's List" few department chairs coveted!

When a president or board hankers for abrupt change to eliminate courses or programs, there typically ensues a collision with faculty in established, endangered departments. This inevitable struggle can easily be taken as evidence that the faculty resists change, or that they are cautious, complacent, and uncooperative. However, we might also choose to read this struggle as a clash between authoritarian and collegial styles of decision-making. And, since faculty in the modern university have relatively little mandate to initiate programs and policies, their primary power by default rests in the collective ability to obstruct what they consider hasty and inappropriate edicts from on high. To the outside analyst this response may seem to indicate faculty sloth – or, their frustrating attitude toward curricular change. But it also could demonstrate a deliberate, albeit imperfect commitment to a system of checks and balances, ensuring that change does not happen too quickly or irresponsibly. This can be an appropriate response as stewards of the curriculum.

The Curricular Banquet Table: Guess Who's Coming to Dinner!

The curriculum certainly has provided "food for thought" to higher education analysts over time. Clark Kerr, legendary president of the University of California, referred to the "cafeteria line curriculum" in his 1960 book, *The Uses of the University*. Another culinary metaphor for campus curriculum deliberations is that of a banquet table with seating for many long-time members and a few guests. Power and prestige – two related but distinct criteria – determine the seating arrangements. It's common knowledge that fields such as women's studies and statistics are newcomers to the table. Less known is that agriculture, engineering, forestry, and business are also recent arrivals since the late 19th and early 20th centuries.[9] It was only a century ago that these "new" professions were able to use their financial resources and popularity with tuition-paying students to gain seats next to the prestigious (but sometimes impoverished) fields of the established liberal arts and the learned professions of law and medicine. Many disciplines often believed to be "old" or "established" – including history, English literature, anthropology, linguistics, geography, economics, and political science – are, in fact, relative newcomers to American higher education. Studio art, music, and other performing arts indicate yet another strand of fields that are established today, but not too long ago were confined to the extracurriculum, without academic degree programs. All initially were obstructed in their quest for academic legitimacy by some college presidents and established departments.

Computer science is another example of seating at the academic table. It's a robust department in the 21st century. This popularity today masks the fact that it was scarcely known by this name 40 years ago. As late as 1975 at many major universities it had no departmental home or degree programs. It took shape as a hybrid field diffused across such disparate departments as electrical engineering, library science, mathematics, linguistics, and philosophy. Statistics, which first surfaced as a discipline sponsored by the College of Agriculture and the Mathematics Department at Iowa State University in the 1930s, now enjoys stature at most campuses as a distinct department – and with almost every academic college having its own statistics faculty and courses.

The history of departmental growth and prestige contains fascinating and antiquated customs, bringing to mind the arranged marriages and prestige posturing in a Henry James novel. For example, the first students in Yale's Sheffield School of Science were required to sit at the back of the campus chapel, a symbolic and mean-spirited gesture that sent the message that intellect did not guarantee social prestige. In the 1890s Dartmouth College used its law school as a haven to enroll football players who lacked the academic rigor necessary for admission to the liberal arts college. Even in the early 20th century most medical schools had minimal admissions standards, with neither a bachelor's degree nor a "pre-med" curriculum as requirements. Obviously, over the next half-century there were some changes made in the curriculum that made both admission and the curriculum in colleges of medicine academically rigorous and selective.

And not the least among important curricular changes was the "elective system" in which an undergraduate declared a "concentration" or "major" field – and completed prescribed courses in that field. This was accompanied by the requirement of a "minor" field, along with elective courses and completion of "general education" requirements to demonstrate breadth of study. It became standard practice and was hardly perfect. It was, however, a distinct innovation based on a logical design, and has endured in the curriculum at colleges and universities nationwide.

Consumer Demand and Students Voting with Their Feet

Was the 19th-century curriculum stagnant? A groundswell of research has recently led scholars to reconsider the allegedly moribund curriculum.[10] In fact, higher education's motto in the antebellum period should have been *caveat emptor!*, translated as "Let the Buyer Beware!" The stereotypical "old-time college" with its fossilized classical course of study was but one of many options available to paying customers. A new undergraduate degree, the "Ph.B.," was added. That was not a typographical error for the prestigious

"Ph.D." Rather, it stood for the "Bachelor of Philosophy" degree. Its distinctive feature was that it included no requirement of Latin or Greek. Meanwhile, the traditional "Bachelor of Arts" degree persisted with its emphasis on classical languages. Both degree tracks overlapped and coexisted – usually joined by the "bachelor of science" degree. It increased options for students and increased enrollments and tuition revenues for the college administration. The financial impact of the Ph.B. receives added attention on page 281 in Chapter 12 on Colleges and Consumerism.

Elsewhere, diploma mills flourished, embodying the American spirit of an enterprising and unregulated society. And in the 1870s when the market slowed, institutions had to become particularly flexible to attract students. Brown University, for instance, would lower its tuition rate the closer one got to the start of the academic year – comparable to airlines offering empty seats to stand-by customers at a discounted fare just prior to flight departure. No college that wished to survive financially had the luxury of unfilled classroom seats and empty dormitories.

Some medical schools in the 19th century took an ingenious approach to keeping expenses down and maintaining efficiency. One did so by having neither faculty nor courses nor laboratories.[11] They simply conferred a certificate or degree, such as the M.D., to students who paid a fee of $300. The school did have the expense of purchasing diplomas, but sheepskin was cheap compared to having to spend on scalpels and salaries. Even the established universities were flexible in their degree offerings. Not until after World War II and the administering of the GI Bill did regional accreditation gain significant presence in monitoring academic standards of degree programs nationwide.

Curricular innovation has never guaranteed consumer satisfaction nor institutional affluence. Some new programs fizzled out despite the best-made plans advanced by academic leaders. College presidents in the 19th century often were surprised to find that new courses designed to connect to the job market – such as engineering and applied science – often had little market appeal to 18-year-olds. And, when the 1862 Morrill Act provided states with resources for such fields as agriculture, in most cases both farmers and prospective students were slow to show much interest in the new offerings. Students as consumers frequently seemed to want a conservative, familiar curriculum that conferred traditional prestige rather than new vocational credentials. In the decades after Yale issued its notoriously stodgy 1828 Report, the college's applications for admissions remained healthy. Indeed, Yale had the largest enrollment of any undergraduate college in the nation.

Has Distance Learning and Online Instruction Transformed the Curriculum?

In 2013 *Inside Higher Ed* published the results of their survey about faculty views of online education. Reporter Steve Kolowich looked over the survey data and noted that for professors, "the rise of online education excites them more than it frightens them." Why some faculty colleagues feared or avoided online education was puzzling. By 2013 it had become an established, expanding, and improving format – and was a part of college teaching and learning that was unlikely to disappear. At a flagship state university, online education is less of a threat to job security than is the administrative penchant to hire adjuncts at a relatively low salary to teach traditional courses. Learning how to teach online probably would be one of the best steps a professor could take to assure viability in the 21st century. The most dysfunctional response by a professor today would be to dismiss or ignore both the technology and the social consequences online learning has acquired.[12]

Online Education Is Neither Simple Nor Sinister

Many professors are not so much low tech as slow tech. They discover that becoming ready to teach an online course takes a long time. But the time lapse falls into two markedly different phases. To convert a course that one had taught in "traditional mode" for many years, one started out in September of the new academic year by seeking advice from the campus's director of distance learning programs offered by the university. This led to sessions with the DL staff for a long series of revision. The DL staff patiently yet firmly showed why and how it was important to understand the logic and logistics of course preparation and presentation. One had to have course materials – including syllabus, weekly content, discussion topics, assignments, and links to materials – clearly in place on the Internet site before starting to teach. Otherwise, one would be scurrying to remain current, let alone ahead of the students and the course calendar, while at the same time having to deal with interactive class discussion threads.

The more one learned about the format of the online technology, the more interesting and effective teaching and learning would be. Best of all, the DL professionals showed how an instructor could use imaginatively digital technology to post historical photographs, old newsreels, and archival documents as visual sources that animated teaching and learning. They also drove home the need to gain copyright permissions and make technical arrangements to "stream" historical films and video clips, and helped new instructors do both. In sum, they combined their stern warnings with interest and assistance. The happy result was that after about two months of practice, course materials had met their standards – and an instructor then could proceed to the second sluicegate: official approval of the new DL course by the university's faculty.

The official academic approval process can be different from the course preparation experience. It combined the slow pace of regular course proposal with added delays in deliberations because it was a distance learning course, especially at the higher levels of university-wide review. Approval and encouragement usually came promptly from the department and college curriculum committee and from the academic dean – all of whom had an interest in having the college venture into online courses. However, at the next levels, the senate committee reviews involved little in the way of acquiring skills or rethinking teaching design or course substance. It was characterized by objections about details and was marked by long periods of waiting for approval to go on to the next step.

After subcommittee review, the surprising finding was that in the faculty senate, often there were obstructionist colleagues. One professor who was a senator raised objections and voted against DL course proposals on the grounds that as a matter of principle he did not approve of distance learning as part of the university's curriculum. The merits of a course topic, contents, proposed presentation, significance of readings and assignments were insufficient to dislodge this dissenting vote. This meant that professors who took initiative to transform existing traditional courses – or create new ones – in online mode faced unreasonable obstacles. One phase promoted thoughtful innovation; the second phase often was filled with delay and distrust. So, one finds simultaneously a tradition of innovation coupled with the infamous "legacy of lethargy."

Online Education Is Neither Inherently Inexpensive Nor Efficient

If university officials embrace distance learning as a quick fix to offer courses at low cost to a large number of students, they are mistaken. Preparation and teaching are labor-intensive. Those "guardians of standards" who are skeptical about the quality of a proposed online course struck me as wrongheaded given that there is great variance in quality among traditional courses as well. There may well be a latent function of fear operating here – namely, some professors are worried that *their* traditional courses may ultimately be in jeopardy with the proliferation of large enrollment online courses. It is doubtful this is a widespread or warranted fear among tenured professors. A more rational concern would be that one's failure to be able or willing to incorporate online learning in blended form with "real" courses would have declining appeal both to prospective students and to deans and provosts.

Budget-minded provosts and deans may dream of online courses as a lucrative source of new revenue streams. However, there is no guarantee that creating an online course or program is inexpensive. To be appealing, the Internet course must have high-quality technology, graphics, production, and software. Relying on a charismatic, respected "academic star" to be the featured speaker for a large enrollment Internet course will command a high salary in the academic market. Nor is there any certainty that a university will lower the tuition price – even if the online course cost were eventually to cost less than a "traditional" course. All the variables of effectiveness, efficiency, cost, and price are subject to the same complexities, adjustments, and vacillations of any higher education program offering.

Established universities would be wise to heed the innovations taking place in all sectors of postsecondary education. Most surprising is to learn how much attention a for-profit institution such as the University of Phoenix pours into the creation and evaluation of its online courses. The focus of its faculty and staff on working with instructors, designing courses, and monitoring student participation has been a source of innovation often under-appreciated by traditional colleges.

Online Education Makes History by Being Part of Higher Education's History

Online education may be new, especially in Internet technology. But what Luddite faculty opponents ought to recognize is that online education is merely the latest in a long succession of teaching innovations fueled by a combination of technological and social changes. In other words, online education is part of higher education's heritage.

New teaching media have long attracted scholars. For example, several years ago my wife came across an old packet of letters in a secondhand store in Washington, D.C. She gave them to me because the envelopes were addressed to a professor. It turns out that the packet contained the exchanges and comments of a correspondence course from 1891. Most spectacular was our finding that the professor reading and grading the correspondence examination essays was Richard Ely – at that time a professor of economics at Johns Hopkins University, who soon would join the University of Wisconsin, where he would lead one of the most influential economics departments. He was no less than a founder and president of the American Economic Association. To discover that Ely found time to teach in a new format and took seriously the evaluation of student correspondence courses was a revelation. It showed that more than a century ago, a famous professor took the plunge to participate in an innovative format for college-level teaching. It would be comparable today to having the Nobel Laureate and syndicated *New York Times* columnist, Princeton professor Paul Krugman, find time to respond individually to an undergraduate's e-mails as part of Krugman's teaching an online course.

Between the end posts of Richard Ely teaching correspondence courses in 1891 and a distinguished professor offering online courses in 2016 there is a heritage of professors who embrace new media as a way of reaching extended student audiences. Today much of the publicity in higher education involves the role of Stanford, Harvard, and MIT venturing into "massive open online courses." Often overlooked is that this is a familiar theme in higher education. It included major network broadcast shows in the 1950s followed by the entrance of the Public Broadcast System into educational programming in the late 1960s. Each decade a handful of outstanding academic scholars have been elevated by electronic media coverage to the rank of what may be termed "educational superstars" – all indicators of the tradition of established colleges and universities making forays into new forms of mass dissemination. The important, residual legacy, however, is that these new forms – including Internet courses and MOOCs – usually coexist with traditional forms of instruction.

Implications for Established Higher Education

The *Inside Higher Ed* survey showed that online education persists as one of many strands that coexist in higher education. In summer 2013, for example, a sub-theme about the forced resignation of the president of the University of Virginia evidently was the Board of Visitors' concern that new innovations such as online courses were being ignored in favor of saving established fields, such as classics offered in the traditional on-campus format. The problem with such characterizations is that they set up false dichotomies – such as the wrongheaded belief that classics are at odds with online learning. For example, at one university the director of distance learning programs who assists faculty with immersion into online education that is both effective and enjoyable brings to her role an academic background in information science – and, in classics! This interesting combination was revealed by the motto at the bottom of her e-mails: "*Fluctuat nec mergitur*" – "She is tossed by the waves, but is not drowned."

That's not a bad motto for dealing with flux in our teaching and learning. For higher education in the 21st century, consideration of online education must be given – plus comparable consideration of lectures, seminars, tutorials, independent studies, internships, and fieldwork, all of which cross-fertilize one another without eliminating any one format. This interdependent mix brings to mind the Latin motto of Claremont Graduate University: "*multi lumina, lux una*" – "many lamps, one light!"

How Has the College Curriculum Become a Forum and Battleground for Polemics and Politics?

Academic departments within a campus always have been a source of rivalries. Some obvious tensions are applied fields such as engineering versus philosophy. This is because each discipline tends to represent a lens for viewing the world. Economists think that market behavior is central. Sociologists emphasize collective behavior and societal relationships. Providing distinct departmental homes is one bureaucratic means to promote coexistence and keep interdepartmental tensions in check.

Some academic rivalries are peculiar because they are grounded in misnomers about various fields of studies. At one university, for example, the field of history is placed within the umbrella of "humanities." Elsewhere, it may be part of "social studies." Departments of economics often are part of the College of Arts and Sciences. But it is also possible to find numerous examples where economics is a department within the

College of Business. Other categorizations of fields are more problematic. One such mischaracterization is that "STEM" (science–technology–engineering–math) fields are apart from the liberal arts. As the president of Harvard wrote to the editor of the *New York Times*, a liberal arts education did, indeed, include mathematics and sciences.

> In representing STEM and liberal arts education as antithetical, "Gap Widening as top Workers Reap the Raises" (front page, July 25, 2015) reproduces a widespread and dangerous misunderstanding. A liberal arts education is one that embraces – indeed requires – broad learning across the fields of natural and social sciences and humanities.
>
> Its goal is to create citizens equipped with habits of mind and analytic capacities to shape human experience within the context of the natural realities and technological forces – and opportunities – we confront.
>
> The world needs scientifically sophisticated humanists and humanistically grounded scientists and engineers who can think beyond the immediate and instrumental to address the bigger picture and the longer term.
>
> Liberal arts learning contrasts itself not with STEM fields, which it encompasses, but with purely vocational education. Its goal is not to ready its students for one particular job, but for many jobs extending over a lifetime and requiring a depth and breadth of understanding that exposure to the range of human knowledge through the liberal arts is uniquely intended to impart.[13]

Although the president of Harvard's clarification about STEM as part of liberal education may temper the tensions at the moment, the curricular debate's dichotomies usually surface again. Within some departments, such as economics or political science, schisms appear to be along lines of methodological research. This might play out as quantitative versus qualitative research, or "big data" analyses as distinguished from "area studies." *Within* academic fields, disputes are less about methodologies and information than about ideas, interpretations, and ideology. All economists may agree that economics is important and even rely on the same key concepts to define their discipline, but they may be sharply divided on "school of thought." The same goes for a history department. One tends to associate these internal disputes with social and behavioral sciences and the humanities. On closer inspection, they surface in most fields – including the natural and physical sciences. In recent years, for example, a biology course may be the site for serious dissent. Should a student whose religion teaches the doctrine of creationism be required to study and answer exam questions based on the instructor's and textbook's presentations on evolution? Conflicts between religious doctrine and academic teaching are perennial features of American higher education, whether in 1715 or 2015. Episodes may be resolved, but the potential for disagreement is never eliminated. To do so most likely would create a static curriculum set outside the figurative marketplace of ideas.

Taken together, one has had for at least 30 years what may be termed the "Campus Curricular Crusades" – battles for the minds and support of constituencies.[14] The term "political correctness" worked its way into the academic and public lexicon, with the implication that in particular fields professors leaned politically to the left and scholarship allegedly had turned from analysis into advocacy. It became associated with academic support for social justice and civil rights. It probably is accurate that at most established colleges and universities, faculty in the social and behavioral sciences do report attitudes and affiliations that are called "Left Coast." On closer inspection one finds that a diverse range of donors and advocates have sponsored endowed professorships, establishment of research centers and "think tanks," and editing of journals that tend to advance their respective political perspectives across the political spectrum.

Whatever signs of radicalism surface from the left, they are joined by a counter-revolutionary move. In the 1990s this included the founding of the NAS – the National Association of Scholars. Also, one finds the emergence of a national group such as the American Council of Trustees and Alumni (ACTA). Based in Washington, D.C., ACTA is an independent, nonprofit organization "committed to academic freedom, excellence, and accountability at America's colleges and universities." It focuses on educating trustees about asserting influence over college governance, with particular focus on liberal education and changes in how history is taught in the nation's colleges and universities – and annually decries the decline in undergraduates' knowledge of what ACTA considers to be essential understandings of liberal arts fields, including American history. It expresses concern when, for example, a university department does not require students majoring in English to have read works by William Shakespeare. Implicit in the ACTA newsletters and publications is that this curricular change has meant deterioration in American principles and essential educational standards and values.

What Are the Relationships Between Teaching and Research?

In the competition for time, attention, and resources in higher education, few issues are more volatile than how faculty research affects teaching. No doubt faculty teaching loads have tended to be reduced over time. A century ago professors typically taught four to five courses per semester. Even at "major" universities, undergraduate instruction was the central obligation of faculty. Outstanding books such as Larry Cuban's *How Scholars Trumped Teachers* document systematically the push by professors to teach fewer courses. Cuban's historical case study of Stanford University focused on two departments with very different cultures and teaching customs – history and medicine. Along with their different departmental characteristics, faculty in both units sought and received reduced teaching loads. Scholarship in the form of research grants and research publications ascended in departmental and institutional priority. Stanford, of course, is hardly a typical American college or university. However, an important legacy is that the primacy of sponsored research and writing for publication as a central part of a professor's working life has tended to diffuse to almost all types of institution in American higher education.

The implications of this trend are not wholly clear. For example, if a president or provost proclaims, "We are committed to teaching undergraduates!" one is hard pressed to decipher what that means. It could be a rationale for increasing faculty's teaching course loads. But that does not necessarily mean that the institution's commitment is to *better* teaching or even *excellence* in teaching. The most one can discern is that it means a commitment to teaching *more* rather than *less*. Conversely, one might argue that having a professor teach two courses per semester rather than three implies the administrative belief that an instructor then might have more time to prepare, to be available to students, and to focus – in other words, to be a *better* teacher. This conjecture about the various scenarios reinforces the point that it is not easy to determine excellence and quality in teaching.

For starters, one must be careful not to presume that teaching and research are antithetical. At best, a professor who is vital in her or his laboratory experiments or archival research may bring fresh scholarship to the syllabus and classroom. Numerous examples of professors who excel in both teaching and research give some credence that the two activities can be reciprocal and even have a multiplier effect. Perhaps the worst-case scenario is if a college happens to have a professor who is not good or even dedicated in *either* teaching or research. What Larry Cuban's historical study of Stanford shows, reinforced by research such as sociologist Burton Clark's *The Academic Life: Small Worlds, Different Worlds*, is that each academic unit, whether at the campus or department level, acquires over time a distinctive culture of teaching.

We do know that the increased availability of outside funded research grants allows a professor to reduce her teaching load by "buying out" courses. This would seem to "prove" that sponsored research drives out teaching. Unfortunately, that is not evident. Deans and department chairs often applaud such "buy-outs" because it may remove the professor-researcher from teaching a course, but in so doing it actually provides increased funding for the dean to hire replacement teachers. What is this sleight of hand that transforms research dollars into teaching scholars? A dean charges the professor 20 percent of his annual salary to "buy out" one course per semester – even though one course actually only represents 12 percent of a professor's full-time workload. And, presuming the professor who lands a major research grant probably has a relatively high salary, this increases the financial advantages to the college or department. This is a good deal for the dean because on the official "distribution of effort" workload form, a single semester course is billed as 12.5 percent of the professor's annual salary. This means the dean and department have discretionary money with which to hire an adjunct instructor or visiting professor – probably at a lower pay rate than the tenured professor. The courses are taught, the classes are filled, the professor does research, and the dean has surplus revenue. Furthermore, research grants typically provide other funds in the form of overhead and indirect costs channeled from the research grant to the provost and dean. The problem with this pragmatic solution is that it is short term and penny-wise. Students forfeit the opportunity to study with and learn from a senior, established scholar in the field.

If time devoted to research is the nemesis of commitment to teaching, a sense of fair play and thorough analysis suggests one must look at other sources that also erode teaching from a professor's workload. One overlooked source is the expansion of administrative assignments – work usually initiated by the dean of the college or the provost. The proliferation of faculty appointments shifted to administrative roles includes department chairs, assistant deans, associate deans, program directors, assistant provosts, and associate provosts. In most instances, these internal appointments are made to tenured or tenure track professors. They retain their faculty appointment and tenure while devoting a substantial percentage of their professional time to administration – with a reduction in effort for teaching and research. It is an expensive practice whose costs in time and money add up.

There is another cost to scholarship: namely, when administrators return to a full-time faculty role, they often carry back with them the increased salary they received as part of the package of being an associate dean or dean. Press conferences traditionally include the emotional statement, "In leaving administration I look forward to returning to my teaching and scholarship." This is possible but often not completely plausible. Henry Rosovsky, legendary Harvard dean and highly regarded economist, observed in *The University: An Owner's Manual* that after an administrator is away from teaching and research for about five years, it is unlikely he or she will truly resume those disciplinary activities. Retiring presidents who "return to the faculty" often have *no* obligations to teach or conduct research. Since they probably retain the lion's share of their presidential salary upon return to an academic department, they raise the statistical mean of their department or college's faculty salaries – but in a way that is disingenuous to their incumbent faculty colleagues who really are teaching. So, the argument that research often trumps teaching should be accompanied by the comparable observation that for professors, administration also trumps teaching.[15] Unfortunately, a convenient way that academic administrators try to buffer this loss is by increasing reliance on hiring low-paid adjunct instructors. This may help balance the books financially, but it does so by neglecting the books that are written and read.

Context on Curriculum

To come full circle on the fundamental question, "Why does curricular change seem so slow?," we need to keep in mind some problems of analysis and evaluation. One inclination is to follow Clark Kerr's observation in *The Uses of the University*: namely, that universities are *conservative* in their internal dealings while *liberal* in their external recommendations for others to follow. Or, one might argue that the distinctive feature of American curricular planning is its grass-roots character. We have in the United States a relatively decentralized arrangement of institutional and even departmental autonomy. It means that innovation is best when it takes place from the ground up.

A less obvious but attractive hypothesis concerns the role of consumerism in American life; whether we look at education or any other sector, consumerism works in antithetical ways. On the one hand, it creates a demand for new, affordable, and accessible programs – a pressure that accelerates curricular change (or, in many cases, curricular "growth"). On the other hand, consumerism can exert a braking action. The public, including prospective students and their parents, as well as state legislators and Congress want protection from bogus claims, shoddy work, inferior teaching, and worthless degrees. One weakness of American higher education stems from the fact that it is so diverse that it resists rational control.

Demands for accountability have increased over the past four decades, along with creation of state postsecondary education coordinating councils, which sometimes hold up curricular changes in order to ensure the effective use of taxpayers' dollars. Further, in many public systems, campus projects must obtain approval from a state agency charged with preventing the unnecessary duplication of courses and programs. Such reviews take time. Whatever lens one adopts, the stereotype of curricular stagnancy should not lead us to overlook how – and how much – change takes place in higher education. For instance, those very same state agencies that obstruct change can also act as catalysts for it, in that they provide funding incentives to develop new academic programs in areas given high priority by state coordinating councils.

Most complex decision-making bodies, whether in higher education or federal agencies approving prescription drugs, are chronically clogged and slow. Is the typical campus deliberation any slower than, say, a legal case that wends its way to the Supreme Court? Sometimes a slow process signals thoroughness – as in government agencies such as the Food and Drug Administration approving a drug for commercial production and sale. Though members of Congress may chide academics for inaction, Congress itself relies on filibusters as standard practice in the legislative process. And things certainly don't move any more quickly in the international arena: simply to agree on the seating arrangements for the Vietnamese peace talks in Paris took three years!

CHARACTERS AND CONSTITUENTS

Turf Wars Between Students and Faculty

According to historian Frederick Rudolph, a good way to understand changes in what is studied is to see it as an orchestrated series of contests between students and the administration.[16] Deliberations over "campus turf" have a distinctive life cycle. First, undergraduates initiate a new subject or activity as an informal extracurricular pursuit. Second, college faculty and administration become upset about the popularity of such informal activities and fear they are "getting out of control" (or, more accurately, "getting out of the control of the college officials"). The faculty and administration then attempt to squelch them because they pose a threat to the "real" mission of college education. Third, administrative failure to abolish a renegade activity is followed by a period of benign neglect. The final stage is for the college administration to adopt formally the new field, in a simultaneous display of surrender to student tastes and their own interest in gaining control of this student activity.

This explains how, for example, a facility such as the campus library and subjects such as modern literature, journalism, music, studio art, and political economy worked their way into the formal curriculum between 1890 and 1950. So, too, does it describe the process by which music, theater, and other fine and performing arts have acquired academic legitimacy – and a place in the degree programs and course offerings of the college curriculum. A good recent example since the early 1990s is "service learning." A recent episode in the coexistence of faculty and students has come about in instructional software used campus-wide for storing and broadcasting each course's syllabus, assignments, discussion threads, and course notes. One newcomer to the field proclaimed that it fixed the bugs and addressed the problems that undergraduates had disliked in an existing product marketed by a rival company. The new curricular software, in contrast, was "designed by students, for students." At tutorials to introduce faculty and staff to the new course software, the 23-year-old instructional technology laboratory assistant started the session by matter-of-factly telling the group, "As an instructor you may find this troublesome at times, but this is what your students want in a course website." Here was 21st-century evidence of the power of student consumerism to set the course and the priorities even for the professional experts: the tenured faculty.

Law and Order

In 1881 disgruntled students at Dartmouth College allied with faculty and alumni to revolt against a curmudgeon president.[17] They literally put him "on trial." What was the president's crime? He was charged with having resisted lively ideas, including curricular innovations. The interesting characteristic of this organized dissent was the consensus among students, faculty, and recent alumni. All agreed that the college should allow for scientific inquiry, scholarly exploration, and the addition of new fields to create a collegiate experience that was both interesting and useful. The president lost and the college won!

External Bodies and the Curriculum

Accrediting agencies warrant distinct note here. It's important to distinguish between the two types: *regional accreditation* refers to an overall review of the entire institution in a range of areas from fiscal procedures to institutional control and autonomy. In contrast, *specialized* accreditation refers to the periodic evaluation by a particular scholarly or professional association selected to monitor curricular standards for that field. Often this refers to some group representing professional certification or licensure – such as nursing, teacher education, physical therapy, social work, or law. The organizational tendency is for a specialized scholarly or professional group to recommend, even require, that a department add courses in the specialty. In other words, the Association to Advance Collegiate Schools of Business (AACSB) may demand that a university's undergraduate degree in business add more courses in accounting or finance to maintain accreditation. If so, there are two likely consequences: first, the number of credit hours a student must complete in order to graduate will go up. Second, the department may formally or informally encourage its students to take fewer electives or courses in the humanities or other fields outside the departmental major. The net result is to make degree completion longer while being characterized by greater specialization. The dilemma for a dean or department chair is that it forfeits some measure of creating its own program of study if it wishes to assure its students that the degree is professionally accredited. The other alternative – for a department to design its own degree requirements while forgoing professional accreditation – is a risky venture that may repel students as well as future employers who recruit at the campus.

Stealth Agents

The campus is usually assumed to be the scene of curricular crimes and achievements, but the momentum for change may come from all sorts of unexpected sources. It's useful to look at "horizontal history" which describes the influence of those organizations that are outside the campus and cut across the higher education landscape. How, for example, have major philanthropic foundations worked to introduce academic innovation at colleges and universities? Using this lens one unearths all sorts of interesting stories, such as the Carnegie Foundation for the Advancement of Teaching (CFAT), which used the incentive of a pension plan in the early 1900s to bring "standards" to college admissions and to the undergraduate course of study.[18] Or, one could point to the decades after World War II when a deliberate program sponsored by the Ford Foundation transformed the content and character of the Master's in Business Administration – the M.B.A. – nationwide by fostering model programs at five selected universities in which such fields as economics, political science, and statistics were infused into the faculty and curriculum in order to transform what was seen as the insularity of incumbent business administration programs.

Technology complicates our ability to decode puzzles of the curriculum, especially when new practices coexist with old ones. It is not unusual for a college instructor to teach in a single classroom that combines the teaching technologies of several eras – a slate blackboard developed in the 19th century; an overhead projector that was novel in 1955; a VCR made available in the 1980s; "compressed video" facilities popular in the early 1990s for interactive teaching at multiple sites; and now a "smart classroom" that combines a computer with a projector and Internet connection. Even the basic hardware of classroom furniture reflects changes, as for one class, chairs are arranged around a table for a seminar, yet in the following class meeting, chairs are rearranged into rows. Illustrative of the flux and confusion is a sign that warns instructors and students to "Restore Chairs to Their Proper Arrangement" – a message that is baffling to a well-intentioned new instructor who has no idea as to what the original configuration was. What exactly is the proper pedagogical arrangement for chairs? Not to beg the question, but a good answer depends on what the teaching material and audience is. To show how terminology goes full circle, on the Internet one can use the software program copyrighted as "Blackboard" or "Canvas" to post all course materials such as syllabi, assignments, and lecture notes, and even to host "discussion threads" for class members. One can use each and all of them in the same course. A more accurate observation is that an instructor may try to use all these – but each tool or medium has its problems that reduce its usefulness. At times there is no chalk for the blackboards, the overhead projector lamp is burned out. The VCR heads need cleaning. The new computer has no DVD capacity. Besides, DVDs by 2016 are becoming obsolete – in favor of Internet streaming. And, in some rare instances, a power outage or hacker causes the campus computer network to shut down temporarily – thus disrupting class instruction. With this array of formats and technological devices, has college instruction changed or not? What one finds in most colleges and universities is *layering* and *blending* – the coexistence of several strands, each originating at a different time, which converge to provide a quiver of teaching styles and tools. An innovation may have a dramatic impact. But it does not necessarily replace existing, older teaching tools.

The Origins of Innovation in Distance Learning

A few years ago the president of a state flagship university urged departmental faculties to create "distance learning" graduate programs. Certainly this could be viewed as an admirable effort by the university's administration to provide advanced degree programs to all parts of a large state. So, too, could it be seen as a shrewd political tactic, meant to alleviate pressure from the governor and from other state college presidents who had challenged the university's monopoly on providing doctoral programs. In the long run it is the faculty's effort to comply that will be watched closely. And it is the faculty who will be left wondering whether they can provide, via computer and the Internet, the sort of advising and mentoring that sets a sound doctoral program apart from a mere collection of courses. Already the university president has received favorable applause and publicity for this bold, innovative use of technology that purportedly extends access to these graduate programs.

The unfinished business, however, is that the faculty are left to manage a task they might not have chosen for themselves. So, how do we interpret this new program? Is it a laudable or dubious effort at change? Is it another case of familiar campus politics? A good example of the pedagogical transformations made possible by the Internet? A failure in the making, destined to be cited as evidence that faculty lack commitment to curricular innovation? Often what happens with quick innovations mandated from the top administration is that the new programs bog down or simply do not have a prompt pedagogical solution to what was an administrative problem. In such cases, top administrators often abandon the initiative. Such has been the case with universities that were relative latecomers to MOOCS and other Internet programs, reinforcing the adage that "nothing is so dated as yesterday's fashions," including curricular innovations.

COMPLEXITIES AND CONFLICTS: IMPLICATIONS FOR DECISION-MAKING

Accountability: The Evaluation of Teachers and Teaching

Where do the time and money go in a college's commitment to teaching and learning? This usually is distilled to a focus on teaching evaluations of instructors. This descends from on high, starting with concerns raised by influential groups outside the campus – such as gubernatorial candidates or a state legislature. For example, the genesis of end-of-course student evaluations of teachers surfaced in the late 1970s during a period of severe campus financial exigency. Here was yet another example where academic officials lagged behind and imitated student initiatives. At Harvard, Berkeley, and some other campuses, undergraduate editors started in the early 1950s to publish "underground guides" to courses and instructors, commentaries that included student evaluations and remarks. By 1978 presidents, provosts, and deans were sensitive to questions from the public and the state legislature about indifferent teaching and "deadwood" faculty because their salaries were high and their (lack of) work was counter-productive. A response was to require each instructor to be evaluated by students near the end of each academic term. The standard format was a sheet of multiple-choice responses to questions about course specifics, usually concluding with omnibus questions about overall evaluation of the course and of the instructor. These were analyzed and presented with a profile, usually using a scale of 1 to 4 or some equivalent – with a 4.0 representing an outstanding mean score. In some cases students also were allowed to write comments to supplement the quantitative evaluations.

Administrators were surprised to find that students gave their instructors high ratings and positive evaluations. Students found teaching to be sound and their teachers to be prepared, effective, and accessible. An unpleasant surprise for the administrative architects of teaching evaluations was that most student discontent gravitated toward such administrative matters as the disrepair of the classroom or limited access to laboratories and libraries. The unexpected consequence was that the academic profession tended to be praised – and vindicated from rumors of teaching malfeasance. What might have been conceived as a tool to root out bad teaching left the impression that administrators may well have been out of touch with students as consumers who were appreciative of dedicated teaching. What was an attempt to root out "bad apples" among college teachers spiraled into a new obligation that really did little to reward or improve teaching. Also awkward was that given budget crises, administrators really could not reward excellent teaching other than through perfunctory and gratuitous symbols. Furthermore, even when deans and department chairs documented cases where a professor was chronically sub-par in student evaluations of course teaching, administrative and legal protocols made it difficult to reform or fire an errant faculty member. Alas, however, there still remained one way in which administrators could use the new data to bring all professors to heel: the so-called "mean of means." According to this strategy, an instructor who received, for example, a teaching evaluation of 3.5 on a 4.0 scale probably would be regarded as very good or excellent. However, if the overall departmental mean teaching evaluation were 3.7, a punitive dean could argue that, statistically at least, the instructor with a 3.5 rating was "sub-par." The residual point is that the information colleges gather – and how they choose to use it in evaluation and decision-making – can reveal the underlying culture of the academic unit.

Apart from the internal student course evaluation data, colleges and universities are fortunate to have access to an impressive body of research about teaching and learning – studies whose findings are the results of sophisticated, imaginative qualitative and quantitative analytic methods and concepts.[19] Alexander Astin, Professor of Higher Education at UCLA, for example, made influential contributions with two books: *Four Critical Years*, published in 1978, and his 1993 sequel, *What Matters in College?* Some consistent findings over several years were that academically selective residential colleges characterized by full-time enrollment tended to show great gains in cognitive skills by undergraduates. What was not readily evident was the chemistry and culture that led to such a favorable finding. Was it the quality of the teaching? Perhaps the students represented a self-selected group that helped make the college experience particularly fulfilling in terms of intellectual development. Also provocative was that Astin's original allusion to "four critical years" as the time period for completing a bachelor's degree had become inaccurate when he undertook his sequel work in the early 1990s. A growing percentage of undergraduates were taking five to seven years to complete their B.A. or B.S.

This "time to degree" change signaled that numerous things were taking place within the undergraduate experience. A partial explanation was that colleges were enrolling an increasing number of non-traditional students who enrolled part time – and, hence, took more years to finish the degree. Another finding in the 1980s, especially at the University of California, Berkeley, was that many undergraduates were making poor course choices because they over-estimated their preparation for advanced courses. As a result they either failed or dropped these courses – a syndrome that meant they would require additional semesters to complete degree requirements.

Probing the causes and sources of good learning lead to some conceptual questions. Consider, for example, the *Atlantic* magazine article, quoted at the start of this chapter, that invoked the practice of "competency-based education." It did not necessarily confine student skills to course attendance. A student could gain course credit by demonstrating knowledge that may have been acquired earlier and outside the formal course. According to this compact, it mattered less how and where a student learned, so long as they could document and display their learning.

In contrast, a rubric in which one tries to figure out what the "value added" from taking a specific course or going to a particular college was for a student produces an interesting dilemma: does one applaud a college for its "value added," or, ultimately, do rewards go to those institutions whose students show the highest scores on various tests used as proxies for achievement? How one frames the system of measuring and giving credit for learning is consequential. The stakes are high. A financially strapped and underfunded HBCU (Historically Black College or University) that does not have the luxury of selective admissions may, in fact, help its students make great gains in learning – yet still lag behind metrics of net academic scores for prestigious, well-endowed institutions whose entering freshmen have had numerous advantages that place them at a high point in learning and achievement whether or not they have taken any college courses. There is no lack of data on student learning and student outcomes. More problematic and important is clearly identifying what one wishes to track and measure and, ultimately celebrate and reward in terms of educational achievement – and to make certain the analyses are significant and valid.

This seems obvious, but it warrants a reminder because there are landmark cases where lack of conceptual clarity and sound measures are disastrous. A prime example has been American higher education's reliance on student scores on the SAT for making decisions about admissions, awards, and placement.[20] For decades the official litany was that the SAT was the "Scholastic *Aptitude* Test" – a construct that allegedly meant a student's score could not be influenced by special preparation courses or practice tests. Eventually, the College Entrance Examination Board, after facing years of studies that questioned this characterization, conceded that the SAT was more accurately described as an *achievement* test in which a student's performance was, indeed, influenced by what one had studied, read, practiced, and so on. At least the acronym of SAT remained intact, although the nature – and consequence – of the nationally administered test changed drastically. Comparable questions of "reasonable doubt" frequently surface, as higher education analysts who study teaching and learning must continually ask, "What are we measuring? Is this significant? Is it accurate? Is it conceptually valid? Is this truly what we wish to reward or punish?"

Effectiveness and Efficiency

The two analytic concepts of effectiveness and efficiency often are used together – and often are viewed as synonymous. But they are not. *Efficiency* tends to deal with expenses (costs) as a ratio of result, with an emphasis on achieving some educational result at a low cost. It is neutral on matters of quality in achievement – how well or how much one learned. Can one educate in a relatively inexpensive way? For example, law school tends to be a relatively *efficient* educational program because a law lecture hall can seat a large number of students while requiring only a single professor per lecture or course. In contrast, the education of future medical doctors is relatively *inefficient* because it requires a large number of professionals, ranging from faculty to staff, plus expensive technology. In some cases within a college of medicine, the student–faculty ratio is inverted, with more faculty than students. Likewise, consider the contrast of a single professor who teaches a lecture class that enrolls 200 students versus a Ph.D. dissertation committee session in which five tenured, senior professors spend hours examining the research and presentation of a single student. Each activity is important – yet each requires human effort and resources in markedly different ways.

Effectiveness, in contrast, focuses on how well some goal has been achieved – regardless of costs. If, for example, our primary concern is for students to learn a lot and complete degrees, this may call for reliance on small class sizes. It also might be promoted by hiring experienced, advanced professors, or, at the very least, adding numerous teaching assistants. All these measures tend to make college education expensive and, hence, *inefficient* as a strategy to be *effective*.

At colleges that have open admission or are not selective in admission, choices deal with how to allocate the professional services of instructors and academic advisors. Working to assure or increase retention and success of students with relatively weak academic preparation costs more in time and professional expertise. Indeed, *retention* and *degree completion* have percolated to the top of college and university concerns about performance by students – and by faculty. Part of the concern is pragmatic in that a student who drops out represents forgone tuition revenue and an empty dormitory space, further compounded by the lost time and energy spent in recruiting that student. Obviously a high retention rate and a high percentage of degree completions, especially in four years, are indicators of a strong academic campus that probably is both effective and efficient. When a college struggles to raise what it considers to be a low retention and graduation rate, it is not easy to discern causes and consequences. Why are students leaving? Were they underprepared? Was teaching indifferent? Retention data, then, serves as a suggestion and estimate for more detailed explorations of what really is taking place within the campus and curriculum.

Most difficult to posit is what exactly is a reasonable expectation for retention? A comprehensive analysis of nationwide databases over 30 years by economists William G. Bowen, Matthew M. Chingos, and Michael S. McPherson in 2009 exhumed good insights on the matter.[21] Disconcerting to campus administrators who had been investing in academic advising and enrollment management was that for all the institutional intervention, undergraduate retention and bachelor's degree completion at flagship state universities had changed very little in the three decades between 1978 and 2008. The typical profile was of about a 60 percent graduation rate in five or six years. Retention, of course, is a gross measure and incomplete proxy for the teaching and learning that is taking place at a campus. It does provide a license and mandate to probe the educational climate and culture deeply to try to dig out the explanation as to why a particular college is high – or, low – in its retention and graduation. Perplexed academic planners today may find some consolation in the often overlooked fact that a century ago even at historic, prestigious colleges with full-time students, dropout rates were high and graduation rates were low.[22]

What Do Students Learn? How Do They Learn? How Do We Know What They Learn?

Gains in the increasing sophistication of evaluation and measurement in the social and behavioral sciences have opened the floodgates for various strategies to decipher the impact of the college experience on student learning.[23] This can be microscopic in systematic efforts to calibrate "value added" in a particular course. Or, to another extreme, psychologists with access to large comprehensive databases on students' standardized test scores work to make estimates on the differences in learning from one field to another, from one campus to another, and within student groups. The paradox of this abundance of resources on learning outcomes is that one has access to more and better deliberations, but little agreement on what the student learning data mean or signal in terms of effective and ineffective pedagogy. National tests such as the SAT, the ACT, the LSAT, the GRE, and the MCAT are readily used for making admissions decisions from one level to another – but are not adequate as sources on student learning in any meaningful way. Studies in cognitive science have been rich and interesting in suggesting the range of learning styles that a college student is likely to encounter, both within the formal curriculum and in other campus settings. On balance, however, there remains little consensus on translating the studies of learning into "best practices" for a department or a campus. Besides, there may be agreement on the efficacy of some arrangements – but implementation is cost-prohibitive and, hence, pretty much out of the question for many colleges. Knowing that college freshmen are more likely to learn well in a calculus class limited to an enrollment of ten students is good to know. It does not follow that a dean or provost is going to rush to adhere to this finding in practice because it is expensive. In a similar vein, if a president and provost glean from numerous studies that having students who enroll full time and live on campus enhances learning, it's still unlikely, perhaps impossible, for a commuter campus without residence halls to heed the research findings because their founding mission and finances probably mean that their destiny and commitment are as a commuter institution, even if this is not the optimally effective pedagogical arrangement.[24]

Further complicating the drawing of inferences from student learning data is the custom of relying on official proxies. Most departments or colleges publish a grading scale, noting that an "A" represents outstanding performance, all the way through to an "F," which signals failure in a course's examinations and graded assignments. But these standards and standardizations, of course, vary greatly from one department to another, and one institution to another. Grade inflation, an allegation that started to surface in the late 1960s, casts further suspicion on the proxy measures of course grades as indicators of how much and how well a student has learned.

CONNECTIONS AND QUESTIONS

Essential questions are clear: "Who is taught? Who teaches? What is taught?" The responses to these are complex because the issues are significant and the resolutions are not obvious. The major problem is not so much to gather data, but rather to try to figure out if information about student learning is either valid and/or significant.

The Hidden Curriculum

Each and every college or university can provide an official paper framework of degree requirements and course catalogs, supplemented by course syllabi to document its curriculum. However, these formal materials often reveal very little about the actual teaching and learning that occurs on that campus. In fact, all sorts of subtle, unwritten compacts govern the everyday behavior of faculty and students, and these compacts can vary widely from one era or place to another. In other words, although the curriculum may seem calm at the surface, changes could be happening in the depths – and out of sight.

At the Massachusetts Institute of Technology (MIT), for example, researchers discovered that a "hidden curriculum" put high priority on research in the "hard" sciences, contrary to the university's mission statement that ostensibly encouraged intellectual breadth. Even within a highly selected and well-prepared student body, classroom sessions were characterized by intense competition often accompanied by professors' predilection for bullying and badgering students in discussions. An implication from psychologist Benson Snyder's study was that the "hidden curriculum" in this variation was pervasive – and, also, often dysfunctional in identifying and educating intellectual talent.[25] Elsewhere, though, the official curriculum might conceal a very different pattern, such as the mutual avoidance common at many schools, where students and professors made the implicit compromise, "I won't bother you if you don't bother me!" Such was the case in the 19th century. Student memoirs from the 1890s indicate that the requirement of daily recitations gave rise to elaborate "cat-and-mouse" games between instructors and students. Both sides obeyed some ground rules of the classroom, with students earning from the instructor marks of "pass," "fail," or "draw" in their responses to the professor's questions. Each tried to trick the other. The one unforgiveable breach of conduct, according to all parties, was for a student to volunteer an earnest, serious intellectual opinion.[26]

Instructors and students may agree on information covered in readings and lectures, but with different understanding of its implications for future behavior. A good example is novelist Irwin Shaw's *Rich Man, Poor Man*, which includes an extended account of a liberal arts classroom around 1950. The instructor, a Professor Denton, emphasized in his lectures that the American economic system perpetuated social class inequities by means of a stilted tax system that favored the wealthy. Everyone agreed on the importance of the information, but with contrasting meanings. As one student, "Rudolph Jordache," recalled:

> The effect on the class, as far as Rudolph could discern, was not the one Denton sought. Rather than firing the students up with indignation and a burning desire to rally forth to do battle for reform, most of the students, Rudolph included, dreamed of the time when they themselves could reach the heights of wealth and power, so that they, too, like J.P. Morgan, could be exempt from what Denton called the legal enslavement of the electorate body.[27]

To an ambitious, business-oriented undergraduate, the responses to the professor's lectures were "not those of a disciple, but rather those of a spy in enemy territory." The professor's earnest lessons that exposed abuse actually perpetuated the inequitable system he had intended to reform!

Academic Ideals and Institutional Realities

The academic prestige or societal reputation of an institution does not always tell us much about the official curriculum's relationship to actual campus practices. Contrary to conventional wisdom, institutional prestige has not always depended on high academic performance. For example, at Yale in the early 1900s each class vied for the honor of having the *lowest* academic rating. In one yearbook, the Class of 1904 boasted "more gentlemen and fewer scholars than any other class in the memory of man." Not to be outdone, the Class of 1905 countered with the self-congratulatory claim:

> Never since the Heavenly Host
> With all the Titans fought
> Saw they a class whose scholarship
> Approached so close to naught.

There are other interesting variations on the "hidden curriculum." Architecture as an undergraduate field of study has a distinctive ethnography. Whatever the course catalog and official memoranda state, it is customary for architecture to be an inclusive, fully demanding course of study. Far beyond course meetings, students majoring in architecture spend night and day at their workshops and laboratory spaces, comparing notes and working on design projects. It is a 24/7 devotion – and socialization into the field means that novitiates accept this commitment which personifies the notion of a genuine vocation as a calling. One off-handed tribute to this distinctive ethos is that architecture often is a field that varsity athletes are either prohibited from or advised not to take as it would be impossible to reconcile with the demands of a sport's practices, group meetings, travel, and games. There are, of course, other distinctive characteristics of fields of study and the example of architecture is illustrative rather than exhaustive. An interesting exercise would be to survey the departments on campus and talk to students, alumni, and faculty about just what is the defining character of that particular field.

Once in a while a college or university is able to incorporate some shared experience that influences the undergraduate experience for all students. A good example of this is the consideration to have a degree requirement that each student must write a senior thesis. This, for example, is the custom at Princeton University. Interestingly, the senior thesis does not carry course credit. According to student accounts, they start thinking and talking with fellow students, seeking advice from upper division students as well as from faculty about potential topics as early as their freshman or sophomore year. By the middle of one's junior year, the senior thesis becomes a pervasive force in how students think about their education and translate it into an approved topic. Given the positive impact of such a requirement, why do many colleges and universities not follow the Princeton model and require a senior thesis? Among the excuses is that it involves a great deal of work, on the part of both students and faculty. Also, it provides no added tuition revenue to the institution nor does it provide added degree course credit to the student. For the faculty member who sponsors a student's senior thesis, it does not "count" on the tally of teaching load. Deliberation over whether to add a senior thesis requirement reveals in stark contrast the difference between *efficiency* and *effectiveness*. In other words, it's a substantial investment of time and resources for all. If not carried out with serious commitment from students and faculty, the mandatory senior thesis runs the risk of being a hollow obligatory activity that has marginal contribution to undergraduate education. Such responses indicate that many activities and forces compete for student and faculty time – and that one curricular option to an added requirement such as the senior thesis is just to say "No!"

The Elective System versus the Effective System

Not all academic problems have solutions. Rather, they do not always have agreeable, good solutions. Consider long-time complaints about the lock-step of letter grades for semester courses. From time to time, a college decides to do away with impersonal, inhumane letter grades. At the University of California, Santa Cruz, one innovation that characterized its curriculum at its founding was to substitute the instructor's narrative evaluation of a student's work in a course – with no letter grade. Starting in 1970 Brown University approved a new curriculum in which a student could opt in each course for a "Pass/No Pass" or a traditional letter grade. The obstacle is it takes a lot of time to write an evaluation for a student's work; it requires the instructor to know and read and listen closely to each student's work in the course; it is an exception to standard reporting; and is difficult for graduate schools to assess a student's transcript.

CONNECTIONS WITH DIVERSITY AND SOCIAL JUSTICE

Starting around 1970 American colleges and universities underwent a slow then persistent development in changing the curriculum to add new fields of study, especially interdisciplinary initiatives, to incorporate under-represented perspectives into a variety of courses: Women's Studies, Gender Studies, African American Studies, Native American Studies, Latino Studies, and Asian Studies are illustrative but not exhaustive of the trend. Typically the sequence is one of temporary and tentative offerings as "special topics" courses, which later progressed to formal status as a "program" and then approval as a degree-granting department. From the perspective of curricular offerings in, for example, 1955 or 1960, this innovation and expansion has been genuinely "transformational."

It has been healthy because it provides a partial remedy to what had been chronic neglect of perspectives, topics, and constituents. Historian Maresi Nerad of the University of Washington, for example, documented the long history of women as students and professors being confined to "the academic kitchen." The problem was not simply that women were quarantined into such fields as home economics, but also that when professors and chairs in this department petitioned for courses and facilities to make the field academically rigorous, they tended to be ignored.[28] Each under-represented student constituency has experienced its own variation on this theme. Academic transformation has included multiple changes. In addition to the creation of new formal departments and programs in, for example, women's studies and African American studies, equally impressive is the changing perspectives in the scholarship and teaching of numerous departments, including history, sociology, political science, English, education, and psychology to include the disciplinary study of under-represented groups. Furthermore, professional and scholarly accrediting agencies increasingly require departments to document how themes related to social justice and equity are included by design in syllabi and program requirements.

One widespread change in college teaching and learning since about 1980 that has significant implications for diversity and social justice has been the increasing awareness of civil behavior in the classroom. Accounts of professors in lecture halls and seminar rooms from earlier decades abound with matter-of-fact episodes of an instructor publicly humiliating a student, or belittling a particular opinion without due cause, or making inappropriate remarks or jokes that were racist, sexist, or discriminatory about ethnicity and religion – all at the expense of a particular individual or group, often with disproportionate impact on students who were members of minority and historically under-represented constituencies. Perhaps once tolerated or overlooked by faculty and administrators, today it is increasingly flagged as an abuse of power in the teacher–student relationship. This may still happen, but probably less so than in the past. And, today there is more codification of responsibilities of instructors and students on public conduct and civil behavior. It entails expansion of bureaucratic measures and procedures with staffing of ombud offices, appeals boards, and so on. Yet such innovations have provided procedural and structural means by which to try to change the academic culture toward one of mutual respect despite myriad differences with the campus curriculum and community.

CONCLUSION

Academic lethargy is to some degree illusory and exaggerated. Many of today's familiar practices were at one time the brave new worlds of teaching and learning: seminars, lectures, lab sessions, libraries, independent studies, field projects, sponsored internships, honors theses – one will not find these often, if at all, in the American undergraduate experience prior to 1890. Majors and minors once were considered innovations. So, too, was the elective system that gave undergraduates unprecedented power, either to satisfy genuine intellectual curiosity or to evade difficult work – or, perhaps, to avoid classes that started before noon! What one does find is that colleges and universities scrutinize what seems to be working – and what does not – in such familiar formats as the introductory science courses. A good example comes from some leading universities, including the University of California, Davis and the University of Colorado, Boulder. The traditional lecture format in some sections of introductory chemistry or physics has been "reinvented" to highly interactive "transformed classes" that still have a large enrollment yet provide a markedly different pedagogical style that forces both students and instructors to interact.[29] Central to this instructional innovation was a fundamental philosophical belief that an aim of introductory courses was to attract and retain student interest in the field – whereas in an earlier era, an aim of faculty might have been to weed out students and to discourage them from advanced study in challenging fields such as chemistry or biology.

One area of innovation often overlooked is the flourishing of interdisciplinary and multidisciplinary courses fields. In the 1960s American studies often brought together professors from such disparate departments as history, English, political science, and sociology. Today, a School of Public Policy draws from economists, lawyers, and political scientists. Nowhere is the synthesis of new combinations more evident than in the health sciences. In addition to "traditional" departments of biology, chemistry, and physics, most research universities also offer courses in biochemistry, biostatistics, bioengineering, and biophysics.

Alongside allegations that colleges and universities are slow to change one must add the counterpoint: namely, since American colleges are ambitious and even alert in competition for prestige, resources, and enrollments, they then are susceptible to expanding programs without great reflection or resources. This has been called "mission creep" and is characterized by a dean or provost who wishes to add advanced degree programs as a source of either prestige or added tuition revenues. A department that has traditionally offered a bachelor's degree aspires to add a master's program. A regional comprehensive university whose highest degree for years had been a master's degree sets out to add new doctoral programs.

A comparable attention to the need for student enrollments has taken place in the humanities. The chair of an English department observes that undergraduate enrollment is declining both in the number of students opting to major in English, and also in the registrations for English courses that satisfied General Education requirements. In response one finds the flourishing of a new graduate degree – the Master of Fine Arts in Writing. It is a prime example of academic consumerism in which English departments sensed a growing demand by both recent graduates and older alumni who wished to become serious writers in fiction, non-fiction, and poetry. The founding programs in the 1930s and 1940s included Stanford and the University of Iowa. But these were exceptional. In contrast, today there are more than 350 full-time accredited, degree-granting writing programs in American colleges and universities.[30] These are attractive to deans because they do not require investment in laboratories or cyclotrons. Expenses are low while student morale and net university tuition revenues are high.

In recent years, when budgeting models emphasize head-count enrollments in courses as sources for a college's revenue, mission creep operates in the reverse direction, i.e., going down rather than up the instructional pyramid. For example, a college of medicine traditionally known for focus on educating future M.D.s sets out to increase its tuition revenue base by adding new courses in physiology or anatomy for undergraduates throughout the university. Another expansion and diversification has been the practice of creating *certificates* – an approved cluster of courses which ascertain that a student has acquired expertise in some specialty. Comparable in some ways to the familiar practice of completing a "minor" field of study, the recent *certificate* phenomenon illustrates how the established curriculum does, indeed, have some resiliency to be mixed and matched to meet the demands of a new generation of undergraduate and graduate students. These combinations coagulate incumbent courses into new, creative syntheses – often accomplished without having to invest in new facilities. Another distinct but related development has been investment in honors colleges at flagship state universities – often decades after such models were initiated at private colleges such as Swarthmore College.[31]

Innovation within a college and university also takes place in teaching formats and styles. Within a single department, one typically has in any semester the following *kinds* of course: lecture, seminar, independent study, internship, practicum, fieldwork, honors seminar, and directed readings. Equally diverse are the kinds of assignment instructors use for students to demonstrate what they have learned. The multiple-choice examination shares the stage with essays, term papers, group projects, field notes, oral presentations, journals, laboratory experiment write-ups, PowerPoint presentations, music recitals for voice or instrument, honors theses, and even joint authored manuscripts that students submit for scholarly publication.

This latter example brings to the fore a counter-intuitive finding: "research universities" are not always the best places for students, especially undergraduates, to learn about and practice the details and delights of advanced scholarly research. And, the corollary is that colleges that do not claim to be "research universities" may, in fact, be a fertile ground for undergraduates to gain high-level experience in research. That is because at a small liberal arts college that does not offer master's or Ph.D. programs, a professor who is committed to both advanced research and teaching may look for talented research assistants from undergraduates – who in turn may be invited to be a partner on a research grant. It can include the student serving as a co-author on a published paper. This estimate is further reinforced by the well-documented fact that strong liberal arts colleges are the alma mater of a disproportionate number and percentage of future Ph.D. students who do enroll as graduate students at research universities. Such are the contours, complexities, and unexpected consequences of the curriculum in American higher education.

NOTES

1. Abraham Flexner, *Universities: American, English, German* (New York and London: Oxford University Press, 1930).
2. Frederick Rudolph, *Curriculum: A History of the American Undergraduate Course of Study since 1636* (San Francisco: Jossey-Bass, 1977) pp. 6–7.
3. Christopher Jencks and David Riesman, *The Academic Revolution* (Garden City, NY: Doubleday Anchor, 1968).
4. John R. Thelin, "A Legacy of Lethargy?: Curricular Change in Historical Perspective," *AAC&U Peer Review* (Summer 2000) vol. 2, no. 4, pp. 9–14.
5. Alana Semuels, "A College without Classes," *The Atlantic* (July 31, 2015).
6. Frederick Rudolph, *Curriculum: A History of the American Undergraduate Course of Study since 1636* (San Francisco: Jossey-Bass, 1977) pp. 12, 17.
7. "The Yale Report of 1828," in Richard Hofstadter and Wilson Smith, Editors, *American Higher Education: A Documentary History*, vol. 1 (Chicago: University of Chicago Press, 1961) pp. 275–291.
8. Rebecca Lowen, *Creating the Cold War University: The Transformation of Stanford* (Berkeley: University of California Press, 1997) pp. 158–160.
9. Earl Cheit, *The Useful Arts and the Liberal Tradition* (New York: McGraw-Hill, 1975).
10. Roger L. Geiger, Editor, *The American College in the Nineteenth Century* (Nashville, TN: Vanderbilt University Press, 2000).
11. Andrew E. Smith, "The Diploma Peddler: Dr. John Cook Bennett and the Christian College, New Albany, Indiana," *Indiana Magazine of History* (March 1994) vol. 90, pp. 26–47.
12. John R. Thelin, "Professors Shouldn't Be Afraid of Online Learning," *Inside Higher Ed* (July 10, 2012).
13. Drew Gilpin Faust, "Letter to the Editor," *New York Times* (July 29, 2015) p. A20.

14. John R. Thelin, "The Curriculum Crusades and the Conservative Backlash," *Change* (January/February 1992) pp. 17–23.
15. Peter Schmidt, "In a Fight for More Funds, Professors Quantify Colleges' Neglect of Instruction," *Chronicle of Higher Education* (July 8, 2014).
16. Frederick Rudolph, "The Extracurriculum," in *The American College and University: A History* (New York: Alfred A. Knopf, 1962) pp. 136–155.
17. Marilyn Tobias, *Old Dartmouth on Trial: The Transformation of the Academic Community in Nineteenth Century America* (New York: New York University Press, 1982).
18. Ellen Condliffe Lagemann, *Private Power for the Public Good: A History of the Carnegie Foundation for the Advancement of Teaching* (Middletown, CT: Wesleyan University Press, 1983).
19. Ernest T. Pascarella and Patrick Terenzini, *How College Affects Students: Findings and Insights from Twenty Years of Research* (San Francisco: Jossey-Bass, 1991). See also, their sequel volume dealing with "A Third Decade of Research," published in 2005.
20. Nicholas Lemann, *The Big Test: The Secret History of the American Meritocracy* (New York: Farrar, Strauss and Giroux, 1999).
21. William G. Bowen, Matthew M. Chingos, and Michael S. McPherson, *Crossing the Finish Line: Completing College at America's Public Universities* (Princeton, NJ and Oxford: Princeton University Press, 2009).
22. John R. Thelin, *The Attrition Tradition in American Higher Education* (Washington, D.C.: The American Enterprise Institute, 2010).
23. Ernest T. Pascarella and Patrick Terenzini, *How College Affects Students: Findings and Insights from Twenty Years of Research* (San Francisco: Jossey-Bass, 1991). See also, their sequel volume dealing with "A Third Decade of Research," published in 2005.
24. Alexander Astin, *What Matters in College?: Four Critical Years Revisited* (San Francisco: Jossey-Bass, 1993).
25. Benson Snyder, *The Hidden Curriculum* (New York: Alfred A. Knopf, 1971).
26. Henry Seidel Canby, *Alma Mater: The Gothic Age of the American College* (New York: Farrar & Rinehart, 1936).
27. Irwin J. Shaw, *Rich Man, Poor Man* (New York: Delacorte Press, 1969) pp. 282–283.
28. Maresi Nerad, *The Academic Kitchen: A Social History of Gender Stratification at the University of California, Berkeley* (Albany: State University of New York Press, 1999).
29. Richard Perez-Pena, "Colleges Reinvent Classes to Keep More Students in Science," *New York Times* (December 27, 2014) pp. A10, A12.
30. Diane Johnson, "They'll Make You a Writer!," *New York Review of Books* (November 7, 2013). See also, Mark McGurl, *The Program Era: Postwar Fiction and the Rise of Creative Writing* (Cambridge, MA: Harvard University Press, 2013).
31. Frank Bruni, "A Prudent College Path," *New York Times* (August 9, 2015) p. SR3.

Additional Readings

Alexander Astin, *What Matters in College?: Four Critical Years Revisited* (San Francisco: Jossey-Bass, 1993).
Mary Burgan, "In Defense of Lecturing," *Change* (November–December 2006) vol. 38, no. 6, pp. 30–34.
Earl Cheit, *The Useful Arts and the Liberal Tradition* (New York: McGraw-Hill, 1975).
Larry Cuban, *How Scholars Trumped Teachers: Change Without Reform in University Curriculum, Teaching, and Research, 1890–1990* (New York and London: Columbia University Teachers College Press, 1999).
Abraham Flexner, *Universities: American, English, German* (New York and London: Oxford University Press, 1930).
Roger Geiger, Editor, *The American College in the Nineteenth Century* (Nashville, TN: Vanderbilt University Press, 2001).
Clark Kerr, *The Uses of the University* (Cambridge, MA: Harvard University Press, 1963).
Ellen Condliffe Lagemann, *Private Power for the Public Good: A History of the Carnegie Foundation for the Advancement of Teaching* (Middletown, CT: Wesleyan University Press, 1983).
Arthur Levine, *Handbook on Undergraduate Curriculum* (San Francisco: Jossey-Bass, 1978) (published for the Carnegie Council on Higher Education).
Rebecca Lowen, *Creating the Cold War University: The Transformation of Stanford* (Berkeley: University of California Press, 1997).
Maresi Nerad, *The Academic Kitchen: A Social History of Gender Stratification at the University of California, Berkeley* (Albany: State University of New York Press, 1999).
Ernest T. Pascarella and Patrick T. Terenzini, *How College Affects Students: Findings and Insights from Twenty Years of Research* (San Francisco: Jossey-Bass, 1991).

Ernest T. Pascarella and Patrick T. Terenzini, *How College Affects Students: A Third Decade of Research* (San Francisco: Jossey-Bass, 2005).

Frederick Rudolph, *Curriculum: A History of the American Undergraduate Course of Study since 1636* (San Francisco: Jossey-Bass, 1977).

Benson Snyder, *The Hidden Curriculum* (New York: Alfred A. Knopf, 1971).

4

STUDENTS AND STUDENT LIFE

SETTING AND OVERVIEW

Each year more than 20 million students enroll at colleges and universities in the United States.[1] To make sense out of this large group, this chapter examines the profiles and patterns of student life – by institutional type, fields of study, and other characteristics. This is an analysis of the differences and complexities associated with universal access to higher education. Consider that on August 10, 2014, newspaper articles reported that minorities were a majority in American public high school enrollments. In a few years this demographic procession would head to college and create yet another new profile of those enrolling in postsecondary education.

Whether parsed by race, gender, ethnicity, religion, age, native language, geography, or social class, it is the diversity of American students that shapes the college experience. At the same time, along with this diversification, there are strands of continuity and privilege in who goes where to college. This chapter provides a glimpse at this fluidity and complexity. It is grounded in the premise that campus life is a setting in which students create worlds on their own terms. Students' interaction with adult groups helps shape the student drama in a mix of cooperation and contention with their elders. The adults include administrators, parents, police, counselors, faculty, and student affairs professionals.

How important are students to American higher education? The first alert is that when the American public and college officials mention students, they are probably referring to undergraduates. Graduate students are a sizeable part of the total student enrollment – but usually are invisible in the general discussions, especially in feature articles and announcements about the arrival of new students. Today just about all college and university presidents give high priority to welcoming undergraduates who are freshmen students and their parents. It often starts with special summer orientation sessions and campus visits, long before the fall semester and classes start. Some universities have freshmen students and their parents join together for a convocation with the director of career planning for a communal commitment to a sustained effort to integrate family, home, classroom, and support services in providing a new student optimal preparation for future job preparation.

About a week prior to the start of fall semester classes, a president and the Vice President for Student Affairs typically send out memos and other public announcements to encourage the entire campus community to join in to welcome and help new students as they move in to dorms – and into the organizations of campus life. This is not just directed at the student affairs professionals or academic advisors. All faculty and staff are implored and enlisted to pitch in as a way of putting a human (and humane) face on life and work within the college. It aims to break down specialization and professional expertise to foster a new holistic dedication to student success. The logic is that the college gains this sense of commitment when the same professor who teaches calculus also shows she can help a student carry suitcases and laptop computers to the new residential suite. One staple of university public relations is to have candid photographs of the president, dressed in casual clothes, welcoming parents and also pitching in to do useful work, especially unloading boxes from a freshman student's family car trunk in front of the state-of-the-art dormitory. The dominant theme is that even the leaders and top administrators are caring – and that *students* are the foremost concern of the entire college or university. A good deal of the socializing and socialization is intended both to make students feel at home and confident – and also to promote integration into the campus, which, one hopes, will increase student retention and prompt graduation.

For an interesting contrast from 130 years earlier, when students often were left to their own initiatives and resourcefulness on campus, consider the following account of the start of the academic year in September 1895:

> When I first saw the college town it was late September and I, a somewhat frightened boy from home, was dragging a suit-case full of books across the exciting spaces of the Green. The books were for the final cram before entrance examinations…. What I saw before me that afternoon across the Green would have been disillusioning if I had been realistic. The rather dingy halls, boxes ornamented with pseudo Gothic or Byzantine, were little like my dream, and the beautifully simple relics of the old college of brick Colonial were much too simple to mean anything to my taste tutored in the nineties. But I was far from being realistic, so that in a second of time, between Green and campus, I had dropped, with the easy inconsequentiality of youth, all illusions of architectural grandeur for the real thing, college life.

The student recalled:

> Close at hand or described from memory, it seemed more like a haven for American youth, a little space of time in which energy had its outlet, and where the young made a world to suit themselves, which, for a while at least, the adult world was to accept at surprisingly near the college estimate.

It was no less than a fantastic voyage in which, "Overnight we were to step through an opening door into tradition, a usable, sympathetic tradition of youth. It was our privilege to be born again, painlessly, and without introspection. All this, which I felt, not spoke, was true." Initiation, baptism, rebirth – all themes one associates with a spiritual transformation were, for a cohort of new college students, no less than induction into citizenship into a new community:

> Therefore, like all that confident generation, I accepted the college as I found it, and believed in its life and its spirit with a fanatic devotion. I saw that the boys

who were strolling that day in the latter nineties down the autumn streets were as easily distinguishable among the town crowds as being from another world. The town was only their background, and I picked them out in their turtle-neck sweaters under the briefest of top coats, as a dog sees only other dogs on a busy road. There was an arrogant and enchanting irresponsibility in their behavior which was intoxicating. I longed to get rid of my suitcase with its irrelevant books, and into a sweater which I saw to be obligatory – to dress like them, to be like them.[2]

College students in 1890, whether at Yale or at the University of Minnesota, at Smith College or elsewhere, would have been incredulous and uncomfortable with having parents and assistant deans of student affairs helping them move into dormitories and have a formal orientation to campus life. Nonetheless, in both the late 19th and early 21st centuries, students entering college is an exciting and important rite of passage in American life. Beyond that commonality, the two contrasting anecdotes about arrival and moving in suggest changes in students and in college officials. One important contribution of this chapter is to explore and perhaps explain those similarities and differences associated with regulations, supervisions, and what might be termed "support systems."

One shared characteristic for those of us who study and work in higher education, whether in the past or present, is that we need to take students seriously. This includes their values, hopes, dreams – and foibles. Failure to do so is a recipe for disaster. Consider the following public statement in 1964 by the late, great Clark Kerr who, as President of the University of California, gave a landmark speech about the university and the emerging "Knowledge Industry." In the aftermath of telling a national audience about the importance of universities for economic growth, he turned to the topic of student activities and student activism, with a world-weary tone:

> One of the most distressful tasks of a university president is to pretend that the protest and outrage of each new generation of undergraduates is really fresh and meaningful. In fact, it is one of the most predictable controversies that we know – the participants go through a ritual of hackneyed complaints almost as ancient as academe, believing that what is said is radical and new.[3]

Clark Kerr was a wise person and great leader. Nonetheless, this was not the kind of attitude one needs in teaching and in working with students. The only credible way to explain his gaffe is that, indeed, sometimes smart and wise people say dumb things. Kerr, who had been featured on the cover of *Time* magazine as the uncontested leader of the new design of a growing American higher education, had earned that accolade. And, even he – or, rather, especially he – paid dearly for his oversight in which he dismissed student concerns and discontents as trite and petulant. Thank goodness, years after his having been fired by Governor Ronald Reagan in 1967, Kerr rebounded and went on to a brilliant role as a thoughtful analyst and leader of higher education values and issues. Important to note is that he grew sideburns along with acknowledging belatedly and good-naturedly that he had misjudged students and their discontents. So, let's learn from Kerr's example – and take students seriously even if their liturgy and rituals of complaint and concern seem naive, obvious, or hackneyed to us.

ISSUES

An enduring depiction of the bittersweet emotions associated with going to college in American life is conveyed by Norman Rockwell's illustration, "Breaking Home Ties," which appeared as a cover for the *Saturday Evening Post* for the September 25, 1954 issue. It struck a chord and a nerve with the readers of the largest circulation magazine in the United States. Today, we would refer to the young man as a "first-generation college student." The term probably was not used in an earlier era – but the deep sentiments are familiar. The father, a hardworking and grizzled rancher, shares with most Americans the belief that a college education is important as a part of and path to a "better life." Yet such a venture by his son may well mean that a child will find other opportunities and explorations that may take him off the farm and far from home.

One may notice the "State University" pennant decal on the young man's suitcase. The illustration meshes well with the following account by historian Frederick Rudolph:

> "State College" would come to have as homely and honest a ring about it as any of the numerous institutions identified with agrarian America. State Fair. Fourth of July picnic. Church social. Saturday night in town. None of these came any closer than "State College" in evoking an appreciation of wholesome rural values – clean, hardworking, honest young men and women, determined to live good lives in a good world, gone down or up to the state college, there to broaden their horizons and to perfect their ingrained common sense.[4]

The realities of going to college certainly have complexities beyond the ideals conveyed by these memoirs. Still, there is a shared American experience in which all families, rich or poor, privileged or impoverished, have both anxieties and hopes for their daughters and sons who enroll at college. In contrast to the rural, first-generation family from years ago, consider the experience of Hollywood actor Rob Lowe in 2014. Coming to terms with parenthood and his own teenage son's going away to college, he described himself as "unprepared" and wrote:

> I'm trying to remember when I felt like this before.... When was the last time my heart was breaking?... Today is my son Matthew's last night home before college. I have been emotionally blindsided. I know that this is a rite many have been through, that this is nothing unique. I know that this is all good news; my son will go to a great school, something we as a family have worked hard at for many years. I know that this is his finest hour. But looking at his suitcases on his bed, his New England Patriots posters on the wall, and his dog watching him pack, sends me out of the room to a hidden corner where I can't stop crying.[5]

Rob Lowe probably would have much in common with the hardworking rancher in 1954 whose own son was headed for "State College." And, in both cases, the family dog was witness to the new college student's packing and departure. Sometimes life mirrors art. Lowe himself three decades earlier starred in the 1984 movie, *Oxford Blues* – the improbable, albeit entertaining, fictional story of a young man who works as a parking attendant at a Las Vegas casino and then finagles his way to Oxford University on the strength of his skill in crew. The interesting twist is that when the topic is going to college, the real stories for *all* families surpass the fiction of Hollywood if you are seeking drama and depth.

This poignant observation is not hyperbole. Consider the comments by the President of the United States, Barack Obama, in May 2016 when news media featured the story that his daughter, Malia Obama, announced that she was accepting Harvard College's admission offer – and planned to enroll after taking off for a "gap year." President Obama politely but firmly declined an invitation to be the commencement speaker at Sidwell Friends School in Washington, D.C., from which his daughter was graduating. President Obama told the press:

> Malia is more than ready to leave, but I'm not ready for her to leave.... And I was asked if I would speak at her graduation and I said, "Absolutely not," because I'm going to be sitting there with dark glasses, sobbing.

Going to college and leaving home persist as an All-American experience, eliciting a range of powerful, even contradictory emotions in all families.[6]

How should one connect these fragmented illustrations and episodes of a shared American experience into context? The late sociologist Martin Trow, a professor at the University of California, Berkeley, wrote a seminal essay in 1970 about the transition from elite to mass to universal higher education. It persists as a tribute to the power of conceptual insight – an example of scholarship that was concise but prescient and enduring. The essence of his argument was that quantitative changes in higher education enrollments carried with them qualitative changes.

What this general claim meant specifically was that between 1900 and 1970, the United States had experienced – and promoted – a remarkable transformation in the number and percentage of late adolescents who would go on to college – or, more precisely, to some form of postsecondary education beyond high school. The summary statistic was that in an era of elite education, about 5 percent of 18- to 21-year-olds went to college – and this characterized the situation in the United States at the start of World War I. A generation later, prior to World War II, access to higher education had expanded to about 33 percent of high school graduates who went on to college. This was described as commitment to "mass higher education." By 1970 some states and institutions had bought into the proposition of universal access to higher education: namely, enrolling 60 percent or more of high school graduates. This is the situation we inherit in the early 21st century, with both prospects and problems.[7]

The major issues involving students deal with the following questions:

Who Goes to College? Where Do They Go? Why Do They Go?

The gulf between what sociologist Martin Trow called "elite higher education" a century ago and "universal higher education" today gains clarity when grounded in data to document the change. In 1900 slightly fewer than 30,000 students were awarded bachelor's degrees. This was about 2 percent of young Americans around age 21. In 2005 the number of bachelor's degree recipients was 1.44 million – 48 times the number of 1900, and now represented about 36 percent of the national 21-year-old age cohort. Furthermore, both the number and kind of institutions have increased.

This massive change in scope presents a problem with generalizations and summaries about student enrollment patterns today because the summaries tease us by presenting categories that create an overview of who goes where to college – with helpful breakdowns by numerous demographic variables of race, ethnicity, and family background matched with institutional types. The risk is that often the exceptions and smaller groupings have disproportionate importance or influence. For example, more than 77 percent of all students are enrolled in public institutions. Keep in mind that in 1950, the split was around 50 percent in state universities and 50 percent in private colleges. That decisive numerical and percentage advantage of public institutions today hardly precludes the presence of the independent (or, private) college sector, which confers an inordinate percentage of bachelor's degrees and includes the most academically selective institutions within all of American higher education. The reapportionment can also be misleading because it might erroneously suggest that the independent colleges have shrunk. In fact, they have expanded enrollments – it's just that the public sector enrollment has grown at a very high rate for many decades. Another important detail is that a large part of the public sector expansion has been via the founding of new two-year community colleges. The insight to carry away just from this one example is that the diversity (and diverse consequences) of college are revealed as one carefully disaggregates the overall summaries.

Consider this disaggregation exercise by focusing on selected variables. A century ago white men, most of whom were Protestant, between the ages of 18 and 22 dominated the American campus. Some of this hegemony persists. Whites, for example, today represent 66 percent of all students. Yet preoccupation with that majority figure turns attention from the important change which shows that each year an increasing percentage of college students are from other under-represented groups. Women, once often excluded from many colleges and overall under-represented, now constitute about 55 percent of college students. Furthermore, most single-gender institutions, whether historically "all men" or "all women," have become coeducational. This demographic change along gender lines becomes more pronounced as one tracks the increasing gains and parity of women in graduate programs and advanced professional schools. Indeed, women represent a majority of students both for higher education overall and with a decided plurality at many campuses. If Rip Van Winkle had been a college student who fell asleep during a lecture in 1900 and then was awakened from his slumber today, he would have been incredulous at the number of women who were his classmates. Given his predilection for sleeping rather than studying, he may have been upset but not surprised that women had substantially higher grade point averages than their male classmates – and carried away a disproportionate number of academic awards such as election to Phi Beta Kappa and admission to graduate programs. When the topic is student life, history matters – as these changes attest.

Another key finding from dissecting the overall profile is that the increases both in numbers and percentages of African American and Hispanic students tend to be concentrated in the public two-year community colleges. Hence, the gross gains in access are not distributed evenly across the spectrum of institutions. What we have in American higher education is a sophisticated sorting machine. As a nation we do well in accommodating somewhere and somehow most students who wish to pursue formal studies beyond high school. These gains in access are far more impressive than our track record in providing all students equity and choice. The public community college, a genuine American innovation, accounts for about one-third of all enrollments. This understates the sector's presence because it is a "two-year" institution. Its main and growing role is that more than half of all college freshmen start their studies at a community college. Furthermore, community colleges seldom offer a residential campus. Their tuition charges are relatively low and their students overwhelmingly come from modest income families and include a large percentage of students from racial and ethnic minorities.

The historical perspective in connecting past and present is that the United States has accommodated diversity in student enrollments primarily by allowing special interest groups to create their own colleges. This was a pragmatic, often convenient, strategy to evade questions of desegregation. And, often, it fulfilled the slogan of "Separate but Unequal," as newcomers often lacked the endowments and donors that the oldest surviving colleges enjoyed. One exception gained momentum in the late 19th century when many of the newly founded colleges for women had brand new campus classrooms, dormitories, libraries, and laboratories whose quality surpassed most established colleges – thanks to the generosity of founding philanthropists.

The most visible example of this was the proliferation of denominational colleges just within Protestantism. Congregationalists, Presbyterians, Episcopalians, Lutherans, Methodists, Baptists, and Quakers were just some of the college builders. Catholic colleges served the dual purpose of providing access both for a religious group that had faced exclusion and discrimination as newcomers and for providing a port of entry for immigrants, such as Irish, Italian, French, and Slavic families. Women were grudgingly allowed to pursue studies beyond high school – but, usually, were limited to what were called "female seminaries" and, then, women's colleges.

Historical change has been a mixed blessing for underserved constituencies and the colleges that traditionally provided access for these students. Good examples are Black colleges and universities. Prior to nationwide racial desegregation, these institutions (sometimes referred to via the acronym "HBCUs" – Historically Black College or University – which included both state and independent colleges) provided access and affordability to African American students either formally excluded or informally shunted aside by predominantly White institutions. However, since the 1970s the reshuffling of recruitment and admissions has meant that traditional matches of students and institutions have changed. A large number of African American students no longer enroll at Black colleges and universities, and Black colleges and universities sometimes now alter their mission and composition toward greater racial inclusion.

This historic model of collegiate accommodation without equity or integration across institutional categories also includes Native American students. In the late 19th century it took the form of the patronizing federally funded "Indian Schools," such as the Carlisle School in Pennsylvania or the Sherman Institute in California. In the 20th century its new category was numerous Tribal Colleges. The 1890 Morrill Act simultaneously increased access overall while it reinforced legal traditions of racial segregation, as those states with dual school systems who did not want to desegregate their existing all-white state colleges were eligible to receive federal land grant monies if they did agree to create state colleges for African Americans.

Another note of caution in perusing the contemporary statistics is that the categories impose, perhaps unconsciously, a simplistic notion of a college student's path from freshman year on. The ideal is a construct in which one presumes a student spends four years at the same campus, declares a major, and completes the bachelor's degree. Or, another variation is that this same student has academic problems as a freshman or sophomore and drops out. However, both the success story and the tale of failure are too simplistic. They represent extremes and miss the nuances of the numerous permutations of students' patterns.

Clifford Adelman, long-time researcher for the U.S. Department of Education, looked at thousands of transcripts as the foundation of a fundamental rethinking of college student's dynamics.[8] What Adelman found was that some conventional categories, such as state of residence, meant little in terms of college choice – especially if one lived in a border area adjacent to several states. Dropping out was joined by stopping out. Many students transfer – often more than one time. Our presumption usually is that a student leaves a college because she or he has low grades. Sometimes, however, students leave a particular college because they find it academically inadequate and seek a better institutional match. Or, they may have trouble paying tuition at Alma Mater and find a more affordable option elsewhere. As research scholars such as Vincent Tinto and John Braxton have shown in thoughtful, systematic analyses, why students leave – and, perhaps, return to – college is not always obvious.[9]

The conventional notion of the four-year undergraduate experience persists – but even registrars and institutional research directors have changed categories to allow for five, six or seven years to degree completion as normal. One explanation for some of the changes in statistical patterns is the changing profile of American college students. For the past three decades the term "non-traditional student" has gained in usage, as it connotes students who are adults, probably older than 24 years, and either delayed or interrupted their college studies in order to focus on family, jobs, or other options. Many opt to be part-time students – a decision that, of course, extends the number of years to bachelor degree completion. On balance, what were once considered the "exceptions" among college students have gained increasing presence as the "new normal."

Reliance on additional, specialized statistical categories provides correlations that may explain differences among institutions in the student experience on their campus. The growth of the "for-profit" sector increases the diversity of college enrollments – and at the same time increases the difficulty of making generalizations about college students. The University of Phoenix, for example, enrolls 600,000 students each year – almost all of whom are non-traditional in that they are older, combining degree studies with full-time jobs, and are taking courses primarily on the Internet. This does not erase the "traditional college campus" student and experience, but creates more of a mosaic.

The best and convenient indicator of modest income is whether a particular student qualifies for a federal Pell Grant. Each college, in turn, can be reviewed in terms of the percentage of its students that are Pell Grant recipients. A low percentage suggests that a college draws from a relatively affluent student application pool. An interesting note on this litmus test is that the correlations are not always obvious. One can find, for example, state universities with less than 10 percent of their student body receiving Pell Grants – despite the national rhetoric of "public" higher education as affordable and accessible.

What Are the Patterns of Student Life?

The term *college culture* refers to patterns of student life within a campus. It encompasses *collective* behaviors and values – as distinguished from the mere compilation of *aggregate* data about numerous individual students. Furthermore, the concept emphasizes continuity of these social patterns, in contrast to transient or haphazard episodes. In sum, a college culture is a complex social network that endures over time through elaborate rituals and symbols. It includes, for example, inviting a student to be a member of a prestigious honor society or extending a pledge of initiation as part of a sorority or fraternity. And, it also includes the scars one acquires when turned down for inclusion in such groups. As such it has become an integral rite of passage for late adolescents in American society. Thanks to the seminal work of sociologist Burton Clark, characterizations of college culture emphasize institutional belief and loyalty as central to affiliation.[10] These help to create and to transmit a college's culture to newcomers over generations, contributing to a legendary memory about campus events, often called the "institutional saga."[11]

An excellent source for a literature review of college culture as explored from a variety of disciplines is the monograph by George Kuh and Elizabeth Whitt, *The Invisible Tapestry* (1988). Placing this concept within research on college students is covered in two classic works: Nevitt Sanford's pioneering 1961 anthology, *The American College: A Psychological and Social Interpretation of the Higher Learning*, and more recently, Ernest Pascarella and Patrick Terenzini's *How College Affects Students: A Third Generation of Research* (2005).

Observation of college culture has a rich tradition first associated with memoirs about the clustering tendencies of students at medieval universities. At the University of Paris and elsewhere in Europe, migrating students in the 13th and 14th centuries formed associations reflecting their national roots. Banding together, they acquired distinctive colors and codes, giving rise to the characterization of "Town versus Gown." This convention of wearing academic gowns distinguished university students and faculty from local citizens. As a result of student clashes with landlords and merchants around charges of price gouging on rents, food, and wine, higher authorities such as popes, bishops, and kings bestowed permanent legal protections on university students. Within this framework of academic rights and responsibilities, student cultures flourished.[12]

In contrast to the urban universities on the European continent and in Scotland, English universities around the 16th century underwent a structural change, and the college cultures within these universities veered in a new direction. At Oxford and Cambridge, the crucial unit became the residential "colleges" that formed a honeycomb within the university framework. So, although the university conferred degrees and administered examinations, undergraduate life and learning took place within a self-contained residential college. Each college had its own charter, endowment, faculty, curriculum, admissions plans, and traditions of student life. Construction of a spacious university campus and its college quadrangles gave rise by the late 19th century to an elaborate array of teams and clubs that were run by students, for students. A student could join with fellow debaters, athletes, or musicians whose shared experience often surpassed the formal course of studies as a source of a student's primary identity.

This "collegiate way" was successfully transplanted to colleges of the American colonies and, later, the United States.[13] Groups formed within the college flourished as extracurricular activities and were a major source of socialization into American life. Faculty accounts of student life in the late 19th century invoked colorful metaphors. Undergraduates at Yale brought to mind thoroughbred ponies at play, cantering and frolicking in the campus meadow.[14] Shifting from turf to surf, another depiction was that of fellow passengers in a boat – a common fate while rowing from freshmen to senior status. Students who had to drop out due to poor grades were mourned as sailors who had fallen overboard and missed all the good times. One archaeologist whose 2010 study focused on campus life at the University of California, Berkeley in the late 19th and early 20th centuries concluded that the masculine subcultures of fraternities and clubs brought to mind a Peter Pan world buffered from adult responsibilities and serious choices, which she called "The Lost Boys of Zeta Psi."[15]

A college culture socializes assorted students into a coherent group. In the United States this usually has focused undergraduates. However, the concept is sufficiently elastic to include other constituencies, including graduate students and professional school students. Indeed, one of the classic studies of college culture is *The Boys in White*, based on an ethnographic study of medical students.[16] Sociologists Burton Clark and Martin Trow in 1967 identified the concept of collegiate "student subcultures." According to their model, a campus was a fluid configuration of subgroups, many of which provided a student with a primary affiliation within the context of the general campus culture. This conceptualization allowed an analyst to impose a loose template on any particular college or university – and then refine the relative strength of each subculture both to confirm the universal model and simultaneously to capture the precise variations for the case study. Also, Clark and Trow's typology was neutral. It did not say that the persistence of a strong subculture of fraternities and sororities was good or bad; rather, the researcher had to identify and interpret on a case-by-case basis. It even allowed for subtle, important distinctions. One might find that a campus had a distinctive subculture – for example, being a place where performing arts enjoyed a strong tradition of prestige – yet there was no imperative that this same subculture would be, or should be, found elsewhere.

A good illustration of the capacity for undergraduates to cluster into groups and to create an elaborate status system of power and influence comes from Henry Seidel Canby's 1936 memoir about his freshman year at Yale in 1895:

> And there were the Strong Silent Men I had read about in the newspapers, the football and crew heroes, calming the crowded field by the full-breasted dignity of the white letters on their blue sweaters. And there were other slighter figures in tiny top coats with upturned collars, who seemed to exercise an equal authority. These, I were told, were the Big Men, the managers, the powers behind college life, more important, because brainier, than the athletes … I felt, in a leap of the imagination, as if I were being naturalized into a new government, more vital than any I had known, as indeed I was.[17]

So, although one can speak generally about a college culture, historians and sociologists have taken such first-hand observations and parsed the broad concept of "student life" into components. Helen Lefkowitz Horowitz characterized campus life, whether in the 17th or 20th century, as having three layers: "insiders," "outsiders," and "rebels." Groupings were related to prestige, power, wealth, race/ethnicity, and gender. She identified what she called the "College Men" as the group with inordinate power to set the tone and reward system for the entire institution. Later, with the emergence of women's colleges as well as coeducation, women negotiated and navigated their distinctive collectivities within each campus.[18]

Horowitz noted that the "College Women" could be added to her original concept. "Rebels" referred to relatively small groups – ranging from reform-minded student editors to innovative clubs – who did not seek the affirmation of the dominant "inside" culture. "Outsiders" typically were those students denied full acceptance into the prestigious groups, suggested today by the social exclusion of "nerds" or racial minorities from fraternities and sororities.

Central to research and theories on college cultures is that students have power to create a world of their own within the institutional regulations and campus environment. One editor of *The Saturday Review* described college cultures to be no less than a "city-state" established by students within the institution. For students in the late 19th century the collective motto was, "Don't Let Your Studies Interfere with Your Education." Implicit in this good-natured banner was the serious fact that college culture was not the same as those of the faculty or administration. College culture demonstrated the ability to defer when necessary to official rules. Yet the enduring college was in the quite separate arena by and for students themselves.

If a dominant college culture has the capacity to resist control by adult groups, it also has the leverage to split the student body into factions. Although admission to a college was supposed to provide entrée to campus citizenship, this usually worked only so long as a college was small and homogeneous. However, when enrollments expanded rapidly and included increasing student diversity in religion, ethnicity, family income, and geography, a major function (often a dysfunction) of college cultures was to break down shared experiences of students and to fragment them by exclusion *within* the campus. This relates closely to historian Horowitz's typology of "insiders" and "outsiders" within a student body. This was controversial when membership in an internal subculture was based less on merit and more on ascribed characteristics. In other words, students were frequently and systematically excluded from membership in eating clubs, fraternities, or student government on the basis of race, gender, ethnicity, or religion – regardless of their academic achievements.

The power of exclusion was a formidable detriment to integration of diversity for women and for racial and ethnic minorities. One partial response was for "outsider" groups to form their own subcultures. Hence, one finds exclusion from established fraternities may have led to creation of Jewish fraternities or African American fraternities as a counterbalance to the dominant Greek letter system. Cultural patterns reinforced by the Greek letter societies were complex. To one extreme, they were hailed for promoting loyalty to fellow members and teamwork. To another extreme, fraternities were often associated with encouraging ritualized student drinking and extended immaturity. In sum, the crucial research question was whether a college culture was inclusive or exclusive in campus life.

If there is an area where there is substantial lag between the composition of the student body and the structures and cultures of campus life it is in the area of gender. Even though women have strong representation as a plurality of enrollments within a college or university, and also receive a disproportionate percentage of merit awards in academic and extracurricular pursuits, many coeducational institutions still convey a decidedly dated masculine tone in terms of power and institutional character. Reconciling this gender gap persists as a major challenge for coeducational institutions.

Research on higher education since the 1950s has drawn heavily from the behavioral sciences. Yet for the serious study of college culture, an appropriate and sorely needed discipline has been anthropology. Perhaps one of the most original and provocative studies of college cultures was the 1989 book by anthropologist Michael Moffat, *Coming of Age in New Jersey*.[19] Relying on strategies of fieldwork usually associated with the analysis of distant cultures, Moffat chose to undertake an ethnographic study of a dormitory at a large state university – his own campus, Rutgers University in New Jersey. An important feature of the campus residence hall was that it was coeducational. Moffat focused on how young women and men cooperated to create an environment with norms and values in the relatively new format where members of both sexes shared living spaces. The findings were counter to fears of concerned parents and clergy. Coeducational dormitories did not promote licentious behavior or rampant promiscuity. To the contrary, students emphasized respect for privacy and mutual concern for the welfare of members of the dormitory community. Instead of amorous relations, men and women tended more toward sibling interactions of brothers and sisters. A promising sign of continued reliance on anthropology to study college culture is the book *My Freshman Year* (Nathan, 2005) and Armstrong and Hamilton's *Paying for the Party* (2013).

The influence of "Greek life" in the form of fraternities and sororities has persisted since the late 19th century. Today, when one visits a college campus in early or mid-August, weeks before classes start, it is not uncommon to see groups of young women wearing formal attire, singing songs and undergoing initiations on lawns in 90-degree heat – all part of sorority rush. Such activities reaffirm the claim that it is in the extracurricular associations that one finds some of the most demanding features of college life. The hegemony of such student organizations as Greek letter fraternities and sororities to dominate American college culture for centuries now faces a new perspective. Whereas selection into a fraternity or sorority was long seen by insiders and outsiders as advantageous to adult success, signs of change have surfaced. At the University of California, Santa Barbara, for example, membership in a fraternity tended to be counter-productive as a base from which to gain campus leadership. And at Yale in the early 1990s there were surprising signs that some seniors who had been "tapped" for membership in elite senior societies were making decisions that would have been unthinkable to earlier generations of undergraduates: some were rejecting membership invitations. One explanation was that exclusive student groups not based on merit are seen as detrimental to adult life, especially public office, where discrimination by gender, race, religion, or ethnicity have become a liability.

How this groundswell of refusal develops in the 21st century will be important. A recent sign of change is that in September 2015 some of Harvard's historically all-male clubs, such as the Spee Club, invited women students to be members. This voluntary act, although perhaps a sign of progressive change, had not come quickly or easily. The Harvard administration had demanded in 1984 that the clubs start admitting women. The response of the clubs was to resist that demand and opt to sever all ties with the university and move off campus.[20]

A fertile area of reconsideration involves attention to students' family affiliations as part of college life, based on criticisms of an earlier model in which a new student who entered college was seen as poised to discard family affiliation to become a citizen in the campus.[21] Many sociologists saw this transitional split as necessary if students were to internalize new cognitive skills, values, curriculum, and networks. It was captured in the expression of "breaking home ties" as a feature of "going away to college." A revised perspective is that a college experience need not require this break. For many students, maintaining family ties has been recast as helpful to navigating the new demands of campus life. This is an important deliberation given concern about undergraduate attrition and alienation.[22]

The diversity of American higher education also has meant that *college culture* requires recognition of new constituencies. Commuter students often have been ignored as marginal or disengaged. This neglect makes little sense if commuters dominate an institution's student profile. One novel study focused on "the commuter's alma mater" to identify how non-traditional students worked among themselves and with campus officials to reconfigure services and facilities to fit their social patterns.[23] Another group of newcomers are "first-generation" college students – those whose parents did not go to college and, hence, for whom there probably is much less "anticipatory socialization" into college life than their fellow classmates.

CHARACTERS AND CONSTITUENTS

A glance at a student handbook today reveals an elaborate system of official college support services. Typically, the Vice President for Student Affairs holds a position on the President's Council and is the administrator to whom numerous offices ultimately report. The elevation and expansion of the Vice President for Student Affairs goes in several, often opposite, directions. To one extreme, it feeds the expectations of parents as well as students that colleges provide services once incidental to the institutional responsibility – career placement, internships, study abroad, and student engagement. On the other hand, it intrudes on students' self-determination in establishing highly legalistic boards of student conduct – often pitting students against students. These also mean the end of informal, intramural hearings – shifting to high stakes, with lawyers on all sides.

The origins of this arrangement stretch back to the early 20th century with the creation of the Dean of Students as a full-time, responsible campus position. As coeducation of men and women within the same campus became more prevalent, a college then had a distinct Dean of Men and a Dean of Women. The division of labor did not include parity, as the Dean of Men emerged as a powerful figure both within and outside the campus. He was no less than the "enforcer" for numerous regulations – including the strict admonition to freshmen that they must heed the warning: "three C's, a D – and keep your name out of the newspapers." Whatever nonchalance male students, especially members of fraternities, might exhibit toward professors, they feared the rules and wrath of the Dean of Men. According to historian Robert Schwartz, the Dean of Men acquired prestige as the primary "face" of the college at ritualized festivities such as "parents' weekend" – often having as much public renown as the president.[24] And, when a male student faced a campus conduct hearing, parents would see the dean's authority clearly – and often with trepidation. This power ascended into the post-World War II era – and then tapered.

The position of Dean of Women has a different story – both in the personality types attracted to the role and to the evolution of the office. Historian Jana Nidiffer's analysis of pioneering Deans of Women finds that they were more than "wise and pious matrons" and hardly fit the popular stereotype as "curmudgeons and house mothers." Most brought strong academic credentials and imaginative skills to the new administrative position. In contrast to the "enforcer" role of the Dean of Men, the Deans of Women were advocates for advancement and extension of higher education for women, including integration of formal academic studies and the extracurriculum. In addition to achieving scholarly respect for their own teaching and research, several were promoted to university positions with responsibilities for the entire campus, not just women – such as academic dean, provost, and president.[25]

Over the past three decades most colleges and universities dissolved the dual "Dean of Men" and "Dean of Women" offices, opting instead for the "Dean of Students" nomenclature, which eventually was elevated to "Vice President for Student Affairs." A familiar figure in student life was the "Baby Dean" – usually a recent alumnus who had been recruited by the senior Dean of Students to join the staff to provide a connection between the administration and the undergraduates. Whether motivated by a concern about discipline of students or a desire to make the campus experience meaningful (and comfortable), expansion of resources and roles under the student affairs umbrella has been the conventional pattern. Whenever a campus admitted a new constituency, creating a specialized office related to student life was a customary organizational response. Today, a campus usually has a vice president for diversity, an associate provost for student success, a director of career planning, an academic ombud, and a financial counselor. Some of the forerunners to these positions existed in an earlier era – but their time commitment, office space, and personnel budgets were limited. At some colleges with a full-time, residential student body, it is not unusual to find such positions as directors of community engagement, coordinator of experiential education, a childcare coordinator, and a spouse/partner employment counselor.[26] Editors of the *New York Times Magazine* in 2015 characterized these innovations and emphases as creating a new world for undergraduates, anointed as "Collegeland."[27] At Brown University the proliferation of student activities led some faculty to talk about the campus as "Camp Bruno."

In addition to the specialization of new student affairs staff positions, professionalization included the growth of national associations representing each administrative niche. Also, the student affairs structure included annual election of a board of student affairs representatives who, in concert with the vice president's office, oversaw distribution of funding for various student activities – revenues made possible by mandatory student fees. These services, combined with a Student Union building and facilities such as bookstores, theaters, and recreation centers, were the visible signs that student life occupied a formal, substantial place within the city-state of the American campus. In the 21st century the appeal and influence of student affairs were sufficiently great that deans of student affairs switched from speaking of their activities as "extracurricular" in favor of the new term "co-curricular."

COMPLEXITIES AND CONFLICTS: IMPLICATIONS FOR DECISION-MAKING

The major complexity of college students is the perception that these are a highly accomplished, self-selected group within the American population. We expect the campus and student life to be different – i.e., safer and better – than the "outside" world. Also, college often is characterized as a time and place where students are given both the latitude and obligation to explore and make choices (and mistakes). But does this become problematic? Is the role of the college to provide a total environment shaped by the principle of *in loco parentis*?

Eventually these concerns include the safety and welfare of students within a student culture. Sexual harassment, physical harm, and bodily injury along with the scars and stigmas of humiliation, exclusion, and rejection were syndromes that caused alarm. In 1986 at Lehigh University one student stalked and eventually raped and murdered a classmate. It not only jarred the popular expectations of a bucolic, self-regulating residential campus – it exposed the vulnerability and liabilities of a campus and its offices to an exceptional but real event. It led to the passage in 1990 of the Jeanne Clery Disclosure of Campus Security Policy and Campus Crime Statistics Act, which requires all colleges and universities receiving federal student financial aid monies to report and keep statistical records on crimes within the campus area.

A complication of this heinous crime was the role of campus counseling and health services. How does a university office that has professional knowledge of a troubled student's health problems mesh with confidentiality of student patient records – and preemptive or preventive measures within campus life? Such criminal acts and allegations, along with sexual harassment, rape, misbehavior related to alcohol, and bullying, also put a spotlight on the strengths and weaknesses of traditional campus structures for hearing cases involving misconduct. The congruence of campus committees and their administering justice is not at all one and the same as procedures and protocol in courts of law in civil society. Reliance on a volunteer board of students, faculty, and student affairs officials can be ill-suited to handling serious charges.

Furthermore, colleges and universities nationwide are facing lawsuits from victims who say schools failed to address student trauma, investigate complaints, or bring charges against alleged attackers. One response is for colleges to bolster their legal counsel and its connection to student life by requiring training programs for student affairs officers involved in campus judiciary cases. Usually this implies increased administrative and legal concern for the rights of students as victims. Yet the increase in litigious patterns also has pressed in another direction – namely, concern over rights and due process for the student charged with the crime. At the same time, in recent years, some colleges are considering what is termed "an alternative approach to campus justice." As an editorial in the *New York Times* noted on September 11, 2015:

> As colleges and universities in the United States, Canada and elsewhere search for ways to handle campus misconduct, some have explored a practice called restorative justice, which focuses on repairing the harm done to the victim and the surrounding community. It has been used as an alternative or a complement to traditional disciplinary processes in cases of sexual harassment, racist behavior, alcohol violations, and other offenses.

In addition (and sometimes related) to student conduct, the issue of student mental health and official college services have gone from being marginal concerns to center stage in campus life. A debate surfaces with questions about the roles and responsibilities of colleges in this domain. By 2015 the *Chronicle of Higher Education* published a report dealing with "An Epidemic of Anguish," and the problem that, "Overwhelmed by demand for mental-health care, colleges face conflicts in choosing how to respond."[28] The genesis of demand for expanded mental health services has multiple sources. First, students today may come from families whose health plans and personal situations allow students to make extended use of therapy and counseling. Parents then expect a college to continue this by providing professional counselors as part of the tuition and fees package. Second, colleges themselves must take some responsibility for the increased student demand. After all, recommendation from student affairs professionals and their national organizations has been to persuade colleges to provide an increasing array of services and resources to students on campus.

Since colleges have taken the initiative in providing recreation centers, elaborate dining halls, career planning offices, financial aid representatives, credit unions on campus, activities, clubs, and health insurance, why, then, shouldn't mental health services follow as a logical extension? Colleges, of course, will vary greatly in what they agree to provide, especially as part of the standard slate of tuition and fees. Should students with self-reported conditions of depression seek help outside campus, through family health plans? Or, should the campus be the locus of mental health services and solutions? If a student reports a serious mental health problem, should college officials favor having the student take a leave from college studies? What ought to be the basis for re-admission? Must a student then provide documentation of having completed therapy or treatment? Who will bear the expenses of mental health services? Each campus will deliberate this bundling of issues within its administrative ranks and with students.

Whatever the resolutions on this cluster of questions, the overriding campus trend is that mental health services will become increasingly familiar in the array of services – and those colleges' liabilities and responsibilities most likely will increase substantially. At some campuses, there will be some constituencies who offer a counter-response along the lines that colleges are drifting toward the "coddling of the American student" and are setting a dangerous precedent for extending college services (and responsibilities) into non-educational areas. In addition to the proliferation of facilities and resources for accommodating mental health services, there is a related concern that "In the name of emotional well-being college students are increasingly demanding protection from words and ideas they don't like."[29]

CONNECTIONS AND QUESTIONS

If one were to rely on the images of students projected by colleges on their websites and view books, the dominant theme would be of late adolescents exuding joy combined with earnest research in laboratories, and participating enthusiastically (and knowledgeably) in class discussions. This image is reinforced nationwide on college football game day as major television network cameras pan across the stadium section reserved for students and then again in the brief promotional videos the colleges are permitted to broadcast during the game's half-time. These are not necessarily inaccurate, but they are incomplete.

Given these exaggerations, how do we learn about student life to gain a more complete perspective? We are fortunate to have readily available and varied sources of data, ranging from databases to student memoirs. Each year the *Chronicle of Higher Education* publishes at the start of the fall semester a comprehensive Almanac, much of which is devoted to analyzing college students. Furthermore, the Almanac's charts and graphs are drawn from numerous detailed studies compiled by the National Center for Educational Statistics – fertile sources for even more insights. Some additional annual reports include Beloit College's Mindset project, which since 1998 has published a survey on what college freshmen know – and do not know:

> Members of the entering college class of 2019 were mostly born in 1997 and have never licked a postage stamp, have assumed that Wi-Fi is an entitlement, and have no first-hand experience of Princess Diana's charismatic celebrity.
>
> Each August since 1998, Beloit College has released the Beloit College Mindset List, providing a look at the cultural touchstones that shape the lives of students entering college this fall. For this year's entering class there has always been Google; Email, informal to previous Millennials, has emerged as "the new formal"

for them, while texting and other social media serve as the wild and wooly mode of exchange. Teachers have had to work overtime encouraging them to move beyond the Web and consult sources in books and journals. And Poland has always been a member of NATO, suggesting that Mr. Putin's heartburn about Western expansion is at least as old as the new college kids are.

According to Charles Westerberg, Director of the Liberal Arts in Practice Center and Brannon-Ballard Professor of Sociology at Beloit College, "The Class of 2019 will enter college with high technology an increasing factor in how and even what they learn," and

> They will encounter difficult discussions about privilege, race, and sexual assault on campus. They may think of the "last century" as the twentieth, not the nineteenth, so they will need ever wider perspectives about the burgeoning mass of information that will be heading their way. And they will need a keen ability to decipher what is the same and what has changed with respect to many of these issues.

This alerts adult readers to the divide across generations in terms of knowledge (and ignorance) based on age group experiences and frames of reference. Another fertile source of insights on college students comes from Indiana University, which sponsors the National Survey of Student Engagement. These reports provide a healthy counter to the superficial images on television and college websites because they remind us that although the American campus is a remarkable place, it is a complex environment and there can, indeed, be "trouble in paradise."

The broadcast of a glossy image in view books, websites, and other mass media and social media may help college presidents and boards – and parents and prospective students – reassure one another that all is well on the American campus. But at some point these dominant images can be dysfunctional and counter-productive because, ultimately, recognition and discovery of exceptions to this imagery become extremely stark and disconcerting. In other words, large percentages of students face myriad problems and frustrations, ranging from avoiding having to drop out due to financial problems, concern about course grades due to lack of adequate academic preparation, or fear of being social outcasts due to rejection by some student organizations.

One change in the connections between American culture and colleges is that many popular magazines used to feature in August or September their annual "back to college" issues for fashions, fads, and trends. These were mass-circulation publications geared to college students as readers and consumers. But this has diminished since about 1990. The implication for this decline is that the American high school has become the locus to set the tone in terms of students' music, fashion, and fads, and its influence is carried by graduating high school seniors from below on to the college campus. If this analysis is correct, it is an interesting reversal of trends. It manifests itself with allegations that some colleges represent an extension of high school in terms of ambience and atmosphere. Yet publications geared toward adults – namely, the parents of college-bound students – show constant, perhaps increasing, scrutiny of college trends and higher education themes.

Worth noting is that college culture is a topic long central to an American tradition of memoirs and fiction.[30] A challenge for social and behavioral scientists is how to give adequate consideration to this genre of American literature as an important source of data as part of their own systematic scholarly research. It could mean reliance on Owen Johnson's 1912 novel, *Stover at Yale*, to describe the round of life and values at Yale and other historic East Coast campuses prior to World War I. In the early 2000s a novel such as Tom Wolfe's *I Am Charlotte Simmons* provided American readers with a dramatized glimpse from an adult perspective on the party culture of the prestigious, expensive "DuPont University" (considered to be a thinly veiled pseudonym for Duke University), with emphasis on the protagonist, a young woman who was a first-generation college student from a modest income family in the North Carolina mountains. Today, one might consider how well or how poorly a popular Hollywood movie such as *Animal House* (1978) provides a reasonably accurate portrayal of fraternities and sororities as strong influences on the college culture of a state university. A limit of popular media, however, is that their need for dramatic effect seldom can be fulfilled by a focus on real students whose activities and lives may not lend themselves to a Hollywood-style depiction.

CONNECTIONS WITH DIVERSITY AND SOCIAL JUSTICE

The central question for probing how a campus promotes diversity and social justice is whether gains in admission and access are followed by comparable advances and opportunities for new students *within* campus life and activities. Earlier we noted that American higher education is a formidable sorting machine at the juncture of admissions. Equally powerful is the sorting mechanism for life inside a campus. And here data are troubling. Consider a 2013 book by Elizabeth A. Armstrong and Laura T. Hamilton, *Paying for the Party: How College Maintains Inequality*. In a study of a Midwestern state university, the authors found a distressing syndrome: undergraduates from affluent and educated families gravitated toward their own orbit – often in sororities. Social class and family income differences were accentuated – as were perks of campus awards, honors, and preparation for adult life after leaving college. Furthermore, such findings often were connected to a larger social trend among high-achieving college students and recent alumni – namely that their long-term aspirations focused on financial success rather than service. As one political scientist concluded, on balance, "They'd Much Rather Be Rich!"[31]

A dilemma with such works is that they may mask other remarkable simultaneous trends and individual exceptions. For example, beginning in the 1990s student-originated philanthropy and service activities started and flourished. Nonprofit groups such as Teach for America has shown sustained effort and success in attracting recent graduates of prestigious colleges to consider teaching in public schools, often in underserved locales. It is not that the data are contradictory, but rather, complex and still not fully understood.

Sociologists Richard Arum and Josipa Roksa's study found that college students who are "meandering," especially those from low-income backgrounds, were "aimless, demoralized and with fewer chances than their more affluent peers to recoup lost opportunities."[32] A critical response is to note that those first-generation college students from modest income families who do flourish and thrive in the educational activities of a prominent college are exceptions to the rule. Such achievement and acceptance are not impossible, but they are difficult and unusual. So, the question is whether a college and its student culture reinforce social class differences. Or, does it provide genuine opportunities to reward and seek out talent from across the entire student body?

These recent sobering studies need to be reconciled with a long line of higher education research that has indicated that college students as alumni show marked gains in civic participation, voting behavior, cognitive skills, and societal concerns, along with the pragmatic concern about enhanced future earnings – all of which have been the foundation for our nation's "investment in learning."[33] A good way to think about and explore the question is to see whether or not a particular campus has made the transition from access to inclusion of newcomers – namely, students from groups that previously were excluded or under-represented. One model is for the campus life, including both students and formal student activities, to promote social justice and civil rights by allowing minority students to be both apart and a part. This has meant, for example, official prohibition of exclusion on the basis of non-merit factors such as race, gender, and religion. And, at the same time, the college and university have a responsibility to assure that the student activities structure provides funding, space, and permissions for, for example, an African American Student Union or a club or association for lesbian, gay, bisexual, transgender (LGBT) students. These dual assurances are an imperative because a campus culture changes slowly, with historic privileges tending to persist despite changes in admissions.

Students with Disabilities

Are colleges leaders or followers in making the campus accessible to traditionally under-represented groups? Nowhere is this more evident than in the provisions and place for students with disabilities. Historically, colleges have resisted – or asked for exemptions and reprieves – in accommodating students who are members of groups already welcomed into public school systems. Special education, with an emphasis on "mainstreaming" in the 1980s, is a good example where policies were pioneered in elementary and high schools – and slow to percolate to colleges and universities. The Americans with Disabilities Act of 1990 was for years reduced to a campus debate on whether a college had the obligation and/or money to install wheelchair ramps to campus buildings. This focus trivialized a broader concern in both the definition and accommodation of disabilities. Today most colleges have created an office of student disabilities to provide services, assistance, counsel, and liaisons with faculty and staff. There's little room for debate or disagreement – it is a matter of compliance with federal law. Most impressive has been how workable many innovations have been.

CONCLUSION

For students, going to college endures as a remarkable opportunity and experience. Yet it is fraught with problems and pitfalls – along with differential benefits. Put another way, data overwhelmingly indicate that failure to go to college and to complete a bachelor's degree puts one at a serious disadvantage in gaining a legitimate place in American life. The disheartening codicil is that opting to go to college – and to complete a degree – is uncertain in guaranteeing a place in our national economy and society. The luster has dulled on some of the expectations and returns, such as a "good job" and a respected place in the community, which for decades had been readily accepted as part of the college experience.

If diversity is a strength of American higher education, then the differential and uneven returns on going to college are its less positive side effect. Today affluent and educated families tend to transmit to their children more affluence and educational achievement at each stage of sorting and selection in the college experience. At best, college provides a multiplier effect in which experiences, associations, contacts, and networks compound both the good times and long-term benefits of higher education. Outside this circle, the experience for a student as part of student life has become uncertain and perplexing to both its participants and observers. College matters – but precisely *how* varies substantially among students and among institutions.

NOTES

1. "Students," in *Almanac of Higher Education, 2015–16* (Washington, D.C.: Chronicle of Higher Education, 2015) p. 33.
2. Henry Seidel Canby, "College Life," in *Alma Mater: The Gothic Age of the American College* (New York: Farrar & Rinehart, 1936) pp. 23–26.
3. Clark Kerr, "The Knowledge Industry" speech of 1964, videotape segment in Mark Kitchell, Director, *Berkeley in the Sixties* (New York: First Run Features, 1990).
4. Frederick Rudolph, *The American College and University: A History* (New York: Alfred A. Knopf, 1962) p. 264.
5. Rob Lowe, "Unprepared: Rob Lowe on Sending His Son off to College," *Slate* (May 15, 2014).
6. Julie Hirschfeld Davis and Nicholas Fandos, "White House Letter: A First Daughter Rebels, Sort of, by Choosing Harvard," *New York Times* (May 2, 2016) p. A13.
7. Martin Trow, "Reflections on the Transition from Elite to Mass to Universal Higher Education," *Daedalus* (Winter 1970) vol. 99, pp. 1–42.
8. Clifford Adelman, *The Tool Box Revisited: Paths to Degree Completion from High School Through College* (Washington, D.C.: United States Department of Education, 2006).
9. Vincent Tinto, *Leaving College: Rethinking Causes and Cures of Student Attrition* (Chicago: University of Chicago Press, 1987); John M. Braxton, Editor, *Reworking the Student Departure Puzzle* (Nashville, TN: Vanderbilt University Press, 2000).
10. Burton R. Clark, "Belief and Loyalty in College Organization," *Journal of Higher Education* (June 1971) vol. 42, no. 6, pp. 499–515.
11. Burton R. Clark, *The Distinctive College: Antioch, Swarthmore, & Reed* (Chicago: Aldine, 1970).
12. Charles Homer Haskins, *The Rise of the Universities* (Ithaca, NY: Cornell University, 1925).
13. Frederick Rudolph, *The American College and University: A History* (New York: Alfred A. Knopf, 1962) pp. 86–109.
14. George Santayana, "A Glimpse of Yale," *Harvard Monthly* (1892) vol. 15, pp. 89–96.
15. Laurie A. Wilkie, *The Lost Boys of Zeta Psi: A Historical Archaeology of Masculinity at a University Fraternity* (Berkeley and Los Angeles: University of California Press, 2010).
16. Howard Becker, Blanche Geer, Everett C. Hughes, and Anselm L. Strauss, *Boys in White: Student Culture in Medical School* (Chicago: University of Chicago Press, 1961).
17. Henry Seidel Canby, "College Life," in *Alma Mater: The Gothic Age of the American College* (New York: Farrar & Rinehart, 1936) pp. 23–26.
18. Helen Lefkowitz Horowitz, *Campus Life: Undergraduate Cultures from the End of the Eighteenth Century to the Present* (New York: Alfred A. Knopf, 1987).
19. Michael J. Moffat, *Coming of Age in New Jersey: College and American Culture* (New Brunswick, NJ: Rutgers University, 1989).
20. Katherine Q. Seelye and Jess Bidgood, "With an Invitation, a Gender Barrier at Harvard Falls," *New York Times* (September 12, 2015) p. A15.
21. Vincent Tinto, *Leaving College: Rethinking Causes and Cures of Student Attrition* (Chicago: University of Chicago Press, 1987).
22. John M. Braxton, Editor, *Reworking the Student Departure Puzzle* (Nashville, TN: Vanderbilt University Press, 2000).
23. Tisa Ann Mason, *The Commuter's Alma Mater: Profiles of College Student Experiences at a Commuter Institution* (Williamsburg, VA: The College of William & Mary Ph.D. Dissertation, 1993).

24. Robert Schwartz, *Deans of Men and the Shaping of Modern College Culture* (New York: Palgrave Macmillan, 2010).
25. Jana Nidiffer, *Pioneering Deans of Women: More Than Wise and Pious Matrons* (New York: Columbia University Teachers College Press, 2000).
26. Andrew Hacker, "They'd Much Rather Be Rich," *New York Review of Books* (October 11, 2007).
27. "The Education Issue: Collegeland," *New York Times Magazine* (September 13, 2015).
28. Robin Wilson, "An Epidemic of Anguish," *Chronicle of Higher Education* (August 31, 2015) (Special Report) pp. A1, A38–A45.
29. Greg Lukianoff, and Jonathan Haidt, "The Coddling of the American Mind," *The Atlantic* (September 2015).
30. John E. Kramer, *The American College Novel: An Annotated Bibliography*, 2nd edn (Lanham, MD: Scarecrow, 2004); Christian K. Anderson and John R. Thelin, "Campus Life Revealed: Tracking Down the Rich Resources of American Collegiate Fiction," *Journal of Higher Education* (January–February 2009) vol. 80, no. 1, pp. 106–113.
31. Andrew Hacker, "They'd Much Rather Be Rich," *New York Review of Books* (October 11, 2007).
32. Richard Arum and Josipa Roksa, *Aspiring Adults Adrift: Tentative Transitions of College Graduates* (Chicago: University of Chicago Press, 2014). See also, Andrew Delbanco, "Our Universities: The Outrageous Reality," *New York Review of Books* (July 9, 2015) pp. 38–41.
33. Howard R. Bowen, *Investment in Learning: The Individual and Social Value of American Higher Education* (San Francisco: Jossey-Bass, 1977); Ernest Pascarella and Patrick Terenzini, *How College Affects Students: A Third Generation of Research* (San Francisco: Jossey-Bass, 2005).

Additional Readings

Clifford Adelman, *The Tool Box Revisited: Paths to Degree Completion from High School Through College* (Washington, D.C.: United States Department of Education, 2006).
Elizabeth A. Armstrong and Laura T. Hamilton, *Paying for the Party: How College Maintains Inequality* (Cambridge, MA: Harvard University Press, 2013).
Richard Arum and Josipa Roksa, *Aspiring Adults: Tentative Transitions of College Graduates* (Chicago: University of Chicago Press, 2014).
Howard Becker, Blanche Geer, Everett C. Hughes, and Anselm L. Strauss, *Boys in White: Student Culture in Medical School* (Chicago: University of Chicago Press, 1961).
John M. Braxton, Editor, *Reworking the Student Departure Puzzle* (Nashville, TN: Vanderbilt University Press, 2000).
Henry Seidel Canby, *Alma Mater: The Gothic Age of the American College* (New York: Farrar & Rinehart, 1936).
Burton R. Clark, "Belief and Loyalty in College Organization," *Journal of Higher Education* (June 1971) vol. 42, no. 6, pp. 499–515.
Burton R. Clark and Martin Trow, *Determinants of College Student Subcultures* (Berkeley, CA: Center for Research and Development in Higher Education, 1967).
Andrew Delbanco, "Our Universities: The Outrageous Reality," *New York Review of Books* (July 9, 2015) pp. 38–41.
Andrew Hacker, "They'd Much Rather Be Rich," *New York Review of Books* (October 11, 2007).
Charles Homer Haskins, *The Rise of the Universities* (Ithaca, NY: Cornell University, 1925).
Helen Lefkowitz Horowitz, *Campus Life: Undergraduate Cultures from the End of the Eighteenth Century to the Present* (New York: Alfred A. Knopf, 1987).
John E. Kramer, *The American College Novel: An Annotated Bibliography*, 2nd edn (Lanham, MD: Scarecrow, 2004).
George D. Kuh and Elizabeth J. Whitt, *The Invisible Tapestry: Culture in American Colleges and Universities* (Washington, D.C.: ASHE-ERIC, 1988).
Greg Lukianoff and Jonathan Haidt, "The Coddling of the American Mind," *The Atlantic* (September 2015).
Julie Lythcott-Haims, *How to Raise an Adult: Break Free of the Over-Parenting Trap and Prepare Your Kid for Success* (New York: Henry Holt and Company, 2015).
Michael J. Moffat, *Coming of Age in New Jersey: College and American Culture* (New Brunswick, NJ: Rutgers University, 1989).
Rebekah Nathan, *My Freshman Year* (Ithaca, NY: Cornell University, 2005).
Jana Nidiffer, *Pioneering Deans of Women: More Than Wise and Pious Matrons* (New York: Columbia University Teachers College Press, 2000).
Ernest Pascarella and Patrick Terenzini, *How College Affects Students: A Third Generation of Research* (San Francisco: Jossey-Bass, 2005).
Frederick Rudolph, *The American College and University: A History* (New York: Alfred A. Knopf, 1962).

Nevitt Sanford, Editor, *The American College: A Psychological and Social Interpretation of the Higher Learning* (New York: Wiley, 1962).

John H. Schuh, Susan R. Jones, Shaun R. Harper, and Associates, *Student Services: A Handbook for the Profession*, 5th edn (San Francisco: Jossey-Bass, 2011).

Robert Schwartz, *Deans of Men and the Shaping of Modern College Culture* (New York: Palgrave Macmillan, 2010).

Benson R. Snyder, *The Hidden Curriculum* (New York: Alfred A. Knopf, 1971).

Vincent Tinto, *Leaving College: Rethinking Causes and Cures of Student Attrition* (Chicago: University of Chicago Press, 1987).

5

FACULTY AND THE ACADEMIC PROFESSION

SETTING AND OVERVIEW

The academic profession has a central place in the academic procession. But precisely *where* remains a source of both mystery and debate. No one denies that professors are important to higher education, yet few can agree as to how they fit – or, *should* fit – into the structure and life of colleges and universities. There also is serious concern about where the academic procession is heading. A 1971 book brought attention to "academics in retreat!"[1] More recently, Jack Schuster wrote in 2011 about "the professoriate's perilous path."[2] Prof. Mary Burgan of Indiana University – a faculty leader and president of the American Association of University Professors (AAUP) – devoted her 1998 book to the question, "Whatever happened to the faculty?"[3] Did they disappear? Are they missing in action? Even Burgan was puzzled by the peculiar absence of her fellows as a collective force. Do the faculty lead the academic procession? Or, perhaps they are muddled in the middle? The consensus was that professors had become symptomatic of "drift and decision making in higher education."

Answering some of those questions will be part of Chapter 6 dealing with *governance and organization* in higher education. The first order of business here is to go to essential questions about faculty *roles*. What do faculty do? What are their commitments? How do they devote their time on a daily, annual, and career basis? What are the reward structures for the academic profession? How do each of these queries vary across categories of colleges and universities? What are the particular rights and responsibilities faculty members face according to their rank or title? To follow from Chapter 3 dealing with teaching and learning, this chapter looks critically and systematically at the characteristics, patterns, power, and behavior of professors. It includes similarities and differences across fields and disciplines across the varied types of colleges and universities that hire (and fire) faculty. It provides attention to defining key concepts and charting features in tenure and promotion and hiring. It focuses on discussion of the growing reliance on part-time and adjunct instructors. Coverage also provides an introduction to the principles and practice of "academic freedom," including discussion of connections with the U.S. Constitution, and the roles of scholarly associations for various disciplines along with such national bodies as the AAUP. It sketches a profile of professional career paths, including potholes, detours, and dead-ends. Finally, the academic guild will be analyzed in comparison and contrast with other learned professions, such as law, business, and medicine.

Analysis includes reconciling images and realities about the faculty in American higher education. That is necessary because popular images of professors are abundant and embellished. Consider what historian Frederick Rudolph wrote in 1962 about professors at colleges in the mid-19th century:

> In the mythology of American education, the old-time college professor, if nothing else, was a character. Beloved or unloved, tyrannical or permissive, stern or playful, tall or short, skinny or fat, young or old – he might be any of these things, but one thing for sure, he was a character. He was someone whom students played tricks on, and if he found a cow in his classroom one morning, somehow he would find some telling way of turning that disaster into a personal advantage. He was probably famous for college generations for that special lecture of his, the one that brought the Battle of Thermopylae right into the classroom. That hat, the one he wore twelve months of the year, too small, too old, too odd, though it was – that made him a character, too.[4]

This historic image persists, often joined with the caricature of the "absent-minded professor." An addition to the depiction of professors would take root starting around 1890 and increasing persistently into the 21st century: namely, the professor as an expert. This was a gradual transformation due to the advanced education of professors, as the Ph.D. degree became increasingly accepted – and expected – as the necessary certification. The professor as "expert" also was a function of specialization. The rise of funded research projects added to the professorial presence. The professionalization of scholarship also was part of a crucial societal change in which journalists, television reporters, and other media relied on interviews and quotes from professors for commentary on issues – all to be read and heard by the American public.

A legacy of World War II was public and congressional gratitude to professors who were effective in harnessing their scholarly skills to solve problems and create weapons and other products as part of the war effort. Most conspicuous would be the physicists, chemists, engineers, and mathematicians involved in developing the atomic bomb and the hydrogen bomb through the teamwork of Los Alamos or the Manhattan Project. Less glamorous, but also crucial, was professorial knowledge of esoteric languages spoken in Asia and Eastern Europe or geographers who were skilled in cartography and cultural details. Professors, far from being "ivory tower recluses," developed intense language training courses and also served as interpreters and translators.

Popular images depicted professors who were goofy, zany, and wacky – personality traits that were simultaneously tolerated and gently ridiculed by the American public. Hollywood made good money off Jerry Lewis's portrayal of "The Nutty Professor" in 1963 – so much so that the remake in 1996 with Eddie Murphy also was a box office hit as a new generation of viewers enjoyed once again the humorous depictions of faculty. Marbled within images of expertise and idiosyncratic behavior were recurrent portrayals of professors as sinister figures who used their knowledge in devious plots as the "mad professor." According to historian Richard Hofstadter, it was indicative of a strand of anti-intellectualism in American life.[5] Most Americans remained wary of those who opted for a life of scholarship. Tenure often was popularly misunderstood as an indulgence in lifetime job security without accountability. Not the least disconcerting (and enviable) to most American adults was the lack of hour-by-hour and daily accountability of professors in the office. This tension was portrayed in the popular television series, *Law and Order*, when the hard-boiled New York City detective barges into the lecture hall at fictional "Hudson University" (most likely based on Columbia) and makes a grandstand show of arresting the professor, handcuffing him and then, turning to the rows of students, announcing, "Class dismissed!"

ISSUES

The reality is that the faculty of American colleges and universities earn high respect worldwide. Indeed, they are considered in international surveys to be the key element in the stature of American universities as the best in the world. This success is pronounced in the high ratings given to professors who are central to Ph.D. programs at top research universities in the United States. The halo effect spreads across all institutional categories, as American professors are viewed as well-educated, dedicated to teaching and scholarship, and productive. At the same time, some politicians, along with assorted business leaders, still add their own sharp criticism of the American academic profession as troublesome. This call for detailed analysis.

What Are Faculty Roles and Responsibilities?

Responsibilities of a professor span three areas: teaching, research, and service. The time one devotes to each varies, based on institutional mission and on individual negotiation of teaching load and of service and research. Some definitions of roles are obvious, but these may be incomplete. Teaching, for example, brings to mind instructing for courses along with face-to-face instruction and/or online or hybrid courses, and sponsoring independent studies, internships, and student research projects. At universities offering advanced degrees, teaching includes chairing doctoral dissertations plus serving on master's and doctoral degree committees. "Research" brings to mind library and laboratory work, collecting data via surveys or field observations, writing up results for scholarly articles and books. Research time also can be devoted to applying for grants.

Among the three faculty roles, "service" goes relatively unnoticed and undefined. It may refer to membership on campus committees that constitute "systems maintenance." Examples of committee appointment include admissions, graduate studies, academic ombudsman, library advisory, tenure and promotion, and the deceptively powerful campus parking committee. Another twist on "service" is extramural – i.e., service to the scholarly profession in such roles as an officer in a national scholarly society or serving on a group's research awards committee, journal editorial board, or conference planning committee. How much or how little these are counted in a faculty member's workload effort and rewards differs from institution to institution.

Faculty also can alter the configuration of their professional work with administrative appointments that coexist with their primary faculty role. Many academic administrative appointments draw their candidates exclusively from the faculty ranks. Department chair, assistant dean, associate dean, vice provost, and research institute director are illustrative of such appointments. When a faculty member's administrative appointment surpasses half of one's professional workload, a professor usually retains faculty appointment but is reclassified as an administrator in terms of salary and evaluation. Academic administrative appointments usually include provision to reduce one's course teaching load. Usually academic administrators retain the right to step aside from administrative appointment and "return to their teaching and research" – while retaining most of their high administrative salary.

Academic custom at most colleges and universities is that a tenured professor is eligible for a sabbatical leave every seven years. Terms are different from one institution to another. For example, at some universities a professor on sabbatical can receive full pay and benefits for one semester. If the professor opts for a full academic year leave, compensation may be reduced to half pay and benefits. If a professor takes a leave of absence to accept an appointment outside the university, regulations stipulate a calendar limit if one wishes to retain the faculty appointment and be able to return. Harvard, for example, has a strict policy that limits leaves to two years – even for such prestigious positions as a Secretary of Defense or as an ambassador. But these vary from one university to another.

Another variable in establishing faculty time includes monitoring research and consulting. A customary allowance is that a faculty member may devote the equivalent of one day per week to outside projects during the academic year, with no limits during the summer months. Equally important, external projects such as research, consulting, or managing a "start-up" company must be approved by one's academic dean, a university advisory committee, and, in some cases, university legal counsel to document that such faculty projects do not represent a conflict of interest with institutional norms and regulations. This oversight becomes important if a particular academic unit or the entire university has a strong presence in enterprising initiatives based on research and development activities.

What Part Are Faculty in the Expenses of a College or University?

Full-time, tenure track professors are well paid and represent a major personnel expense for any college or university. In 2013–2014, for example, at a doctoral-granting university, mean annual salaries were $140,000 for a full professor, $95,000 for an associate professor, and $80,000 for an assistant professor. These would be about $20,000 lower in each category at institutions whose highest conferred degree was a master's degree. Community college salaries by rank were $80,000 for full professors, $60,000 for associate professors, and $44,000 for assistant professors. Later on, however, national data about adjunct and part-time faculty at the public two-year colleges will drastically alter the profile of the total community college faculty.

This proportional presence of faculty salaries as an expense in the overall annual budget, however, has declined as most campuses have steadily added administration and staff professionals since about 1970. Also, since salaries of mid- and top-level administrators have risen at a higher annual rate than that of faculty, the place of professors as an expense in the university budget has shrunk even more than the head-count tallies of faculty and administrators. Furthermore, hiring of part-time adjuncts and instructors and utilizing graduate students as teaching assistants has tended to taper the number of new full-time professors added – even when student enrollments are increasing.

What Is Tenure? How Does It Fit into Terms of Employment for Professors?

"Tenure" is an academic protocol or status that, if conferred by the president and trustees on a faculty member, provides that professor with protection against arbitrary firing or punishment by the employing college or university. A tenured faculty member cannot be dismissed for the legitimate scholarly pursuit and presentation of knowledge in such activities as classroom teaching and scholarship.

A popular misconception is that a professor who has been granted tenure enjoys lifetime job security and cannot be fired. This is not accurate. Tenure applies only to well-defined, limited aspects of what one teaches and writes. It does not provide protection against misconduct, malpractice, dereliction of professional duties, harassment of colleagues and staff, or abuse of power with students. Failure to show up for teaching classes is dubious conduct wholly apart from tenure. A professor who commits a felony may put her or his job in jeopardy – and has no grounds to invoke tenure as some protective buffer. All such offenses can be grounds for institutional and administrative review leading to reprimands and, perhaps, to dismissal. But dismissal of any professional employee in a complex organization such as a university, a state agency, or a business corporation usually is time-consuming and difficult. And this is the part of the procedure that in higher education often is erroneously attributed to some exaggerated notion about protections provided by tenure. The reality is that a department chair, dean, and provost probably dread the laborious task of documenting a professor's professional or personal misbehavior, which must be presented as a discernible pattern and then can lead to internal hearings, appeals, and, if not resolved within the campus, to civil lawsuits by the accused professor against the administrators and institution. The path of least resistance for an administrator is to shrug one's shoulders, focus on positive things, acquiesce, and allow the errant professor to continue on – and then blame the stalemate on the inertia of tenure. In this script, tenure becomes a convenient, albeit undeserving scapegoat for dubious professional performance of academic duties.

How Is "Academic Freedom" Defined and Derived, Both Inside and Outside a Campus?

"Academic freedom" usually is mentioned in concert with the protections of "tenure," discussed above. The linkage is important because faculty who work under limited contracts and do not have tenure have few safeguards provided by a college's internal regulations and protocols. When one shifts from "academic freedom" to the highly related but still distinct issue of "free speech," one finds some important, perhaps surprising, nuances. According to legal scholar Scott Bauries, the First Amendment of the U.S. Constitution does *not* give special protection of free speech to professors.[6] This is contrary to supposition, as one would expect there would be numerous court cases in which professors petitioned for (and were granted) freedom of speech on the basis of their official position as a college professor. In fact, according to Bauries, the Constitution gives no more and no less protection to professors than it would to any citizen. Furthermore, if one looks at professors as institutional employees, the divide is along public and private lines. Faculty at state colleges and universities and at community colleges are categorized as "public employees" – and their rights and restraints on free speech rest with civil service staff, police, fire marshals, bailiffs, coroners, clerks, and other positions one finds in a local, state, or federal bureaucracy. Faculty employed at private or independent colleges essentially have no special protections or privileges conferred by the First Amendment and are subject to their employing college's internal regulations.

This interpretation hardly exhausts the principles and complexities of academic freedom in American higher education. There is a growing body of scholarship that also looks at academic freedom as having textures and dimensions that are more than an individual right. It can be viewed, for example, as an essential feature of organized, collective scholarship. Robert Post, Dean of Yale Law School, makes the compelling argument that academe is distinctive in the need for protection of freedom of speech because professors and their scholarly associations and journals deals largely with the "production of expert knowledge" and the "reproduction of expertise," both of which are protected by academic freedom.[7] The logic is that one cannot simply ignore the codification, synthesis, reconsideration, and discovery of arguments within scholarly disciplines and their protocols of peer review in understanding free speech and its treatment in the First Amendment. In other words, on matters of scholarly analysis and inquiry, not all opinions are of equal weight. One may be free to pontificate on a topic, ranging from biology to arithmetics, but at some point these must be reconciled with the rigorous, established theories and interpretations that constitute *informed* discussion. And, by this line of analysis, a professor's affiliation with a bona fide academic group or discipline gains by association a measure of special consideration.

Legal scholar Michael Olivas's book, *Suing Alma Mater*, brings attention to the growing role of what he calls "purposive organizations" – formal groups whose advocacy of beliefs and points of view enter into college and university forums, including classroom discussions.[8] These span the political and religious spectrum. Illustrative of the tension is a biology class in which a professor is lecturing on evolution. A student, for example, asserts that the instructor should present the perspective of creationism – and that, furthermore, since the lecture on evolution as a theory conflicts with personal religious beliefs, the student should be exempted from accepting it as fact and from, for example, writing about it in an examination. Such claims introduce an extreme relativism into scholarly discussion that jeopardizes scholarly expertise. Furthermore, examination of scholarly topics indicates that debates within a discipline already include a wide, varied range of perspectives and arguments subjected to peer review and debate.

Another variation on these clashes is that of "trigger warnings" in which instructors are expected to send advance alerts to students about course materials whose themes and content might be painful or controversial. Since college officials fear litigation from disgruntled students, the campus most likely will continue to be fertile ground for these kinds of complaints and whose net impact is to provide continual questions about academic freedom.

One sign of pushback by professors who oppose succumbing to the internal pressures of students' stifling of uncomfortable and unpopular scholarly themes and arguments is the group known as FIRE – short for the Foundation for Individual Rights in Education – which in September 2015 launched a national campaign "asking colleges and universities to adopt the free speech policy statement drafted by the University of Chicago's Committee on Freedom of Expression." The statement guarantees "all members of the University community the broadest possible latitude to speak, write, listen, challenge, and learn" and makes clear that "it is not the proper role of the University to attempt to shield individuals from ideas and opinions they find unwelcome, disagreeable, or even deeply offensive."[9]

These initiatives do not exhaust other sources that may provide faculty certain measures of academic freedom and freedom of speech. A crucial source of documents will be the codes officially adopted within each college and university – found in documents called the *general regulations* (and abbreviated as the "GRs") and the *administrative regulations* (popularly called the "ARs"). If, for example, the board of trustees has approved adherence to the AAUP's guidelines on tenure and promotion, and drafted commensurate language into the GRs and ARs, this is an important commitment for both the board and administration as well as for hired faculty. It provides the script and procedures, all approved by the university legal counsel. If a board of trustees and president or provost do not follow the AAUP guidelines or the ARs and GRs or some other approved protocol or regulation, the faculty member will have grounds for internal appeal; and, if that does not provide relief, it leaves room for the faculty member to file suit against the college or university. In the latter category, the merit of the grievance will be based on selected criteria that must be clearly stated. A grievance based on allegations of gender discrimination, for example, would be significantly different than one in which the plaintiff professor focuses on the institutional review process's failure to document decisions about lack of scholarship or other criteria or failure to adhere to institutional procedures.

How Is Hiring Handled for the Academic Profession?

Hiring a permanent, career path professor is an extended, detailed endeavor fraught with legal, institutional, and customary procedures that must be obeyed. The multiple stages represent a ritual best described as a mating dance in which participants follow detailed rules and roles. Overseeing the process, especially the formal hiring, is the institution's board of trustees, who must approve any offer and signed contract. In almost all cases, the board of trustees relies on the recommendations made by the search committee, the departmental faculty, the dean, the provost, and, finally, perhaps the president. Ratification is customary, often pro forma. However, although the departures from this are rare, when they do happen they are highly visible and volatile. This is because such extraordinary attention and interference usually are seen as involving a political or personal dimension – whether as an advantage or as vengeance – on criteria outside academic and scholarly merit.

As prelude to dissecting the academic hiring process, it is worthwhile to acknowledge the extraordinary preparation and certification candidates for faculty appointments bring to the table. Most candidates will have completed a bachelor's degree, a master's degree, and a terminal degree – usually the Ph.D. This totals at least nine or ten years of advanced study beyond high school – or, five or six years following completion of college. Usually the candidate will have acquired formal college-level teaching experience, written journal articles and book reviews, participated in a major research grant project, and perhaps received research grant funding. Many candidates for an assistant professorship also will have received and completed post-doctoral appointments – a prestigious and demanding research role for one or more years, working with a senior scholar and research team.

Applicants for faculty appointments to teach in the advanced professional schools of law and medicine usually do not have the Ph.D. degree, as the J.D. and M.D. are considered to be the customary terminal degrees in those fields. However, an increasing number of these do also earn a Ph.D., compounding both their expertise and the years and expense of advanced degree education. Furthermore, both law and medicine faculty applicants are required to devote added years to particular kinds of professional service and experience. An M.D. will have an internship and residency, and, perhaps, a research post-doctoral stint. Yet important to note is that a substantial percentage of tenured or tenure track professors in academic colleges of medicine are not M.D.s. Rather, medical education requires the expertise in both teaching and research of faculty who hold the Ph.D. in such fields as biochemistry, physiology, anthropology, bioengineering, and numerous other "bio" combination specialties.

Law professors are noteworthy in that although their potential earnings as a professor are dwarfed by those of classmates who go into corporate law or private practice with major firms, contenders for law faculty appointments are universally regarded by their classmates and professors as especially talented and dedicated within the field of law. Most have served as editors of the law review – among the highest academic honors one can achieve in a law school class. And, before applying for a faculty position, it is customary to have clerked for a federal judge and then worked in a private firm or government agency. In short, there is a long, competitive grooming and screening of applicants for law faculty positions.

In contrast to hiring for most jobs, including those for "professional" level positions and staff appointments, faculty hiring is laborious and serpentine. For a department to gain permission even to "search" for a faculty member, it must persuade the academic dean and provost that the proposed specialty is worthy and needed – and that it fits well with the priorities of the college and perhaps the entire campus. Other considerations are whether the position warrants a tenure track appointment and also the rank – assistant, associate, or full professor – for which the search is approved. Position descriptions must be posted both with the university Human Resources office, local newspapers and media, and in scholarly trade journals, including the *Chronicle of Higher Education* and *Inside Higher Ed*. Faculty members in the department also usually arrange to make appointments at major academic conferences to talk with applicants. Candidates are expected to file a detailed letter about their teaching and scholarly experience plus proposed future agenda. They will either include reference letters from respected scholars in the field or, at least, provide the search committee chair a roster of references that the search committee is invited to contact. Even if there is consensus on this among the search committee members, it must be reviewed by Human Resources for compliance with Title IX and Affirmative Action guidelines to ascertain there has been a conscientious effort to attract a pool of applicants that is diverse in matters of gender, race, and ethnicity along with compliance on various other federal, state, local, and institutional regulations.

One expensive part of a faculty search is arranging for a small number of finalists to visit campus for about two days, to make a formal presentation, to meet with departmental faculty, student groups, research staff, along with courtesy talks with the dean and provost. It is a grueling schedule that leaves both candidates and departmental hosts exhausted. Most search committees arrange to have candidates reimbursed for travel and lodging – although in a buyer's market and during lean times, search committees sometimes may opt not to defray candidate expenses. The customary procedure is for the search committee and department chair to make a recommendation to the dean about the candidate to whom they wish the college to make a formal offer. Formal terms such as salary, teaching load, research support, laboratory space, and research travel monies are determined and negotiated by the dean with the candidate. The candidate, of course, has a right of refusal and can suggest counter-offers – just as parties do in purchasing and selling a car. If the deal falls through, the dean confers with the department chair and perhaps the search committee chair to see if they then wish to proceed down the list of finalists and extend an offer to one of them. The permutations are numerous. If offers bog down, the dean and department may opt to abandon the search and start over another time – if the provost approves.

This is a best-case scenario and represents at least about a six-month venture. For optimal position in the academic market, a search committee must harmonize with the academic calendar and the dates of major conferences. Usually it is best to start searching early in the fall semester, with the target of making a firm offer and closing the deal by spring – before faculty members in the department break for summer.

Another side dimension is that of terms within a faculty offer. Contrary to conventional belief, the salary range usually is not controversial. That's because nationwide databases provide comprehensive information on salary and compensation according to discipline, rank, institutional category – and, sometimes, even for a particular college or university. A salary offer may go up if the search committee is trying to attract an established professor who they think is in high demand or may be reluctant to move. At the same time, a search committee might estimate that they can offer a below-market salary because it is offset by the hiring institution's prestige or desirable location – or, low cost of living. In hiring junior faculty – i.e., assistant professors – search committees often encounter the issue of *salary compression* in which new Ph.D.s in a dazzling field may command higher salaries and compensation than tenured, established senior professors. All these factors are fair play in a department's planning and strategies.

More uncertain than salary range will be such discretionary items as the amount of a research start-up fund or kinds of laboratory space and facilities a searching university will offer to a candidate. This is crucial and expensive in such fields as physical sciences, medicine, biochemistry, and other applied sciences. Often a department, in concert with the dean and provost, may determine that they can stake a new assistant professor to about three years of funding for laboratory space, equipment, and research assistants – after which it is both implicit and explicit that the faculty member as scientist will be responsible for bringing in their own fresh grant money to continue research projects. If a hiring university has identified a field and a professor as part of their "steeples of excellence" plan for institutional greatness, the amount offered will increase – on the condition that the dean and provost think that the candidate they are pursuing could really make a difference in future institutional reputation and research grants. These discussions become increasingly important if the proposed faculty hire is in a new field that would require a massive new venture in terms of construction and resources – as distinguished from replacing a retired senior professor in an already established field.

How Does Promotion in Faculty Rank and Conferral of Tenure Take Place?

One of the most distinctive, complex episodes in an academic career involves deliberations about granting promotion and tenure. It is a detailed algorithm. An assistant professor with a tenure track appointment typically has a seven-year contract, at the end of which she or he "moves up or out." This means that the trustees and president shall have rendered a decision to confer promotion to the rank of associate professor with tenure or to deny tenure and promotion, offering the failed candidate a single terminal year contract.

The seven-year period is in practice much shorter than seven years because the faculty candidate must file all dossier materials for committee review early in the assistant professor's fifth year of university employment. The review process takes at least a full academic year. The dossier includes solicited letters from external professors in the field. The external reviewers usually are divided among those suggested by the candidate and those selected by the department chair and dean. They must have what the dean considers to be appropriate scholarly achievements and be tenured professors at benchmark colleges and universities. These provisions are yet another example of the importance of "peer review" in academic deliberations.

The first stage of dossier review is in the professor's department. All tenured professors are required to write an analysis and make a recommendation. The department chair then tallies the votes and writes a detailed summative letter. All these materials are then forwarded to a college-wide faculty review committee and to the unit's academic dean. An important difference from one university to another is how votes and recommendations are bundled for forwarding to the next and higher level – university-wide area committees for tenure and promotion review. Meanwhile, the faculty candidate has access to the various evaluation and recommendation letters. At some institutions, the college faculty committee and the dean each make independent recommendations. Under this arrangement, then, if the two are not in agreement on recommendation, *both* go forward – and the university-wide faculty review committee, which represents several departments and academic units, is left to sort out and make its own independent evaluation, followed by its recommendation to the provost.

A contentious situation arises if university regulations state that the college dean's recommendation prevails as the single vote from the college. If the college faculty votes in favor of promotion and the dean does not, the dossier stops and the candidate is, essentially, denied. Conversely, a dean could favor approval of a candidate that the faculty committee deemed unworthy of promotion and tenure. This procedure places inordinate power in the academic dean – and strips the college's faculty of significant decision-making. It means that a faculty candidate who does not have the favor of the dean has little recourse regardless of how strong the record of scholarly accomplishment, teaching evaluations, and service may be. To another extreme, it allows a dean to champion a faculty candidate even though the college's faculty peers have determined the candidate to lack adequate achievements. Structure matters, as these arrangements can make or break academic careers.

If a faculty candidate's dossier is forwarded to the university-wide faculty committee with either consensus or a split vote for promotion and tenure, then the committee makes a *recommendation* to the provost. The provost in turn reads the dossier and makes a recommendation to the president and the board of trustees. It is rare for a president or board to overturn a recommendation for promotion. But it does happen. In such instances the alert is that there may be some political or personal consideration, since several preceding layers of scholarly review, including those filed by external experts, had accumulated for a strong recommendation of promotion and tenure. It calls for explanation and investigation. These cases usually attract attention from media and press. In summer 2015, for example, the University of Illinois board of trustees rescinded a faculty appointment letter, which led to protest by academic deans and campus faculty because the board action went counter to recommendations from the search committee and dean. The incident was sufficiently acrimonious that it led to the retirement and/or resignation of the chancellor of the flagship state university campus. The extended incident was news because it was unusual – and demonstrated the informal influence of faculty and deans who thought the board of trustees had not followed customs and protocols.

How Does the Academic Profession Participate in Curricular Policies?

Educational policies and programs are the right and responsibility of the faculty. When professors claim they are "the heart of the university," it may be hyperbole. But educational policies and programs are their rightful turf. They teach – and they determine what courses and programs shall be taught. Most course and degree program proposals originate at the grass-roots level of an academic department and work their way upward through a college and then on to consideration by the university-wide faculty. And, collective bodies such as the faculty senate usually have official jurisdiction over review and recommendation on educational policy proposals. This educational policy power can be muted, however, by a provost and president who retain authority over funding decisions about program proposals.

Another variation and source of tension is when an academic program is proposed from on high by a president, provost, or dean – as distinguished from originating with professors. Top academic administrators would argue that they have a perspective that departments and professors may lack – and that moving promptly into a new field is necessary and advantageous. Even if these claims are warranted, professors tend to be wary of such impositions. It is seen as comparable to "cutting in line" at the movies – usurping faculty prerogatives and patience.

Accountability for Academics

Faculty are subject to numerous checks and balances during a given semester and academic year. In addition to the five-year dossier one compiles for tenure and promotion review, typically each faculty member regardless of rank undergoes a biennial evaluation typically conducted by the department chair who then forwards the data and recommended evaluation for approval by the dean. Also, at the end of each academic term, students fill out course evaluations. Another source of discipline is that a college may establish criteria for enrollments. A class must have some set minimum enrollment if it is to be offered. When enrollment falls short, the class may be canceled – and the instructor is given alternative assignments. If a faculty member shows a persistent pattern of low enrollment classes that are then canceled, it triggers an alert from the associate dean. A professor who has a chronic track record of canceled classes then has some explaining to do to the department chair.

Colleges and universities increasingly make use of standardized "digital measures" features for each faculty member, available at their employee website. This compiles all records on courses taught, student evaluations of teaching, sponsored research, along with sections where the faculty member enters self-reported data on research, publications, advising, campus committee service, and other professional activities. Biennial evaluation made by the department chair is forwarded to the dean, who then makes an independent evaluation. The faculty being reviewed then has an opportunity to review the materials and recommendations. These periodic reviews provide the basis for annual salary raises.

Periodic review of faculty also includes formal, strict attention to signs of professional misconduct, such as plagiarism, fabrication of research data, inappropriate spending of university research funds, unauthorized research on human subjects, mistreatment of animals in experiments, and even research espionage. Most research universities have in place a committee called the Institutional Review Board (commonly called "The IRB"), which reviews and then approves, disapproves, or suggests modifications to faculty research projects and proposals. These are serious concerns of the university administration because failure to comply with federal regulations on one federally sponsored research grant project could jeopardize receipt of any and all federal funding to the entire university.

CHARACTERS AND CONSTITUENTS

A Profile of the Profession

According to the *Chronicle of Higher Education's Almanac of Higher Education for 2015–16*, the broad contours of the faculty as a profession employed at colleges and universities include the following data for fall 2013: 703,150 faculty members, about 40 percent of whom (303,618) hold positions at a relatively small number of large research universities. Colleges whose highest degree is the bachelor's degree accounted for a little over 9 percent of the total. Community colleges conferring the two-year associate's degree employed 133,308 (19 percent). Master's degree-granting institutions, meanwhile, represented 150,802 faculty members (22 percent). The remainder were diffused through varied, sometimes unclear, institutional affiliations.

The limit of this summary is that it does not readily convey configurations within each institutional category in regard to the number and percentage of faculty members who are outside the full-time appointments eligible for tenure. For example, a snapshot of the entire faculty for all institutions shows that 504,168 (a little over 70 percent) hold appointments as either professor, associate professor, or assistant professor. This means that among all colleges and universities, 30 percent of the faculty are appointed either as instructors, lecturers, or without academic rank. Furthermore, most of these latter categories are part-time assignments. It reinforces the significant point that a large and growing number of college faculty members do not have full-time, long-term career appointments. The proportion of college and university courses taught by instructors other than tenure track professors probably is understated because the preceding data do *not* include the large number of graduate students at research universities who are classified as "teaching assistants" for a large number of undergraduate courses. Most are actually more than "teaching assistants," as they are responsible for being the primary instructor for "sections" of large courses. Their compensation usually is in the form of a graduate assistantship, as distinguished from a salary.

At the very least, these data and side commentaries make meaningful generalizations about "the faculty" difficult because the profession is split and dispersed along the lines of a defining characteristic. As a general rule, the most established, well-endowed, and academically prestigious colleges and universities have maintained a faculty composition of tenure track, full-time appointments. Yet even this observation warrants careful note: this "best-case scenario" for professional employment and career fulfillment relies on a large number of adjuncts, instructors, and lecturers. Furthermore, looking at faculty data over time, the percentage of faculty appointments that are full time and tenure eligible is shrinking year by year. The baccalaureate colleges devoted to the liberal arts and sciences display a profile that decidedly favors traditional tenure track appointments. And, these are evenly divided among full professors, associate professors, and assistant professors. But this is increasingly rare.

Full Professors

A full professor with tenure represents the high point of rank, seniority, and usually salary. The long apprenticeship and advanced studies of a faculty member mean that it's unlikely for one to be promoted to full professor before age 40. Since there is no mandatory retirement age for professors, the mean age of full professors is old – and getting older. A key datum is the percentage of tenure track professors within a department who are full professors. When that percentage goes above half, it suggests an aging, clogging faculty group. In the late 1970s, Stanford and other prestigious research universities reported that among their full-time professors, about 80 percent had tenure. The policy implication was that the faculty pyramid was top-heavy – and prospects for many vacancies due to retirement were slim. Hence, there would not be a great number of new positions open at the entry-level assistant professor rank. It was a statistical profile of the "graying of the faculty."

Associate Professors

Members of this group represent those who have persevered and prevailed in the academic sweepstakes. They have completed a lengthy socialization, initiation, and inspection by senior faculty colleagues – and the provost and board of trustees. Having achieved tenure, there is less formal obligation or pressure to write for publication or conduct research. However, for many professors, gaining associate professor and tenure status represents a productive period in teaching and research and service. Joining this group gives an opportunity to rethink and reorder priorities and projects, with a measure of confidence and seniority. On a less positive note, one syndrome is complacency and coasting, in which some tenured associate professors either do not seek or are not granted promotion to the rank of full professor. The "career" associate professor who persists as relatively indifferent to or disengaged from scholarly research and publication is a source of concern for energy and morale within a department and college.

Assistant Professors

These are the newly hired faculty members who are on tenure track and have about five years to establish a record of achievement in teaching, research, and service that will qualify them for promotion with tenure to associate professor. Many departments recognize the pressures of adjusting to a new job with the specter of tenure and promotion review coming due in a few years. Hence, assistant professors sometimes are given reduced teaching loads and are exempted from service assignments. However, department chairs can abuse the power they hold over untenured assistant professors by requesting they take on assignments that will not count in the all-important career path of tenure review. It is hard for a new assistant professor to "just say no" to a department chair who has to solve a staffing problem for teaching a course. The untenured assistant professor is "whiplashed" by immediate departmental needs in conflict with research and scholarly publications essential to long-term career advancement.

Research Professors

"Research universities" that rely on substantial funding in sponsored research from federal agencies and private foundations acknowledge this institutional priority by creating a special faculty category. A "research professor" is one who is not obligated to teach classes and devotes full attention to research projects. Employment is based on a research faculty member's success in landing adequate funding for salary, benefits, indirect costs, laboratory expenses, and other items connected with a major research grant. This works well so long as a research professor lands new grants or has existing projects that receive renewed funding.

Less clear is the situation when the research professor has done excellent research and has published articles – but the funding agency changes its priorities and the research professor no longer brings in the requisite external funding. Does a provost or dean "float" the unfunded research professor with cross-subsidies from elsewhere in the academic budget, in the hope or belief that the lack of research grants is temporary? Also central to the consideration is the fact of organizational life that "tooling up" for research projects and grants by talented Ph.D.s takes a long time. Hence, pulling the plug on a research center and its faculty could be a false sense of savings. On the other hand, if sponsored research is literally the "coin of the realm" of high-stakes research, lack of funding can be decisive in not renewing a research faculty professor's contract.

Clinical Professors

In professional schools such as medicine and allied health, where providing expertise and services to paying clients is integral to the mission and operation of the academic unit, a university often creates a special faculty status for practicing clinicians, known as "clinical professor." Since a clinical professor brings in fees from patients or clients – and is expected to do so – a dean must negotiate specific terms of salary, workload, and eligibility for promotion and tenure. At universities with a health sciences campus, clinical professors may constitute somewhere between a quarter and a third of the entire faculty.

Lecturers

Lecturers usually have a term contract along with responsibility for being the instructor of record for assigned courses. Contracts can be from one year to five years, perhaps eligible for renewal. The position provides an intermediate resolution with more stability and even benefits along with a salary than is the case with adjunct faculty. Yet the lecturer position is not eligible for tenure without special allowance by the dean or provost. It is not always certain or clear whether a lecturer is eligible to serve on graduate committees for master's degree examinations or on doctoral dissertation committees.

Instructors

The designation of "instructor" is, along with "lecturer," a catch-all category for limited-term appointments. The formal and official definitions and distinctions vary from one university to another. Unless expressly stated otherwise, instructors teach undergraduate-level courses – often introductory courses primarily for freshmen and sophomore students.

Adjunct Faculty

This represents one of the largest categories of faculty at colleges and university. Appointments are limited and specific – and contracts usually expire at the end of a semester. Seldom do adjunct faculty receive the benefits of full-time professors such as health insurance, a retirement plan, or job security. Often the contracts lead to piecemeal work so that many adjuncts cobble together a slate of courses at different institutions, in which case they become higher education's itinerant or gypsy faculty – which translates into demanding work, low pay, and little job security.

Teaching Assistants

At institutions that enroll graduate students, a large percentage of undergraduate teaching is handled by graduate students who are appointed and employed as teaching assistants. Typically, teaching assistants receive less compensation, respect, and eligibility for departmental resources than do instructors, adjuncts, and professors. Teaching assistants, known as "TAs," who aspire to faculty careers face much the same challenges as assistant professors – for example, pressure to publish, along with the need to balance teaching and research – but they do so at only a small fraction of the salary while they enjoy few if any of the professional benefits (such as conference travel funding or course releases) that a formal academic appointment affords. Little wonder, then, that at some large research universities the TAs have sometimes been characterized as the academic profession's equivalent of apprentices and/or indentured servants.

Scholarly Organizations and Associations

Even though a typical American university is depicted as a "knowledge factory," its monolithic image is quickly broken down into small units, such as an academic department, in terms of curriculum, teaching, prestige, and values. A professor's particular field or department is where rewards and value systems are determined. In addition to the college or university that employs a professor, each professor has a strong affiliation with their respective disciplines. And each discipline has its national association that sponsors an annual research conference, a scholarly journal, and confers awards for research and scholarship in the field. Illustrative organizations include the Organization of American Historians, the American Sociological Association, the Association for the Study of Higher Education, and the American Psychological Association.

Differences from one scholarly field to another are idiosyncratic yet important. For example, in some fields the "coin of the realm" may be the ability to land sponsored research grants from a particular federal agency, such as the National Science Foundation or the National Institutes of Health. In another field, research grants may hold less prestige than one's success in having a refereed article published in certain established journals. A discipline may allow and even encourage multiple authors on articles, indicative of the cooperative nature of research in the field. Yet other disciplines may discount co-authorship, with a strong preference for solo-authored books and articles. Each field has its customs and ground rules on place and pride of authorship. In one field, multiple authors may be listed with the senior or primary author first, followed by listings according to rank or contribution. Yet in another department, the practice may be to list co-authors alphabetically. These nuances may seem insignificant to the outside observer, but they are consequential for scholars in the midst of an academic career. Field-by-field differences can be problematic at the all-university faculty review stage. To promote equitable and fair evaluation, a crucial role of the chair of the review is to educate committee members drawn from disparate departments about the customs and standards of the candidate's particular discipline.

The American Association of University Professors (AAUP)

The AAUP is the membership association for professors nationwide. It has a long record for over a century of providing support for celebrated landmark cases involving abuses of academic freedom. Its 1915 statement of principles on tenure and promotion and academic freedom sets the standard for individual faculty rights and responsibilities – and commensurate college and university compliance. However, during the so-called McCarthy Era of the early 1950s, the AAUP was deluged with cases involving loyalty oaths at numerous universities and was not effective in responding to many of the challenges.[10] In recent decades, its sound principles and advocacy have been bruised by declining membership among faculty, especially new professors. One of its major resources and tools is that of institutional censure for those colleges and universities who flagrantly defy AAUP principles. The threat of censure, however, has been uneven and uncertain in its ability to prompt college and university presidents and boards to play by the AAUP rules. As a result, the AAUP leadership has a place at the table in Washington, D.C. in various national policy deliberations – but, due to waning campus membership and the historic strength of presidents and boards of trustees, the AAUP does not provide a guarantee of strong influence on individual cases of faculty grievances.

Faculty Unions

Whereas the AAUP is a professional association, many higher education systems participate in faculty unions. These tend to have greatest presence at public institutions, especially at regional state college and university systems.

COMPLEXITIES AND CONFLICTS: IMPLICATIONS FOR DECISION-MAKING

Teaching versus Research

Implicit in this dichotomy is that a faculty member's time and priorities are stretched between the two essential activities. Often it is presented with *versus* rather than *and*. This casts the pair as inherently in conflict, whereas in some cases they may be in harmony where one enhances the other. In fact, a characteristic of a "complete professor" is one who excels in both teaching and research. However, there is a saturation point in which competition for a faculty member's working time calls for decisions about proportions to devote to each category. Over the past century the tendency has been for professors to have had their required teaching loads reduced. Prestigious research universities have been in the vanguard of this drift.[11] Yet over time it has been observed and emulated at liberal arts colleges and most state universities.

Publish or Perish

This historic slogan refers to the "up or out" code in which a professor is obligated to demonstrate scholarly publications in the form of books or journal articles. Failure to do so means that promotion and tenure are unlikely, leaving one to "perish" by losing one's job. The standards of what constitutes a satisfactory quantity and quality of scholarly publications varies from one institutional category to another – and within scholarly disciplines. Whatever those numbers or terms are, it's fairly safe to say that professors – especially assistant professors who are coming up for promotion review – are cognizant of the publication litmus test.

Departmental Cultures

Membership in an academic department is comparable to socialization into an academic tribe. Village elders – namely, the senior professors – wield great power in the affairs considered at councils. As sociologist Burton Clark observed, the academic life consists of "small worlds, different worlds."[12] Hence, each department has its own culture and its own rewards and penalties. At best, a department's priorities (e.g., strong commitment to undergraduate teaching) are congruent with those of the academic college in which it is based – and with the overall campus mission.

One syndrome, especially at research universities where scholarly prestige and productivity is the paramount value, is the persistence of a "culture of mediocrity" within some departments.[13] According to sociologist Joseph Hermanowicz, this cultural dysfunction is most likely to take root at a doctoral-granting research university that may aspire to national stature, but probably is outside the prestigious circle of the Association of American Universities and its 62-member top caliber research institutions – and also outside the orbit of academically selective liberal arts colleges. The scenario within the second-tier research university is thus: all departments have a range of achievement and scholarly engagement among their departmental faculty members. However, the curious phenomenon is that in many cases, those professors who best fulfill the primary goal of achievement in scholarship and research tend to be marginalized by what he calls the "mediocre" members of the department, who have acquired influence and even power in group deliberations and in handing out rewards and raises. It plays out as a form of hazing, with a collective regression to the mean. The high-achieving colleague, whom one would expect to be praised and rewarded by colleagues for having brought individual prestige for the overall good of the department, is ignored or even ridiculed – i.e., "cut down to size." Since it is part of the insular departmental culture, it is difficult to monitor and even more difficult to root out of the departmental patterns of life.

The Barter System of Faculty Life

The formal structures in place for faculty advancement are accurate yet incomplete in understanding the rewards system of colleges and universities and how professors make decisions about allocating their time and commitments. Presume that a professor is on track for promotion and tenure, or has achieved it. This builds in a structural stability and self-confidence in which fulfillment of one's annual obligations in teaching then leaves a great deal of discretionary time. Furthermore, most colleges and universities rely on annual or biennial salary increases that usually are modest. The differential annual salary increase between a high achiever and a moderate performer usually is minuscule, especially when a dean is given only a 2 percent salary pool for merit increases. Why, then, do some professors opt to do many things either at the campus or regional or local level that have no discernible direct compensation?

At first glance the explanation might seem to be that professors make irrational choices. Or, a more cynical view is that volunteering to serve on a task force or accepting an invitation to give a guest talk for a college across campus exemplify "smart people doing dumb things." Perhaps so, but if one understands the culture of a campus, these faculty members' voluntary commitments can make sense. Even a large research university really is a small academic village. And the college or university as a village only works well if its citizens, especially its highly regarded professors, pitch in on projects and committees. Within the campus, there is no financial gain or loss because the coin of the realm among colleagues is goodwill, reciprocity, and interdependence.

Often university regulations require a departmental committee, such as a doctoral dissertation defense or a search committee, to have an outside member. To invoke the Ghostbusters' query, "Who ya gonna call?" Or, more important, "Who will take your call and say, 'Yes!'?" These are the informal networks of cooperation and collaboration that make a campus healthy and vital. Crucial to this dynamic is that faculty feel that they are full citizens of the academic city-state. And that is why tenure and academic rank can be important. Part-time or non-tenure track faculty are less likely to feel the allegiance and affiliation of such voluntary participation. So, steering away from tenure track and tenured faculty appointments may save on salary and benefits and give deans and provosts a malleable "labor force," but it is penny-wise and pound foolish in shaping a college or university as a working community. Important to note is that administrators – presidents, provosts, vice presidents, and deans – often are major beneficiaries of the academic "barter system." That's because senior administrators usually are the ones who create the myriad task forces, ad hoc committees, strategic planning work groups, budget advisory committees, and honorary degree committees that are the heart of a college or university as a complex, rich community. What one finds is that in each campus there is a significant minority of high-achieving professors who illustrate a "multiplier effect" in which excellence and dedication in one area do not preclude comparable excellence and availability in several other activities. Many professors have strong allegiance and loyalty to their campus. Understanding this code, unfortunately, often is overlooked or under-valued by senior administrators. The "barter economy" of academic life extends beyond the campus to faculty members' voluntary involvement in national-level scholarly associations, journals and publications, and service groups.

Rivalries for Resources: Departmental Differences in Customs and Competition

A glance at a college catalog or organizational chart imposes a misleading sense of standardization, suggesting equality and equity across the numerous academic units. Power and prestige, combined with differential funding demands, create pronounced differences in faculty salaries and in departmental operating expenses and budgets. Historians Rebecca Lowen and Roger Geiger have documented in their respective works that in American research universities since the 1930s the deliberate strategies used by presidents and boards has been to identify and then to fund and create "steeples of excellence."[14] These are selected programs within a campus that command special treatment because they are seen as crucial to a college or university's reputation and rankings. These vary from institution to institution, but as a general rule, some fields such as medicine, physics, engineering, and biochemistry tend to be both prestigious and expensive. Mathematics requires little in the way of laboratories or special equipment. Law often is prestigious and its professors are relatively expensive in the salaries they command. However, law school facilities are relatively inexpensive when compared to the physical sciences and health sciences. An interesting yet difficult task is to figure out how a particular campus positions itself – does it build from existing strengths or does it stake out new, emerging fields as objects of prestige? What ambitious presidents and boards of trustees need to keep in mind is that most national and international rankings of university prestige place primary emphasis on faculty research and scholarship as the key indicator of status. Quite apart from prestige and reputation, the decision to offer a course of study and to hire faculty in some fields is, by definition, expensive.

Power and Priorities

Within the academic profession, there is increasing tension between the administrative leadership and the collective faculty. This probably is less pronounced at the most prestigious academic institutions with substantial financial resources and selective admissions. At worst, the tensions give rise to what might be termed a "management versus labor" schism – a characterization that is anathema to the tradition of professors as a learned profession and constituting a self-determining academic guild.

Professors are a problem. Or, at the very least, professors are problematic. Some university presidents, such as Donald Kennedy of Stanford in the late 1980s and early 1990s, were exasperated with stalemates in attempts to reach decisions and take actions on various university programs. He cited a cluster of Stanford professors as "the problem."[15] According to this scenario, professors tend to be spoiled, whining, or devious. They obstruct administrative initiatives. They are the academic equivalent of the prima donna soprano in an opera company – indispensable and at the same time insufferable. Furthermore, these troublesome professors know every trick of the trade in how to get lighter teaching loads, higher travel allowances, and other institutional perks.

So, how does one unravel this mess? The paradox is that professors often have more prestige than power both inside and outside the campus. The American public, boards of trustees, presidents, students, and alumni give professors respect – but hold them suspect – for their authority and influence within academic institutions. From time to time some governors see professors as *the* problem bedeviling state universities. However, such tirades that professors are expensive and lazy often do not stand the test of systematic cost–benefit analysis, at least for the total or collective faculty record in teaching, research, and service. The code of conduct that defines professors is both a part and apart from most occupations. It makes professors hard to place within the world of jobs, employees, and companies. For politicians running for office, this tends to make the faculty at state colleges and universities a convenient, easy target. Making sense out of the faculty requires some careful dissection of a new version of the "three Rs" – rights, responsibilities, and regulations.

CONNECTIONS AND QUESTIONS

How Does the Academic Profession Compare and Contrast with Other Learned Professions?

Historically the academic profession has lagged behind medicine, law, and business in salaries and compensation. Illustrative of this was Andrew Carnegie's surprise at finding that steel-mill workers and railroad clerks in his employ often had pension plans that surpassed those of college and university professors. To remedy the situation and to bring stature and standards to the academic profession, he provided the funding and created the retirement and pension funds we know today as TIAA-CREF in the early 1900s, a generous plan available to many colleges and universities nationwide provided they agreed to explicit provisions on hiring and curriculum. By the early 1960s economists tracked substantial gains in salaries for professors, especially those at academically selective institutions. The rule of thumb is that tenured professors have comfortable salaries – but the tipping point that often made the academic profession attractive was the autonomy and freedom of movement, along with choice of research and teaching topics.

When one looks at the top or high end of learned professions, professors tend to lag behind those who are practicing law and medicine or are business executives and bankers. And this is a readily accepted fact of American life, taken in stride. A handful of superstar professors command celebrity status as syndicated columnists, as consulting experts, and as "public intellectuals." But this number is minuscule. Usually the highest salary for a professor at a university goes to a specialist in the medical center – for example, a thoracic surgeon who is in high demand and who also shoulders an excruciating schedule in terms of readiness and service.

The area of greatest change among the learned professions has been at the entry level. The academic profession has experienced a deflated and stagnant labor market in most fields since the early 1970s – a sufficiently long period that has become more or less accepted as the normal and enduring condition. By 2015, though, the news was that the academic profession had company. Recent graduates of medical school and law school were facing a changed professional market. Many top law firms had reduced the prospects for conferring partnership to younger attorneys in their ranks. Private medical practice had become prohibitive in start-up expenses, as a young medical doctor would have to pay hundreds of thousands of dollars to "buy" or "buy into" an established specialty private practice. The most likely projection was that a large number of young medical doctors would become salaried members of the professional staff of a health maintenance organization or hospital – a good salary to be sure, but a far cry from the once widespread expectations of lucrative private practice.

The linkage of advanced studies and professional certification to the future character of learned professions in the United States is tightened by a disconcerting trend that has crystallized into a fact of professional life: both law students and medical students enter their professional work with increasing student loan debt. The sobering alert was that these changes in the professional market were not temporary aberrations. Rather, they signaled a fundamental, wrenching change in the place of learned professionals in the American economy. Recent Ph.D.s who were chronically under-employed now could say to a cohort of colleagues in medicine and law who faced "de-professionalization," "Welcome to the club!"

What Are the Connections Between the Academic Labor Market and University Graduate Schools?

Between 1944 and 1967 analysts repeatedly warned of a shortage of qualified, well-prepared recruits into the academic profession. The challenge after World War II was for universities to expand and energize their various Ph.D. programs to ensure that there was a viable succession of professors to stock and staff colleges and universities at all levels and in all regions nationwide. Sociologists Theodore Caplow and Reese McGee's pioneering study, *The Academic Marketplace*, provided both narrative and systematic analysis of a competitive, robust environment of faculty hiring in the late 1950s.[16] Nevitt Sanford's anthology on the American College included studies that indicated professors had made significant gains both in income and public respect by 1960.[17] Sociologists Christopher Jencks and David Riesman's 1968 encyclopedic analysis of American higher education emphasized that the "academic revolution" that had started after World War I had ascended to no less than the triumph of the faculty – and faculty values – on the American campus and in the larger context of American society.[18] Dorothy Finnegan's research has documented that in the mid-1960s someone who received a Ph.D. from a reputable research university typically had four to five tenure track job offers. However, the number and ratio subsided year by year, from 4 to 1, then 3 to 1, toward a dismal end. By 1972 the bottom had dropped out of the academic market, as enrollments stopped expanding.[19]

The implication was that an extended period from 1945 to 1970, often hailed as "higher education's golden age," had a lifespan that had now ended.[20] The myopia of many academic advocates was that they mistook an episode that was both exciting and finite as the situation that would be "business as usual" for some extended period. The sobering realization was that the period of growth, expansion, and professorial advantage had subsided and was over. This paralysis revealed a distinctive feature of academic hiring: a tenure track or tenured professor represented a major investment – and often was a compact or partnership for about 20 to 30 years. Professors might show lateral and institutional mobility, jumping to a more prestigious institution or taking a salary increase elsewhere. On the whole, however, there was little exodus out of the academic profession. A large number of professors stayed put for their entire career at a single institution. The bowl of faculty hiring was full – and was going to be slow to drain. Department chairs grew frustrated with unsolicited inquiries about faculty vacancies and sometimes sent out brief postcards with the message, "We do not anticipate any hiring for the next three decades." And they were not kidding!

A good grounding in data for this observation comes from a case study of academic vacancies at one prominent research university. Sociologists Neil Smelser and Robin Content's case study of the hiring process for two tenure track assistant professorships at the University of California, Berkeley in the 1980s indicated that more than 200 applicants filed dossiers – and almost all of the applicants were well qualified.[21] In traditional fields, especially those that faced declining numbers and percentages of student majors, departmental faculty numbers remained static at best for several decades. Between 1980 and 2015 there was substantial new faculty hiring in attractive fields that promised connection with jobs and the national economy. This included computer science and business administration, among many. Health-related fields such as nursing, pharmacy, and physical therapy also boomed. In such fields as history, English, or anthropology, however, even retirements of senior professors offered little room for a new generation of scholars to become full-time faculty.

What Are the Prospects for the Future Profile and Prestige of the Academic Profession?

Scholars who are defenders and advocates of the academic profession tend to foresee a bleak future for professors. Howard Bowen and Jack Schuster concluded in 1986 that professors were "a national resource imperiled."[22] In subsequent studies drawn from national databases they both reaffirmed that finding and also warned that the problems facing professors had become even worse than their original research indicated. In 2009 the Institute of Higher Education at the University of Georgia hosted a symposium of analysts and scholars representing multiple perspectives, including economists, sociologists, political scientists, and university professors, to examine the American academic profession.[23] Their findings, published as an anthology edited by sociologist Joseph C.

Hermanowicz, echoed the storm warnings posted by such scholars as Howard Bowen, Jack Schuster, and Martin Feldstein – with new, added analyses of the impact of high-tech changes on the professoriate. The overwhelming theme from disparate disciplines was that individual and collective faculty in colleges and universities in the United States were undergoing a fundamental transformation – and it constituted a crisis that had done no less than imperil a national resource.[24]

How did this "faculty crisis" come about? Presidents and trustees from time to time – and for a long time – have floated the idea of eliminating tenure as an antidote to faculty excesses and excess faculty. This has been difficult to achieve, in part due to the tenacity of faculty and academic culture, allied by the AAUP and by accrediting standards. What presidents and provosts discovered about 20 years ago, especially after having been rebuffed in initiatives to eliminate tenure, was that there was little need to launch a formal, frontal attack on faculty tenure. One could break the logjam simply by an end-around run. For example, the job description for a position vacated by a retiring senior tenured full professor could be reclassified by administrative fiat as a five-year-term appointment without tenure or slicing it into three adjunct appointments, which were available options that incumbent faculty might not like, but could not reject. Or, one could shift a vacancy in the Classics Department to a new appointment in Accounting offered by the School of Business.

One result at the very least is a reconfiguration of the faculty in terms of its distribution by fields and by ranks. It has been a "silent revolution" by administrative action – with changes in practice but few changes in academic policies.[25] Tenure and promotion are intact. The change, however, is that what one might call the "real faculty" have over time become a more malleable and shrinking portion of the overall faculty membership within the campus. The result is that when one is asked to take stock of the American academic profession in the 21st century, it is fair to say that life and work are very good for those who have tenured, full-time positions – especially at institutions with high academic prestige and healthy revenues and endowments. Outside that important, prestigious circle, however, the academic profession has become increasingly marginalized while showing a tendency toward more work, less pay, and even less certainty in terms of professional security and stability. These latter trends run counter to the operational definitions of a genuine profession.

What Are Changes in the Socialization, Preparation, and Recruitment into the Academic Profession?

Preparing Future Faculty (PFF) programs, offered by the Dean of Graduate Studies at many universities, attracted doctoral students from numerous disciplines who wished to explore teaching as a career – and to acquire both skills and certification to confirm that commitment. Such programs represented the irony of better preparation as the academic labor market subsided. Professors and department chairs at research universities who once had the luxury of having their doctoral students focus on research and dissertations increasingly came to the realization that to be attractive on the academic labor market required conscious attention and programs to provide Ph.D. candidates with teaching experience and orientation into the world of campus work.[26]

CONNECTIONS WITH DIVERSITY AND SOCIAL JUSTICE

The academic profession in the United States has historically been dominated, both in numbers and perspectives, by white males from middle-class and upper-middle-class families. At times and at some institutions a significant exception to this was the staffing of faculty at women's colleges and historically black colleges and universities – although even at these institutions with a specific constituency of students, white men still had a strong presence in faculty roles. Since eligibility for a faculty vacancy required an applicant to have completed the Ph.D. or other appropriate advanced degree, academic standards and the lengthy time required for graduate studies tended to delay and even discourage diversification. Changing the composition of the American professoriate to include women, African Americans, Latinos, Native Americans, and Asian Americans was slow and belated so long as graduate programs remained relatively homogeneous, exclusive, and expensive.

Only around 1970 were there serious initiatives to open up the academic profession. Laura Nader recalled how, as one of the few tenure track female professors at the University of California, Berkeley in the early 1960s, she and another female colleague literally had to climb through a bathroom window in the Berkeley faculty club in order to gain entrance to university faculty meetings, all held in the men-only faculty club.[27] Her individual memoir was reinforced by the 1972 Newman Report's extensive coverage of barriers to women in higher education.[28] Another problem in diversifying the professoriate, along with incumbent faculty inertia and discrimination, was bad timing with the academic job market. Logistically the best time to apply to be a professor was from about 1955 to 1970. Minorities, however, were not poised to be faculty candidates in any substantial numbers until about 1975 – by which time the bountiful years of faculty hiring nationwide had reached a halt.

Despite the obstacles of inertia, discrimination, and unfortunate timing, the academic profession has gradually shown some signs of hiring and promoting new professors from traditionally underserved groups. For all higher education institutions in the United States, scholars of color represent about 19 percent of the faculty. African Americans constitute 9 percent and Asian Americans about 7 percent. Women have been the most successful among historically excluded groups in completing advanced graduate degrees and then starting successful academic careers. More important to note is that gradually this included obtaining faculty appointments in disciplines and departments that traditionally had been closed or discouraging to women and other minorities. In other words, some fields had been slotted as the "academic kitchen," stigmatized as "women's work" – namely, teacher education, home economics, library science, social work, and nursing.

Signs of substantive transformation included a growing number of women as professors in history, sociology, English, modern languages, mathematics, statistics, anthropology, psychology, biology, and law. In 2015, for example, nationwide women represented about half or more of the law students and medical students as well as the Ph.D. recipients in biology, anthropology, and English – an encouraging signal for eventual changes in the gender composition of faculty appointments. More resistant to change were such fields as engineering, business, and physics. However, since about 1995 women's representation as professors of law, medicine, psychology, biology, history, anthropology, and literature have ascended substantially, as has their presence as academic deans, provosts, and presidents.

Progressive change that included racial and ethnic minorities as tenure track professors has been extremely slow. One impediment is that minority students who had the academic ability to pursue a Ph.D. and apply for professorships may have been deterred by the dismal job market and relatively low salaries and long ascent to senior status. Hence, professional fields such as law, banking, business, and politics often were seen as having better prospects and fewer student loan debts than did completing the Ph.D. necessary for academe after 1970. New fields of topical and area studies, including African American Studies, Hispanic Studies, Asian American Studies, and Women and Gender Studies perhaps provided a cluster of new faculty positions – but the end game was to achieve diversity throughout the entire slate of academic programs and departments. If progress in hiring increases were disappointing, the socialization and acceptance of minorities who did receive faculty appointments into the professoriate was equally bleak in its net achievements in changing the traditional, dominant faculty culture.

Social Class and Politics

Most surveys of the American professoriate suggest a slightly leftward political leaning. However, this varies greatly from field to field. The most "liberal" faculty clusters tend to be in the social and behavioral sciences. Schools of business and engineering, in contrast, show self-reported data that are centrist or to the political right. In terms of social class and income group, professors tend to have been drawn from the middle and upper middle class, with some recent signs of growing diversity. Whatever the socio-economic origins of faculty, most professors are almost by definition in the upper middle class in terms of income and acculturation.

CONCLUSION

Perhaps the ideal professor is found in the example of Jeremy Bentham. A distinguished faculty member at the University of London, and a world-famous philosopher of Utilitarianism, also was generous as a philanthropist, as he left a substantial gift to the University of London after he died in 1832. According to one widespread and highly exaggerated legend, his one condition was that he would attend all faculty meetings for perpetuity. So the legend goes, University of London officials dutifully wheeled in a glass case with his embalmed corpse, in full formal dress, to each and every faculty meeting. And, to further embellish this "campus myth," the recording secretary allegedly noted in the official minutes: "Dr. Bentham: present. Did not speak. Did not vote."[29] He also did not receive a salary. All these heroic actions and personal characteristics, whether historically accurate or embellished, probably made him the prototype of a provost's dream candidate for professor.

The late Dr. Bentham's model of the professor as a recognized scholar, generous donor, and silent supporter of the university may be attractive to presidents and trustees. But his single case is inadequate to address the widespread crises facing professors. The recent transformation of the academic profession has not been good news. In 2002 Roger Baldwin and Jay Chronister reported a problem with colleges relying increasingly on teachers without tenure.[30] An editorial in the *New York Times* on April 14, 2014 announced no less than "The College Faculty Crisis." Drawing on systematic data from a study of 71,000 public community college instructors conducted by researchers at the University of Texas, the editorial expressed concern about the "invisible faculty" of adjuncts and part-timers who are paid about $3,000 per course and treated "almost like transient workers" with little support system, few opportunities to engage in campus planning or activities, and often without the courtesy of reasonable advance notice about teaching assignments.[31]

How derelict was the low pay for the "invisible faculty"? The best-case scenario would be for an adjunct professor to teach four courses per semester, with another four courses during the summer session – for a total of 12 courses in a calendar year. At the stated rate of $3,000 per course, this means that the optimal salary would be $36,000 per year – without a pension plan, health benefits, or paid vacation. For comparison, in 2015 in Kentucky – a relatively poor state – a county clerk in a remote, rural county received an annual salary of $80,000 per year plus retirement and health plan benefits. The inequity of faculty pay for adjuncts was further illustrated by the fact that most community college instructors had master's degrees and many had doctorates – whereas the county clerk position had no educational or academic degree requirements. Improving the compensation and treatment of these academic professionals was both crucial and expensive. The editorial concluded:

> All of this will require more money for higher salaries and professional development. College degrees worth having don't come cheap. Public officials who determine community college budgets should know full well that colleges, like other institutions, only get what they pay for.

The editorial was refreshing in that it brought attention to readers nationwide about the plight of many community college faculty. And, by extension, the shortfalls that characterized faculty hiring and faculty development in the public two-year colleges also were found in all categories of colleges and universities, such as four-year comprehensive campuses and research universities. So, if professors were a "problem," it was not that they were slackers or trouble-makers. Rather, they were under-paid and under-respected members of the academic profession who were central to any institutional, state, or national goals of sending Americans to college for a substantive course of study and a worthwhile college degree. In other words, if the academic profession were to receive reasonable respect, compensation, and professional development rather than being cast as a "problem," the faculty then could provide a "solution" to many of American higher education's genuine "problems" in the 21st century.

NOTES

1. Steven E. Deutsch and Joseph Fashings, *Academics in Retreat* (Albuquerque: University of New Mexico Press, 1971).
2. Jack Schuster, "Introduction: The Professoriate's Perilous Path," in Joseph C. Hermanowicz, Editor, *The American Academic Profession: Transformation in Contemporary Higher Education* (Baltimore, MD and London: Johns Hopkins University Press, 2011) pp. 1–20.
3. Mary Burgan, *What Ever Happened to the Faculty?: Drift and Decision in Higher Education* (Baltimore, MD: Johns Hopkins University Press, 2006).
4. Frederick Rudolph, "Academic Man," in *The American College and University: A History* (New York: Alfred A. Knopf, 1962) see esp. pp. 394–395.
5. Richard Hofstadter, "On the Unpopularity of Intellect," in *Anti-Intellectualism in American Life* (New York: Random House, 1962) pp. 24–54.
6. Scott R. Bauries, "Individual Academic Freedom: An Ordinary Concern of the First Amendment," *Mississippi Law Journal* (2014) vol. 83, no. 4, pp. 677–744.

7. Robert Post, *Democracy, Expertise, Academic Freedom* (New Haven, CT: Yale University Press, 2011). See also, Scott McLemee's review of Post's book in *Inside Higher Ed* (January 18, 2012).
8. Michael A. Olivas, *Suing Alma Mater: The Courts and Higher Education* (Baltimore, MD and London: Johns Hopkins University Press, 2011).
9. Greg Lukianoff, "FIRE Launches Campaign in Support of University of Chicago Free Speech Statement," Foundation for Individual Rights in Education, press release of September 28, 2015.
10. Ellen W. Schrecker, *No Ivory Tower: McCarthyism and the Universities* (New York: Oxford University Press, 1986).
11. Larry Cuban, *How Scholars Trumped Teachers: Change Without Reform in University Curriculum, Teaching and Research, 1890–1990* (New York: Teachers College Press, 1999).
12. Burton R. Clark, *The Academic Life: Small Worlds, Different Worlds* (Princeton, NJ: Princeton University Press, 1987) (Special Report for the Carnegie Foundation for the Advancement of Teaching).
13. Joseph C. Hermanowicz, "The Culture of Mediocrity," *Minerva* (June 13, 2013) pp. 363–387.
14. Rebecca S. Lowen, "Building Steeples of Excellence," in *Creating the Cold War University: The Transformation of Stanford* (Berkeley: University of California Press, 1997) pp. 147–190. See also, Roger L. Geiger, *Research and Relevant Knowledge: American Research Universities since World War II* (New York: Oxford University Press, 1993).
15. Donald Kennedy, *Academic Duty* (Cambridge, MA: Harvard University Press, 1997).
16. Theodore Caplow and Reese J. McGee, *The Academic Marketplace* (New York: Basic Books, 1958).
17. Anthony Ostroff, "Economic Pressures and the Professor," in Nevitt Sanford, Editor, *The American College: A Psychological and Social Interpretation of the Higher Learning* (New York: John Wiley & Sons, 1962) pp. 445–462.
18. Christopher Jencks and David Riesman, *The Academic Revolution* (Garden City, NY: Doubleday Anchor, 1968).
19. Dorothy E. Finnegan, "Segmentation in the Academic Labor Market: Hiring Cohorts in Comprehensive Universities," *Journal of Higher Education* (1993) vol. 64, pp. 621–656.
20. Richard M. Freeland, *Academia's Golden Age: Universities in Massachusetts, 1945–1970* (New York: Oxford University Press, 1992).
21. Neil J. Smelser and Robin Content, *The Changing Academic Marketplace: General Trends and a Berkeley Case Study* (Berkeley: University of California Press, 1980).
22. Howard R. Bowen and Jack H. Schuster, *The American Professoriate: A National Resource Imperiled* (New York: Oxford University Press, 1986).
23. Joseph C. Hermanowicz, Editor, *The American Academic Profession: Transformation in Contemporary Higher Education* (Baltimore, MD and London: Johns Hopkins University Press, 2011).
24. Howard R. Bowen and Jack H. Schuster, *The American Professoriate: A National Resource Imperiled* (New York: Oxford University Press, 1986); Martin J. Finkelstein, *The Academic Profession: The Professoriate in Crisis* (London: Routledge, 1997); Martin J. Finkelstein, Robert K. Seal, and Jack H. Schuster, *The New Academic Generation: A Profession in Transformation* (Baltimore, MD: Johns Hopkins University Press, 1998).
25. Benjamin Ginsberg, *The Fall of the Faculty: The Rise of the All-Administrative University and Why It Matters* (New York: Oxford University Press, 2011).
26. Ann E. Austin, "The Socialization of Faculty in a Changing Context: Traditions, Challenges and Possibilities," in Joseph C. Hermanowicz, Editor, *The American Academic Profession: Transformation in Contemporary Higher Education* (Baltimore, MD and London: Johns Hopkins University Press, 2011) pp. 145–167.
27. "Document 9.3: Faculty Memoir – An Interview with Professor Laura Nader," in John R. Thelin, Editor, *Essential Documents in the History of American Higher Education* (Baltimore, MD and London: Johns Hopkins University Press, 2014) pp. 334–443. This interview by Russell Schoch was originally published in *California Monthly* (November 2000) pp. 28–32.
28. Frank Newman, Chair, *Report on Higher Education* (Washington, D.C.: Task Force of the U.S. Department of Health, Education and Welfare, 1971).
29. The late Professor Bentham endures as an intriguing, problematic character who has fused fact and fiction. Even critics of the legend concede that he has, indeed, attended some faculty meetings – in 1976, for example. In setting the record straight, literalists are insistent that Professor Bentham did not preside over the meetings – but whoever claimed that he did? As part of organizational saga, the legendary academic figure does convey the qualities a provost would welcome in a professor.
30. Roger G. Baldwin and Jay L. Chronister, *Teaching Without Tenure: Policies and Practices for a New Era* (Baltimore, MD: Johns Hopkins University Press, 2002).
31. "The College Faculty Crisis," *New York Times* (April 14, 2014) p. A18.

Additional Readings

Roger G. Baldwin and Jay L. Chronister, *Teaching Without Tenure: Policies and Practices for a New Era* (Baltimore, MD: Johns Hopkins University Press, 2002).

Scott R. Bauries, "Individual Academic Freedom: An Ordinary Concern of the First Amendment," *Mississippi Law Journal* (2014) vol. 83, no. 4, pp. 677–744.

Howard R. Bowen and Jack H. Schuster, *The American Professoriate: A National Resource Imperiled* (New York: Oxford University Press, 1986).

Mary Burgan, *What Ever Happened to the Faculty? Drift and Decision in Higher Education* (Baltimore, MD: Johns Hopkins University Press, 2006).

Theodore Caplow and Reese J. McGee, *The Academic Marketplace* (New York: Basic Books, 1958).

Burton R. Clark, *The Academic Life: Small Worlds, Different Worlds* (Princeton, NJ: Princeton University Press, 1987) (Special Report for the Carnegie Foundation for the Advancement of Teaching).

Larry Cuban, *How Scholars Trumped Teachers: Change Without Reform in University Curriculum, Teaching and Research, 1890–1990* (New York: Teachers College Press, 1999).

Steven E. Deutsch and Joseph Fashings, *Academics in Retreat* (Albuquerque: University of New Mexico Press, 1971).

Martin J. Finkelstein, *The Academic Profession: The Professoriate in Crisis* (London: Routledge, 1997).

Martin J. Finkelstein, Robert K. Seal, and Jack H. Schuster, *The New Academic Generation: A Profession in Transformation* (Baltimore, MD: Johns Hopkins University Press, 1998).

Dorothy E. Finnegan, "Segmentation in the Academic Labor Market: Hiring Cohorts in Comprehensive Universities," *Journal of Higher Education* (1993) vol. 64, pp. 621–656.

Richard M. Freeland. *Academia's Golden Age: Universities in Massachusetts, 1945–1970* (New York: Oxford University Press, 1992).

Roger L. Geiger, *Research and Relevant Knowledge: American Research Universities since World War II* (New York: Oxford University Press, 1993).

Benjamin Ginsberg, *The Fall of the Faculty: The Rise of the All-Administrative University and Why It Matters* (New York: Oxford University Press, 2011).

Joseph C. Hermanowicz, Editor, *The American Academic Profession: Transformation in Contemporary Higher Education* (Baltimore, MD: Johns Hopkins University Press, 2011).

Joseph C. Hermanowicz, "The Culture of Mediocrity," *Minerva* (June 13, 2013) pp. 363–387.

Christopher Jencks and David Riesman, *The Academic Revolution* (Garden City, NY: Doubleday Anchor, 1968).

Donald Kennedy, *Academic Duty* (Cambridge, MA: Harvard University Press, 1997).

Rebecca S. Lowen, *Creating the Cold War University: The Transformation of Stanford* (Berkeley: University of California Press, 1997).

Michael A. Olivas, *Suing Alma Mater: Higher Education and the Courts* (Baltimore, MD and London: Johns Hopkins University Press, 2011).

Robert Post, *Democracy, Expertise, Academic Freedom* (New Haven, CT: Yale University Press, 2012).

Nevitt Sanford, Editor, *The American College: A Psychological and Social Interpretation of the Higher Learning* (New York: John Wiley & Sons, 1962).

Jack H. Schuster and Martin J. Finkelstein, *The American Faculty: The Restructuring of Academic Work and Careers* (Baltimore, MD: Johns Hopkins University Press, 2008).

Ellen W. Schrecker, *No Ivory Tower: McCarthyism and the Universities* (New York: Oxford University Press, 1986).

Edward Shils, *The Academic Ethic* (Chicago: University of Chicago Press, 1984).

6

GOVERNANCE AND ORGANIZATION

Structures and Cultures

SETTING AND OVERVIEW

"Why can't a college be run more like a business?" This chapter responds to that criticism and query by looking at the decision-making, administrative structure, and culture of colleges and universities. It then sets forth comparison and contrast with their counterpart business and industrial corporations. Chapter 7, dealing with "fiscal fitness," will continue to respond to the rhetorical "business" question, but with a different focus: to analyze both colleges' and corporations' financial profile and performance.

Decision-making in higher education is best understood by providing a guide to the structure and ground rules associated with the distinctive "shared governance" model usually associated with colleges and universities.[1] Emphasis is on the interaction of major stakeholders. Boards of trustees, presidents, provosts and vice presidents, faculty, students, alumni, as well as donors and legislators each may have distinctive powers and divisions of labor – but each and all respect one another informally and formally. What this means is that the institutional culture of shared mission, cooperation, and civility animates the organizational structures.

Although comparison with the "business corporation" is at the top of the agenda, why be confined to that one model? Equally intriguing is to search and scrutinize additional models and metaphors. Therefore, analysis of higher education governance will include comparisons with other options, including city and state governments, as well as a range of nonprofit organizations.

First, let's turn to the familiar contemporary business model analogy. A glance at organizational charts shows remarkable overlap between academic institutions and commercial corporations in the United States. One legacy is that the early colonial colleges shared a bold structural innovation that set them apart from the established English universities – Oxford and Cambridge. Even though the American colonial college founders relied on the established English universities as inspirations, they made deliberate adjustments. The American college founders were forthright in establishing a strong office of president. This went hand in glove with their deliberate act of creating an *external board of trustees* that had ultimate legal power and responsibility for the institution.[2]

This structure joins colleges and businesses in the United States. In fact, business tended to borrow this arrangement from the colleges who were ahead of the curve in the 17th century by having charters that provided incorporation for perpetuity with a locus of power in the president and board! This structural tradition has been persistent for four centuries. Given this shared emphasis on a strong executive and external board, with top-down authority to oversee a pyramid of staff and employees, how is it that colleges and companies have become perceived by some as wholly different organizational creatures? If one takes seriously the suggestion that "colleges should be run more like a business," we are left with additional puzzles. First, why is this a good idea? What is the problem in higher education that emulating business decision-making would solve or improve? Do businesses "meet a payroll," while colleges do not? Is corporate executive leadership decisive, whereas college and university presidents are less so? Second, which business corporations in particular are good to emulate? In 1959 General Motors might have been a wise choice – but not so a half-century later in 2009 when it faced bankruptcy.

ISSUES

Concerns about academic governance have been generated by an escalation of questions about the efficacy of "shared governance." This is the distinctive model in which a complex academic organization, ranging from a liberal arts college to a multi-purpose research university, can respect and include various constituencies of faculty, students, alumni, donors, and staff. It is an unusual, even daring model because it contrasts markedly with the hierarchy of authority and decisions in a business or commercial organization. And, the academic ideal of "shared governance" also stands apart from the civil service structure of bureaucratic offices one associates with many local, state, and federal agencies.

In fact, academia's "shared governance" is neither simplistic nor standardized. Within each campus there are structures and customs of deference and cooperation. Even in a college or university with a strong tradition of faculty influence, professors ultimately defer to the decisions made by the board of trustees and carried out by the president. To understand the strengths and limits of "shared governance" it is essential to survey the cast of groups and offices that interact formally and informally within a campus setting.

CHARACTERS AND CONSTITUENTS

The apex of an academic organizational chart is the president – the functional equivalent of a business's chief executive officer, or "CEO." She reports directly to the board of trustees, who are in charge of hiring, firing, and evaluating the president. The pyramid descending from the president's office links to a gallery of vice presidents. Almost all institutions, large or small – public or private – have the following vice presidential officers: academic affairs, business affairs, development and external relations, and student life. Universities with large enrollments, diverse missions, and complex interactions inside and outside the campus usually have added vice presidencies to show that they are committed to some new function or activity. Added vice presidencies include auxiliary services, government relations, research, medical center and health campus, enrollment management, and institutional diversity. On paper, vice presidents all report directly to the president. In practice, the priorities (and crises) particular to a college or university modify this.

Proximity to the throne, the executive suite, or the boardroom confers status and privilege for academic office-holders. At colleges and universities with commitment to academics, the academic vice president may also be designated as "Provost" and enjoy the status of being "first among equals" of the vice presidents. Elsewhere, it varies. It may well be that the hospital, parking, an industrial park, and other enterprising ventures are most central to the university priorities – in which case the Vice President for Auxiliary Services is favored. For an institution heavily dependent on sponsored research projects from federal agencies, the Vice President for Research gains an edge. If private fundraising is the lifeblood of a college, then the Vice President for Development may be the favored courtier.

In some instances an administrative position acquires the status of direct reporting to the president. This is the case with the Director of Athletics, especially if the intercollegiate athletics program is high profile. One provision for law school accreditation is that the Dean of the Law School reports directly to the president. Otherwise, there usually are institutional layers that spare the president from direct access by all constituencies, even in a culture of cooperation. That is hardly a sinister or aloof characteristic – but often a reasonable, pragmatic design that minimizes the odds that the president's time will be nibbled away, imprisoned by the erroneous notion that all issues are equally worthy of presidential attention. The corollary is that in the shared governance institution, individuals and groups need to learn how to navigate the labyrinth of offices and services. This, of course, is easier said than done.

If educational instruction and degree programs are central to the mission of a university, then the key unit is the *academic college*. The college is essentially an academic city-state with its own rites and regulations of courtesy, pecking orders, and protocols. Presidents and provosts ultimately have power over each academic dean. However, the crucial juncture is at the hiring stage where a provost more or less gets to select the dean-elect; provosts will have numerous university-wide directives and mandates with which an academic dean must comply. But there is a customary invisible fence that provosts are reluctant to cross so as to not be seen as meddling in the dean's college pasture.

The Board of Trustees

Boards are baffling. They represent an extraordinary concentration of power and trust into an appointed body that serves on a voluntary basis and has relatively little proximity to or involvement in the various life and activities of the college or university. Furthermore, most board members are appointed on the basis of accomplishments in fields other than higher education. Be on the alert for variations in terminology. "Board of Trustees" is most familiar, but one also finds in American higher education a "Board of Visitors," "Board of Curators," "Overseers," and "Fellows of the Corporation." A board typically has between 15 and 30 members. Independent (private) colleges and universities usually have more board members than do state or public institutions.

At state institutions, most board members are appointed by the governor – usually in staggered, four-year terms. This allows for continuity while avoiding abrupt turnover in a single year. The Regents of the University of California have a 16-year term. They have been called "the world's largest unhappy family," indicative of factions that have included lawsuits filed by one Regent against another. In states where the governor has the power to appoint to hundreds of boards and commissions, being tapped to serve as trustee at a flagship state university is often a repayment of a political favor and a nod of thanks for a job well done. Its perks include free tickets and good seats at intercollegiate athletic contests – often highly coveted and a source of envy from state legislators who are in the bleachers or on their way out of office.

Trustees at independent (private) colleges and universities carry multiple burdens of responsibility. Independent colleges and universities seldom have assurances of state appropriations or per student subsidies or state-backed bonding authority, which means that the college relies almost exclusively on student tuition revenues, federal Pell Grant payments carried by eligible students, and funds brought in via private fund-raising. Since there is less margin for error or prospect for state assistance, board members are often expected to lead by example as generous donors. Furthermore, they are expected to cultivate prospective donors from the circle of their peers. The CEO who is appointed to the board of Alma Mater accepts the signal that she or he should invite fellow CEOs into the donor's circle, using one's own substantial gift as a model of service. All college and university board members are expected to chair or serve on one or more major committees as appointed by the chair of the board.

Unlike the custom with corporate boards, college and university trustees are not compensated handsomely. Reimbursements for travel and lodging usually are the financial limits. Symbolic awards to recognize distinguished board service are usually the ultimate honor – as dedicated former chairs and rectors often are conferred honorary degrees at commencement. Serving on a college or university board is a labor of love – sprinkled with measures of frustration as well as quiet accomplishment and contribution, and, in recent years, an increasing workload.[3]

Initiation into the ranks of college and university boards can be enhanced through membership in such organizations as the Association of Governing Boards (AGB) and the American Council of Trustees and Alumni (ACTA) – each with national headquarters in Washington, D.C. Membership in these groups, however, is voluntary. Only a minority of trustees nationwide make use of the materials and conferences sponsored by AGB and ACTA.

About a century ago the composition of college boards shifted drastically from clergy to corporate executives.[4] This may explain the contemporary invocation of business models in attempts to reform higher education. The demographics of board composition have changed gradually yet persistently over the past half-century. In 1969, 88 percent of trustees were men – overwhelmingly white men. Women constituted 1 percent of boards; 1 percent were African American; and there was no indication of Hispanic or Latino trustees. In 2010 women were 30 percent of board members, 7.4 percent were African American, and 2.4 percent were Latino. A large percentage of trustees are alumni, especially at independent colleges and universities.

Some institutions have special seats, elected by designated groups. The faculty, for example, may be allotted the right to elect one or two of their colleagues to serve on the board. The staff employee association also often has representation by electing a board member from its ranks. The alumni association has some designated representatives. The president of the student government association usually is an *ex officio* member of the university board. Hence, over time, colleges have gained some diversification in representing constituencies.

In contrast to boards with appointments by the governor, many institutions – especially independent colleges and universities – have self-perpetuating boards. This means that as a member's term expires, the chair of the board holds an election of appointment, and perhaps re-appointment. And, as often is the case with generalizations about higher education, there are important exceptions. The University of Delaware, for example, is a flagship state university. And, its board of trustees is selected by means of appointments from a self-selecting board.

With this overview as introduction, we now can go into detail about each of the major participants and constituencies.

The President

Presidents are the leaders and conspicuous figures in American colleges and universities.[5] They command respect, power, prestige, privilege, and visibility by dint of their office. College and university presidents' leadership often is acknowledged by leaders in such spheres as business and government. This is demonstrated by invitations for a college president to serve on corporate boards, boards of other philanthropic foundations, along with appointment to task forces assembled by the President of the United States, state governors, and metropolitan mayors. College and university presidents are center stage in the American Establishment.

Serving as the president of a college or university carries demands of time, energy, and attention. These are multiplied by the diverse, often conflicting, constituencies who claim affiliation with a campus. So, in addition to being the CEO of a central campus staff and, by extension, over a large service bureaucracy, a president is expected to meet with and speak to prospective donors, the alumni association, chamber of commerce, and athletics boosters. And, the president also serves as the real and symbolic presence of the institution at command performance public events. Each campus group, whether the Dean of Agriculture or the university choral director, the president of the Interfraternity Council, the Friends of Alma Mater Basketball, or the African American Student Association, seeks for the president to grace their particular event by a guest appearance. Expectations extend to the presidential spouse – so much so that some universities, such as UCLA, formalized the presidential partner role into a salaried position.

Review of a typical day in the life of a president indicates a dizzying calendar, starting with, for example, a breakfast meeting through a succession of ceremonial events, public speaking engagements, staff meetings, and availability to respond promptly to unexpected campus crises involving students, staff, and community groups. Few college or university presidents today would recognize the daily regimen of the President of the United States Calvin Coolidge who, despite constantly alluding to his vaunted New England parsimony and work ethic, found time each day for a leisurely lunch followed by a nap. Nor do academic presidents today have the luxury of President Coolidge's three-month vacation to the Dakotas and other U.S. territories. The contemporary college and university president works long and hard – and seldom, if ever, is truly "off duty."

Since colleges and universities and their related groups constitute a "loosely coupled" network and federation of constituencies, the character of a president's work brings to mind that of a large city mayor or, perhaps, a governor of a state. The myriad issues and events are never-ending. On the other hand, this potential roster of obligations means that a president has the right and necessity to "just say no!" to an invitation or request.

Sending a proxy as emissary is customary – however, making those decisions to attend or not are delicate matters of power and diplomacy. A campus president might be compared to an unelected politician – constantly running for office, playing off numerous partisan groups to maintain institutional priorities. Knowledgeable analysts of the presidential workload – along with the job descriptions posted in a presidential search – marvel at the range of skills one must bring to the presidential office if one is to be successful and effective. Public speaking, diplomacy, a cast-iron stomach to endure numerous banquets – all these are concluded with the good-natured quip that the ideal college president most likely should have the ability to "walk on water."

Evaluating the performance of a college or university president is simultaneously high stakes and difficult to do in a meaningful way. The ultimate decision to hire or fire is made by the board of trustees. But it is preceded by the ritualized year-long exercise of consulting with numerous institutional groups. More accurately, the board should *appear* to confer. Faculty usually are miffed to learn that their voice is not central, compressed in with staff and alumni. But even a well-intentioned board finds that it is not easy to know whether or not a president is doing a good job. Hiring – or, firing – a president involves a great deal of time and energy. It is not done lightly or capriciously. The entire institution suffers great trauma if a president is fired or forced to resign after a short tenure and/or for capricious, superficial reasons.

What might be a flashpoint wherein a board of trustees moves to oust a president? Often it is some conduct that is symbolically offensive – or, which is galvanized by such a gaffe. At one flagship state university whose colors are orange and white, a new president raised trustee and alumni eyebrows shortly after moving in to the lavish presidential house. Ripping out the orange wall-to-wall carpet in favor of new crimson carpeting signaled a fundamental ignorance or disrespect for the university colors. Trustees might be patient with budget shortfalls, accreditation problems, uncertainty on starting a new program in the college of medicine – but the color of carpeting is visible and visceral. Some accounts note that when the offending president was fired, the board quickly arranged for the crimson carpet to be picked up and then shipped at no charge to a rival university whose true color was crimson.

Disloyalty can also take the form of not heeding the cues of an institution's priorities. A president most certainly has the right to reserve the university jet for fund-raising calls. And, a board might even overlook a president whose frequent jet flights allegedly involved trips for personal dalliances. Where the board did look askance was when such a presidential jet trip happened to bump the football coach's scheduled flight to land a prized quarterback recruit. This reinforces the message that academic presidents ought to heed Mark Twain's advice that "It is all right to break laws so long as one obeys customs."

Turn-about is fair play in university leadership. Often overlooked is that presidents, especially those who are confident and ascending in stature, can "fire their board." Or, put another way, a good president usually is in demand elsewhere and just might have a great job offer and pay raise plus pledges of support from a more prestigious college or university elsewhere.

Boards want presidents to have the resources, ranging from salary to staff, to excel at the job upon which the board and president agreed. What a board chair probably cannot accommodate is if a relatively new president whines about a salary increase – tantamount to holding an entire institution hostage over a petty, personal, and selfish matter that the board thought had been mutually and amicably settled at the contract signing.

In such rare instances, boards move quickly to remove an ill-fitting president. Equally volatile is when a president messes up the highly visible role as spokesperson in the public media. Off-color jokes, sexism, and gender and racial stereotypes do not have a high tolerance threshold in an era of widespread press and social media coverage. If the President of the Ohio State University makes jokes about Catholic priests in speaking to Buckeye Boosters a few days before their game with Notre Dame, recordings and videos of the speech probably will be diffused to the press via social media. Such remarks, perhaps once permissible because private and contained, provide the negative publicity that can be harmful, perhaps fatal, to an offending president.

To communicate – or, perhaps, the failure or inability to communicate – in a tense public setting is an infrequent but important experience for presidents. And, as suggested by the November 2015 events at the University of Missouri in which both the president and chancellor resigned due to dissatisfaction with their lack of attention to racial tensions on campus, high-level administrators who are ill-at-ease with the fluidity and complexity of organized student demonstrations and grievances run the risk of losing support not only from dissident student groups, but also, eventually, from their board of curators or board of directors. Since presidents often are shielded by their staff from controversy, recent generations of presidents probably have lost facility with genuine public speaking, especially if it involves spontaneity and debate on significant public issues. It signals an historic decline in the oratory skills that characterized American leaders, whether as politicians or college presidents, a century ago.

The typical presidential pattern is that the new leader is allowed a generous honeymoon period, followed by several years in which to "make a mark," with the one condition that he or she avoid a scandal. Estimates on length of presidential service are about five to ten years. But this may be determined by different performances and evaluations. An outstanding president – or, more specifically, a president who is perceived as outstanding – may gain a following nationwide, be in demand, and leave a college in order to accept another presidency elsewhere – perhaps at a more prestigious institution. If one does serve as president for about five to seven years, trustees keep tabs on whether a president has fulfilled the institutional promises made as a candidate and then reaffirmed at the inauguration ceremony. If the perception among board members, and perhaps by an inquisitive governor or a major donor, is that the institution is stalled, one hears such phrases as, "we need to go in a different direction," or, "I can't put my finger on it, but the fit no longer seems right," or, "It's not you, it's me..."

This administrative death knell drags out until one day there is the ritualized press conference in which the president announces one or more of the following: "I want to spend more time with my family," or "I want to return to my teaching and research." A third prevalent outcome is that the exiting president is named to head up a foundation or some special task force initiative. Farewell packages usually are robust. In 2015 the retiring president of Yale University, who had served over 20 years, received a gesture of thanks from the Yale Board – namely, $8.5 million for a job well done. When a president does opt to "return to the faculty," the terms usually are generous – maintaining most of the presidential salary, granted a fund for research, often a free year of sabbatical at full pay, a spacious office and research lab, and minimal teaching obligations. Deferred compensation and insurance policies are customary.

Who becomes a college or university president? Some claim the job is so demanding that a candidate must be a glutton for punishment along with the long days and endless commitments. Perhaps so. Equally plausible is that to be a president – just as with running for mayor or governor – one will fare well if one has a propensity for the kinds of activities that are standard for the job. A good match in terms of personality and president can mean that the role can be downright enjoyable. Conversely, if one does acknowledge that such activities are standard fare, no amount of salary compensation can bring a reluctant or timid president up to par.

Some presidents thrive on the challenges. All the obligations of the office are accompanied by a constellation of professionals and administrative staff to carry out presidential requests for information, reports, drafts of speeches, security patrols, chauffeurs, a director of public relations, a vice president for government relations, and other invaluable support. Although the job has great responsibility and demands, no one becomes a president without deliberate quest and ambition.

First-hand familiarity with colleges and universities is almost always a requirement for a successful presidential applicant. Usually this includes experience moving up through academic ranks as a professor, with advancement into such campus administrative appointments as a department chair, dean, or academic vice president. However, there is no imperative that a president must have been a faculty member or even have earned a Ph.D. To the contrary, a college or university presidency is one of the few academic positions where the paramount criterion is leadership potential that might be conveyed by any number of prior positions. From time to time there are discernible patterns where lawyers were in demand as presidents – and this did not necessarily mean one had to have been a law professor. Leadership in military, politics, government, or business at a high level can be seen by search committees as good connections to lead a college or university. General Dwight D. Eisenhower was hand-picked by the chair of the Columbia University board to lead that institution after World War II – a five-year tenure prior to Eisenhower's election as the President of the United States. At one time Dartmouth selected an alumnus who had been CEO of the John Deere Corporation as its president. In 2013 Purdue University's new president held no faculty appointment, but had been governor of Indiana. He did hold a Ph.D. and had a strong academic record. In 2015 presidential selections at the University of Iowa and the University of North Carolina attracted attention – and created some tension – given the limited academic credentials and experience of the appointees. Other examples surface, such as the President of the University of Missouri system who came to his academic leadership role from private industry, where he had been the CEO of a successful high-tech company. And, crucial to note is that he had grown up as a "faculty brat" on the campus where he returned to serve – a strong indicator of sustained loyalty and familiarity with Alma Mater. What any new president does need to keep in mind is that preoccupation with the "bottom line" of budgets and fund-raising should not blind a president to the fact that a college or university is a community with its own culture. Working with and talking to various groups, plus listening to concerns, is essential for the well-being of an institution – and its president. Management skills may be necessary, but are not sufficient to create respected academic leadership.

Rising through the campus ranks can also provide numerous administrative avenues to being selected as a president. The increasing importance of administrative vice presidencies means that one who was successful as, for example, a vice president for development could be a viable candidate as president of a college that sorely needed expertise and experience in fund-raising. A former U.S. senator or governor could be competitive if those experiences in either Washington, D.C. or the statehouse are timely credentials for a particular college. More urgent and uncertain, however, is how much importance a presidential search committee places on prior presidential experience. The code words in job ads emphasize that priority will be given to "a sitting president." The subtext is that deans and provosts will face obstacles in ousting a candidate who has presidential experience elsewhere. Newly selected presidents have some support systems, such as Harvard's special (and expensive) summer seminar for new presidents.

The gravity of being a college and university president is widely acknowledged and respected. Nobody wants a president to fail. Presidents – especially at complex universities with a large range of academic programs – are expected to focus on issues and constituencies external to the campus. Here, potential donors, major foundations, federal agencies, prominent alumni, and lobbying groups represent the main event. The trade-off is that the academic vice president or provost is the CAO – Chief Academic Officer – who oversees curricular innovations and academic programs. These lines of demarcation are not indelible – just as any substantive academic initiative will overlap with numerous campus offices – ranging from construction to philanthropy. Most likely the board of trustees will acquiesce to a president who does choose to be involved in academic affairs.

The research literature on college and university presidents is itself a testimony to the power affiliated with the office. Among the research questions that have gained prominence in recent years include: "Do presidents make a difference? And, if so, how much?" "What or who is the counterpart of a college president in other professions?" In 1960 Clark Kerr observed that with the evolution of the multiversity and the multi-campus system, the possibility of a university president being authoritarian or patriarchal had passed. Kerr thought that presidents increasingly were cast in the role of a mediator. A check of job ads over the years shows some discernible trends: increasing specific requirements for management experience, fund-raising acumen, and external relations. As noted earlier, prior service as a professor seems necessary in most cases, as does experience as a dean or perhaps also as a provost. On close inspection, these are neither necessary nor sufficient for one to prevail as a president.

Within American higher education, a question that surfaces is whether serving as president of a large university – or, a university system – is more difficult than the role of president of a college, which probably is relatively small in size and clear in degree programs and mission. There is no single answer. Worth considering, however, is what may be termed the presidential "margin of difference." Whereas the president of a large university has numerous layers of support systems and professional offices, the president of a college has an immediate presence and has little allowance for delegating or deferring responsibility. This builds in decisiveness to the round of presidential life that probably is under-appreciated by presidents at a multiversity.

The Provost

Provosts are problematic. The late Clark Kerr, legendary President of the University of California and, later, Chair of the Carnegie Commission on Higher Education, noted in 1986 that in his opinion being a provost was one of the great jobs one could have. However, a provost had to see herself or himself as first among equals among the faculty. And that is increasingly difficult to do in the college or university of the 21st century. A more realistic definition is that a provost, who also is usually the academic vice president, is the customary leader among the growing ranks of university vice presidents. That might have once been almost a sure thing, but it is uncertain – and declining in likelihood. In general, provosts have lost power and prestige. First, they are almost always lieutenants to the president. If by chance a particular president extends priority to academic matters, this intrudes on the provost's primary authority and responsibility. But there is little room for protest. Second, it's possible for other vice presidencies to assert inordinate power. The Vice President for Development or the Vice President for Research are potential candidates. Nor is it likely that a provost has much power over the Vice President of the Medical Center.

The provost does have a crucial role as the leader of numerous academic deans. Although the office of the provost has considerable power of coercion and top-down authority, the role really is more like mediator among a federation of academic chieftains. If the president and/or the board decide on some transformational strategy in terms of curricular programs, the provost ideally should have a strong voice in the deliberations. After all, it is the provost who will have the obligation to break the news and implement the "new academic vision" or the new educational budgeting model to the assorted deans and colleges.

One source of internal power provosts have involves evaluation and dismissal of academic deans. At one time and at some campuses, the academic dean was considered to be the "first among equals" for the faculty in a college. In recent years, however, the center of authority has shifted away from a collegial model toward a more hierarchical arrangement. Academic deans increasingly have become lieutenants and subordinates to the provost. This drift toward top-down governance is especially evident in the periodic evaluations of academic deans about every five years or so. The provost typically controls the membership of the evaluation committee, increasingly diluting faculty slots with other constituencies. Furthermore, the faculty advisory group probably has to sign a confidentiality form in which each agrees not to discuss the faculty group's deliberations or recommendations. When the faculty advisory group for a college does file its recommendations to the provost, there is little assurance that the provost will heed or even publicize the recommendations. The caveat is that the provost ultimately is a lieutenant, not a leader. That is because the provost, either formally or informally, serves at the pleasure of the president.

Vice Presidents

A college or university probably has between five and 15 vice presidents. This number, which represents a sizeable increase over the past three decades, is due to two factors: first, some administrative offices have been elevated to the rank of vice president. A Dean of Student Affairs in 1990 often now is a Vice President for Student Affairs – without elimination of the earlier, incumbent dean position. Instead of, or perhaps in addition to, a Dean of Admissions, one now has a Vice President for Enrollment Management. Another explanation is that colleges and universities have created new vice presidencies to reflect the addition of new functions and responsibilities at the top of the administrative chart. Vice President for Institutional Diversity would be a good example, as would be a Vice President for Planning. The one-time Business Officer has been transformed into the Vice President for Business Affairs. At universities with a medical center, the typical arrangement used to be to have a dean of the college of medicine and a director of the university hospital. Both positions may still exist, but the important news is that they each and both report now to a Vice President for Health Services.

On paper, all vice presidents report directly to the president. This, of course, is a bit of a paper tiger because not all vice presidencies are equal. The president probably has an Executive Council in which selected, prestigious, and/or powerful vice presidents are part of the inner sanctum. Even though the official organizational chart may depict the numerous vice presidential offices in a uniform, horizontal row, in reality there is an informal pecking order. If a campus has an academic medical center, its Vice President for Health Services most likely is powerful within the circle of vice presidents – and, in some cases, may have power and resources that can trump those of the university president.

Academic Deans

In glancing at a campus organizational chart, an initial impression is to place deans as the institution's "middle managers."[6] Although visually and structurally correct, this understates and misreads both the importance and autonomy of academic deans. At a liberal arts college whose primary mission is undergraduate education, the academic dean may double as the provost, in either title or responsibilities – or both. With the exception of the president, the academic dean at a college is the single most important leader. Within a university whose educational enterprise is distributed among a galaxy of academic colleges, each college dean has both responsibility for and leadership of a crucial, complex, self-contained educational unit that is central to the institutional mission. At a land grant institution, the Dean of the College of Agriculture may inherit extraordinary influence and resources because the unit includes extension services to all counties in the state along with an array of academic and educational degree programs.

The academic college is home of educational programs. Departments, courses, majors, concentrations along with their instruction, evaluation, delivery, tuition revenues, awards, and honors all take place foremost in a college. This means that the dean of a college is in charge of student recruitment and enrollment, curricular programs, degree completion, faculty hiring and evaluation, staffing support offices, monitoring and paying for building renovations, troubleshooting various problems. And, a dean is in charge of private fund-raising – a responsibility that may take up between 25 and 50 percent of a dean's time. The exhaustive list of internal responsibilities is supplemented by the external roles of the academic dean in deliberations with special accrediting agencies, federal research offices, state government units, alumni associations, extension agents, and outreach activities. And, perhaps most important, the academic dean represents the college in decision-making and engagement with the provost and, in many cases, with the president and the board of trustees.[7]

Generic profiles of a dean are complicated by the fact that within each campus there are pecking orders of privilege and priority. A School of Business with robust undergraduate enrollments and a prestigious Executive M.B.A. program and generous donors will tend to have internal prerogatives and privileges over the College of Social Work or the College of Education. But this is subject to change, as both resources and glamour are fickle. What is intriguing and perplexing about the advice manuals and testimonials by and for academic deans in 2016 is that most accounts emphasize the kinds of innovations and changes in structure and alliances a new, dynamic dean implements.[8] These are for the most part "inputs" – and their connection, if any, with the "outputs" of the college's achievements remains vague, resistant to coherent evaluation.

What this means is that academic deans have to pay attention to data and indices of rankings and ratings within their particular field – and within their own total university. News coverage in such professional trade journals as the *Chronicle of Higher Education* gravitates to cover those institutions whose deans and colleges are dramatic and innovative. The difficulty is that much of the coverage represents some blend of self-promotional public relations announcements or interviews – usually as pronouncement of a dean's "vision" and goals. These have only incidental connection with subsequent follow-up as to whether such bold new measures are successful and effective. Ribbon-cutting ceremonies and groundbreaking events are all at the front end.

An academic dean presses for autonomy and self-determination without hindrance from a provost, president, or alumni. Autonomy, however, does not mean isolation, as a dean will lobby persistently for favored trade status within the provost's tent. At the same time, academic deans usually join together to meet as a council with the provost. These gatherings have twofold importance: first, for the dean to achieve or retain high status within the provost's priorities; and, second, to form alliances with other deans for whom such cooperation is mutually beneficial. It can include several deans of varying kinds of colleges complementing one another to form a comprehensive coalition within university discussions. Or, it could be a place to carry out a strategy to vote in a bloc against a powerful college whose dean is seen by other deans as an academic bully.

Meanwhile, no matter how intriguing such external relations may be, a dean must tend to the smooth operation and prestigious innovations, along with revenue sources, within the home college. It is what Mimi Wolverton and Walter Gmelch have described as "leadership from within."[9] Whatever regulations and committees the university has in place, each academic college is a microcosm with its own distinctive codes, handbooks, mission statements, rules of eligibility for faculty voting, and network of committees to oversee the annual round of academic life. All these must be in harmony with the overriding university handbook and codes, but within that boundary, the college grows its own systems and structures. Factions and disputes within an academic college are especially problematic to a dean for two reasons. First, disparate departments must be either placated or put on notice to prevent intramural brushfires from becoming major catastrophes that impede the overall standing or success of the whole college. Second, provosts who like to have time to attend to the overall mission of the entire campus do not at all appreciate word of intramural disputes. It's often interpreted as a dean having "lost control" of people and programs. College disputes are distractions from large, positive initiatives.

Assistants and Associates within the Administration

Increased attention to planning and budgets, along with vice presidential specialization, has meant a proliferation of professional staff throughout the academic structure. A provost's office, for example, may be subdivided between two associate or vice provosts: one for graduate studies, another for undergraduate education. A good example of a position that has gained in influence and compensation is that of the president's chief of staff. In some cases a chief of staff earns a salary double that of many full professors. When presidents and provosts make such administrative appointments there is little fuss; justification is self-evident in the eyes of the senior administrator. However, ascertaining one way or the other the "value added" of such new, enhanced staff support positions is neither obvious nor inevitable.

Faculty Senate

Many colleges and universities have in place as part of their administrative regulations and faculty handbook formal provision for academic governance. Usually this carries the name "Faculty Senate" or "Faculty Assembly." The typical format is for each academic unit to be allotted, on the basis of number of full-time faculty, a number of "seats" in the Faculty Senate. Elections are held within the home unit. The collective body of elected senators, then, elects a president, a vice president and president-elect, and assorted officers. Let's say the full Faculty Senate has 100 delegates. Its officers and a small number of at-large seats will constitute the steering committee, which is the focal point of initial deliberations. Monthly meetings of the full Faculty Senate are supplemented by weekly meetings of the steering committee or faculty council. In a spirit of shared governance, several seats in the Faculty Senate are reserved *ex officio* for selected high-level administrators. The president of the university, for example, may be designated in some central role to which the senate ultimately serves as an advisory body. One customary arrangement at some campuses is for the president of the university to preside over the opening Faculty Senate meeting – with the ritualized handing of the gavel to the professor who is chair or president of the senate.

The charge of the Faculty Senate varies in formal definition from one campus to another. Usually it pertains to matters of educational policy. This often includes curricular matters – but also has broader operational definitions. However, regulations also state that body's restrictions. For example, the Faculty Senate may have first, even exclusive, right to consider and make recommendations on a new educational program that is intended ultimately for consideration by the board of trustees. Yet this may be parsed so that power over any decisions about allotment of funding or resources is retained by the provost or president. The result is that the Faculty Senate and the top administration continually go through exercises in presentation, discussion, and attempted resolution on major proposals.

Parliamentary procedure along with practices borrowed from other deliberative, elected bodies such as Congress and state legislatures instill a protocol that leans toward extensive consideration and accommodation of multiple constituencies. Therefore, it tends to be slow. As suggested earlier on page 47 in Chapter 3, it gives rise to the quip attributed to Henry Kissinger and others, "Academic politics are so vicious because the stakes are so low." A better characterization would be to say, "The reason academic politics are so *viscous* is that the stakes are so low...."[10] This resurrects a concept of liquids one might have studied in high school chemistry – or, more likely, when being a savvy consumer for the type or grade of motor oil one selects during winter months versus summer months of driving. Viscosity refers to the "ability to resist flow." It's a conceptualization that makes sense to anyone who endures watchful waiting as a course or program proposal wends its way through the labyrinth of academic approval.

Kissinger's quip certainly has much familiarity and even some truth to it. But it also is a bum rap. Speed and efficiency, often hailed by change agents and program advocates, coexist with the less spectacular but sometimes worthy features of carefulness and thoughtful review. First, courses and programs are major investments of time and resources – and should be built to last. Second, one reason that the Faculty Senate gives attention to educational policy matters is that the faculty often have been either prohibited or blocked from decision-making in other areas of institutional initiatives. There is always some level of trust and distrust. Also, institutions vary in the strength of their faculty bodies. Princeton University goes through a monthly ritual in which the call for agenda items for a regularly scheduled faculty meeting attracts no interest – and, like clockwork, the monthly faculty meeting is canceled. Yale University has no formal faculty senate. And, Yale professors were surprised in 2012 that the Yale president, with support of the board, announced the opening of a new Yale College campus in Asia – the Yale–National University of Singapore College. The slow character of faculty senates can provide some well-needed scrutiny of presidential initiatives. Presidents and provosts often rail about faculty senate's insistence on rules and regulations. And a complete story is that the same presidents and provosts are masters at invoking rules and regulations if a group is proposing some project to which the administration is opposed.

According to Robert Birnbaum, criticisms of faculty senates tend to overlook why this formal entity is invaluable, even if the senate is seen as obstructive or limited in its formal deliberations.[11] Faculty senates can be useful to a president or provost who is stymied by distracting nuisance problems. The executive solution is to delegate respons-ibility to the Faculty Senate to discuss it, set up a task force, and at the very least ensure that the president and the board of trustees will not have to deal with the problem for a long time. Professors are put in a bind. Even if they see that the presidential issue is part of a stalling tactic, they would be seen as discourteous or uncooperative if they did not accept the presidential invitation to set up such a special committee. The president and provost, in turn, score a double coup in that by sending the Faculty Senate off on what is often a fool's errand or an inconsequential project, this may help remove the Faculty Senate from a more meaningful role on a substantive topic.

No one denies the importance of "shared governance" in an academic community. Disagreement occurs, however, on how much faculty should participate in certain deci-sions. The search for and selection of a new president is a good example. In recent years the drift has been for the faculty to be muted and evaded. Board tactics to minimize faculty involvement include stacking the deck with search committee delegates from numerous other campus constituencies – such as alumni, community, and students – all of which proportionally dilute the faculty representative's vote and voice. Another ploy is to bring only one candidate to campus for interviews and a public forum – the finalist who is the top choice of the search committee.[12]

The balance of courtesy and cooperation between presidents and elected faculty bodies has been declining. It is signaled on the national level by the declining faculty membership in the Association of American University Professors (AAUP). Also, as more faculty vacancies are filled with adjunct appointments, the collective voice of tenured and tenure track full-time professors tends to be both shrinking and aging. At many institutions, what once might have leaned toward or aspired to collegial govern-ance increasingly resembles a "management versus labor" arrangement.

What are some individual rewards for those professors who do devote considerable time over the years to participation, especially in leadership positions, to the Faculty Senate? One hypothesis is that the Faculty Senate serves as an incubator or boot camp for future, ascending campus academic leaders. However, what Robert Birnbaum found was that usually this was not the case. A faculty leader who demonstrated such skills more often than not was seen as a threat or nemesis to the incumbent president or provost. Independent thought combined with the grass-roots support of faculty across many units were antithetical to the kinds of loyalty and affiliation a president or provost expects in their administrative groups, such as the council of deans. The irony is that an effective Faculty Senate president is likely to be observed and acknowledged – but primarily so that the president can pass such individuals over, opting instead for those Faculty Senators who have demonstrated the requisite traits of agreement and uncritical loyalty to the superior administrator. It is a sorting machine that leads to sponsored promotion – but according to the particular qualities useful in a top-down organization, not one of shared decision-making. The ironic result is that faculty senates can become entities that do not work, but because of their latent functions do not go away.[13]

The ability of professors to influence institutional decisions and leadership often takes place most effectively, although unexpectedly, at colleges and universities with a strong academic culture – regardless of how strong or how weak the formal faculty bodies may be. Two examples in the early 21st century come from trustees' decisions to fire presidents – at Harvard University and the University of Virginia. At Harvard, the board reluctantly decided to fire President Lawrence Summers in the wake of informal but strong faculty anger with his treatment of faculty in his discussions and queries at departments across the university. At the University of Virginia, faculty showed a spontaneous and widespread support for President Teresa Sullivan, when she was abruptly fired by the Board of Visitors. This grass-roots public gathering of faculty on the historic Lawn was sufficiently visible and influential to lead the Rector of the Board of Visitors to rescind the presidential firing. Such episodes are important, but highly unusual. In most cases and at most colleges and universities, collective faculty will tend to be muted or diffused by the administrative machinery and strategy.

Staff Senate

Inclusion as part of shared governance often extends to the campus staff – a group that probably constitutes the largest number of college or university employees. Ranging from grounds crew and custodians to administrative assistants and professional support such as computer programmers, this constituency elects its own senate and also elects one of its members to serve on the university board of trustees. Usually it is a group whose role is under-appreciated. Important to monitor is the extent to which the Staff Senate and the Faculty Senate collaborate, cooperate, and share information. Also, at institutions that have unions, overlap with the Staff Senate will be strong.

Associations and Foundations

For a few important functions, colleges and universities opt to create incorporated foundations that reside within the university structure – and which may have an overlap of a foundation board and director plus perhaps appointment within the administrative structure of the university. For those universities that have committed seriously to sponsored research, it means the creation of a University Research Foundation, with its own board and charter. It usually includes formal provision for the university president to be a board member or perhaps even chair of the board. This accomplishes two goals: first, it helps incorporate the University Research Foundation into the discussions and decisions of all vice presidents and the president's council. Second, it enables the president and board of the university to maintain ultimate oversight and control over the Research Foundation. In practice, however, a powerful vice president who also heads up the affiliated foundation may behave and lead in an autonomous style. Foundations affiliated with a university medical center stand out. Their quasi-autonomous status can be convenient for a state university president and board who do not wish to release detailed financial data about the hospital billings and clinical doctors' fees – justified on the grounds that the foundation is a separate incorporated entity. However, courts usually rule that since the host university is required to have ultimate control over its affiliated foundation, the foundation records are ultimately part of university records – and subject to the Freedom of Information Act.

Another, opposite variation on the connections of foundations and a university comes from the case of the University of Georgia where the University Foundation, which had its own endowment, often was a source of salary supplements to the president and was also the prime manager of university real estate. In some instances, deference to the university president and board were not always maintained. When a university sets up a foundation as a source for receiving and then disbursing large amounts of money – whether through federal research grants, donors gifts, or other sources – the separation from the university leaves the possibility of tension and conflicts.

Students

One legacy of the student unrest between 1963 and 1973 has been the concession by boards of trustees to allow students (usually, undergraduates) to elect delegates who serve as members of the university board of trustees. In some instances, delegates to university-wide governance are drawn from the student government association. The president of the SGA, for example, may be *ex officio* designated to represent students on the board of trustees. Students demand services or attention that compete with faculty priorities. An example where this split is evident is in differential views on academic freedom and students' rights. Students have substantial leverage in campus governance because the president and board of trustees know that students are future alumni and potential donors. Furthermore, they may well be the daughters and sons of current donors and alumni. In 1999 at the University of Chicago, undergraduates resented and resisted a presidential initiative to change the curriculum, student services, and admissions criteria. Students, both in groups and in campus newspaper editorials, denounced the proposed changes both in the procedure (top-down) and in its real and symbolic dimensions. In other words, the undergraduates ridiculed it as "Chicago Lite." Eventually, the student push-back gained interest and support from faculty and alumni – and the reforms were seen as counter to the university's student culture. This led the president to resign.

A landmark case came in 2015 when student protests over racial tensions and allegations of administrative lethargy led the President of the University of Missouri to resign his system-wide leadership role.[14] As noted in detail in a later section on social justice and campus governance, such organized student activism has been relatively rare in the 21st century. However, by 2016 these kinds of demonstrations were taking place with increasing frequency at campuses nationwide – and usually were unexpected by campus presidents and boards.

Alumni

Alumni represent a large, loyal constituency. Their influential role in institutional matters is a distinctively American phenomenon, not found elsewhere in colleges and universities worldwide. They are supportive as donors and as participants and spectators at numerous campus events, ranging from concerts and guest lectures to intercollegiate athletic contests. Their formal presence is demonstrated by creation and staffing of an alumni association. This typically includes an executive director and professional and clerical staff. Many alumni associations have incorporated as a nonprofit organization whose by-laws included affiliation with the host college or university. From time to time this supportive structure is frayed. If so, the governance question arises about accountability, control, and funds of the alumni association. Are they ultimately part of the university? What happens in a case where the alumni association board wants to support a particular program, but the university president does not? Such episodes are contentious and litigious, as associations have gone to court to protect their organization from what they consider to be undue intrusion by the president and board of trustees. Often such disputes represent generational differences: for example, the alumni association tends to be composed of a large number of older alumni who are generous donors and who favor retaining the university's traditional mascot, even though a group of students finds it politically incorrect and offensive.

Donors

Donors represent a large, informal, and perhaps disorganized group who nonetheless exert great influence via the power of the purse. They are symmetrical partners in the fund-raising ritual with the Office of Development and, often, the president. In a positive sense, this could mean that if a donor supports an institutional initiative by way of gifts and pledges, this promotes success. Conversely, deliberately withholding a gift to make a statement in opposing some university proposal could act as a block. Obviously, a major donor who agrees to a "transformational gift" can be a partner to a president in creating a bold new institutional direction. Meddling, restrictions, and conditions are potential prices a president must pay.

COMPLEXITIES AND CONFLICTS: IMPLICATIONS FOR DECISION-MAKING

Transplants from Business to the Campus

Robert Birnbaum, who has served as a university president and provost as well as professor, has made an influential contribution to higher education with his book, *How Colleges Work.*[15] His 2001 book, *Management Fads in Higher Education*, traces the succession of acclaimed innovations that have caught the attention of college and university boards and leaders over the past half-century. Planning Program Budget Systems (PPBS), Total Quality Management (TQM), Management by Objectives (MBO), Zero-Based Budgeting, Strategic Planning, Benchmarking, and, most recently, Creative Disruption – each was center stage at one time. And, each has either exited or been partially grafted onto the way a campus works. For all the invocation of rational decision-making and concern with effectiveness, what Birnbaum found was that each of these "fads" was based on charismatic or messianic appeal. Not only did a campus have to adopt a plan, it had to *embrace* it. It could not be done piecemeal; it had to be incorporated into the fabric of the institution. Furthermore, the message of urgency included the warning that to be incomplete was to be vulnerable to problems and mistakes. These once-bold initiatives seldom reached their potential or promises.

A problem, for example, with "Strategic Plans" is that the commitment involves dedication and coordination over several years. Certainly this makes sense for a provost and an administrative team whose primary assignment is to shepherd the Strategic Planning initiative through the campus committees and units. In contrast, for professors whose focus is on teaching, research, and service, the trade-off is that participation at the department, college, or campus level requires a time commitment into what often is seen as administrative work. Strategic Planning also carries the baggage of its association with the former Soviet Union and its five-year plans for production of tractors and crops. Most of the proposed innovations run the risk of making administration become an end in itself. This makes more sense to administrators, of course, than to other members of the campus community. The failure of Strategic Planning also can be due to turnover in high-level administration. A new president or provost announces a plan (what Birnbaum calls a "management fad") comparable to a new head football coach whose first move is to insist on new decals and colors as part of the football helmet design. Yet if a new president (or, coach) is hired in midstream, the prior president's initiative is quickly set aside and probably not mentioned. When one of these fads is implemented, it may have numerous unexpected consequences or latent functions – some of which may be counter-productive.

Loyalty and Belief versus Rational Data

One problem in making sense of presidential service – and that of deans and provosts as well – is that most innovations in terms of structure or administrative models are not readily testable. How does one know that embracing a new governance model or mission statement will make the campus "better?" Perhaps, though, that is the wrong way to think about leadership mandates and invitations. In an organization based on services and human relations – as characterizes a college or university – the foremost standard is that of loyalty and affiliation. Just as new football coaches insist on changing players' uniforms or the logos on the football helmets, so do administrative reorganizations signal a "new era" and, of course, a "new regime." So, it really matters little to the incumbents in the faculty and administration whether a massive change is plausibly "good" or bad" – rather, it is a question of whether one will show fealty to the new leader who introduces and invites constituencies to "buy in" to the new plan. It is a ribbon-cutting ceremony. In fact, colleges are not unlike corporations – most major business decisions are based on some belief and/or leap of faith.

One prescription for increasing faculty loyalty and respect has been to invite professors to try their hands at simulations of campus problem solving – problems and issues that typically a president and provost would face. When this exercise was tried out at independent colleges in the Great Lakes Consortium, the promising result was that faculty acknowledged that they did not have experience in such demanding situations – and there was a learning curve in the burdens of decision-making.[16] What might be a good complement to this exercise would be for high-level administrators to sample the demands on faculty to balance teaching, research, and service.

Many high-level administrators, of course, have had extensive experience in teaching and research as part of their earlier faculty appointments. But these experiences may be distant and hazy. Furthermore, many vice presidents have little if any experience in teaching or academic advising. One underrated feature of college teaching is that although professors have great autonomy, course meetings are inflexible. A president or vice president who has become accustomed to having an administrative assistant set her calendar, or cancel meetings in favor of an unexpected important appointment, is startled at the planning that goes into a course, along with the balancing act to schedule administrative meetings around class meetings – which are, after all, central to the mission of the institution and an important source of tuition revenues. One finds that few presidents or provosts are willing or able to teach a solo class that meets two to three times per week. Furthermore, the time needed for class preparation, office hours, and grading papers usually is underestimated by the top administrators who do dare to rediscover the demands of serious college-level teaching.

Presidents versus Deans

The conventional practice is for academic deans to defer to the provost and president. The big news comes about in those rare cases that depart from this script. For example, in 1998 at Georgetown University the president designed a plan to bail out the university medical center, which was hemorrhaging red ink and running an alarming deficit. The presidential solution was to "tax" other academic units – with a sharp eye on the prestigious, prosperous School of Law and School of Business. Instead of the "Robin Hood" phenomenon of taking from the rich to give to the poor, such a move probably could be best seen as the governing and financing model one would associate with the tactics of Prince John and the Sheriff of Nottingham. The deans of the targeted colleges to be plucked objected, arguing that the tax was unfair because it penalized their own academic success and fiduciary responsibilities. And, the president responded by firing the resistant Dean of the Law School. To apply the laws of physics to academic institutions, the action led to a reaction – namely, effective objection and protest by law school alumni. The dean was reinstated and vindicated, and the taxed monies were restored.[17] A lesson was that decentralized budgeting and respect for academic colleges is a serious matter for presidents as well as for deans and professors.

The Curious Case of Creative Disruptions

Earlier in this chapter, focus was on the place of management fads in higher education governance. A particular and important case study on this note is the case of "Creative Disruption." Starting in the late 1990s the world of business – and university M.B.A. programs – gave attention and applause to the "Creative Disruption" theories of business success and failure, as advanced by Clayton Christensen, Professor at the Harvard School of Business. His books sold in the hundreds of thousands and Christensen commanded a speaking fee of $40,000 per talk – and was in great demand at business conventions. He emphasized a counter-intuitive explanation about the jockeying among high-tech start-up companies, with the seemingly paradoxical explanation why some companies that pioneered high-quality computer-related hardware, software, and services tended to be outflanked in the long-term sales market. In step with a long tradition of businesses asking colleges to adopt business practices (and colleges choosing to mimic business practices), Christensen's "Creative Disruption" arrived at the campus in pilot projects adopted by high-level college and university administrators. Furthermore, many universities adopted new curricula and programs dedicated to "disruption," conveying the sense that here were a theory and strategy that were enduring and powerful. One implication, according to Christensen's speeches and articles, was that established colleges were in danger of losing out to lower-priced innovations, such as those that emphasized massive open online courses (MOOCs) and Internet instruction.[18]

At the height of its popularity, Christensen's "Creative Disruption" movement started to unravel due to its critical dissection by his fellow scholars in business – including corridor colleagues at Harvard Business School. The most influential critique that cast doubt on Christensen's credibility came in July 2014 from an historian at Harvard, Prof. Jill Lepore, who was highly regarded as a regular author for *The New Yorker*.[19] The bill of particulars was that Christensen had rushed to establish a "theory" of organizational behavior, based on selected case studies. Grating to historians and economists was that much of Christensen's key terms were derived from the influential, graceful writings of Austrian-born Joseph Schumpeter, who was a legendary professor of economics at Harvard from the 1930s and into the post-World War II years.[20] Christensen's principles were suspect in explaining the past – and did not work when he and his associates used them to guide their own corporate investment ventures. The high-quality practices at prestigious, established institutions that were pegged as the Achilles heel over the long run were not dysfunctional and continued to add to the academic and financial health of the university – contrary to the "Creative Disruption" projections. Some amazing (and amazingly candid) characterizations followed, with one of Christensen's Harvard Business School colleagues stating in print that it was "the latest example of snake oil" and other volatile indictments.[21] Christensen, of course, responded with disclaimers and charges of "foul!" But the opinion of critical analysts had shifted from applause to doubt.

Unfortunately, many academic administrations now were stuck with a flawed "work in progress" to convert their colleges to the gospel of "Creative Disruption." The problem was that Christensen's meteoric rise as a scholar and analyst who could predict crises and solve organizational problems had crashed. He had made a lot of money in consulting, but, ultimately, he had forfeited an enduring stellar scholarly reputation. And, the legacy of management fads in providing false promises to resolve problems in higher education continued.

CONNECTIONS AND QUESTIONS

Is the Campus a Bureaucracy?

The answer is a resounding "Yes!" All too often this descriptor is presumed to be a pejorative. However, equally important is to consider that it is good news and a very good thing that a campus is a bureaucracy.[22] Bringing order and systematic behavior to a campus with thousands of students and staff is desirable and not easy.

Legendary political scientist, the late James Q. Wilson, took seriously the stereotypes attributed to bureaucracy, especially in government organizations.[23] His detailed response was to find significant differences within bureaucracies across particular fields. He looked at numerous public institutions – prisons, Social Security agencies, departments of motor vehicles, schools – and colleges and universities. The differences in morale, effectiveness, and efficiency were substantial. Foremost was the disconnect between top administration and the professional corps – a graphic example was a police department. The administrative mandate was for officers to write more tickets – both as a source of revenue and to provide statistics to document that the police force was "tough on crime." The professional ethos among police officers, however, was commitment to resolving disputes such as domestic violence without arresting anyone. Academic counterparts might be that a dean or provost attempts to decree some behavior or pattern in grading. So, which value system do instructors follow? And, which responses indicate a healthy organization or campus?

Closely related to the lore and motifs of "bureaucracy" is that of "red tape." Again, this usually has a pejorative connotation. Often overlooked is the origin of the term as the ribbon used to tie a scroll of some important, official document to be hand delivered – and only later to be associated with the morass of bureaucratic delays and labyrinths, with a quest for the bureaucrat who could solve the problem by "cutting red tape."[24] What is crucial in analyzing an academic institution is to distinguish the "systems maintenance" work of internal routines that are not spectacular, but necessary – and especially helpful if done effectively and efficiently. Payroll offices and budget administrators along with research grant administrators and registrars who are organized and prompt make a great difference in organizational life. Unfortunately, their job well done gets taken for granted – with the atypical snafus getting magnified. An excellent bureaucracy, far from being a hindrance to academic work, is essential. Robert Scott compared directors of financial aid, admissions, and other mid-level administrative positions to the "lords, squires and yeomen" of medieval life. His general observation was that they received more acknowledgments in national associations than at home on their own campus.[25]

Is the Campus Disorganized and Dysfunctional?

In contrast to the characterization of the campus as a slow bureaucracy, an equally critical depiction is that colleges and universities are dysfunctional because they are disorganized and incoherent. This view from the outside, particularly from the CEO of a company that manufactures a single product, is understandable. And, it calls for close inspection as part of its explanation. Organizational theorists have, indeed, called American colleges and universities a site for "organized anarchy."[26] This includes the so-called "garbage can model" of decision-making in which administrators identify solutions and then sort through the institutional flotsam and jetsam to identify problems that are a good match for their proposed solutions. At the heart of this organizational setting is that higher education institutions are home to numerous groups, each of which has multiple and often disparate goals. One graphic description was that a campus was comparable to a round soccer field in which each player brought her or his own goal net, balls, rules, and scoreboard. Furthermore, the round soccer field was on a tilt. By extension it showed why attempts to compare the modern university to a "knowledge factory" were incomplete and simplistic. But such simultaneous activities and pursuits hardly means that individuals and groups are not doing good things or accomplishing worthwhile goals. It gives credence to the metaphor of the campus as a marketplace of ideas – and activities.

How Has Campus Administration Changed? The Managerial Revolution

One of the most significant organizational changes in higher education took place between about 1975 and 1985 – namely, the professionalization of administration.[27] During a period of extended financial exigency, colleges and universities sought out a new cohort of high-level and mid-level administrators who tended to be proactive and systematically informed in carrying out their offices' charges. Admissions, financial aid, fund-raising and development, and institutional research were among the foremost offices to be energized.

The transformation was essentially to go from being passive to proactive and dynamic. At many colleges and universities admissions had been coupled with the registrar's office

– a combination that tended to emphasize enrollment and record keeping. Continuing a trend started by a handful of colleges in the early 1960s, by 1975 a growing number of campuses were seeking out more and better applicants by using mailing lists, visiting high school campuses and holding "college nights" in school gymnasia. View books, brochures, and telephone calls were used to keep in touch with potential students. Awards for student financial aid were changed by the creation of federal programs in 1972, including Pell Grants (originally known as BEOG – Basic Educational Opportunity Grants), SEOG (Supplementary Educational Opportunity Grants), and numerous student loan programs. Since most of these sources of federal student aid were "portable," the designated award was attached to the particular student applicant, who then could "transport" the aid to the college of his or her choice. It gave great incentive for college admissions offices to have an alert director of financial aid who would keep track of federal programs and then keep equally vigilant monitoring of potential students who might enroll – and bring those federal aid funds to the college's bursar office.

A dramatic transformation took place in fund-raising, where the development office expanded from fairly routine annual fund drives among alumni to intense cultivation of prospective donors from numerous constituencies as well as from the traditional alumni base. Prospect research represented a growing use of databases, census records, and marketing reports to identify and track potential contributors.

Underlying all these initiatives was a reliance on systematic information. Hence, the office of institutional research and its branches became increasingly important in the daily, annual, and long-term decisions of each and all campus offices. With the introduction of accessible computer systems into many campuses by the mid-1980s, institutional research evolved from unwieldy, large volumes published once per year with a compendium of facts and figures into interactive databases that could shape strategic planning and immediate considerations.

Within a college or university, the managerial revolution had its foremost impact on financial accountability. Where did the money come from? Where did it go? Traditionally these questions were tantamount to higher education's Riddle of the Sphinx. By 1990 campus financial officers knew the answer to that accounting riddle with growing speed and accuracy of information access. And, in some selected cases, more constituencies within a campus gained at least partial access to the budgetary information. Often, however, broad categories and summaries glossed over the details and disaggregation that are essential to any meaningful analyses of budgets. It was a gradual, partial gain for financial transparency.

The Exaltation of Transparency: Public Relations and Internal Relations

Contemporary colleges and universities embrace as a fact of organizational life that publicity and media coverage of campus figures and events are desirable. Furthermore, strong working relations and cooperation by and with news media are cultivated consciously and strategically. Newspaper, radio, and television coverage represent a windfall of inexpensive exposure, especially when it is favorable. It permeates every category of newspaper and news broadcasts, ranging from politics to sports to student life, feature stories on college outreach and human relations stories. Hard to imagine today is that this emphasis and success was not always a fixture – and not necessarily pursued by college and university officials. A few robust universities a century ago, particularly the University of Chicago, understood early the imperative of staffing a news bureau, putting up billboards around the metropolitan area, and holding presidential press conferences. By 1970 these had become standard fare nationwide. The move of colleges and universities into the media was part of a "graphics revolution" made possible by gains in the technology of mass circulation and rapid printing and distribution of magazines and newspapers.[28] It was supplemented by a broadcasting wave, first with radio, then followed by television and, in the 21st century, the Internet and social media.

Closely related to publicity and news releases were public and government demands for accountability by higher education officials and their institutions. "Sunshine laws" in some states introduced requirements that board meetings, committee deliberations, and presidential search committees be subject to press coverage and open records searches. The resultant watchword of the 21st century has been "transparency," which connotes visibility and openness. One is hard pressed to imagine any president who does not extol "transparency," regardless of how much or how little the institution genuinely implements these principles in practice. A realistic appraisal is that in matters of substantive information about the inner workings and decisions of a college or university, the campus was a fortress – and the site of an ongoing cat-and-mouse game between news reporters and college officials in determining the level and detail of information that was revealed and shared.

For audiences both inside and outside the campus the watchword is "caveat emptor!" Official announcements on admissions predictably proclaim "Our best class yet!", with selected details on high school grade point averages, SAT scores, and National Merit Scholarship recipients. But profiles are predictably selective, with silence on numerous substantive questions. Fund-raising campaigns, usually not publicized until completion of the so-called "quiet period," are always successful eventually – even if it means extending the closing date of the campaign or even modifying the dollar goal. And, of course, public relations directors usually can invoke the protective clause, "We're not at liberty to talk about that at this time." In sum the press releases may be intriguing and partially informative, but seldom exhaustive. They constitute the empty calories of higher education analysis in which independent digging usually reveals more interesting details that somehow got left out of official publicity.

The president persists as the central figure, as official spokesperson for the college or university. Presidential press conferences and speeches are buoyed by a formidable arsenal, including a Vice President for University Relations, a Director of Government Relations, a Director of Public Relations, and university legal counsel. Most of these media initiatives are promotional – and self-promoting. And, frequently local media and newspapers publish or broadcast at face value the press releases and video clips produced and distributed by the college or university. In other words, public relations rather than substantive news reporting dominate coverage. Yet this genre is marbled with some strands of investigative news reporting. Presidents and boards are torn in that they, of course, want publicity – but are wary if and when the coverage is critical or questioning. Also, most local newspaper editors allow the local president and presidential staff generous access to write op-ed pieces to rebut any public criticism the newspaper or other constituencies have leveled at the campus and its leaders. So although presidents may whine about "living under a microscope and microphone," on the whole they and their campus receive a pretty good deal in the world of media coverage.

Since about 2000 academic media coverage has been dominated by the rise of institutional "branding." For almost a century colleges and universities had devoted some attention and received some publicity from symbols of institutional pride, often generated from intercollegiate athletics mascots. The difference has been that college and university legal counsel and marketing offices have cooperated in high-powered campaigns to identify royalty payments while increasing signage and broadcast of campus logos. Proactive dissemination of institutional branding has been accompanied by equal vigilance to make certain that Alma Mater is not usurped by unauthorized, renegade sales of T-shirts, mugs, and product names that skirt the legal measures for royalties and permissions. The net result is that colleges and universities are covetous and concerned about the images conveyed about their institution.

The Question of Administrative Bloat

No doubt there has been a managerial revolution and administrative expansion in higher education in the past three decades. It has enhanced the ability of colleges and universities to be more professional and effective in a range of administrative decisions and planning. And, this has been accompanied by the fact that administrative salaries have soared ahead of faculty salaries. It has included expansion of office space, and clerical staff.[29] Vice presidents, along with their assistant vice presidents and associate vice presidents, often received highly preferred perks in health benefits, travel allowances, and salary bonuses. One explanation was the organizational behavior in which any new problem was "solved" by creating a new, high-level administrative office. Particularly offensive to faculty and staff is when, for example, in a lean year, the Faculty Senate voluntarily passes a resolution for faculty to forgo salary increases. Then, a few weeks later, the president announces that he will be accepting his salary increase and bonus, because, after all "he earned it." Is there a point at which such expenditures on new, enhanced positions cease to be both effective and efficient? A frequent claim by boards of trustees is that in selecting a president, "You get what you pay for...." This explanation is not wholly convincing. It leaves room for reasonable doubt. For example, a study in 2015 reported that enhanced salary and compensation for presidents did *not* demonstrate significant change in presidential performance in institutional fund-raising at over 100 state universities.[30]

CONNECTIONS WITH DIVERSITY AND SOCIAL JUSTICE

One of many indices of campus concern for social justice is to track the establishment of new offices whose foremost purpose is to deal with diversity and inequities. A good example is the Vice President for Diversity – or, some comparable nomenclature – which is now a fixture at most colleges and universities, but was relatively unknown 20 years ago. Even though such administrative additions signal priority and institutional commitment, they are best seen as a surface change whose potential still needs to be tested.

Another approach to organizational change in diversity and social justice is to track the composition over time of administrative positions, especially those of president, provost, vice presidents, and academic deans. This lens, of course, can be extended throughout the entire organizational chart. In 1996, for example, the *Chronicle of Higher Education* featured a front-page story on prospects for women to become provosts. Illustrative of a pattern or trend, the article featured the recent announcements of women appointed as provosts at three prestigious institutions – Brown, Princeton, and the University of Michigan. Whether these were real or symbolic breakthroughs, they were important. Mentorship and sponsorship remain crucial to administrative leadership career routes. Women made substantial gains in completing Ph.D.s by the late 1970s and early 1980s. The residual question was whether this would eventually lead to breaking or even cracking the "glass ceiling" in academe – or, put another way, would college and university boards and search committees someday turn up the thermostat to reduce what had long been called the "chilly climate for women"?

Gains in gender representation within higher education administration, including leadership, are strong – and getting stronger. One datum worth consideration and debate is the Ivy League – eight historic universities – many of which remained exclusively or largely male in composition and character through the late 1960s and even into the 1970s. In 2010 women were presidents of four of the eight Ivy League institutions. This included one president who also was African American. This was yet another example of a partial triumph of meritocracy. Perhaps most important for watchful waiting was that these were high-profile, powerful, and academically prestigious institutions whose actions and innovations are watched, even emulated, nationwide.

Preoccupation with top-level leadership as the genesis of deep institutional change, however, is woefully incomplete. Often overlooked is the potential energy and power of associations and alliances developed at the grass-roots level of the campus by minority students. A good example came about on November 9, 2015, when both the President and Chancellor of the University of Missouri held a press conference to announce their respective resignations. It was the culmination of months of activism by African American students, preceded by years of expressing concern over racial slurs and tensions on campus. These grievances fused with discontent over such decisions as the closing of the University of Missouri Press and abruptly eliminating health insurance programs for graduate students. A striking feature of the announcements and events was how uncomfortable and ineffective the president and chancellor were in handling questions and comments from students in the public forum.

A tendency for presidents has been to cite their accomplishments in strategic planning, task forces, and budget reviews – all of which represent formal and structural initiatives, usually coming from the top down. Yet these can be usurped in public relations and governance decisions by being inarticulate and inflexible when encountering a groundswell of organized student statements and demonstrations combined with that constituency's effective use of social media to spread their message and grievances. According to numerous reporters and media coverage, the African American student movement gained visibility and influence when African American student-athletes proposed a boycott of football practices and football games. Furthermore, the student-athletes on the football squad had the public support of both the athletic director and the football coach. Such effective organization by students has been relatively rare on American campuses – with some important exceptions, such as the student activism of the late 1960s. Yet at certain crucial junctures, the chemistry is timely and effective in sending a message to the board of curators and to the president and chancellor.[31]

The student groups were able to bring attention to long-term concerns, ranging from the low percentage (less than 7 percent) of African American students at the flagship state university campus, followed by low representation of African Americans as presidents, provosts, deans, and professors. On balance, it was a *cultural* dimension of campus life in which "outsiders" overrode the *structural* features of the top administration by prompting institutional self-scrutiny and some measure of leadership change.

CONCLUSION

A college or university fuses several organizational models simultaneously – the political model, the bureaucratic model, the collegial model, and even the autocratic model. The crucial distillation is that each institution has its own particular and peculiar mix of these various models. Deciphering the proportions and balances is an important exercise that hardly is an exact calculation. And, even though academic institutions are historic entities, colleges and universities can – and sometimes do – change their ways of making decisions.

The opening question for this chapter was, "Why can't a college be run more like a business?" Exploration of how colleges and universities actually work suggests both the foibles and strengths of academic governance. An added consideration in the comparison of corporations. Colleges have been resilient, and usually it is big news and bad news when a college or university closes its doors. In contrast, the lifespan of most new businesses is little more than a year. Sixty years ago Americans confidently exclaimed that "What was good for General Motors is good for America!" The postscript is that General Motors went bankrupt, as have Amtrak, United States Steel, Arthur Andersen, Lehman Brothers Financial Services, and Enron Corporation. These icons of American business were focused on making profits and sometimes were thought to be "too big to fail." Just as the expression "sound as a dollar" has changing connotations depending on the era, so has the success of business corporations been in flux. It's fair to answer a question with a good question. Perhaps in the 21st century one can look at the forlorn industrial landscape of Detroit and the "Rust Belt" and also ask, "Why can't a business be run more like a college?"[32]

NOTES

1. Robert Birnbaum, *How Colleges Work: The Cybernetics of Academic Organization and Leadership* (San Francisco and London: Jossey-Bass, 1988) (published for the National Center for Postsecondary Governance and Finance). See also, Henry Rosovsky, *The University: An Owner's Manual* (Cambridge, MA: Harvard University Press, 1991).
2. W.H. Cowley, *Presidents, Professors and Trustees: The Evolution of American Academic Government*, edited by Donald T. Williams (San Francisco: Jossey-Bass, 1980). See also, John R. Thelin, "Colleges, Colleagues, and Cowley: An Essay Review," *Review of Higher Education* (Fall 1980) vol. 4, no. 1, pp. 33–38.
3. Robert Strauss, "Bigger Expectations for College Trustees," *New York Times* (November 8, 2015) p. F7.
4. Clyde Barrows, *Universities and the Capitalist State: Corporate Liberalism and the Reconstruction of Higher Education, 1894 to 1928* (Madison: University of Wisconsin Press, 1990). See also, Thorstein Veblen, *The Higher Learning in America: A Memorandum on the Conduct of Universities by Business Men* (Baltimore, MD: Johns Hopkins University Press, new edition, 2013; originally published 1918).
5. William G. Bowen and Harold T. Shapiro, Editors, *Universities and Their Leadership* (Princeton, NJ: Princeton University Press, 1998).
6. Gary S. Krahenbuhl, *Building the Academic Deanship: Strategies for Success* (Washington, D.C.: American Council on Education and Westport, CT: Praeger, 2004).
7. Jeffrey L. Buller, *The Essential Academic Dean: A Practical Guide to College Leadership* (San Francisco: Jossey-Bass, 2007).
8. Audrey Williams, "To Change a Campus, Talk to the Dean," *Chronicle of Higher Education* (November 24, 2014) pp. A1, A13.
9. Mimi Wolverton with Walter H. Gmelch, *College Deans: Leading from Within* (Westport, CT: American Council on Education and Oryx Press, 2002).
10. John R. Thelin, "A Legacy of Lethargy?: Curricular Change in Historical Perspective," *Peer Review* (Journal of the Association of American Colleges & Universities) (Summer 2000) vol. 2, no. 4, pp. 9–14.
11. Robert Birnbaum, "The Latent Organizational Functions of the Academic Senate: Why Senates Do Not Work But Will Not Go Away," *Journal of Higher Education* (August 1989) vol. 60, no. 4, pp. 423–443.

12. Kellie Woodhouse, "UNC Presidential Search in Chaos amid Charges of Politicization and Secrecy," *Inside Higher Ed* (October 19, 2015).
13. Robert Birnbaum, "The Latent Organizational Functions of the Academic Senate: Why Senates Do Not Work But Will Not Go Away," *Journal of Higher Education* (August 1989) vol. 60, no. 4, pp. 423–443.
14. Andy Thomason, "Embattled U. of Missouri President Resigns after Mounting Protests over Racism," *Chronicle of Higher Education* (November 9, 2015) p. A1.
15. Robert Birnbaum, *How Colleges Work: The Cybernetics of Academic Organization and Leadership* (San Francisco and London: Jossey-Bass, 1988) (published for the National Center for Postsecondary Education Governance and Finance).
16. Lee Gardner, "Faculty Leaders Try Their Hand at Running a College," *Chronicle of Higher Education* (December 15, 2014) pp. A1, A16.
17. Katherine S. Mangan, "An Unfair Tax?: Law and Business Schools Object to Bailing out Medical Centers," *Chronicle of Higher Education* (March 15, 1998) p. A1.
18. Clayton M. Christensen and Henry J. Eyring, *The Innovative University: Changing the DNA of Higher Education from the Inside Out* (San Francisco: Jossey-Bass, 2011).
19. Jill Lepore, "The Disruption Machine: What the Gospel of Innovation Gets Wrong," *The New Yorker* (June 23, 2014).
20. Joseph Schumpeter, *Capitalism, Socialism, and Democracy*, 3rd edn (New York: Harper & Row, 1950); Herbert Kaufman, *Red Tape: Its Origins, Uses and Abuses* (Washington, D.C.: The Brookings Institution, 1977).
21. Evan R. Goldstein, "The Undoing of Disruption: Clayton Christensen and His Critics," *The Chronicle Review* (October 2, 2015) pp. B6–B9.
22. Harold L. Hodgkinson, "Bureaucratic Structure and Personality," in *Education, Interaction, and Social Change* (Englewood Cliffs, NJ: Prentice-Hall, Inc., 1967) pp. 25–47.
23. James Q. Wilson, *Bureaucracy: What Government Agencies Do and Why They Do It* (New York: Basic Books, 1989).
24. Herbert Kaufman, *Red Tape: Its Origins, Uses and Abuses* (Washington, D.C.: The Brookings Institution, 1977).
25. Robert Scott, *Lords, Squires and Yeomen: Middle Managers and Their Organizations* (Washington, D.C.: ASHE-ERIC Report No. 7, 1978).
26. Michael D. Cohen, James G. March, and Johan Olsen, "A Garbage Can Model of Organizational Choice," *Administrative Science Quarterly* (March 1972) vol. 17, no. 1, pp. 1–25.
27. George Keller, *Academic Strategy: The Management Revolution in American Higher Education* (Baltimore, MD and London: Johns Hopkins University Press, 1983); John R. Thelin, "Institutional History in Our Own Time: Higher Education's Shift from Managerial Revolution to Enterprising Evolution," *CASE International Journal of Educational Advancement* (June 2000) vol. 1, no. 1, pp. 9–23.
28. Daniel J. Boorstin, *The Image: A Guide to Pseudo-Events in America* (New York: Harper Colophon, 1964).
29. Benjamin Ginsberg, *The Fall of the Faculty: The Rise of the All-Administrative University and Why It Matters* (New York: Oxford University Press, 2011).
30. Peter Schmidt, "High Pay for Presidents Is Not Shown to Yield Any Fund-Raising Payoff," *Chronicle of Higher Education* (November 7, 2015) p. A1.
31. Douglas Belkin and Melissa Korn, "University of Missouri System President Tim Wolfe Resigns," *Wall Street Journal* (November 9, 2015) p. 1; Jack Stripling, "Thrust into a National Debate on Race, 2 Missouri Chiefs Resign," *Chronicle of Higher Education* (November 10, 2015) p. A1.
32. John R. Thelin, "Why Can't a Business Be Run More Like a College?," *Planning for Higher Education* (Spring 1996) vol. 24, no. 3, pp. 57–60.

Additional Readings

Clyde Barrows, *Universities and the Capitalist State: Corporate Liberalism and the Reconstruction of Higher Education, 1894 to 1928* (Madison: University of Wisconsin Press, 1990).

Robert Birnbaum, *How Colleges Work: The Cybernetics of Academic Organization and Leadership* (San Francisco and London: Jossey-Bass, 1988) (published for the National Center for Postsecondary Governance and Finance).

Robert Birnbaum, *Management Fads in Higher Education: Where They Come from, What They Do, Why They Fail* (San Francisco: Jossey-Bass, 2001).

William G. Bowen and Harold T. Shapiro, Editors, *Universities and Their Leadership* (Princeton, NJ: Princeton University Press, 1998).

Jeffrey L. Buller, *The Essential Academic Dean: A Practical Guide to College Leadership* (San Francisco: Jossey-Bass, 2007).

Clayton M. Christensen and Henry J. Eyring, *The Innovative University: Changing the DNA of Higher Education from the Inside Out* (San Francisco: Jossey-Bass, 2011).

Michael D. Cohen, James G. March, and Johan Olsen, "A Garbage Can Model of Organizational Choice," *Administrative Science Quarterly* (March 1972) vol. 17, no. 1, pp. 1–25.

W.H. Cowley, *Presidents, Professors and Trustees: The Evolution of American Academic Government*, edited by Donald T. Williams (San Francisco: Jossey-Bass, 1980).

Benjamin Ginsberg, *The Fall of the Faculty: The Rise of the All-Administrative University and Why It Matters* (New York: Oxford University Press, 2011).

George Keller, *Academic Strategy: The Management Revolution in American Higher Education* (Baltimore, MD and London: Johns Hopkins University Press, 1983).

John Lombardi, *How Universities Work* (Baltimore, MD: Johns Hopkins University Press, 2013).

Henry Rosovsky, *The University: An Owner's Manual* (Cambridge, MA: Harvard University Press, 1991).

John R. Thelin, "Why Can't a Business Be Run More Like a College?" *Planning for Higher Education* (Spring 1996) vol. 24, no. 3, pp. 57–60.

Thorstein Veblen, *The Higher Learning in America: A Memorandum on the Conduct of Universities by Business Men* (Baltimore, MD: Johns Hopkins University Press, new edition, 2013; originally published 1918).

James Q. Wilson, *Bureaucracy: What Government Agencies Do and Why They Do It* (New York: Basic Books, 1989).

7

FISCAL FITNESS

Budgets and Finances

SETTING AND OVERVIEW

This chapter provides a guide to where money comes from – and where it goes – within colleges and universities. Just as in Chapter 3, which offered the caution that an obvious, important document – namely, a college catalog – was limited in understanding teaching and learning, the counterpart for this chapter is that a university's formal budget is an important document, yet still requires supplementary information if it is to lead to significant interpretation. It needs, for example, to be understood in conjunction with the institutional mission statement and such practices as Strategic Planning, Responsibility Centered Management (RCM), and state and federal restrictions on spending.[1] The budget gains in analytic strength when considered along with other documents such as an end-of-year operating statement and balance sheet. Campus spending documents will be analyzed from the perspective of ongoing national reports and databases, including the Delta Cost Project and the federal government's Integrated Postsecondary Education Data System (IPEDS).[2]

The budget is the most philosophical of statements about institutional priorities. In colloquial terms, it documents the adage, "You get what you pay for...." Vague, general statements and facile promises made in college brochures, annual reports, and press releases are ultimately grounded in dollar commitments. At the same time, the paradox of the budget is that the document one has in hand often is sufficiently incomplete and unexplained. Often it is presented to audiences in a whirlwind of Power-Point slides that transform it into a remarkable work of fantasy and fiction. In such cases it raises more questions than it answers. This chapter attempts to go from fiction to fact in understanding college income and expenditures and investments to carry out missions of teaching, research, and service. Once having established this foundation, the focus will be on the stories about how different institutions – and kinds of institution – go about surviving the present and planning for their respective futures. This requires exploration of *academic strategies*. These, in turn, will be explained in terms of some *theories* about the *costs of higher education* provided by thoughtful economists.[3]

The issues and concepts introduced here lean heavily toward an exploration of the financing of higher education from the perspective of leaders within institutions. It is confined to nonprofit colleges and universities, whereas analysis of for-profit institutions will be covered later in Chapter 11, "Research and Development: The Enterprising Campus." It provides a prelude and complement as many of the concepts and findings presented in this chapter will resurface in Chapter 12, dealing with "Colleges and Consumerism," where the emphasis will be on how students and their families consider the complexities of higher education costs and prices as part of accessibility and affordability.

The Heritage of Higher Education's Bottom Line

Fiction is a good place to start to understand American higher education finances and budget. Going back to 19th-century England, to Charles Dickens' account of young Oliver Twist, the orphan in a London slum who, having finished his meager bowl of oatmeal, went back for a second serving, explaining to the master, "Please, sir, I want some more!" College presidents everywhere, past and present, can identify with this insatiable appetite for resources. This is not hyperbole. In 1996 the President of Cornell University addressed a gathering of fellow presidents of established universities and noted matter-of-factly that, after all, university presidents are "beggars who live in big houses."[4]

The perennial search for funds to run the campus is a tradition that has deep roots in American higher education. It is the means necessary for pursuing the laudable ends and goals of higher education. Probably the best institutional type today for understanding this heritage is the small, independent liberal arts college.[5] Its mission is clear – and so are its challenges in continual hunting and gathering for its academic tribe. It has many characteristics similar to those that faced American colleges in the 18th and 19th centuries. How each year – and over the years – does a president and board of trustees acquire adequate revenues to meet the expenses of educating undergraduates, meeting the payroll, and maintaining the physical plant of the campus? This was no abstract matter, as colleges frequently cut their offerings or even closed their doors if tuition revenues fell short.[6] One consequence of these repeated financial struggles was that over time historic colleges changed their categorical affiliation. The College of William & Mary in Virginia, for example, was in the late 19th century essentially an underfunded private institution with Episcopal Church affiliation. Faced with financial insolvency, it increasingly relied on state scholarship funds for students who pledged to be teachers – and early in the 20th century became a "state" or "public" institution. Dartmouth College, in contrast, early in the 19th century weaned itself from standing as a "state institution" and in a landmark case asserted its identity as an "independent" or "private" college. Indeed, during the 1970s the precedent held true, as such financially stressed private institutions such as the University of Pittsburgh and the University of Louisville became part of their respective state postsecondary education systems.

Certainly this historical model of the 19th-century small private college does not suffice to explain completely the financing complexities of a modern comprehensive and multi-purpose university. But even research universities have much in common with small colleges of 1816 and 2016 in going about the business of meeting the costs and then providing the services of undergraduate education. Both the large research university budget and that of a small college can be divided into separate components that are largely autonomous. These include, for example, student services, parking, auxiliary enterprises, its hospital, and its research and grants activities, its foundation, and perhaps intercollegiate athletics. These stand apart from what often is called the "E&G" portion – short for "education and general expenses." The "E&G" is usually what is meant when deans and provosts talk about the "academic budget" or the "educational budget." Later in this chapter and in subsequent, specialized chapters we will analyze research grants, teaching hospitals, and other advanced expensive units of a university. Meanwhile the basics of the budget still rest with the prototypical undergraduate college.

All institutions of higher education in the United States share the common feature of a "pay as you go" approach in operating the college, meeting the payroll, and paying bills on a year-to-year basis. Almost all colleges and universities, then and now, have relied heavily on income from students' tuition payments. With perhaps the exception of such specialized and generously endowed institutions such as Rockefeller University, whose mission is advanced medical research, colleges and universities need to enroll students – and to collect their payments of tuition and fees, or, some proxy such as per student subsidies from the state government. An institution that forgets this risks poverty. And, without students, it faces the prospect of becoming a campus that resembles a ghost town. Johns Hopkins University in 1909 is a good example: it was the foremost American university of the 1890s, but then suffered a persistent decline when it decided to try to de-emphasize its undergraduate college while focusing on its medical students and its Ph.D. and master's degree programs. Its total enrollment for all programs shrank from a high of about 3,000 to less than 700. This was not a good trajectory.[7]

If it is risky to run a college without students, what about another bold variation? Namely, can a college dare to enroll students without charging tuition? The basic reliance on student tuition payments also is illustrated by those few examples where a college simply did not charge tuition. Memorable cases in the late 19th and early 20th centuries were Stanford University and Rice Institute. Both relied on their endowments to meet the costs of providing undergraduate education. By the early 1900s Stanford's experiment with affordability drained its reserves. At one point only the generosity of Jane Stanford, widow of Leland Stanford, in writing checks from her personal bank account helped the university meet its payroll and fend off merchants and craftsmen whose bills were overdue. Rice Institute, later Rice University, was "tuition free" for over half a century in compliance with conditions in the will of its benefactor and namesake, William Marsh Rice. But in 1965 the Rice Board successfully petitioned the courts for permission to depart from the will and to charge tuition. Most recently, Cooper Union in New York City faced financial crisis, in part due to its honoring the conditions of its historic trust that it be tuition-free. Berea College in Kentucky is one of a handful of American institutions that remains tuition-free as part of its distinctive mission to serve a modest income student constituency – but it is able to do so only because it has put into place some distinctive arrangements, including a strong endowment and a work study requirement, that makes the no-tuition principle feasible. The state of California endorsed a "no tuition" policy for in-state students enrolled at the University of California, the California State University and Colleges, and at the California community colleges.[8] After several decades, however, this ceased to be tenable and was over time changed to adding mandatory fees and, finally, to charging tuition. This is a story whose details we will analyze later in the chapter.

The basic ground rule, then, is that a college collects tuition from each student – and, hypothetically, this cumulative collection each semester provides the foundation of meeting the college's costs of educating students. One must even accept hypothetically that each student's tuition revenues pay for the instruction and services she or he receives. It means that the cost and the price of a college education are the same dollar figure. This direct, simple notion of tuition as a "user's fee" may work in some cases, but often it quickly unravels and becomes more complicated even at a single-purpose institution. So, the analytic challenge is to track and explain any departure from the basic equation.

One answer is the concept of *cross-subsidies* in which the revenues generated in one unit are partially transferred to another unit. It brings to mind the adage, "robbing Peter to pay Paul." Another variation is when a department or program on a campus is recognized as a "cash cow." To extend the agrarian analogy, some units are expected to be a "golden goose." There is nothing sinister or cynical about these characterizations, however, so long as all parties involved understand the ground rules of who is doing what to whom – and abide by them.

For each college and university, the "budget" provides a snapshot of its projected financial condition. Typically this includes such major sections as "income," "revenues," and "investments." These in turn are separated into two major categories: "restricted" and "unrestricted." This then leads to disaggregating the large, central university into its sub-units. Fortunately, such groups as the National Education Association (NEA) and the National Association of College and University Business Officers (NACUBO) provide faculty, boards, and other campus constituencies excellent primers and handbooks on the budget both as a document and tool.[9]

The budget as presented in the agenda for boards can be misleading. It seems so permanent, set in stone. It is not. A better way to understand the budget is to accept its fluidity – a perspective acquired by participating in its creation and editing over time. Usually, when one questions pieces of the budget after it is in place, it is not necessarily "too late" to change – but to try to do so is confining and limited. Predictable responses from the Vice President for Business Affairs include the following liturgies: "But the budget has already been set for the year." Or, "But we cannot do that because it is not in the budget." Each of these responses, of course, often is a delay or evasion. In addition to focusing on the figures presented in the Annual Report version of the budget, there are some good ways to test out the fluidity and transparency of a campus budget. First, go to some particular unit – it could be the provost's office or, perhaps, the dean's office of an academic college. Ask the budget officer for the current *detailed* budget summary and statement. Ask for a careful explanation about expenditure or a category – and its details. Be prepared to wait. Be prepared to be puzzled and, perhaps, disappointed.

The eulogy for such budget inquiries often will be, "too little, too late." The summary sheets are superficial because the categories are broad. And, requesting any level of information beyond the most general summaries usually entails waiting. In some cases, budget offices will require the requesting person to submit a Freedom of Information Act request. Understanding budget documents may be difficult and can be enhanced by a trained eye guided by information about accounting and budget principles. But even more difficult is simply obtaining meaningful budget data, whether for the institution as a whole or one of its member components. The irony is that such delays and blockages take place in an era when the technology of interactive budget databases should make such requested data readily accessible.

The major limit of the budget document is that the version one usually receives lacks adequate detail to probe discerning questions and concerns. Second, it is static. As such it masks the drama of its story. Higher education analysts might take a cue from political science, where Aaron Wildavsky, in his 1964 book, *The Politics of the Budgetary Process*, describes the "mating dance of the budget."[10] What then is the higher education variation on the dance floor of resource allocation? Who are its dancing stars? As partners, who leads and who follows in the minuet? Who are the higher education wallflowers left to sit on the sidelines to watch, with little influence or involvement? Only when one starts to ask these kinds of questions does discussion of budgets and finance in higher education acquire substantive meaning and animation.

ISSUES

Learning to read budgets and financial operating statements is, of course, useful for making sense out of higher education's fiscal fitness. Equally important is to become conversant with some of the essential principles of institutional mission and some of the analytic concepts that help one ask significant questions about how a college is doing – and where it is going.

The Mission Statement

Finances disconnected from core college principles are meaningless. A first good step, then, is for stakeholders to understand the institutional mission statement. This probably exists as a formal document drafted by the president, preceded by open forums across campus, then ultimately presented to and approved by the board of trustees. One caveat is that in recent years such formal statements have tended to be inflated and subject to what is called the "omnibus fallacy." The good feelings and optimism lead to well-intentioned but vague proclamations. Another pitfall is the temptation of what is called "mission creep" in which a president or board keeps extending its domains.[11] Furthermore, given the competitive and ambitious character of American higher education, the "mission creep" tends to push an institution upward, into more prestigious and more expensive kinds of programs. A regional comprehensive university, bolstered by optimism and alumni pride, considers adding doctoral programs – as a potential source of both added revenues and added academic stature. Yet its actual contribution may also be added expenses.

Some universities use their heritage to justify lateral expansion. The best example of this license comes from "land grant institutions." In the 1980s the "land grant" designation had actually fallen into disuse and even disfavor, as some major state universities referred to their new identity as the "post-land grant university." The elaboration was that emphasis on crop yields, mechanical engineering, home economics, and ROTC – historical elements of the Morrill Act that created the land grant funding model and institutional categories in 1862 and in 1890 – was tired and not well suited to the late 20th century.[12] An interesting twist of fate is that around 2000 many state universities rediscovered the "land grant mission" and reinvigorated it to justify adding any new programs. After all, one ostensibly could argue that creating a new School of Public Health or a Robotics Institute were consistent with the historic "land grant mission."

Extending the operational definition of specific programs as part of the institutional mission ultimately faces building a budget. What is crucial at this juncture is that members of the campus community – perhaps senior faculty who are experienced and loyal – provide reminders of the institutional gyroscope. Regardless of what the formal mission statement proclaims, one must keep in mind that it is in large part a public relations item that can be readily altered one way or the other by the administration and board. The more thoughtful and clear the institutional mission remains, the more likely an institution will have some principles to guide decisions about spending and cutting.

One situation where this foundation is helpful is when an influential figure, whether a president or a trustee or a donor, puts forward a proposal for a new program because it is touted as being a "money maker." First, that is not a good reason to add a program if it does not mesh with the institutional mission. Second, most proposals for lucrative, new initiatives tend to *underestimate* the start-up costs and unexpected expenses for maintaining the program, complying with regulations, and paying for construction of new facilities. It leads to what has been called "the over-investment crisis."[13] One contribution of the mission statement is to prompt campus decision-makers to ask thoughtfully whether or not they really would want this program as part of the whole institution even if it did not make money – or, even if it did make money.

The mission statement also provides a reminder about essential versus peripheral activities. In times of a budget crunch, a state legislator, trustee, or provost might recommend that the university phase out a department that they think is obsolete. The philosophy department, for example, is a familiar target. Quite apart from budget matters, an appropriate question to ask is whether a college or university could be legitimate without this department. Can one have a genuine university without a philosophy department? How about the importance of a biology department? After gathering information and discussing this question, one then could ask secondary questions about minimal and maximum departmental size, teaching expectations, and enrollment goals. But this second round of questions only surfaces after a program or department passes review on questions of its essential importance to creating a bona fide college or university.

Having grounded budgetary discussions in the authentic mission of the college or university, one then can turn to critical analysis of present and future investments in learning. Here, for example, are some concepts and analytic tools economists use:

Cost versus Price

These two terms are often used as synonyms. Although closely related, they are distinct. College "costs" refers to the money an institution spends to provide instruction and services and to construct buildings and campus facilities. The "price" of college, in contrast, refers to what a student pays for a college education. In this chapter focus is on institutional costs. In Chapter 12, attention shifts to prices and how students figure out what they can and will pay. "Cost" and "price" have no single, set relationship. Depending on institutional strategies, a college or university can peg its "price" as higher, lower, or equal to its "costs."

Efficiency versus Effectiveness

These two terms also are often mixed and matched, or used interchangeably. In fact, they represent markedly different concepts in terms of spending and allocation of resources. A college can be "efficient" if it educates students while keeping costs low. It is comparable to being inexpensive. This might mean having lean facilities, a high ratio of students to faculty, low salaries, and no campus landscaping. To be "effective" as a college, however, indicates that a college does well in terms of its educational goals, such as having students learn, complete courses, earn degrees – all at a high rate. Stepping aside from higher education, automobiles provide a good illustration of the conceptual differences. A nondescript sedan that gets 40 miles per gallon despite a maximum speed of 25 miles per hour is "efficient." A race car that wins the Indianapolis 500 is "effective" because it is very fast – but its pit crew and sponsors have little care about how much or how little gasoline it consumes, so long as it wins. Obviously, in higher education, one would like to have an institution that is simultaneously effective and efficient. How each college fares in that dual performance leads to an interesting balancing act.

Cost–Benefit Analysis

Following close behind deliberations over efficiency and effectiveness is the ratio of cost–benefit. In other words, academic planners who are considering new projects will try to estimate whether an investment is worthwhile. In a money-making venture, this can be plotted readily: if sponsors spend $100 will they get a return of $200? Or, perhaps $300? And, of course, there is the possibility of losing money. Although the ratio approach is comparable, the estimates or even measurement of results are less clear when the aim is to achieve some goal associated with prestige or award, not money. Consider an academically ambitious university where the question is which new professor to hire – with the goal of hoping to attract, keep, and nurture a future Nobel laureate. Is hiring a physicist who is highly regarded internationally and whose work will require millions of dollars of laboratory space and equipment a "better" choice than a geneticist whose major expense will be drosophilae or an economist who needs a computer and subscriptions to databases? Another scenario in which this plays out may involve a scholar's career path – does one opt for a young, promising researcher whose salary is relatively low and who has many years to do her scholarly work? Or, does one break the bank for an established scholarly "star" who brings immediate prestige to the institution, yet who may already have peaked in terms of scholarly achievements while also commanding a high salary? Long before the Oakland A's General Manager became famous for developing the financial strategy known as "Money Ball" in Major League Baseball personnel decisions, academic deans and provosts were sifting and sorting their odds for prestige and prosperity among numerous departments and academic all-stars.

Merit versus Worth

The conceptual distinction between "merit" and "worth" is among the most important and perplexing trade-offs in college spending decisions. Consider the situation in which a president must choose between paying a high salary for a chief of staff versus that of hiring an outstanding biological sciences professor who has landed major grants from the National Institutes of Health. One might protest that the two positions are not comparable. But if resources are limited, a president may have to choose one or the other. The appeal of paying a high salary for a chief of staff is that, of course, the president has a valued, loyal assistant whose staff skills can reduce the burden of administrative tasks, absorb flak from pesky reporters, get the president to meetings and trips on time, and provide expertise in institutional planning. In contrast, the scientist will be of no use, obviously, in administrative planning or running the institution – and, as such, will not help the president in solving immediate problems and facing day-to-day demands. But she might bring in a great deal of sponsored research grant dollars, favorable publicity with national research awards, be a mentor to outstanding doctoral students, and be a magnet for attracting other outstanding new professors.

Administrative Justification of Expensive and Expansive Programs

Department chairs, deans, and professors are used to being turned down by provosts and presidents in requests for added funding for new or existing programs. What about the reverse situation? How do presidents and provosts justify approving expensive new programs – or enhanced existing programs – that they favor? One interesting, frequent ploy is to shrink its presence by folding it into the overall institutional budget. Consider the case in which the president and provost recommend starting a new academic unit that is estimated to cost $20 million per year. Or, the president and board approve an enhanced football program that will increase the intercollegiate athletics department budget by $20 million per year. A way to deflect criticism is to say, "After all, this is only three percent of the total annual university budget. That's a very small percentage of the pie!" Critics are defused by being made to feel foolish, perhaps petty, for questioning such an "obviously" small percentage amount. But this can be disingenuous on the part of the president. In sum, 3 percent of a university budget is a lot, in real and relative terms.

Accountability: The Faculty

Presidents and their budget analysts often preface their reports on financial health with the reminder that personnel costs are both a substantial part of expenses, and they are intractable. Faculty, for example, represents one of the largest and most expensive personnel categories. Ineffective and indifferent teaching by professors can be monitored and then tied to decisions on salaries, promotion, retention, and termination if a college or university implements a comprehensive faculty performance data-collection system. One of many such plans was developed by Richard O'Donnell in his role as an advisor to the University of Texas system who conducted a study of faculty productivity that was intended to be implemented at Texas A&M University and the University of Texas in 2011 as the university regents sought to make public higher education accountable.[14] In one phase of the initiative, the university published reports that listed each faculty member in terms of a "profit-or-loss" statement. The subsequent criticism was that the accountability template tended to be simplistic in that it did not include faculty roles in advising, sponsoring research, chairing master's and doctoral degree programs, or supervising Ph.D. dissertations.

An added complication is that long-term national studies conducted by university administrators elsewhere, such as the Delaware Study (formally, the National Study of Instructional Costs & Productivity), have led to the finding that "faculty pay is not part of academe's cost crisis." Michael Middaugh, Assistant Vice President for Institutional Research and Planning at the University of Delaware, told reporters in 2006 that "Faculty instruction has been managed and managed well," and that spikes in the costs of health care, energy, and complying with federal laws constituted the "other stuff that's killing us."[15] As another analyst concluded, the university president and trustees' focus on professors as the source of financial problems was the "wrong kind of accountability."[16]

One proposed solution to rising expenses is to eliminate faculty tenure. If professors with tenure are seen by the president and provost as a liability in keeping a college or university vital in its hiring and teaching, eliminating tenure is an attractive option. Yet changing faculty handbooks and then dealing with such external groups as the American Association of University Professors (AAUP) is arduous. Rather than eliminate a tenure policy, what already has happened at many institutions is that the president is evading tenure appointments. This is done by offering contracts to new faculty hires that have term limits and are not tenure eligible. Increased reliance on adjuncts and part-time instructors along with graduate teaching assistants and lecturers means that in 2011 professors who had tenure or were eligible for tenure constituted a shrinking proportion of the teaching faculty.[17]

Eliminating – or avoiding – tenure track faculty appointments may cause problems for the long-term operation and character of an academically strong college or university in that fewer permanent, full-time professors would then be available for customary roles in advising undergraduate and graduate students as well as serving on the numerous university committees that constitute shared governance in numerous aspects of institutional decisions and operations. Implicit in these concerns is that faculty – and their various contributions to teaching, research, and service – are central to the academic mission and campus community.

CHARACTERS AND CONSTITUENTS

Trustees

A reasonable assumption is that college and university trustees have detailed knowledge about their institution's budget and finances. After all, the board of trustees has ultimate responsibility for a college or university – and they must approve all expenditures. Fiduciary responsibility combined with an ethos of good stewardship implies that the boards of trustees are integral to planning and resource allocation. In fact, there is good reason to believe that trustees often are not well informed – and often are not provided good, thorough information. The American Council of Trustees and Alumni (ACTA), a Washington, D.C.-based association, has identified this situation as problematic. Its remedy has been to provide trustees with timely information on questions to ask about budgets and financial planning. This has included a former Regent of the University of Colorado who prepared materials dealing with the topic of "Getting to the Data: Questions Trustees Should Ask." The essential four questions are as follows: "How much cash do we as a university have? Who has it? What is the money for? Have we as trustees approved this expenditure?"[18]

The implication is that even boards of trustees are not exempt from lack of good data. If so, is it little wonder that numerous other campus constituencies are either bewildered or concerned about lack of access to essential budgetary information?

Presidents

Presidents command respect and deference. As noted in earlier chapters, few if any colleges or universities elect a candidate to fill the presidency who is not privy to the important decisions about mission, institutional choices, and how (and how much) the institution should allocate to it. Most likely a president will advance support for new initiatives and priorities, after which vice presidents and staff will analyze estimated costs and perhaps possible funding sources and strategies. The president will be knowledgeable about the budget – but will rely on the detailed professional expertise of the Vice President for Business Affairs and other budget officers and academic deans.

Vice President for Business Affairs

An increasingly visible and powerful figure in the academic structure is the Vice President for Business Affairs. Terminology varies from institution to institution – and, in some cases, the role has become sufficiently important that it demands creation of *multiple* vice presidencies. The highest office, for example, is an *Executive Vice President for Finance and Administration.* Offices reporting included the Treasurer, the Vice President for Facilities Management, the Vice President for Human Resources, and a distinct *Vice President for Financial Planning and Chief Budgetary Officer.* For this latter vice presidency, the role is to be chief executive for the University Budget Office, whose charge is to coordinate and provide leadership for university-wide financial and resource planning, budgeting, and policy analysis. All this expansion of personnel – at high salaries and with generous benefits of retirement, health care, and insurance – attests to the importance of budget and finance and planning in the structure and strategies of the modern campus. This profile of the upper-level central administration of finances understates the offices and personnel a contemporary university devotes to these functions. The roots and branches extend to every college, department, program, and center – each of which has its designated budget officer.

Despite, or perhaps because of, such concentration and extension of financial expertise, caution must be exercised to not take budget reports at face value. Strategies of presentation are sophisticated, especially at academic institutions with relatively thorough financial accounting systems. In 1992, for example, Harvard University's public reports noted that despite an endowment of almost $5 billion (worth $8.5 billion in 2015 when indexed for inflation), its annual operating budget was $42 million in the red. One reason for this profile was the university's use of "fund-accounting" reports, suggesting that Harvard was:

> managing its bottom line in such a way as to appear poorer than it really is. The university is in the midst of a plan to reportedly raise $2.5 billion on top of what is already the world's largest private endowment. Harvard is a bit like the rich man who wears scuffed shoes and a frayed collar when he visits his doctor.[19]

Conversely, some universities present a deceptively glossy financial profile when doing so is expedient. This tactic reassures worried alumni, legislators, and donors that the president and board can balance the university's budget and that the administration's vision for the college's future is bright.

The University Hospital and Academic Medical Center (AMC)

If a university is home to a hospital and an academic medical center, this is central to the institutional mission and overall university budget. About 100 institutions fall into this distinctive category. It will be a focus of analysis in Chapter 11, "Research and Development: The Enterprising Campus."

Intercollegiate Athletics Department

College sports are highly visible both in real and symbolic terms for many American colleges and universities. If a university is home to a big-time program geared toward large crowds and television audiences, most likely the department of intercollegiate athletics will be free-standing and is expected to be self-supporting.[20] If, as is the case at most colleges and small universities, the varsity sports program is considered to be part of student life and educational programs, it most likely will be marbled into the planning and budgetary decisions in which academic chairs and all programs participate. The complications and consequences of college sports for these two categories will be covered in Chapter 8, "Intercollegiate Athletics."

The University Foundation

Many colleges and universities establish a special, incorporated entity that receives and disburses funds received from such external groups as donors, grants from federal agencies, awards from philanthropic foundations, and, perhaps, rents and revenues from real estate holdings. It means the quasi-autonomous foundation has substantial oversight and control of the sluice gates as to where these receipts are then distributed throughout the institution. Just as was the case with our earlier example of tuition revenues, there is no certainty that an external dollar that flows into the foundation will then be disbursed to a specified source for a specified purpose. The foundation officials have some discretion on redistribution. This allowance ties in to the practice mentioned earlier – cross-subsidization.

The Endowment

Most colleges and universities have established an endowment fund or trust in which private donations designated as perpetual gifts are placed. A good analogy for this is a large mutual fund in which each component has its respective monies, conditions, restrictions, and arrangements for investment. The conventional practice is that a college or university spends the interest or dividends received from a particular fund's investment – but does not touch the principal, which is expected to grow over time. The Internal Revenue Service requires that a college spend at least 4 percent of its endowment each year. The relative importance and size of endowments vary greatly across institutions. An obvious measure of strength is the gross or total endowment. Harvard University, for example, has the largest endowment in 2015 – worth about $38 billion. Another important way to gauge the strength of a college's endowment is its *per capita* amount per student. By this litmus Princeton University comes out on top. Even though it has a smaller endowment than Harvard, it has far fewer students. Its per capita endowment is over $1,800,000 per student. About 96 colleges and universities reported an endowment worth more than $1 billion in 2015. Central to administering the endowment is the fund manager. At institutions with large endowments this is a high-stakes appointment and commands a high salary – and, in some cases, comparable to a hedge fund manager in business, compensation may include some percentage of the annual returns. The reality, however, is that for most colleges and universities, endowments are not large. Their interest and dividends may provide some annual margin of purchasing power – but not enough to transform institutions or even ease their worries about paying annual bills.

Federal Agencies

Colleges and universities guard their autonomy. But often they must share their information by complying with government reporting requirements. The central federal agency for this is the United States Department of Education. It also includes such research granting agencies as the National Institutes of Health (NIH), the National Science

Foundation, the National Endowment for the Humanities, and the National Endowment for the Arts. The prod to institutional compliance is that they are requirements if a college or university wishes to be eligible to receive federal funds from any number of federal agencies and programs. This leads to the federal government pushing for two distinct but related features: *standards* and *standardization*. Nowhere is this more pronounced than in accountability for finances, enrollments, and especially for spending using federal grant dollars. It means that although a college is free to use whatever accounting procedures and protocols it wishes, it must also report essential financial data in the nationwide format that is part of the database known as Integrated Postsecondary Education Data Systems. Abbreviated and made into an acronym, IPEDS (pronounced "Eye-Peds") is the database that gathers and then publishes various figures from each institution. It is the successor to the original federal database created in 1967 – the Higher Education General Information Survey (HEGIS). These in turn can be analyzed in an interactive way in any number of collective displays – peer institutions, benchmarks by geography, by enrollment size, degrees conferred, and so on.

COMPLEXITIES AND CONFLICTS: IMPLICATIONS FOR DECISION-MAKING

Inflation

How do annual increases in a college or university's operating expenses compare with the national economy's rate of inflation? To answer this probably brings to mind using the Consumer Price Index (CPI) as the standard. Higher education officials object, however, because the CPI tends to measure increases in the cost of recurring goods and services, such as selected market basket items. To accommodate colleges and universities, economists devised the Higher Education Price Index (HEPI). The logic is that a college education is an extraordinary item – and should be compared with large purchases such as a house or an automobile rather than with groceries. Concern expressed by external audiences over the allegedly high inflation rate of college costs started around 1984 and has continued ever since. In August 1996, for example, the General Accounting Office (GAO) released a report, *Higher Education: Tuition Increasing Faster than Household Income and Public Colleges' Costs.*[21] The report, which looked at both increasing institutional expenditures (costs) and rising tuition charges (price), has had numerous sequels over the past three decades – with little change in the tone of concern. Left out is that in the years 1972 to 1980, when most colleges faced severe financial problems, college tuition and charges showed increases *below* that of the CPI. That was not good for colleges, as it meant they deferred maintenance and on-campus repairs and also resisted adding new programs and reduced spending on student services. It also was symptomatic of an extended period of *stagflation* – in which annual inflation rates exceeded 10 percent for over a decade while at the same time the economy remained sluggish.

Taxes

The welcomed news for colleges and universities is that many, perhaps most, of their income and property are tax exempt – which saves them a great deal of money. IRS status as a 501c3 educational and charitable institution is the key to exemption from federal income tax. An exception to this is what the IRS calls "UBIT" – unrelated business income tax. If a college engages in a business that is not part of its educational services and mission, goods and services may be subject to federal income tax.

State and local governments usually confer property tax exemptions to colleges and universities, whether public or private. However, this benefit often is subject to review. In some metropolitan areas where large portions of property are owned by nonprofit institutions – including museums, foundations, symphonies, schools, as well as colleges and universities – city councils tend to scrutinize how a college actually uses its real estate. A university-owned golf course, a performing arts center, or a hospital may be designated as subject to property tax because its primary purpose is recreational or commercial, rather than educational. Often colleges and universities negotiate with their host city to determine a voluntary payment in lieu of taxes.

Compliance Costs

Since colleges and universities receive numerous external funds, especially from federal agencies, they are obligated to document their adherence to various regulations and laws.[22] To do so means hiring staff who carry out this work in numerous departments and units. Foremost is compliance with Title IX to monitor equity in hiring and to monitor allegations of discrimination. Compliance costs can also include systematic data on safety and health procedures, not for humans as subjects and employees. It also pertains to laboratory animals used in trials and experiments. This latter example may sound frivolous, but, if you pay a visit to the numerous animal laboratory sites on a campus and consider that colleges and universities are the nation's largest purveyors of laboratory mice, rats and other animal subjects, and then check the budgets of such units as the department of physiology or psychology, the high costs will be evident. They also will understate the expense, as one must also include professional staff to take care of and monitor the health, feeding, and sanitation of the lab animals. When laboratory space is at a premium, the expense of square footage rental areas for the cages adds to the already formidable budgets.

Liabilities and Security

Although colleges and universities often receive exemptions from some government items, such as taxation, these same institutions are held to a high standard on conditions of safety and numerous health risks for students, staff, employees, and visitors. This means that insurance policies are extensive and expensive. It represents a thankless, hidden expense that adds little to the active pursuit of excellence in teaching, research, and service. But it is necessary and pervasive. In addition to insurance costs, since a campus is an intensive living and learning environment, it is densely populated. This magnifies the need for campus security and safety, ranging from police personnel to security cameras, building access, and technology protections on software and computer files. As noted in Chapter 4 dealing with students and the campus student culture, a college and its officials are subject to accountability and lawsuits from parents if a child who is a student is injured or is killed on campus.

Privatization

"Privatization" has two markedly different meanings in higher education. Its original meaning referred to the practice of a college outsourcing services that at one time might have been conducted by in-house staff. This referred, for example, to dining halls and custodial services. It was comparable to the practice in many cities whereby local government contracted with a private company to handle garbage collection. The second connotation cuts deep into the meaning of public higher education. It referred to a growing tendency of state governments to expect students and their families to bear a great and increasing percentage of paying for costs. It was best shown by the inordinate increase in tuition charges at state colleges and universities.[23]

CONNECTIONS AND QUESTIONS

Why Do College Costs Rise?

Once a college establishes a course of study, a research institute, or some other activity, it is hard to eliminate it. The tendency is toward proliferation of programs – and their endurance. According to political scientist Aaron Wildavsky, this phenomenon across many kinds of organization and agency is termed *incrementalism*. The best predictor of an upcoming institutional budget is to look at its past year's version, with scattered additions within this established base. It is difficult, almost impossible, for a college to reduce costs – apart from catastrophic situations that signal impending closure. On a more positive note, if a college or university wishes to be competitive in regional or national rankings and reputation, it must plan to increase its spending.[24] This is the theme labor economist Ronald Ehrenberg developed in his book, *Tuition Rising*. Using Cornell University as his reference point, he provides a guided tour of campus facilities and meetings where at every turn the message is that staying even and getting ahead are expensive propositions.[25]

In the same vein, Charles Clotfelter of Duke University used case studies of several colleges and universities to explain the strategies and investments made around 1985. The common denominator was that all the selected cases were academically selective and had ample resources. Over the next 20 years the story was that of "Buying the Best" – in terms of the quality of undergraduate applicants, graduate student fellowships, and recruiting outstanding professors.[26] The immediate result was that this small circle of institutions soared in prestige. The secondary consequence was that they set a pattern and a pace that all colleges envied – and tried to imitate. It kindled an academic arms race. The institutions studied by Ehrenberg and Clotfelter provided graphic illustrations of both Howard Bowen's "revenue theory" of college costs and William Baumol and William Bowen's "disease theory" of increased spending at prestigious nonprofit organizations.

The Revenue Theory of Higher Education Costs

According to economist Howard Bowen, colleges pursuing excellence "raise all the money they can, and spend all the money they raise."[27] Bowen's finding was a dispassionate conclusion based on data. The implication was that colleges always seemed to be able to find a "good use" for whatever funds they acquired. Their work was never done, their education could be improved, and, hence, seldom was their thirst for resources exhausted. The situation was not that a college president or board did not want to save money or reduce expenses, but rather, the open-ended nature of improving quality or extending services tended to lead to immediate "good" spending on programs. This phenomenon would be particularly pronounced at colleges and universities that were chronically underfunded and malnourished in their efforts to keep up and catch up with peers and rival institutions. And, as noted in Ehrenberg's book, *Tuition Rising*, institutions that were on the move upward in terms of prestige and selectivity also were predisposed to spend – and spend more – in the academic arms race.

The Disease Theory of Higher Education Costs

Economists William Baumol and William Bowen relied on their studies of such non-profit organizations as performing arts groups and highly skilled professional practices, and then turned their attention to colleges and universities. The essence of the "disease theory" was that spending, especially on expensive personnel and equipment, tended to spread. It was infectious. Furthermore, it was unlikely costs could be reduced. A chamber music quartet could never be expected to reduce its membership to three in a cost-cutting exercise for the obvious reason that it would then cease to be a quartet.

Meanwhile, the pursuit of excellence meant that in the performing arts or universities the quest for improvement meant paying high salaries for, for example, an outstanding cellist (for the chamber music quartet) and top-quality professionals in designated fields. Furthermore, adding talent in all aspects of production and services was undeniable and unavoidable. Hence, costs in such selective institutions tended to go up higher than in, for example, a manufacturing company. For colleges and universities, which are in some ways a federation of numerous high-performance units, the syndrome is continually repeated, whether in the College of Fine Arts' opera program, in the varsity football team and coaching staff, the medical center's heart replacement surgical unit, or the nationally ranked English department.[28] Each university has discretion to subsidize activities that its trustees and president deem important.

What Is the RCM Budgeting Model?

RCM is the acronym for *Responsibility Centered Management*. This model of campus budget planning was adopted by selected universities in the early 1990s and has persisted over two decades as an appealing innovation nationwide. It has been characterized as a public college model that allows them to work more like a private or independent college or university. Its roots derive from a concept of decentralized fiduciary responsibility first developed at Harvard in the early 19th century, whose motto was, "Every tub on its own bottom." The essential principle is that within an organization, each component unit is expected to pay its own way.

When RCM is transplanted into a university it carries with it a detailed tracking system of income and expenditures. And, as befits a campus where students, teachers, and courses are central, it includes student enrollment tracking. The idea is that a department or college can show if it is filling its classroom seats, along with other measures such as graduating its fair share of students. What often is not mentioned is that RCM in practice centralizes oversight of all the parts. It also provides an opportunity for the provost or president to build in a taxation system. It could be, for example, that each unit, such as an academic college, must send back to the central administration a certain percentage of its revenue dollars.

Also central to RCM is a lens by which each unit is designated as *revenue producing* – or, not! This alone creates uneasiness among units. And for good reason, because a thorough adoption of RCM would reveal for each unit where money comes from and where it goes. An obvious source of intramural curiosity is to probe how each unit manages to fund its activities. Furthermore, just within the ranks of the *revenue produc-ing units* there is an added level of scrutiny, not unlike farmers who peer over the fence at their neighbor's crops and try to decipher why their neighbor's harvest is so bountiful – or, so meager. RCM data, if fully available, places in bold relief what may be termed "givers" and "takers" among academic departments, campus offices, and other units. One can find out, for example, if an academic department brings in more federal research grant money than it receives in funding from the university's research foundation.

Why is this important? Because with university funds, often the popular image blurs spending and receiving dollars so that the two categories become indistinguishable, at least in the public eye and popular reputation. A physics department, for example, must spend a lot in terms of highly paid physicists, laboratory support staff, and a cyclotron. And, understandably, the inference is that this expensive department therefore must land a lot of research grants. That may well be the case. But, what RCM data reveal is that at many universities, a department such as physics or other high-powered science pro-grams are better at spending than they are at being successful in competition for grants from the National Science Foundation. Furthermore, federal grant money, no matter how abundant, cannot be used to pay for faculty salaries or laboratory construction – expenses that must be paid from other university sources. And, whatever power or pres-tige high-level physics may have, at many universities it attracts relatively few undergraduate majors and their tuition revenues – and does not graduate a large number of Ph.D.s. So, from where is the cross-subsidy to prop up the physics department origi-nating? In contrast, some academic departments have been maligned as being unat-tractive, unpopular, and not very lucrative. The classics department is the usual suspect cited in hearings hosted by state legislators or in newspaper columns about academic excess.

On close inspection with RCM data what one often finds is that the classics depart-ment is truly self-supporting. Its faculty are few in number and their salaries are relat-ively low. The department requires little in the way of expensive equipment or laboratory space, nor are its journal subscriptions expensive. Furthermore, the RCM records indi-cate that the so-called "dead languages" of Latin and Greek have come back to life as competitors for sponsored research funding from private foundations and several federal agencies, ranging from the National Science Foundation to the National Endowment for Humanities and the National Endowment for the Arts. The classics department's faculty has expertise in software development for archaeology, salvaging and translating ancient manuscripts and other codification projects. One member of the department also has developed syndicated Internet courses about the mysteries and marvels of antiquity that attracts paying students nationwide – and is under consideration for a contract for a television series on PBS. Contrary to the popular image, it pays its own way and gener-ates surplus revenues from both tuition enrollments and external grants.

The RCM reality of the two departments is counter-intuitive. It is contrary to image and innuendo – a gulf that sends a shock through the academic system of prestige and rewards. A hallmark of the RCM is that it promotes and relies on *transparency*. This gives it a mixed reception, depending on the academic unit one scrutinizes. It also opens the door to making public the records for comparison and contrast of all units – and the institution as a whole. This is potentially embarrassing to those departments that are found to be "takers."

One might argue that RCM ultimately is more of a governance process than a budgeting model. What is not clear is exactly how RCM changes decision-making by a provost or president. There is no mandate that a provost must translate RCM data into a particular decision. Provosts and presidents often continue to provide full funding to academic units that are expensive – and some that run a deficit. With genuine RCM data available to all campus constituents, however, such propping up becomes painful to justify. Little wonder, then, that even though many research universities once adopted RCM, many eventually abandoned it.

How Do Colleges and Universities Set Tuition?

Each college sets a tuition charge that it thinks the market will bear. This sounds cold and bold. In fact, it is a delicate decision that gains from sound information and candor about the strengths and weaknesses of one's own campus. One interesting phenomenon discovered by some colleges in the late 1970s was that raising tuition to levels higher than that charged by traditional peers and rivals had the unexpected consequence of increasing both the number of applicants and their academic profiles. As discussed in some detail in a later section, "How Does a College Set Enrollment Targets?," academic leaders compare data and projections on total costs for the coming year and tend to "back in" to what the total amount left would then be covered by tuition receipts. A rough approximation then would be to divide the gross amount needed by the number of students one planned to enroll.

Setting tuition includes awareness of what one's competitors are charging. At times it may include cooperation as well as competition. In 1991 the United States Treasury Department filed an anti-trust lawsuit against the eight Ivy League institutions plus Stanford and the Massachusetts Institute of Technology.[29] The grounds of the lawsuit was that when presidents of these ten institutions convened to compare notes on tuition charges plus anticipated financial aid packages to accepted students, this constituted some approximation of price fixing. Only the Massachusetts Institute of Technology refused to settle out of court. The incident illustrated graphically the high-stakes nature of the academic marketplace.

How Do Private versus Public Institutions Differ in Financial Planning?

Almost all colleges and universities, whether public or private (independent) are dependent on undergraduate enrollments – and the related undergraduate tuition payments. Also, both categories of institution try to maximize the practice of students receiving portable federal student aid, either as Pell Grants or federal student loans, which go directly to the campus treasurer's office as receipts.

A difference between public and private institutions is that in many states the legislature provides subsidies to the state colleges and universities. These appropriations can take several forms, ranging from block grants to dedicated line item special project support. However, indelibly linked to state support of higher education is the practice and policy of *per capita subsidy*. What does this mean and why is it important, even controversial? One answer is that it helps explain the origins and changes in how states view their responsibility to provide students with affordable education at public colleges and universities. According to Clark Kerr, after World War II in states with robust economies and growing populations, state governments wanted to expand higher education and had few qualms about allocating tax revenues to do so.[30] Their concern was whether state universities could build necessary classrooms, dormitories, and lecture halls fast enough to accommodate the large number of sons and daughters of taxpayers who had graduated from high school and were ready to go to college. The question was not about money, but rather, how could the state transfer the money to state institutions in a way that was effective? The policy solution was per capita student funding. The more students a state university enrolled, the more state money it received. Furthermore, state universities could reap the benefit of decreasing unit costs, as each subsequent student brought in the base subsidy even though each added student cost the institution less to educate. If all these goals (construction, enrollment, and funding) were accomplished on time, everyone – students, parents, governors, legislators, and state university officials – went away happy.

What was left to determine was exactly how much per student a state university should receive from the state government. This required calculation of the *cost of attendance*. Known as the COA, this meant the total expense to educate an undergraduate for a year. The state then determined what dollar amount and/or percentage of the COA it would subsidize, with the remainder being left as the tuition the state university would charge the student. In California, the remarkable policy was that state government would provide a full subsidy – and the University of California, the California State University and Colleges, and the California Community Colleges would each and all charge no tuition. Across the nation, state governments varied in the proportion they would subsidize. If a state either had a philosophy of low taxation and/or a weak economy, the per student subsidy might be relatively low, and the tuition charge relatively high.

This compact worked reasonably well into the 1980s. Tensions surfaced between state university presidents and state legislatures in the early 1990s that dealt with the issue of who determined the COA along with the state's responsibility for part of that expense. In contrast to the mutually beneficial agreements of the 1950s and 1960s, by 1990 some state university presidents feared that state legislatures were year by year reducing the dollar amount they would contribute to the COA, leaving the state university to charge an increasingly high tuition – an expense borne by students and their families.[31] The controversy increased when state legislatures placed a cap on tuition charges. It meant that a state university was put in a lose–lose situation where the sum of its maximum tuition charge plus a reduced state subsidy meant it lacked adequate resources to educate students. This was particularly hard on state colleges and universities that were not the research or flagship or land grant institutions – and which tended to have small reserves from which to draw. The irony was that state per capita subsidies that rewarded state universities during years of economic prosperity and enrollment growth had become counter-productive, even punitive, to state colleges by the early 1990s.[32]

Private colleges faced their own set of challenges in setting tuition. First, they argued that unlike state universities, they received no state subsidy and, hence, had to charge tuition that was close to the full COA. This led independent colleges to use the concept of the *tuition gap* to mark the difference between a private college tuition charge and what they thought was an artificially low, misleading state tuition charge. Many parents and taxpayers, for example, would read that the state university charged, for example, $1,000 for tuition while the private college tuition was $15,000. This led to the uninformed but widespread response, "How come private colleges are so expensive?" In fact, most independent colleges worked hard to keep costs and tuition charges down.[33]

How Does Student Financial Aid Fit into Costs and Prices?

Student financial aid is a large part of a college or university budget and is central to how an institution positions itself in terms of enrollment, revenues, and expenditures.[34] It has a mercurial character in that at times it surfaces in one category and, later, in another. For example, if a college receives a gift from a donor earmarked for establishing a scholarship fund, the money (whether its principal or its annual interest) is designated as *income*. And, when the scholarship moneys are awarded to a student recipient, it is designated as an *expense*.

From time to time academic officers meet to decide how much of the institutional funds should be dedicated to student financial aid.[35] An important distinction and decision is how much of this should be used for *need-based aid* and how much should be designated for *merit-based aid*.[36] The distinction is consequential because need-based aid serves the purpose of making the college's tuition price affordable to applicants who have been offered admission, yet whose family and personal income record calculations indicate the student most likely cannot afford to pay full tuition. The college then turns to financial aid *packaging* to compile a layered arrangement of institutional grants, federal grants, federal loans, state loans, and state grants that results in a reasonable, realistic financial aid package for the student. It is a means by which a college seeks out academic talent and makes the college affordable to applicants from modest and low income families.

In contrast, merit-based financial aid awarded by the college does not include any requirement that the recipient has financial need. It is based on some ranking of the student's merit in some special category, such as performing arts, journalism, science research, volleyball, or leadership – just to name a few. The recipient might be from a modest income family or, perhaps, from an affluent family. Many merit scholarships are especially attractive because they serve as magnets to attract and enroll students with skills that add to the college's prestige and hold the promise of future achievement and honors. As such, it is the college's "talent hunt."

The differences between the two kinds of student aid reinforce the earlier discussion of the importance of institutional mission and principles. That is because need-based and merit-based scholarships set markedly different priorities, although there may be overlap if, for example, the college enrolls a highly accomplished student who won the national cello competition and also has high financial need. Usually, however, how much a president and provost place into one category versus the other reveals a great deal about the institution's priorities. Merit-based scholarships are especially attractive to colleges whose leadership has grown weary of having outstanding applicants who choose to go elsewhere because rival colleges are academically more prestigious and/or the financial aid award is generous. Merit scholarships carry some distinctive risks. What if, for example, a college's top-ranked candidates for a "full ride" merit scholarship opt to go to other colleges? How far down the list of talent does one go in offering these expensive scholarships to students who may not need the money and also may not be especially excellent in the designated talent area? Above all, merit scholarships are silent on the matters of affordability and access.

How Does a College Set Enrollment Targets?

A provost, in conjunction with other academic deans and student affairs officers, has an informed estimate on the college's capacity for student enrollment – a calculation that combines classroom space, number of faculty, dormitory rooms, parking spaces, and other variables. This is a step that starts to fuse budget decisions with the expertise of enrollment management. Any consideration of increasing enrollment size usually takes into account whether the campus can accommodate the added number of students. Economists refer to increasing returns to margin – often using the example of a class-room with 100 seats. Obviously, if a college last year had students who filled 95 of those seats, it has some room for enrollment expansion. But what about when 101 students show up? Does the college turn that student away from enrolling in that class section because it is filled up? Or, does the college perhaps consider building an additional class-room that can readily accommodate the 101st student – and many more?[37] This delib-eration reverberates through all aspects of campus capacity planning.

The aim for the college is to estimate what it needs in terms of tuition revenues paid by students to meet projected educational expenses. Going back to the preceding section on student financial aid, a dean or bursar cannot presume that each added student will bring in a full tuition payment. To the contrary, the student who receives a grant from the institution represents both partial income and partial expense for the college. If the student's financial aid is in the form of some external award – such as the federal Pell Grant of about $3,000 – it will be counted completely as revenue, part of tuition, with no reduction from the college's own financial aid funds.

Projections by the college are complicated by the fact of organizational life that there is no guarantee that a student who is offered admission – even with financial aid – will choose to enroll. Using previous years' data as a base, deans of admissions and provosts will then try to project what they think the percentage of admitted applicants will actu-ally enroll. This crucial calculation is called the *yield*. Prestigious, academically strong institutions with abundant financial aid tend to have the highest yield. Moving across the spectrum, some colleges have to face the fact that they are "second choice" institu-tions, or what high school seniors call "safety" or "fall back" schools. Such categories reinforce the sobering fact that running a college is a highly demanding, competitive activity – with serious financial consequences.

The temptation to use enrollment increases as a means to increasing institutional resources is risky. If, as colleges often proclaimed to the public, a college subsidizes the costs of a student's education beyond the tuition price, it means that each added student will drain institutional reserves. And, ultimately, substantial expansion creates the need to build more dormitories, laboratories, and classroom buildings – along with adding professional personnel to provide academic services and instruction to the large student body. Increased student enrollments also add costs if the expanded cohort of students shows an academic profile that is weaker than preceding years entering classes. That is because students with lower high school grade point averages than preceding years probably will require more services in terms of academic counseling, remediation courses, and other educational support services.

CONNECTIONS WITH DIVERSITY AND SOCIAL JUSTICE

One indicator of a college's commitment to diversity and social justice is to identify budget items that are intended to provide personnel and services in this area. The most visible sign would be the creation of a Vice President for Institutional Diversity, who is well paid among the ranks of all vice presidents, has adequate office space and support personnel, and is a member of the President's Council and the Provost's Council. Related investments might include having an Assistant Dean of Admissions whose particular charge is minority student recruitment. The staffing of a compliance officer for Title IX in the human resources division, along with lieutenants in key areas throughout campus, is one measure. In the academic programs, signs of substance include departments of African American Studies, Hispanic Studies, and Gender and Women's Studies. Student affairs budgets might include a range of student organizations and clubs for under-represented student constituencies.

A college or university that places social justice and serving underserved and first-generation students as a high priority will be effective in reaching these goals only if it stakes out a large portion of its budget for *need-based student financial aid*. This observation is based on the premise that underserved students tend to come from modest income families. There may be exceptions to that generalization, but for most institutions it stands as a reasonable correlation. Decisions within an institution that give priority to need-based student financial aid will tend to promote social justice and diversity far more than would opting for merit scholarships. Furthermore, financial aid provided by the college will be most effective in attracting and retaining minority students if it reflects a policy of awarding student grants that need not be repaid – as distinguished from loans.

CONCLUSION

Attempts to assess the fiscal fitness of a particular college or university are enhanced when it is depicted in the context of national databases. We have been fortunate in the 21st century to have periodic detailed reports from the Delta Cost Project – a Washington, D.C.-based research institute sponsored in part by the AIR. In trying to answer the fundamental higher education questions, "Where does the money come from? Where does the money go?" the Delta Cost Project reports present compelling evidence that the persistent, cumulative trend is that the dollars a college takes in as tuition revenues have been shifting away from academic programs and educational spending, increasingly toward non-instructional and administrative costs.[38]

There is, of course, variation from institution to institution in proportional changes. But the general finding holds up with remarkable consistency. Are these shifts in spending due to drift or to deliberate decisions? Each institution will have to probe that on its own – and then evaluate whether such trends have been efficient or effective. The gravity of these hard questions is grounded in some important historical trends. First, according to economist Earl Cheit, around 1973 American colleges and universities were cast into a traumatic period of financial peril.[39] The situation was exacerbated by lack of reliable data and analytic tools to diagnose financial crises and stake out realistic solutions. The good news was that college and university officials did acquire the information to scrutinize their own financial planning and missions. This helped deter what had been projected as somewhere between 25 and 33 percent of colleges facing closure. The sequel was the good news that between 1985 and 2016 higher education in the United States has overall enjoyed growing enrollments and reasonably good resources. It is not likely that such largesse and good fortune will continue indefinitely.[40]

Already in this chapter we have invoked literature to provide insight into the essential workings of budget and finance at a campus. Given the labyrinth of offices, decisions, and rationales for what is included in – and excluded from – a college's expenses, it is also fitting to compare exploration of the budget process to Lewis Carroll's *Alice in Wonderland*. Distorting mirrors, rabbit holes, strange rules for games of croquet, a mixture of loyalty and royalty in setting priorities, and rooms in which things are not as they seem. For those at colleges and universities, all these provide shocks of recognition for deciphering the decisions in costs and prices of higher education.

NOTES

1. George Keller, *Academic Strategy: The Management Revolution in American Higher Education* (Baltimore, MD and London: Johns Hopkins University Press, 1983).
2. Donna M. Desrochers and Jane V. Wellman, *Trends in College Spending, 1999–2009: Where Does the Money Come From? Where Does It Go? What Does It Buy?* (Washington, D.C.: Delta Cost Project, 2010).
3. Howard R. Bowen, *Investment in Learning: The Individual and Social Value of American Higher Education* (San Francisco: Jossey-Bass for the Sloan Foundation and the Carnegie Council on Policy Studies in Higher Education, 1978); Howard R. Bowen, *The Costs of Higher Education: How Much Do Colleges and Universities Spend per Student and How Much Should They Spend?* (San Francisco: Jossey-Bass for the Carnegie Council on Policy Studies in Higher Education, 1986); William J. Baumol and Sue Anne Blackman, "How to Think about Rising College Costs," *Planning for Higher Education* (Summer 1995) no. 23, pp. 1–7.
4. President Frank Rhodes of Cornell University, quoted in William G. Bowen and Harold T. Shapiro, Editors, *Universities and Their Leadership* (Princeton, NJ: Princeton University Press, 1998).
5. Steven Koblik and Stephen R. Graubard, Editors, *Distinctively American: The Residential Liberal Arts Colleges* (New Brunswick, NJ: Transaction Publishers, 2000).
6. Frederick Rudolph, "Financing the Colleges," in *The American College and University: A History* (New York: Alfred A. Knopf, 1962) pp. 177–200.
7. John R. Thelin, "Why Did College Cost So Little?: Affordability and Higher Education a Century Ago," *Society* (November–December 2015) pp. 1–9.
8. John Aubrey Douglass, *The California Idea and American Higher Education: 1850 to the 1960 Master Plan* (Stanford, CA: Stanford University Press, 2000).
9. Leroy W. Dubeck, *Budget Handbook for Association Leaders in Higher Education Units: Budget Analysis for Faculty and Staff* (Washington, D.C.: National Education Association, 2002).
10. Aaron Wildavsky, *The Federal Budgetary Process* (Boston: Little, Brown, 1964).
11. Gordon K. Davies, "The Importance of Being General: Philosophy, Politics, and Institutional Mission Statements," in John C. Smart, Editor, *Higher Education: Handbook of Theory and Research*, vol. 2 (New York: Agathon Press, 1986) pp. 85–102.
12. Malcolm Moos, *The Post-Land Grant University: The University of Maryland Report* (College Park: University of Maryland Long Range Planning Study, 1981).
13. Bruce Vladek, "Buildings and Budgets: The Over-Investment Crisis," *Change* (December 1978–January 1979) p. 39.
14. Richard F. O'Donnell, *Higher Education's Faculty Productivity Gap: The Cost to Students, Parents and Taxpayers* (Austin: Report for University of Texas System, 2011); Rick O'Donnell, "Why Productivity Data Matter," *Inside Higher Ed* (July 20, 2011). Online: www.insidehighered.com/views/2011/07/20/o_donnell_on_faculty_productivity_data.
15. Michael Middaugh as quoted in Paul Fain, "Faculty Pay Is Not Part of Academe's Cost Crisis, Expert Tells Trustees' Conference," *Chronicle of Higher Education* (April 4, 2006) p. A1. See also, Michael F. Middaugh, *Understanding Faculty Productivity: Standards and Benchmarks for Colleges and Universities* (San Francisco: Jossey-Bass, 2001).
16. Dan Berrett, "Wrong Kind of Accountability?," *Inside Higher Ed* (May 10, 2011).
17. Joseph C. Hermanowicz, Editor, *The American Academic Profession: Transformation in Contemporary Higher Education* (Baltimore, MD: Johns Hopkins University Press, 2011). See also, Roger G. Baldwin and Jay L. Chronister, *Teaching without Tenure: Policies and Practice for a New Era* (Baltimore, MD: Johns Hopkins University Press, 2001).
18. Stephen C. Ludwig, *Getting to the Data: Questions Trustees Should Ask* (Washington, D.C.: American Council of Trustees and Alumni, November 2015).
19. Rhoula Khalaf, "Customized Accounting," *Forbes* (May 25, 1992) p. 50.

20. Murray Sperber, *College Sports Inc.: The Athletic Department vs. the University* (New York: Henry Holt and Company, 1990).
21. Carlotta C. Joyner, Director, *Higher Education: Tuition Increasing Faster than Household Income and Public Colleges' Costs* (Washington, D.C.: General Accounting Office, August 1996).
22. Nathan Glazar, "Regulating Business and the Universities: One Problem or Two?," *Public Interest* (Summer 1979) pp. 42–65. See also, Carnegie Foundation for the Advancement of Teaching, *The Control of the Campus: A Report on the Governance of Higher Education* (Princeton, NJ: Carnegie Foundation for the Advancement of Teaching, 1982). See also, Robert M. Rosenzweig, *The Political University: Policy, Politics, and Presidential Leadership in the American University* (Baltimore, MD and London: Johns Hopkins University Press, 1998).
23. Edward St. John and Michael D. Parsons, Editors, *Public Funding of Higher Education: Changing Contexts and New Rationales* (Baltimore, MD and London: Johns Hopkins University Press, 2004); Andrew Policano and Gary Fethke, *Public No More: A New Path to Excellence for America's Public Universities* (Stanford, CA: Stanford Business Books, 2012).
24. Gaye Tuchman, *Wannabe U: Inside the Corporate University* (Chicago and London: University of Chicago Press, 2009).
25. Ronald Ehrenberg, *Tuition Rising: Why College Costs So Much* (Cambridge, MA and London: Harvard University Press, 2000). See also, Robert B. Archibald and David Feldman, *Why Does College Cost So Much?* (New York: Oxford University Press, 2010).
26. Charles T. Clotfelter, *Buying the Best: Cost Escalation and Elite Higher Education* (Princeton, NJ: Princeton University Press for the National Board of Economic Research, 1996).
27. Howard R. Bowen, *Investment in Learning: The Individual and Social Value of American Higher Education* (San Francisco: Jossey-Bass for the Sloan Foundation and the Carnegie Council on Policy Studies in Higher Education, 1978); Howard R. Bowen, *The Costs of Higher Education: How Much Do Colleges and Universities Spend per Student and How Much Should They Spend?* (San Francisco: Jossey-Bass for the Carnegie Council on Policy Studies in Higher Education, 1986).
28. William J. Baumol and William G. Bowen, *Performing Arts: The Economic Dilemma* (Washington, D.C.: Twentieth Century Fund, 1966); William J. Baumol and Sue Anne Blackman, "How to Think about Rising College Costs," *Planning for Higher Education* (Summer 1995) no. 23, pp. 1–7.
29. Michelle Healy, "Ivy League Settles Price-Fixing Suit on Aid," *USA Today* (May 23, 1991) p. 1A.
30. Clark Kerr, *The Uses of the University* (Cambridge, MA: Harvard University Press, 1963).
31. Ronald Ehrenberg, Editor, *What's Happening to Public Higher Education?: The Shifting Financial Burden* (Baltimore, MD: Johns Hopkins University Press, 2006). See also, Donald E. Heller, Editor, *The States and Public Higher Education Policy: Affordability, Access, and Accountability* (Baltimore, MD and London: Johns Hopkins University Press, 2001).
32. Thomas Wallace, "The Age of the Dinosaur Persists," *Change* (July–August 1992) vol. 25, pp. 56–63.
33. Alvin P. Sanoff, "Serving Students Well: Independent Colleges Today," in *Meeting the Challenge: America's Independent Colleges and Universities since 1956* (Washington, D.C.: Council of Independent Colleges, 2006) pp. 37–62.
34. Michael McPherson, Morton Owen Shapiro, and Gordon Winston, *Paying the Piper: Productivity, Incentives, and Financing in U.S. Higher Education* (Ann Arbor: University of Michigan Press, 1993); Michael B. Paulsen and John C. Smart, Editors, *The Finance of Higher Education: Theory Research, Policy and Practice* (New York: Agathon Press, 2001).
35. Frederick M. Hess, Editor, *Footing the Tuition Bill: The New Student Loan Sector* (Washington, D.C.: American Enterprise Institute, 2007).
36. Chester E. Finn, Jr., *Scholars, Dollars and Bureaucrats* (Washington, D.C.: Brookings Institution, 1978).
37. Bruce Vladek, "Buildings and Budgets: The Over-Investment Crisis," *Change* (December 1978–January 1979) p. 39.
38. Donna M. Desrochers and Jane V. Wellman, *Trends in College Spending, 1999–2009: Where Does the Money Come From? Where Does It Go? What Does It Buy?* (Washington, D.C.: Delta Cost Project, 2010).
39. Earl F. Cheit, *The New Depression in Higher Education: A Study of the Financial Conditions at 41 Colleges and Universities* (New York: McGraw-Hill for the Carnegie Council, 1971).
40. Andrew Delbanco, "The Universities in Trouble," *New York Review of Books* (May 14, 2009) no. 56.

Additional Readings

Robert B. Archibald and David Feldman, *Why Does College Cost So Much?* (New York: Oxford University Press, 2010).
William J. Baumol and Sue Anne Blackman, "How to Think about Rising College Costs," *Planning for Higher Education* (Summer 1995) no. 23, pp. 1–7.

William J. Baumol and William G. Bowen, *Performing Arts: The Economic Dilemma* (Washington, D.C.: Twentieth Century Fund, 1966).

Howard R. Bowen, *Investment in Learning: The Individual and Social Value of American Higher Education* (San Francisco: Jossey-Bass for the Sloan Foundation and the Carnegie Council on Policy Studies in Higher Education, 1978).

Howard R. Bowen, *The Costs of Higher Education: How Much Do Colleges and Universities Spend per Student and How Much Should They Spend?* (San Francisco: Jossey-Bass for the Carnegie Council on Policy Studies in Higher Education, 1986).

Howard R. Bowen and Jack H. Schuster, *American Professors: A National Resource Imperiled* (New York and Oxford: Oxford University Press, 1980).

David W. Breneman, Larry L. Leslie, and Richard E. Anderson, Editors, *ASHE Reader on Finance in Higher Education* (Needham Heights, MA: Simon & Schuster for the Association for the Study of Higher Education, 1996).

Patrick M. Callan and Joni E. Finney, Editors, *Public and Private Financing of Higher Education: Shaping Public Policy for the Future* (Phoenix, AZ: American Council on Education and the Oryx Press, 1997).

Earl F. Cheit, *The New Depression in Higher Education: A Study of the Financial Conditions at 41 Colleges and Universities* (New York: McGraw-Hill for the Carnegie Council, 1971).

Charles T. Clotfelter, *Buying the Best: Cost Escalation and Elite Higher Education* (Princeton, NJ: Princeton University Press for the National Board of Economic Research, 1996).

Charles T. Clotfelter, Ronald G. Ehrenberg, Malcolm Getz, and John J. Siegfried, *Economic Challenges in Higher Education* (Chicago: University of Chicago Press, 1992).

Donna M. Desrochers and Jane V. Wellman, *Trends in College Spending, 1999–2009: Where Does the Money Come From? Where Does It Go? What Does It Buy?* (Washington, D.C.: Delta Cost Project, 2010).

Leroy W. Dubeck, *Budget Handbook for Association Leaders in Higher Education Units: Budget Analysis for Faculty and Staff* (Washington, D.C.: National Education Association, 2002).

Ronald Ehrenberg, *Tuition Rising: Why College Costs So Much* (Cambridge, MA and London: Harvard University Press, 2000).

Ronald Ehrenberg, Editor, *What's Happening to Public Higher Education?: The Shifting Financial Burden* (Baltimore, MD: Johns Hopkins University Press, 2006).

Chester E. Finn, Jr., *Scholars, Dollars and Bureaucrats* (Washington, D.C.: Brookings Institution, 1978).

Roger L. Geiger, *Knowledge and Money: Research Universities and the Paradox of the Marketplace* (Stanford, CA: Stanford University Press, 2004).

Nathan Glazar, "Regulating Business and the Universities," *Public Interest* (Summer 1979) pp. 42–65.

Donald E. Heller, Editor, *The States and Public Higher Education Policy: Affordability, Access, and Accountability* (Baltimore, MD and London: Johns Hopkins University Press, 2001).

Frederick M. Hess, Editor, *Footing the Tuition Bill: The New Student Loan Sector* (Washington, D.C.: American Enterprise Institute, 2007).

D. Bruce Johnstone and Pamela Marcucci, *Financing Higher Education Worldwide: Who Pays? Who Should Pay?* (Baltimore, MD: Johns Hopkins University Press, 2010).

Carlotta C. Joyner, Director, *Higher Education: Tuition Increasing Faster than Household Income and Public Colleges' Costs* (Washington, D.C.: General Accounting Office, August 1996).

George Keller, *Academic Strategy: The Management Revolution in American Higher Education* (Baltimore, MD and London: Johns Hopkins University Press, 1983).

Steven Koblik and Stephen R. Graubard, Editors, *Distinctively American: The Residential Liberal Arts Colleges* (New Brunswick, NJ: Transaction Publishers, 2000).

Arthur Levine, "Higher Education's New Status as a Mature Industry," *Chronicle of Higher Education* (January 31, 1997) p. A48.

Stephen C. Ludwig, *Getting to the Data: Questions Trustees Should Ask* (Washington, D.C.: American Council of Trustees and Alumni, November 2015).

Michael McPherson, Morton Owen Shapiro, and Gordon Winston, *Paying the Piper: Productivity, Incentives, and Financing in U.S. Higher Education* (Ann Arbor: University of Michigan Press, 1993).

Michael F. Middaugh, *Understanding Faculty Productivity: Standards and Benchmarks for Colleges and Universities* (San Francisco: Jossey-Bass, 2001).

Richard F. O'Donnell, *Higher Education's Faculty Productivity Gap: The Cost to Students, Parents and Taxpayers* (Austin: Report for University of Texas System, 2011).

Rick O'Donnell, "Why Productivity Data Matter," *Inside Higher Ed* (July 20, 2011). Online: www.insidehighered.com/views/2011/07/20/o_donnell_on_faculty_productivity_data.

Michael O'Keefe, "Where Does the Money Really Go?: Case Studies of Six Institutions," *Change* (November–December 1987) pp. 12–34.

Michael B. Paulsen and John C. Smart, Editors, *The Finance of Higher Education: Theory Research, Policy and Practice* (New York: Agathon Press, 2001).

Andrew Policano and Gary Fethke, *Public No More: A New Path to Excellence for America's Public Universities* (Stanford, CA: Stanford Business Books, 2012).

Henry Rosovsky, *The University: An Owner's Manual* (New York and London: W.W. Norton, 1990).

Edward St. John and Michael D. Parsons, Editors, *Public Funding of Higher Education: Changing Contexts and New Rationales* (Baltimore, MD and London: Johns Hopkins University Press, 2004).

Alvin P. Sanoff, "Serving Students Well: Independent Colleges Today," in *Meeting the Challenge: America's Independent Colleges and Universities since 1956* (Washington, D.C.: Council of Independent Colleges, 2006) pp. 37–62.

John R. Thelin, "Why Did College Cost So Little?: Affordability and Higher Education a Century Ago," *Society* (November–December 2015) pp. 1–9.

Gaye Tuchman, *Wannabe U: Inside the Corporate University* (Chicago and London: University of Chicago Press, 2009).

Bruce Vladek, "Buildings and Budgets: The Over-Investment Crisis," *Change* (December 1978–January 1979) p. 39.

Thomas Wallace, "The Age of the Dinosaur Persists," *Change* (July–August 1992) vol. 25, pp. 56–63.

Aaron Wildavsky, *The Federal Budgetary Process* (Boston: Little, Brown, 1964).

8

INTERCOLLEGIATE ATHLETICS

Higher Education's Peculiar Institution

SETTING AND OVERVIEW

No college or university in the United States lists intercollegiate sports as a central mission or purpose. Yet this "untruth in advertising" belies the remarkable fact that college sports are at the heart of many colleges' and universities' presence and priorities. This takes place not only at universities with "big-time" commercialized sports teams, but also through all American higher education, encompassing small liberal arts colleges, regional comprehensive universities, and community colleges. It is inclusive, as student-athlete participation cuts across categories of gender, family income, race and ethnicity. Intercollegiate sports are formally classified as an *educational* activity that is part of *student extracurricular offerings* – and whose players are *student-athletes* enrolled full time in degree programs. These definitions and distinctions will be central to the questions about both the present and future character and even the legal status of intercollegiate athletics.

College sports are hailed as the "front porch" of a college or university. What does that mean? It does mean that college sports in the public forum and popular culture exude a "halo effect" that often shapes the general image and reputation of a campus. It also means that intercollegiate sports are associated with television broadcast contracts, news coverage in the media, ticket sales, and other income.

One connotation of the campus "front porch" is suggested by the vital statistics of intercollegiate athletics in number of institutions, sports, contests, spectators, and participating student-athletes. For example, member institutions of the National Collegiate Athletic Association (NCAA) accounted for championships in 24 varsity sports in 2016. In addition to the obvious ones such as football and basketball, the roster includes field hockey, lacrosse, wrestling, soccer, rowing, bowling, golf, ice hockey, cross-country, track and field (both indoor and outdoor seasons), women's gymnastics, tennis, volleyball, softball, baseball, fencing, rifle, and skiing. Furthermore, several sports have their own national collegiate championships *outside* NCAA sponsorship. The number of colleges participating in the NCAA is large, with 1,092 member institutions. NCAA games were played by more than 460,000 student-athletes nationwide. In football, one of the major sports, 655 teams played 3,693 games, with a total attendance of more than 49 million spectators. In men's basketball, more than 32 million fans attended. Total revenues for all NCAA college sports in 2013 were $14 billion.

Even this profile tends to understate the pervasiveness of college sports. All the numbers increase when one adds to the NCAA summaries the comparable data for institutions belonging to the National Association of Intercollegiate Athletics (NAIA), which has over 250 member institutions and championships in 25 sports, the national association of junior and community colleges, along with the more than 100 California community colleges.

The spotlight on the campus "front porch" shines each year on the showcased championship games, especially in football and basketball for the high-powered NCAA Division I category whose institutional membership is 345 – of which 250 have varsity football programs. Within this group, the top-tier division of the Football Bowl Series, its 125 college teams accounted for just under 35 million attendance in 2014, with an average game attendance of a little more than 44,000. Thirty football teams reported an average attendance of more than 57,000 per game. The highest average attendance for home games included the Ohio State University at 106,296; Texas A&M, 105,123; University of Michigan, 104,909; Louisiana State University, 101,723; Pennsylvania State University, 101,623; and Alabama at 101,534.

In men's basketball, the 345 institutions playing in NCAA Division I had an average attendance of 4,754. At the highest level, 41 colleges averaged more than 10,000 spectators per game. College teams with the highest attendance per game included Syracuse University with 23,854; the University of Kentucky, 23,572; the University of Louisville, 21,386; the University of North Carolina at Chapel Hill, 19,582; and the University of Wisconsin at 17,279.

Broadcasts and branding make intercollegiate athletics pervasive in the nation's spectator sports. For example, on a typical Saturday in October a sports fan has the opportunity to watch 12 college football games broadcast on major television networks, namely, ABC, NBC, CBS, and ESPN. These viewing opportunities could be expanded to at least another ten games if one were willing to pay a modest subscription or pay-per-view charge. Saturday, of course, has long been the premier day for college football. It starts with ESPN's *Game Day* program – one of the most sophisticated and successful television shows, which provides viewers a festival of campus visits and interview shows hosted by college sports announcers and commentators who have become media celebrities.[1]

Starting on December 20 each year, after the finish of the "regular" college football season that had started in August, television networks broadcast 40 post-season bowl games, culminating in January with the playoff quarter-finals and, then, the championship game. These latter games attract television viewing audiences of about 28 million per game. The 2015 championship game between the Ohio State University and the University of Oregon attracted about 34 million viewers.

Football may be the favorite college sport for the American public, but it is not the whole story of college sports broadcasts. On a January weekend in 2015 a typical slate of intercollegiate basketball games available to a television viewer was 32 men's games and four women's games. Whereas college football tends to be concentrated into weekend games, college basketball broadcasts regularly tally six games per night during the week. Playing college sports – and broadcasting big-time college games – is a 24/7 feature in

American popular culture and an activity that is a blend of educational-commercial-cultural activity.

This quantitative profile of spectator college sports in the early 21st century extends beyond attendance at the games and the media viewing audiences to include the financial impact on intercollegiate athletics programs. The 40 post-season Football Bowl Series (FBS) games distributed $505.9 million to the participating conferences and schools. These same participating institutions and their conferences spent $100.2 million to take part in the bowl games, leading to a net gain of over $400 million for the college programs. College football bowl revenues of $509 million had increased dramatically – from $310 million in 2013–2014 and $301 million pay-outs for the 2012–2013 bowl seasons.[2] One result of these recent developments is the emergence of five "super conferences" that have acquired lucrative television contracts. For the Southeastern Conference in 2014–2015 this meant distribution of more than $455 million, which breaks down to $31.2 million to each of its 14 member institutions, plus an additional $10 million from football bowl revenues.[3]

If this extended survey of facts and figures seems overwhelming and perhaps tedious, that is neither a mistake nor an exaggeration. However, it may be an illusion – or, at least, misleading. Although a small number of institutions report substantial net income from their athletics enterprise, most college sports programs, even in the "big-time" arena and in powerful conferences, run a deficit and require cross-subsidies from their institution. Such contradictions add to the appeal of the story of college sports as higher education's "peculiar institution."

This chapter topic is important because the United States is the only nation in the world that showcases intercollegiate sports as a visible institutional activity geared toward popular audiences and commercial broadcast contracts. International visitors to American campuses are surprised and fascinated by the amount of space and buildings we devote to facilities and fields for varsity sports. Since college sports are "intercollegiate" it means that competition against other institutions has fostered group associations and conferences. These are highly structured, formal collective bodies with governing by-laws, a commissioner, and contractual obligations. Analysis of college sports will include not only exploration at the campus level but also will provide an introduction to such organizations as the NCAA, the Knight Commission on the Future of Intercollegiate Athletics, the Drake Commission, and various other conferences and associations to which institutions belong.

ISSUES

Is College Sports an Educational Activity?

The historical root of college sports is that they were developed by and for students. Student teams and their games against rival colleges often were renegade activities prohibited by presidents and professors. By World War I, however, their persistence and popularity made them fixtures at most American campuses. As such, they were placed under the supervision of a campus administrative office. Characterization of college sports as *educational* in nature comes from the observation that students who participate learn significant lessons in teamwork, leadership, cooperation, fair play, good sportsmanship, and decision-making. One acquires the discipline helpful to achieve a goal such as winning a game or a conference championship. Furthermore, a student-athlete learns time management to balance the demands of academics and athletics, course work and practice. These statements, however, are best understood as *beliefs* rather than *facts* about the benefits of playing college sports. These may be achieved and acquired – but are not necessarily universal.

Social and behavioral scientists, along with historians and economists, have undertaken numerous studies to test out the claims of the positive impact of sports participation by students. William Bowen, former president and provost of Princeton and, later, president of the Mellon Foundation, teamed with co-authors James Shulman and, in a sequel study, Sarah Levin, to analyze comprehensive databases on undergraduates and their academic performance profiles in order to discern how student-athletes fare within their cohort of classmates.[4] In one study, the focus was on universities that were academically selective and also played intercollegiate sports in the most competitive, commercial orbit – NCAA Division I. This meant analysis of college sports at Stanford, Duke, Northwestern, the University of Michigan, Vanderbilt, Tulane, the University of California, Berkeley, UCLA, and their kindred institutions. The study deliberately excluded institutions with relatively low admissions standards for all students and which also hosted big-time sports programs. Bowen and Shulman cited data to indicate that student-athletes at their selected universities tended to have grade point averages lower than non-athletes – and they under-performed in college on the basis of combined predictors such as Scholastic Aptitude Test scores and high school transcripts. A large number opted for concentration in the social sciences – as distinguished from the natural sciences, engineering, architecture, history, or mathematics. Furthermore, this profile persisted when student-athletes' academic records were contrasted with fellow students who held leadership roles in demanding extracurricular activities, such as editor of the campus newspaper or president of the student body.

At the same time, within this select circle of academic institutions, student-athletes' grades were not much lower than the general student body and did have grade point averages and graduation rates that were relatively solid when charted against nationwide norms for all higher education. When Bowen and Levin later focused on a different, significant group of institutions in their subsequent 2003 study, *Reclaiming the Game*, namely, prestigious, selective independent colleges that did not offer athletic grants-in-aid, their findings were comparable. This sample included institutions that were members of the Ivy League along with liberal arts colleges such as Amherst, Williams, Wesleyan, Bucknell, Colgate, Holy Cross, West Point, the United States Naval Academy, and Washington University of St. Louis.

When one looks at colleges and universities that are less academically selective in admissions than those Bowen considered, the gap between students and student-athletes becomes less pronounced. On the one hand, student-athletes in the revenue sports of football and men's basketball usually live and play in a secluded campus enclave; they have numerous benefits and advantages usually not available to the general student body. This includes academic support services, nutritionists, and psychological counselors, along with staff who assist with course selection, career counseling, tutoring, and sometimes with purchasing textbooks. What one finds in data from the NCAA is that, overall, student-athletes have higher grade point averages than the general student body. One partial explanation for this edge is that the academic services provided to a scholarship athlete often are significantly greater than those available to a "regular" student. Furthermore, scholarship student-athletes do not hold down part-time jobs, unlike many undergraduates who are working their way through college. Student-athletes on scholarships also are going to college full time – whereas many students are part time. Such relatively higher graduation rates by student-athletes suggest that playing varsity sports can be a positive dimension of the undergraduate collegiate experience, especially if it is accompanied by academic support services – and if student-athletes have good academic records and skills when they enter college.

By 2009 the NCAA data indicated that for student-athletes nationwide and in all levels of NCAA competition, the mean hours per week spent on activities related to one's varsity sport was about 40 hours. Apart from the NCAA studies, some estimates for student-athletes in the revenue sports is that participation entails between 60 and 70 hours per week when one factors in time spent for travel to and from games, voluntary breakfast meetings, voluntary summer training sessions, and myriad sport-related activities.

On balance, it is fair to say that a student-athlete who receives a full grant-in-aid receives many resources and benefits – many of which can make college a special experience and even promote academic achievement and degree completion. And, one also can report with comparable reliability that the demands of varsity competition are formidable – and the role of being a varsity athlete often trumps that of being a student. Even if student-athletes do well in their academic grade point averages, often their curricular options are restricted. Can one, for example, pursue a concentration in architecture – an intensive field of study where students often work around the clock and in groups on demanding projects – while competing in a high-level varsity sport? Or, put another way, if laboratory sessions for chemistry customarily take place in the afternoon, how can one logistically meet that obligation if varsity team practices run from 1 p.m. to 6 p.m.? A reasonable observation is that achieving excellence in both academics and athletics is not impossible – but it is difficult. Furthermore, if student-athletes have high school academic records lower than that of the entering class as a whole, balanced academic and athletic achievement tends to be unlikely.

College officials historically recognized the demands of varsity sports on students and built in measures to reduce competitive pressures on entering freshmen. An undergraduate was not allowed to play a varsity sport during the freshman year – and almost all colleges and universities had both freshmen teams and varsity teams for each sport. Furthermore, varsity eligibility was limited to three seasons. Starting gradually in the early 1970s, the NCAA allowed freshmen to compete as varsity athletes in the so-called "Olympic sports" or "minor sports." Furthermore, a student was granted four years of varsity eligibility, an increase over the three-year limit. Eventually the four-year immediate eligibility allowance was extended to all sports, including football and men's basketball. One justification was that the skill level of high school seniors who then entered college had risen – and many had the maturity and ability to play on the varsity right away. Another consideration from the point of view of athletic directors was the prospect of maximizing grants-in-aid. First, freshmen eligibility eliminated the expenses of coaching staff, equipment, and travel for freshmen squads. Second, it weeded out freshman players who were not likely to have the talent to play on the varsity. Third, it meant that for an outstanding athlete, the coaches now could count on four years of playing, spread over five years, whereas under the old arrangement, the athletic department was paying for a grant-in-aid without varsity performance by the freshman athlete. Whether or not this was consequential for a student-athlete's academic adjustment and participation in campus life faded as a consideration in the cost–benefit calculations.

In recent years the NCAA has devoted a great deal of public relations effort to dispelling the stereotype of the student-athlete as a "dumb jock" or that going to college is used by some outstanding athletes as primarily a springboard to future professional athletic success. The NCAA motto has been something along the lines of the proclamation, "Ninety percent of our athletes are going pro – in something other than sports!" And, this is accurate. The record of academic and athletic achievement among all student-athletes in all sports and all institutions is impressive. The sticking point, however, is that this masks the profiles and performances of students who play in the major revenue sports – the small subset who are the overwhelming focus of most media attention and sports page coverage. These are student-athletes most important to the power and prestige of an athletic department's overall reputation. The NCAA and some athletic conferences also have worked deliberately to expand the activities and horizons of student-athletes by providing sponsorship for NCAA community service projects – innovative programs that suggest that athletic directors and NCAA officials have been responsive to concerns about the confining nature of varsity sport participation.

Is College Sports a Business?

Even though the preceding discussion staked out the rationale for characterizing college sports as an educational activity, this does not exhaust the additional, potentially accurate depictions. College sports have gone from informal to increasingly formal recognition as a "big business." Consider the following judicial brief: On June 4, 2015 in the case of *Javon Marshall, et al.* v. *ESPN, Inc. et al.* and several other broadcasting corporations and the NCAA, Judge Kevin H. Sharp wrote, "College basketball and football, particularly at the Division I and FBS levels, is big business. Of that there can be little doubt."[5] What were the kinds of data that would lead a Federal District Judge to make this observation? What are the financial and commercial revenues associated with the amateur athletics programs of our colleges and universities in the 21st century?

One answer is that broadcast of games associated with "March Madness" has led to a related "Advertising Madness." An article in the Business section of the *New York Times* on April 6, 2015 reported that ten corporations spent a total of $267 million for advertising. These top spenders were joined by others. According to Shelly Freierman of the *New York Times*:

> Between the start of the N.C.A.A. men's basketball tournament on March 19th, and the Final Four games on Saturday, companies spent an estimated $870 million to broadcast TV commercials 5,349 times. Still to come, of course, is the Wisconsin-Duke final on Monday. By comparison, the advertising spent on the 2015 Super Bowl was $432 million, and on the Oscars, $147 million.[6]

When one looks at national cable television ratings between March 23 and March 29, 2015, NCAA college basketball game broadcasts represented seven of the top ten rated shows.

The heightened stature of college sports for spectators today gains clarity when contrasted to their counterparts about a half-century ago. In 1965 a television viewer probably could watch, at most, a total of two college football games on a Saturday, one with a kick-off time at noon, with a second game scheduled for 3 p.m. Broadcasts were confined to regional audiences – two games targeted within each of four regions nationwide, a total of eight broadcasts. College basketball had few if any nationwide broadcasts during the regular season.

CHARACTERS AND CONSTITUENTS

Student-Athletes

As noted in the opening profile, college students who play a varsity sport constitute a significant segment of full-time student enrollments. This is most evident at small enrollment colleges and universities. A college whose athletic department offers a large number of sports for both men and women probably has between 300 and 500 varsity athletes. Today a college student who wishes to be eligible to compete in an NCAA sport must fulfill formal requirements ranging from approved high school transcripts with a satisfactory grade point average and test scores, documentation of progress toward the bachelor's degree, and passing periodic drug and substance tests. Furthermore, as a condition of receiving an athletic grant-in-aid to play a varsity sport, a potential student-athlete must agree to conditions on personal conduct – including waiving some rights granted to all students in the college. Student-athletes often must sign agreements that they will not speak to the press or other media without explicit permission of the athletic department. Nor may student-athletes place on retainer an agent or accept royalties or payment for endorsement of products. Failure to sign such agreements – or failure to comply – carries high penalties, including forfeiting eligibility to play.

Athletic scholarships – formally called "grants-in-aids" – are regulated by the institution, the conference, and the NCAA. A complete grant-in-aid – known as a "full ride" – covers tuition and includes meals, access to well-stocked "snack bars," textbooks, and other academic expenses. Beyond such items, however, additional payments for travel home, extra meals, and entertainment and taking on jobs or employment are prohibited. In 2015 the NCAA made changes allowing each conference to expand the grant-in-aid to cover the "COA" – the cost of attendance for a full-time student.

Being a college student-athlete is neither a casual nor a haphazard activity – for either the individual or the institution. This contrasts markedly with the lack of regulation or monitoring in college sports a century ago, when nicknames such as "muckers" and "ringers" designated young men whose brawn was more in demand by colleges than their brains, and admission was easily accomplished, as were under-the-table payments for athletic services rendered.[7] To the contrary, in recent years the implementation of academic requirements (such as the NCAA's Proposition 48) has sometimes been criticized as too intrusive, with a side effect of becoming an inordinate hurdle for prospective student-athletes who are from modest income families and racial and ethnic minorities.

Integration of student-athletes into campus life remains uneven and sometimes problematic, especially with the revenue sports at large universities. The NCAA expressly prohibits separate dormitories for student-athletes. Yet the practice persists because athletic directors can readily comply with the letter of the law while evading its spirit. Operationalized regulations call for some fixed percentage of non-athletes to live in a dormitory. And, coaches and athletic officials satisfy the standard by arranging for student managers, athletic tutors, and other non-athletes to reside in the dormitories. But who are we kidding? These are athletic dormitories.

Gradually yet persistently over several years, the demands of college sport participation combined with the high level of skills displayed by recruited athletes has led to lawsuits and court cases with disputes over the legal status of student-athletes. Economist Andrew Zimbalist concluded that the high-profile basketball and football players were "unpaid professionals."[8] In 2014 football players at Northwestern University petitioned the regional National Labor Relations Board to have them categorized as university "employees." This ruling was not upheld in courts in August 2015 – a decision that was hailed as a "victory for the college sports establishment." Despite this setback, the players' initiative did send a message that reconsideration of the time, work, and expertise of student-athletes was an issue that would gain increasing scrutiny.

Furthermore, during the same years, in what would lead to a landmark court case, a former UCLA basketball player, Ed O'Bannon, noticed that his likeness, including his UCLA jersey and number, were featured in NCAA-sponsored video games – a commercial product. O'Bannon was successful in petitioning for compensation, leading the NCAA to discontinue its forays into commercial video game licensing. Elsewhere, from time to time, an injured college student-athlete has filed for workmen's compensation. Even the former president of the NCAA, Walter Byer, devoted his retirement years to advocating against excesses and abuses of what he felt was the exploitation of college athletes.[9]

Mascots

Including college sports team mascots in the company of student-athletes, coaches, athletic directors, deans, and presidents at first glance seems to be a silly, frivolous choice. On close inspection, however, one finds that these have been personified to be the "face" not only of college sports but also of the entire institution. At first, mascots were confined to the stadium or basketball arena during the game or at pep rallies. However, with the rise of national television broadcasts, especially shows and promotionals by ESPN, college mascots literally are "for real." They also provide some insight into the heritage and legacies of a university. Consider, for example, the University of Texas "Longhorns," the Indiana University "Hoosiers," Purdue University "Boiler Makers," the Oklahoma State University "Cowboys," the Ohio State University "Buckeyes," the MIT "Engineers," the University of Virginia "Cavaliers," and the University of Tennessee "Volunteers." Mascots can turn a college football rivalry into a morality play, as one waits in awe to see if Duke's "Blue Devils" will prevail over Wake Forest's "Demon Deacons." Often the mascots pay homage to founders and major donors, as illustrated by Vanderbilt and its Commodores, or Stetson University and its "Hatters." The University of Notre Dame has for over 70 years invoked a characterization of its heritage with the mascot of a leprechaun who represents the historical "Fightin' Irish."

The mascots and their connotations and symbolism are serious business as matters of state pride and institutional mission. Amidst the menagerie of lions, tigers, and bears, one has to take serious note of the University of Pennsylvania's "Fightin' Quakers" as part of institutional roots, even if it scrambles historical accuracy. And, in some cases, conflicts and disputes over historical figures as team mascots have cost presidents their jobs and alienated potential major donors. As we shall discuss in greater length in a later section on social justice, the naming – and renaming – of sports team mascots has been visible and central to matters of institutional identity and inclusion.

Coaches

College coaches are the key adult professionals in the conduct of intercollegiate athletics. As such, they are the most influential figures both in working with student-athletes and in the role of public figures, even popular celebrities. In a typical American college and university where requirements on academic degrees and other credentials are the norm for faculty and professional staff, college coaches seldom encounter any standards of professional certification or licensure. Whereas the typical search and hiring for an academic position takes close to a calendar year, coaching vacancies are filled quickly – sometimes in a matter of days or a few weeks. Athletic directors often are brazen and so confident of their privileges in hiring that they frequently announce the sole finalist for a coaching position – with the disclaimer that it is not yet officially approved by campus human resources. One dysfunction of this efficiency is lack of procedural accountability that would document whether or not applicants from historically under-represented minority groups have been vetted and given fair consideration.

USA Today has devoted considerable research and writing to coverage of college coaching salary trends since 2006. In 46 states, the highest paid state employee is a head coach at one of the state's public universities. In the NCAA Division "FBS" category, head football coaches received on average a salary of more than $2 million per year. The highest paid head football coaches each received more than $7 million per year. At the same time, the highest paid university presidents in the nation received, respectively, $4 million and $3 million – with an average presidential salary being about $460,000. Furthermore, for head football coaches the average annual bonus was $95,000 for having met performance goals such as winning a conference championship or going to a post-season bowl game, and even more for then winning that bowl game.

Coaches also were eligible for substantial bonuses on non-athletic matters, including grade point averages and graduation rates by student-athletes – even though there is little clear evidence that a head coach had much if anything to do with classroom matters. Assistant football coaches in this group are relatively well paid – about 500 assistant football coaches had annual salaries surpassing $200,000 per year. Within that group, 152 had salaries of more than $400,000 per year. Nine were paid more than $1 million per year.

A comparable profile accompanies head coaches of men's varsity basketball teams in NCAA Division I. The highest compensation packages surpass $7 million per year. In 2015, 40 basketball coaches received salaries of more than $1 million per year. Not only have head coaching salaries at big-time programs ascended, so has the proliferation of well-paid staff personnel outside the "coach" category. Directors of recruiting, strength coordinators, team psychologists, nutritionists, and numerous other specialists indicate an athletics staff arms race, at least at the top of the college sports pyramid. One strategy for institutions has been to endow head coaching positions, funded by athletics donors.

Hiring leads to firing when discussing college head football coaches' compensation. Most big-time coaches have elaborate contracts, complete with "roll over" provisions. In other words, if a coach has a five-year "roll over contract," after completing a year, another is automatically added on. This is important and expensive because a coach who is fired then is eligible for numerous years' salary compensation. In some cases an athletics director and board of trustees must pay a coach a "buy out" severance package of several million dollars. According to reporters for the *Washington Post*, in 2014, 48 public universities spent $28.5 million on severance deals with former coaches – an increase of 120 percent since 2004.[10]

Consistent with other practices in college sports, these are outliers because they are considered to be coaches at the most competitive, high-pressured programs. The implication is that their high compensation packages are justified on the basis of job pressures and "market forces." Ironically, if one surveys the entire landscape of college sports, college coaching in NCAA Division III in most sports probably stands as an endangered profession in which an aspiring college coach faces bleak prospects for a long career in which one could reasonably afford to buy a home and support a family. These disparities make valid generalizations across college sports difficult if they are to be meaningful.

For some powerful athletics programs a goal is to be a contender for what is called the "Director's Cup" – an award for the best comprehensive varsity program across ten selected sports. Stanford in NCAA Division I and Williams College in Division III have been perennial winners in this annual competition. Some ambitious institutions such as the University of Florida showed commitment to contending for the Directors' Cup by increasing revenues to numerous Olympic sports. To attract outstanding leadership across the board, the athletic director raised salaries outside the customary money sports of football and men's basketball by offering salaries of $300,000, for example, to the coach of women's volleyball. It suggests some gradual movement toward parity across all intercollegiate sports, as distinguished from having high salaries and resources confined only to the major revenue sports. At several big-time sports universities, there is an interesting compromise of sorts. The coach of the men's basketball team and the coach of the women's basketball team have comparable base salaries as paid by the university. The difference, however, is that the coach of the men's team usually has contracts for external compensation from radio stations. Again, however, such practices remain the exception rather than the rule.

A head coach of a high-profile college sports program often becomes a public figure and, perhaps, a popular celebrity. A standard feature in a coaching contract is for a television show, a post-game radio interview show, product endorsement fees, and other perks. College coaches often appear and are well compensated for appearances in television commercials for, for example, Taco Bell fast food restaurants, automobile showrooms, and banks. In some cases a coach receives a lucrative payment from a sports shoe manufacturer on the condition that the manufacturer has exclusive rights to the shoes and other uniform apparel worn by team players. In other industries this is known as a "sweetheart contract" and may represent either self-dealing or a conflict of interest. In higher education's peculiar institution of college sports, however, it is "business as usual."

Women's college sports have enjoyed some gains in being assimilated into the unified campus athletics department, but on balance they have had mixed results. This is most glaring in the gender composition of head coaches. Whereas historically women were almost always the coaches for women's teams, since 1990 there has been a persistent trend, especially at universities with high-profile championship teams, to hire a man as the coach of a women's varsity team. Disparities in composition of college coaching staffs are also evident in matters of race and ethnicity. Even though African American students represent a large percentage of players in the revenue sports of football and men's basketball, few major university programs have African Americans as head coaches.

Athletics Directors

Athletics directors orchestrate the total operation and multiple sports of the varsity sports program. They also can include providing leadership and oversight for numerous auxiliary services, such as the academic-athletic tutoring center, numerous profitable summer camps for high school players, public relations, and special events. To place their budgetary responsibilities in perspective, in 2002 the highest annual operating expenses for an NCAA Division I sports program was those of the Ohio State University at $79 million.[11] In 2015 the top figure was claimed by the University of Oregon, with revenues of slightly more than $196 million and expenditures of $110 million.

Well into the 1970s a common practice was for a highly successful football coach to hold a dual appointment as athletics director. Such an arrangement may have acknowledged coaching success on the field, but skirted over the logical and legal problems of how a single person could, in effect, report to himself. Increasing specialization of both the athletic directorship and that of major coaches, combined with the appearance of a conflict of interest, have ended this organizational arrangement. Up until about 1980 most campuses had a dual athletic program and directorships – one for women, and one for men. When these were consolidated, most directors of the women's athletics program – who at that time were women – were not promoted to the single directorship, but usually were reassigned to being an associate director. Gradually a small number of women have been selected to serve as overall athletics director at major coeducational university sports programs.

The highest paid university athletics director in 2015 was at Vanderbilt, at $3.2 million. This was substantially higher than others; usually the range was from $1.8 million to $500,000 in NCAA Division I. In terms of power and institutional position, it is useful to look at the campus organizational chart. At universities where the athletics department is both powerful and problematic, the director of athletics reports directly to the president. Often this signals more presidential access than that enjoyed by the provost and various vice presidents and academic deans.

Presidents

College and university presidents are both obligated and expected to serve as the ultimate institutional officers responsible for university programs. Failure to do so has serious consequences, such as verdicts of "loss of institutional control" for regional accreditation. This holds true in intercollegiate sports where, for example, an institution's delegate to the NCAA is not the director of athletics, but rather, the president. Despite this paramount leadership status and responsibility, presidents often lag far behind head football coaches in salary, which is perhaps indicative of the prestige and priority of college sports within a campus. Even though intercollegiate athletics are seldom part of the official institutional mission, estimates are that a modern university president devotes as much as 20 percent of her time to athletics matters. Since sports events such as football games and basketball tournaments attract alumni and prospective donors, presidents often use these as opportunities for fund-raising and spreading institutional goodwill. Some college and university presidents take time to write perceptive analyses of the condition and issues presidents face with intercollegiate athletics. Timing, however, is crucial – and, unfortunately, most of these books and articles are published *after* the president as author has left office, forfeiting their opportunity to make a difference among influential, active presidents and trustees.[12]

A university president, regardless of how much or how little athletic skill or participation she or he demonstrated as a student, always tends to be center stage as "number one fan" for the photo shoot in joining with players and the coach to cut down the basketball net when the varsity team wins the conference or national championship. In contrast to such joyous publicity rituals, one of the dread episodes in the tenure of a president is the press conferences with the somber response to the periodic news stories involving some variation of scandal in the athletic department. The hiring and firing of high-profile head coaches also includes the melodrama of the grim press conference announcing that "We have decided to go in a different direction – and wish Coach Gasman the best in her future endeavors." This liturgy is followed a few weeks later, introducing new Coach St. John, with the president enthusiastically exclaiming to the press, alumni, and fans that this hiring "marks a new, great day in university athletics!" Both episodes, whether somber or happy, share the common feature that it means the university will be spending a lot of money on coaches past and present.

Boards of Trustees

College and university trustees are simultaneously powerful and silent in the governance of intercollegiate athletics. As with all institutional policies, they are the ultimate arbiters on recommendations made by the president and even the athletics director. At some universities, the board retains the direct power to hire and fire head coaches – an unusual and important exception that defuses presidential power and respect.

In college sports matters the trustees are comparable to a sleeping lion who really would prefer not to be disturbed – but is loud and assertive when roused from slumber. In fact, they received such a wakeup call in 1989 when the Association of Governing Boards (AGB) commissioned L. Jay Oliva, Vice Chancellor of New York University, to write a special report, *What Trustees Should Know about Intercollegiate Athletics*. It was a model of forthright insights and information to guide reasonable questions and provide a framework and lens for responsible oversight of athletics. In the Introduction, Oliva noted to trustees, "In the area of intercollegiate athletics, you have a power you must use. Tradition or external pressures may make all of us reluctant to wrestle with the problem." He went on to elaborate:

> But be assured: in the current state of intercollegiate athletics, there is no such thing as benign neglect. By getting involved in your sport program, you can protect and even salvage, institutional relationships with parents, donors, taxpayers, and the general public. Even more important you can protect the lives and futures of the young men and women entrusted to your care. But trustee involvement in athletics need not be limited to "damage control." There is an affirmative role you can play. Your sports program is the most visible sign of how your institution views itself. Thus, a controlled athletic program that reflects your institution's values can be one of the finest vehicles for communicating institutional strength. With your help, the image of the entire university can be permanently enhanced, without danger and disaster always hovering in the wings.[13]

Oliva, who went on to become President of New York University, provided trustees the map to master the thickets of college sports. Its principles were supplemented with pragmatic guides to analyzing data. Trustees were urged to be informed and interested. Whether trustees have made use of such invaluable resources remains uncertain, but the publication of this remarkable report by the AGB meant that henceforth trustees would be hard pressed to claim they had not been alerted.

Provosts and Deans

At many universities with NCAA Division I programs, academic deans and academic vice presidents have little, if any, voice in intercollegiate athletics. This seems peculiar in that intercollegiate sports are described as a student activity and as integrated into the educational experience. Few provosts or academic deans probably would want the responsibility to oversee intercollegiate athletics, as it usually is perceived as a juggernaut that at the very least distracts from a primary focus on academics and educational degree programs and research and development.

Faculty

Historically, faculty attempted to gain control of intercollegiate athletics both at the campus and conference level. However, this stature was never pervasive or persuasive – and has tended to be thwarted and then wane. At large universities, governing regulations tend to separate intercollegiate athletics from educational policy matters. The result is that faculty bodies such as the Academic Senate are either restricted or even prohibited from any substantive governance role in college sports.

For NCAA member institutions, there is the appointed position of Faculty Athletic Representative (FAR). The limit of this is that the FAR usually is not selected by some faculty governance body such as the Academic Senate. Rather, the FAR is appointed by the president.

Conferences and their Commissioners

Perhaps the most influential collective unit in shaping intercollegiate athletics is the *conference*. Its institutional membership, heritage, and priorities often acquire a broad imagery and symbolism that help define the entire college or university. It's a manageable critical mass of about eight to 14 member institutions usually within geographic proximity of one another – and which ascribe to some common academic and athletic goals. When the presidents of incumbent members in a conference discuss possible invitations for new members, deliberations include a candidate's academic standards, research reputation, along with geographic location and potential spectator base. The ideal is for a conference to bring together colleges and universities that share academic values as well as athletic records.

Historic conferences that today constitute the "Power Five" of big-time college sports include The Big Ten, The Pacific Twelve (aka "PAC Twelve"), The Atlantic Coast Conference, The Southeastern Conference, and the Big Twelve Conference. For all the similarities across conferences, each of these has a particular saga in university marriages – and divorces.

The Big Ten heritage connotes large Midwestern universities committed to Big Sports and Academics. Their tradition of combined academic and athletic excellence was demonstrated by their pride in the fact that all member institutions in the conference also belonged to the Association of American Universities (AAU) – the prestigious group of 62 top research universities. The PAC Twelve, which evolved from the historic Pacific Coast Conference, went through debilitating scandals in the 1950s and several reconstitutions, until settling on the name of the PAC Eight – whose members included the University of California, Berkeley; Stanford; the University of Washington; Washington State University; UCLA; the University of Southern California; the University of Oregon; and Oregon State University. In 1970 the conference became the PAC Ten, with the addition of the University of Arizona and Arizona State University. The recent addition of the University of Colorado and the University of Utah expanded the membership and name to Twelve, and provide a generous geographical map of how far inland the Pacific Coast can spread.

The Big Ten conference truly is a very Big Ten because today it has 14 members, yet retains its historic name along with peculiar counting. Its charter members as the "Western Conference" in the late 19th century included the University of Chicago, the University of Iowa, the University of Illinois, the University of Michigan, the Ohio State University, Indiana University, Purdue University, the University of Wisconsin, Northwestern University, and the University of Minnesota. In the 1990s the Big Ten added Pennsylvania State University. Its recent additions include the University of Nebraska, Rutgers University, and the University of Maryland.

The Southeastern Conference (SEC) was formed in the early 1930s as a correctional measure in light of a 1929 Carnegie Foundation study of college sports abuses. Originally it was an unwieldy federation of more than 30 universities. By 2000 it had evolved into its classic composition of 12 large Southern universities – all but one of which were state universities. The roster included Vanderbilt, the University of Georgia, the University of Tennessee, the University of Florida, the University of Alabama, the University of South Carolina, the University of Mississippi, Mississippi State University, the University of Kentucky, Auburn University, Louisiana State University, and the University of Arkansas. Recent additions have been Texas A&M University and the University of Missouri, bringing total membership to 14. Returning to the earlier suggestion that academic as well as athletic stature should shape membership, the SEC contrasts markedly with the Big Ten. Whereas all Big Ten institutions are members of the AAU, only four out of 14 SEC universities belong to the Association.

Reviewing the historically changing composition of these conferences is worthwhile because it suggests that although historical affiliations in college sports are important, they do not always resist changes from financial and political considerations. The University of Maryland was a charter member of the Atlantic Coast Conference, but opted to bolt and join the Big Ten – despite almost 70 years of annual rivalries with regional counterparts such as the University of North Carolina and the University of Virginia. The most dramatic change in college sports conferences was the dissolution of the strong, historical Southwest Conference in 1996.

A prestigious conference outside this circle of the "Power Five" is the Ivy League (formally named "The Ivy Group"), whose teams all play in NCAA Division I but do not offer athletic grants-in-aid and also prohibit their member institutions' football teams from playing in post-season bowl games. Harvard, Yale, Princeton, Brown, Cornell, Pennsylvania, Dartmouth, and Columbia are sometimes called "The Ancient Eight" by sportswriters and newscasters. In fact, although these institutions individually pioneered big-time college sports in the late 19th century, they did not create a formal conference until 1954. The Ivy League stands out as an anomaly within NCAA Division I. On the one hand, it is viewed as less committed to college sports because it opts not to offer grants-in-aid or play in post-season football games. On the other hand, Ivy League members offer a high number of varsity sports and provide outstanding facilities and support systems. Furthermore, conference champions do well in NCAA tournaments and competition, with a fair share of individual and team championships. Harvard University sponsors 39 varsity sports – the highest number among all NCAA Division I institutions. Attention by boards and presidents to the importance of college sports is not limited to the state flagship universities. In November 2014 the *Wall Street Journal* featured a full-page story on both the success and finances of football at Harvard.[14]

National Collegiate Athletic Association (NCAA)

The NCAA stands as the premier governing body of college sports in the United States. Its headquarters in Indianapolis provides for coordination of over 1,200 member colleges and universities. The NCAA is distinctive in its dual roles of regulating college sports and promoting their championship events and profitable activities. Starting around 2000 the NCAA also took on the role of reviewing and certifying academic programs at member institutions. The NCAA generates more than a billion dollars in revenue per year – with most of it coming from its "March Madness" men's national basketball tournament. The president of the NCAA has great real and symbolic power. Ultimately, however, the NCAA is a voluntary nonprofit association whose policies and practices are determined by the voting membership of college and university presidents.

The NCAA's position as the "voice of college sports" came about by chance in the early 1950s.[15] The U.S. Congress wished to avoid federal oversight of intercollegiate sports and its numerous scandals, but was unable to persuade any national association of academic leaders and presidents to take on the task. The NCAA was a small unit, occupying a suite of three rooms in a Chicago office building. Its main activity was sponsoring national championship tournaments in selected sports. Even in this role it was not dominant, as its men's basketball tournament lagged behind the separate National Invitational Tournament held in Madison Square Garden in New York City as the premier college post-season championship. The NCAA had tried in vain after World War II to get member institutions to agree on what was called the "Sanity Code" of educational standards and amateurism for college athletes. When the American Council on Education was unable to reach agreement on its proposed role in controlling college sports, by default Congress asked the NCAA to take on the task. It did so and elicited both fear and respect when it placed such showcased programs as the University of Kentucky basketball team off-limits for college games in the 1952–1953 season.[16] Over the next three decades the NCAA extended its regulations and review of programs – all marked by the growing number of regulations and penalties in its handbook.[17]

Television, which originally was thought to be the death of college football attendance, ended up ironically as the lever by which the NCAA enhanced its control and influence. From 1956 to 1982 the NCAA enjoyed a virtual cartel on televised college games. This was challenged before the Supreme Court in a case filed by the University of Georgia and the University of Oklahoma. The NCAA narrowly averted secession by numerous high-profile colleges that had formed the College Football Association (CFA). The resolution was that colleges and conferences henceforth were free to negotiate their own television broadcast contracts. The NCAA's gains in revenues, power, and influence have at the same time created problems of publicity. It has become the organization that college sports fans love to hate – in part due to its regulatory powers and periodic penalties for college programs found to be out of compliance with NCAA regulations.

NCAA governance by institutional presidents resembles the bicameral arrangement in federal politics. "One institution, one vote" is comparable to the United States Senate. A resolution within the NCAA is increasingly to distinguish top-tier programs, with their own privileges and regulations. What maintains the NCAA's executive power is that, at least for now, all institutions stand to gain from the distribution of profits from such money-making events as the "March Madness" basketball tournament. Thus far the NCAA has prevailed against plaintiffs in lawsuits who have alleged that the NCAA should not be classified as a nonprofit educational organization. Although the NCAA's primary focus is on promoting and advancing college sports – and bringing in revenues – a lesser-known role is that of constraining some expensive practices among member institutions. For example, the NCAA by-laws discourage an ambitious coach or president from taking a new football or basketball program as a vehicle for national fame. The NCAA does so by requiring any institutional candidate for NCAA Division I membership to fulfill demanding criteria. An institution must offer at least seven sports for men and seven sports for women. It must provide a prescribed number of athletic scholarships across sports – an antidote to funding football grants-in-aid while other sports, including women's sports, are malnourished. Furthermore, an aspiring NCAA Division I football program must have demonstrated average home capacity of at least 35,000 attendance for several consecutive years.

The NCAA also tries to reduce the "athletics arms race" among rival college programs. After World War II, a college was free to offer as many athletic scholarships as it wished. Today, NCAA Division I programs are limited to a ceiling of 85 football scholarships, with an even lower number for conferences outside the FBS elite group. The intent is to help less successful, less affluent football programs literally "stay in the game." It also curbs programs from stockpiling athletic talent. The NCAA also has mandated scholarship limits for all other varsity sports in order to placate athletic directors whose programs are financially strapped. Such restrictive policies provide the battleground between "haves" and "have nots" in NCAA Division I.[18] Meanwhile, NCAA Division III colleges watch from the sidelines, as they are outside the debate since they are not allowed to offer athletic scholarships. The NCAA also limits the number of coaches per sport – another concession to providing a more or less level playing field. Otherwise, some affluent programs would have large numbers of coaches, conditioners, and assistant or associate athletic directors.

Alumni, Booster, and Athletic Associations

Non-academic groups, such as the Alumni Association, as well as "boosters" and donors have a long history of influence and involvement with a college's varsity sports program. In the early 1900s some university presidents were wary of incorporating the athletics program into the central university structure and sought to place sports loosely under the sponsorship and support of alumni groups. Even after the athletics department was shifted into the institutional core, the quasi-external groups retained involvement through financial support – and at times the threat of withholding financial support. A highly organized, devoted association of alumni and major donors often has the political and financial strength to influence the hiring and firing of coaches and athletics directors.

Many large state universities opt for incorporation of a "University Athletic Association," or the "UAA." It has its own board of directors and chair and can be set up as the recipient of donations. It is joined at the hip with the university, with by-laws requiring that the university president be *ex officio* chair of the association. Such associations originally were set up in the late 1930s and 1940s at the University of Georgia and the University of Kentucky as a way of separating the athletics program from the protocols and procedures of the university.

COMPLEXITIES AND CONFLICTS: IMPLICATIONS FOR DECISION-MAKING

Institutional Differences

Much of this chapter has understandably gravitated toward the high-profile big-time university athletics departments and their coaches, sports, and highly recruited student-athletes. But this is lopsided and should be leavened with perspective on the varied categories and kinds of colleges and their sports programs. Just within NCAA Division I there is a growing chasm between "haves" and "have nots."[19] This gap is most pronounced within the circle of NCAA Division I universities whose conferences do not command lucrative television contracts and whose spectator ticket sales are consistently below 35,000.

A solution for such revenue shortfalls is for an athletics program that is supposed to be self-supporting to balance its budget by reliance on mandatory student fees. An interesting case study is the College of William & Mary in Virginia – an academically prestigious state university with a comprehensive slate of 23 NCAA Division I varsity sports. Tuition for an in-state student per academic year in 2015–2016 was $13,978. But this is incomplete because an added category of "mandatory student fees" totaling $2,081 is tacked on. Included within this is a student athletic fee of $1,759 per student. Furthermore, graduate students – who seldom are eligible for or interested in playing a varsity sport – are charged this fee. With an undergraduate enrollment of 8,437 students combined with graduate students, a grand total of about 10,000 students will be paying the mandatory $1,759 fee. This means that cross-subsidies for the intercollegiate athletics program increase mandatory student payments by more than 12 percent. The athletics fee provides the athletics department more than $17.5 million per year.

Elsewhere in NCAA Division I, at universities such as Tulane and Vanderbilt, both of which are private universities with relatively high tuition charges, a custom has been for the university's general fund to be the source of transfers that cover athletics grants-in-aid. Using a base figure of $50,000 for a grant-in-aid, this would calculate to about a $15 million per year subsidy from the provost's office and academic programs to the athletics department.

When one considers NCAA Division III, finances and practices represent a markedly different environment than NCAA Division I. By definition and according to NCAA guidelines, a Division III program is not expected to be self-supporting. A president and provost, working in conjunction with a council of administrators, including deans and department chairs and the athletics directors, allocate resources from tuition and donations on educational priorities. Where there is competition, this is not in financial aid – because there are no athletics grants-in-aid – but rather, in allotments for admissions slots. In an academically selective college, each advocate for some special group – including performing arts, music, studio art, science departments, modern languages, alumni legacies, and intercollegiate athletics – negotiates with the dean some number of slots in which an academically qualified applicant is guaranteed admission. Intercollegiate athletics represents a substantial admissions investment.

From the perspective of NCAA Division I problems, it is tempting to characterize NCAA Division III as a trouble-free zone for college sports. In fact, it has its own distinctive tensions and challenges.[20] Today, most varsity athletes in Division III are serious, accomplished high school athletes who probably have been recruited or at least designated for playing potential by a head coach. In the case of a liberal arts college with a total enrollment of 1,500 students, students playing varsity sports may constitute somewhere between 25 and 50 percent of the student body. A concern raised by faculty, as well as by disgruntled parents whose academically strong children were not offered admission, is that skill and promise in a varsity sport provides an applicant a substantial edge in the admissions sweepstakes. Furthermore, a college's commitment to a broad-based coeducational varsity sports program tends to foster a strong athletics presence within the overall campus culture. This is neither inherently good nor bad, but it is consequential. At one point faculty at Amherst College expressed concern that the numerous conference championships won by the intercollegiate teams meant that post-season championships and NCAA tournaments were prompting student-athletes to miss a large number of classes. The residual point is that even though the NCAA Division III model of college sports is spared the commercial excess of NCAA Division I, it holds its own distinctive challenges of priorities and balance within small, academically selective colleges.

NCAA Division II Institutions and Policies

Most discussions about philosophies of academics and athletics tend to polarize between NCAA Division I and NCAA Division III. This is attractive because it places in dramatic contrast the high-octane programs that utilize grants-in-aid for varsity student-athletes versus the predominantly small colleges that do not give athletic scholarships and treat varsity sports as just one of many student activities. Often overlooked, then, is another category with its own characteristics and emphases – NCAA Division II. Members of this category tend to be public colleges and universities of medium size in enrollments, not highly selective in undergraduate academic admissions, and unlikely to generate large sports revenues. A central feature of this category is that the athletic department does confer athletic grants-in-aid. These colleges offer a large slate of sports for men and women and have a relatively large percentage of their student body on athletics scholarships.

CONNECTIONS AND QUESTIONS

Do College Sports Enhance an Institution's Educational Stature and Ranking?

The University of Alabama and its football program since 2007 stand as the "best-case scenario" for indications that an outstanding and visible intercollegiate athletics program can enhance a university's educational stature and national ranking. Under head coach Nick Saban, the Alabama Crimson Tide football team has won several national championships. In 2012 the athletics department had total revenues of $124.5 million, with a surplus of $19.4 million. This surplus grew to $33 million in 2014–2015. This represented an increase from the 2007 athletics budget of $67.7 million, with a $7.1 million surplus. According to articles in *Forbes Magazine* in 2013 and then a front-page article in November 2015 in the *New York Times*, the football championships and revenues have had benefits for the entire university, including admissions, educational programs, and faculty salaries. As Joe Drape wrote in his *New York Times* article, "Rolling in Cash, Crimson Tide Lifts All Boats," the football program is regarded as a "powerful engine for the university's economic and academic growth, a standout among other large public universities with similar zests for capitalizing on their sports programs."[21] Over the past decade enrollments have increased by more than 55 percent, up to 37,100 students. At the same time, the increase in applicants has meant more academic selectivity, going from a 72 percent acceptance rate to 54 percent. The 174 National Merit and National Achievement finalists rank Alabama among the top five public universities for this metric. Both the applicants and eventual enrolling students have increasingly come from out of state.

Responses to the glowing tributes note that for all its academic gains from athletics, the University of Alabama is not a member of the AAU – the premiere designation for an outstanding research university. Despite gains in the number and quality of applicants and enrolling students, the University of Alabama is less selective and less prestigious than several flagship state universities, not to mention numerous independent universities such as Stanford, Northwestern, Vanderbilt, and the eight members of the Ivy League. But, who knows? This may change with time. More problematic is deciphering the message that the Alabama model holds for other state universities. One is hard pressed to name any other institutions that have reported the multiple gains of increased sports revenues, an athletics department surplus, and a gain in support for educational programs. So, the model is inspiring and intriguing – and also difficult to achieve.

A glance at university development office annual reports often indicates that donations to intercollegiate athletics ranks among the highest of all giving categories in the campus. Trustees, alumni, and major donors often endorse increased commitment to big-time college sports as a key to overall institutional reputation. A good example of this initiative – and its controversies – was provided in Joe Nocera's May 12, 2015 column in the *New York Times* about Rutgers University's "books vs. ballgames" debates, as the university positioned itself to succeed in its new affiliation as a member of the Big Ten conference. The Chair of the Rutgers Board of Governors, joining in support of Rutgers alumnus and State Senator Raymond Lesniak's bill that would give Rutgers $25 million in tax credits for infrastructure projects, led him to announce, "We weren't interested in joining the Big Ten. We were interested in competing and winning in the Big Ten" – a goal that requires spending money.[22] The front-page news about Rutgers became increasingly disturbing over the years. On December 9, 2015, for example, a front-page story in the *New York Times* noted that since Rutgers had joined the Big Ten conference its main feature was "big headaches" in terms of financial losses, controversies over student-athlete conduct, misbehavior by coaches, and, to add insult to injury, very few winning teams.[23]

It is no accident that in an August 3, 2013 feature article in the *New York Times*, reporter Greg Bishop provided a detailed headline account of how the University of Oregon has embraced its identity as "University of Nike" – a sign of the influence of college sports, donors, and sports marketing in the overall persona of a university. However, in contrast to the claims of academic gains made by the University of Alabama's athletics department, there does not seem to be comparable correlation between athletics and academics at the University of Oregon. In September 2015 the *Chronicle of Higher Education*'s front-page feature story focused on how the University of Oregon's academic reputation was at risk. It had dropped substantially and persistently in national academic rankings and ratings among its fellow AAU universities.[24] This was during the same years of its athletic ascent as the "University of Nike."[25]

When intercollegiate athletics news goes from the sports page to the front page it usually means serious problems for the entire institution. Scandals associated with intercollegiate athletics can tarnish the academic reputation of an outstanding university. Such was the case starting in 2013 at the University of North Carolina, Chapel Hill, with headline news stories about a long-running abuse of grading in selected courses and departments, all of which enrolled a disproportionately high number of student-athletes.[26] In addition to academic abuses, the case of Pennsylvania State University in 2013, in which a long-time former assistant coach was charged and convicted of sexually assaulting children, attracted sustained headlines. These cases were not merely college sports incidents, as they each and all had repercussions for the president, the trustees, and the reputation of the entire university, all described as a campus culture of accommodation and then denial. A predictable question that spread across these episodes was whether the president and board were knowledgeable about and in control of the disparate situations.[27]

Do College Sports Make Money or Lose Money?

The summary statistics presented at the start of this chapter documented the high gross revenues of college sports as a nationwide activity across all regions and institutional categories. This would seem to indicate that, on the whole, college sports "make money." A close look, however, questions this for any and all categories of institution.

For most institutions – for example, NCAA Division III – college sports is an educational expense that is neither expected nor able to be financially self-supporting. More surprising, according to a detailed December 2015 report by the *Washington Post*, is that even within the high-profile, highly commercialized teams and conferences, college sports run deficits.[28] Within the "Power Five" conferences, 28 universities ran deficits despite all the benefits of television contracts and conference revenue sharing. This included Auburn; the University of California, Berkeley; Rutgers; Louisiana State University; and the University of Maryland.

To compound disputes over the detailed data compiled by the NCAA, even many big-time college *football* programs – the alleged "golden goose" – lose money. What one has is a small number of football programs that make a lot of money – and an even smaller number of host athletics programs that operate in the black. The Knight Commission and other research agencies have documented, going back to the 1980s, that year after year only about 15 to 20 intercollegiate athletics programs consistently operate with a net financial gain.

Does a Strong College Sports Program Increase University Fund-Raising?

The rationale for this question is to test the proposition by college sports advocates that the entire university benefits from increased gifts by donors when the athletics department has championship teams, especially in the major sports. Arithmetically, this may be true in that any money donated to athletics does increase the cumulative, running total for institution-wide fund-raising. This can be disingenuous because usually most, if not all, of such gifts remain confined to the athletics department and its program. The athletics department is getting long-term use of valuable campus land at no expense. At most universities large donations have not been sufficient to help the athletics department balance its budget. Decades of analyses by economists have been equivocal on the benefits of winning teams for overall fund-raising.

Do College and University Presidents Have Control of College Sports?

According to a 2010 study by the Knight Commission on Intercollegiate Athletics, presidents at universities with big-time college sports programs had little control over the spending or direction of those varsity sports programs. To reinforce this statement, on July 15, 2015 retiring Chancellor of the University of Maryland, Brit Kirwan – himself a long-time leader in the Knight Commission panels and studies – emphasized in his farewell interview with reporters from *Inside Higher Ed* that one of the major regrets of his having served as president of the University of Maryland and the Ohio State University was that university presidents had lost control of intercollegiate athletics. He included himself as a member of the presidential group. The University of Maryland athletics department in 2015 reported $95 million in debt, including $31 million owed to the Atlantic Coast Conference for leaving the conference. Despite such debts, the athletics department is planning to spend $155 million to convert its old basketball arena into a football practice facility. Kirwan noted that intercollegiate athletics "is the one area of a university where presidents are not really in control."[29] He continued, "There's sort of the face of their being in control, but can you imagine a president of a big-time football power announcing they were going to de-emphasize intercollegiate athletics and concentrate more resources on academics?" And yet, according to the *Inside Higher Ed* reporter:

> for all of the money at stake, the attention paid to college athletics and the enormous impact an athletic program can have on an institution's reputation, Kirwan says university presidents have little ability to control them or rein in spending.

Kirwan concluded, "It's a really sad state of affairs, but short of some intervention by a powerful outside source, I don't see how we move off this trajectory."

Where Should College Sports Fit in the Campus Organizational Chart?

Intercollegiate athletics often is placed on the organizational chart as an "auxiliary service." But this is misleading and understates the significance of big-time sports, at least at many universities. Could one imagine a flagship state university without a prestigious program? Furthermore, at most universities – and many colleges – the athletics director reports directly to the president. This accessibility is not extended to academic deans, who traditionally report to the academic vice president. Compensation provides clues to institutional priorities and rewards. According to annual surveys by *USA Today*, in almost every state the state employee with the highest salary is a college head coach – usually either football or basketball. To send the message that athletics was in harmony with academics, have the athletic director report to the provost. Or, if a university views intercollegiate athletics as a commercial enterprise, have the athletics director report to the Vice President for Business Affairs.

CONNECTIONS WITH DIVERSITY AND SOCIAL JUSTICE

Few topics in higher education match intercollegiate athletics for connections and complexity with diversity and social justice. This pertains both to race and to gender. For both foci it is a tale of mixed results in terms of exclusion and access.

Gender and Title IX Legislation of 1972

The greatest and most unexpected transformation in American intercollegiate athletics has been the increasing presence of women as student-athletes, coaches, and athletic directors on campuses nationwide. Much of this is due to the eventual enforcement of Title IX legislation passed in 1972. It represents what Welch Suggs has analyzed as women's extended quest for "a place on the team."[30] Ironically, those drafting the legislation in the early 1970s focused on equal opportunities in academic programs, with little discussion of college sports. After 1972 application of the law to include gender equity increased. In 1978 the NCAA reversed its firm stand against including women's sports in its organizational umbrella. However, the Justice Department and other federal agencies were generous and patient in giving established college sports programs reasonable time to comply with reasonable accommodation of women as varsity athletes. Many athletics directors at coeducational institutions dragged their heels, and often used women sports as a convenient target for budget cuts in times of austerity. A succession of United States Supreme Court decisions between 1985 and 1997, involving suits brought against Colgate University and Brown University by women student-athletes as plaintiffs, however, changed enforcement to include a three-pronged metric by which institutions were required to demonstrate their record or patterns of providing athletic opportunities for their female students.

Eventually the NCAA contributed to gains for women by requiring its member institutions to comply with new standards that promoted parity in, for example, grants-in-aid across men's and women's sports, resources for uniforms and travel, and reasonable facilities. Yet some systemic inequities persist. Varsity football requires large squads and, hence, large coaching staffs and an inordinate investment in grants-in-aid. If an athletics department sponsors a football team, achieving cumulative equity across the entire men's and women's sports offerings is difficult.

Racial Expansion and Exploitation

College sports in America has a tradition of self-congratulation in promoting itself as a source of educational and social mobility regardless of race or social class. Since about 1890 one can readily trace the demographics of highly recruited college athletes and find a trail that mirrors immigration passage through Ellis Island. First, Irish Catholics, then Swedes, Slavs, and Italians were the fortunate few who as football players found a place on campus – thanks to their athletic talent rather than their academic record or family lineage. African Americans were latecomers, with sporadic representation on college teams in the Northeast, the Midwest, and Pacific Coast. In 16 states, however, stretching from Delaware to Texas, African Americans were not allowed to enroll, let alone play sports, at historically White institutions.

In the South, even though state laws mandating racially segregated colleges were outlawed in 1956, followed by African Americans being admitted as students in the late 1950s and early 1960s, for years they were prohibited by university coaches and athletic directors from playing varsity sports. It was a world turned upside down, or, at least, criss-crossed, in which academics surpassed athletics as a forum for merit and an arena opened to talent. Legendary coaches such as Bear Bryant at Alabama were converts to equal opportunity only after their segregated white teams lost, for example, to the racially integrated football squad of the University of Southern California. In some instances African Americans were quarantined to college sports enclaves within their campus. In 1976 James Michener described in *Sports in America* the perplexing spectacle of Georgetown University basketball games in Washington, D.C. where an upper-middle-class, all-white student body and alumni watched a championship Georgetown basketball team whose roster consisted of 13 African Americans and one white player.[31]

A ploy by college coaches in recruiting outstanding African American high school players was the pitch that, after all, an athletic scholarship was the only way, the best way, to go to college. In fact, it often was a bad deal. It also was deliberately misleading, as a number of federal financial aid programs such as Pell Grants, along with academic support systems, were focused on identifying and assisting promising minority students in making college affordable and accessible. This syndrome of athletic abuse came to a head at the University of Minnesota in the 1970s when a student-athlete on the basketball team, Mark Hall, sued the academic dean as well as the athletics department. The university had allowed Hall to play for two seasons despite his poor academic preparation and college course record. When no department would accept him as a major, he was forced to drop out. Fortunately, an attorney represented him to prevail in the courts that Hall was the victim of a revolving door. The University of Minnesota had little if any interest or intent to help him develop as a student, but did make good use of his basketball skills at least for two seasons.

The disproportionate presence of academically underprepared and under-achieving college football and basketball players was an epidemic whose subtext included differences by race. When the NCAA introduced its Prop 48 standards, in which a combination of test scores plus high school grades determined sports eligibility in the late 1980s, it was hailed as a triumph of academic standards. Analysis of the differential impact, however, indicated that minority students – many of whom were from modest income families – represented a large percentage of college student-athletes who had not satisfied the new academic requirements. So, in solving the problem of academically deficient athletes, the NCAA also had to face the data that showed colleges had willingly and knowingly recruited large numbers of high school players who were not ready for college studies. One partial resolution has been since 1980 the proliferation of special academic athletic centers that provide tutoring and academic assistance. Despite such measures, grade point averages and graduation rates of modest income minority students lag behind student-athletes in many sports and, often, behind that of the general student body.[32]

Another peculiarity of intercollegiate athletics in terms of shortfalls in social justice is that although minority students, especially African Americans, represent a disproportionate number of varsity athletes in football and men's basketball, there has been little transfer in proportionality for African Americans as head coaches in these same collegiate sports. In December 2015, there were ten African American head coaches among the 128 NCAA FBS college teams.

CONCLUSION

Only in America does higher education gain public recognition with such varsity sports headlines as "March Madness," the "Road to the Final Four," the "College Football

Playoffs," and the "College World Series." No other nation looks to colleges and universities for spectator sports. And our colleges fulfill this expectation enthusiastically and effectively.

A college's intercollegiate athletics program provides a good lens by which to view the institution's academic mission and educational philosophy. It brings into the spotlight the best and worst aspects of American higher education. Using the 1989 founding of the Knight Commission as the starting point, one finds simultaneously a record of reforms in the conduct of intercollegiate sports programs at all levels. At the same time college sports have literally been reformed in new alliances that often perpetuate the excesses they were intended to reduce. These dilemmas have led some to call for external mediation, perhaps by the U.S. Congress or even the formation of a Presidential Commission.[33] We are witness to history in our own time regarding a transformation of college sports. It is the consolidation of a commercial model that has scant integration into the educational structures or culture of colleges and universities.

NOTES

1. Jeff Benedict and Armen Keteyian, "Game Day: The Genius of ESPN," in *The System: The Glory and Scandal of Big-Time College Football* (New York: Doubleday, 2013) pp. 355–373.
2. Press Services, "CFP Debut: Bowl Payout up $200M to Record $500M" (April 15, 2015).
3. Marc Tracy and Tim Rohan, "What Made College Ball More Like Pros? $7.3 Billion, for a Start," *New York Times* (December 23, 2014) pp. A1, B12.
4. James L. Shulman and William G. Bowen, *The Game of Life: College Sports and Educational Values* (Princeton, NJ and Oxford: Princeton University Press, 2001); William G. Bowen and Sarah A. Levin, *Reclaiming the Game: College Sports and Educational Values* (Princeton, NJ and Oxford: Princeton University Press, 2003).
5. Judge Kevin H. Sharp, "III. Conclusion," in *Memorandum*, for *Marshall, et al. v. ESPN, Inc.* et al. (United States District Court, Middle District of Tennessee, Nashville Division) (Case 3:14-cv-01945, Document 284, Filed 06/24/15, page 2 of 33 PageID#2627).
6. Shelly Freierman, "Advertising Madness," *New York Times* (April 6, 2015) p. B6.
7. John R. Thelin, *Games Colleges Play: Scandal and Reform in Intercollegiate Athletics* (Baltimore, MD and London: Johns Hopkins University Press, 1994 and 1997).
8. Andrew Zimbalist, *Unpaid Professionals: Commercialism and Conflict in Big-Time College Sports* (Princeton, NJ: Princeton University Press, 1999).
9. Walter Byers with Charles Hammer, *Unsportsmanlike Conduct: Exploiting College Athletes* (Ann Arbor: University of Michigan Press, 1995).
10. Will Hobson and Steven Rich, "College Sports' Fastest-Rising Expense: Paying Coaches Not to Work," *Washington Post* (December 11, 2015). Scott Jaschik, "Golden Parachutes for Coaches at Public Universities," *Inside Higher Ed* (December 14, 2015).
11. Welch Suggs, "How Gears Turn at a Sports Factory," *Chronicle of Higher Education* (November 29, 2002) pp. A1, A32–A37.
12. James J. Duderdstadt, *Intercollegiate Athletics and the American University: A University President's Perspective* (Ann Arbor: University of Michigan Press, 2000).
13. L. Jay Oliva, *What Trustees Should Know About Intercollegiate Athletics* (Washington, D.C.: Association of Governing Boards, 1989).
14. Matthew Futterman, "How Harvard Became 'Harvard' of Harvard Football," *Wall Street Journal* (November 20, 2014).
15. Jack Falla, *NCAA: The Voice of College Sports – A Diamond Anniversary History, 1906–1981* (Mission, KS: National Collegiate Athletic Association, 1981).
16. John R. Thelin, *Games Colleges Play* (Baltimore, MD and London: Johns Hopkins University Press, 1997).
17. Paul Lawrence, *Unsportsmanlike Conduct: The National Collegiate Athletic Association and the Business of College Football* (New York: Praeger, 1987).
18. Joe Nocera, "Playing College Moneyball," *New York Times* (January 15, 2015) p. A23.
19. Marc Tracy, "In N.C.A.A.'s Varied Landscape, Some Open Floodgates While Others Fear Drought," *New York Times* (January 19, 2015) p. D7.

20. Alan Draper, "Innocence Lost: Division III Sports Programs," *Change: The Magazine of Higher Education* (December 1996) pp. 32–34.

21. Joe Drape, "Rolling in Cash, Crimson Tide Lifts All Boats," *New York Times* (November 6, 2015) p. A1.

22. Joe Nocera, "At Rutgers, It's Books vs. Ballgames," *New York Times* (May 12, 2015) p. A23.

23. Kate Zernike, "Few Wins But Much Chaos at Rutgers After Move to the Big Ten," *New York Times* (December 9, 2015) pp. A1, A27.

24. Jack Stripling, "An Academic Reputation at Risk: The University of Oregon's Big Brand Masks Its Fragile Standing," *Chronicle of Higher Education* (September 14, 2015) p. A1.

25. Greg Bishop, "Oregon Embraces 'University of Nike' Image," *New York Times* (August 3, 2013) p. D1.

26. Sarah Lyall, "U.N.C. Investigation Reveals Athletes Took Fake Classes," *New York Times* (October 23, 2014) p. B12. For academic problems elsewhere, see Charles Huckabee, "Auburn Reversed Course on Cutting a Major Favored by Athletes," *Chronicle of Higher Education* (August 27, 2015).

27. John R. Thelin, "College Presidents, at Any Level, Face Sports Challenges," *Inside Higher Ed* (May 21, 2013).

28. Will Hobson and Stephen Rich, "Operating in the Red: Big Time College Sports Programs Are Taking in More Money Than Ever – And Spending It Just as Fast," *Washington Post* (November 23, 2015).

29. Kellie Woodhouse, "Brit Kirwan on the 'Troubling Transformation of College Athletics'," *Inside Higher Ed* (July 14, 2015).

30. Welch Suggs, *A Place on the Team: The Triumph and Tragedy of Title IX* (Princeton, NJ: Princeton University Press, 2009).

31. James Michener, *Sports in America* (New York: Random House, 1976).

32. Donald Yee, "Commentary: College Football Is Rigged Against Black Head Coaches," Special to the *Washington Post*, published in the *Lexington Herald-Leader* (December 14, 2015) p. C3.

33. Andrew Zimbalist, "Time for a Presidential Panel to Investigate College Sports," *Chronicle of Higher Education Commentary* (January 13, 2015) p. A1.

Additional Readings

William G. Bowen and Sarah A. Levin, *Reclaiming the Game: College Sports and Educational Values* (Princeton, NJ and Oxford: Princeton University Press, 2003).

Charles T. Clotfelter, *Big-Time Sports in American Universities* (Cambridge and New York: Cambridge University Press, 2011).

Eddie Comeaux, Editor, *Introduction to Intercollegiate Athletics* (Baltimore, MD: Johns Hopkins University Press, 2015).

James J. Duderdstadt, *Intercollegiate Athletics and the American University: A University President's Perspective* (Ann Arbor: University of Michigan Press, 2000).

Arthur A. Fleisher III, Brian L. Goff, and Robert D. Tollison, *The National Collegiate Athletic Association: A Study in Cartel Behavior* (Chicago and London: University of Chicago Press, 1992).

L. Jay Oliva, *What Trustees Should Know About Intercollegiate Athletics* (Washington, D.C.: Association of Governing Boards, 1989).

William J. Oriard, *Bowled Over: Big-Time College Football from the Sixties to the BCS Era* (Chapel Hill: University of North Carolina Press, 2009).

James L. Shulman and William G. Bowen, *The Game of Life: College Sports and Educational Values* (Princeton, NJ and Oxford: Princeton University Press, 2001).

Murray Sperber, *College Sports, Inc.: The Athletic Department vs. the University* (New York: Henry Holt and Company, 1990).

Murray Sperber, *Beer and Circuses: How Big-Time College Sports Is Crippling Undergraduate Education* (New York: Henry Holt and Company, 2000).

Welch Suggs, *A Place on the Team: The Triumph and Tragedy of Title IX* (Princeton, NJ: Princeton University Press, 2009).

John R. Thelin, *Games Colleges Play: Scandal and Reform in Intercollegiate Athletics* (Baltimore, MD and London: Johns Hopkins University Press, 1994 and 1997).

John R. Thelin and Lawrence Wiseman, *The Old College Try: Balancing Academics and Athletics in Higher Education* (Washington, D.C.: ASHE-ERIC, 1989).

J. Douglas Toma, *Football U.: Spectator Sports in the Life of the American University* (Ann Arbor: University of Michigan Press, 2003).

Andrew Zimbalist, *Unpaid Professionals: Commercialism and Conflict in Big-Time College Sports* (Princeton, NJ: Princeton University Press, 1999).

9

PUBLIC POLICIES

The Campus and Federal, State, and Local Governments

SETTING AND OVERVIEW

For those who work in higher education, the campus is understandably the center of the cosmos. This chapter, however, aims to temper such myopia. It calls for a different perspective in which colleges and universities are seen as just one of many institutions whose priorities and urgent issues cut *horizontally* across the nation's legislative agenda. The aim is to analyze the politics of higher education by showing how colleges and universities interact with various layers and levels of government and other related organizations. These include federal, state, and local agencies in such matters as legislation, lobbying, policy formulation, program delivery, regulation, and court cases.

This profile analyzes higher education in terms of government and public policy. It is a diverse, complicated mosaic. When one watches a political ceremony, such as the President of the United States signing a bill into law about student financial aid or a governor's speech at the dedication of a library at the state university, its memorable drama imposes a false sense of coherence on what probably was a long, convoluted series of events. An illustration of the symbolism and liturgy in the politics of American education was the 1989 front-page headline story in the *Washington Post* in which President George Bush assembled governors and education leaders nationwide at the University of Virginia in Charlottesville, invoking the heritage of Thomas Jefferson for an "education summit."[1] The smiling dignitaries included the U.S. Secretary of Education and a young "Education Governor" from Arkansas, Bill Clinton – himself a model figure to illustrate how affordable higher education could be a source of opportunity and upward mobility for talented youth from a modest income family. Three years later Clinton, a former Rhodes Scholar, would be elected President of the United States and move education from a state to a national priority. Along with agreement on ambitious goals, the mix of governors and the President all took care to "steer clear of the federal aid issue" and discussing costs. The motto for the politics of American higher education could be, "All's well that ends well!"

Although President Bush's 1989 "education summit" commanded national headlines, education policies often are secondary in policy agenda – making our schools and colleges innocent bystanders in some other political fracas. For example, in 1978 when California citizens voted in favor of Proposition 13 to lower property taxes statewide, it did not signal public animosity toward public education. Yet the unexpected consequence of tax reform depleted funding for public libraries, schools, and community colleges.

How has our national political heritage shaped higher education policies? We are distinctive, perhaps unique, among modern nations in that the United States has never had a central ministry of education.[2] Elsewhere, in the nations of Europe, Asia, Africa, and Latin America, the ministry of education is powerful. Absence of a strong federal organizing authority for higher education policies in the United States is rooted in the tradition that powers not expressly vested by the Constitution to the national government remain under the domain of the states.[3] Starting with the creation of a new nation in 1781 there has been federal government deference to state governments as the source of granting charters to colleges and universities. Yet sometimes this too gets muddled, because even though the state grants a charter it has never been completely or clearly defined what is meant by "state control." Colleges and universities in the 19th, 20th, and 21st centuries have included a large number of "private" or "independent" institutions.

One legacy, then, is the coexistence of "public" and "private" colleges and universities, characterized by varied and changing definitions over time.[4] What we do not find, whether in 1816 or 2016, is that the federal government is granting charters to degree-granting academic institutions – with the important exceptions of the United States Military Academy at West Point and the United States Naval Academy at Annapolis. Education is not mentioned in the United States Constitution. Despite this lack of a clear federal source of national policies for colleges and universities, higher education from the colonial era to the present has been an enterprise in American life. We are a nation of college builders – sometimes to a fault, as higher education in the United States has a tendency to overexpansion and underfunding.

A fundamental political change took place in the shift in status from the American colonies to the new United States. The original colonial colleges followed the English custom of restraint in the granting of a royal charter. Each petition for founding a new college was scrutinized by the Crown or by a colonial government in order to avoid over-proliferation of degree-granting academic institutions. However, a group of petitioners who were granted a charter by the Crown were then assured generous, continuous funding. Colonial governments emulated this English practice – usually limiting college charters to one per colony. The colonial governments also honored the royal practice of support for their chartered colleges. In contrast, by 1810 state governments conferred numerous college charters as a form of political patronage – but without assurance that the legislature would provide sustained funding.[5] The result was that by 1870 there were hundreds of chartered colleges, especially in the newer states of the South and the West, most of which were in precarious financial condition. In contrast, England confined its chartered degree-granting universities to three – Oxford, Cambridge, and the University of London. State government funding for the American colleges was haphazard and uneven, ranging from proceeds from a state lottery to giving a college some cheap land. Thus, American higher education was from the start a highly competitive field since it was dependent on student tuition payments along with support from private donors.

Some federal legislation was memorable. The Northwest Ordinance built in both rewards and obligations on townships establishing schools. The Morrill Act of 1862, which utilized the sale of western lands as a source for directing federal monies to state governments, was significant because it stimulated creation of instructional programs in the "useful arts" such as agriculture, mechanics, mining, and military, as well as liberal education and classics. It showed how the federal government could be a partner with states and colleges to stimulate innovation in higher education. In this legislation, higher education was a secondary concern, and sometimes used as a means to achieving some other national goal.

Illustrative of the federal "hands-off" relationship with the states and higher education was the variety of institutions state legislatures identified as their land grant partners. Initially, numerous historic liberal arts colleges such as Dartmouth, Transylvania, and Yale were the designated institutions for hosting the new programs in such fields as civil engineering and agriculture. Yet soon thereafter, many state governments opted to build new state agricultural or engineering colleges. In each of these various, sporadic federal programs, the U.S. Congress was careful to be a voluntary and supplementary partner with state governments. Perhaps the most striking example of this federal deference to state law was the second Morrill Act of 1890, which extended land grant funding to states that had earlier seceded from the Union to join the Confederate States of America. Congress gave these states two choices for compliance with federal law and, hence, eligibility for the land grant funding. The first option was to open the state's single land grant college to all qualified students in the state regardless of race. This, of course, was unattractive to the 17 states with legally segregated school systems. The second option provided an accommodation by which the federal government could be fainthearted in civil rights and avoid angering or offending Southern states. The federal fallback position was that if a state did not wish to allow enrollment of the races together, a state could qualify for the 1890 second land grant Act funds by establishing a distinct state college for African American students.

Since the Morrill Acts of 1862 and 1890 have been celebrated in recent years for creating the "land grant legacy," it's worthwhile to note what the legislation accomplished – and what it did not. First, the federal government was not in the business of building federal colleges or state colleges. It provided a voluntary incentive system whereby states could qualify for funding but were then free to set up programs of agriculture and mechanics, along with arts and sciences, either at existing colleges or by the state establishing new ones. Second, the Morrill Acts did not quickly transform American higher education with a new era of affordable, utilitarian degree programs. With the important exceptions of New York and its land grant institution, Cornell University, and Wisconsin's University of Wisconsin, most of the land grant colleges and programs sputtered for at least 40 years. George W. Atherton, President of Pennsylvania State College, had the foresight to rally his fellow land grant college presidents to form a lobbying group that gave them an effective presence in Washington, D.C.[6] Only subsequent legislation pushed by Atherton – such as the Smith–Lever Act (1914), which provided federal funding for extension services and for agricultural research stations – provided the necessary catalyst to be influential in promoting new priorities in American colleges and universities.

The same strategy held with later large federal initiatives. The Servicemen's Readjustment Act of 1944 (popularly known as The GI Bill) included college financial aid for veterans as only one of about a dozen services or programs such as small business loans and mustering out bonuses to assist in adjusting to domestic life in a postwar society.

The main aim of the bill was not to increase access and affordability for going to college. This was something of an afterthought – and a program the bill's sponsors did not think would have widespread appeal to returning soldiers and sailors. Rather, the bill's aim was to defuse the potential for discontent and protest marches by unemployed veterans. Even with the federal legislation on student financial aid between 1964 and 1972, Congressional priority was to increase civil rights. Going to college happened to be viewed as a good vehicle to promote opportunity and equity.

The 1944 GI Bill illustrated the principle that generous federal funding for higher education carried with it some requirements for colleges and universities to comply with federal guidelines. Congress's obvious and foremost concern was consumer protection for returning GIs who were using the scholarship vouchers. Hundreds of diploma mills and fly-by-night educational institutions mushroomed, with the intent of enrolling gullible military veterans. How did Congress and federal agencies know that federal dollars were being spent appropriately? A dilemma was that Congress – and the American public – liked and trusted established colleges and did not really wish to get into the role of monitoring their financial and educational activities. The solution for regulation and accountability was that Congress accepted as a proxy for federal certification of academic institutions the good faith designation that a college that was in good standing with a regional accreditation body, such as the Southern Association of Colleges and Schools or the Western Association of Colleges and Schools, was, then, eligible to receive federal scholarship payments carried by enrolling veterans.

In the 1972 reauthorization of the Higher Education Act it used financial incentives to state governments for them to establish what were called "1202 commissions" – designated agencies in each state that would be eligible for substantial federal funding to be used exclusively for the purpose of building coordinating mechanisms to promote statewide planning among colleges, the state agency, and the federal government. States were not required to participate, but the financial incentives of federal funding were effective magnets. It was yet another stage in the succession of measures for mutual cooperation and planning among the state, federal, and institutional levels.

Since the United States did not have a national ministry of education, in the early 20th century a new entity – the well-funded private foundation – filled this void and set out to promote two goals – standards and standardization – in both secondary and higher education. The foremost example of this was the Carnegie Foundation for the Advancement of Teaching (CFAT). Its strategy was to provide a qualifying college with a pension plan on the condition that the college would agree to abide by certain admissions standards and high school transcript conventions, along with a commitment to having the college's enrollment be at least 300 students and, finally, to show evidence that the college's curriculum was void of a religious denomination's orthodoxy or indoctrination. A legacy of this foundation reform initiative is TIAA-CREF – today, the largest pension fund in the United States. As we shall discuss in detail in Chapter 10, on philanthropy, some other foundations that represented "private resources for the public good" included the Rockefeller Foundation, the General Education Board, the Russell Sage Foundation, and, later, the Ford Foundation, which continued this distinctive American approach to large-scale national higher education projects – in large part because the federal government had such a limited role in these years.

Although state legislatures had provided sporadic funding for public higher education well into the 20th century, following World War I several states in the Midwest and on the Pacific Coast relied on tax revenues for stable annual appropriations to their respective state colleges and universities. After World War II the state funding became generous, especially in California, which adopted a policy of charging no tuition to any in-state student. Its umbrella of institutions included the University of California, with ten campuses enrolling over 190,000 students, the California State University and colleges with 450,000 students enrolled at 19 campuses, and over 100 community colleges with 2.5 million students, along with 64 independent colleges and universities.

To another extreme, many states were not comparably committed to being simultaneously extensive and inexpensive for students. In some states in the Northeast, such as New Hampshire, state governments would assist in building state university and college campuses, but tended to view tuition as a user's fee in which students and their families were expected to pay a high percentage of costs, without benefit of a large taxpayer subsidy. In the South, a stagnant regional economy meant that many states simply did not have much funding for public higher education, even if this were a high priority. In a state such as Georgia, the president of the struggling University of Georgia lobbied hard over many years following World War I to have both the legislature and voters see the state university as the capstone of an interdependent, rational system of public education, but progress was slow and dollars were low. What this meant was that state-by-state variations were significant, and higher education practices reflected each state's distinctive traditions on taxation and revenues. Despite these state differences, it is accurate and fair to say that up until about 1990 state support for higher education had been strong and enduring.

A convergence of state support, private foundations, and selected large federal programs made the period 1945–1970 American higher education's "Golden Age." At the federal level, it included creation of the National Institutes for Health (NIH) and the National Science Foundation (NSF) – and later, and lesser funded, the National Endowment for the Humanities and the National Endowment for the Arts. Establishing these formidable federal research agencies, however, still confirmed the general precedent that the federal government was not primarily concerned with directly boosting colleges and universities. Once again, colleges and universities were the available vehicle by which federal agencies fulfilled their own independent goals. For example, for the NSF the goal might be to develop a nuclear accelerator or stimulate, as was the case in the 1990s, genome research. It did not matter so much *who* received NSF funding to accomplish this so long as there was reasonable certainty that they *could* deliver the goods. At the same time in the post-World War II era it so happened that a small number of universities had the combination of scientific talent, a track record of industrial applied research projects, and available laboratories and buildings who then were positioned to undertake the particular high-stakes project. To assure favorable results, the NSF and the NIH relied on what was known as "peer review" decision-making on grant proposals.

NSF and NIH provided the sponsored research grant resources that spawned the "federal grant university." According to Clark Kerr, President of the University of California, in 1960 about 15 to 18 universities received more than 80 percent of all NSF-sponsored research grant funding. In December 2013 the federal government announced it was devoting $140.82 billion for research and development spending in the coming fiscal year. About 96 percent of this was concentrated in five federal departments, with 51 percent to the Department of Defense and just under 23 percent to the Department of Health and Human Services. There was no mandate that these monies had to go to university-based research. However, universities did well in competing for federal grants. For example, for 2013 about 50 percent of the Department of Defense research and development grants were awarded to university-based academic research units. To illustrate the concentration of federal research dollars into a relatively small number of highly regarded universities, for 2012 ten universities reported more than $1 billion each on federal research expenditures. Johns Hopkins University, with $2.1 billion (which included $1.1 billion in applied physics), was ranked first, far ahead of the second-ranked institution, the University of Michigan. The University of Wisconsin, the University of Washington, the University of California, San Diego, the University of California at San Francisco, Duke, UCLA, Stanford, and Columbia rounded out the top ten.

In contrast to the flourishing of federal research funds being awarded to universities by the early 1950s, there was no immediate counterpart success story of federal funding designated for the second plank – student financial aid programs. Despite the recommendations for federal aid to make college affordable, as emphasized in the 1947 report of the Truman Commission dealing with higher education in a democracy, the 1944 GI Bill was not followed by any counterpart for Congress to provide scholarships or tuition vouchers in the peacetime economy. These programs would show some signs of life with the Higher Education Act of 1965, but did not really materialize until 1972. State governments would be the backbone of making postsecondary education accessible and affordable to a growing number and percentage of late adolescent Americans.

Meanwhile, added to the founding and funding of federal agencies was the National Defense Education Act of 1958, popularly known as the NDEA. Once again the focal point was not enhancing education per se, but rather for an embarrassed U.S. Congress and citizenry to try to catch up in scientific and technological achievement in light of the 1957 Sputnik triumph of the Soviet Union. The NDEA's numerous programs included support for research as well as for graduate education and teacher preparation.

A peril of prosperity and expansion of higher education, especially public higher education, between 1945 and 1970 was the problem of conflict and duplication across colleges and their systems. One solution pioneered in California and hailed worldwide was the 1960 Master Plan in which the state universities, the regional state colleges, the public junior colleges, and independent colleges and universities agreed to coordination and cooperation. The California Master Plan, for example, staked out some ground rules in which the prestigious University of California aimed to enroll the top 10 percent of high school graduates, with the California State University and Colleges to focus on the next 33 percent, and the state's junior colleges serving the roles of open admission and transfer institutions. Furthermore, the University of California retained exclusive right among the public institutions to confer doctoral degrees. Under this arrangement, not all students enrolled in public institutions were treated equally, as the state subsidy per student was highest for those at the University of California, with substantial drops to the state colleges and even more per capita compression for junior college enrollees.

The so-called "golden age" of American higher education became tarnished by the 1970s when state governments faced the double jeopardy of tapering state revenues coupled with increasing demand that the state subsidize other, new services ranging from health care to senior citizens programs, road construction, and tax exemptions for some industries and business corporations. State university presidents and trustees were faced with new era in which their customary "most privileged status" for state appropriations now was subject to renegotiation by legislators and governors. Part of the price to pay was a demand from legislatures and courts for accountability in academic affairs, ranging from treatment of students to procedural fairness in faculty tenure deliberations, and new standards for student retention and degree completion. It included some limited measures to tie part of an institution's state subsidies to what was called "performance-based funding." All these were areas of institutional activity that historically had been out of bounds for external scrutiny by the state. At the same time state governments expected public institutions to enroll a growing percentage of high school graduates, which meant that colleges were expected to do more with less.

The foremost legacy since 1980 is that as a nation we remain more or less committed to access and affordability for all Americans who wish to go to college. However, this goal, which once seemed a source of clarity, optimism, and abundance – and with consensus across parties and voters in 1960 – now seems to have lost energy and direction, leading it to fall short of the goal. Yet it remains unclear as to who is to blame for this unfulfilled pledge. It leaves us with numerous issues and unresolved business in the 21st century.

ISSUES

Transparency: Laws and Sausages

A truism in political science, drawn from Chancellor Otto von Bismarck's reunification of Germany in 1876, is that there are two things one should never watch being made: namely, laws and sausages. The late Alan Rosenthal, a distinguished professor at Rutgers University who was director of the Eagleton Institute of Politics, devoted several years to testing out this claim.[7] What he found was that sausage factories tended to be well-managed, goal-oriented, concerned about safety and health ordinances, and aimed to provide consumers with reliable, desirable goods – sausages! In contrast, Rosenthal made site visits and scoured budgets and documents from numerous state legislatures, and concluded that the sausage factories had cleaned up their act whereas state legislatures remain mired in disputes, delays, conflicts of interest, and an inability to meet deadlines.

So, the political adage linking sausages and law-making now required reconsideration – and politics, including the politics of higher education, remained dubious in visibility and character. On the one hand, political quips echoed fast food restaurant television advertisements, as constituents looking for substantive programs would ask legislators, "Where's the beef?" And, frequently, a reasonably good answer was that successful members of Congress "brought home the pork," whether in construction of highways or new state university facilities.

The Saga of Federal Student Financial Aid, 1965 to 2016

One of the more bizarre stories in the evolution of federal student financial aid programs over the past half-century involves the deliberations and legislation on loans and grants as tools to promote affordability and choice in going to college. The programs were latecomers to the Washington, D.C. forum – yet once they surfaced starting around 1965, student financial aid proposals enjoyed widespread bipartisan support in both the U.S. Senate and in the House of Representatives. The most reluctant participants were banks – even though bankers stood much to gain and little to lose in the alliance.[8]

Both Democrats and Republicans in Congress agreed on the social goals and national benefits of expanding access and affordability for going to college. Grants – which later would be known as Pell Grants – were the primary plank and had the goal of reaching financially needy students, many of whom were from minority groups. The supplement was to then build in federal student loan programs to provide low interest rates for students who probably did not have the financial need to qualify for Pell Grants, but who still needed assistance to afford college. Between 1968 and 1978 Congressional subcommittees made the suggestion, then pleaded, that commercial banks should become a partner. The bank resistance stemmed from a reluctance or inability to see human achievement and individual potential as collateral on loans. It was good banking practice to take a chance on a restaurant or a shoe repair shop or a new corporate office, but still risky to approve a loan, even with federal backing, on a bright undergraduate's future citizenship and earning power. Eventually, major banks came around – but only after being promised little risk and favorable terms in the backing of the federal government. The banking boom took place in 1978 with congressional approval of the Guaranteed Student Loan (GSL) program. According to program terms, a college student could apply to receive an annual loan of $2,000 – up to a maximum of $4,000 over three years, at a low interest rate. There was no requirement in which a student applicant had to show financial need. Private banks who signed the loan were backed by the federal government in case a student defaulted. Everybody went away happy, especially students from upper-middle-income families who understood the use of loans – which often they used to pay college tuition, but, equally probably, to help purchase a vacation home.

Americans whose children were going to college eventually would pay dearly for this 1978 bonanza. Eventually it meant that the federal government financial aid programs relied on loans rather than grants. For the short term, both an enrolling student and the college were well served. The college student was able to pay tuition and fees, the college received its payments, and the partnership worked smoothly. The presumption was that a college student who completed a bachelor's degree would in reasonable time land a good job and be able to repay the federal government's college loan. In fact, by 2000 what became evident was that American college graduates would be burdened with a large, growing student loan debt that was unforgiving. And, for Congress and banks, this state of affairs was unforgiveable.

But what about grants? Federal Pell Grants persisted as a mainstay student aid program – no less than an entitlement for student applicants who met specified guidelines of demonstrated financial need and bona fide college enrollment. A problem, however, was that although the total dollars spent by Congress on Pell Grants was impressively large, the Pell Grant program was not fully effective in making college affordable for modest income students. One reason was a lag in Congressional perceptions about the price of going to college – and about family income.

The maximum Pell Grant award for a student in 2014–2015 was $4,800. Given that the price to go to a state university for a year was about $25,000 and its counterpart at a private or independent college was between $30,000 and $60,000, then the maximum Pell Grant award did not cover a large percentage of college charges. The artificially low cap on family income screened out numerous applicants who had genuine financial need. So, as Pell Grants declined in eligibility and in net contribution to meeting the price of college, student loans increased as a source of student financial aid. This was an expedient short-term solution with bad consequences over the long run. The result was that by 2015 average student loan indebtedness of college graduates rose to about $29,000.

The Federal Role in Research

Research and development sponsored by the federal government has been powerful and successful since World War II. And, research universities in the United States have been both contributors and recipients in the large-scale research efforts. A price of this success is intense competition for federal grant funding. Reliance on scientists' peer review has promoted keen scrutiny of research proposals. And, it also has led to complaints by both universities and individual scientists who think their excellent proposals should have been funded. An increased number of aspiring newcomers to the ranks of research universities has combined in the past 20 years with a leveling in available federal research funds. The result is persistent discontent. In recent years an added dimension to the criticisms of the large-scale research programs sponsored by the federal government is that screening, paperwork, and other selection criteria can be counter-productive in that they discourage or work against new talent with truly innovative ideas. The issue, then, is whether decades of funding and achievement have unwittingly left the research establishment funded by the NSF and NIH mortgaged into crystallized priorities.

Regulation

One signal of changing federal government attitudes toward colleges and universities was Harvard President Derek Bok's 1980 article about federal regulation, published in *The Public Interest*. Bok took on the role of spokesperson for all American higher education and used his own university as a pivotal case study. He sounded the alarm that colleges and universities were deluged with red tape, filling out periodic reports. The customary invocation by presidents and boards was that colleges and universities have the traditional right to determine who they shall teach, what they will teach, and who will teach. Intrusion of government agencies was considered a new and unfair usurpation.

One historical analysis of these contemporary complaints about over-regulation is that since about 1890 colleges and corporations have switched places in how the respective organizations are viewed by federal agencies and the U.S. Congress. According to this interpretation, colleges were definitely and deliberately exempted from the oversight and regulation that Congress directed at railroads, banks, and businesses. It included tax exemptions and also leniency on such workplace ordinances as providing clean drinking water, affirmative action, overtime pay, the university's obligation to pay into social security plans, and other employee rights. However, by 1979 the pendulum had swung markedly in the other direction.[9] Business corporations, for example, were often granted tax forgiveness along with incentive subsidies to develop new products. Colleges and universities, meanwhile, felt that they were subjected to increasing regulation to the point of government intrusion.

Privatization

A controversial development in public support of higher education since World War II has been the appearance, spread, and then acceptance of "privatization" as an acceptable philosophy and strategy. The term can be confusing because it has multiple connotations for government services. For cities and metropolitan governments, its most basic meaning is that the city manager signs a contract with a private company which then agrees to provide specified services, such as weekly trash collection or janitorial service for government office buildings. Sometimes it is defined by the term "outsourcing." It's a way in which a government can avoid investing in permanent civil service staff and expensive equipment, such as trash-collection trucks, while still making certain that taxpayers receive municipal services.

"Privatization of public higher education," however, carries with it implications that go to the heart of compacts and charters about the state's role in providing affordable, accessible college education to what might be termed a mass, even universal, constituency of potential students. One scenario is that since the reluctance of state governments and taxpayers to provide ample support for public higher education is not a temporary suspension, but a permanent, new reality, then institutions themselves must respond to this new, harsh public policy environment. This could mean charging differential tuition, so that programs that are prestigious and/or expensive to operate could – and should – then charge significantly higher tuitions than, for example, admission to undergraduate general studies. Many of these campus-based institutional strategies, including arguments for "running a university more like a business," already have been discussed in Chapter 6. But in this chapter, the concern is less on university presidents and boards looking from the inside out to external constituencies and more with the reverse: what seems to be in store for the ways in which governments, especially state legislatures, have been viewing their public colleges and universities, along with the entire higher education umbrella.

A succession of self-proclaimed "Education Governors" from 1980 through 2000 got good mileage and won elections campaigning on a platform that included the promise that an investment in public higher education would lead to job creation because the state's higher education system was no less than an "economic engine." The immediate appeal of such a campaign was that it could include all segments of public higher education, ranging from the high-tech inventions and patents from the state flagship university, to the agricultural extension services of the land grant campus, and extending to the resiliency of the state's community and technical colleges to "meet workforce demands" in preparing job-ready skilled craftspeople and technicians for entry-level manufacturing and production. The problem is that this was a risky projection whose central flaw was its misunderstanding of an educated citizenry and a complex modern economy. Many state university presidents and trustees were partners in this liturgy that seemed to have been persuasive both for gubernatorial candidates, state legislators up for re-election, and newly inaugurated state university presidents. But, if a nationwide or state economy is sagging, higher education is a poor candidate to lead a rescue mission.

At the same time, if a state government experiences several years of declining tax revenues it's unreasonable and unlikely that prior levels of funding for public higher education can be maintained. Consider a prevalent situation – a governor and many state legislators are alumni of one of the state's universities. They enjoy the goodwill and prestige that higher education brings to the entire state and they most certainly use the perks of college athletics tickets and invitations to campus receptions and celebrations as part of their administration. State universities continue to pump up optimistic public relations broadcasts and news releases about how higher education contributes to the "quality of life" and economy and physical health of its citizens. So, neither side – state government or state universities – seems to have renegotiated relations with the other.

Since about 1980 the recurrent public statements by harried state university presidents is to make the somber observation, "We used to be state supported. Then we were state assisted. Now we are state located." The problem with such a tale of woe is that it's not clear what responses it is expected to elicit. It also in some states and at some times tends to be exaggerated. One strategy state university presidents and provosts use to "document" declining state support is to select a peak year in which state funding spiked, perhaps due to a retroactive goodwill initiative by the state to reinstate funding that had dipped during a preceding multi-year period of state revenue shortfalls. Using this selected year as the base, it is little wonder that funding in subsequent years probably will decline. Furthermore, in some years that ostensibly indicate a decline in state funding, it's important to be clear whether the charts and graphs present actual dollars or dollars that have been indexed for inflation. Also interesting, perhaps puzzling, about state university lobbying is that the institution's expenditures for government relations have tended to increase – even after several years' indication that state appropriations may level or even taper.

When presidents of flagship state universities emphasize historical declines in state support for public higher education they often rely on a precarious use of historical data: namely, the dangers of relying on percentages without ordinal numbers to track institutional budget changes. Assume that in 1916 the state provided 90 percent of the annual operating budget for "Flagship State U." A century later, the proportions have changed drastically, leading the president to complain, "Do you realize we now only receive 20 percent of our annual operating budget from the state?" Well, this may indicate some serious decline in state dollars for biennial appropriations over several decades. But then again, it may not. The change over a century from 90 percent state funding to 20 percent state funding could equally signal that the flagship state university has both expanded and diversified its overall budget to include units that did not exist – or, which were inexpensive – in 1916.

The size of the university budget pie has expanded many times over the past century. The portion of the pie pertaining to state support for operating budgets often has increased in actual dollars while still declining as a percentage of the whole. This is likely to take place with new, expensive programs and facilities outside state appropriation support: for example, the addition of a self-contained academic medical center and its hospital, a veterinary medicine school, a university research park and accelerator funded by federal grants, a Free Enterprise Institute named in honor of a successful alumnus and funded by corporate donations, and a new athletics complex whose generous funding comes through the privately incorporated University Athletic Association, including its television contracts plus booster club donations. Furthermore, state universities tend to overlook and underestimate numerous other indirect and direct benefits they receive from state governments, ranging from state bonding for capital projects, special state appropriations for construction apart from annual per student subsidies, and power of eminent domain for procuring real estate.

Governors and legislators in turn respond to criticisms of allegations that they are remiss in support by noting that colleges and universities probably will expect more funding regardless of how much the state provides. Adding to the unreasonable expectation is a governor's explanation that the state economy is sluggish and that public higher education leaders often have internal control over their funds – and opt voluntarily to spend on facilities and programs that stray from the central core. And this echoes several years of analysis from the Delta Cost Project reports that indicate a persistent shift in each institutional dollar toward more spending on non-educational services and personnel. If one visits a flagship state university in 2016 it's not always easy to see signs of financial distress or income malnutrition.

External analysts of state university budgets often identify pockets of largesse within a campus. From the standpoint of public relations and public appearances, how destitute can a state university be if it is able to pay an assistant coach $500,000 per year? How prudent is it in its hiring and firing decisions if, for example, the board votes to buy out the contract of the remaining four years' salary of an academic who after a year was considered "not to be the right fit"? What if an NCAA Division I football program loses money and does not fill its stadium for numerous consecutive years? How is that enduring shortfall subsidized – and at whose expense? Why does a state university with a Vice President for Business Affairs and an elaborate professional support staff need to spend over $1 million to hire a private consulting firm to suggest a new budgeting model? If a state university is supposed to be committed to providing accessibility and affordability for students within its state, how does one explain a provost's deliberate decision to shift scarce student financial aid funds into "merit scholarships" targeted at students from out-of-state who may not have any financial need?

A subsequent question from these assorted incidents is how might the lump sum from these cumulative expensive decisions be used more appropriately? University officials often object, responding, "But you don't understand! That's different! We're just responding to market forces!" The problem is that appearances do count in public policy. Universities, including state universities, present an image to the public in which universities usually find the money and justification to pay what they wish for selected individuals and services.

The eulogy from this highly ritualized stand-off of state governments and state universities blaming the other is that somewhere in the late 20th century an historic compact of commitment to educational opportunity, especially for the underserved and modest income families of a state and the nation, eroded. A problem with this insight is that it does not necessarily lead to a good resolution. Consider a state policy that represents an extreme, generous gesture toward affordability: namely, charging no tuition, with the state government providing adequate per capita financial subsidy to cover realistic college costs. Unless a state economy has unlimited resources, the zero tuition policy probably will be inefficient, ineffective, and, worst of all, inequitable. This is because it often provides generous subsidy to students from affluent families who have no financial need and who could readily pay a reasonable, realistic tuition charge. If so, that would save either the state government or the state university substantial money – revenues that then could be directed to provide funding for specific, worthy programs or constituencies.

An example of a flawed resolution of state funding limits comes about when the state legislature simultaneously reduces its per capita student subsidy combined with placing a severe limit on the tuition that a state university is allowed to charge prospective students. The result is a false economy in which tuition is kept artificially low with curricular offerings and student services starved. State university officials are then caught in a bind. They are tuition sensitive in that they do not want to price themselves out of the market for applicants, yet at the same time their lowered state subsidies means that revenues have to come from tuition or other sources in order to provide quality instruction and other services.

An explanation, and perhaps a partial solution, is that state universities have over time drifted into a new model. Although a state university's tuition may be raised to accommodate annual inflation, perhaps more consequential is that each year state legislatures are shifting an increasing percentage of costs away from a state subsidy and toward the student as consumer, thus increasing the price of going to a state university but not necessarily the cost. This is a tuition pricing model long used by independent or private colleges. And, the decision to charge a relatively high tuition price usually introduces a commitment to enhance need-based financial aid. What it suggests is that many of the important components and units of a public institution are not much different, if at all, from an independent or private college or university. All research universities, whether public or private, seek and depend on federal research grants. All prestigious universities, whether private or public, pursue private donors. Indeed, flagship universities are sufficiently historic and celebrated among alumni and business corporations that they are able to compete for major gifts alongside their counterparts among independent colleges and universities. In fact, the real schism in potential funding is not so much public versus private institutions, but rather, differences *within* public higher education. UCLA, for example, has the benefits of heritage, neighborhood, alumni, endowment, medical center, law school, and political ties that render it more comparable to the University of Southern California than to a neighboring state campus such as California State University, Dominguez Hills.

CHARACTERS AND CONSTITUENTS

Vice President for Government Relations

Today almost every college and university has a Vice President for Government Relations. The nomenclature may vary from campus to campus, in some cases being a Vice President for College Relations or a Vice President for External Relations. What is consistent is that modern academic administration puts a high priority on making certain that a senior official deals with the lobbying and conversations with federal, state, and local government representatives. Failure to do so places an institution at risk in the high-stakes negotiations with legislators, governors, members of Congress, as well as mayors and city council. And, the Vice President for Government Relations often represents the institution in its meetings with various higher education trade associations as well as with the state postsecondary education coordinating council. Furthermore, this vice president probably also meets with delegates from business and industry – who, in turn, meet with government representatives. The result is a network of influential representatives and officials that connect campus, community, corporations, and governments.

But, the nagging question is, to what end do universities become involved in such government relations? One goal is to land federal research grants from any number of various government agencies. The other aim is less positive yet still pervasive: to derail or block legislation whose regulations would cause problems for a college or university.

Federal Government

The federal government's role in higher education is a paradox: it is both large and small. It is large because it deals with a great deal of funding in the aggregate for all colleges and universities – and large for a relatively small handful of prestigious research universities who are able to compete effectively for sponsored research and development grants. At the start of the 21st century the federal government was the source of about 60 percent of all spending on research and development by colleges and universities – $33 billion out of a total spend of $55 billion. In student financial aid, the federal government also looms large as the major funding source. In 2010, for example, this included $2.2 billion for Pell Grants and total undergraduate aid of just under $12 billion.

At the same time the federal government's role is small in that it is limited to these two areas: student financial aid programs and sponsored research programs. Furthermore, these two domains are disconnected, as each is autonomous from the other, hosted by disparate federal agencies and departments.

The third area where the federal government presence in higher education is large is in regulation. The thread that ties federal support for colleges and universities to regulation is that an institution that accepts federal dollars, whether through a federal agency's research project grant or through using federal student financial aid grants and loans, explicitly agrees then to abide by numerous federal standards. Failure to comply with federal regulations in one area of university activity can jeopardize receipt of federal funds for *all* campus programs. For example, if a college is found to be in violation of Title IX provisions for gender equity in athletics, it could lead to suspension of all federal research grants elsewhere on campus. Another example is that if university researchers put children in inner-city housing projects at risk to lead paint exposure, the grant funding may be suspended – and all campus-wide programs ranging from receipt of student financial aid loans and grant payments and various research grant project funding could be shut down. These are extreme examples, but they do illustrate the federal government strategy by which it can extend its power to impose and then enforce regulations on colleges and universities.

State Legislatures

State legislatures have been the linchpin of strong government relations with colleges and universities. In the opening section of this chapter we discussed the historic power of state governments to confer charters, without which a college or university cannot grant academic degrees. In addition to this power, state governments also have been the foremost funding source for public higher education, such as state colleges, state universities, and public community colleges. The primacy of state government for funding public higher education provided $80 billion for higher education operating expenses, and also $11 billion on student financial aid in 2011. State governments also are generous in their support of college and university construction projects by issuing bonds.

From time to time an ambitious governor focuses on the state university as an acute problem because it has become out of touch with the voters and taxpayers of the state. A good example of the recent negative spin comes from Wisconsin in 2014–2015, which included state university budget cuts and, most troubling, attempts to alter quickly, and some would say capriciously, the historic language of the distinctive, admirable state charter that brought to American higher education what was known as "The Wisconsin Idea." The shift in the formal language of the mission statement was from an educational mission of service, teaching, and research, to specific language about "workforce development." From 2012 through 2014 the Governor of Texas relied on this streak of populism to conduct analyses of faculty productivity at the University of Texas and Texas

A&M University, even though both institutions were among the most academically prestigious in the nation.

State Postsecondary Education Councils

Since public policy formulation calls for continual actions and reactions among governors, state legislators, and the presidents and vice presidents of colleges and universities, there exists a need for mediation. This has been a role of state coordinating councils over the past 50 years. The key national organization is the State Higher Education Executive Officers (SHEEO). There is some variation from state to state on how the leadership position is designed and filled, depending on the structural arrangements for the various public higher education segments. But the general principle is similar: state coordinating councils represent higher education to the legislature, and they represent the governor and legislature to the colleges' presidents and boards. The price of this buffering role is that each side probably tries to use the state coordinating council to its own advantage and persuasion. State council staff collect systematic data on state higher education issues. It is a presence and role that allows and encourages the state council to raise questions about the future of higher education in the state and nationwide that college and university presidents are unlikely to have the time or inclination to investigate when left on their own. In some states the higher education coordinating council administers statewide grant and loan funds, whose student financial aid supplements both federal and institutional programs. Also, the statewide data collection and analyses that include all institutions provide a good counter and context to the use and abuse of data by individual colleges and universities. Above all, a good state council leadership and research director makes an invaluable contribution to thoughtful state planning by providing informed analyses to avoid duplication of academic programs across the state and other extravagances.

The problem is that politics ultimately tends to trump research analysis in the state politics of higher education. For example, in one state with a population of about six million, there already existed seven law schools – four at state universities and three at independent or private universities. Indeed, the adult population of the state's major metropolitan area was top-heavy with licensed attorneys. Nonetheless, the president of a relatively young, ambitious, and popular state campus lobbied his local state delegates to push for the state to create yet another law school – at his own campus. Analyses by the state council staff led to the recommendation that there was already a glut of law school graduates and there was no demand for another law school. Nonetheless, the state university president, buoyed by his local state legislators, prevailed and got their own new law school.

Local Government

The role of local government – such as municipal or county – in American higher education tends to be overshadowed by the dominance of state and federal programs and regulations. This oversight is unfortunate because it glosses over the importance of what may be termed the "Town and Gown" legacy. Or, at times, disputes modify this to "Town versus Gown." Stretching back to the medieval universities of the 13th century, which included bloody riots between scholars (wearing academic gowns) and landlords, merchants, and other "town" people over student complaints about bad food, spoiled wine, and high rents for squalid lodgings, the relation of an academic institution to its immediate, surrounding host community has been crucial both in the past and present. One of the critical, enduring legacies was legal standing for the academic institution and its campus, with its own codes of conduct and regulations. Sheriffs, constables, and police officers were required by the king, or, today, by the governor, to respect the academic community as a city-state.

The "Town versus Gown" customs are especially pertinent to contemporary student affairs professionals. Students residing in campus dormitories, for example, usually are the major user of fire alarms within a community. What adds to the ill feelings between municipal fire departments and the campus is that most of the alarms are false alarms – most likely, expressions of juvenile misbehavior among undergraduates. This seems trivial, but it is a nuisance that also can drain city budgets. Perhaps a larger legal issue is that of jurisdiction in alleged criminal offenses. Most colleges and universities now have full-fledged police forces whose officers are permitted to carry firearms and make arrests. But the coordination and priorities of jurisdiction between campus and community remains complex.

Town and gown issues surface when, for example, a college or university expands its student enrollment while at the same time not building commensurate on-campus dormitories. The influx of new students who pay rent might be music to the ears of local landlords, but if such student enrollment growth is not coordinated with city planners and city council, it is havoc for neighborhoods and adult residents, along with zoning problems caused by overcrowding per apartment, inadequate parking spaces, loud parties and music, increased trash collection, and post-game celebrations and riots. Yet often colleges and universities are oblivious or even cavalier in their lack of consideration for such environmental impact of their own campus decisions. Colleges and universities also have a disproportionate influence on their communities in razing blocks of houses, tearing down historic buildings without collaborating with local historic preservation groups, or adding such monumental structures as a new hospital wing.

In addition to these campus turf wars, local government is pertinent to higher education policies in such matters as property taxation.[10] The widespread practice in the United States was that city councils exempt colleges and universities from local property taxes. It usually means that the city government has then forfeited substantial property tax revenues to assist one educational institution, thus reducing its ability to provide funding for another educational system – namely, the city or county public schools. As shall be a focus in greater detail in Chapter 13, in many cases a college or university is the largest landowner and largest employer within a metropolitan community. When cities have been strapped for tax revenues a compromise in many communities has been for the local college or university to make a voluntary payment to the city government – but without calling it a tax payment.

The Courts

The custom in federal courts has been to show keen restraint in becoming involved in academic affairs.[11] This has meant that federal courts were reluctant to hear cases involving a college or university as a defendant in lawsuits involving academic freedom, including denial of faculty tenure or promotion. Gradually, yet persistently, courts have allowed such lawsuits to be heard in civil cases – pulling colleges and universities into the legal forum to be held accountable for some internal regulations and decisions.

Recent scholarship has revisited the claim that courts and colleges have not been frequently engaged. In fact, state and local courts in the United States have heard cases stretching back into the late 19th century involving students' grievances about mistreatment by college officials.[12] Following the 1954 *Brown* v. *Board of Education of Topeka* case on racially segregated school systems, over time colleges and universities have been involved in cases about admissions and affirmative action. This has included the *Regents of the University of California* v. *Bakke* case and, since the 1990s, cases involving undergraduate admissions at the University of Texas, the University of Michigan, and the University of Michigan law school.

Higher Education Associations

Starting in the late 19th century colleges and universities have had a tradition of "banding together" for scholarly alliances and, for political initiatives, to form trade associations.[13] In Washington, D.C. a huge monolithic office building at One DuPont Circle is home to hundreds of higher education associations – each of which stakes out a presence in the nation's capital for access to congressional staff and to talk with one another in the higher education ranks. What exactly the purposes and achievements of many of these trade associations are is unclear. Foremost higher education groups include the American Council on Education (ACE), the Association of American Universities (AAU), the National Association of Independent Colleges and Universities (NAICU), and the American Association of State Colleges and Universities (AASCU).

Each association usually is funded by subscription fees paid each year by institutional members. Understanding the financing requires some thoughtful strategies. Educational nonprofit organizations usually are prohibited from political lobbying as a condition of their federal tax-exempt status. But this is not quite accurate. A college is allowed to spend up to 5 percent of its annual operating budget for lobbying and educational activities. At a university with an annual budget of, say, $3 billion, this means $150 million can be legally earmarked for lobbying activities. And, when dues are collected from a membership of, for example, 100 colleges and universities, the potential funding for a higher education association is substantial. Presidents of the higher education trade associations are comparable to – and in terms of compensation sometimes surpass – top-paid college presidents.[14] The proliferation of higher education trade associations with large staffs and high salaries understandably raise questions about exactly what they do.

Lobbying in higher education is peculiar among trade groups and industries in that it is characterized by in-fighting. State universities competing with independent colleges and universities is one scenario. Another pits the for-profit colleges such as the University of Phoenix, Kaplan University, and Corinthian College versus the established non-profit associations such as the ACE. This often is counter-productive because the model that Senators and congressional staffers prefer is when an industry – whether banking, manufacturing, or higher education – presents a united front.

No overview of higher education associations in Washington, D.C. would be complete without explicit mention of the fifth estate representation – namely, the weekly and daily higher education journalism provided by the editors and writers of the *Chronicle of Higher Education* and *Inside Higher Ed*. These two publications, which provide both print and electronic coverage on a daily and weekly basis, contribute a high level of investigative reporting along with databases, discussion of long-term trends, as well as daily news releases – all of which have helped transform analysis of higher education issues into an increasingly respected and analytic pursuit.

COMPLEXITIES AND CONFLICTS: IMPLICATIONS FOR DECISION-MAKING

Access versus Choice in Policy Priorities

The United States has been relatively successful in making postsecondary education accessible to almost all potential students who seek formal education beyond high school. But this is a limited accomplishment because it begs the question of affordability and choice. Persuading first-generation college students and their families to apply for federal and state financial aid programs that would lower tuition charges often is met with skepticism by the constituents the programs were intended to serve.

Academic Accountability

Congress and state legislators increasingly ask for higher education to provide systematic data on the effectiveness and efficiency of academic programs. The demand is for measurable outcomes of student performance, along with data on faculty productivity. Collecting and analyzing student assessment data have become standard features of institutional research. However, the politics of data analysis often create a level of mistrust between academic officials and faculty versus external constituents.[15]

Loans versus Grants in Federal Student Financial Aid Programs

By 2006 the drift toward student loans as the dominant form of federal student aid turned into a tidal wave.[16] Furthermore, graduate students, including those enrolling in law, business, and medical schools, started taking on an increasing amount of student loans – often piled on top of existing loans from undergraduate studies. The imbalance was made more disconcerting by debates over who the student lenders should be. Commercial banks liked being eligible for this role, especially when federal guarantees and rising interest rates provided the banks a good return. In the 2006 elections, however, the tide turned – as Democratic victories for Congress led to reinstatement of the federal government as the primary lending agent.[17] Amidst these vacillations and flurries, American families and taxpayers were left with an unresolved question of who should pay – and how much – for going to college.

Young adults who had substantial loan indebtedness and who were entering a stagnant job market were cast into a hard situation.

Private versus Public Institutions

Within the ranks of traditional not-for-profit higher education, the major split is that of private versus public institutions. Or, more accurately, it is that of "independent" institutions versus state colleges and universities. Placing institutions into one of the two categories is for the most part straightforward and obvious, although at times there are some hybrid cases and some exceptional situations that complicate this. But for public policies with various levels of government this is not always clear. A major obstacle to effective higher education lobbying in Washington, D.C. is the repeated inability of higher education to show a united front. Often, proposed legislation to favor higher education is mired in contentious family quarrels, pitting state universities against independent colleges and universities. This has surfaced in deliberations with congressional staff over provisions in proposed student financial aid programs.[18]

At one time, state universities assumed that public funding from the federal government would and should, of course, be directed exclusively to public institutions at the state level. In the early 1970s during the transformational discussions about creating massive federal student financial aid programs, independent colleges through such associations as the NAICU made the effective case that independent colleges and universities should be just as eligible for student financial aid dollars as were state colleges and universities. Their argument made good sense – a college chartered by a state government and accredited by a regional accreditation agency served the public good and national welfare, whether it was private or public.

One result of these heated deliberations was that Congress made all regionally accredited institutions eligible to receive federal student aid funds. Second, in a gesture to accommodate voters and to promote student choice rather than colleges, student financial aid funds such as Pell Grants and federal student loans were made "portable." A federal grant or loan was awarded directly to the individual student, who then would carry these to the approved institution where the student enrolled. This disappointed colleges and universities and almost all of their trade associations and lobbyists, most of whom had been confident in the early 1970s that direct funding to institutions was imminent. The decision to veer from direct institutional subsidies toward students as recipients provided an incentive for colleges to work to be attractive to federal grant recipients. It also made many incumbent Congressmen popular with taxpayers and voters who also were parents of college students.

Not-for-Profit versus For-Profit Colleges

For-profit colleges and universities (FPCUs) represent a formidable presence in American higher education. For example, in 2010 their students were the largest bloc of federal student loan recipients. Furthermore, students at "for-profit" colleges represented 26 percent of all undergraduate enrollments at four-year colleges in the United States. Not-for-profit colleges, which usually are considered the "real" and established colleges, argue that for-profit colleges are different and often have displayed an alarming trend of high student loan debt. A weakness of this argument is that in the early 1970s when Congress was deliberating potential new student aid programs, the lobbying groups for proprietary and trade schools – forerunner to the name "for-profit" sector – were organized and effective. They made certain that students at their institutions would be eligible for many federal student aid programs. Furthermore, many of the proprietary schools, including the University of Phoenix, were serving student constituencies such as re-entering older students – working adults who in the late 1970s and early 1980s often were not especially welcomed or accommodated by established nonprofit colleges and universities. In contrast, lobbying by the higher education establishment often had been ineffective or indifferent, in large part because college and university presidents were over-confident and underprepared in making the case for their institutions.[19]

Elementary and Secondary Education versus Postsecondary Education

Even though the various levels of education are interdependent, their relationship in lobbying for resources from state government remains mixed – and contentious. In times of economic prosperity, where a state has a culture of support for education, tax support for both elementary and secondary education and higher education has had a multiplier effect. A strong secondary school system provides a state's public and private colleges and universities a well-prepared source of potential students. Enrollment followed by retention and then graduation propel one another. This partnership breaks down, however, in lean times. What one finds is a checkered legacy varying from state to state. State support for prestigious public universities, for example, can take place even if the base of K-12 education is relatively weak or uneven. Conversely, some states show a pattern of supporting elementary and secondary education, while remaining relatively indifferent to the number and quality of colleges and universities. Most unfortunate is when public support for education is cast as a zero-sum game with the false dichotomy that support for one level of schooling drains support for the other.[20] This has been the political reality in many states over the past three decades.

State versus Federal Government

There is no imperative that higher education policies from states be coordinated with those from the federal government. What one finds is some disconnects and some coincidence, even cooperation, along with confusion and conflict. In the early 1970s state governments were in reasonably good financial shape, often leading them to be a friendly partner which assumed the debts in transforming a beleaguered private university into a new identity as a state university. And by 1980 state governments had stepped up in responsible funding for higher education nationwide, at a time when the federal government role had declined. By 2000, however, this reversed as overextended state budgets stopped increasing, leading to reliance on federal bailouts to assist beleaguered state universities.[21]

CONNECTIONS AND QUESTIONS

Equality and Excellence

The balancing act for public policies in American society is to achieve equality and excellence in higher education. The ledger sheet as of 2016 leans toward high marks in academic excellence at the best institutions and programs – but inconsistency and disappointment in fusing this with equity in access and degree completion across family income groups. All data on quality of life, health, professional achievement, earnings, and civic participation indicate the benefits that accrue to individuals and communities where college education and degree completion are high. This leads to general agreement that public investment in higher education is the base of sound policies.

The message leads educated, prosperous, and achievement-oriented families to transmit this ethos to their children who eventually apply to college. As a result, the educated and advantaged tend to become more so, despite a substantial investment by federal and state governments to extend access to higher education. Consider the following programs offered by the *New York Times* on December 24, 2015:[22]

Weekend Courses for High School Students Taught By the School of the
New York Times
Providing a deep dive into topics not readily available in high school, these courses allow students to pursue their passions, engage experts in the field and produce a

portfolio of exemplary work, while exploring how academic subjects are realized in real-world careers. Courses are taught by award-winning *New York Times* staff and experts across several fields.

Courses run for five weekends starting January 23–24 held at the *New York Times* building. Cost: $525.

According to the advertisement, course offerings included the following:

Writing the Big City: Reporting New York: Learn how to capture New York City in words, pictures and sounds and think like a reporter at a major news site.

Write Your Way Into College: Perfecting the Personal Essay: Craft an authentic, memorable and effective personal statement, a crucial differentiating factor in the college admissions process.

Additional courses over the five weekend sessions included the following:

Sustain What?: Dive into the world of environmental sustainability and hear from experts who are shaping this vital field.

Sports Management and Sports Media: Take your game to the next level and explore the business side of sports. Meet owners, agents, players' union reps and league officials.

Build Your Business: A Toolkit for Launching Your Start-Up: Make your idea a reality. Learn how to start a business with a focus on current-day tech start-ups, leveraging the rapidly growing start-up community of New York City as a guide.

The Numbers Game: Sports, Statistics and Fantasy: Explore the statistics behind sports, from player performance to the increasingly popular world of fantasy sports leagues.

Broadway to Bushwick: Theater in New York City: Go behind the scenes as we raise the curtain on theater life in New York City.

Creative Writing: discover the art of fiction writing – from scripts to short stories – and begin crafting the story you've always wanted to write.

Movies and Journalism: Explore how journalism, a subject focused on truth, is represented in film – a media steeped in fictional narratives.

Daily readership of the *New York Times* already is a select audience. The price actually is not prohibitive. American families typically spend more than $5,000 per year on a high-school-age student's sports, so $525 for five weekends of these advanced courses is a bargain. But most likely the response will be disproportionately from a highly educated family clientele in the immediate New York City metropolitan area.

So, the irony is that this extracurricular program tends to confirm the belief that intense educational programs work. In fact, they work so well that they increase the education and opportunity gap in American society. Who can blame American families who devote the time, money, and initiative for their own children to partake of such programs? Yet it leaves a nagging public policy question about the extent to which federal programs can – or, should – attempt to "level the playing field."

CONNECTIONS WITH DIVERSITY AND SOCIAL JUSTICE

Today concern with diversity and social justice could and should be a high priority of public policies, especially at the federal and state levels. However, raising this proposition is only about a century old at best. Well into the late 19th and early 20th centuries there was scant indication that higher education policies either from the federal government or various state governments exhibited much commitment to equity and reasonable opportunity for underserved and disenfranchised groups, such as racial minorities and women. Most likely what one finds are "separate but unequal" provisions. The federal government was timid and reluctant to intrude on state laws and customs, often which accommodated both de facto and de jure racial segregation.

Looking at the historical spectrum from about 1947 to the present, one finds a gradual yet grudging accommodation of civil rights and social justice in the various layers of government policies and programs. The 1947 Truman Commission Report dealing with higher education in a democracy probably was one of the first documents to support these goals. Yet its commitments in principle were not immediately effective, as the Commission Report was not linked to any legislation. It also was vague on whether it advocated racial desegregation, let alone racial integration. Between 1957 and 1967 it is clear that the federal government, often through the Office of Civil Rights, was proactive in enforcing federal law in the racial desegregation of public school systems, such as Little Rock, Arkansas, and at historically segregated state universities, including the University of Alabama and the University of Mississippi. Even though such campus episodes were volatile and violent, most state colleges and universities in the South underwent voluntary racial desegregation that was uneventful. Racial desegregation of state campuses, which for decades had been de jure racially exclusive, did not mean racial integration in the campus curriculum and round of life.

The partial gains of American colleges and universities in extending opportunities lead to a paradox. On the one hand, American higher education has been reasonably successful in providing access for students who seek to enroll in some program in post-secondary education. But both federal and national planning has not done well in avoiding institutional tracking. Within most states, for example, the flagship state university tends to enroll a fairly affluent student body – with varying degrees of academic strength depending on the particular campus. Meanwhile, most high school students from modest income families and especially those who are "first-generation" college students end up enrolling in the academically less prestigious community colleges and state comprehensive regional campuses. Since about 2000 there has been a fundamental reframing of the economic and political environment that has led to affordability and student access being drastically curtailed. Since 1978 increased federal emphasis on student loans – moving away from grants as financial aid – has been inseparable from growing student loan debt.[23] During the same years many state legislatures shifted increasing dollars and percentages of the cost of state universities toward students and their families in the form of higher tuition charges and lower state per student subsidies.[24] It has been a double jeopardy that hampers first-generation college students and those from modest income families.

Federally sponsored research grant programs rely on peer review and merit-based selection. Although this approach may be reasonably accurate in selecting the "best among the best" in research proposals, it also has perpetuated imbalances in distribution of research resources. From time to time federal sponsored research programs came under fire for their exclusion of new groups – perhaps an artifact of the peer review system in which science experts selected other science experts whose work was familiar for grant awards. The NSF made some concession to this by dedicating some monies to its EPSCoR program – a category of research grants where eligibility was confined to researchers at colleges and universities in states that had not been competitive in nation-wide grant competition. This was a partial solution to stark regional imbalances across regions and states. It did not, however, provide a lasting resolution to questions by dis-gruntled Senators and members of Congress who were upset that research funds were not coming to their home state.

In the area of gender, especially women, and equity, the 1972 Title IX stands foremost for gains in reducing imbalances in access and achievement in a range of educational programs. One interesting way to think about public policies and federally initiated pro-grams is that they prompt colleges and universities to act in ways that they were unlikely to do when left to their own initiatives and resources – and traditions. In 1969 women represented less than 5 percent of medical school students and less than 10 percent of law school students, even though women had demonstrated high undergraduate enroll-ment, retention, degree completion, and academic honors. By 2016 nationwide women had made substantial gains, as they were more than 50 percent of the students in these two advanced professional schools. What would the profile and percentages have been without the push and pull of Title IX and other external programs? Raising this question gives no cause for complacence or self-congratulation because today within colleges and universities, pockets of academic programs still show signs of exclusion and gross under-representation.

CONCLUSION

Over the course of the 20th century higher education became a significant concern in public policies and court cases at the state, federal, and local levels.[25] Although there has been an American consensus that going to college is important, there is far less agree-ment on the particulars of what appropriate, effective government programs should be. These differences may be masked in periods of economic abundance when there are adequate tax revenues to avoid hard choices. But this strategy has eroded in the harsh economic and political climate of the early 21st century. Many higher education pro-grams at the policy level are gridlocked and marked by internal tensions, churning, and a great deal of lobbying and legislative effort, along with lawsuits that often are focused on obstructing adversaries on programs and constituents. Ironically, the expansion and excellence of colleges and universities nationwide have made them the object of atten-tion among competing groups, whether the focus is on eligibility for advanced research funding or the right of an applicant to admission to a prestigious program. This scarcity value now means that higher education advocates need to draft a new agenda and find new alliances of cooperation if higher education is to be a vital part of public policies. The paradox of public policies is that in the 21st century, programs have achieved excel-lence while at the same time signaling that fulfilling excellence with equality and equity remains increasingly elusive, as gaps in affordability and choice have tended to widen rather than shrink.

NOTES

1. David S. Broder and David Hoffman, "School Days: President Bush, Governors Chart Ambitious School Goals," *Washington Post* (September 28, 1989) pp. A1, A4.
2. John R. Thelin, "Higher Education," in Paul J. Quirk and William Cunion, Editors, *Governing America: Major Decisions of Federal, State and Local Governments from 1789 to the Present* (New York: Facts on File, Inc., 2011) pp. 481–488.
3. Chester E. Finn, Jr., *Scholars, Dollars and Bureaucrats* (Washington, D.C.: Brookings Institution Press, 1978).
4. John Whitehead, *The Separation of College and State* (New Haven, CT: Yale University Press, 1973).
5. John R. Thelin, "Higher Education," in Paul J. Quirk and William Cunion, Editors, *Governing America: Major Decisions of Federal, State and Local Governments from 1789 to the Present* (New York: Facts on File, Inc., 2011) pp. 481–488.
6. Roger L. Williams, *The Origins of Federal Support for Higher Education: George W. Atherton and the Land-Grant College Movement* (University Park: Pennsylvania State University Press, 1991).
7. Rate Zernike, "Alan Rosenthal Who Reshaped Legislatures, Dies at 81," *New York Times* (July 11, 2013). See also, Robert Pear, "If Only Laws Were Like Sausages," *New York Times* (November 4, 2010).
8. John R. Thelin, "Higher Education's Student Financial Aid Enterprise in Historical Perspective," in Frederick M. Hess, Editor, *Footing the Tuition Bill: The New Student Loan Sector* (Washington, D.C.: The American Enterprise Institute, 2007) pp. 19–41.
9. Nathan Glazer, "Regulating Business and the Universities: One Problem or Two?" *The Public Interest* (Summer 1979) pp. 42–65.
10. Lois Therrien, "Getting Joe College to Pay for City Services," *Business Week* (July 16, 1990) p. 37.
11. Walter C. Hobbs, "The Courts," in Philip Altbach, Robert O. Berdahl, and Patricia Gumport, Editors, *Higher Education in American Society*, 3rd edn (Amherst, NY: Prometheus Books, 1994) pp. 181–198.
12. Scott Gelber, *Courtrooms and Classrooms: A Legal History of American College Access, 1890–1960* (Baltimore, MD and London: Johns Hopkins University Press, 2015).
13. Hugh Hawkins, *Banding Together: The Rise of National Associations in American Higher Education, 1887–1950* (Baltimore, MD: Johns Hopkins University Press, 1992).
14. Ry Rivard, "Higher Education Trade Group Presidents Make More Than Many College Presidents," *Inside Higher Ed* (October 24, 2014).
15. Gilbert Cruz, "Holding Colleges Accountable: Is Success Measurable?," *Time* (January 7, 2010).
16. James C. Hearn and Janet Holdsworth, "Federal Student Aid: The Shift from Grants to Loans," in Edward P. St. John and Michael D. Parsons, Editors, *Public Funding of Higher Education: Changing Contexts and New Rationales* (Baltimore, MD and London: Johns Hopkins University Press, 2004) pp. 40–59. John R. Thelin, "Higher Education's Student Financial Aid Enterprise in Historical Perspective," in Frederick M. Hess, Editor, *Footing the Tuition Bill: The New Student Loan Sector* (Washington, D.C.: The American Enterprise Institute, 2007) pp. 19–41.
17. Nick Anderson, "Bill Would End U.S. Subsidy for Lenders of College Aid," *Washington Post* (September 17, 2009) p. A3.
18. Samuel Halperin, "Politicians and Educators: Two World Views," *Phi Delta Kappan* (November 1974) pp. 189–190.
19. Constance Cook, *Lobbying for Higher Education: How Colleges and Universities Influence Federal Policy* (Nashville, TN: Vanderbilt Issues in Higher Education Series, 1998).
20. See, for example, the front-page headline story on high school graduation trends and "college readiness": Motoko Rich, "As Graduation Rates Rise, a Fear High School Diplomas Fall Short," *New York Times* (December 27, 2015) pp. A1, A19.
21. Donald E. Heller, Editor, *The States and Public Higher Education Policy: Affordability, Access, and Accountability* (Baltimore, MD: Johns Hopkins University Press, 2001); Ronald G. Ehrenberg, Editor, *What's Happening to Public Higher Education?: The Shifting Financial Burden* (Baltimore, MD: Johns Hopkins University Press, 2006).
22. "Weekend Courses for High School Students Taught by the School of the New York Times," *New York Times* (December 24, 2015) p. A8.
23. Edward P. St. John, Nathan Daun-Barnett, and Karen Moronski-Chapman, *Public Policy and Higher Education: Reframing Strategies for Preparation, Access, and College Success* (New York: Routledge, 2013); James C. Hearn and Janet Holdsworth, "Federal Student Aid: The Shift from Grants to Loans," in Edward P. St. John and Michael D. Parsons, Editors, *Public Funding of Higher Education: Changing Contexts and New Rationales* (Baltimore, MD and London: Johns Hopkins University Press, 2004) pp. 40–59.

24. Donald E. Heller, Editor, *The States and Public Higher Education Policy: Affordability, Access, and Accountability* (Baltimore, MD: Johns Hopkins University Press, 2001); Ronald G. Ehrenberg, Editor, *What's Happening to Public Higher Education?: The Shifting Financial Burden* (Baltimore, MD: Johns Hopkins University Press, 2006).
25. Christopher P. Loss, *Between Citizens and the State: The Politics of American Higher Education in the 20th Century* (Princeton, NJ and Oxford: Princeton University Press, 2012).

Additional Readings

Philip G. Altbach, Robert O. Berdahl, and Patricia J. Gumport, Editors, *Higher Education in American Society* (Amherst, NY: Prometheus Press, 1994).

Derek Bok, "The Federal Government and the University," *The Public Interest* (Winter 1980) pp. 80–81.

Carnegie Foundation for the Advancement of Teaching, *The Control of the Campus: A Report on the Governance of Higher Education* (Princeton, NJ: Carnegie Foundation for the Advancement of Teaching, 1982).

Constance Cook, *Lobbying for Higher Education: How Colleges and Universities Influence Federal Policy* (Nashville, TN: Vanderbilt Issues in Higher Education Series, 1998).

Ronald G. Ehrenberg, Editor, *What's Happening to Public Higher Education?: The Shifting Financial Burden* (Baltimore, MD: Johns Hopkins University Press, 2006).

David H. Finifter, Roger G. Baldwin, and John R. Thelin, Editors, *The Uneasy Public Policy Triangle in Higher Education: Quality, Diversity, and Budgetary Efficiency* (New York: Macmillan for the American Council on Education, 1991).

Chester E. Finn, Jr., *Scholars, Dollars and Bureaucrats* (Washington, D.C.: Brookings Institution Press, 1978).

Scott Gelber, *Courtrooms and Classrooms: A Legal History of American College Access, 1890–1960* (Baltimore, MD and London: Johns Hopkins University Press, 2015).

Lawrence Gladieux and Thomas R. Wolanin, *Congress and the Colleges: The National Politics of Higher Education* (Lexington, MA: D.C. Heath, 1976).

Nathan Glazer, "Regulating Business and the Universities: One Problem or Two?," *The Public Interest* (Summer 1979) pp. 42–65.

Hugh Hawkins, *Banding Together: The Rise of National Associations in American Higher Education, 1887–1950* (Baltimore, MD: Johns Hopkins University Press, 1992).

Donald E. Heller, Editor, *The States and Public Higher Education Policy: Affordability, Access, and Accountability* (Baltimore, MD: Johns Hopkins University Press, 2001).

Christopher P. Loss, *Between Citizens and the State: The Politics of American Higher Education in the 20th Century* (Princeton, NJ and Oxford: Princeton University Press, 2012).

Edward P. St. John and Michael D. Parsons, Editors, *Public Funding of Higher Education: Changing Contexts and New Rationale* (Baltimore, MD and London: Johns Hopkins University Press, 2004).

Edward P. St. John, Nathan Daun-Barnett, and Karen Moronski-Chapman, *Public Policy and Higher Education: Reframing Strategies for Preparation, Access, and College Success* (New York: Routledge, 2013).

John R. Thelin, "Higher Education," in Paul J. Quirk and William Cunion, Editors, *Governing America: Major Decisions of Federal, State and Local Governments from 1789 to the Present* (New York: Facts on File, Inc., 2011) pp. 481–488.

John Whitehead, *The Separation of College and State* (New Haven, CT: Yale University Press, 1973).

Roger L. Williams, *The Origins of Federal Support for Higher Education: George W. Atherton and the Land-Grant College Movement* (University Park: Pennsylvania State University Press, 1991).

10

FUND-RAISING AND PHILANTHROPY

The Nonprofit Sector

SETTING AND OVERVIEW

America is both a nation of joiners and a nation of givers.[1] And, colleges and universities in the United States have always been active in – and dependent on – the interplay of joining and giving. These are central to *philanthropy*, which can be defined as "voluntary giving for the public good."[2] The result is that higher education is part of a continual, complex dynamic of this American ritual of "give and take."[3]

This chapter provides an account of how colleges and universities in the 21st century have defined and carried out the historic practices of fund-raising. It includes the broad field of philanthropy. At each campus it requires analysis of the college and university development offices. It extends beyond the campus to the *nonprofit sector*. It includes orbits of foundations with which colleges interact in a variety of roles, ranging from recipient to contributor of program resources. The reminder is that higher education is just one of many worthy causes and coexists – and even competes – with, for example, health care, fine arts, performing arts, museums, and social welfare.[4]

How private monies and donations for higher education ultimately work as part of an institution's internal allocation of resources and decisions is central to the story of fund-raising and philanthropy. So, in addition to charting the ways in which colleges and universities go about seeking donors and raising money, this chapter will include discussion of the deliberations academic officials undertake in mapping strategies for their endowments and investment practices.

For colleges and universities, a big change is when giving is transformed from individual, scattered gifts into *organized* and *systematic* gifts that provide collective strength combined with strategic focus so that philanthropy becomes consequential. Americans as a nation of joiners often banded together to cooperate on good works, often at the local level of township or county. Local, voluntary initiatives included creation of community campaigns, foundations, and nonprofit boards. This organizational transformation increased the complexity and influence of philanthropy in a nation that was undergoing population growth, urbanization, and commercialization.[5]

Nonprofit groups often have been both givers and receivers. Churches, for example, consistently received tithes and donations. At the same time, either by volition or statute, churches were then expected to distribute philanthropy. At times their philanthropic role could be as the major institutional source of social services, welfare, alms, and emergency relief. In such cases, the *parish* was the administrative unit. It also could be in the form of a particular denomination soliciting for donations, which it would deposit in a scholarship society and then award as financial aid to needy, academically able students. All this took place outside state or federal services. In a similar vein, a *foundation* may be established with the express mission of drawing from its own endowment to support some charitable activity. And, at the same time, the foundation may solicit and receive donations that it then plows back into its endowment. There's an important, fundamental principle illustrated in this: namely, that in the United States a *nonprofit* organization or institution often is expected to reciprocate through good works and money the opportunities and privileges it has acquired as part of its nonprofit, tax-exempt legal status.

Colleges in the American colonies relied on a mixture of government support and private donations. Even when funding from the Crown or from the colonial government was generous, American college founders and presidents beat the bushes for donors. Local citizens often gave gifts in what was called "country pay," more familiar to us as "gifts in kind." Crops, animals, silver candlesticks, crockery, and other useful items literally helped Harvard College and other new institutions set up housekeeping. Even today university athletic departments still are pleased to accept gifts of livestock from grateful ranchers who also are football fans – especially since their gifts will make their way to the training table where the beef will literally beef up the stalwart football linemen who play for Alma Mater.

Fund-raising included pilgrimages by college delegations back to England. Saving the souls of either indigenous American tribes or young Anglo scholars had great appeal. One finds establishment of "Indian Schools" at William & Mary, Harvard, and Dartmouth – all of which were great failures despite great funding.[6] These collegiate "Indian Schools" provided an enduring lesson of "worst practices." First, money without a thoughtful plan and appropriate mission reduced the possibility for effective education. Second, imposing one society's values and culture on another was both inappropriate and ineffective. Third, once the colonial college officials abandoned their ill-fated "Indian Schools," they were left with a legal and financial quandary: what to do with the unspent endowment that had been earmarked for this particular educational program that was now eliminated? Herein surfaced both ingenuity and deception. At the College of William & Mary, the president petitioned the courts for permission to use the endowment not for the education of Native Americans, but for the education of students who perhaps *might* someday educate Native Americans. This was expedient and pragmatic, but not necessarily ethical.

Another innovation in philanthropy was when a major donor opted to endow a professorship or "chair" dedicated to some designated field of study. These rare bequests allowed a college to attract scholarly talent to the faculty without draining the regular operating budget. From the start, however, endowed professorships often represented a battle of wills between the college president and the donor. The benefactor wanted not only to designate the field of scholarship and teaching, but also to select *who* would be named to the professorship. Presidents bristled at this as an intrusion that compromised the right of the college to be autonomous.

With the creation of the new United States in 1787 fund-raising became increasingly important (and urgent) for college officials. As noted in Chapter 9 dealing with "Public Policies," state legislatures seldom provided regular appropriations for their colleges. To make matters worse, most college students could not afford to pay high tuition charges. Hence, most colleges worked hard to keep prices low – and campus expenses lean. Even with such frugality, most colleges in the 19th century had trouble meeting their payrolls. Whether in 1816 or 2016, philanthropy was viewed by the trustees as a means of survival. It also could be a dual source of salvation in that a gift could save the donor's soul while also helping to save the college financially. Since most college presidents also were clergy, they were experienced in passing the hat and putting the squeeze of good works or guilt on parishioners and any other potential donors they could corner.

Each college scrapped and scraped to pay its bills and maintain its campus year by year – thanks to the philanthropy of supporters and alumni. Institutional survival was important, but it was not the whole story of giving to higher education. By 1815 a new strategy had evolved to make philanthropy focused and effective. Some religious denominations committed to having an educated clergy, especially the Congregationalists and Presbyterians, sought donations to create scholarship funds. The charitable dollars did not go directly to a college. Rather, donors gave to a scholarship fund that had its own administrative staff. Students, meanwhile, applied to the scholarship foundation. Often the awards were impressive – four years of tuition, room, board, and books. A college gained enrolled students plus the scholarship payment. The condition was that the scholarship recipient had to be enrolled at a college affiliated with the scholarship fund's denomination. Furthermore, upon completing the Bachelor of Arts degree, the young college graduate had to agree to accept a scholarship at a seminary, and then be ordained as a minister. Following ordination, the college-educated clergyman had to get married, after which the couple agreed to go as missionaries to an underserved region assigned by church elders. A good example of this is the missionary destination of Hawaii, where Yale alumni who were Congregationalist ministers built churches and schools – including founding the prestigious Punahou School in 1841 – which sent its alumni back to Yale and other colleges.

The scholarship funds established by a group, such as a church, laid the groundwork for an interesting philanthropic strategy. Those who were rewarded by the charitable foundation received good funding along with the opportunity for education and professional advancement. They helped a special interest group resolve a problem: namely, how to ensure a flow of new talent into a particular profession. This model was emulated in the 20th century when, for example, some foundation board wished to compete for students who will commit to some particular service field or area. The early-19th-century Congregationalists used it to attract future ministers, but elsewhere it could be shaped to focus on attracting students to become nurses and medical doctors or some other professional specialty.

Philanthropy also was used in the 19th century to create specialized professional service institutions: for example, a school for the blind or a school for the deaf. One discovery, however, was that single institutions were inadequate to address large-scale social problems. Wars often turned out to have influences on philanthropy – including higher education. During the Civil War, for example, numerous colleges in the South and some in the North became hospitals near battlefields. The impact of war was to illuminate the gravity and logistical problems of large-scale suffering. Two exemplary nonprofit voluntary private initiatives included the American Red Cross and the United States Sanitary Commission. They distanced themselves from government agencies such as the United States Surgeon General, which the private philanthropic organizations viewed as either corrupt and/or inept. The leadership of the private philanthropies was drawn from the "responsible elites" of Boston and New York – most of whom were college alumni and many of whom had served as college presidents or trustees.

This created the so-called "private sector" of philanthropy.[7] One of the sobering lessons from battlefields was the need for orderliness and organization. These voluntary associations also insisted on strict record keeping on income and expenditures for accountability to minimize financial waste and corruption. Eventually, such Red Cross sponsors and board members as Charles Eliot would serve as academic presidents – and in the late 19th century would help define private institutions, whether a college or a hospital, from government agencies.

Great family fortunes changed the scope of charitable giving. Consider the familiar names of some of the oldest colleges: Harvard, Brown, and Yale. Philanthropists helped found and/or transform these hearty institutions. Brown and Yale are most illustrative of the power of mercantile wealth in the 18th and early 19th century. The United States was not much involved in manufacturing or industrial production, but its shipping fleet was among the strongest in the world. The Brown family of Providence, Rhode Island made this New England coastal colony and state one of the busiest, most lucrative destinations for shipping and selling. It combined sugar cane, rum, and slaves in a golden triangle of trade. It was legal. But was it ethical or moral? Colleges were the beneficiaries, as John Nicholas Brown and his sons gave large gifts that prompted the trustees of the College of Rhode Island and Providence Plantations to change the name to honor the donor family – Brown University. The connection of family wealth and college building persisted – and would blossom between 1870 and 1910 with the advent of unprecedented industrial fortunes.

Familiar, prestigious names of colleges today include Cornell, Johns Hopkins, Vassar, Stanford, Tulane, Vanderbilt, Carnegie, Rice, Rockefeller, Duke, Stetson, and Scripps, among others. Their founders who transformed American philanthropy starting in the late 19th century did so by drawing from their commercial wealth to make major gifts. One historical puzzle is to explain how and why founding and funding for colleges gained such popularity among the new wealth – whose members were for the most part lacking in formal education. Creating a grand campus in 1890, for example, was just one of many possibilities facing a steel mogul. Libraries, museums, city parks, theaters, opera halls, and hospitals, for example, were just as likely to be choices for architectural monuments. For whatever reasons, it was creating a university that captured the fancy – and funding – of what were known as "captains of industry" – the same group criticized by muckraking journalists as "robber barons."

Since the availability of great wealth was increasing dramatically in the 1890s it was not surprising to see the emergence of fund-raising as a pursuit that evolved into a profession. Heroic figures such as Frederick Gates wrote manuals and memos that gave advice to young men who were "canvassers" or "agents." The unabashed name for what we call "fund-raisers" of the era was "Honorable Beggars." The strategies and courtesies were pragmatic, even stern, covering every detail from how to make appointments to see a prospective donor to ways to engage the donor in conversation. Young men who entered the field were energetic, even brash. So, they had to learn the lessons of patience along with advice on wearing clean linen each day. The candor of the advice manuals was colorful, as prospective donors were referred to as "trout" who were "heavy with gift" and "ready to be reeled in." The professional fund-raiser became a fixture in American society, the one character who could work effectively in the university trustees' boardroom as well as in the corporate president's boardroom.[8]

Yet for every action there was a comparable reaction – whether in physics or philanthropy. At the same time that fund-raising was morphing into a profession with its codes and conduct, the great industrialists hired trusted assistants and officials to serve as the screening agents who would meet and talk with the legion of supplicant individuals and institutions seeking philanthropic gifts. Ironically, the aforementioned Frederick Gates switched sides and changed hats to go from being the one who had persuaded John D. Rockefeller to give money to Gates' churches and groups, to the new role of being the advisor who saved the senior Rockefeller from sob stories and opportunists. Procedures became more formalized, with interviews, screening, and application forms. The early, unregulated days had saturated the offices of the new wealth who discovered too late that giving away money was harder than making it.

Building the great new American universities between 1890 and 1910 involved the three Ms of money, monuments, and memorials. It was a grand era for historical revival architecture, as one magazine editor noted in 1909 that "the American campus seems to look older as it gets newer." Gothic spires and Georgian red brick were most popular. Stanford University and Rice Institute opted for a Mediterranean style, suitable to their warm climates.

Around 1910 the campus construction boom subsided for two reasons: first, many of the wealthy industrialists had exhausted their philanthropic budgets; and second, wealthy industrialists had grown weary of campus building as a way to make a lasting influence on American higher education. A new strategy for effective, efficient large-scale philanthropy was to create a chartered foundation that then would consider projects cutting across a region or the nation, rather than focused on a single campus. There were, of course, some important exceptions in the 1920s and 1930s, such as Duke University, the University of Pittsburgh, and magnificent new buildings at such old, established universities as Harvard, Yale, and Princeton. And, following World War II, family money from the Coca-Cola founders led to a transformational gift to Atlanta's Emory University.[9] On balance, however, grandiose buildings declined because wealthy donors no longer relied on a university as the optimal investment to achieve philanthropic goals.

Foundations, rather than universities, became the favored institution for philanthropists.[10] Among the prominent organizational names were the Carnegie Foundation for the Advancement of Teaching (CFAT), the General Education Board, the Russell Sage Foundation, and the Rosenwald Fund.[11] Several decades later, the Ford Foundation would emerge as the formalized philanthropy of automobile pioneer Henry Ford – a foundation whose inaugural grants were deliberately delayed by the Ford family to avoid income taxes.[12]

The primacy of foundations was both good news and bad news for American higher education. For the great new universities, it was traumatic. Mortgaged with expensive, high-maintenance campus architecture and grounds, combined with low tuition revenues and no dynamic investment strategies, little of the generous donations had worked their way into educational programs or academic initiatives. For the new, well-endowed foundations it was a golden opportunity to solve problems and extend their influence nationwide, free from the collegiate preoccupation with bricks and mortar. The CFAT combined the offer of a faculty pension plan (familiar today as TIAA-CREF) as an incentive for a college to agree to some serious terms: increase enrollment to at least 300 per student; strengthen college preparation from high school applicants via transcripts utilizing the "Carnegie Unit"; and, third, pledging to purge the college's undergraduate curriculum of exclusively denominational influences. Once an industrialist gave approval to creating a namesake foundation, it could mean a loss of individual control. Andrew Carnegie, for example, realized too late that the foundation named in his honor was not out of control, but it certainly was out of *his* control.[13]

The President of the new CFAT, Henry Pritchett, had previously served as President of the Massachusetts Institute of Technology. Educated as an engineer, Pritchett favored efficiency and a commitment to "standards and standardization" as the panacea for the ills of a sprawling, unregulated American higher education whose academic degrees often were regarded with disdain by professors at universities in Europe. The result was that the CFAT tried to enhance recruitment and retention of talented scholars into faculty positions by providing the funding for a pension plan. And, by encouraging cooperation between secondary schools and college admissions offices, set out to raise the threshold of academic preparation for undergraduate studies. It was an example where a private foundation was a close approximation functionally to a national ministry of education. Eventually the CFAT plan to fund college pensions dissolved, and the foundation redirected its focus to the role of conducting studies of school systems, college sports, professional education, and other topics.[14]

When the large founding gifts to create great new universities had run dry after about four decades of extravagance, most colleges had to learn to be administratively organized to undertake serious, unspectacular but systematic fund-raising. Harvard University was ahead of the pack in part because it had never been spoiled by having received a huge transformational gift from a single donor. Harvard had affluent, loyal alumni – and presidents and board members worked persistently and effectively to build a good financial base without the flamboyance of a Cornelius Vanderbilt or a John D. Rockefeller as a major donor. The Harvard approach developed under President Charles Eliot was that of annual campaigns, alumni mailing lists, and the attention to detail that established a sustainable development office.[15]

By 1920 a number of professional agencies had sprouted, especially in New York City and Chicago, to provide underprepared colleges and universities with help on effective fund-raising campaigns and offices. Professionalization of development in higher education and other educational institutions had come of age. A major component of this was that the large foundations assumed the role of stimulating advanced research capabilities that individual colleges were either unwilling or unable to support. The Social Science Research Council, funded by the Rockefeller Foundation, was a good example of a foundation priming the pump for applied research, especially in economics, with nationwide statistical data that were useful to Congress and industry, as well as to university scholars.[16]

Following World War II memorable foundations included the Ford Foundation and the Hewlett Foundation, joined by numerous other, albeit smaller, endowed trusts and foundations. Here the agenda prompted colleges and universities to engage in activities that were beyond business as usual. It involved selecting five great universities that would receive sufficient gifts to undertake transformation of their M.B.A. programs as part of a larger aim to integrate schools of business into the mainstream of top-flight academic research, scholarship, and teaching. International topics also loomed large for the Ford and Rockefeller Foundations.

Contributions of business corporations to philanthropy for higher education made legal gains in public policies after World War II. Today we take for granted corporate and individual tax deductions for donations to colleges. In fact, they are relatively new and came about only because of changes in federal laws that imposed income taxes and, three decades later, a deliberate lobbying effort by some corporations and colleges to make college donations legal at the corporate level and then deductible both for corporations and individual tax filers.

At times colleges, foundations, and business corporations intersected in public policies. An important innovation that surfaced between World War I and World War II was the federal government's favorable rulings on relations between private business and private colleges. Sustained, systematic contributions from business corporations started around 1936 and gained momentum as an important addition to the philanthropy of higher education.[17] According to historians Merle Curti and Roderick Nash, the first step in this extended campaign was led by Frank Abrams, corporate executive for Standard Oil of New Jersey in 1948. He urged companies to make charitable contributions to private colleges and universities. Soon thereafter, however, Abrams' efforts were stalled when his company's legal counsel warned that the state's corporate charter forbade such contributions to higher education unless all stockholders approved. But this restriction was removed when the State of New Jersey amended its corporation law to "empower corporations chartered in the state to contribute, as public policy, to educational institutions." Elsewhere, other New Jersey corporate boards tested the restrictions. In one high-stakes court case dealing with the constitutionality of corporate gifts to private colleges, the board of the A.P. Smith Company made a contribution to Princeton University, which was promptly blocked by stockholders who argued that the state amendment was unconstitutional if applied to an historic, existing corporate charter. Fortunately for independent colleges, the courts upheld the company's right to contribute to private higher education. As a superior court judge in New Jersey wrote in his 1951 opinion:

> I am strongly persuaded by the evidence that the only hope for the survival of the privately supported American colleges and universities lies in the willingness of corporate wealth to furnish in moderation some support to institutions which are so essential to public welfare and therefore, of necessity, to corporate welfare ... I cannot conceive of any greater benefit to corporations in this country than to build and continue to build, respect for and adherence to a system of free enterprise and democratic government, the serious impairment of either of which may well spell the destruction of all corporate enterprise.[18]

This opinion carried the day in the court's decision. As such, it cleared the way for a period of generous support of independent colleges from corporations and foundations. And, eventually, state colleges and universities were folded in to the beneficiaries. Not only were corporate barriers to donating to higher education removed, incentives to do so were enhanced. Heretofore, when corporations contributed to independent colleges, their company initiatives usually had been confined to scholarships for the children of employees. There was little consciousness among executives or board members about long-term or large-scale support of colleges as an endangered, important national resource for the public good. However, this changed dramatically in the early 1950s when major corporate leaders, including Frank Abrams of Standard Oil and Alfred P. Sloan of General Motors, worked persistently among chief executive officers and board members of companies nationwide to overcome the conventional view that a corporation ought not, or need not, support independent colleges and universities unless there was some direct benefit to the company.

This informal movement eventually led to creation of formal agencies that provided the dynamic structure and leadership for systematic, ongoing financial support of independent colleges as a collective entity. The landmark event was the founding of the Associated Colleges of Indiana in 1948, called the "first of the regional college fund-raising cooperatives." Its founder was Frank Sparks, the founder and former executive of the Indianapolis Pump and Tube Company, who at the age of 40 had earned a Ph.D. in order to fulfill his own self-imposed criteria as to what entailed being qualified to serve as a college president. As president of Wabash College in Indiana from 1941 to 1956 he combined his commitment to his own campus with attention to the larger sphere of higher education philanthropy and the business community.

After World War II Sparks led an ambitious plan to create a "Greater Wabash" that had far greater implications as a model and precedent for public policies and academic institutions nationwide. It was foremost a model of a small college's self-revitalization. Sparks as college president emphasized multiple initiatives. These included healing schisms between college officials and old-guard alumni; reconstructing the board of trustees into a powerful body of prominent, wealthy individuals; recruiting nationally distinguished professors to the college; renovating and expanding the campus and physical plant; and attracting sustained large-scale financial support. The convergence of these emphases would, then, give Wabash College national visibility as a "pillar of strength" in the private sector. And, the aim was for the college to be associated in the public mind with the philosophy of independence and self-reliance characteristic of the American private business sector. Philanthropic support from alumni, citizens, and private foundations were integral to this plan.

President Sparks' vision for his own Wabash College provided a base for his larger commitment to the character and health of all independent colleges in Indiana and nationwide. It sprang from his concern after World War II that the recent, growing entrance of state and federal government support of higher education also carried the threat of government control of higher education. He wrote, "Federal aid to education almost certainly will mean the disappearance from our educational system of the independent, privately financed, liberal arts colleges." President Sparks talked with leaders from business and industry as well as with board members and presidents at other colleges in the state. He gained a strong ally in the president of Earlham College. Their efforts were persuasive and led to creation of the Associated Colleges of Indiana – the first cooperative statewide association of independent colleges in the nation – which stood as the enduring, formal product of Sparks' ideas and groundwork. This pioneering association in Indiana fostered counterparts elsewhere, particularly in Ohio, Michigan, New York, and California. The hallmark of the associations was their partnership of college presidents and corporate leaders. Historians Merle Curti and Roderick Nash observed that Sparks' campaign emphasized that "liberal arts colleges preserve freedom; they produce many essential scientists and business executives; tax laws make it inexpensive to give, since corporations could deduct up to five percent of their net income for contributions to charitable institutions and causes."[19]

Creation of state associations to support independent colleges eventually led to national initiatives. The Council for Financial Aid to Education was incorporated in 1952 "with funds supplied by the General Education Board, the Alfred P. Sloan Foundation, the Carnegie Corporation, and the Ford Foundation's Fund for the Advancement of Education." Similarly, in 1957 business and academic leaders formed the Informal Committee for Corporate Aid to American Universities. And, in 1962, the Council for Financial Aid to Education reported more than $42 million in corporate contributions.

One interesting, unforeseen consequence of the successful efforts of private businesses working to support private colleges and universities was that ultimately it benefited *all* colleges and universities, whether private (aka, independent) or public (i.e., state-supported). This would become especially evident by the 1970s as state universities stepped up their own private fund-raising campaigns. Another significant result of these cumulative efforts was that *donors* to colleges and universities who filed itemized tax returns were allowed to declare college gifts as income tax *deductions*. This allowance gave colleges and other nonprofit sector organizations added magnetism in attracting donations from an expanded, diverse constituency.

Meanwhile, the large philanthropic foundations once again faced criticism from the public and from Congress. Most prominent were the congressional hearings about the new Ford Foundation. Another extended round of hearings started a decade later, and concluded with the Tax Reform Act of 1969 in which the large foundations received a scolding of sorts for alleged political lobbying as well as being disingenuous in the shifting of business and philanthropic funds as a tax ploy. In looking over these periodic congressional hearings the irony is that the private foundations were at one time criticized by Democrats and, later, by Republicans – a vacillation that had the net effect of neutralizing partisan attacks and, thus, over the long haul allowed foundations to gain congressional acquiescence if not in their declining relative financial strength whenever federal agencies entered into some shared area of research and development, such as the health sciences and medicine. To exacerbate this schism, in the period between 1970 and 1990, the established foundations' endowments were eroded by declines in the value of their stock market holdings.[20]

The success of colleges and universities as part of the nonprofit sector to gain federal tax exemptions along with tax incentives has been integral to the flourishing of higher education nationwide. The price of this success was excess, as the nonprofit sector became a relatively easy mark for groups that sought inclusion.[21]

ISSUES

A central issue is to analyze and explore the issues and ideas associated with charitable giving. The various legal and philosophical concepts ultimately conclude with recent attention to the topic of *donor motivation*. This seemingly straightforward concept tends to become more, not less, complicated as one probes its variations and implications.

What Is the Definition of Philanthropy?

As noted at the start of this chapter, the basic definition of philanthropy from which other connotations and variations emanate is "voluntary giving for the public good."

This is distinguished from services and projects reliant on tax revenues because for these a citizen paying taxes is obligatory, not voluntary. One complication comes about in policies and legal regulation is defining and then sorting out activities or services that may seem inappropriate as the objects of charitable giving.

The success of colleges and universities in fund-raising has skewed the popular conception of philanthropy as being defined in dollars. Since the early 1990s, however, college campuses have become the fertile ground for a markedly different notion of philanthropy, one that recommends direct voluntarism. Initiated by undergraduates, often met by opposition or indifference by professors and administrators, "service learning" and "civic engagement" have persisted and flourished as a meaningful strand in philanthropy originating on the campus yet reaching into communities in numerous forms and places.[22]

What Is an Eleemosynary Institution?

An *eleemosynary institution* is one associated with charitable acts and projects. The root word derives from Latin used in the medieval period, referring to *alms*. In the early 19th century the term *eleemosynary* was central to the legal definition and categorization of colleges as being part of a larger category of educational and charitable organizations. This included the Supreme Court ruling in the case of *Dartmouth v. Woodward*.

What Are Connections Between Religion and Philanthropy?

Many, perhaps most, formal religions give explicit attention to encouraging and even requiring the faithful to embrace and engage in charitable giving.[23] An essential tenet of Islam is *zakat*, in which wealth carries the obligation to give. From Protestantism comes ongoing discussions about the varied relations between good works and salvation. Where some interesting differences in practice and interpretation arise are in the relationship and role of the recipients of charity. If, for example, giving a gift is, perhaps, a sign of grace, is receiving charity stigmatic as a source of guilt or weakness?

Where Do Gifts Come From?

The historical analysis of American society and colleges from the 17th through 19th centuries indicates the primacy of individual donors. There also are collective and corporate sources of philanthropy. In Renaissance Italy wealthy merchants made certain to enter their income and expenditures in ledgers – including the notation "Domini Deo," which meant "given to God." Anthropologists, historians, philosophers, and behavioral scientists in recent years have given a great deal of attention to analyzing the delicate protocol of giving and receiving gifts.[24] In addition to gifts from individuals, other sources can be collective entities – such as a corporation, a trust, or a fund.

Where Do Gifts Go?

Philanthropic gifts overwhelmingly go to colleges and universities. Although true, it begs questions on both the macro and micro levels. From a macro or larger perspective, many gifts do not go directly to colleges and universities. In fact, they go into trust funds or to foundations – often, so-called "family foundations" – which then make decisions about awarding grants among a range of potential recipients, including colleges, but also museums, hospitals, think tanks, centers, or institutes. At a micro level, when gifts do go to colleges and universities, there are major differences as to precisely where they are directed. One can distinguish, for example, building and capital construction as a major recipient. Or, there are differences among academic fields – with medicine and sciences usually having high priority.

What Are Motivations for Donors?

Why do people give? The reasons are varied.[25] Some obvious explanations include the following: care, guilt, optimism, pessimism, obligation, duty. The notion of *stewardship*, whereby one carries out a commitment to taking care of individuals or institutions, is central. Tax policies often play a role, such as the prospect of a tax write-off for a charitable contribution. Or, business corporations as well as foundations may be required by law to donate a certain percentage of profits each year. Associated with these various motives was that Americans *like* colleges and universities. Belief and loyalty are the principles that define the distinctively American affiliation with higher education. Even for donors who were not alumni, many communities embraced the idea that being home to a campus made a city complete.

CHARACTERS AND CONSTITUENTS

Donors

Major donors such as Bill and Melinda Gates, John D. Rockefeller, Jane Stanford, and William Hewlett predictably are magnetic figures who attract our attention – and, perhaps, our envy. However, the diversity of philanthropy in the United States is such that preoccupation with iconic figures glosses over equally interesting groups and types of donors. What most colleges and universities have found over time is that a large base of persistent, loyal donors whose gifts vary in amounts is essential. It may be even more consequential than the sporadic big gifts of a charismatic industrialist. One indicator of fund-raising success for a college is the percentage of alumni who give. Research in recent years has focused on recent alumni and young donors, testimony to the importance of setting a pattern of caring and sharing.[26]

Since about 1990 development offices at colleges and universities, along with other nonprofit organizations, have acquired increasingly sophisticated tools to gather and then analyze data on what is called *prospect research*.[27] Correlations and connections allow development officers to try to make informed estimates on who might be interested in supporting a college – and, more specifically, particular areas or programs within an institution.

Successful business executives and investors do not necessarily give exclusively to schools of business at their alma mater. A good example is Michael Bloomberg, who has emerged in the 21st century as one of the most generous philanthropists to colleges and universities, having donated an estimated $1.1 billion. Bloomberg had been an engineering major at Johns Hopkins University and went on to be successful in designing software for financial systems – and, then, on to mayoral elections in his adopted city of New York. In 2013 one of Bloomberg's major gifts to his alma mater, Johns Hopkins, was not for its engineering department but rather for enhancing the residential campus. Bloomberg was thoughtful and inspiring as he recalled the opportunities for leadership, service, and camaraderie he enjoyed as a fraternity member and as a leader in student government in the early 1960s.

Endowments

An *endowment* is a formal, permanent legal account in which a college or university places charitable gifts for safekeeping and investment. As varied and numerous charitable gifts to the college are received, they are deposited into the endowment. The result is comparable to a complex mutual fund. Although endowment gross or total accumulations are listed as a single figure, this can be misleading. Each sub-account within the endowment is subject to particular conditions and restrictions on withdrawals. The concept is to both protect and promote accumulated earnings, applying them to specified projects each year. A college's endowment usually is one of the institution's major sources of year-by-year income. Interests and dividends are cycled back into the endowment, allowing it to grow – supplemented, of course, by new charitable gifts from alumni and other groups. By regulating the spending down, an institution can simultaneously free up some monies for immediate use, while growing the principal of the endowment.

An endowment of a billion dollars is relatively large.[28] In 2013, 83 colleges and universities reported an endowment surpassing $1 billion. Harvard University ranks first in total endowment, at about $38 billion.[29] Impressive as this is, it actually is lower than Harvard reported in 2007 before the severe decline in the stock market. Total endowments drop off sharply, as the second place institution is Yale, with slightly under $21 billion, the University of Texas system at $20.5 billion, and Stanford and Princeton with more than $18 billion each. This cluster is followed by abrupt decline – and one finds such institutions as the Massachusetts Institute of Technology, Texas A&M, Michigan, Columbia, Northwestern, Penn, Notre Dame, Chicago, the University of California, Duke, Brown, Emory, Washington University, Cornell, the University of Virginia, and Rice University in the range of $9 billion to $4 billion.

Economists also rely on per capita endowment of an institution based on the size of its student enrollment. Princeton, for example, usually emerges at the top of the per capita rankings. Its $19 billion endowment is ranked fifth overall – but it is a relatively small institution. With $2.6 million endowment per student it can undertake just about any educational initiative it so desires. Eleven institutions have an endowment of $1 million or more per student.[30]

Foundations

A foundation is a legal entity in which philanthropic activities are formalized by grant of a charter. Most foundations are chartered by a state government. Also, an incorporated foundation is subject to Internal Revenue Service guidelines and regulations. Although the visible, well-endowed foundations such as Ford, Rockefeller, Carnegie, Lilly, and, later, Bill and Melinda Gates are foremost, they are atypical. One estimate is that in 2015 there were 72,000 foundations incorporated in the United States. Many of these are relatively small in holdings, set up for an individual or a family, with no more physical presence than a file folder in an attorney's office.

The Nonprofit Sector

Alliances and associations of educational, philanthropic, and charitable organizations have led to the distinct but related terms, *independent sector* and *nonprofit sector*. These grew out of initiatives by the late John Gardner, an influential university president and foundation executive, in the late 20th century. The two terms were closely related, almost synonymous. The distinction was one of emphasis, as "independent sector" underscored separation from a government agency.

The scope of the nonprofit sector in the United States is large. According to Editor Lewis Lapham, relying on data from the Urban Institute in Washington, D.C., the profile as of summer 2015 is as follows: for the 1.5 million nonprofit organizations in the United States, the profile includes $4.18 trillion in total assets, $2.16 trillion in total revenues, and $2.03 trillion in total expenditures. This accounted for 5.4 percent of the United States' gross domestic product, about 10 percent of all wages and salaries, and $887 million in annual spending. Total annual private giving from individuals, foundations, and businesses was $335 billion. The service component of volunteers is estimated at 8.1 billion hours per year, an estimated worth of $163 billion.

The idea and organization of nonprofits and philanthropy is not unique to the United States, but it is distinctive and unmatched in scope in any other nation. The place of colleges and other nonprofits in the national economy is about 4 percent.[31]

College and University Presidents

Presidents persist as the principal figure in college and university fund-raising. This legacy is so strong that in their own clubs and conferences presidents refer good-naturedly to themselves as "beggars who live in big houses." The expression "making the ask" refers to the highly personal, ritualized act in which the president confirms the request and bequest from a donor – especially from a major donor. One of the more interesting challenges in being a president is to make the transition from "raising money" to that of genuinely seeing oneself as "educating prospective donors" about opportunities to make a difference. Presidents, along with academic deans, probably spend at least half their professional time in some aspect of development and fund-raising.[32]

Vice President for Development

A fixture in the organizational chart of almost every college and university in the United States is that of the *Vice President for Development*. Sometimes the terminology varies, perhaps as the *Vice President for University Advancement* or the *Vice President for College Relations*. Nonetheless, the role is comparable – namely, to oversee, lead, and coordinate the disparate fund-raising and development activities marbled throughout an institution. Typically the Vice President for Development reports to and advises the president, providing the background, strategy, and information that are essential for the president to be effective in landing major gifts. The vice president also plays a crucial role in helping to set priorities across numerous academic units – at times, adjudicating disputes over prospects and, ultimately, working to avoid multiple, uncoordinated requests of the same potential donor.

Vice presidents oversee such initiatives as the *annual campaign*, which solicits alumni and recurrent donors for year-by-year support pledges. From time to time – perhaps once a decade – the Vice President for Development orchestrates a *capital campaign*. This is a complex, lengthy project with a high goal – sometimes as high as $1 billion to $7 billion among the most prestigious universities. Originally universities and hospitals showcased a capital campaign to raise money for bricks and mortar projects – a new research laboratory, a hospital wing, or an art museum. But this has changed over time to include a range of other potential emphases, such as scholarships, endowed faculty chairs, and other campus facilities and functions. The success of capital campaigns has led to their popularity at almost all colleges and universities. Standard procedure is to start with a "quiet period" in which the president and vice president work with staff to gain about 20 to 25 percent of the campaign goal. This in turn is followed by a campaign kick-off and highly public (and publicized) campaign.

Professionalization of fund-raising has increased, especially by the founding and growth of the Council for the Advancement and Support of Education (CASE), whose national headquarters are in Washington, D.C. The aim of such groups, in addition to professional affiliation and cohesion, is to promote a sense of professionalism in ethics and knowledge, along with technical and organizational skills. Expertise in development and fund-raising is in high demand and stands as a high priority for boards and presidents.[33]

Perhaps the most significant change in the campus Office of Development has been the rise of the *investment fund manager* as a highly paid and highly influential figure in college and university administration. Orchestrating the diverse portfolio and endowments of an academic institution holds out the prospect (but not promise) of double-digit investment returns.[34] It is as if Wall Street runs through the campus, as high-risk and high-return hedge funds whose overseers are professional investment experts chart the campus course. This is not hyperbole, as many of the investment managers at great universities did come from Wall Street!

COMPLEXITIES AND CONFLICTS: IMPLICATIONS FOR DECISION-MAKING

Conditions on Donations and Bequests

American traditions and laws leave to the discretion of donors to specify terms and restrictions on the use of their charitable gifts. However, freedom to give coexists with the equally established freedom of institutions and organizations to reject gifts. In the 21st century, where commerce is strong as a priority, the question of donor control is more likely to deal with large gifts tied to business beliefs.

New buildings are popular with donors – but eventually they cost a lot in terms of maintenance and renovation. Initial funding for a research center appears to make good sense – but, years later, the university may be saddled with topics and projects that have lost their intellectual vitality and currency.[35]

Perpetual Gifts and Endowments

One line of argument that has shaped the legal terms of philanthropy in England and the United States has been the principle that sound stewardship of wealth calls for endowments to colleges and universities to be *perpetual*. In other words, the recipient institution is pledged to invest the donated sum, drawing its annual interest or dividends for expenditures, all the while leaving the gift principal intact so that it lasts forever. This discipline builds in endurance so that the endowment literally makes a lasting, perpetual contribution to the mission and projects of a college. It provides a guard against squandering, or, to draw from nautical lore, "spending like sailors on leave." Compliance with the terms of a perpetual endowment prevents an opportunistic president or board of trustees from "breaking the bank" for immediate, expensive projects that deplete the institutional reserves. There are, however, good objections to perpetual endowments as infallible elements of prudent philanthropy. First, insistence on a perpetual endowment can lead to hoarding. This could be violating the spirit of charitable giving – i.e., they are not working or being put to use actively and wholly to make a genuine difference in achieving the donor's or institution's goals.[36]

Some goals may take five years to achieve, whereas others may be 15 or 50 years. As John D. Rockefeller exclaimed as he objected to making a large gift in the form of a perpetual endowment, "Forever is a long, long time…" In contrast to our Anglo-Saxon and American traditions that favor perpetual endowments, one finds in some important cases – such as France in the 17th century – government policies that moved deliberately to dissolve perpetual endowments. Gifts had to be spent within five years – this would stimulate spending into the national economy – to counter the logjam of funds being tied up in perpetual endowments.[37]

Competition and Imbalances within Educational and Charitable Recipient Groups

Philanthropy ultimately converges on questions of values, priorities, and worth. To one extreme, in the United States donors are, of course, quite free to choose the objects of their giving. Ethicists sometimes undertake the exercise of attempting to rate or rank which issues or causes are "most worthy" – or, at least, "more worthy" than others. Peter Singer, Professor of Bioethics at Princeton University, has argued that gifts to medical and health fields that deal with "life and death" programs are of paramount importance. That is plausible, but it becomes unconvincing when subjected to reasonable queries. What if, for example, some non-medical program was set up to save lives? Might not food relief for infants be a rather unscientific, non-medical solution to a serious problem of starvation or malnutrition? If so, would it surpass or lag behind medical research and development in the rankings of life and death?

Another complication with ratings and rankings of philanthropic "worthiness" is that it may unwittingly suggest a "winner takes all" fallacy. Presume, for example, that providing funding which allows medical researchers to work on cures for various forms of cancer or for alleviating muscular dystrophy is of paramount worth. Does it necessarily follow that such paramount causes should receive all philanthropic funding? To do so would be silly and selfish. One reason is that some problems or issues may be insoluble and, hence, could devour any and all charitable giving – and still have no prospect of success or achievement.

The irony is that this message often worked well, perhaps too well, in some situations. It is especially pronounced in metropolitan areas such as New York City. The performing arts of opera and the symphony, along with art museums and other established civic institutions, have acquired high status among donors who aspire to be appointed as trustees and, hence, lead to funding. Affiliation with such notable programs and institutions has higher social cachet and prestige than, for example, funding for a food bank or soup kitchen.[38]

Imbalances within Colleges and Universities

Many colleges and universities have a central office of development or an institutional foundation into which all donations are placed. This does not mask the fact that certain departments and fields perennially attract more donors and dollars than do others. The sweepstakes for campus prestige, always present, have accelerated since about 1985.[39] Intercollegiate athletics has a presence and priority that almost always will dwarf the department of social work. Some universities may have specialty programs, such as opera at Indiana University, in which a tradition of excellence and national recognition propels generous external financial support. Within academic fields, medical and health specialties are magnets for gifts that support an expensive, extensive research and development agenda.

Distribution of charitable giving to colleges and universities is controversial when one scans the roster of annual rankings of such indices as total endowment, endowment per student, and annual total of gifts received. There is a pronounced tendency for rich colleges and universities to become richer. Old, prestigious, and wealthy institutions may have alumni who are simultaneously successful in professional life and investments and who are loyal to Alma Mater.

Conflicts of Interest and Institutional Self-Determination

If, as suggested in the preceding section, fund-raising amounts and proportions are at odds with a college or university's strategic plan or mission statement, a crucial role of academic leaders is to set the institutional gyroscope aright. Most egregious is when major gifts even appear to compromise institutional integrity in terms of decisions about curricula or educational programs. As reinforced by regional accreditation standards, an institutional board and the president are expected to maintain control over decision-making and institutional directions despite the temptations of large gifts.

Conflict of Interest and Donor Discontent

College officials dating back to the 17th century have been periodically concerned (and always vigilant) to make certain that a donor does not abuse the academic institution. Equally plausible is the concern by major donors and their heirs that a college be faithful to the letter and spirit of the family's gift. The William Randolph Hearst family gave generously to establish programs and departments in mining engineering at the University of California in the early 20th century. After World War II, however, the demand for expertise and research in the field dwindled. How, then, does the university comply? Another conflict came about early in the 21st century at Princeton University, where the heirs of family donors expressed vehement concern that their endowment for the Woodrow Wilson School of Public and International Affairs had been compromised. The family argued that resources intended to attract talent into the Foreign Service had been neglected, with increasing attention to the professional education of future international corporate executives. In such cases the host college or university can face lawsuits, to explain how money is being spent – and whether new emphases are consistent with the historical endowment.

A highly publicized incident in January 2016 brings dramatic attention to tensions between donors and colleges. Eric Suder, a prosperous Texas entrepreneur, was committed to creating scholarships and opportunities for "first-generation" college students. To this end he arranged for his family foundation to establish a program called "First Scholars," and invited universities to apply to participate, eventually giving multi-million-dollar grants to seven universities.[40] One condition of the First Scholars gifts was that after four years and receipt of the final payment promised as part of the "First Scholars" grant, the university then agreed to continue the program using its own resources. In one instance, Suder discontinued the grant at a university that he felt had not complied with the terms during its initial years. And, in 2016, Suder sued the University of

Alabama for having canceled its program even though it had received agreed-upon monies over four years. At the very least the case illustrates the potential for friction and legal disputes between donors and colleges and universities.

The Changing Role of Major Foundations

Foundations gained presence and power in the late 19th and early 20th centuries.[41] Given their large endowments – usually thanks to familial corporate wealth in new industries such as oil refining, steel production, coal mining, railroads, timber, and manufacturing – the major foundations were in the right place at the right time to build and then shape American higher education. This leverage as "the Big Foundations" and "the Golden Donors" was especially high up until 1915 because there was no federal income tax that would drain off corporate profits. And, over the next three decades, in the absence of strong federal or state higher education funding or directives, the private foundations were probably the strongest organizational force in higher education.[42] The historical change was that by increments the federal government and its numerous agencies and presidential cabinet positions moved into increased involvement in providing either resources or regulations that determined what colleges could – and could not – do.

The federal government was slow to enter into educational policies, but once it did opt for a particular activity, it would be dominant. Even though private foundations had been relatively strong in science and medical research for decades, after World War II when Congress provided sustained funding for the National Science Foundation (NSF) and the National Institutes of Health (NIH), these federal agencies would be the prime movers in setting as well as funding the academic science agenda. Even though a private foundation might increase its funding for academic research, by 1970 it would be out-paced by a federal agency. In 2015 the wealthiest foundation in the United States spent about $472 million from 2006 through 2013 on projects related to higher education. Among the largest annual budgets for distribution by foundations on all projects are amounts ranging from $122 million to about $600 million. In contrast, the annual budgets for the two major federal research agencies dealing with academic science are, respectively, $31 billion for the NIH and $7.7 billion for the NSF.

A new generation of wealthy commercial entrepreneurs in high-tech industries have become philanthropists. The notions of "mega gifts" and "transformational gifts" pervade the new vocabulary.[43] They are distinctive for having added a new strategy that represents a change from providing programs to lobbying for policies – dealing with influence rather than bricks and mortar. Whereas historical foundations, such as the CFAT or the General Education Board, would fund and build programs and institutions about a century ago, a major foundation such as the Gates Foundation or the Lumina Foundation behaves differently. In many cases with higher education – especially some initiative such as "college readiness" for students in the connection between secondary school and college enrollment – the foundation awards money to numerous other foundations, research institutes, centers, and to colleges and universities to pursue policy research and advocacy. In other words, a new emphasis is to be architects of the next wave of federal policies and legislation. It is an expensive agenda – but has the advantage of leveraging foundation monies. In other words, if a foundation ultimately succeeds in having Congress and federal agencies adopt the foundation's favored policies, the resultant federal dollars authorized for the new programs far surpass the resources the foundation could have mustered on its own.

Tax Policies: Incentives for Higher Education and Philanthropy

Federal and state governments often have been encouraging and supportive of academic fund-raising. An example of *direct support* is matching grant programs. Some state legislatures have established what have been termed "Bucks for Brains" programs in which the state provides a dollar-for-dollar match for each private dollar the state research university raises. It exemplifies a public–private partnership as a way to attract outstanding faculty members.

More widespread have been indirect enhancements. Donors to colleges and universities are granted a charitable gift tax deduction.[44] And, the recipient academic institutions do not have to pay income tax on the contributions they receive. There has also been a reverse twist on this – the prospect that perhaps academic institutions, especially those with large endowments, might forfeit some of their federal tax exemptions unless they adopt practices and policies conducive to the public welfare.[45]

CONNECTIONS AND QUESTIONS

How Does Philanthropy Coexist and/or Conflict with Other Funding Sources?

Financial planning in higher education continually gravitates to questions of multiplier effects. In other words, do private gifts to a college set into motion increased returns to margin? Or, perhaps philanthropy merely leads to some funding sources being reduced? This concern surfaces in public institutions where sometimes the logic of legislators is that if a campus can raise private monies, this then releases the legislature from some of its customary support obligations. In recent years the more prevalent institutional rationale has been that since state appropriations will continue to decline, all colleges need to invest more in private fund-raising.

How Do Groups Compete and Cooperate within the Nonprofit Sector?

Associations such as Nonprofit Sector indicate that varied educational and charitable organizations have much to gain via cooperation in both administering services and in advocating for public policies. Ultimately, however, this consensus breaks down as each area and, then, each organization is compelled to attract its own donors. A compromise approach is the model pioneered by the United Way. Instead of having disparate, numerous community agencies and charities competing in a chaotic year-round melee, the reform approach has been to collaborate on a single, coherent annual campaign. An executive director and central staff then orchestrate budget hearings and criteria by which the gross proceeds are allocated. Such an approach usually assists less established, smaller organizations to gain some reasonable funding. A single strong, dominant organization or campus, however, may decide that it can do better on its own in targeting donors and cultivating constituencies.

How Does Higher Education Fit into the Scheme and Ethos of Philanthropy?

Colleges and universities historically have been favored institutions in the eyes of individual donors and major foundations. Although this still holds in the main, over the past 20 years other and new organizations and issues have made relative gains in philanthropic giving. In part this signals that colleges and universities have declined in their appeal. When asked, "Why have foundations cut back on higher education?"

a university development officer in 2003 warned college and university officials that foundations had the following bill of concerns: first, colleges and universities tended to lack common goals and cooperation for innovation; second, campuses had not been persuasive in showing systematic innovation or measurable results. Foundations also tend to think that established colleges do not need extra help. What foundations do not like to do is fund what they consider to be the college's "business as usual."[46]

Favored targets within a college or university also elicit mixed feelings from Vice Presidents for Development. Intercollegiate athletics tends to draw a large number of donors whose gifts range from modest to mammoth. In 2015, for example, intercollegiate athletics accounted for $1.2 billion donations out of the total of $40 billion that colleges in the United States raised. Furthermore, major donations were concentrated in a relatively small number of sports-minded universities, with Texas A&M totaling $67 million and the University of Oregon reporting $54 million for intercollegiate sports.[47] So, the real gain for institution-wide program support is uncertain.

CONNECTIONS WITH DIVERSITY AND SOCIAL JUSTICE

The historical charters that codified philanthropy and eleemosynary institutions made commitment to social justice a defining purpose and priority. The overwhelming intent was to extend help and resources to the underserved. And, in the main, donors and philanthropic foundations have carried out this charge. Following the Civil War and into the early 20th century one finds a groundswell of charities committed to establishing schools for African Americans, especially in the segregated South. These were called "dangerous donations" because they were substantive in changing the societal order of civil life in the Southern states; and, in a second connotation, dangerous for their advocates who were subject to threats, harassment, and even legal prohibitions.[48]

One of the most significant, effective initiatives in harnessing organized philanthropy to social justice emerged in the 1940s: the United Negro College Fund (UNCF). Prof. Marybeth Gasman's *Envisioning Black Colleges* reconstructs the historical development of this distinctive philanthropy in its full complexity. The paradox of the UNCF is that simultaneously it illustrates the high mark of fund-raising achievement by the Black Colleges in a competitive environment, yet dramatically conveys the difficult task these institutions face individually or collectively in acquiring private donations. Racial exclusion and discrimination, even in New York City and other Northern states, impeded the UNCF leaders – until a group of white women who were the wives of the heads of national corporations – pressured and prompted their husbands to take seriously and give generously to the Black colleges.[49] In more recent years scholars have become increasingly cognizant that the dynamics and patterns of philanthropy in the African American community and institutions are potent – but distinctive and different than those of the Ivy League or the flagship state universities.[50] When one focuses on donated dollars exclusively, it is evident that in matters of social justice and racial equity, the gains attributed to mainstream philanthropy are partial gains – and the Achilles heel of American philanthropy is that the institutions with high need, committed to providing affordable access for needy students, seldom gain much ground on the most affluent, academically prestigious colleges and universities.

This observation may be offset at least in part by acknowledging a drastic change in the scope, strategy, and targets by such contemporary philanthropists as the Bill and

Melinda Gates Foundation, the Ford Foundation, and the Soros Foundation. Whereas an individual college or university defines its work and success in terms of its own campus and activities, the new philanthropy has less loyalty or deference to the campus for tackling problems of social justice. In 2016, for example, the re-energized Ford Foundation led by President Darren Walker has "set out to conquer inequality."[51] Such a commitment may in part include colleges and universities, but increasingly the foundation portfolio is to look beyond a campus and deal with numerous constituents and grant applicants who seek to work on global hunger, illness, financial instabilities, lack of clean water, limited access to loans and credit, distribution of health and medical supplies and treatments, and improving elementary and secondary education. Higher education, then, must work longer and harder to maintain a place in line for foundation support.

Going back to the early 19th century, the contributions of women as philanthropists in higher education have been underestimated and overlooked. Since much of their contributions were through service and donated time rather than money, the ledger sheets are misleading. By the late 19th century women as donors who set up trusts for the founding of women's colleges along with establishing scholarship funds were significant. Consider such heroic figures as Sophia Smith, Sophie Newcomb, Ellen Browning Scripps, and Jane Stanford, to name just a few examples of college builders. Today women in higher education probably fare better than the Black Colleges and Tribal Colleges in the private philanthropic activities. This can be disaggregated into two distinct categories. First, although the number of colleges exclusively for women has declined over the past 40 years, those that have retained their historical mission gain the advantage of commitment and loyalty, both by alumni and prospective students. This strength is enhanced by the disproportionate accomplishments in professional and public life by the women who graduate from these colleges. Second, across all higher education, the increasing opportunities and achievements of women has kindled scholarship and fellowship funds designed to attract and retain women as top students and aspiring professionals.[52]

CONCLUSION

Philanthropy and American higher education is an enduring success story with deep roots – and deep pockets. It remains central to the general field of fund-raising and philanthropy. And, the systematic study of philanthropy has gained a healthy place within American universities.[53] In 2015 colleges and universities in the United States raised a total of $40 billion. About 20 percent of all the money raised went to just 20 colleges. According to the Council for Aid to Education's annual Voluntary Support of Education Survey, the universities that were top in the rankings were as follows: Stanford, $1.63 billion; Harvard University, $1.05 billion; University of Southern California, $653 million; the University of California at San Francisco, $608 million; and Cornell University, $591 million.[54] This illustrates a continuing trend among institutions in which the rich get richer – increasing differences within and among colleges and universities nationwide.

For all these accomplishments, the celebration is muted by some sobering insights. An impressive, provocative recent work is Lewis Lapham's anthology on *Philanthropy* published as the Summer 2015 issue of *Lapham's Quarterly*. The sheer magnitude of increases in "philanthropic largesse" in the United States over the past half-century led Lapham and numerous other thoughtful analysts to raise serious questions about motives and results in our charitable giving.[55] He noted in his essay, "Pennies from Heaven," that increasingly philanthropy is seen by many as a "big business," a "false front" for a variety of ploys ranging from tax evasion to lobbying to funding political campaigns. Drawing from an abundant historical literature, Lapham hints at a tradition of criticism bordering on cynicism. In 1862, for example, novelist Anthony Trollope made the acid comment, "I have sometimes thought that there is no being so venomous, so blood-thirsty as a professional philanthropist."

Lapham is not alone in critical scrutiny of philanthropy and the major foundations. Michael Massing, former Executive Editor of the *Columbia Journalism Review*, argued in 2016 that the most influential philanthropists are members of what has been termed "The One Percent." One might hope that with great wealth comes great responsibility. But it also confers great autonomy. What has been called "philanthrocapitalism" can take the form of Mark Zuckerberg, who made his fortune with Facebook, announcing at a national press conference that he had decided to give $100 million to the Newark, New Jersey public school system. It was a gift that was both generous and generally thoughtless. Elsewhere, the most significant recent characteristic of the philanthrocapitalists is that they are less likely to ask nonprofit organizations how they as donors might be of help – opting instead to advance their own independent agenda and ascertaining whether a university or other nonprofit can be of help to the granting foundation. The philanthropists often give large donations to their own family foundations. Another attractive approach has been to use foundation grants to shape the public policy research agenda at established think tanks such as the Brookings Institution. The new, large foundations interact with universities both in awarding grants to researchers and in gaining seats as members of university boards of trustees.[56]

Colleges and universities probably will continue to do well in attracting a high proportion of donations for the annual fund, for special class gifts, and for both small and large gifts from appreciative alumni. Large donations, however, will be increasingly difficult given the acceleration of the very wealthy to create their own family foundations and to be aggressive in their strategies and goals. College and university presidents and their development officers have to work hard to make their case persuasive to the bold "philanthrocapitalists." Explaining the connection between good intentions and ultimate good works remains less certain – and, hence, calls for more informed reconsideration in the 21st century.

NOTES

1. Robert H. Bremner, *American Philanthropy*, 2nd edn (Chicago: University of Chicago Press, 1988); Lawrence J. Friedman and Mark D. McGarvie, Editors, *Charity, Philanthropy, and Civility in American History* (Cambridge: Cambridge University Press, 2003); Olivier Zunz, *Philanthropy in America: A History* (Princeton, NJ: Princeton University Press, 2011).

2. Robert L. Payton, *Philanthropy: Voluntary Action for the Public Good* (New York: American Council on Education/Macmillan Publishing Company, 1988).

3. Merle Curti and Roderick Nash, *Philanthropy in the Shaping of American Higher Education* (New Brunswick, NJ: Rutgers University Press, 1965); Michael Rothschild, "Philanthropy and American Higher Education," in Charles T. Clotfelter and Thomas Ehrlich, Editors, *Philanthropy and the Nonprofit Sector in a Changing America* (Bloomington: Indiana University Press, 1999).

4. Burton A. Weisbrod, *The Nonprofit Economy* (Cambridge, MA: Harvard University Press, 1988).

5. Deni Elliott, *The Kindness of Strangers: Philanthropy and Higher Education* (New York: Rowman & Little-field, 2006).

6. James Axtell, "Dr. Wheelock's Little Red School," in *The European and the Indian: Essay in the Ethnohistory of Colonial North America* (New York: Oxford University Press, 1981) pp. 87–109.
7. John Whitehead, *The Separation of College and State* (New Haven, CT: Yale University Press, 1973).
8. James Howell Smith, *Honorable Beggars: The Middlemen of American Philanthropy* (Madison: University of Wisconsin Ph.D. Dissertation, 1968).
9. Nancy Diamond, "Catching Up: The Advance of Emory University Since World War II," in Roger L. Geiger with Susan Richardson, Editors, *History of Higher Education Annual 1999: Southern Higher Education in the Twentieth Century* (1999) vol. 19, pp. 149–183; Peter M. Ascoli, *Julius Rosenwald: The Man Who Built Sears, Roebuck and Advanced the Cause of Black Education in the American South* (Bloomington: Indiana University Press, 2006).
10. Barry D. Karl and Stanley N. Katz, "The American Private Philanthropic Foundation and the Public Sphere, 1890–1930," *Minerva* (June 1981) vol. 19, no. 2, pp. 236–270.
11. Edwin R. Embree and Julia Waxman, *Investment in People: The Story of the Julius Rosenwald Fund* (New York: Harper, 1949).
12. Dwight McDonald, *The Ford Foundation: The Men and the Millions* (New York: Reynal, 1956).
13. Ellen Condliffe Lagemann, *The Politics of Knowledge: The Carnegie Corporation, Philanthropy, and Public Policy* (Chicago: University of Chicago Press, 1989).
14. Ellen Condliffe Lagemann, *Private Power for the Public Good: A History of the Carnegie Foundation for the Advancement of Teaching* (Middletown, CT: Wesleyan University Press, 1983).
15. Bruce Kimball with Benjamin A. Johnson, "The Beginning of 'Free Money' Ideology in American Universities: Charles W. Eliot at Harvard, 1869–1909," *History of Education Quarterly* (2012) vol. 52, pp. 222–250.
16. Donald Fisher, *Fundamental Development of the Social Sciences: Rockefeller Philanthropy and the United States Social Science Research Council* (Ann Arbor: University of Michigan Press, 1993).
17. Merle Curti and Roderick Nash, "Corporations and Higher Learning," in *Philanthropy in the Shaping of American Higher Education* (New Brunswick, NJ: Rutgers University Press, 1965) pp. 238–258.
18. New Jersey Superior Judge Alfred P. Stein (1951) as quoted in John R. Thelin, "Small by Design: Resilience in an Era of Mass Higher Education," in *Meeting the Challenge: America's Independent Colleges and Universities Since 1956* (Washington, D.C.: Council of Independent Colleges, 2006) p. 12.
19. Merle Curti and Roderick Nash, *Philanthropy in the Shaping of American Higher Education* (New Brunswick, NJ: Rutgers University Press, 1965).
20. Waldemar A. Nielsen, "The Crisis of the Nonprofits," *Change* (1980) vol. 12, no. 1, pp. 23–29.
21. Rob Reich, Lacey Dorn, and Stefanie Sutton, *Any Thing Goes: Approval of Nonprofit Status by the IRS* (Stanford, CA: Stanford University Center on Philanthropy and Civil Society, 2009).
22. Erin Strout, "Universities Try to Serve a Generation of Those Who Seek to Do Good: Institutions Add Courses and Degree Programs in Nonprofit Management," *Chronicle of Higher Education* (April 3, 2008).
23. James R. Wood and James G. Houghland, Jr., "The Role of Religion in Philanthropy," in J. Van Til and Associates, Editors, *Critical Issues in American Philanthropy* (San Francisco: Jossey-Bass, 1990).
24. William T. Sturtevant, *The Artful Journey: Cultivating and Soliciting the Major Gift* (Chicago: Bonus Books, Inc., 1997); Natalie Zeman Davis, *The Gift in Sixteenth-Century France* (Madison: University of Wisconsin Press, 2000); Richard M. Titmuss, *The Gift Relationship: From Human Blood to Social Policy* (New York: The New Press, 1997); Marcel Mauss, *The Gift: The Form and Reason for Exchange in Archaic Societies*, translated by W.D. Halls (New York: W.W. Norton, 1990).
25. Richard B. Gunderman, *We Make a Life by What We Give* (Bloomington: Indiana University Press, 2008) pp. 21–22.
26. J. Travis McDearmon, "Hail to Thee, Our Alma Mater: Alumni Role Identity and the Relationship to Institutional Support Behaviors," *Research in Higher Education* (2013) vol. 54, pp. 288–302.
27. Peter Frumkin, *Strategic Giving: The Art and Science of Philanthropy* (Chicago: University of Chicago Press, 2006).
28. Robert S. Shepard, "The Credibility of Big Fund-Raising Campaigns," *Chronicle of Higher Education* (January 12, 1994).
29. Carl A. Vigeland, *Great Good Fortune: How Harvard Makes Its Money* (New York: Houghton Mifflin, 1986).
30. John R. Thelin, "Small by Design: Resilience in an Era of Mass Higher Education," in *Meeting the Challenge: America's Independent Colleges and Universities since 1956* (Washington, D.C.: Council of Independent Colleges, 2006).
31. Peter D. Hall, *Inventing the Nonprofit Sector: And Other Essays on Philanthropy, Voluntarism, and Nonprofit Organizations* (Baltimore, MD: Johns Hopkins University Press, 1992); David C. Hammack, Editor, *Making the Nonprofit Sector in the United States* (Bloomington: Indiana University Press, 1998).

32. Barbara Brittingham and Thomas Pezzullo, *The Campus Green: Fund Raising in Higher Education* (Washington, D.C.: ASHE ERIC, 1990); Margaret Rooney, *The Dean's Role in Fund Raising* (Baltimore, MD and London: Johns Hopkins University Press, 1993); Michael Worth and James W. Asp, *The Development Officer in Higher Education: Toward an Understanding of the Role* (Washington, D.C.: ASHE ERIC, 1994); Francis C. Pray, General Editor, *Handbook for Educational Fund Raising: A Guide to Successful Principles and Practices for Colleges, Universities, and Schools* (San Francisco: Jossey-Bass, 1981).
33. Frank T. Rhodes, Editor, *Successful Fund Raising for Higher Education: The Advancement of Learning* (Washington, D.C.: American Council on Education and Oryx Press sponsored by Council for Advancement and Support of Education, 1997) (Series on Higher Education); Patrice A. Welch, Editor, "Increasing Annual Giving," in *New Directions for Institutional Advancement No. 7* (San Francisco: Jossey-Bass, 1980); A. Westley Rowland, General Editor, *Handbook of Institutional Advancement: A Modern Guide to Executive Management, Institutional Relations, Fund-Raising, Alumni Administration, Government Relations, Publications, Periodicals, and Enrollment Management*, 2nd edn (San Francisco: Jossey-Bass Inc., 1986); Michael Worth and James W. Asp, *The Development Officer in Higher Education: Toward an Understanding of the Role* (Washington, D.C.: ASHE ERIC, 1994); Ralph Lowenstein, *Pragmatic Fund Raising for College Administrators and Development Officers* (Gainesville: University Press of Florida, 1997).
34. David F. Swensen, *Pioneering Portfolio Management: An Unconventional Approach to Institutional Investment* (New York: Free Press, 2000).
35. Bruce B. Vladek, "The Over-Investment Crisis in Higher Education," *Change* (1979) vol. 10, no. 11, p. 39.
36. Henry Hansmann, "Why Do Universities Have Endowments?" *Journal of Legal Studies* (January 1990) vol. 19, pp. 3–42; John R. Thelin and Richard W. Trollinger, *Time Is of the Essence: Foundations and the Policies of Limited Life and Endowment Spend-Down* (Washington, D.C.: Aspen Institute Program on Philanthropy and Social Innovation, 2009).
37. John R. Thelin and Richard W. Trollinger, "Forever Is a Long Time: Reconsidering Universities' Perpetual Endowment Policies in the Twenty First Century," *History of Intellectual Culture* (2010/2011) vol. 9, no. 1, pp. 1–17; Jack A. Clark, "Turgot's Critique of Perpetual Endowments," *French Historical Studies* (Autumn 1964) vol. 3, no. 4, pp. 495–506; Waldemar A. Nielsen, "The Pitfalls of Perpetuity," in *Inside American Philanthropy: The Dramas of Donorship* (Norman and London: University of Oklahoma Press, 1996) pp. 245–252; Francie Ostrower, *Limited Life Foundations: Motivations, Experiences, and Strategies* (The Urban Institute: Center on Nonprofits and Philanthropy, February 2009).
38. John Hawk, *For a Good Cause?: How Charitable Institutions Become Powerful Economic Bullies* (Secaucus, NJ: The Carol Publishing Group, 1997).
39. Dominic J. Brewer, Susan M. Gates, and Charles A. Goldman, *In Pursuit of Prestige: Strategy and Competition in U.S. Higher Education* (New Brunswick, NJ: Transaction Publishers, 2002); Gaye Tuchman, *Wanna Be U: Inside the Corporate University* (Chicago and London: University of Chicago Press, 2009); Marts & Lundy, *Special Report: 2013 Giving to Higher Education – The Big Gift Revival* (New York: Marts & Lundy, February 2014).
40. Paul Sullivan, "A Scholarship Program Is Dropped, and a Benefactor Sues," *New York Times* (January 23, 2016) p. B4.
41. Joel L. Fleishman, J. Scott Kohler, and Steven Schindler, *Casebook for the Foundation: A Great American Secret – How Private Wealth Is Changing the World* (New York: Public Affairs, 2007); Barry D. Karl and Stanley N. Katz, "The American Private Philanthropic Foundation and the Public Sphere, 1890–1930," *Minerva* (June 1981) vol. 19, no. 2, pp. 236–270.
42. Waldemar A. Nielsen, *The Big Foundations* (New York and London: Columbia University Press, 1972); Ellen Condliffe Lagemann, Editor, *Philanthropic Foundations: New Scholarship, New Possibilities* (Bloomington: Indiana University Press, 1999); Waldemar A. Nielsen, *The Golden Donors: A New Anatomy of the Great Foundations* (New York: Truman Talley Books of E.P. Dutton, 1985).
43. Gary A. Tobin and Aryeh K. Weinberg, *Mega-Gifts in American Philanthropy: Giving Patterns, 2001–2003* (San Francisco: Institute for Jewish & Community Research, 2007); Jerold Panas, *Mega Gifts: Who Gives Them, Who Gets Them*, 2nd edn (Medford, MA: Emerson & Church Publishers, 2005).
44. John D. Colombo and Mark A. Hall, *The Charitable Tax Exemption* (Boulder, CO: Westview Press, 2005).
45. Suzanne Perry, "Charities Get Tough Questions on Tax Breaks – and Can Expect More," *Chronicle of Higher Education* (February 15, 2013).
46. Mary B. Marcy, "Why Foundations Have Cut Back in Higher Education," *Chronicle of Higher Education* (July 23, 2003) p. A24.
47. Brad Wolverton and Sandhya Kambhampati, "Colleges Raised $1.2 Billion in Donations for Sports in 2015," *Chronicle of Higher Education* (January 27, 2016).
48. Eric Anderson and Alfred A. Moss, *Dangerous Donations: Northern Philanthropy and Southern Black Education, 1902–1930* (Columbia: University of Missouri Press, 2003).

49. Marybeth Gasman, *Envisioning Black Colleges: A History of the United Negro College Fund* (Baltimore, MD: Johns Hopkins University Press, 2007).
50. Marybeth Gasman, Benjamin Baez, and Caroline Sotello Vierennes Turner, Editors, *Understanding Minority Serving Institutions* (Albany, NY: State University of New York Press, 2008); Marybeth Gasman and Noah D. Drezner, "A Maverick in the Field: The Oram Group and Fundraising in the Black College Community During the 1970s," *History of Education Quarterly* (November 2009) vol. 49, no. 4, pp. 465–506.
51. Larissa MacFarquhar, "What Money Can Buy," *The New Yorker* (January 4, 2016) pp. 38–51.
52. Andrea Walton, Editor. *Women and Philanthropy in Education* (Bloomington and Indianapolis: Indiana University Press, 2005).
53. Noah Drezner, *Philanthropy and Fund Raising in American Higher Education* (New York: Wiley, 2011); Robert L. Payton and Michael P. Moody, *Understanding Philanthropy: Its Meaning and Mission* (Bloomington: Indiana University Press, 2008); Dwight F. Burlingame and Lamont J. Hulse, Editors, *Taking Fund Raising Seriously: Advancing the Profession and Practice of Raising Money* (San Francisco: Jossey-Bass, 1992); Dwight F. Burlingame, Editor, *Critical Issues in Fund Raising* (New York: John Wiley & Sons, Inc., 1997) p. 146.
54. Rebecca Koenig, "U.S. Colleges Raise $40 Billion; Stanford Tops List at $1.6 Billion," *Chronicle of Higher Education* (January 27, 2016).
55. Francie Ostrower, *Why the Wealthy Give: The Culture of Elite Philanthropy* (Princeton, NJ: Princeton University Press, 1995); Paul G. Schervish, "Major Donors, Major Motives: The People and the Purpose Behind Major Gifts," in Lilya Wagner and Timothy L. Seiler, Editors, *Reprising Timeless Topics* (San Francisco: Jossey-Bass, 2005), New Directions for Philanthropic Fundraising vol. 47.
56. Michael Massing, "How to Cover the One Percent," *New York Review of Books* (January 14, 2016) pp. 74–76.

Additional Readings

Robert H. Bremner, *American Philanthropy*, 2nd edn (Chicago: University of Chicago Press, 1988).
Dwight F. Burlingame, Editor, *The Responsibilities of Wealth* (Bloomington: Indiana University Press, 1992).
Dwight F. Burlingame, Editor, *Critical Issues in Fund Raising* (New York: John Wiley & Sons, Inc., 1997).
Dwight F. Burlingame and Lamont J. Hulse, Editors, *Taking Fund Raising Seriously: Advancing the Profession and Practice of Raising Money* (San Francisco: Jossey-Bass, 1992).
Charles T. Clotfelter and Thomas Ehrlich, Editors, *Philanthropy and the Nonprofit Sector in a Changing America* (Bloomington: Indiana University Press, 1999).
Scott M. Cutlip, *Fund Raising in the United States: Its Role in America's Philanthropy* (New Brunswick, NJ: Transaction Publishers, 1965, 1990).
Merle Curti and Roderick Nash, *Philanthropy in the Shaping of American Higher Education* (New Brunswick, NJ: Rutgers University Press, 1965).
Noah Drezner, *Philanthropy and Fund Raising in American Higher Education* (New York: Wiley, 2011).
Lee A. Dugatkin, *The Altruism Equation: Seven Scientists Search for the Origins of Goodness* (Princeton, NJ: Princeton University Press, 2006).
Deni Elliott, *The Kindness of Strangers: Philanthropy and Higher Education* (New York: Rowman & Littlefield, 2006).
Joel L. Fleishman, J. Scott Kohler, and Steven Schindler, *Casebook for the Foundation: A Great American Secret – How Private Wealth Is Changing the World* (New York: Public Affairs, 2007).
Claire Gaudiani, *The Greater Good: How Philanthropy Drives the American Economy and Can Save Capitalism* (New York: Henry Holt and Company, 2003).
Kay Sprinkel Grace, *Beyond Fund Raising: New Strategies for Nonprofit Innovation and Investment* (New York: John Wiley & Sons, Inc., 1997).
Kay Sprinkel Grace and Alan L. Wendroff, *High Impact Philanthropy: How Donors, Boards, and Nonprofit Organizations can Transform Communities* (New York: John Wiley & Sons, Inc., 2001).
Peter D. Hall, *Inventing the Nonprofit Sector: And Other Essays on Philanthropy, Voluntarism, and Nonprofit Organizations* (Baltimore, MD: Johns Hopkins University Press, 1992).
Margaret Rooney Hall, *The Dean's Role in Fund Raising* (Baltimore, MD and London: Johns Hopkins University Press, 1993).
David C. Hammack, Editor, *Making the Nonprofit Sector in the United States* (Bloomington: Indiana University Press, 1998).
John Hawks, *For a Good Cause?: How Charitable Institutions Become Powerful Economic Bullies* (Secaucus, NJ: The Carol Publishing Group, 1997).
Ann E. Kaplan, Editor, *Giving USA: The Annual Report on Philanthropy for the Years 1992, 2000, 2005, and 2012* (New York: The AAFRC Trust for Philanthropy, 1993).

H. Peter Karoff, Editor, *Just Money: A Critique of Contemporary American Philanthropy* (Boston: TPI Editions, 2004).

Ellen Condliffe Lagemann, *Private Power for the Public Good: A History of the Carnegie Foundation for the Advancement of Teaching* (Middletown, CT: Wesleyan University Press, 1983).

Ellen Condliffe Lagemann, *The Politics of Knowledge: The Carnegie Corporation, Philanthropy, and Public Policy* (Chicago: University of Chicago Press, 1989).

Ellen Condliffe Lagemann, Editor, *Philanthropic Foundations: New Scholarship, New Possibilities* (Bloomington: Indiana University Press, 1999).

Ralph Lowenstein, *Pragmatic Fund Raising for College Administrators and Development Officers* (Gainesville: University Press of Florida, 1997).

Waldemar A. Nielsen, *The Big Foundations* (New York and London: Columbia University Press, 1972).

Waldemar A. Nielsen, *The Golden Donors: A New Anatomy of the Great Foundations* (New York: Truman Talley Books of E.P. Dutton, 1985).

Robert L. Payton and Michael P. Moody, *Understanding Philanthropy: Its Meaning and Mission* (Bloomington: Indiana University Press, 2008).

Francis C. Pray, General Editor, *Handbook for Educational Fund Raising: A Guide to Successful Principles and Practices for Colleges, Universities, and Schools* (San Francisco: Jossey-Bass, 1981).

A. Wesley Rowland, General Editor, *Handbook of Institutional Advancement: A Modern Guide to Executive Management, Institutional Relations, Fund-Raising, Alumni Administration, Government Relations, Publications, Periodicals, and Enrollment Management*, 2nd edn (San Francisco: Jossey-Bass, 1986).

Harold J. Seymour, *Designs for Fund-Raising: Principles, Patterns, Techniques* (New York: McGraw-Hill Book Company, 1966).

John R. Thelin and Richard W. Trollinger, *Philanthropy and American Higher Education* (New York: Palgrave Macmillan, 2014).

Andrea Walton, Editor, *Women and Philanthropy in Education* (Bloomington and Indianapolis: Indiana University Press, 2005).

Andrea Walton and Marybeth Gasman, Editors, *Philanthropy, Volunteerism & Fundraising in Higher Education* (Boston: Pearson Publishing, 2008) (Association for the Study of Higher Education, ASHE Reader Series).

Burton A. Weisbrod, *The Nonprofit Economy* (Cambridge, MA: Harvard University Press, 1988).

Michael Worth and James W. Asp, *The Development Officer in Higher Education: Toward an Understanding of the Role* (Washington, D.C.: ASHE ERIC, 1994).

Olivier Zunz, *Philanthropy in America: A History* (Princeton, NJ: Princeton University Press, 2011).

11

RESEARCH AND DEVELOPMENT

The Enterprising Campus

SETTING AND OVERVIEW

The chief business of the American people is business! They are profoundly concerned with producing, buying, selling, investing and prospering in the world. I am strongly of the opinion that the great majority of people will always find these the moving impulses of our life.[1]

So observed Calvin Coolidge when he was President of the United States in 1925, in addressing a national group of newspaper editors. Little wonder, then, that the enterprising spirit associated with business has over time spread to our colleges and universities. In 1960, for example, Clark Kerr depicted the modern American university as the "Knowledge Factory."[2] Today, research universities are hailed as "Engines of Innovation."[3] Between these two end points is the story of the commercialization of higher education. Derek Bok, President Emeritus of Harvard University, has critically called it "universities in the marketplace."[4] This chapter analyzes the developments that have shaped alliances of campus and commerce over the past 60 years.

The point of entry for American universities into high-stakes enterprises was the unexpected discovery in the early 20th century that professors, especially at land grant institutions, could solve problems and devise products that boosted agricultural and industrial production. These breakthroughs, however, were sporadic and limited. A turning point was the competition for large research grants sponsored by federal agencies starting after World War II. About 20 institutions defined themselves as "federal grant universities" in which external research funding became a major source of their annual operating budgets distinct from tuition, state appropriations, and private gifts. And, over the next half-century, dozens of other aspiring universities followed their example in applying for research and development dollars, popularly known as "R&D." An added development in this era is that universities have extended their outside alliances to ventures with business and industry as well as contracting with the federal government.

How have enterprising activities by academic institutions played out among business corporations, federal agencies, Congress, private foundations, and units within universities? The answer includes analyzing the proliferation of campus-based research centers and institutes as well as affiliated start-up companies. This leaves questions about the cost–benefit trade-off of an institution's decision to enter into the R&D sweepstakes, including distinctions between "soft money" and "hard money." No account of the business of higher education would be complete without studying hospitals and clinics and the modern Academic Medical Center (AMC) as fixtures in the university structure and in the health care industry.

Professors are encouraged by their universities and the federal government to seek patents and create start-up companies. This seems to be at odds with canons of academic life. Since 1985 colleges and universities have moved into commercialization. Branding, marketing, and royalties now are part of the vocabulary of the campus as well corporations. The business of higher education has become no less than "a whole new ball game." Graduate programs are central to the business of higher education because they are linked with sponsored research. Faculty forays into patents and commercialization of applied scholarship draw from graduate students and doctoral programs for their influx of new talent as post-doctoral fellows, research associates, and laboratory assistants. Which universities persistently are outstanding in landing sponsored research grants? A list for 2014 compiled by the National Science Foundation is as follows:

Johns Hopkins University	$2,242,478,000
University of Michigan	$1,349,262,000
University of Wisconsin	$1,176,340,000
University of California, San Francisco	$1,084,031,000
University of California, San Diego	$1,067,000,000
Duke University	$1,036,813,000
University of North Carolina, Chapel Hill	$989,766,000
Stanford University	$959,247,000
University of California, Los Angeles	$948,197,000
Harvard University	$933,975,000
Massachusetts Institute of Technology	$908,807,000
Columbia University	$890,642,000
Cornell University	$883,292,000
University of Minnesota	$876,870,000
University of Pittsburgh	$856,808,000
Texas A&M University	$854,214,000
University of Pennsylvania	$828,350,000
Ohio State University	$815,075,000
Pennsylvania State University	$800,773,000
University of Texas	$794,980,000
Yale University	$772,840,000
University of California, Berkeley	$744,343,000
Georgia Institute of Technology	$725,550,000
University of California, Davis	$725,734,000
University of Florida	$708,526,000
University of Southern California	$687,222,000
Vanderbilt University	$683,890,000
Washington University of St. Louis	$664,752,000

Northwestern University	$645,333,000
Rutgers University	$644,116,000
University of Illinois	$621,733,000

Total annual federal funding for university-based research is more than $45 billion per year. The top 100 recipients represented over 80 percent of federal research spending by academic institutions. Ten universities accounted for 20 percent of all research spending. This represents the height of what Clark Kerr had called the emergence of the "federal grant university."

How does an ambitious university become part of this elite club? Institutional size is an interesting characteristic. One finding from Hugh Graham and Nancy Diamond is that large enrollment is not by itself an especially reliable indicator of research strength.[5] Some relatively small universities – such as Johns Hopkins, Vanderbilt, Caltech, the University of Chicago, and the University of California, San Diego – are among the top tier in gross federal research spending. And, using a ratio of federal grant dollars per faculty member, their intensity and effectiveness becomes more evident. A significant historical change is geographical balance. In 1950 one would be hard pressed to find a university in the South that was competitive. In the 21st century, however, this has changed dramatically with Duke, Emory, Georgia Tech, Vanderbilt, Rice, University of Texas at Austin, Texas A&M, the University of Florida, Tulane, and the University of Virginia as members of the prestigious Association of American Universities.

Do established or historic universities have an edge over newcomers? The answer is that the 20 universities who got in on the ground floor of federal grants between 1950 and 1960 have tended to stay there. There has been room for some relatively young campuses to make their mark in serious research. A good example is the University of California system in which relatively young campuses at San Diego, Davis, Irvine, and Santa Barbara have joined the older flagship campuses of Berkeley and UCLA. The University of California at Davis is yet another rising star in serious research funding. And, an additional example is the University of California, San Francisco (a campus for health sciences and medicine), which is fourth in the national rankings and illustrates the importance of medical research in federal grants.

A signal of success in the federal grant dollars sweepstakes is having a medical school where sponsored research is a high priority characterized by collaborations and alliances with such essential sciences as biology, chemistry, physics, and engineering, as well as with the social and behavioral sciences. Also, a university demonstrates a commitment to advanced graduate education, with annual conferral of 300 or more Ph.D. degrees.

Perusal of the top 100 universities in the research spending rankings indicates that a number of institutions have attempted to stake out a place and then rise in the rankings. However, since 2009 the split between the top research universities and the aspirants has increased. Many of the universities in the top ten have doubled their research grant dollars between 2009 and 2014. Outside the top 50 universities, in contrast, federal research dollars have tapered. In research, as with endowments, successful universities have become more successful over time.

How did universities acquire a strong sponsored research presence? One of the most important cases is that of Stanford University. In 1930 Stanford was a comfortable, perhaps complacent, university whose medical college was in San Francisco – geographically and psychologically apart from the main campus in Palo Alto. When the president made the decision to relocate the medical school to the main campus, it met with skepticism and even ridicule. Over time, it turned out to be a fortunate move. In addition to positioning its medical school to be a partner with science programs in biology, chemistry, and engineering, Stanford administrators made some other innovations in the 1930s and 1940s. Physicists and engineers were encouraged to cooperate across departmental lines and to seek external funding for applied research projects sponsored by nearby industrial corporations in aerospace and engineering. Thus the habit of applied research tied to outside contracts was instilled into the Stanford campus ethos before World War II. Stanford was then poised to compete for federal research grants announced by the National Science Foundation and the National Institutes of Health in the early 1950s.[6]

Each ambitious university had to write its own script for research and resources. What seems incomprehensible in retrospect is that as late as 1951 faculty and academic administrators at Harvard still had serious debates about the problems that might surface if professors as researchers were to accept federal grant dollars. One would be hard pressed to find a research university in the United States today that could envision its work without heavy reliance on federal research grants. According to historian Roger Geiger, the effective strategy over the past half-century is for an aspiring university to identify "steeples of excellence" within its campus – and then concentrate on programs and units to succeed in applying for federal research grants.[7]

ISSUES

Monetization

One distinctive characteristic of the modern enterprising university is its strong ties with word improvisation and dubious word usage. These give little pause because the prospect of massive funding usually trumps grammar. Corporate executives, governors, and university presidents now frequently use as a verb the word *incentivize* – ostensibly to build in attention to goals and rewards. Most crucial in the new lexicon is the primacy of the word *monetization*. This comes to the fore in policy planning discussions. It even includes faculty and tenure promotion guidelines at some universities, where the crucial question is not only whether a particular line of applied research has brought in external funding; rather, an equally important consideration is whether this funded research project also will lead to a *product*, which in turn connects to a measurable flow of profits back into the university department and the researcher who initiated the research.[8]

Corporate and Industrial Alliances in Research

Universities with engineering programs and other applied sciences have relied on contract projects with local and regional industries since the early 1900s. The Massachusetts Institute of Technology, Georgia Institute of Technology, and California Institute of Technology (originally known as "Throop Institute") were among early pioneers. Their projects were not glamorous and provided necessary supplements to tuition income. In the 1930s Stanford University was successful in taking on projects with Northern California aeronautical companies. Since the early 1980s "biotech" fields have increased presence. Today university-based pharmaceuticals in applied research has moved to center stage.

Branding

"Branding" in higher education is a tradition that has deep roots at American colleges and universities, most of which are tied to honoring major donors whose fortunes were made in commercial enterprises. Consider the following roster of high-profile college and university names:

Yale
Brown
Duke
Vanderbilt
Tulane
Cornell
Harvard
Stanford
Rice
Johns Hopkins
Clark
Stetson

Each and all represent the naming of an institution of higher learning in honor of a major donor. It reaches back to the 18th century when the governing board of "The College of Rhode Island and Providence Plantations," which had been chartered in 1764, announced in 1803 that the institution would be renamed if a benefactor were to contribute $5,000 dollars. Nicholas Brown, Jr., an alumnus of the Class of 1786, was a prosperous merchant from a prominent Providence family who accepted the challenge and made the pledge. The rest is history – and the institution endures and prospers by its changed official name, "Brown University."

Branding Brown University was distinctive but not unique, as the preceding honor roll of family names and institutions indicates. All these benefactors were indelibly linked to commercial and industrial wealth. Hence, the names set precedents for both "institutional branding" and "corporate sponsorship" – even though those terms were not used specifically a century ago. Duke University was based on and associated in the public eye with fortunes in tobacco and utilities. Rice University (originally chartered as Rice Institute in 1910) was beholden to the wealth made by William Marsh Rice in oil, timber, and merchandising. Commodore Vanderbilt had made his fortune in ship lines and railroads. Stetson University, with the appropriate nickname of the "Hatters," came out of the famous (and lucrative) hat manufacturing company. Other sources of business wealth that led to branding at colleges included oil refining, steel manufacturing, department stores, telegraph lines, and brewing. On balance, the American tradition in supporting colleges was that the "Captains of Industry" often were "Captains of Erudition." Connections between campus and commerce were celebrated as part of institutional saga and heritage. Emory University in Atlanta, for example, has songs and annual gatherings in which freshmen students celebrate their new alma mater as the "Coca-Cola School!"

The logos, pennants, decals, and television promotionals initiated by university intercollegiate athletics teams have been the driver in serious academic branding. First, starting around 2000 university athletics departments edged away from a benign, laissez-faire attitude toward unauthorized usage of university athletic logos by various manufacturers of T-shirts and other sports paraphernalia. Athletics departments obtained and enforced copyright and trademark rights. University administration followed the example of intercollegiate athletics and launched systematic branding campaigns, including licensure and trademark registration. The result was both lucrative and protective, ensuring that seals and symbols would be broadcast in the media and on products – and that universities would receive royalties for use of their trademarks.

One thinks of commercial products and industrial organizations as the dominant force in branding as part of American life. Kleenex, Xerox, Google, IBM, RCA, Starbucks, Kentucky Fried Chicken, CBS, NBC, ABC, Yahoo, Amazon, and numerous other brand names are familiar and recognized by the American public. Trademark infringement is prosecuted vigorously – and "knock off" products are outright illegal. So, the conventional wisdom is that once again higher education belatedly imitated businesses. In fact, elevating "branding" to a sophisticated, comprehensive, and expensive organizational strategy owes much of its prominence to academe. David Aaker, Professor of Business at the University of California, Berkeley, has been considered the guru of corporate branding. And, eventually, his own campus and others enlisted his services – and those of other consulting firms – to undertake comprehensive institutional branding strategies. The University of Oregon, for example, harnessed its gifts from and ties to Nike athletics to market and copyright its distinctive yellow "O" branding initiative, which was estimated to have a total cost of $20 million – and which had been "seeded" by a $5 million gift. In 2016 this included the university's multi-year contract with 16over90, a Philadelphia-based branding agency, which was estimated to cost $3.4 million. By 2016 "branding" and "marketing" were fixtures in college and university budgets for promotions and public relations. The new organizational belief is that this is necessary if a university wishes to be competitive for students, funds, and reputation.[9]

Revenue-Producing Academic Programs and Projects

The model for high-powered, high-stakes university enterprise in the late 20th and early 21st centuries is a chain that starts with campus-based faculty research, leading to discovery, validation and confirmation, and then commercialization and investment for the host university. At best, a university's incorporated URF (university research foundation) employs its patenting and licensing efforts, which enables university innovations to advance from the campus research laboratory to the marketplace. This ideal imposes a "best-case scenario" algorithm that understates the detours and disappointments. It is, however, the model to which most research universities ascribe. How did it develop?

The two most fertile sources for early ventures in the late 19th and early 20th centuries came from the "A&M" side of the land grant universities. Agriculture and mechanics (engineering) lent themselves to problem solving and practical applications associated with economic productivity. They also were among the few campus units that could count on any external funds through federal legislation for experimental stations. One of the leaders in outreach and economic innovation was the University of Wisconsin, committed to the "Wisconsin Idea" of statewide service. Starting around 1894 agricultural chemists turned their attention to problems of fair trade and marketing in the state's large dairy industry. Their various and collective efforts culminated in the early 1900s with University of Wisconsin chemist Stephen Babcock's test for determining quickly the percentage of butterfat in a container of milk – a pioneering example where applied science improved the standards and productions of the dairy industry, and also promoted fair compensation for sellers.

The University of Wisconsin once again was central to formalizing applied research into the campus via incorporation. The Wisconsin Alumni Research Foundation – well known by its acronym, WARF – was founded in 1925 to manage a discovery by a university professor, Harry Steenbock, who invented the process for using ultraviolet radiation to add vitamin D to milk and other foods. In this era the standard practice for college and university professors and researchers was simply to leave their inventions unpatented. Rather than leaving the invention unpatented, Steenbock used $300 of his own money to file for a patent. He received commercial interest from Quaker Oats but declined the company's initial offer. Instead, Steenbock sought a way to protect discoveries made by UW–Madison faculty, ensure use of the ideas for public benefit, and bring any financial gains back to the university. His concept gained support from the dean of the College of Agriculture, and the dean of the Graduate School. This included a dean soliciting the interest and financial support of wealthy university alumni in Chicago and New York. Eventually the strategy was to gain verbal pledges from a number of alumni, nine of whom would eventually contribute $100 each. According to the WARF website,

> The UW Board of Regents approved the plan on June 22, 1925, and the organization's charter was filed with the Secretary of State of Wisconsin on November 14 that same year. The organization was named the Wisconsin Alumni Research Foundation to reflect both its governing body of five alumni and its mission to promote, encourage and aid scientific investigation and research at UW–Madison. Each year, WARF contributes more than $70 million to fund additional UW–Madison research. The university refers to WARF's annual gifts as its "margin of excellence" funding. WARF currently licenses nearly 100 UW–Madison technologies each year. As of 2014, WARF had an endowment of $2.6 billion. WARF also works in partnership with a variety of other entities including WiSys Technology Foundation, WiCell Research Institute and the Morgridge Institute for Research.

WARF represents a best-case scenario for an historical, enduring university research foundation. Elsewhere, a number of universities have moved into the research product development arena. An early example of commercial success that has become popular with the American public is "Gatorade." It was originally formulated in 1965 by a team of scientists at the University of Florida College of Medicine. Following a request from the Florida Gators football head coach, Gatorade was created to help athletes by acting as a replacement for body fluids lost during physical exertion. The earliest versions of the beverage consisted of a mixture of water, sodium, sugar, potassium, phosphate, and lemon juice. According to institutional lore, the story is that "Ten players on the University of Florida football team tested the first version of Gatorade during practices and games in 1965, and the tests were deemed successful." The new product benefited from members of the football team who credited Gatorade for helping them to their first Orange Bowl win over the Georgia Tech Yellow Jackets in 1967, at which point the drink gained traction within the athletic community. That hardly satisfied Food and Drug Administration protocols, but it was persuasive in the marketplace.[10]

Crest toothpaste also stands out as an icon in the connection of American product development and research originated at a university campus. It was introduced in the United States in 1953. At first it used stannous fluoride, marketed as "Fluoristan" (which was also the original brand name it was sold under when first introduced in 1954 – the name of the product was later changed from "Fluoristan" to "Crest *with* Fluoristan"). The composition of the toothpaste had been developed by three professors at Indiana University and was patented by one of them. Procter & Gamble paid royalties for use of the patent and thus financed a new university dental research institute. Initial funding for the professors' research came from a modest seed money grant for summer research awarded by the IU Foundation, which had been incorporated in 1937 and directed by an Indiana University alumnus best known as a star baseball player, William Armstrong. The IU Foundation clearly states that its mission is to "maximize private support for Indiana University by fostering lifelong relationships with key stakeholders and providing advancement leadership and fundraising services for campuses and units across the university." Closely related is the IU Foundation's statement of its vision: "As leaders among our peers in higher education and philanthropy, Indiana University and the Indiana University Foundation are partners in marshalling resources to provide the university with the philanthropic assets necessary to achieve its aspirations."

The progression of commercial implications and applications started with agricultural extension services and their innovations in genetics and crop yields. At times, agricultural extension services were both lucrative and basic, as in the case of state fertilizer law, requiring farmers to subject the fertilizer they were planning to sell to chemical composition tests conducted by university agronomists. And, a university stood to gain when a team of their faculty scientists developed a rat poison that was marketable and effective. The presence of applied research with economic benefits eventually extended to mechanical engineering. Later, a big change was the emergence of electrical engineering as an applied field. Foremost in American iconography were William Hewlett and David Packard, young Stanford graduates who set up a workshop and laboratory in a garage not far from the Stanford campus. Illustrative of the changes in state and local economies – and their relations with universities – is that as late as 1960 the Santa Clara Valley's major economy was in orchards of fruit trees – notably apricots and plums. Over time, this subsided, being replaced by electrical engineers and microchips, leading to the flourishing of "Silicon Valley."

This displacement from prunes to microchips did not necessarily mean the demise of Northern California agriculture. Across the Bay in Berkeley, the University of California's College of Agriculture was world-renowned for its scientific research – much of which would provide the patents and processes central to the development of California's "Agribusiness" based in the state's Central Valley.

Another heralded success story of campus and community and corporate cooperation was the creation of the electronics belt in the greater Boston area. After World War II Boston faced the loss of traditional manufacturing and industries – ranging from textile mills that moved to the South to publishing houses relocated to New York City. Alumni and professors from the Massachusetts Institute of Technology, joined eventually by new talent and other colleges, led to the creation of numerous high-tech corporations – many housed along Route 128.[11]

Research Parks

A landmark event in campus and commercialization is investing in off-campus research parks. The "Research Triangle" of the Raleigh–Durham–Chapel Hill region of North Carolina stands out as the most enduring and prosperous. However, elsewhere the research park movement seldom fulfilled its promises. Land and features such as water systems, sewers, electricity, sidewalks, and roads meant a huge investment, usually shared by the state university and its state government. Often, after limited success in attracting viable commercial companies, many have either folded or been turned into retirement villages or other real estate developments.[12] The campus research park was, perhaps, a plausible idea. Over time, however, their cost–benefit in joining campus and commerce has been scant and disappointing.

CHARACTERS AND CONSTITUENTS

Colleges of Medicine, Hospitals, and Academic Medical Centers

The single most important development in academic structure and pursuits since World War II has been the fusion of medical schools with advanced scientific research in a variety of fields. It is dramatized by the proliferation of relatively new departments with the prefix of "bio" – as in biochemistry, bioengineering, and biophysics – to name just a few central examples. In most cases these new academic units, whether departments or research institutes, have their home in the College of Medicine of the Academic Medical Centers (AMCs). The net result is multiple. It has transformed the preparation and then education of medical doctors – long the staple of colleges of medicine. Furthermore, it has closed the historical gap that separated professional education in the health sciences from Ph.D. programs in biology, chemistry, physics, and engineering. At a university with an AMC it is not unusual to have one-third to one-half of all faculty appointments in the health sciences or medical campus. It means that medical centers either start or annex such fields as toxicology, nutrition, rehabilitation sciences, and early childhood development. Professional education and pursuits often face a rough split between the research side and the clinical side – each with their distinctive strengths and foibles. In both cases, financial accounting becomes increasingly prevalent. A researcher who fails to land adequate outside grant funding will have trouble affording the square footage fees for laboratory space. Meanwhile, clinicians such as primary care physicians will be expected to meet a certain number of patients per day whose fees pay clinic salaries and other operating costs. The enterprising side of AMCs often has led to structural innovations. For example, quite apart from most educational programs and departments, university medical centers often create their own endowments along with a foundation for billing and receiving clinical fees. Typically this is named the "UMSF" – standing for "University Medical Services Foundation" – a private corporation affiliated with yet distinct from the public or private university.

The high visibility and marketing of AMCs and medical colleges is suggested by the series of full-page advertisements that Mount Sinai Hospital and Medical Center ran in 2015 in the *New York Times*. These projected a bold new model of the M.D. program. Drawing inspiration from Silicon Valley and its high-tech start-up companies, medical education for changing the world emphasized now that failure was part of success, that impatience was a good characteristic when the aim was to solve big problems. The message for a new generation of medical pioneers was that the need was for a culture of innovation, which often included disruption.

These advertisements are both exhilarating and expensive. No doubt they are inspiring and serve to attract individuals who are energetic and talented. One also suspects that a full-page advertisement in the *New York Times* carries out goals other than trying to reach prospective medical students and researchers. It probably was cast as an effective, dramatic way to acquire prestige and a following among leaders in New York City as a public relations vehicle rather than as a student recruitment tool.

Among the 125 major American colleges of medicine, governance is divided into several categories – a placement that is consequential for the academic life of faculty, students, and administrators. A crucial question is how a teaching hospital is joined with a college of medicine. Does the college of medicine oversee the hospital? Or, in marked contrast, is the teaching hospital owned by the state government? Are the two units separate?

At a flagship state university with an Academic Medical Center, the teaching hospital alone may constitute as much as 25 to 33 percent of the total university operating budget. This is apart from the academic budget for, for example, the colleges of medicine, nursing, allied health, dentistry, and pharmacy. John A. Kastor, a distinguished medical doctor, has undertaken detailed case studies of administrative tensions at teaching hospitals, including those of the University of Pennsylvania and Johns Hopkins University.[13] Kastor cautions that generalizations about AMCs are difficult due to the distinctive culture and structure of each one. His case study of Penn suggests that massive financial problems gave the university president a reason to rein in the medical center and its affiliated hospitals and clinics. In contrast, at Johns Hopkins University, a combination of customary and structural arrangements buffered its medical center from over-spending and other financial problems. Yet deliberations between the university president and the head of the medical center eventually led to dissolution of an historical arrangement in which the hospital and the medical college were separate.

Law Schools

Law schools have traditionally been a source of prestige, revenue, and robust enrollments. In 2016 the American Bar Association accredited 205 law schools, which offered the Juris Doctor (J.D.) degree. Typically about 46,000 law students receive their degrees each year. Although there is no formalized "pre-law" curriculum, law schools have an advantage in academic selectivity in that applicants must have a bachelor's degree and in most cases rank fairly high in their graduating class. Additional screening and selectivity come from the requirement that applicants take the LSAT (Law School Admissions Test) offered by the Educational Testing Service.

Classes taught at law schools typically rely on lecture format, which can enroll additional paying students without driving up faculty salary expenses – until the lecture hall is full. Unlike counterparts in medicine or the sciences, law schools do not require expensive laboratories or technology. A law school does not have to offer small seminars. Furthermore, the law curriculum is set and often selective – the J.D. degree is a three-year course of study. It contrasts drastically with the open-ended nature of a Ph.D. program in which many students require between six and ten years to complete their dissertations.

Little wonder, then, that many universities added a new law school or expanded enrollment in their existing one. By 2005, however, there were signs of student market saturation. Some partial estimates are that the proliferation of new, unselective law schools had graduated a large number of job candidates in what was already a buyer's market. Second, availability of affordable software for conducting computerized tasks such as searching case law reduced some of the need for law clerks and entry-level lawyers in law firms. Third, many law firms moved away from the custom of a pyramid-shaped organizational structure, where the top tier was reserved for those selected for partnership. Fourth, a few high-profile episodes – such as the bankruptcy of the large, prestigious New York City firm of Dewey and LeBoeuf – added to a growing crisis of confidence within the profession.

Business Schools

Starting in the 1970s the Master's in Business Administration (M.B.A.) degree has been a success story in enrollment growth, revenues for universities, and professional benefits for new degree recipients. For 2011–2012 there were 191,530 master's degrees in business conferred – slightly more than 25 percent of all master's degrees completed that year. Often companies and firms pay the tuition and expenses for promising members of their management team. This has led to the popularity of "Executive M.B.A." programs that streamline the time to degree completion while minimizing time spent away from the workplace. Over time these have included "weekend" formats, and by the early 1980s, reliance on interactive television broadcasts, and, since around 2000, Internet-based degree programs – all of which coexist with traditional, on-campus full-time residency programs that take about two years of full-time study. Part of this success story is its dependency on belief and loyalty with only incidental connection to documented learning or skills. An M.B.A. degree is not tied to any professional certification or licensure. There is no professional standards board. Nor is there any agreement as to what exactly completing an M.B.A. degree imparts to its recipients. All this pales alongside the public and business perception around 2000 that an M.B.A. degree was prestigious! However, in the past decade the public image and employer views of the M.B.A. have changed. The proliferation of online M.B.A. degree programs extended access but at the same time tended to dilute the perceived prestige of the degree. The abundance of new M.B.A. degree recipients on the job market meant that some employers could hire an M.B.A. at no more expense than they previously would have paid for a job applicant with a bachelor's degree in business administration.

Master's Degree Programs

Although the M.B.A. probably is the most successful master's degree program, it is hardly alone. Paramount prestige goes to Ph.D. programs, a phenomenon that has masked the extraordinary appeal and success of master's degree programs offered by a wide range of institutions – and whose enrollment of both full-time and part-time students has substantially extended affordable access to graduate education. In addition to the aforementioned 191,530 M.B.A. degrees, other fields accounted for 563,251 degrees – a grand total of 754,781. Leaders among master's degrees included Education with 178,029 and health professions with 83,882, followed by Engineering with 40,230 and Public Administration and Social Services Administration at 41,680. Credentialing and professional licensure in a range of professional fields has been a driver in these enrollments.

Ph.D. Programs

Ph.D. programs at colleges and universities in the United States persist as a success story in both their productivity and quality. They are the most respected and prestigious in the world. What a difference a century makes! On the eve of World War I, only about 14 or 15 institutions were regarded as "Great American Universities." Even within this small cluster, advanced scholarship and mentoring of graduate students was a marginal activity. Looking at the period from 1898 to 1908, Columbia, Harvard, and the University of Chicago each conferred about four to five Ph.D.s per year. Universities responded to the "national need" for Ph.D.s after World War II so that from the decade 1960–1970, the annual number of doctorates awarded rose persistently, reaching about 170,000 in 2011–2012. Universities that consistently have conferred the most Ph.D.s each year include a roster of 36 institutions, each of which had at least 400 Ph.D.s completed in 2011–2012:

University of California, Berkeley	834
University of Michigan, Ann Arbor	825
University of Illinois at Urbana-Champaign	811
University of Texas, Austin	807
University of Wisconsin, Madison	793
University of Minnesota, Twin Cities	721
Stanford University	706
Harvard University	694
University of Florida	692
The Ohio State University	691
UCLA	687
Texas A&M, College Station	653
Pennsylvania State University	651
Purdue University	645
University of Maryland	587
University of Washington	580
Massachusetts Institute of Technology	573
University of California, Davis	553
University of California, San Diego	513
Cornell University	503
Michigan State University	478
Georgia Institute of Technology	473
University of North Carolina, Chapel Hill	472
Johns Hopkins University	456
Columbia University	454
University of Southern California	448
Virginia Tech University	444
Arizona State University	442
University of Pennsylvania	442
City University of New York	427
University of Arizona	415
University of Georgia	413
University of California, Irvine	409
North Carolina State University	407
Indiana University, Bloomington	402
University of Chicago	401

If one extends the roster to the top 50 doctoral degree-granting universities, a number of prestigious institutions crop up – such as Yale with 379, University of Virginia with 374, Princeton University with 351, the University of Colorado, Boulder with 343, and Duke University with 342. It's a formidable group that shows distribution across all regions of the United States, a mix of private and public institutions, and inclusion of numerous relatively young institutions and newcomers to doctoral education. Extending the list from, for example, the top 10 or 20 to the top 50 is important because it brings into the profile some prestigious universities with relatively small enrollments – at which graduate education enjoys priority and prestige.

The top 50 account for about 16,000 Ph.D.s. One is left with the riddle: how do we account for the remaining 154,000 doctorates awarded in a year? Using the Carnegie Classification of 2014, an estimated 300 institutions confer at least 20 doctorates per year. These are roughly partitioned into three clusters – those that combine doctoral programs with very high research spending (109), a second tier with "high" research spending (99), and a remaining group that confer doctorates but do not show large-scale federal grant activity (90). If you exclude the 48,000 law degrees and the health science doctorates (M.D.s and Pharm.D.s, Doctors of Veterinary Medicine, et al.) that used to be classified as "first professional" degrees, you are left with 51,000 "research doctorates" conferred in 2012 and distributed as follows:

Life Sciences	12,045	(23.6%)
Physical Sciences	8,952	(17.6%)
Social Sciences	8,353	(16.4%)
Engineering	8,427	(16.5%)
Education	4,802	(9.4%)
Humanities	5,503	(10.8%)
Other	2,926	(5.7%)

It leaves a large distribution across hundreds of marginal doctoral-granting institutions. "Mission creep" lures presidents and provosts to be tempted to introduce one or two programs so that their institution can henceforth be in the ranks of "doctoral-granting universities." Second, newcomers tend to add doctoral programs in inexpensive and less prestigious fields. It's unlikely one is going to find a university new to graduate studies deciding to add a Ph.D. program in physics. Laboratories, faculty salaries, facilities, journal subscriptions, and research start-up packages are expensive – and the field is well established elsewhere. A new phenomenon that partially explains the distribution of scattered new doctoral degrees has been the proliferation of online doctoral programs.

A traditional reward for outstanding graduate students in highly competitive fields, especially in the sciences, has been post-doctoral fellowships. They conferred both prestige and an adequate stipend that allowed a new Ph.D. recipient to have two or three years working as the junior researcher for an established senior professor in a laboratory. This customary accolade has been tarnished in recent years so that its "rewards" are increasingly suspect. In the arena of high-stakes funded research, there is increasing concern that "post-docs" are abused. Consider, for example, a case in which a post-doc in biological sciences receives $34,000 per year as a research assistant for a professor at a university in New York or Chicago. The arrangement works largely because of the student's belief that such experience eventually will lead to a tenure track faculty appointment at a good university. Today, however, there is no guarantee that this will be the outcome. At the same time, there is warranted concern that the sponsoring professor can keep the new Ph.D. in suspension indefinitely as an apprentice, beholden and subservient, especially if one is dependent on a favorable reference for future job applications.

COMPLEXITIES AND CONFLICTS: IMPLICATIONS FOR DECISION-MAKING

Corporations versus Campus

Thorstein Veblen was foremost in a long tradition of criticism about intrusion of corporate values into the American campus. First, he pointed out the preponderance of business executives appointed to college boards of trustees. Second, starting in the 1890s there were numerous examples of board and business censorship of scholars, especially in economics and public policy analyses. Third, this kind of board composition weighted heavily toward corporate executives tended to favor proactive movement into research initiatives that held out the promise of product development and profits.[14] These emphases in turn have left university research units and their professors susceptible to temptations and abuses.

Research Fraud

One impetus for research fraud has been the high stakes of a professor getting tenure or promotion. Dependence on external funding means that young researchers are under pressure to conduct and then quickly publish research that shows dramatic new findings. The impression among federal agencies is that such pressures have led to increased incidents – or, at least, increased reports – of research fraud. In 2009, for example, at the University of Kentucky Medical Center, a faculty researcher at the Pediatric Research Institute was working with a lab technician to prepare materials for a presentation. As part of the scientific report, the researcher reviewed the 2005 federal grant and happened to notice that the principal investigator at the university had made a commitment to use special genetically altered mice for the research on childhood diabetes. The principal investigator had not had the special mice ready until 2007 or 2008 – years after the grant had started. The faculty researcher reported the incident to university administrators. The principal investigator cast blame on the faculty researcher who had raised the question. Subsequent investigations by both the university and federal authorities concluded that false information in the project had then "spiraled out to numerous scientific papers, progress reports and other applications." According to reporters, the faculty researcher who was the "whistle-blower" lost his job and his research career was permanently damaged.[15] The newspaper's editorial emphasized that the university's top research value was money – and that it and other universities did not do enough to protect or reward whistle-blowers. It elaborated:

> Indeed, the picture that arises is of a research community driven not by scientific inquiry, but by ability to bring in money, of research assistants who rely upon the success and favor of their superstar bosses to advance, so much so that they're reluctant to complain about long hours, harassment, or even fudging the data.

The particulars of this incident at one university were hardly isolated, as a 2004 paper in the *Journal of Medical Ethics* noted that "medical schools have policies and committees about ethics, but that rubber rarely meets the road." In sum, for many universities, the "Research system was 'Badly Broken'."[16]

The prospect of commercial support for academic research from time to time has led to dubious research practices. Comparable to point shaving in college basketball scandals, the temptation is not necessarily for blatant fraud. Rather, it is subtle, with emphasis on having research be equivocal in its findings. A case that made national front-page headlines in 2015 involved Coca-Cola's substantial funding at a university research center. According to articles in the *New York Times* published in August 2015, Coca-Cola, "the world's largest producer of sugary beverages," provided substantial financial support for researchers at several university institutes and centers for studies which direct attention to exercise rather than sugar consumption and diet, as a primary source of obesity.[17] This included the University of South Carolina, the University of Colorado School of Medicine, and the West Virginia University School of Public Health. An editorial in the *New York Times* brought attention to "Coke's Sugarcoated Research," noting that

> respected scientists … say Coca-Cola will have no control over what they study or say, but corporate sponsorship tends to affect a study's results. An analysis published in PLOS Medicine found that studies financed by Coca-Cola, PepsiCo, the American Beverage Association and the sugar industry were five times more likely to find no link between sugary drinks and weight gain than studies reporting no industry sponsorship or financial conflicts of interest.[18]

Furthermore, these industrial associations sponsored paid speakers for conventions or educational courses of dieticians and nutritionists to offset research that had reported that sugar and diet had a disproportionate impact on weight gain nationwide.

Financial Abuse in Applied Academic Research

In addition to research fraud that involves fabrication of data and results, high-stakes projects with grant and/or corporate funding have increased the susceptibility of university researchers to financial fraud. For example, in 2015 a "former high-profile electrical engineering professor" was indicted on racketeering charges, nearly five years after his career at the Georgia Institute of Technology collapsed over a wireless chip start-up company he founded. The former professor was indicted on two counts of racketeering and was accused of a scheme that robbed the university of more than $1 million. In allegedly mismanaging university funds and other research to benefit his start-up wireless company, the professor stood as "an especially vivid illustration of the volatile reaction that can occur when professors mix academic and entrepreneurial ambitions." He had been considered a "star" and one of the most successful members of the university faculty upon whom the university aspired to build "its reputation as a hotbed of start-ups that would spin out from the university with ideas and technologies gestated there by students and professors."[19]

This high-profile case at Georgia Tech is hardly typical of university researchers involved in commercial applications. At the same time it is not isolated. Rather, it provides an alert to a widespread opportunity and a recurrent syndrome of misconduct that does, indeed, take place at many research universities. For example, in August 2014, at the University of Kentucky a mining engineering professor was accused of (and eventually pled guilty to) fraud. Graduate students filed allegations that he required them to work without compensation on his private clients' projects. Additional records from the university included allegations that the professor had created fake invoices for $62,000 for travel, hotels, and meals and $9,000 for equipment – all of which he had double billed, one set to the university and one set to private clients. He also fabricated consulting invoices for $31,000 and then paid research assistants more than $312,000 from university grants even though the work was done for his private consulting clients.[20]

Research Abuse of Human Subjects

The high stature of modern university-based scientific research also makes it susceptible to abuses. Reporters have uncovered examples of flagrant abuses in ethics, especially in the poor treatment of human subjects. Infamous cases include the Tuskegee study on penicillin and syphilis, which deliberately used a group of African American men who were imprisoned as a "control group" and given placebo treatments. In the years immediately following World War II, one instance of human subjects abuse took place at a residential school for special needs children in Massachusetts in which the Quaker Oats company sponsored a study of the effects of radioactive iodine. And, from 1946 to 1948 a federally funded experiment on venereal disease whose principal researchers were at the University of Pittsburgh knowingly and flagrantly abused inmates in Guatemalan prisons in their experiments.[21] In 2001 Johns Hopkins University was ordered to cease all federally funded research on humans following disclosure of the death of a volunteer in an asthma experiment.[22] In another research project dealing with the effects of lead paint on health, Johns Hopkins University researchers had allowed inner-city children living in old apartment buildings whose walls were knowingly painted with lead paint years before to be subjects in the research experiment. It leaves open to serious reconsideration who and how human subjects are recruited, advised, and compensated in "big science" research. Consider, for example, the following poster on a public bulletin board in the lobby of a university hospital:

RESEARCH OPPORTUNITY FOR OPIATE USERS

One might think plausibly that this was an invitation to participate in research as, well, a researcher. After all, it was posted in an Academic Medical Center. In smaller print, however, the poster states:

> If you currently use Lortab, Percocet, OxyContin and/or prescription opiates recreationally (for nonmedical reasons) and are interested in participating in a research study, please call the Center for Human Behavioral Sciences for a confidential interview and to see if you qualify.... The purpose of this study is to learn more about the strength and effects of prescription opioids. You must be able to make several visits over a period of about 7 weeks. You will be paid for your participation.

This is the proverbial deal that sounds too good to be true. It attracts an unwitting hospital visitor's attention on misleading grounds. It is disingenuous because its headline resembles an announcement for students as research assistants. It has no intention of providing opiate users a research opportunity. It cultivates and then exploits individuals who are vulnerable, unwitting – and probably are not going to get much pay or other benefit from this alleged "research opportunity." It provides a mild example of how for years medical research has sought out subjects, whether inmates or unemployed

– and even university students. Such recruitment probably leads to the explanation and justification that, after all, how else will medical researchers get the subjects they need? That is a good question and a big problem – but it does not excuse the path of least resistance strategy of enticing those who are at risk to be subjects in research projects that can be harmful.

Beyond this graphic, individual incident of the bulletin board poster, one finds numerous examples of recurrent problems in the ethics of how subjects and patients are treated in university-based research studies. According to a professor writing an op-ed essay in the *New York Times*, the University of Minnesota Medical School (where he taught medical ethics) had long tolerated concerns about alleged research scandals. This had included a felony conviction and a Food and Drug Administration research disqualification for a faculty member in the psychiatry department and other abuses over a 25-year period.[23]

A question that surfaces for consideration by all AMCs is whether customary university reliance on an institutional review board (widely known at universities as "the IRB") composed of academic volunteers is adequate. A concern is that the IRB protocols are more of an honor code than a rigorous, ongoing review of medical studies and experiments. Some argue that often this reliance is inadequate given the pressures for obtaining external grants and publishing findings that face university researchers.

University Hospitals as Businesses

The line between nonprofit organizations and commercial businesses often is blurred in the contemporary era of enterprising universities. At best this fluidity may indicate that universities are responsive to the marketplace along with "meeting societal needs." At worst, they have drifted from their historic roles of serving the public and carrying out educational goals. The commercial character and financial volume of the health care industry associated with the AMCs has not gone unnoticed by county and municipal governments, especially when these urban units face declining local tax revenues.

The question is whether hospitals, especially university hospitals, are fulfilling their obligations as charitable organizations. The city of Pittsburgh filed suit challenging the University of Pittsburgh's Medical Center's tax-exempt status, "saying that the medical center should pay some payroll taxes and more property taxes, estimated to total about $20 million annually." The city's lead lawyer on the case wrote to the city solicitor, "Its commitment to charity is dwarfed by its preoccupation with profits."[24] According to official reports, the university hospital had excess operating revenues of nearly $1 billion and reserves of nearly $3 billion. Twenty of its executives were paid salaries of more than $1 million annually. The city attorney claimed that the university hospital spent only about 2 percent of its net patient revenues on charity care. These proportions led to the recommendation to the city that such a hospital did not deserve its customary tax-exempt status. This led to predictable protest and defensiveness from hospital boards and executives. Despite their objections and denials, the AMC officials in this case had to acknowledge the dictum that if a nonprofit institution acts like a business, the likelihood increases that it will be treated and categorized as a business. The same principles also can be applied to a wide range of academic enterprises and centers and institutes, especially in cities where nonprofits are large landowners and also where traditional industries such as commercial manufacturing have moved out, leaving the municipal tax base depleted.

Setting University Priorities

Larry Cuban's 1999 case study of Stanford University documented the unplanned but decisive transformation in the balance of teaching and research at Stanford, with the conclusion that research and scholarship trumped teaching. Not far from Stanford University, the University of California administration approved its new College of Natural Resources (formerly, the College of Agriculture) to enter into a long-term contract with a commercial company, Novartis, whose substantial financial support for faculty and research carried with it provisions for Novartis to have first access to many of the faculty's research findings – and, in part, to determine funding priorities on faculty research projects. The result is that as colleges and universities become more entrepreneurial in a post-industrial economy, they focus on knowledge less as a public good and more as a commodity to be capitalized on in profit-oriented activities. In *Academic Capitalism and the New Economy*, higher education scholars Sheila Slaughter and Gary Rhoades detail the aggressive engagement of higher education institutions in the United States in what is called the knowledge-based economy. They analyzed the efforts of colleges and universities to develop, market, and sell research products, educational services, and consumer goods in the private marketplace. A challenge was that universities still wanted to maintain customary and legal status as educational, not-for-profit educational and charitable organizations that receive federal, state, and local tax exemptions. Slaughter and Rhoades tracked changes in both policy and practice, revealing new social networks and circuits of knowledge creation and dissemination, as well as new organizational structures and expanded managerial capacity to link higher education institutions and markets. They depict an ascendant academic capitalist knowledge/learning regime expressed in its operationalization and accounting of faculty work, departmental activity, and administrative behavior. Clarifying the regime's internal contradictions, they note the public subsidies embedded in new revenue streams and this shift in emphasis from serving student customers to leveraging resources from them.

CONNECTIONS AND QUESTIONS

Entrepreneurship as a Field of Study in the University

Thanks to numerous large bequests nationwide, centers and institutes for student enterprise and creativity have sprouted. The intent is to increase the odds of the future equivalent of the microchip or Gatorade by formalizing the creative technology that once had been left to chance or individual initiative. One way to cast the situation is that a college or university asks, with a combination of longing and curiosity, how might it be the alma mater of the next Mark Zuckerberg?

This has led to a groundswell of initiatives in which some colleges and universities have created formal programs and structures to attract and encourage undergraduates to be enterprising. Stanford University, indelibly linked to Silicon Valley, focused both its student recruitment and faculty relations so that it has come to be hailed as "Start Up U." Drawing from its legacy of alumni Hewlett and Packard and alumni who have been enterprising leaders in the digital and electronic transformation of new American companies, both the faculty culture and the formal course and facilities have welcomed risk-taking and innovation for students in all departments and fields. These efforts are not confined to electrical engineering or computer science, even though those particular majors remain popular and potent.[25]

Elsewhere, numerous colleges and universities are raising and spending large amounts of money to create programs and facilities that do not leave to chance the education of entrepreneurs. Rice University, long famous worldwide for its engineering and physics programs, announced in December 2015 its emphasis on recruiting students who have "entrepreneurial aspirations," working to persuade them that Rice University was a good campus for them to realize their ambitions. New York University, Princeton, Brown, the University of Southern California, among others, have worked to fulfill such goals by establishing curricula, workshops, seminars, institutes, and centers whose multidisciplinary aim is to accommodate and encourage innovative thinking.

Comparable projects took place at New York University, where a trustee who was founder of a successful software company and his wife were donors for construction of a 5,900-square-foot lab "to provide space for budding entrepreneurs to network, attend events, and make prototypes of their products."[26] The founder of "Papa John's Pizza" corporation partnered with the Charles Koch Foundation in a grant of $10 million to the University of Kentucky's College of Business to create an "Institute for the Study of Free Enterprise." Its purpose is to offer students and scholars "the opportunity to engage in classes and research that explore the role of free enterprise in advancing a free and prosperous society that benefits everyone." According to the major donor, "free enterprise is the greatest mechanism mankind has ever created to eliminate poverty, enhance prosperity and enable the 'pursuit of happiness' spoken of in the Declaration of Independence." Participants will be "contributing to a better world for everyone, especially the least fortunate." And, "Unleashing the power of entrepreneurship is a critical part of restoring Americans' belief that the future will be better than the past."[27]

What remains to be analyzed is how one ultimately measures the effectiveness of these new programs. One irony is that some of the paragons of 21st-century entrepreneurship, such as Steve Jobs of Apple and Bill Gates of Microsoft, were college dropouts. Does that mean their undergraduate colleges, Reed and Harvard, were inhospitable to imagination and enterprise? Conversely, what assurance do we have that the new programs at Stanford and New York University will retain the interests of a future Steve Jobs or Bill Gates? Will these colleges have "failed" if their alumni are not successful entrepreneurs?

The initial administrative response is to report that the "buzz" of student activity in the enterprise labs and work stations are signs of success. In fact, they are at best indicative of a good start in appealing to new students – but tell little more than that. As one professor noted, "Real innovation is rooted in knowledge and durable concern and interest, not just 'I thought of something that nobody ever thought of before.' That's not educating people, frankly." A different concern is that professors committed to entrepreneurship as a field or academic endeavor "say that some universities are not ensuring that students learn the fundamentals of starting, running, and sustaining a business." One professor elaborated, "Just because you have a nice space and a laundry list of entrepreneurship activities doesn't mean there is an effective story around that program, or that students know how to navigate their way around those resources."[28]

Rethinking the Sponsored Research Model

Is the classic system of peer review for federal grants obsolete or even dysfunctional? Another question is the hegemony of the major federal agencies. If, for example, leaders at the NIH decide that genome research is to be the showcased research priority for coming years, this has a domino effect through and across not only universities, but also the numerous small businesses and commercial research laboratories.

A serious question is whether the established system of selection and rewards has crystallized – or, as some critics are apt to say, fossilized? In 1948–1949 analysts worried that there were not enough Ph.D.s to carry out the post-World War II scientific research agenda. The opposite is true in 2016, where the number of highly qualified, educated, and experienced researchers who apply for federal research grants far outstrips available grants.

The liability of linking university scientific research with grant funding and, later, with profits and patents is that financial records allow one to track with minute detail whether or not a particular researcher or department is "paying its own way." Sometimes the findings are surprising. Expensive departments in the life sciences and physical sciences require a high initial investment, especially the "start-up" packages for new faculty. What does a dean or provost do or say if, for example, a physics department or a pharmacology program fails to bring in subsistence grants to carry out research in the present – and little evidence of patents or marketable services or products in the future? Is cost–benefit the appropriate litmus for keeping or curtailing an advanced field of study?

Rethinking the Education and Professionalization of Medical Doctors

The success of AMCs, including expansion of research programs, is problematic. One national report on training doctors referred to the situation as "The Current Crisis." At the entry level to medical school, one problem is that the "pre-med" model of undergraduate education, which packs in a high number of required courses in the sciences and mathematics, may at some point be dysfunctional. First, it may unwittingly screen out or dissuade students who have the intelligence and aptitude to be excellent and caring physicians. Second, medical college faculty in recent years have urged that more emphasis be given to having first-year medical students be immersed healing and caring, all of which requires involvement with patients. An interesting finding is that medical students whose undergraduate majors were in the humanities and social sciences had academic performance in medical school that equaled and sometimes surpassed those of their counterparts who had concentrated in the traditional "pre-med" curriculum that emphasized biological sciences, mathematics, and chemistry.[29]

These curricular reforms are crucial because medical education is labor-intensive. Unlike law school with large lecture halls and a single professor, in colleges of medicine it is not at all unusual to have more instructors and professional support staff than there are medical students. The four-year M.D. curriculum includes team teaching by numerous instructors who hold Ph.D. degrees in such fields as physiology, anatomy, toxicology, biochemistry, biostatistics, and other advanced research specialties, apart from mentoring and teaching by medical doctors. Tolerance for high attrition is untenable for several reasons: first, students admitted to the M.D. program are typically well prepared, diligent, and highly motivated – indicators that they should not do poorly in their medical studies. Furthermore, the institutional investment in time, faculty oversight, and advising, combined with the societal demand for new doctors, reinforce the imperative that medical education be effective even though its expenditures tend to make it systemically expensive and, hence, inefficient.

A second source of concern pertains to the graduate education of medical doctors. Foremost is the 2015 book by Kenneth M. Ludmerer, *Let Me Heal: The Opportunity to*

Preserve Excellence in American Medicine. The gist of his analysis is that the AMC emphasis on research grants has a serious trade-off for young doctors and their senior sponsoring physicians, called "attending." Medical college graduates who are residents along with their fellows number about 120,000 in what is called "GME" – graduate medical education. Transformation of teaching hospitals and colleges of medicine by emphasis on commercialization has changed the financing and, hence, character of hospital care and advanced medical education.[30] Changes in Medicare repayments prompt hospitals to get patients in and out as fast as possible.

The casualty in this new model was erosion of emphasis on teaching. It has induced "time management" pressures on clinical doctors and their resident students to have a high number of regulated, short visits with a large number of patients per day. As Dr. Lara Goitein wrote in the *New York Review of Books*, "Being an attending physician was once considered a great honor, but increasingly programs had trouble finding faculty willing to do the job. The demotion and marginalizing of teaching was not lost on residents." It led to what they described as "the physical and emotional abandonment of the house staff by the senior faculty. Quite suddenly, the important mentoring relationships that characterized graduate medical education over most of the last century were the exception, rather than the rule."[31]

The conventional wisdom is that doctors in residency suffered from long shifts. Indeed, regulations put into place in 2003 have codified measures to reform this practice. However, traditions of the teaching hospital and mentoring relations among supervising senior doctors as professors and novitiates actually made for thoughtful teaching and good medicine. Long shifts are not the essential problem. The real threat to both the professional education and socialization of doctors as residents comes from the frenetic pressure of billable hours and short visits with patients. The preponderance of concern over the detriments to the careful education of a new generation of physicians is attributed in large part to the characteristics of health care as a business in Academic Medical Centers.

CONNECTIONS WITH DIVERSITY AND SOCIAL JUSTICE

Among all the chapter topics in this book, this chapter probably is the most removed from and oblivious to social justice and diversity. This is because the institutional pursuit of prestige and profit tends to ride roughshod over other considerations. For example, in the 1950s and 1960s the premier private, academically prestigious research universities in the South – Vanderbilt, Rice, Emory, and Duke Universities – each showed through their boards of trustees little concern for racial desegregation.[32] A few academic administrative leaders cried out, but in vain. President Kenneth Pitzer of Rice University – himself a world-famous chemist – made diversity a priority, but was not able to persuade his board. This was one influential factor in 1969 when he left Rice to become President of Stanford University. The party line he and others faced was that, after all, these academically prestigious – and rising – universities should be exempted from concerns about equity and equality because their focus on excellence pushes out time for equity. The ironic sequel was that eventually these prestigious research universities learned a hard lesson: their preoccupation with being competitive for federal research grants led to scrutiny – and the warning from federal officials that racial exclusion, whether formal or informal, was grounds for denial on federal research grant applications.

If one turns from issues of race and ethnicity to gender, one finds that since 1975 women have made substantial gains in enrolling in and completing Ph.D.s in such traditionally male-dominated fields as computer science, engineering, physics, chemistry, biology, and medicine. In a landmark study conducted by the Dean of the Graduate School at the University of California, Berkeley in 1974, analysts probed the question as to why women were under-enrolled in the sciences. The hypothesis was that women faced discrimination at the admissions stage into Ph.D. programs. This *appeared* to be the case when one looked at the number of applications and number of acceptances for *all* Ph.D. programs across the university. However, when one went through admissions data department by department, no such pattern of discrimination emerged – leaving the analysts with a perplexing riddle. One explanation was that women tended to apply inordinately to Ph.D. programs that had a high number of applicants per admission slot. And these tended to be in fields such as English, modern languages, and history. The relatively few women who applied, for example, to a Ph.D. program in physics or engineering were accepted at the same rate as men who applied. But the problem was that few women were applying to these programs in the sciences and engineering.[33]

The long-term solution has been to encourage women to enroll in science, technology, and mathematics fields starting in high school and continuing through undergraduate studies – and, then, on to graduate school.[34] The measures and strategies have worked reasonably well over the past 40 years when one looks at the changing gender proportions of enrollment in medical school, veterinary school, and in some Ph.D. programs in the sciences. Despite such gains, in 2015 a number of studies by psychologists – and reinforced by women who were Ph.D. recipients and researchers in science and mathematics – provided additional data on "what really keeps women out of tech." The findings indicated that pervasive stereotypes in media and movies, reinforced within academic departments themselves, were that women as scientists were taken aback by the preponderance of the all-male juvenile "departmental culture." Star Wars posters, sexist jokes at the water cooler, emphasis on drinking beer after hours, and "nerd" and "geek" male stereotypes accumulated to prompt women to seek professional research work elsewhere in a professional and scholarly culture that was less stilted and unwelcoming.[35]

There are numerous other examples where the public good falls outside the campus–corporate university research agenda. In the aftermath of the toxic infiltration of the water supply in the city of Flint, Michigan, a professor of civil engineering at Virginia Tech who had been central to revealing problems in public utilities, including water, expressed concern that academic science had veered toward neglect of the public welfare. He noted:

I am very concerned about the culture of academia in this country and the perverse incentives that are given to young faculty. The pressures to get funding are just extraordinary. We're all on this hedonistic treadmill – pursuing funding, pursuing fame, pursuing h-index – and the idea of science as a public good is being lost.[36]

CONCLUSION

The fusion of campus and commerce in the United States that accelerated in the early 21st century has been a source of both celebration and consternation. For university presidents and boards, the prospect of abundant revenues, favorable publicity, and being a good partner in state and national economic development has been attractive. When corporations and campuses collaborate in research projects, the self-congratulatory pronouncements are not modest.

Corporate sponsors and universities are quick to celebrate and/or defend their investments in the research enterprise. Even the hint of reductions or tapering in federal research funding leads to alarmist headlines that "future medical advances are in real danger" because "dwindling federal funds threaten research and lives."[37] But this alarm coexists with the fact that many achievements in health have had little connection with advanced, expensive research and have been the result of such basics as requiring physicians to wash their hands – a practice that was strongly opposed for years by the medical establishment, yet was crucial to reducing deaths in childbirth and other treatments in hospitals. Probably the greatest deterrent to high death rates and illness has been the availability of clean drinking water for the general public. This accomplishment has been known for over a century and perhaps has either been forgotten or taken for granted. Yet its legacy resurfaced in 2016 as a timely reminder with the Virginia Tech team of professors and students in environmental engineering taking their own initiative to solve serious health problems in Flint, Michigan due to a faulty water system – problems that had been ignored or dismissed by state and city officials.[38]

The weaknesses of the campus–corporate research model for pharmaceuticals and medicine are evident in cases such as the 2012 national headlines about Dr. Sidney Gilman of the University of Michigan, a neurologist known as a top Alzheimer's researcher, who crossed the line into criminal conduct and conflicts of interest when connecting his research findings with Wall Street investors and the manufacturers Elan and Wyeth. According to the *New York Times*:

> While he appeared a grandfatherly academic, Dr. Gilman, 80, was living a parallel life one in which he regularly advised a wide network of Wall Street traders through a professional match-making system. Those relationships afforded him payments of $100,000 or more per year – on top of his $285,000 pay from the University of Michigan – and travels with limousines, luxury hotels and private jets.

The article went on to elaborate:

> What is clear is that Dr. Gilman made a sharp shift in his late 60s, from a life dedicated to academic research to one in which he accumulated a growing list of financial firms willing to pay him $1,000 an hour for his medical expertise, while he was overseeing drug trials for various pharmaceutical makers.[39]

For companies whose stock hinged on scientific research and drug trials, an investor who had exclusive or advanced access to scientific expertise – often ahead of the public – could be profitable. It also could be illegal. So, the question is how is the public good served when a university scholar's expertise is the basis for the professor to advise the financial sector?

How to explain susceptibilities to university research abuse? Part of the problem is that academic scholarship and practice in medicine often overlaps with the commercial dimensions of pharmaceutical corporations and other health product manufacturers. Professors as researchers are in a situation where the success or failure of their studies can be subsequently related to success or failure in the marketplace. The result is the pressure of temptation and potential academic and ethical dilemmas increased by the priority of financial success.[40]

Acknowledging the successes of the enterprising instinct in higher education has also elicited warnings about abdication of essential academic values. And the case of Dr. Gilman and the University of Michigan brings scrutiny because it involves an eminent researcher and an elite, established university. Nor can it be dismissed as a minor aberration. Historian Roger Geiger's 2004 book, *Knowledge and Money* presents a reasoned, balanced analysis of the trade-offs enterprising universities have faced in hosting the rise of commercialized research and development. Other critics claim we are in an era of the "Dawn of McScience," a situation that increases the likelihood of research abuses.[41] Nobel laureate physicist Steven Weinberg in 2012 focused his public essays on what he called the "Crisis of Big Science."[42] One response is to argue that the traditional academic ethos is archaic and should be changed. In fact, essential academic principles are well suited to the new challenges provided by campus and corporate research alliances – but the principles must be persistently and thoughtfully applied to new cases and episodes that have defined the American research university in the 21st century.

NOTES

1. President Calvin Coolidge's thoughtful speech has persistently been misquoted and misrepresented as a glib statement – paraphrased as, "The business of America is business." The conventional, erroneous interpretation of this misquotation is that he was justifying the use of business standards in application to other, perhaps all, activities. In fact, his speech was measured and presented a critical observation of a pervasive phenomenon rather than advocacy for the business model as the American measure of all things.
2. Clark Kerr, *The Uses of the University* (Cambridge, MA: Harvard University Press, 1960).
3. Holden Thorp and Buck Goldstein, *Engines of Innovation: The Entrepreneurial University in the Twenty-First Century* (Chapel Hill: University of North Carolina Press, 2010).
4. Derek Bok, *Universities in the Marketplace: The Commercialization of Higher Education* (Princeton, NJ and Oxford: Princeton University Press, 2003). See also, David L. Kirp, *Shakespeare, Einstein, and the Bottom Line: The Marketing of Higher Education* (Cambridge, MA and London: Harvard University Press, 2003).
5. Hugh Davis Graham and Nancy Diamond, *The Rise of American Research Universities: Elites and Challengers in the Postwar Era* (Baltimore, MD and London: Johns Hopkins University Press, 1997).
6. Rebecca S. Lowen, *Creating the Cold War University: The Transformation of Stanford* (Berkeley and Los Angeles: University of California Press, 1997); Larry Cuban, *How Scholars Trumped Teachers: Chang Without Reform in University Curriculum, Teaching, and Research, 1890–1990* (New York: Teachers College Press of Columbia University, 1999).
7. Roger L. Geiger, *Research and Relevant Knowledge: American Research Universities Since World War II* (New York and Oxford: Oxford University Press, 1993).
8. Paul Basken, "Is University Research Missing What Matters Most?," *Chronicle of Higher Education* (January 24, 2016).
9. Lee Gardner, "Oregon's Step Back from a Branding Contract Doesn't Mean Branding Is Dead," *Chronicle of Higher Education* (January 28, 2016).
10. Darren Rovell, *First in Thirst: How Gatorade Turned the Science of Sweat into a Cultural Phenomenon* (New York: AMACOM, 2005).
11. Richard Freeland, *Higher Education's Golden Age: Universities in Massachusetts, 1945 to 1970* (New York and Oxford: Oxford University Press, 1992).

12. Michael I. Luger and Harvey Goldstein, *Technology in the Garden: Research Parks and Regional Economic Development* (Chapel Hill: University of North Carolina Press, 1991).

13. John A. Kastor, *Governance of Teaching Hospitals: Turmoil at Penn and Hopkins* (Baltimore, MD and London: Johns Hopkins University Press, 2004).

14. Christopher Newfield, "Professorial Anger, Then and Now: What Thorstein Veblen Got Right," *The Chronicle Review* (October 30, 2015) pp. B11–B13.

15. Linda B. Blackford, "Research System 'Badly Broken'," *Lexington Herald-Leader* (December 9, 2012) pp. A1, A2.

16. Editorial, "Research Value No. 1: Money: UK, Other Schools Don't Do Enough to Protect, Reward Whistle-Blowers," *Lexington Herald-Leader* (December 16, 2012) p. F1.

17. Anahad O'Connor, "Coca-Cola Funds Efforts to Alter Obesity Battle," *New York Times* (August 10, 2015) pp. A1, A12.

18. Editorial, "Coke's Sugarcoated Research," *New York Times* (August 14, 2015) p. A22.

19. Nick Wingfield, "Former Georgia Tech Engineering Professor Indicted on Racketeering Charges," *New York Times* (January 8, 2015).

20. Linda B. Blackford, "Former UK Professor Accused of Fraud: School Alleges Misuse of $400,000, Students' Time," *Lexington Herald-Leader* (August 21, 2014) pp. A1, A2.

21. Donald G. McNeil, Jr., "U.S. Apologizes for Syphilis Tests in Guatemala," *New York Times* (October 1, 2010).

22. A. Zitner, "U.S. Cuts off Johns Hopkins University Research Funding," *Lexington Herald-Leader* (July 20, 2001) p. A12. See also, John R. Thelin, "Higher Education and the Public Trough: A Historical Perspective," in Edward P. St. John and Michael D. Parsons, Editors, *Public Funding of Higher Education: Changing Contexts and New Rationales* (Baltimore, MD and London: Johns Hopkins University Press, 2004) pp. 21–39.

23. Carl Elliott, "The University of Minnesota's Medical Research Mess," *New York Times* (May 26, 2015) p. A7.

24. Elizabeth Rosenthal, "Benefits Questioned in Tax Breaks for Nonprofit Hospitals," *New York Times* (December 16, 2013) pp. A12, A20. See also, John R. Thelin and Richard W. Trollinger, *Philanthropy and American Higher Education* (New York: Palgrave Macmillan, 2014) p. 140.

25. Beth McMurtrie, "Inside Startup U: How Stanford Develops Entrepreneurial Students," *Chronicle of Higher Education* (October 30, 2015) pp. A30–A34.

26. Natasha Singer, "Colleges Rush to Embolden Entrepreneurs," *New York Times* (December 29, 2015) pp. A1, B2.

27. John H. Schnatter, "UK Center to Unleash Power, Benefits of Entrepreneurship," *Lexington Herald-Leader* (December 29, 2015) p. A7.

28. Professor Heidi Neck, Entrepreneurial Studies, Babson College, as quoted in Natasha Singer, "Colleges Rush to Embolden Entrepreneurs," *New York Times* (December 29, 2015) pp. A1, B2.

29. Molly Cook, David M. Irby, and Bridget C. O'Brien, *Educating Physicians: A Call for Reform of Medical School and Residency* (Stanford, CA: Carnegie Foundation for the Advancement of Teaching, 2010). See also, national front-page news coverage, including Anemona Hartocollis, "In Medical School Shift, Meeting Patients on Day One," *New York Times* (September 2, 2010) pp. A1, A12.

30. Kenneth M. Ludmerer, *Let Me Heal: The Opportunity to Preserve Excellence in American Medicine* (New York and London: Oxford University Press, 2015).

31. Lara Goitein, "Training Young Doctors: The Current Crisis," *New York Review of Books* (June 4, 2015). See also, Jerome Groopman, *How Doctors Think* (New York: Houghton Mifflin, 2007); Richard Horton, "What's Wrong With Doctors," *New York Review of Books* (May 31, 2007).

32. Melissa Kean, *Desegregating Private Higher Education in the South: Duke, Emory, Rice, Tulane, and Vanderbilt* (Baton Rouge, LA: Louisiana State University Press, 2008).

33. P.J. Bickel, E.A. Hammel, and J.W. O'Connell, "Sex Bias in Graduate Admissions: Data from Berkeley," *Science* (February 7, 1975) vol. 182, pp. 393–404.

34. Sheila M. Tobias, *Overcoming Math Anxiety* (New York: W.W. Norton and Company, 1978).

35. Eileen Pollack, "What Really Keeps Women Out of Tech," *New York Times* (October 11, 2015) p. SR3.

36. Steve Kolowich, "The Water Next Time: Professor Who Helped Expose Crisis in Flint Says Public Science Is Broken," *Chronicle of Higher Education* (February 2, 2016); Mitch Smith, "As Flint Fought to Be Heard, Distant Lab Team Sounded Alarm: Virginia Tech Scientists Who Confirmed Fears Now Advise Officials," *Chronicle of Higher Education* (February 7, 2016) p. 12.

37. John D'Orazio, "Future Medical Advances in Real Danger: Dwindling Federal Funds Threatens Research, Lives," *Lexington Herald-Leader* (December 2, 2012) p. E1.

38. Steve Kolowich, "The Water Next Time: Professor Who Helped Expose Crisis in Flint Says Public Science Is Broken," *Chronicle of Higher Education* (February 2, 2016); Mitch Smith, "As Flint Fought to Be Heard,

Distant Lab Team Sounded Alarm: Virginia Tech Scientists Who Confirmed Fears Now Advise Officials," *Chronicle of Higher Education* (February 7, 2016) p. 12.
39. Nathaniel Popper and Bill Vlasic, "Quiet Doctor, Lavish Insider: A Parallel Life," *New York Times* (December 16, 2012) pp. A1, A20.
40. Carl Elliott, "The University of Minnesota's Medical Research Mess," *New York Times* (May 26, 2015) p. A7.
41. Richard Horton, "The Dawn of McScience," *New York Review of Books* (March 11, 2004) pp. 7–9.
42. Steven Weinberg, "The Crisis of Big Science," *New York Review of Books* (May 10, 2012) pp. 59–62.

Additional Readings

David A. Aaker, *Building Strong Brands* (New York: The Free Press, 1996).
Derek Bok, *Universities in the Marketplace: The Commercialization of Higher Education* (Princeton and Oxford: Princeton University Press, 2003).
Larry Cuban, *How Scholars Trumped Teachers: Chang Without Reform in University Curriculum, Teaching, and Research, 1890–1990* (New York: Teachers College Press of Columbia University, 1999).
Roger L. Geiger, *Research and Relevant Knowledge: American Research Universities Since World War II* (New York and Oxford: Oxford University Press, 1993).
Roger L. Geiger, *Knowledge and Money: Research Universities and the Paradox of the Marketplace* (Stanford, CA: Stanford University Press, 2014).
Hugh Davis Graham and Nancy Diamond, *The Rise of American Research Universities: Elites and Challengers in the Postwar Era* (Baltimore, MD and London: Johns Hopkins University Press, 1997).
John A. Kastor, *Governance of Teaching Hospitals: Turmoil at Penn and Hopkins* (Baltimore, MD and London: Johns Hopkins University Press, 2004).
David L. Kirp, *Shakespeare, Einstein, and the Bottom Line: The Marketing of Higher Education* (Cambridge, MA and London: Harvard University Press, 2003).
Rebecca S. Lowen, *Creating the Cold War University: The Transformation of Stanford* (Berkeley and Los Angeles: University of California Press, 1997).
Kenneth M. Ludmerer, *Let Me Heal: The Opportunity to Preserve Excellence in American Medicine* (New York and London: Oxford University Press, 2015).
Edward P. St. John and Michael D. Parsons, Editors, *Public Funding of Higher Education: Changing Contexts and New Rationales* (Baltimore, MD and London: Johns Hopkins University Press, 2004).
Sheila Slaughter and Gary Rhoades, *Academic Capitalism and the New Economy: Markets, State, and Higher Education* (Baltimore, MD and London: Johns Hopkins University Press, 2009).
Holden Thorp and Buck Goldstein, *Engines of Innovation: The Entrepreneurial University in the Twenty-First Century* (Chapel Hill: University of North Carolina Press, 2010).

12

COLLEGES AND CONSUMERISM

Cost and Price of Higher Education

SETTING AND OVERVIEW

"Why does college cost so much?" has become a pervasive, volatile question in the public forum of American life. It has commanded the attention of parents and students, of legislatures, Congress, political candidates, and even the President of the United States.[1] This chapter looks beyond the contentious rhetoric to provide an introduction to the context and concepts that frame this question. It includes defining and distinguishing such concepts as "cost" versus "price" and "access" versus "choice" as factors in how students choose to apply to a college. It extends to the vocabulary of student financial aid by parsing the distinction between *need-based* and *merit-based* awards. It decodes the alphabet soup of terms such as FAFSA, COA, GSL, COFHE, SALLIE MAE, CEEB, SAT, ETS, BEOG, and SEOG as a guide to understanding federal and state programs. As such, its commentary provides explanations of the changing status of various costs and prices within the sprawling American higher education landscape.

Our focus in this chapter will be on students and their families as *consumers*. This builds on the foundation set forth in two earlier chapters – Chapter 7: "Fiscal Fitness: Budgets and Finances" and Chapter 9: "Public Policies." But ultimately the emphasis is on discerning how American families and their children navigate the marketplace of applying to colleges, choosing a college, and then figuring out how to pay for that college experience.

It's crucial to start by defining the two basic concepts: *cost* and *price*. This sounds so elementary as to be patronizing. But it is not. Often the terms are used interchangeably or as synonyms. Almost all journalists, legislators, political candidates, guidance counselors, and, hence, parents and prospective students predominantly use the term "cost" of college when, in fact, they probably mean the "price of college." That's understandable and may appear to be nit-picking. But getting things clear is essential if one is going to wade through the issues.

The *cost* of college is the sum of all the expenses by a college to *provide* instruction, recreational facilities, dormitories, dining halls, libraries, and administrative services that make up college education. The *price* of college is what the college publishes for the charges students and their parents *pay* to the college for tuition, fees, room and board, books, supplies, and clothing. An added concept is *net price* – what a particular student actually pays. It varies, depending on grants, loans, and discounts a student receives from various sources. These initial definitions provide a common ground, which is good to have given all the arguments that soon will unfold.

Prospective students, of course, consider their college options as part of an intricate drama of limited choices and confusing information. These issues facing individual students will be connected to policy questions of federal and state legislation as well as institutional practices in admissions and affordability in determining who goes where to college in the United States. This includes the new "three Rs" in American higher education – rankings, ratings, and rivalries. The focus will be on college as an undergraduate experience, whereas graduate and advanced professional studies were discussed in Chapter 11.

Going to college has long been an important rite of passage in American life.[2] It has always conferred prestige, even when (or, perhaps, especially when) only a small number and percentage of late adolescent Americans had the opportunity to go to college. The historical pattern has been the story of how this scarce or elite experience has been extended from a relatively small percentage of young Americans to a large percentage. This is known as the transition from elite to mass to universal higher education.[3] The paradox is that despite this growth in students who applied, whether in 1816 or 1916 or 2016, most colleges have always depended on students enrolling and paying tuition.

To increase academic headaches, most college staff face the worry every year that they will not have enough students who pay their tuition. If there is a universal condition that provides a bond among colleges, it is this recognition that they are ultimately dependent on students as consumers. This claim seems outrageous because it is contrary to the ritualized angst of college applications and decisions. So, let's subject it to some detailed historical scrutiny along with a hard look at the current situations in college admissions – and paying for college.

The college marketplace is complex and peculiar. In the United States one enduring spring event is the day in early April when high school seniors wait for the postal service – or their e-mail provider – to deliver the official letters from colleges to which each has applied. Will it be a thin envelope or a thick one? Which is good news? Which is bad news? Dousing lighter fluid onto this combustible topic are numerous stories with the headline news that, for example, Stanford University accepts only one out of 20 applicants. And, Princeton, Duke, Williams, Wellesley, Pomona, Vanderbilt, Davidson, and Northwestern are equally exclusive. It extends to some flagship state universities, such as the University of Michigan, the University of California, Berkeley, and the University of North Carolina at Chapel Hill. But, these prestigious institutions are exceptional. Most colleges have trouble filling their lecture halls. So, getting a complete view of the admissions and enrollment phenomenon is complicated by distortions, smoke, and a great deal of hot air. The annual ritual of college applications, acceptances, rejections, and wait lists is complicated by its overlay with the peculiar economics of higher education.

In many market transactions a customer who is willing and able to pay the listed price simply acquires the goods or service without filling out questionnaires or being screened. This breaks down in certain situations when there is a shortage of goods compared to the abundance of money – which leads to inflation. And, prices go up. Goods then may be rationed, with waiting lists and long lines. This was so after World War II when families had made good money from working in factories that manufactured military vehicles, which meant suspending assembly lines on "civilian" American cars. No matter how much one was willing to pay for a new Buick, they simply were not available because consumers who also were producers were busy cranking out armored tanks. The years 1944–1945 were a very good time to get a bargain on an olive green US Army Jeep, but a terrible time to get a fashionable maroon and cream Studebaker sedan.

Elsewhere in purchasing, there may be some episodic crunches. Getting great seats for an opening night show on Broadway or 50-yard-line seats for the Super Bowl game represent intractable limits where customers who are willing to pay still are turned away. But in the main the marketplace of college price and cost is very different than most purchases. It is an extraordinarily large expense and it involves at least two steps on the part of the institution – an offer of admission and an offer of financial aid – in order for a student to enroll. It is complicated by a third step – namely, competing offers and options a student must weigh, all in a relatively short period. What usually gets left out of the journalistic coverage of the anxiety about getting into college is the sequel: the uncertainty and worry that deans of admissions face, waiting to hear whether admitted students will choose to enroll at their institution. This often is then followed by jilted admissions officers scrambling on the telephone or Twitter to persuade applicants on the waiting list that, indeed, the college has a place for them.

One might think that there is a clear logic and symmetry of what colleges pay to provide an education – and what students and their families pay then to partake of that education and campus experience. In fact, it is convoluted and does not follow conventional wisdom. So, the story of college choices and consumerism already has become more interesting as the plot thickens with idiosyncrasies.

In the 19th century colleges did not charge high tuition for several reasons. Few American boys or girls graduated from high school – and, even fewer gave much thought to going to college. Most American families, whether on farms or operating small businesses, could not spare adolescents from working at home. Finally, a college degree was neither necessary nor even helpful in earning a living. To practice law or medicine might require passing the bar exam or medical licensure – but these were quite apart from having earned a bachelor's degree. Yes, there were medical colleges – but these often siphoned off potential students from the liberal arts colleges. That was because the medical schools were free-standing and did not require a bachelor's degree or "premed" curriculum. As a result the potential pool of college students was spread thin.

Two centuries ago there was a rough split between students who could afford to pay full tuition and other expenses, and students who depended on financial aid along with their earnings from work to meet college bills. Going back to England's Oxford and Cambridge Universities, and transplanted to the historical American colonial colleges, an example was a student who was a "servitor" – comparable to a work study student today – who served other students working as a waiter in the dining hall.

Undergraduates who worked their way through college were frugal and resourceful. In an era before public school teaching had achieved status as a full-fledged profession, many towns in rural areas depended on college students to be teachers. College students also had an option to consider various private loan and grant offers whose providers were independent agencies outside the college.[4] And, although most colleges had little to offer in financial aid, a thriving private loan industry took root, especially in the Mid-Atlantic region.

When prospective students chose a college, a major consideration was proximity. Was a college located close to home? Most American students went to college near their home town. After the Civil War, as colleges sought paying students who could pass the admissions examinations, marketing and consumerism took on a peculiar twist. The later a student applied to a college, the less likely he or she would be required to pay. It was comparable to airlines offering half-fare tickets to stand-by passengers just before flight departure; colleges were relatively passive and resigned themselves to this marginal status.

A marketing strategy used by colleges was recognition that the lack of high schools meant that some potential college applicants might wish to fill in the gaps in their secondary school record and college preparation. So, if a student from a community that did not have a public high school wanted to go to a particular college, she or he simply relocated to the campus community and paid for courses and tutoring in the "preparatory department." From time to time one comes across incidents where ambitious young men started to view going to college as a strategic move. Harvard offered a session of its admission examination in cities far from Boston. When a history professor asked a young man from the Midwest why he had uprooted from his family and home state, the undergraduate replied matter-of-factly, "Why, a degree from Harvard is worth money in Chicago!"[5] Indeed, young college graduates flocked to cities to carve out careers.

Between 1890 and 1910 "college life" became fashionable and popular – both for students, who were its main characters, but also the America public, who became its enthusiastic spectators.[6] Surprisingly, this new consumer demand was not really exploited by colleges. Despite booms and busts in the national and regional economies over this two-decade period, the price of going to college remained stable – and relatively affordable. If a college by chance was in a metropolitan area that had experienced high population increases, it usually meant more local students applied to college. Such was the case with Columbia University in New York City, the University of Pennsylvania in Philadelphia, and Harvard in the greater Boston area. The limp, lackluster response of the colleges was simply to admit more students. There seemed to be little initiative to raise tuition prices in response to the changing consumer demand.

Ironically, those private metropolitan universities, such as Columbia and Harvard, which were large and ethnically diverse in their undergraduate enrollments became the battleground for acrimonious disagreements over equitable treatment of students within campus life. The schisms were sufficiently bitter that the presidents of Harvard and Columbia approved implementation of "selective admissions" procedures, based on non-merit criteria of race, ethnicity, and religion, rather than academic records. It heralded an era of quotas that led to deliberate exclusion and discrimination, especially among applicants who were Jewish or Catholic.

By 1930 the tuition price differential between public and private institutions widened. According to economists Claudia Goldin and Lawrence Katz in 1999, "The average (listed) in-state tuition plus fees for under-graduates at public sectors in 1933 was $61 ($753 in 1999 dollars), as compared with $265 ($3,272 in 1997 dollars) in the private sector."[7] An early example of a dramatic change in the balancing of price and cost in a college education came about, ironically, during the Great Depression. A small number of socially elite (albeit not necessarily academically strong) colleges assessed their marketing position, leading to the decision that they would raise tuition to an unprecedentedly high level simply because they were aiming to enroll students from affluent families. According to a 1937 study published in the *Journal of Higher Education*:

> Amherst, Williams, and Wesleyan all charge tuition fees of $400, while women's colleges of comparable type in the same geographical area charge $500. State universities, such as those in Wisconsin, Illinois, and Michigan charge from incidentals to $100 per annum, while large independent universities in the same area tend to charge $300.[8]

Vassar College's tuition was $1,200 in 1931. Bennington College in Vermont charged $1,650 for tuition in 1936. When one indexes for inflation, figures for 2015 are about $19,000 and $28,500, respectively.

The expansion of state colleges and universities often included a commitment to taxpayer subsidy for tuition. For over a century in California, for example, public higher education maintained a policy of no tuition charges. State legislatures, governors, and taxpayers in the Midwest and on the Pacific Coast supported the argument made by university presidents. The result was that from about 1920 to 1970, public higher education enjoyed growth and a generous flow of state resources. By 1950, enrollments in public higher education were equal to those in private (i.e., independent) colleges and universities. This expansion continued such that by 1990, public higher education enrolled about 80 percent of college students.

What certain groups of students did enjoy was the option of vouchers and choice. The GI Bill from 1944 to 1952 provided eligible military veterans with subsidies for an institution's tuition along with living expenses, and additional subsidies if one had a spouse and dependent children. Since the GI Bill was "portable" and could be used at any accredited college, it did not shift the balance of student choice to any sector – i.e., state universities were not necessarily any more desirable or affordable than were private colleges. It provided the model for a college consumerism that tilted increasingly toward student choice.

The dynamics of student consumerism changed due to the increase in the number of high school graduates – and the percentage within that group who now considered going to college as a realistic option. Demography was destiny – and also an early signal of what was in store for aspiring college students. During the early and mid-1950s, especially in states where the population was young and growing, elementary and secondary schools were overcrowded – leading to split daily half sessions to accommodate all pupils. Predictably and eventually this cohort graduated from high school and applied to college. For once, one had an imbalance skewed toward the advantage of colleges.

Factors other than a high-priced tuition usually were responsible for encouraging one group of applicants – and discouraging another. Admissions in American higher education have been largely characterized by student self-selection and what sociologists later would call "institutional fit." A student applies to a college that fits a profile which is compatible and attractive – or, frequently, an obvious choice because it is the path of least resistance. A college's religious affiliation often was central to college choice. Relatively few African American students enrolled at predominantly white colleges. This was due in some cases to formal policies of racial exclusion or informal indifference. Most colleges were racially homogeneous. In the aggregate, colleges represented some diversity across institutions – but usually diversity within a college was limited, often characterized by marginalizing minority subcultures. Students were pragmatic in their college choices. In a student account from 1909 the University of Pennsylvania was hailed as having "the democracy of the street car" because it was affordable, flexible, and accessible for sons and daughters of immigrant families who took some courses and did not live on campus in university dormitories.[9]

Student choices often bewildered college officials. In the first quarter of the 19th century some forward-looking college presidents established separate tracks for what were called "scientific schools" with "practical" and "technical" studies – all to attract bright students who wanted to be surveyors, bridge builders, inventors, or engineers. But few applicants showed interest. Later, the land grant colleges were set up in large part to promote affordable advanced education in practical fields, such as agriculture and engineering. Yet in the first three decades that these colleges put in place the new offerings in the "useful arts," still relatively few applicants showed much interest. One explanation was that for ambitious and upwardly mobile students, college was the way to get off the farm and away from agriculture. Eventually this would change, and after World War II state university enrollments surged, with growing numbers of students majoring in the relatively new vocational and professional fields. And, as noted earlier on page 49 in Chapter 3 on Teaching and Learning, the curricular change that did seize the attention of many high school seniors who wanted "college life" without academic rigor was the new "Ph.B." curriculum – the Bachelor of Philosophy. The degree sounded impressive and, best of all, it did not require studying the ancient languages Greek or Latin.

The important sequel to the popularity of going to college as well as the related campus visits and family deliberations about college choices is that as late as 1960, even the most prestigious, affluent colleges did not give a great deal of student financial aid.[10] Families were expected to make their own arrangements by dipping into savings or borrowing from uncles or grandparents. And most available student aid from a college or university financial aid office was in the form of loans.

Independent colleges and universities started to rethink their traditional frugality around 1960 by taking the initiative to draw from their institutional endowments to provide need-based student financial aid in the form of scholarships. The terminology was financial aid "packaging," that is, a tier of scholarship, work study, and loans. The amount and type of award was calculated by college officials who relied on information that a student provided via a standardized form – the parent's confidential statement on income known as the *FAF* (Financial Aid Form) – administered through the College Entrance Examination Board's *CSS* (College Scholarship Service). The effective change in making academically prestigious private colleges affordable was the implementation of a two-step procedure. First, at Ivy League colleges and other academically strong institutions, admissions decisions were *need blind*. This meant that admissions officers read applications and made decisions about acceptance without regard to financial need. Admissions committees did not know whether an applicant could afford to pay the college's tuition. Second, student financial aid awarded by the college was *need based*. This meant that if an applicant were granted admission, the college guaranteed that the admission offer would be accompanied by a financial aid package – a combination of scholarships, loans, and work study – that met the student's financial need required to pay for attending the college. This was a bold move for colleges because it was expensive. It also showed that colleges were increasingly serious about casting their nets wide to attract academic talent regardless of family income. It signaled a genuine academic revolution in American life that sociologists hailed as the "partial triumph of the meritocracy."[11]

Starting after World War II and then gaining momentum, one finds a new pattern of behavior by high school seniors: they frequently were applying to more than one college. This was a residual effect of the standardized Scholastic Aptitude Test, in which a student could designate to have test scores sent to multiple colleges. Heretofore, many colleges had their own entrance examination, based on a prescribed curriculum. The Scholastic Aptitude Test, although criticized widely by the 1960s for its reliance on examination questions which had systematic social class biases that worked against students from low-income families, for many years did serve to expand options for students in public high schools nationwide who had outstanding grade point averages and high SAT scores. Such records, when reviewed by prestigious colleges especially in New England, established a new connection to a talent pipeline. It provided a lever with which to break the hegemony of the expensive New England prep schools whose academic counselors and college applicants had heretofore enjoyed disproportionate advantages in gaining access to Harvard, Yale, and Princeton. One way the SAT accomplished this breakthrough was that it was a nationwide, standardized examination in which an applicant's scores could be sent to and reviewed by deans of admissions at many colleges. This contrasted dramatically to the old format of each college offering its own entrance examination, usually on campus.

By 1960 one also sees the flourishing of a new publishing industry: namely, guides to college applications for prospective students and their parents. "How to get in to the college of your choice" became an attractive topic and title for high school students to buy who wanted to go to a "good" college. The editors of *The New Yorker* commissioned Katherine Kinkead to research and write an in-depth case study of the Yale admissions office – a series of articles that was so popular it was soon published as a best-selling book, *How an Ivy League College Decides on Admissions*. Reading audiences included not only high school students looking at colleges, but also guidance counselors, admissions consultants, and the concerned parents of students. In the late 1970s, Richard Moll, who had been Director of Admissions at Vassar College, gained a great deal of attention and readers with *Playing the Private College Admissions Game*. A few years later, to supplement his earlier attention on private colleges, he wrote and edited profiles of selective public colleges and universities, which he dubbed *The Public Ivys*.

College admissions offices devoted increasing time and resources to mailing "view books," brochures, and pamphlets with photographs of campus scenes and student activities. Admissions offices' reliance on media to reach prospective applicants tended to mirror technological innovations in marketing and advertisement. There was some humor in the Madison Avenue marketing in college brochure prose.

The clichés and calculated photographs of campus life eventually led some innovative undergraduates to counter these marketing and publishing aids by creating their own sources of advice and information – written by and for students. An example of a local campus publication that acquired a nationwide audience (and customers) was the *Insider's Guide to Colleges* written, edited, and published by the editorial staff of the *Yale Daily News* starting in 1970. The profiles of numerous colleges, divided by such major criteria as selectivity and geography, were refreshing in their candor. They contrasted dramatically with the self-congratulations and vague images conveyed by official college catalogs and view books. From our perspective today, the guides tended to show a strong bias (and myopia) that favored the selective private liberal arts colleges, especially those on the East Coast. So, on balance, prospective students had markedly contrasting sources of images and information to guide, and perhaps complicate, their college choices.

Admissions offices became higher education's counterpart to a manufacturer's sales force. This meant attention to marketing innovations. Northwestern University, for example, decided upon a daring strategy in the early 1970s: they opted to rely almost exclusively on direct mail campaigns, while greatly reducing the custom of joining with admissions representatives from numerous colleges to go to "college fairs" hosted by high schools throughout the state, region, and nation. Another ploy came from new nonprofit organizations such as the National Merit Scholarship Corporation, which combed the lists of high school juniors who scored well on the Preliminary Scholastic Aptitude Test (PSAT) and then collaborated with subscribing colleges to coordinate on a marketing plan for each college to persuade high-achieving students to apply to their campus.

Another part of the access and admission mosaic was the emergence of federal student aid programs starting in 1972. The growth of the Pell Grant program was impressive. In its first year, the program received an appropriation of $122 million and awarded grants to 176,000 full-time undergraduates. Two years later, appropriations jumped fourfold, to $475 million, with 567,000 student grant recipients. By 1990, the program served three million undergraduates, with an appropriation of $4 billion per year (worth about $7.3 billion in 2015 dollars). In 1997 and 1998, those figures had increased to 3.8 million students, with an average Pell Grant award of $1,923 each (about $2,800 in 2015 dollars) for a total funding of $3.8 billion (worth $5.6 billion in 2015 dollars).

Despite the infusion of federal student financial aid, many colleges faced declining applicant pools and budgets starting around 1973. A decade of financial constraints forced even academically prestigious institutions to rethink some of their historic priorities and commitments. Most precarious was the sanctity of the bold policy of need-blind admissions coupled with need-based financial aid. At Brown University, campus officials doubted whether the institution could continue indefinitely to fulfill its financial aid admissions pledge.[12] The situation facing a private college was that about 70 percent of admitted students were paying a high tuition price that enabled the financial aid office to provide scholarships for the remaining 30 percent of the entering class. Some students who were paying "full freight" objected to this redistribution strategy. Even admissions officers who were in favor of the need-based financial aid policy faced a dilemma: when considering applicants in a ranked order, for the final remaining admissions slots, could the university afford not to consider how much was at stake for the university's costs in terms of a student's financial aid award? For example, if the applicant whose academic ranking was 800th in the applicant pool would require the financial aid office to award a scholarship of $10,000, and the 801st-ranked applicant had no financial need, was the university justified in passing over the high-need applicant in favor of the next candidate, who had no financial aid need?

One beleaguered college admissions dean seeking to attract good high school students in a competitive region discovered that offering low tuition was not an effective strategy. The surprise finding was that when the college raised tuition to a level higher than that of its traditional college rivals, the number and quality of its applicants increased. This practice has persisted, as researchers reported in a 2016 article that the "Chivas Regal" effect of high pricing as a counter to declining applications was widespread between 2006 and 2012.[13]

Around 1985 a small number of academically selective private colleges and universities gained confidence through new levels of energetic, effective fund-raising and admissions recruitment, so much so that they embarked on campaigns to "buy the best" – whether this meant offering high salaries to outstanding faculty recruits or providing generous scholarships to highly talented students at both the undergraduate and graduate levels.[14] These enterprising institutions initiated an enduring pattern of *cost escalation* in American higher education. One salient example of this was an increased emphasis on *merit scholarships*, which are grants aimed at attracting highly talented students, with no requirement that a student has demonstrated financial need.

Submitting multiple applications grew in popularity in 1972 with the availability of the BEOG federal grants, soon renamed as Pell Grants. The genius of the Pell Grants was that they heralded a major gain for students in shaping college choice. A condition of the federal grant was that they were awarded to the student rather than the institution. They were portable to the college at which the grant recipient chose to enroll. This meant that deans of admissions, aided by directors of financial aid, proactively recruited students who, if enrolled, would bring their Pell Grant tuition dollars to the college bursar. It represented a new era of college admissions increasingly controlled by prospective students as consumers who now had substantial power and choices.

In congressional elections of 1978 families and students transplanted their college consumerism to the ballot box, and incumbent candidates settled on the effective re-election strategy of providing student financial aid in the form of readily available, low interest loans. Voters, especially families with college-bound children, liked this. Initial terms were that a family could obtain a loan of $2,000 per year for up to four renewed years with interest charged below market rate. Most banks qualified as lenders – with the federal government serving as the guarantor. Bankers were happy. Middle income families were happy. Colleges were happy, especially since the number of high school graduates applying to college had started to decline around 1977.

The sweet deal of student loans – which families often used for purchasing a car or to pay for the down payment on a vacation cabin – took on a very different character by around 2002. Student loan debt soared as more students applied. By 2015 the average student loan debt of a college graduate was about $30,000. Starting around 2009 the popular press was continually peppered with articles about the alarm of student debt and its companion rising college costs. By 2005 private lenders, such as *My Rich Uncle*, used the Internet to provide students with interactive loan applications – with the pledge that paperwork would be processed and loans confirmed often within a matter of hours. Prospective college students enjoyed a cornucopia of advertisements and enticements for student financial aid. Banks, once reluctant to advertise services and not interested in loaning to college students, orchestrated expensive campaigns. One flyer mailed out by a bank depicted a smiling, tanned student, wearing sunglasses and driving a sporty car, with the caption, "You have choices!" Students also had toll-free numbers for an array of services, ranging from college loans to computer purchases and debt consolidation as part of the particular bank's *Education One Loans* program. Either students or parents could borrow up to $25,000 per year for these loans that were based on credit, not need. Applying students could be either full-time or part-time enrollees. Drawing from this same bank's flyer, illustrative of the bank's attention to consumer appeal was its pledge that a check would be mailed within 24 hours after it received a qualified application.

The corollary to this good news about student loan choices was a growing concern by colleges and federal agencies that the shift from grants to loans had become dangerously lopsided. Furthermore, proposals in the reauthorization of the Higher Education Act included students henceforth being subject to a repayment rate of 6.8 percent on federal student loans, leading one major metropolitan newspaper to title an editorial, "Robbing Joe College to Pay Sallie Mae." The residual problem of these student aid issues was the indication that students from modest income families, even if academically strong, represented a small and declining proportion of undergraduate enrollments at prestigious private and public universities. Particularly alarming was a 2006 report sponsored by the Education Trust that characterized flagship state universities as "engines of inequality" as the earning gap separating students from low and modest income families from more affluent classmates increased.[15] From the perspective of institutional differences among the nation's colleges and universities, there were disturbing signs of increasing disparities between rich and poor institutions in their respective spending levels for undergraduate education.[16]

Cost escalation was tolerable as long as there was an overall increase in national prosperity and academic endowments and, of course, increases in student financial aid that kept prices reasonable. However, starting around 1985, there were complaints by the American public, by Congress, and by federal agencies that for many colleges, the annual tuition increases surpassed the inflationary rate as measured by the *Consumer Price Index (CPI)*. One allegation was that colleges were too often oblivious to the burden high tuition charges imposed on American families. In fact, long before outside critics raised the question, many academically selective and prestigious colleges and universities started as early as 1973 to initiate their own systematic studies on the effect of rising costs on college choice. The studies were not in response to external critics, but rather, long before even Congressional criticisms surfaced, the self-analyses were prompted by concern that rising college costs eventually would be harmful by "pricing them out of the market" in an effort to attract academically superior students. This was a particularly urgent concern in what was called an "era of student consumerism," because many states' prestigious flagship universities had either low or no tuition charge.[17]

Government and public concerns over tuition charges and college policies came to a head between 1989 and 1993 in a case involving the Justice Department's investigation of 55 private colleges and universities.[18] The concerns were twofold: first, charges for tuition plus room and board were high, having surpassed $19,000 in 1989 (indexed for inflation, nearly $36,000 in 2015 dollars), and had for over a decade increased at a rate that outpaced the CPI; and second, the Justice Department alleged that some colleges were banding together as a cartel to fix tuition prices.

Primary focus was on the Ivy League and its eight institutional members whose presidents met each year to share information on financial aid, applications, and tuition. The U.S. Attorney General told reporters, "This collegiate cartel denied (students) the right to compare prices and discounts among schools just as they would in shopping for any service."[19] Under the terms of a consent decree announced on May 23, 1991, the Ivy League presidents agreed to stop their "overlap" practice of sharing information. Princeton's Vice President for Public Affairs, speaking for the Ivy Group presidents, defended the overlap as a means to ensure that optimal student financial aid was awarded to students with financial need and to curb the possibility of a student "shopping" and playing one college off against another.[20]

Although the Ivy Group agreed to this settlement, the Massachusetts Institute of Technology (MIT) – an institution included in the initial suit – declined to go along. Two years later, the U.S. Court of Appeals for the Third Circuit in Philadelphia set aside the highly publicized ruling that held that MIT conspired with the colleges in the Ivy League to violate the Sherman Antitrust Act. MIT was exonerated from the accusation of "price fixing" because for many years it had followed a common financial aid policy. Writing in the *Chronicle of Higher Education*, two attorneys (one of whom was general counsel for the American Council on Education) who had filed a friend-of-the-court brief on behalf of the private colleges argued that the flaw in the Justice Department's case was a reductionist fallacy in which a college education and student financial aid were cast as merely another business activity, without regard for the non-economic justifications of what is meant in being a college or a college student.[21]

College and university presidents responded to criticisms about the rate of tuition increases by noting that the conventional inflationary measure – the CPI – was inappropriate because it was tilted toward certain kinds of daily and weekly purchases. As such, they argued, it was a poor choice by which to track changes in a major once-in-a-lifetime cost (e.g., a college education). The resolution was the creation of a new inflationary measure – *HEPI*, the Higher Education Price Index. Introducing the HEPI did not end the debates, as its net contribution was to complicate the allegations. These exchanges in the decades since the MIT ruling took place in a period of rising college costs and the increasing dominance of federal loans as a form of student financial aid.

ISSUES

Cost

What a college spends on all its activities and facilities varies according to its mission along with its relative frugality or generosity. The major issue for college applicants is trying to figure out what this means for an undergraduate student. Are expenses such as advanced research facilities or new venture programs consuming a great deal of institutional resources that may be relatively incidental to an undergraduate – yet whose costs are passed on to the undergraduate?

Price

The amount a student is charged for, for example, a year of college is influenced by such factors as kinds and quality of service. Tuition varies from one college to another – as does the charge for meals, books, and other incidentals. A college determines if it wishes to subsidize some expenses from its endowment. Also, there can be mandatory student fees for various services along with discretionary, optional fees – all of which mount up, increasing cost and price. The term *sticker price* refers to the "full" price – comparable to a car sales lot, with charges for all extras – whether floor mats or a laptop computer are included in the package. Parents whose academically talented children were undergraduates at expensive and prestigious private universities often complained that a high-powered Ph.D. program in the sciences had little to do with the courses and student activities their children pursued. So, why should their tuition payments subsidize these allegedly unrelated advanced programs?

There was a perverse equality in these consumer complaints by undergraduates and their families. Why should undergraduate tuition, for example, help subsidize a university's football team that was losing both games and money? Once again this seemingly rhetorical question elicited markedly different responses. Parents of students, for example, gravitated toward seeing tuition charges as comparable to a user's fee. College officials, in contrast, regarded tuition revenues as resembling tax revenues with the central administration and board retaining power on how to distribute income to meet overall institutional goals and missions.

COA

This acronym for "Cost of Attendance," used by college scholarship offices and federal agencies, along with the National Collegiate Athletic Association (NCAA), is a calculation intended to provide the realistic, full expenses of a college student for one year. Campus officials and groups such as the NCAA use the term because the United States Department of Education defines and uses it, making its usage and compliance a condition of receipt of federal student aid. It is called the "COA" because cost often includes only tuition, as room and board depend on whether a student lives in a dormitory or at home or in an off-campus apartment. It also illustrates the use and abuse of "cost" and "price" because it really refers to "price" – and probably should have been called the "POA."

Access

Access refers to the reasonable likelihood that a particular college is available and within reach of a particular student. As a policy matter, the question includes space: can a college or group of colleges offer classroom seats and dormitories to accommodate all applicants? When one looks at the complete expanse of all colleges and all applicants, the indication is that as a nation we do reasonably well in providing all students some access. But how this plays out in terms of *choice* is a distinct, different matter.[22] A sobering, important reality is that those potential students who have multiple "college choices" are "typical" students.

Affordability

Will a student be able to pay the price charged for college expenses? This is calculated by making reasonable estimates of a student's resources from her or his family, from summer jobs, from academic year jobs, and other income. This, then, is combined with the estimate on what the same student might expect in terms of student aid, such as a grant or from loans. If the sum matches the price, then, this signals "affordability." A crucial, helpful tool for students is the *FAFSA – the Free Application for Federal Student Aid* form.

Choice

Is a high school student applying to colleges able to pick from among several possible colleges and enroll at the particular college she or he chooses to attend? This is an important, often overlooked consideration in that for many federal and state legislators and policy-makers, the primary concern is that each student has *access*. And, in the United States we have been reasonably effective in accomplishing that goal. *College choice*, however, is a much more exacting student consumer goal to achieve. One complication derived from the American preoccupation with reputation and ratings is that a relatively small number of prestigious colleges receives a disproportionate number of applications. In fact, only a small percentage of first-time students apply to more than one college – making the concept of "college choice" a misnomer or an exaggeration. According to higher education policy analyst Edward St. John:

> We are in a period of universal college preparation in most states yet where the price of colleges limits genuine access. Most college applicants from poor or modest income families who have reasonable high school academic records cannot afford in-state public four year college expenses given current policies. "Choice" as a policy goal really only came about in 1972 with Pell Grants – and only lasted until 1978.[23]

Student Financial Aid

This refers to money from a variety of sources – the federal government, state government, private lenders, and from a college's scholarship fund. Among the most important types of student financial aid programs and awards provided by the federal government are Pell Grants, originally known as the Basic Educational Opportunity Grant (BEOG) and the Supplementary Educational Opportunity Grant (SEOG). Federal loan programs include the Guaranteed Student Loan (GSL) and the Perkins Loans. Although federal student financial aid programs have been large in allocated dollars and visible in terms of media publicity, equally important is each college's commitment of its resources for institutional grants and aid. Furthermore, numerous states have substantial student financial aid programs in both grants and loans. An important concept and term, then, is *packaging*, in which an individual student receives financial aid from multiple sources, which then are bundled to form the *financial aid package*. The strategy is that the coordination and cooperation of student financial aid from various sources meets a student's full financial need to pay for the college of choice.

Need-Based Aid

Are student financial aid dollars awarded on the basis of what a student can reasonably afford to pay? This usually is calculated by subtracting a student's contribution to the annual expenses, which then are subtracted from the total price, leaving the balance as the "need" figure. This policy usually is most frequently cited as promoting a widespread talent hunt across the socio-economic spectrum. Embedded in the need-based aid policy is the philosophical statement that students from families who can afford to pay tuition and other college bills should be expected to do so – according to systematic needs-based formulas and calculations. Implicit in this is the rhetorical question, "Why should a college direct some of its scarce financial aid dollars to students who do not have financial need?"

Merit-Based Aid

Is a grant awarded on the basis of a student's particular talents regardless of family income or financial need? Talent categories vary, ranging from academic promise to musical ability or athletic skill. The justification is that a college could and should seek high-level talent and reward it, regardless of student family income. The principle is widely used in fellowships for graduate studies, but has an uneven reception and application within undergraduate admissions. The Ivy Group, for example, prohibits its eight member universities from offering merit scholarships to undergraduates. For most high school graduates making college plans, "need-based" aid comes from federal and state scholarship programs. These represent a partial gain in choice and affordability.

Need-Blind Admissions

Does a college admissions office make a decision to admit or deny an applicant without looking at financial records that show how much – or, how little – a student could afford to pay? This pledge is intended to encourage promising applicants to consider a college without consideration of price. The corollary is if a college also pledges that it will meet an applicant's full financial need if the student is academically qualified and offered admission.

Selective Admissions

Does a college admissions office receive more applicants than it has room to enroll? A second question is whether all or most of the applicants qualify for academic admission and probably could succeed in course work. This second question scrapes away mismatches in which some applications inflate the pool of qualified applicants.

A complication in selective admissions is the ease and low price for high school seniors to apply to many colleges. This is promoted in part by the online "Common Application." At times it encourages multiple applications, where a student applies to 15 colleges. One dysfunction is that it may artificially inflate the size of a college's applicant pool, leaving a dean of admissions to decipher whether or not an applicant is merely "going fishing." It may make the college-bound high school pool seem deceptively large. The counterpart is that some deans of admission work deliberately to enhance a college's image of selectivity by inflating the applicant pool – often done by mass campaigns encouraging high school seniors to apply even though the dean knows that the students in fact have little chance of being admitted.

Even when academic achievement as measured by high school grades and high scores on the SAT or ACT are central to selective admissions, few colleges rely exclusively on grades and test scores for all or most of their admission decisions. First, these indicators may be insufficient to identify all expressions of talent in all fields. Second, most colleges look to their entering freshman class to stock numerous activities that make a campus complete and vital. A good way to characterize selective admissions is that each application is scrutinized for some designation of a specialized, particular source of admissions appeal. It may well be that of general academic achievement and potential. But that probably is just one category among, for example, 15 or 20 possibilities. A high school senior who applies to college will increase her or his chance of admission (and merit grant award) if she or he demonstrates a high level of excellence in a particular pursuit that is highly valued by that college.

For applicants, college admissions is a calculated contest to persuade the admissions office and perhaps the financial aid office that one has talents the college values highly. It might be a goalie for the varsity hockey team, an accomplished violinist for the orchestra, or a champion debater to represent the college in national competition. Some applicants warrant special consideration because of non-merit factors, such as the daughter of a major donor or the son of a prominent alumnus. Among all the categories associated with special consideration for admission, the student who is placed in the "general" category faces the toughest competition to get the prized offer of admission.

Ratings and Rankings and Rivalries

What does an applicant find when comparing a particular college to others with criteria used to assign some score to such characteristics as academic strength, selectivity, prestige, and benchmark institutions? Since 1989 the annual college rankings published in a special edition of *U.S. News and World Report* have provided a form of "consumer information" for college applicants. The caution is that one has to understand and accept the indicators that the report editors have chosen to be both significant and valid. These reports are used disproportionately by educated, affluent families. Colleges and universities take the reports seriously, making certain to complete questionnaires and forms to ensure that their institution is included and that the institutional profile is complete and accurate.

Retention

Do students stay at a college after the first year? The second year, and so on? If they tend to leave, what is the reason? Is it due to poor academic performance? Lack of resources and inability to pay tuition and bills? Or, perhaps, dissatisfaction with some aspect of studies and life at this institution? This is an important consideration for students who are considering enrolling at a particular college. However, pondering the implications of allegedly "high" or "low" retention rates has lacked context that linked past and present. For example, often overlooked is that historically colleges and universities in the United States were characterized by a "tradition of attrition."[24] Case studies of colleges nationwide in the early 20th century indicate a high dropout rate and a relatively low completion rate for bachelor's degree conferral. On the one hand this was a manifestation of administrative indifference as to whether students persisted or dropped out. After 1970, however, colleges were increasingly concerned about student departure. College officials acquired increased awareness of and compassion for the human and societal cost of "lost students" who might have succeeded academically if the college had provided adequate support through counseling, academic advising, and other services. Some of this institutional compassion was pragmatic and financial in nature, because administrators realized that each student who left college meant the college forfeited some tuition revenues.

For students as consumers, the decision to drop out, stop out or to transfer to another institution often represented a conscious, informed decision. Colleges were surprised to find that some of their transfers or dropouts were not necessarily academically low-achieving students. Often they were successful and high achieving – and were bored or dissatisfied with the curriculum and teaching at their college. In some cases the decision to transfer was simply a student's recognition that another institution offered a specialty not found at their original college. Another explanation that gained increasing attention was that students dropped out for lack of money – a factor that should have been obvious from the start. Finally, many students who were academically capable were ill-at-ease at a particular college due to the unfamiliarity of navigating the complex maze of course schedules, requirements, and other logistics – combined with lack of cohesion or affiliation with fellow students in activities or residence halls. These latter factors were especially pronounced in first-generation students and for students who did not fit the dominant profile of the college's student body in terms of family income or other social factors. Research by economist Susan Dynarksi in 2016 suggested that lack of familiarity with academic protocols and the absence of an immediate friend or family member who experienced college life often could be overcome with provision of academic counselors and informal advisors – resources that were familiar to educated, affluent families but often alien to first-generation college students.[25]

CHARACTERS AND CONSTITUENTS

College Applicants and their Parents

This large, diverse group is a loose assembly that ironically has little in the way of organized advocacy even though it is a central constituency in college marketing. What one finds are clusters of small groups often defined by secondary school affiliation or social class. One historic exception to this took place between 1970 and 1972 when organized student rights coalitions worked effectively in lobbying on behalf of students as consumers in the drafting of landmark 1972 federal student financial aid legislation. These student rights groups' proposals, most of which succeeded, were in marked opposition to the priorities endorsed by the higher education establishment and its national associations.

Guidance Counselors

These professionals, usually employed as part of a secondary school staff, face some difficult, thankless situations. At most public high schools, the caseload is enormous and advising college prep students about applications coexists with responsibilities for truancies, classroom misconduct, vandalism, and theft. Putting out brushfires of day-to-day student misbehavior tends to trump clear focus on the subtleties of college admissions. Meanwhile, at private schools – ranging from boarding schools and prep schools to country day schools – the college advisors endure pressure from the head of the school along with ambitious, worried parents, not to mention students, for writing effective reference letters and making recommendations, all of which are expected to ensure acceptance letters from prestigious colleges. The popular image of private secondary schools is that they are "feeders" with a direct pipeline to admissions at prestigious colleges. This may be true for a small number with prestige, high academic entrance and graduation requirements. In fact, many private schools are beleaguered by having a large number of students who display some mix of indifference, insolence, and entitlement without a great academic transcript.

The Dean of Admissions

This official role historically served as the gatekeeper and recruiter for colleges in annual assignments to fill an entering freshman class. Starting slowly in the 1920s and accelerating after World War II, the dean of admissions changed from a relatively passive, clerical function often combined with serving as registrar to tending to admissions examinations, reviewing applications, and then enrolling admitted students. For some selective colleges during the decades 1910 to 1930 the dean of admissions sometimes served an exclusionary purpose to limit with quotas what the college president and board considered over-representation of applicants of certain racial, ethnic, or religious groups.[26] By the 1970s the watchword of admissions, especially at colleges with more qualified applicants than admission slots, was that the challenge was to "craft a class" in which admitted students adequately filled all the needs of campus activities, ranging from sports teams to musical groups.

The Vice President for Enrollment Management

Colleges and universities, in response to the competitive external environment, have created a new campus administrative position – the Vice President for Enrollment Management. Reliance on a dean of admissions no longer sufficed as the new, elevated vice presidential position involved oversight of traditional admissions and recruitment activities along with coordination with the university offices of public relations and government relations. It also meant increased attention to analyzing the flow of students – including concern to reduce dropouts and transfer-outs.

Institute for Higher Education Policy

This nonprofit policy research organization based in Washington, D.C., is popularly known by its acronym *IHEP*. Its flow of timely research papers and presentations constitute one of the foremost "voices" for first-generation college students and prospective college applicants from underserved groups.

Student Loan Marketing Association

Popularly known as "Sallie Mae," the Student Loan Marketing Association does two things: first, it buys student loans from banks and other lenders, thereby becoming the owner of the loan and the one responsible for collecting it when due; and, second, it lends money to banks, up to 80 percent of the face value of the student loans made by that bank, with those loans being the collateral to ensure that Sallie Mae will be repaid. In either case, the effect is that the bank funds are no longer tied up in its student loan portfolio, and the funds received from Sallie Mae then can be turned into more student loans or other kinds of investments a bank may want to make.[27]

COMPLEXITIES AND CONFLICTS: IMPLICATIONS FOR DECISION-MAKING

Concealing College Costs and Prices

The U.S. Department of Education announced on June 30, 2011 a new federal regulation that required colleges to provide student consumer information for a "net price" calculator. The legislation includes provisions for a website on which consumers can find out which colleges are most expensive, and which are least expensive. This "college navigator" feature is part of the Higher Education Opportunity Act Information on College Costs. Popular interest in the initiative increased as the "new web tool helps both experts and public grasp colleges' costs."[28]

The federal mandate has resulted in many colleges providing more and better information for prospective students. However, some start-up groups such as *Abacus* have pushed colleges to collaborate with their initiative to provide comparisons of costs across many colleges in a website format that is easy to navigate and accessible for prospective students. Just as many colleges bristled at the 2011 federal requirement for cost transparency public information, one finds in 2016 that *Abacus* from time to time jousts with deans of admissions to cooperate on the *Abacus* nonprofit collective Internet database.[29]

Need-Based versus Merit Scholarships

Colleges and universities commit a great deal of money to student financial aid. This is necessary for reducing the "sticker price" (or, full price) for many students. How does the college partition student grant money between merit scholarships and need-based scholarship? Usually institutions that lean toward merit scholarships do so to attract academically strong students who typically would choose to enroll elsewhere.

Grants versus Loans in Federal Student Financial Aid Program

The Pell Grant program, started in 1972, gained attention from college officials, prospective students and their families, and from the press, due to its emphasis on scholarship grants that a student recipient did not have to repay. The constituency to whom the program was directed from the start was high school students with good academic grades and high financial need. This did not necessarily mean that recipients were from impoverished families. The calculations to determine need, for example, took into account how many children from a family were attending college at the same time – a kind of consideration that reasonably could allow a middle income family to qualify for a Pell Grant. The grant program fused federal financial aid with social justice and civil rights. For other students, student loan programs apart from the Pell Grants were central to the strategy for the federal government in providing college financial aid in the form of attractive student loans.

Bankers showed little interest in taking on the risk of lending to students. As a result, Congress continually revised the terms of lending proposals so that they were increasingly attractive to banks. The capstone of this initiative was creation of the *Student Loan Marketing Agency*, whose abbreviation of SLMA led to the popular nickname of *Sallie Mae*. The essential strategy was for Sallie Mae, as a federal agency, to provide a *GSL (Guaranteed Student Loan)*.

In 1978, Congress favored a shift in federal student financial aid programs, characterized by a new emphasis on easily available loans and a simultaneous lessening of attention to providing grants to students with financial need. The result was the *Middle Income Student Assistance Act (MISAA)*. According to a Brookings Institution analysis, it "brought college loans to the middle class by removing the income limit for participation in federal aid programs."[30]

By the late 1970s, the era of consensus for support of higher education started to weaken due to the weight of current and projected expenditures – both from Pell Grant and student loan programs. Citing data showing that the amount of Pell Grant awards had not kept pace with rising college costs, college officials, in turn, raised concerns that Congress had retreated from its 1972 commitment to college access and affordability. By 2010, the average amount of loan indebtedness for recent college graduates was more than $17,000. This increased to about $30,000 five years later.

CONNECTIONS AND QUESTIONS

Why Does College Cost So Much?

The rising costs of higher education gained persistent news coverage. Consider, for example, the range of national media coverage that college costs attracted during the summer of 2011 and which continued to escalate in 2012. At a White House briefing for personal finance writers, President Barack Obama emphasized his concern over high college costs, noting that both the First Lady and he had acquired substantial student loan debts so that they could attend law school. This personal matter had policy implications because his experience (and debt) shaped his thinking on federal student financial aid legislation. The CNN evening television show *In the Arena* featured commentator Eliot Spitzer's report "The High Cost of College." His concluding message to viewers was:

> As states are increasingly financially stressed, raising tuition at public universities is becoming more and more common. While still a bargain compared to private universities, public higher ed is no longer the cost-free avenue to education it once was.[31]

To gain a sense of how pervasive and persistent articles about paying for college became in the national media, consider that the *New York Times*' Sunday Review section featured a "Room for Debate" forum on the topic, "College: Is It Worth the Cost?"[32] At about the same time, National Public Radio's *Here and Now* talk show focused on the question, "Will Today's Generation Be Less Educated than Their Parents?"[33] One implication was that rising college costs in the United States have become unbearable for many students and are lowering graduation rates. The lead story on NBC's *Evening News* on September 16, 2011, was, "Is College Still a Good Investment?" The report noted that "since 1980 the price of college tuition had gone up 800 percent more than the rate of inflation and that student loan debt is projected to pass the $1 trillion mark this year."

Rising college costs reached high tide in national political news in January 2012 when the President of the United States mentioned the topic in his State of the Union Address. Then two days later, on January 27, in an address in Ann Arbor on the campus of the University of Michigan, he called for linking federal aid to tuition costs. According to the Associated Press coverage, "President Barack Obama fired a warning at the nation's colleges and universities on Friday, threatening to strip their federal aid if they 'jack up tuition' every year and to give the money instead to schools showing restraint and value."[34]

Discerning the source of rising college prices and costs has led to intricate surgery on college and university budgets. As narrated in detail in other chapters, there were multiple reasons a student had to pay more and more in tuition. In the public sector, tapering state legislative appropriations for state universities meant that students as consumers were being required to pay an increased percentage of costs, which meant that this was shifted from a state subsidy to a consumer-borne "price."

This shift, however, was not the whole story. If, for example, students wanted small class sizes, nationally known professors, state-of-the-art laboratories, and libraries stocked with current scholarly journals and new books, these added institutional costs would in some measure be reflected in the rising price of tuition. Furthermore, academic fields varied significantly in their respective costs to educate a student who chose to major in that department. Physics, chemistry, engineering, and computer science were expensive in part due to the quick obsolescence of their equipment and facilities, as well as the high salaries of their faculty.

One question that resulted both from students and college officials was that of differential tuition. Should a student who chooses to major in an expensive field be expected to pay more than a student in an inexpensive field? Predictably, the answers depended on a student's personal situation. Advocates for a single tuition invoked the idea that a campus was, indeed, a marketplace of ideas – and that differential tuition intruded on a student choosing the academic field for which she was best suited. Also, an extraordinarily high tuition charge might discourage talented students from modest income families. A predictable counter was from some students who happened to be majoring in relatively inexpensive fields – such as history, English, or sociology. Why should they be subsidizing classmates who opted for expensive fields such as physics or chemistry? The questions were financial, but the discussions and decisions were philosophical.

Why Did College Cost So Little?

If, in fact, many Americans think that today college "costs too much," the implication is that college expenses are out of whack and probably have strayed from some time when the price of going to college was reasonable. So, if the situation is deplorable today, when was going to college reasonable and affordable? A problem is that many comprehensive databases on college students and enrollments are limited in the eras they cover. Few of the major college data were gathered by the federal government prior to 1970, so one has to make estimates and take core samples to gain an estimate of college prices and costs from, for example, about a century ago. What one finds is that college tuition charges everywhere tended to be low, both in terms of the prices of 1910 and also when indexed for inflation when compared to the tuition charges of today. For example, such historic, prestigious East Coast metropolitan universities as Harvard and Brown charged about $120 to $150 per year for tuition – a price that had changed little over the preceding 20 years. Indexing for inflation, this would be equivalent to about $4,000 in 2015. Room and board and other living expenses varied depending on "lifestyle," in some cases stretching as high as $500 to $600 for affluent students, and, when indexed for inflation, was far below the equivalent of the $50,000 price paid by a student today at an academically prestigious private college or university.[35]

On the face of it this appears to be a golden mean marked by a happy convergence of low price and low cost. In fact, it was "fool's gold." Unfortunately, on closer inspection one finds that colleges provided little in the way of financial aid to students with high financial need. There were some loans and a few prizes and small scholarships. If today's students were transported back in time to be consumers a century ago they would be surprised by the lack of academic support services, the characteristically frugal provisions for student activities, and essentially what was a barebones campus operation. Despite high dropout rates, there is little indication that college officials were concerned about either a student's lack of money or poor academic performance. If a college had charged a higher tuition, it could have had multiple sources of leverage: students from affluent families easily could afford more than $150 per year in tuition. Meanwhile, prospective students from modest income families could have received institutional grants and other financial aid as incentives to enroll and persist – most of which was not available. It was not a very good model for students. It was an example where low price was a false sense of economy.

Why Not Make College "Free" as a Federal Policy?

At first glance one is tempted to ask, "Who could oppose such an attractive offer?" Unfortunately, it is an offer that may be too good to be true. College cannot really be "free" because eventually someone has to pick up the tab for the *cost*. And, if this were a federal policy, it would be U.S. taxpayers. One controversial feature of this presidential campaign proposal in 2016 is that its details note that it applies only to "public" (i.e., state) colleges and universities. Why would sound policy exclude the nation's independent colleges and universities? They have long been a source of access and affordability, either by keeping tuition down and/or by providing institutional funds for financial aid. Federal student financial aid policies, such as Pell Grants, are applicable to all accredited colleges, whether public or private. Furthermore, numerous analyses over the years show that most independent colleges charge reasonable tuitions and work hard to provide need-based financial aid.[36] This "free college" proposal, if confined to public institutions, would limit student choice. Furthermore, it begs the question that voters and taxpayers and legislatures in many states have repeatedly sent the message that in their state they have no strong interest in providing state funds that would lower the price of college.

In states that did have a "no tuition" policy for decades, such as California, there was no guarantee that such a policy promoted access and enrollment across the family income spectrum. Hence, one potential dysfunction is that state college education would be "free" in price to numerous students from affluent families. An alternative proposal is that students with financial need be provided more financial aid.[37]

CONNECTIONS WITH DIVERSITY AND SOCIAL JUSTICE

Access to colleges and universities in the United States today seldom is defined and confined by the formal exclusions and segregations based on race, ethnicity, and gender that were widespread 50 or 60 years ago. Despite substantial gains in diversity and accessibility, many of the historical tendencies of inequity persist because there remains a high degree of association based on social class and family income. This is especially evident when one acknowledges that students from families of color fall disproportionately into modest and lower-income categories. This means that the costs and prices of higher education stand out as an example where economics intersects directly with significant issues of diversity and social justice. Most glaring is that the appeal of "going to college" has made American higher education often function as an "engine of inequality."[38]

One way to think about this in terms of divisions by family income is that for a reasonably affluent, education-minded and education-savvy family, going to college (especially a prestigious college) is "priceless." In other words, such a family will spare no expense to make certain that a daughter or son has optimal leverage in the college admissions and financial aid quest. An affluent and education-minded family usually is willing to pay more so long as it increases the prospects for admissions and academic prestige, perhaps with a long-term view on positioning for later admission to law school or medical school. In contrast, a modest income family with little experience with higher education, including applications and financial aid forms, often will back away from any uncertain expenditure or investment in programs that are pitched to enhance college accessibility and affordability. And that hesitancy is understandable.

This bifurcation along family income lines helps explain why even programs that provide need-based financial aid do not always completely gain acceptance. One partial solution is to provide first-generation college applicants with readily accessible information and assistance. A good example is the microfinancing online service called "Raise. me," which connects high school students with a tracking and point system connected to subscribing colleges and universities to allow a student to know how their decisions are helping – or hurting – both their odds of admission and financial aid. It operational-izes the economic strategy of "nudging" in which an accumulation of junctures and decisions tell an applicant whether they are making good moves in the path to college admission and affordability.[39] But even such promising nudges in the right direction probably pale in comparison to the kinds of advantages that affluent, college-savvy fam-ilies know about and pay for, such as college prep summer camps, private tutoring, or study abroad programs.

If one knows that such pre-college socialization and programs make a difference in who goes where to college and how well they are prepared, does one then include college prep camp and other activities in a plan for compensatory programs that promote genuine equity and access? Sociologists Christopher Jencks and David Riesman observed in their 1968 work, *The Academic Revolution*, that for the children of education-minded American families, going to college is not a sprint, but a marathon. Some competitive families start the preliminary heats of this race early, with kindergarten admission and, then, summer camp as the racer's edge. Forty years ago John Gardner, in his 1961 book, *Excellence*, asked, "Can we be equal – and excellent, too?" High prices at camp and campus signal that this has been difficult to achieve.

CONCLUSION

The terms "cost" and "price" in higher education are misleading in that their literal con-notation of finances tends to mask the profound social fact that going to college ulti-mately is about expectations and reality in American life.[40] One explanation for the persistent newsworthiness of rising costs of higher education is that "going to college" is serious business for Americans, and it is inseparable from paying for college. So although making college accessible and affordable is widely praised as part of the American Dream, this national commitment quickly leads to serious questions about what is reas-onable and what has gotten out of hand in determining college costs. It is a volatile topic that usually generates more heat than light. To reverse the trend – away from heat and toward illumination – one needs to consider college costs from a variety of perspectives so as to provide students, parents, taxpayers, and other citizens, along with college and university leaders and state and national legislators, with clarity about the implications of various higher education practices and policies.

Why is this further clarification of terms and issues important? Since the end of World War II, we as a nation have aspired to provide mass and even universal access to post-secondary education.[41] In 1910, for example, less than 5 percent of late adolescents between the ages of 18 and 22 attended college. Today, more than 60 percent in that age cohort enroll in a college, university, or institute – an achievement that has fulfilled pro-jections made by sociologists in 1970. Furthermore, college enrollments now include adults older than the "traditional college age" of 18 to 24.

Yet these gains in college enrollment kindle rather than temper heated debates about who should pay for college – and how much. To speak of higher education as an "invest-ment in learning" underscores that for most American families, it (along with buying a house) is one of the largest expenses one faces over a lifetime. Yet this individual or private consumerism coexists with the conviction that investment in higher education also is a "public good."[42]

Students' keen awareness about what they perceive to be the costs and benefits of colleges has, in turn, prompted American colleges and universities to be perpetually vigilant about tuition charges and balanced budgets, while at the same time making certain to provide programs and features that college officials think (or, rather, hope) will be attractive. These simultaneous demands have created an institutional behavior animated by the realization that each college has to compete vigorously to enroll students – especially students who can pay their bills. An illustration of this dependence on paying students is a 2011 survey reported by the *New York Times* that noted that universities were "seeking out students of means," with the elaboration:

> More than half the admissions officers at public research universities, and more than a third at four-year colleges, said that they had been working harder in the past year to recruit students who need no financial aid and can pay full price, according to the survey of 462 admissions directors and enrollment managers conducted in August and early September.[43]

In contrast, a report from Harvard in 2016 recommended that deans of admissions nationwide give increasing attention to non-academic factors and to have compassion and concern for values and character as part of deliberations on applicants.[44]

The result is a living history that plays out as a tradition of consumerism in which students and colleges each year go through an elaborate ritual of application, acceptance, and rejection and, then, enrollment. And, as with all buying and selling in America, the pervasive warning for students and their families who are shopping for colleges is *caveat emptor!*

NOTES

1. See, for example, Robert Archibald and David Feldman, *Why Does College Cost So Much?* (New York: Oxford University Press, 2010); Ronald G. Ehrenberg, *Tuition Rising: Why College Costs So Much* (Cambridge, MA: Harvard University Press, 2001); John R. Thelin, *The Rising Costs of Higher Education* (Santa Barbara, CA: ABC-CLIO, 2013).
2. Helen Lefkowitz Horowitz, *Campus Life: Undergraduate Cultures from the End of the Eighteenth Century to the Present* (New York: Alfred A. Knopf, 1987).
3. Martin Trow, "Reflections on the Transformation from Elite to Mass to Universal Higher Education," *Daedalus* (Winter 1970) vol. 40, pp. 1–42.
4. Rupert Wilkinson, *Attracting Students, Buying Students: Financial Aid in America* (Nashville, TN: Vanderbilt University Press, 2005).
5. Laurence Veysey, *The Emergence of the American University* (Chicago: University of Chicago Press, 1965) p. 274.
6. Henry Seidel Canby, *Alma Mater: The Gothic Age of the American College* (New York: Farrar & Rinehart, 1936).
7. Claudia Goldin and Lawrence F. Katz, "The Shaping of Higher Education: The Formative Years in the United States, 1890 to 1940," *Journal of Economic Perspectives* (Winter 1999) vol. 13, pp. 37–62.
8. Stuart M. Stoke, "What Price Tuition?" *Journal of Higher Education* (1937) pp. 297–303.
9. Richard Angelo, "The Social Transformation of American Higher Education," in Konrad H. Jarausch, Editor, *The Transformation of Higher Learning, 1860–1930* (Chicago: University of Chicago Press, 1983) pp. 261–292.
10. Jerome Karabel, *The Chosen: The Hidden History of Admission and Exclusion at Harvard, Yale, and Princeton* (New York: Houghton Mifflin, 2005); Debra Shore, "What Price Egalitarianism?" *Brown Alumni Monthly* (February 1981) pp. 12–19.
11. Christopher Jencks and David Riesman, *The Academic Revolution* (Garden City, NY: Doubleday Anchor, 1968) p. 12.
12. Debra Shore, "What Price Egalitarianism?" *Brown Alumni Monthly* (February 1981) pp. 12–19.

13. Noah Askin and Matthew S. Bothner, "Status-Aspirational Pricing: The 'Chivas Regal' Strategy in U.S. Higher Education, 2006–2012," *Administrative Science Quarterly* (2016) pp. 1–37.
14. Paul Clotfelter, *Buying the Best: Cost Escalation in Elite Higher Education* (Princeton, NJ: National Bureau of Economic Research Monograph with Princeton University Press, 1996).
15. Dannette Gerald and Katie Haycock, *Engines of Inequality: Diminishing Equity in the Nation's Premier Public Universities* (Washington, D.C.: Education Trust, 2006).
16. Goldie Blumenstyk, "Data Show Wider Gaps in Spending on Students," *Chronicle of Higher Education* (September 23, 2011) pp. A1, A12.
17. David Riesman, *On Higher Education: The Academic Enterprise in an Era of Student Consumerism* (San Francisco: Jossey-Bass, 1981).
18. Associated Press, "College Tuition Survey Spurs Government Probe," *Newport News* (Virginia) *Daily Press* (October 22, 1989) p. A1.
19. Associated Press, "College Tuition Survey Spurs Government Probe," *Newport News* (Virginia) *Daily Press* (October 22, 1989) p. A1.
20. Michelle Healy, "Ivy League Settles Price-Fixing Suit on Aid," *USA Today* (May 23, 1991) p. A1.
21. Eugene D. Gulland and Sheldon E. Steinbach, "Antitrust Law and Financial Aid: The MIT Decision," *Chronicle of Higher Education* (October 6, 1993) p. B3.
22. Chester E. Finn, Jr., *Scholars, Dollars and Bureaucrats* (Washington, D.C.: The Brookings Institution, 1978).
23. Edward P. St. John, personal communication with the author, November 26, 2015.
24. John R. Thelin, *American Higher Education's Tradition of Attrition* (Washington, D.C.: American Enterprise Institute, 2009).
25. Susan M. Dynarski, "Personalized Tips from a Counselor? That's Priceless," *New York Times* (February 21, 2016) p. BU3.
26. Jerome Karabel, *The Chosen: The Hidden History of Admission and Exclusion at Harvard, Yale, and Princeton* (Boston and New York: Houghton Mifflin, 2005).
27. U.S. House of Representatives Committee on Education and Labor, Subcommittee on Postsecondary Education, "Statement of Alfred B. Fitt." See also, John R. Thelin, "Higher Education's Student Financial Aid Enterprise in Historical Perspective," in Frederick M. Hess, Editor, *Footing the Tuition Bill: The New Student Loan Sector* (Washington, D.C.: The American Enterprise Institute, 2007) pp. 19–41.
28. Paul Fain, "New Web Tool Helps Both Experts and Public Grasp Colleges' Costs," *Chronicle of Higher Education* (July 9, 2010); John R. Thelin, "A Bumpy Road to Reforming College," *Inside Higher Ed* (September 20, 2013).
29. Ron Lieber, "Your Money: Concealing the Calculus of Higher Education," *New York Times* (January 16, 2016) pp. B1, B5.
30. Paul Light, "Increase Access to Postsecondary Education," in *Government's 50 Greatest Achievements: From Civil Rights to Homeland Security* (Washington, D.C.: The Brookings Institution, 2002) p. 22.
31. Eliot Spitzer, "Reporting the High Cost of College," *In the Arena* (CNN Broadcast, June 30, 2011).
32. "College: Is It Worth the Cost?" *New York Times* Sunday Review (August 28, 2011) p. SR 12.
33. Robin Young, "Will Today's Generation Be Less Educated Than Parents?" *Here and Now* (NPR, August 30, 2011); Eliot Spitzer, "Reporting the High Cost of College," *In the Arena* (CNN Broadcast, June 30, 2011).
34. Jim Kuhnhen and Kimberly Hefling (Associated Press), "Obama Calls for Linking Federal Aid to Tuition Costs," *Lexington Herald-Leader* (January 28, 2012) p. A15.
35. John R. Thelin, "Why Did College Cost So Little?: Affordability and Higher Education a Century Ago," *Society* (November–December 2015) vol. 52, no. 6, pp. 585–590.
36. Richard R. Spies, *The Future of Private Colleges: The Effect of Rising Costs on College Choice* (Princeton, NJ: Princeton University Industrial Relations Section, 1973); Harold T. Shapiro, "What Price College?," *Washington Post* (February 9, 1993) p. A16; Alex Petros, "McConnell Wrong: Prestigious Colleges Often Are More Affordable," *Lexington Herald-Leader* (July 22, 2014) p. A11.
37. Catharine Hill, "Free Tuition Is Not the Answer," *New York Times* (November 30, 2015) p. A21.
38. Danette Gerald and Katie Haycock, *Engines of Inequality: Diminishing Equity in the Nation's Premier Public Universities* (Washington, D.C.: Education Trust, 2006). See also, Suzanne Mettler, *Degrees of Inequality: How the Politics of Higher Education Sabotaged the American Dream* (New York: Basic Books, 2014).
39. Natasha Singer, "Got an A in Algebra? That's Worth $120: A Microfinance Site Offers an Inventive Nudge to Low-Income Students to Apply for College," *New York Times* (February 21, 2016) p. BU3.
40. John R. Thelin, "Expectations and Reality in American Higher Education," *Thought & Action: Journal of the National Education Association* (Fall 2007) pp. 59–69.
41. Claudia Goldin and Lawrence F. Katz, "The Shaping of Higher Education: The Formative Years in the United States, 1890 to 1940," *Journal of Economic Perspectives* (Winter 1999) vol. 13, pp. 37–62.

42. Howard R. Bowen, et al., *Investment in Learning: The Individual and Social Value of American Higher Education* (San Francisco: Jossey-Bass, 1977); Howard R. Bowen, *The Costs of Higher Education: How Much Do Colleges and Universities Spend Per Student and How Much Should They Spend?* (San Francisco: Jossey-Bass, 1980).

43. Tamar Lewin, "Universities Seeking out Students of Means," *New York Times* (September 21, 2011) p. A18.

44. Steve Cohen, "Real Compassion in College Admissions," *New York Times* Sunday Review (February 7, 2016) p. SR4.

Additional Readings

Robert Archibald and David Feldman, *Why Does College Cost So Much?* (New York: Oxford University Press, 2010).

Howard. R. Bowen, *The Costs of Higher Education: How Much Do Colleges and Universities Spend Per Student and How Much Should They Spend?* (San Francisco: Jossey-Bass, 1980).

Howard R. Bowen, et al. *Investment in Learning: The Individual and Social Value of American Higher Education* (San Francisco: Jossey-Bass, 1977).

Charles Clotfelter, *Buying the Best: Cost Escalation in Elite Higher Education* (Princeton, NJ: National Bureau of Economic Research Monograph with Princeton University Press, 1996).

Ronald G. Ehrenberg, *Tuition Rising: Why College Costs So Much* (Cambridge, MA: Harvard University Press, 2001).

Chester E. Finn, Jr., *Scholars, Dollars, and Bureaucrats* (Washington, D.C.: The Brookings Institution, 1978).

John W. Gardner, *Excellence: Can We Be Equal and Excellent Too?* (New York: Norton, 1961).

Dannette Gerald and Katie Haycock, *Engines of Inequality: Diminishing Equity in the Nation's Premier Public Universities* (Washington, D.C.: Education Trust, 2006).

Jerome Karabel, *The Chosen: The Hidden History of Admission and Exclusion at Harvard, Yale, and Princeton* (Boston and New York: Houghton Mifflin, 2005).

Michael McPherson, Morton Owen Schapiro, and Gordon C. Winston, *Paying the Piper: Productivity, Incentives, and Financing in U.S. Higher Education* (Ann Arbor: University of Michigan Press, 1993).

Suzanne Mettler, *Degrees of Inequality: How the Politics of Higher Education Sabotaged the American Dream* (New York: Basic Books, 2014).

Richard Moll, *Playing the Private College Admissions Game* (New York: Times Books, 1979).

Richard Moll, *The Public Ivies: A Guide to America's Best Public Undergraduate Colleges and Universities* (New York: Viking Press, 1985).

David Riesman, *On Higher Education: The Academic Enterprise in an Era of Student Consumerism* (San Francisco: Jossey-Bass, 1981).

Edward P. St. John, Nathan Daun-Barnett, and Karen Moronski-Chapman, *Public Policy and Higher Education: Reframing Strategies for Preparation, Access, and College Success* (New York: Routledge, 2013).

John R. Thelin, *The Rising Costs of Higher Education* (Santa Barbara, CA: ABC-CLIO, 2013).

Martin Trow, "Reflections on the Transformation from Elite to Mass to Universal Higher Education," *Daedalus* (Winter 1970) vol. 40, pp. 1–42.

Rupert Wilkinson, *Attracting Students, Buying Students: Financial Aid in America* (Nashville, TN: Vanderbilt University Press, 2005).

13

INNOVATIONS AND INTERNATIONALIZATION IN AMERICAN HIGHER EDUCATION

SETTING AND OVERVIEW

Innovation runs deep in the fabric and structure of American higher education. Contrary to the facile stereotypes of an insular, isolated "Ivory Tower," colleges and universities in the United States have long been hungry and vigilant in order to survive financially and to fulfill their various missions. And, at least in recent memory since about 1980, most colleges have continually considered options as they scanned the horizon for new approaches to academic programs and new enterprises. These are all part of a "managerial revolution" that took place and took root starting in the late 1970s. They may coexist with traditional curricular formats and historic buildings, but the net result is a continual synthesis of institutions that are simultaneously existing, exploring, expanding, and innovating.

Since 2000 there also has been a "marketing revolution" in these academic enterprises and services – ranging from student recruitment to branding of college logos and merchandise and establishing satellite campuses and centers. These ventures are indelibly linked to commercialization coupled with aggressive promotion and marketing.[1] We already considered a substantial dimension of this in Chapter 11, dealing with the *enterprising institution in research and development*. In this chapter we build from that base and look to numerous other activities and functions – and locations – where higher education institutions continually consider and sometimes act on decisive experiments and changes. Central to the analysis of higher education innovation are the following themes, many of which often overlap: *internationalization, institutional imperialism and expansion, Internet instruction and programs, "for-profit" institutions*, and *local "town and gown" initiatives*.

Innovation in the 21st century has included internationalization. Whether this means sending students and faculty abroad, enrolling students from other nations, project collaboration with universities in other nations, or building new sites abroad, international themes are present in the agenda for American higher education. The related concept of "globalization" has surfaced in the past decade as a charismatic slogan to describe initiatives by U.S. colleges and universities to alter their relations with other nations.

It includes sending students abroad, and recruiting students to one's campus from other nations. It also can refer to ventures such as building a new campus in another country, or pursuing research and development compacts and partnerships with universities and governments abroad. According to Ben Wildavsky, the result has been "the great brain race" in which global universities are purportedly "reshaping the world."[2]

Media coverage of "globalization" and "internationalization" represents an array of both opportunities and problems for colleges and universities in the United States. Ultimately, "globalization" works in numerous directions – and is hardly confined to initiatives that originate in the colleges and universities of the United States. Essential to the concept is recognition of interdependence, in which the economy and institutions of one nation are intertwined with counterparts elsewhere. The underlying message is that the United States and its higher education cannot afford to be oblivious to their counterparts worldwide. Implicit in all the considerations is the gnawing question, "How does the quality of higher education in the United States fare in comparison with developments and expansions in universities elsewhere?"

International Relations

From the start colonial colleges had obligatory "international relations" in that their charters came either from the Crown of England and/or from colonial governors appointed by the Crown. Furthermore, if a college such as William & Mary in Virginia established a divinity school whose intent was to provide advanced studies for future Anglican (Episcopalian) priests, the novitiates had to travel from North America back to England because ordination had to be conducted by a Bishop of the Church of England – and there were none to be found in Virginia, and certainly not in the New England colonies that were Protestant in ecclesiastic alignment. Another source of college building in North America came from Jesuits, primarily from France, who established seminaries and colleges in the area associated with the Louisiana Purchase.

In the mid-19th century a small but steady trickle of aspiring, adventurous scholars who had graduated from American colleges sought advanced degrees and graduate instruction at universities in Europe, especially at the numerous German universities. These Americans were "innocents abroad" who, having finished their Bachelor of Arts degrees, felt confined by the lack of advanced programs in the United States. Their spirit of academic adventure set a precedent for outreach and exploration – and brought home lessons of academic cross-fertilization. These American scholars were definitely Eurocentric, and had little travel or study at universities in, for example, China or India.

One new opportunity for young American men who had excelled in studies and demonstrated strong character in "manly" sports at American colleges came about in 1902, when British diamond mogul Cecil Rhodes established the Rhodes Scholarships. Each year 32 recent graduates from colleges in the United States were selected to join with counterparts from universities in Canada, New Zealand, Australia, and other nations part of the British Commonwealth for a two-year all-expenses-paid fellowship at Oxford. At the same time, there were signs of life in international programs offered at campuses in the United States. Between 1900 and 1940 students from a variety of nations worldwide enrolled at colleges and universities in the United States. Starting in 1924 the Rockefeller Foundation established several "International Houses" at selected, prestigious American universities to promote interaction of students from abroad and indigenous U.S. students, especially at New York City, Berkeley, and Chicago – with the eventual addition of other sites. Memoirs of International House alumni from numerous nations, many of whom went on to national and international fame and achievement as political leaders and scholars, attested to the remarkable experiences these residences provided.

Internationalism in American higher education may be characterized as a phoenix, resembling the mythical bird rising up from the ashes of the adversity of World War II. One source from 1942 to 1945 was professors at colleges and universities throughout the United States who rallied to the war effort by providing knowledge and instruction in a range of relatively esoteric and under-appreciated languages and cultural studies that had quickly become part of military operations and diplomatic relations. The U.S. Congress acknowledged these useful scholarly contributions in international studies by approving funding for numerous activities as part of the domestic, non-wartime economy. A combination of federal programs and private foundations encouraged American academics to go abroad and to welcome foreign scholars to the United States. This included the Fulbright Scholarship, the Danforth Scholarships, and Marshall Scholarships. These were elite in that they dealt with advanced scholars at top universities in both the United States and cooperating nations. And they were effective and appreciated. They also signaled a maturity and respect given to American colleges and universities.

One attractive arrangement was for governments in developing nations to send their outstanding students to the United States for master's and Ph.D. programs with full funding, based on the understanding that these students would then return to their home nation. This was a success, as the number of academic, government, and political leaders worldwide who experienced and applauded their graduate studies in the United States provided one of the strongest endorsements for the coming of age of American higher education, especially its graduate programs.

International interaction also worked in other arrangements. Foundations such as the Ford Foundation sponsored research projects for U.S. university-based scholars in a variety of fields, ranging from agriculture and engineering to humanities and history. There was little disagreement on the success and impact of such exchanges and programs. However, criticism from scholars such as Robert Arnove was that it led to a transplant of academic and cultural imperialism.[3] It included the "Green Revolution" in agricultural practices and policies. What was undeniable was that higher education in the United States gained unprecedented stature for its expertise and the high quality of its academic programs, especially its Ph.D. programs.

By 1970 a large number of colleges and universities had established "study abroad" programs for their undergraduates. These usually focused on literature and language studies in France, England, and other European countries. Also, since the programs were expensive, their realistic accessibility for most students was limited. Elsewhere, programs such as the nonprofit Experiment in International Living provided college prep high school students as well as undergraduates and recent alumni with learning and language studies in an increasingly varied range of countries.

A major trend since 1970 has been the persistent flow both of students from the United States to colleges abroad, and of students from numerous countries worldwide opting to enroll in academic degree programs offered by colleges and universities in the United States. Important to note is that this trend has extended to all levels of degree programs, whereas years earlier, international student enrollment at American colleges and universities tended to be concentrated in graduate and advanced professional degree programs. Conversely, the number of colleges and students in the United States who participated in various forms of study abroad expanded substantially, so as to be a basic offering at most colleges.

The United States became an international leader in postsecondary education planning following World War II. Since the continental United States had not suffered physical or economic devastation during World War II, the United States was relatively well positioned in terms of financial resources to give high priority to educational funding and expansion. Coincidentally, the expansion of public secondary education combined with returning military veterans and an increasing number of high school graduates meant that several tiers – individual institutions, state governments, and the federal government – were ready to commit to long-term investment in higher education access and construction. The master plans and new higher education systems that appeared between 1950 and 1970 would become a blueprint of sorts for other nations worldwide, especially in Europe, as various nations gradually experienced economic and structural recovery from World War II. For developing nations massive investment in and political control of universities became central to political and economic development.

For-Profit Colleges and Universities

For-profit colleges and universities (whose popular acronym is FPCUs) have long been a part of American higher education – but often have been overlooked in writings about American higher education. Proprietary schools, especially for such professions as medicine, law, and teaching, were staples as free-standing institutions in the 19th century. In the 20th century, with a growing need for business and industry employees, the growth of commercial schools and secretarial schools flourished, often with massive advertising for recruitment and admissions in popular magazines nationwide. The GI Bill, passed in 1944, helped the proprietary colleges in a wide range of academic and vocational subjects, including trades and crafts training, because if a school were accredited, it then qualified for receipt of federal funds to cover tuition and other expenses for enrolling veterans.

Proprietary colleges also benefited in the landmark 1972 federal legislation creating massive student aid programs, thanks in large measure to the success of their national associations and lobbyists in making certain that they were included along with "real" colleges and universities in being eligible to receive federal student financial aid funds. The important point is that although for-profit higher education has attracted both large enrollments and media coverage in the 21st century, this spotlight obscures their long-time presence in postsecondary education. A good example of this is illustrated by the case of the University of Phoenix, founded in 1976 by John Sperling, a former professor of history at San Jose State University in California. The purpose of the original University of Phoenix was to provide college courses and bachelor degree programs to underserved constituencies – namely, working adults who often were not welcomed or accepted at traditional four-year colleges, whether private or public. Classes were held at night and other convenient times for adults in a variety of accessible, non-traditional locations, including shopping malls, office buildings, and military bases. It was an institution whose mission expressed a commitment to what can best be described as the American belief in extending postsecondary education opportunity, especially in academic degree programs, for constituencies that had traditionally been underserved.[4]

Although the University of Phoenix, once called "Drive Thru U" in 1997 by a writer for *The New Yorker*, grew to be one of the most visible and successful institutions in the for-profit sector, it was hardly alone.[5] Other prominent for-profit college and university networks or systems included Kaplan, DeVry University, ITT, Pearson, National Business Colleges, and Sullivan University, to name just a few. History, however, also is the art of omission. What is left out may be one of the most important characteristics of the FPCU sector: the sudden disappearance and short lifespan of many of its one-time member institutions. Whereas the closing of a traditional nonprofit college or university tends to be unusual and often unexpected, it appears to be expected and commonplace in the associations of FPCUs – not unlike the high rate of closures among new small businesses. An important but long-forgotten case was that of LaCaze-Gardner Business School in Washington, D.C., which literally "closed its doors" without notice to students in November 1978. They abruptly fired all 21 instructors and closed its downtown administrative office. Most of its students were from modest income families without higher education experience. The owner, the subject of an FBI investigation, was charged with fraud and misappropriation of $2 million in federal student financial aid that his institution had received the preceding year. Beyond this case study, the larger story was that FPCUs accounted for about 44 percent of all federal student financial aid by 2004, even though they enrolled only 11 percent of all postsecondary education students nationwide.[6]

Thanks to exemplary new research by historian A.J. Angulo, this broad survey of FPCUs and proprietary schools is fleshed out by detailed, documented episodes of campus openings and closures. Using the dramatic, perhaps volatile organizing term of "diploma mills," Angulo provides accounts and historical details to bring to life allegations about dubious educational and financial practices stretching back into the late 19th century and extending into the 21st century. The general criticism of FPCUs is that they have been opportunistic and enterprising to excess whenever federal funds have been available for enrolling students. Furthermore, critics claim that FPCUs frequently have preyed on academically weak and financially impoverished students in their advertisements and recruitments. According to this line of historical analysis, FPCUs have held out the prospect of educational opportunity and career advancement – overtures that have all too often been followed by a profile of students who show high dropout rates, low degree completion, and high student loan indebtedness. Lack of sound data on job placement and professional career paths of FPCU students and alumni emerges as a recurrent source of concern – and external investigation. Graphic cases of a for-profit college abruptly closing up shop and leaving hundreds of students out of money and out of luck surface in newspaper accounts. Comprehensive task forces and investigations looking at the records of FPCUs included federal agencies in the 1930s and, again, in the late 1940s and early 1950s. There was another round of hearings in the late 1970s, with a growing momentum of federal investigation and court cases starting around 2010.

Central to the periodic charges are the data that show that FPCUs have relied heavily on federal student aid as their primary source of institutional income. An added source of financial and legal concern since about 2000 has been the simultaneous entry of FPCUs into the high-stakes, volatile arena of the Wall Street stock market and hedge fund investment strategies. Bankruptcy, as illustrated by the case of Corinthian Colleges, adds to the portrait of a sector characterized by allegations of financial risks and student exploitation, including predatory lending practices. At the same time that such records have surfaced, however, these same FPCUs – and their national associations – have been effective and forceful in lobbying congressional staff on federal policies and programs.[7]

Distance Learning

Starting in the 1990s, "distance learning" came to be strongly associated with college-level courses and degree programs offered on the Internet. This surge of popularity tended to mask the fact that American higher education has long made use of innovative media and technology to provide instruction, examination, and certification to students who were not physically present on campus.[8] Correspondence schools, relying on the United States Postal Service, flourished, starting in the late 19th century. Often overlooked is that many established colleges and universities, including highly regarded professors, participated enthusiastically. Another format was lyceum lectures and the Chautauqua Circuit of courses and lectures at sites far from campus, and sometimes geared toward what we consider lifelong learning. Extension services were another format, especially in agriculture and home economics. Many universities accepted as part of their outreach and service mission a responsibility to take the college to distant sites and underserved constituencies.

So, although digital and electronic innovations accelerated in the late 20th century, they drew from a legacy of media programs that had been in place for decades. In 1956 a national television network, ABC, devoted two hours each Sunday afternoon to broadcasting a series produced by Bell Laboratories Science Series that featured as host Prof. Frank Baxter of the University of Southern California, cast in the role of "Dr. Research." Some years later PBS attracted a large audience in 1969 and 1970 when it broadcast each Sunday evening an episode of Prof. Kenneth Clarke's *Civilisation* – a series so popular that it compelled viewers to look forward to the television equivalent of "Western Civ" instead of watching sitcoms and professional sports on major networks.

By 1980 several colleges and universities were collaborating with their state higher education coordinating councils to offer closed circuit television instruction beamed from a major campus studio to seminar rooms at company headquarters in rural areas for such programs as master's degrees in engineering or M.B.A. programs. In the mid-1990s "compressed video" technology allowed a state university to provide interactive, live classes at multiple sites statewide. These "distance education programs" also crossed state lines and raised questions about what a college education or degree program actually was. It raised questions of regional accreditation. Was a course under the jurisdiction of the state that broadcast the courses, or, perhaps, at the site where students received the images and information? MOOCs (massive open online courses), which surfaced early in the 21st century, were the latest variation on this theme of distance learning involving the sophisticated technology of the Internet. The real gains in enterprising success and Internet innovation may not be colleges and universities. Rather, spin-off corporations such as Coursera – often developed by university professors – offer to colleges as clients high-tech Internet courses and networks that colleges themselves cannot or choose not to develop.

Town and Gown: Local Initiatives

Colleges and universities have been interdependent with their host communities since the 12th and 13th centuries when academic institutions sprouted in such European cities as Bologna, Paris, and Oxford. At best, local vendors for food, wine, and beer, along with landlords who marketed student rental lodgings, benefited greatly from a university that enrolled students and employed faculty – all of whom were paying customers for local goods and services. Their proximity, however, was periodically a source of tension – with accusations of improper conduct volleying back and forth. Riots, often marked by injuries and even deaths, transformed "Town and Gown" into "Town versus Gown" – with "gowns" referring to academic regalia that scholars always wore as a distinguishing costume. An important change took place when some universities moved from merely renting local buildings for lecture halls while students rented apartments to the more enduring presence of the academic institution buying land for its own permanent buildings.

For Oxford and Cambridge Universities in England and, later, for colleges and universities in the American colonies, and eventually in the United States, this meant that colleges and universities had a formal presence in the politics, economy, and real estate of towns and cities. In many small towns and also in large cities, colleges and universities often stand out as the largest landowner and largest employer in the community and county.

ISSUES

Town and Gown: Local Innovation and Expansion

Accounts and memoirs of higher education from the late 19th and early 20th centuries have provided a rich legacy of strong images about the archetypal "college town." Henry Seidel Canby's accounts of Yale University and New Haven in the 1890s indicated that the campus was often a "state within a state" – with its own territory, regulations, and culture distinct from Main Street. Interesting is geographer Blake Gumprecht's 2009 comprehensive study indicating a new model for the American "college town" – the large state university in a relatively small-sized community, with intercollegiate sports stadiums and arenas providing the dynamism and magnet for joining town and gown.[9]

New York City has in the 21st century been a fertile site for innovation. An important case is that of the mayor inviting universities to bid to create a new model high-tech engineering campus. The winning selection for this ambitious innovation was Cornell University pairing with Technion-Israel Institute of Technology to create "Cornell Tech" as an applied sciences graduate school in 2013.[10] This case stands out as a high-risk, high-stakes venture that is both expensive and makes good sense. First, Cornell University's main campus in Ithaca is geographically distant from the energy and population of the state's major metropolitan center, New York City. A new Tech campus in New York City would help Cornell, as the state's land grant institution, truly serve the entire state with the mutual benefit of gaining from the talent, resources, and investment capital concentrated in the New York City area. Second, the new Tech college would add to Cornell's strong cluster of its medical school, labor relations school, and school of architecture already located in New York City. Third, collaboration and encouragement from the New York City mayor's office has been serious – including prospects of free land. In the Cornell case it meant Roosevelt Island – a space that heretofore has been underutilized. The City's commitment is estimated at $400 million and Cornell's investment is about $200 million. Furthermore, cooperation among Cornell, the city, and Technion-Israel Institute of Technology enhances the interdependence of institutions and communities. Public incentives were joined with private philanthropy, including $100 million from Bloomberg Philanthropies and $350 million from a Cornell alumnus.

The project has been competitive both in terms of academic rigor and financial investment, having included a serious proposal from Stanford University as well as bids from Columbia University and New York University. The new campus has the combination of resources, talent, pedagogical experimentation, supportive universities, and a cooperative albeit demanding host city government. By April 2013, a little over a year after having won the prize in competition for the right to create a new school, Cornell Tech was "up and running" with a "nondescript third-floor loft in the Chelsea neighborhood of Manhattan" providing the initial site until the new campus on Roosevelt Island is constructed. The pilot group of eight graduate students in an innovative computer science program combines information technology, business administration, along with mentors from the private corporate sector. Instead of "departments" the new program is based on three "hubs" – "connective media," "healthier life" systems, and what is called the "built environment" component. The layout of the physical space eschews separate offices in order to foster continual interaction. Cornell University, a member of the Association of American Universities, provides both legitimacy and financial commitment to the experiment. Cornell Tech stands out as an example where academic innovation is a serious business in town and gown alliances.

Elsewhere in New York City, in 2016 the New York City Economic Development Council undertook a markedly different approach than the Cornell Tech project. Instead of campus building, the Council is collaborating with the City University of New York to attract diverse groups of talent. The approach is to sponsor a visa program that will bring 80 immigrant entrepreneurs to the city and university. Called IN2NYC, the visiting entrepreneurs are expected to "set up shop" on various CUNY campuses to advise professors and students on how to build start-up companies. The magnet is that the selected entrepreneurs will qualify for a "skilled worker visa," known as an H-1B. The intent is to provide a path and place to overcome difficulties in allowing talented newcomers to come to – and then stay in – the city.[11]

The chemistry of town and gown continues to fascinate analysts and economic development advocates. Looking across the globe, one author sought to identify the most distinguished cities and universities that showcased the "geography of genius."[12] Another variation on the theme – but confined to the continental United States – that surfaced around 2015 is the new construct of "The University City."[13] Its operational definition and components are as follows:

> Each city has a metropolitan population of between 250,000 and 1 million and is closely tied to a major public research university. They all share characteristics that make them ripe for success in a 21st century knowledge-based economy:
>
> - A highly educated population;
> - Local talent and entrepreneurship;
> - An openness to new ideas; and
> - A lot of arts and culture.[14]

Advocates also emphasize that

> University cities also have other advantages: low violent crime rates, high quality of life, and relatively low cost of living. And, unlike many smaller college towns, they are in a good position to leverage the university for economic development and retain talent.

Furthermore, "That all combines to make them places where people want to live and work, which is important in a knowledge-based economy where jobs now often go where the talent is, rather than the other way around."

Based on these criteria the six members of the "University City" designation are as follows:

- Fort Collins, Colorado and Colorado State University
- Lincoln, Nebraska and the University of Nebraska flagship campus
- Madison, Wisconsin and the University of Wisconsin flagship campus
- Ann Arbor, Michigan and the University of Michigan
- Lexington, Kentucky and the University of Kentucky
- Durham–Chapel Hill, North Carolina and the University of North Carolina flagship campus.

Publicists for the "University City" group concluded, "Place matters because people can live where they want to now." All this is intriguing, even exhilarating. It is a new version of the 19th century "booster college" euphoria that animated the founding of towns and campuses, moving from the Midwest to the Pacific Coast. The enduring question is whether the "University City" is a *construct* in search of a following and members. Why, for example, does the operational definition include a public university – and not a private (or, independent) university? What is defining and necessary about that criterion? It would be difficult to consider the economic and creative magnetism of the Durham–Chapel Hill area without the roles and contributions of Duke University. Furthermore, identifying Durham–Chapel Hill as the metropolitan unit seems peculiar given that the "North Carolina Research Triangle" has for well over a half-century been defined by three cities – Chapel Hill, Durham, and Raleigh – as a celebrated pioneer of prosperous campus and community partnerships.

If the criteria simply designated the presence of a "university" or a "research university," one would expect to find numerous good candidates for "University City" designation: namely, for starters, Palo Alto, California and Stanford University; Providence, Rhode Island and Brown University; and Pasadena, California and the California Institute of Technology.

Cost of living differences within the group of six designated "University Cities" is substantial. Ann Arbor, Michigan is very expensive – so much so that new tenure track faculty have trouble affording rental prices, let alone buying a home. Furthermore, ultimately talent gravitates to a locale regardless of the cost of living – as suggested by the continual flow of highly educated talent into New York City, Washington, D.C., Los Angeles, San Francisco, and Chicago.

Interesting is that these recent concepts and depictions tend to overlook historical, classic college communities such as Princeton, New Jersey or Claremont, California. Most surprising is their tendency to omit inclusion of Boston. This seems wrongheaded given that Boston has long been the home of a large number of public and private colleges and their companion institutes, centers, museums, and workshops, with college and university students along with faculty and staff providing a substantial portion of the city's residents and revenue sources. If one were to identify a new model of campus and community a good candidate would be Worcester, Massachusetts.[15] Located about 40 miles outside Boston, Worcester represents a medium-sized unpretentious American city that has evolved slowly but persistently from its late-19th- and early-20th-century identity as an industrial city. Indeed, as its original industries have moved out or closed down, one finds that the various academic institutions in the city have increasingly cooperated to create a new network of "town and gown." Instead of building expensive, flashy campus dining halls, the city's colleges have devised an imaginative meal plan that encourages students to eat at restaurants in the city. The College of the Holy Cross, Worcester Polytechnic Institute, and the University of Massachusetts Medical Campus, along with other campus-related organizations, represent a collective force within the economy and social ecology of the greater metropolitan community.

CHARACTERS AND CONSTITUENTS

The Bologna Process

Created in 1999 this formal alliance of 24 European nations has been committed to advocacy and support of postsecondary education as a central component of European planning and development.[16] It is intertwined with the European Union's organization, the *European Higher Education Area*. One significant residual feature of the Bologna Process has been to reinforce development of universities and other higher education systems as an incentive for nations who seek membership in the European Union. Also related to the Bologna Process has been the development of innovations in access and enrollment in higher education programs across national boundaries. This has included the *Erasmus Plan*, which has served as an academic common market with ease of entry and admission for undergraduate students.

Organisation for Economic and Cooperative Development (OECD)

Created in 1961 as a successor to the 1948 *Organisation for European Economic Cooperation*, this formal group of 34 European countries focuses on strategic planning and economic development – including data collection and research reports. Its importance for higher education and the European Union has been its emphasis in the 21st century on advocating national investment in higher education as a primary feature of national and continental planning.

For-Profit Colleges and Universities (FPCU)

For-profit colleges and universities combine the mission of offering educational courses, programs, and academic degrees through a variety of formats along with financial and governance structures usually associated with commercial business corporations. These include investors and shareholders. Its distinction within American higher education is that by definition and custom a primary aim of the college is to make a profit and pay dividends to investors. Students enrolling at FPCUs are eligible to apply for and receive federal student financial aid. Most FPCUs are members of the Accrediting Council for Independent Colleges and Schools to satisfy regional accreditation requirements.

Higher Education Learning Commission (HLC)

This regional accrediting commission for postsecondary education programs conferring degrees traces its origins to 1895 as the *North Central Association*. With the dissolution of the North Central Association, authorization was transferred to the HLC. As one of six historical regional accrediting bodies, the HLC jurisdiction includes 19 states – from the Southwest through the Midwest.

Accrediting Council for Independent Colleges and Schools (ACICS)

This accrediting body has had in its membership, and subject to its review and approval, a large number of for-profit colleges and universities. The scope of ACICS recognition by the Department of Education and CHEA (Council for Higher Education Accreditation) is defined as accreditation of private postsecondary institutions offering non-degree programs or associate's, bachelor's, and master's degrees in programs that are "designed to train and educate persons for professional, technical, or occupational careers." As an accreditor for many for-profit colleges, ACICS provided information during U.S. Congressional investigations of for-profit education in 2010. ACICS reported that the institutions it accredits are required to demonstrate a student retention rate of at least 75 percent, to be calculated within a single academic year. In 2015–2016 ACICS was subject to scrutiny and reprimand from the U.S. Department of Education for its alleged laxness in oversight of educational programs and financial condition of several member institutions. It is not to be mistaken for the National Association of Independent Colleges (NAICU), a consortium and trade association of traditional not-for-profit independent colleges and universities.[17]

United States Department of Education

This federal agency is central to regulation of postsecondary education, including oversight of accreditation bodies. The latter is important because it is a determinant in whether or not an educational institution qualifies to be eligible for its enrolling students to receive federal student financial aid.

Confucius Institute

The Confucius Institute is a nonprofit public educational organization affiliated with the Ministry of Education of the People's Republic of China, whose aim is to promote Chinese language and culture support to local Chinese teaching internationally, and to facilitate cultural exchanges. The Confucius Institute is sometimes compared to language and culture promotion organizations such as Britain's British Council, France's Alliance Française, Spain's Instituto Cervantes, and Germany's Goethe-Institut. Unlike these organizations Confucius Institutes operate within established universities, colleges, and secondary schools around the world, providing funding, teachers, and educational materials. This has raised concerns over their influence on academic freedom, the possibility of industrial espionage, and concerns that the institutes present a selective, politicized view of China as a means of advancing public relations internationally.

The Confucius Institute program began in 2004 and is overseen by Hanban (officially the "Office of Chinese Language Council International"). The program is governed by a council whose top-level members are drawn from the Communist Party of China's leadership and various state ministries. The institutes operate in cooperation with local affiliate colleges and universities around the world, and financing is shared between Hanban and the host institutions. The related Confucius Classroom program partners with local secondary schools or school districts to provide teachers and instructional materials.

Community-Based Organizations

A central part of relations between a campus and community is the relationship of local nonprofits, charities, and services known by the acronym *CBO*. Unlike start-up companies and for-profit ventures, the CBOs usually are committed to increasing information and assistance on admissions for underserved high school students within an academic metropolitan community.

Consulting Firms

A relatively new and growing source of influence on higher education innovation has come from a small number of private consulting firms. Bain and Huron are prominent names. They serve as the de facto brokers and liaisons in both internal reorganizations and outside strategies. Since 2000 a hybrid organization has emerged that draws from the legacy of "R&D" think tanks. Data driven, these are used both in lobbying initiatives and in institutional planning.[18]

COMPLEXITIES AND CONFLICTS: IMPLICATIONS FOR DECISION-MAKING

Criticisms of Academic Imperialism: Internationalization and U.S. Expansion Overseas

Between 1995 and 2005 numerous major universities in the United States invested in construction of their own branch campuses in nations overseas. Typically this happened in places relatively new to the American university, areas such as the Middle East and Asia. Dubai, for example, was for several years a favorite site for establishing an American academic presence. However, several of these initiatives faced serious setbacks – due to a combination of financial problems, unexpected expenses, conflicts over academic freedom, and other sources of cultural tension that came to a head within what was intended to be an American-style campus. This meant that several American universities withdrew from their overseas campus-building ventures.

In the 21st century, however, a new slate of overseas campus expansion has taken place. One can readily understand the argument that such institutions as Yale and New York University have the resources and stature to build new campuses overseas as part of an extended, serious commitment to the internationalization of higher education. Since 2011 Yale has joined in partnership with the National University of Singapore to create a new small college that confers the bachelor's degree, in which one of its aims is "globalizing the liberal arts." It has been an accomplishment that Yale hails as the first time an Ivy League university has established a new college in Asia.

Cases such as Yale–NUS and New York University's international campuses are both the pinnacle of planning and success. However, the recurrent syndrome in American higher education is for numerous institutions to imitate belatedly these powerful pacesetters. Is it sound educational priority and policy, for example, for a public regional comprehensive university to invoke the same goals? Consider the case of the University of Akron, which was described by one higher education reporter as "a struggling regional, [which] hopes to expand worldwide." The case study is especially pertinent to the multiple themes introduced in this chapter because internationalization is combined with a not-for-profit college's reliance on contracts and outsourcing with "for-profit" organizations.

The University of Akron's President, Scott Scarborough, announced in 2016 that it was becoming a "national university" – a "university to develop a national presence with an international reach, through a proposed network of satellite campuses." Evidently fulfilling this vision included engaging Higher Education Partners, a for-profit company. Plans also included the possibility that the University of Akron might attempt to take over some campuses owned by ITT Tech, a for-profit chain that had been charged with fraud. According to Ellen Wexler of *Inside Higher Ed*, the plans for expansion of sites and mission came at a time when the university had cut 200 jobs at its historic campus and the president had been criticized for spending $1 million on renovating the president's house. The president said of his plans, "It feels uncomfortable at the moment because we are making a transition in character." His hope was that nationwide expansion would help bring the University of Akron out of its financial distress.[19]

Criticism of Internationalization as a Student Recruitment Strategy

On April 20, 2016 a front-page feature story in the *New York Times* focused on a disturbing practice: public comprehensive universities in the United States who were relying on paid foreign companies to recruit students from overseas to fill seats while not meeting regular university admissions standards. Recruiting companies such as Global Tree Overseas Education Consultants represented a thriving industry in which the American university pays a commission of 15 percent of the first year's tuition of students who enrolled – a fee estimated at about $2,000 per student. According to Prof. Philip G. Altbach, founding director of the Center for International Higher Education at Boston College, "There are some incentives for not delivering complete clunkers, but the underlying motivation for both the university and the agent is to get warm bodies in the door."

One campus highlighted in the article, Western Kentucky University, describes itself as "A leading American university with international reach." Its new building for the Honors College and International Center has a sign proclaiming, "Gateway to the World." The critical question, however, is that 106 of the 132 students admitted through the recruitment effort scored below the university's requirement on an English skills test. Such campus initiatives are described by university officials as exposing local students to global cultures. This motive coexists with economic necessity in which public colleges look at foreign students who pay full tuition as a source of institutional financial salvation. Reliance on agents who are paid a bonus, commission, or other incentive payment on the basis of the number of students who are recruited and/or enrolled was criticized by the National Association for College Admission Counseling as a potential source of "misrepresentation" where conflicts of interest were unavoidable. International recruiters often rely on "spot assessment" and "spot admission" to persuade students in, for example, India to enroll at a U.S. campus of which they have little knowledge. Marketing websites urge students to act immediately.[20]

Criticism of University Expansion within a Community

More conspicuous have been such cases as the place of New York University within Greenwich Village and Washington Square. Consistent with NYU's expansion in international programs and building overseas sites, its local initiatives in Manhattan have elicited objections from neighborhood groups and even from campus constituencies of faculty and staff. Disruption and dislocation, invoking eminent domain, and tearing down historic buildings are among the concerns about aggressive campus expansion.

Criticisms of FPCUs

The earlier section providing a summary of developments and trends in innovation included a bill of particulars in which FPCUs were cited, usually critically and negatively, for disproportionate reliance on federal student aid funding, followed often by little indication of effective training and placement for jobs. A predictable counter to such allegations by advocates and leaders among FPCUs is simply to ask detractors for comparable evidence of efficient, effective, and appropriate performance by traditional colleges and universities. One possible result is that even if FPCUs have fallen short, the counter claim is that so have nonprofit colleges and universities. Established colleges and universities are careless when they proclaim or imply their own record of achievement without compelling data. Furthermore, there is a great deal of mimicry that takes place in both directions between the FPCUs and the nonprofit colleges and universities. Perhaps the most comparable unit for the FPCUs could be public community colleges in that both enroll a high percentage of first-generation, modest income students who have little experience with navigating the maze of higher education and professional careers. In sum, any shortfall attributed to the FPCUs might also be found in, for example, the community colleges and perhaps in some regional comprehensive public universities, which are characterized by open admission and show a high dependence on students with Pell Grants, low retention and even lower graduation rates, and lack of data on job placement. In 1981, for example, the Council on Postsecondary Education (CPEC) in California conducted a study of enrollment, graduation, and transfer and degree completion at the state's massive network of more than 100 public community colleges. Many of the "missions" (plural) taken on by the community colleges were largely untestable in terms of such measures as "value added" to be "job ready" or "work preparedness."

The lines between the FPCUs and the nonprofit colleges and universities are increasingly blurred. The televised promotional for SNHU – Southern New Hampshire University – is a good example.[21] Originally founded as a business school in downtown Manchester, New Hampshire, SNHU eventually became formally registered as a not-for-profit degree-granting accredited academic institution. During the past decade SNHU has expanded its relatively small traditional campus of about 2,500 annual enrollees to include nationwide television marketing for its online programs – which typically enroll 25,000 students per year. Its president and academic leaders are forthright in noting that the FPCU University of Phoenix provided both a model and inspiration for SNHU's transformation. The television advertisements, often featuring an SNHU bus that travels across the United States, emphasize accessibility for working adults. Self-improvement and self-esteem are fused with the autonomy of online computer learning along with traditional commencement ceremonies in a full auditorium with graduates in caps and gowns, cheered on by family and friends. The television slogans are attractive, urging prospective students to consider SNHU and "See Yourself Succeed." On balance, one finds that *both* traditional and for-profit colleges gear their online degree programs to non-traditional students, with curricular emphasis on degrees that are perceived as practical and "employable." Traditional academic terminology for sites and services, such as "campus," "faculty," "library" are used in reference to new structures and formats.

FPCUs stand out in higher education because of their "business model" operations that include reliance on investors who seek a profit and management which is associated with distinctively swift decisions on staffing and closures. Consider the headline article on April 7, 2016: "University of Phoenix Lays off Nearly 500 Employees":

> The University of Phoenix laid off 470 employees on Tuesday, according to *The Arizona Republic*. The move comes after Phoenix's parent company, Apollo Group, announced in February that it was in the process of selling the company to a group of private investors for $1.1 billion.
>
> "A significant workforce reduction was announced today in departments across the university. I support the decisions and am gratified by the planning that ensures a seamless student experience with minimal disruption. I also am grateful for the work of our human resources leaders to ensure our colleagues affected by the restructuring receive severance and outplacement services," said Timothy Slottow, president of the for-profit institution, in a statement. "This difficult decision came after careful deliberation and analysis with a focus on stream-lined workflow serving fewer students than in years past, improved use of technology and ultimately an approach that ensures our students have the transformative experience that leads to higher retention and improved learning outcomes."[22]

However, it's not clear that FPCUs are unique in their abrupt staffing cuts. Shortly after the University of Phoenix news release, the University of California, Berkeley announced in April 2016 that it was laying off 500 campus staff. It was another example of where the sectors often shared behaviors.

If FPCUs and traditional colleges are often blurred in their form and function, there are pronounced differences in their respective governance, accreditation, and funding models. In some landmark cases, governing bodies have drawn a formal line between an FPCU and a nonprofit college. An interesting counter to this blurring came about in 2016 when an FPCU was denied in its petition to shift its legal charter to that of a non-profit institution. On March 4, 2016 a news release from Credit Suisse announced that Grand Canyon University terminated its bid to convert the university to not-for-profit status. The release elaborated: "Expressing surprise and dismay at the outright denial by the governing body of its accreditor," the Higher Education Learning Commission (HLC), the company announced that its 18-month effort to convert the university has ended. It simultaneously announced a new $100-million share repurchase program. The analysis provided investors the good news that the unexpected decision actually represented a "positive development for investors" because

> The debt burden on GCU contemplated in the proposed transaction [to become a not-for-profit] would have effectively prevented the university from expanding into new states and potentially relegated the services company to the status of a micro-cap orphaned stock with no compelling peers. While the return of several hundred million dollars of shareholders' capital would have been welcome, the company seems ready to substitute for this loss through share repurchases.[23]

The HLC used the case to issue new policy guidance regarding the practice of a college "outsourcing" services with the following statement:

> In addition, the Board concluded that the current Eligibility Requirements and Criteria do not allow for an institution to outsource all or the majority of its basic

functions related to academic and student support services and curriculum development, even where the contract between the parties indicates that the accredited institution provides oversight of those services.

Grand Canyon University objected, as it felt that "this policy had not been consistently enforced previously." Prohibiting or restricting an accredited college from outsourcing vital functions, they felt, was likely to have a dampening effect on reform efforts in curbing college costs. Credit Suisse concluded that "For-profit schools are not going to easily escape their model," Urdan said in a written statement. "Creative efforts to unlock value by separating profit making from regulatory oversight may find that goal increasingly difficult to achieve."[24] However, Credit Suisse did not see the ruling as a threat to the online program management (OPM) model.

Town versus Gown

For city, county, and metropolitan governments, local colleges and universities represent a combination of prospects and problems for urban vitality. An obvious source of concern that has surfaced with increasing frequency is that of property taxation. Yet many metropolitan governments are likely to overlook or downplay this direct issue if the sense is that a local campus is behaving like a good partner in major economic initiatives crucial to both the community and campus. An example of conflict coming from proximity is when a civic sports arena that has long depended on the university's championship team as major tenant looks elsewhere. What ensues may be skirmishes over zoning or veiled threats of retaliation: for example, in which the city council implies that it might refuse a university request to close a street near its medical center so long as the university delays renewing its downtown lease for its basketball games.[25] Colleges and universities become more important to a city when industrial manufacturing moves out, leaving many downtowns dependent on service organizations, government agencies, banks, and law offices – all of which are desirable, but probably not sufficient to provide either the volume of jobs or the property taxes of a major manufacturing plant.

Do academic institutions in the "University City" category participate in civic advancement? There is some evidence that town and gown cooperation is not always in place. In Lexington, Kentucky, a group of business and community leaders formed an initiative called "Together Lexington" in April 2016 to energize the community by creating a marketing campaign and funding project that aims to improve quality of life. This would appear to be a perfect match with the "University City" announcements earlier in the same week. Founding members of the alliance included leaders from a home construction firm, a telecommunications corporation, the CEO of the local United Way, the president of the local newspaper, the president of a bank, several corporate executives, along with representatives of a heating and air conditioning company, the marketing director of a major medical insurance group, the president of the local community and technical college, and the CEO of a prominent horse racing track. "Together Lexington will build pride by promoting the unique assets of the community."[26] There was no mention of the state university, which a week earlier had been hailed in the same newspaper as the "economic engine" and "cultural center" of this metropolitan area. So, readers were left to guess about the role of a flagship state university in the overall life of the community.

The kind of economic development and job creation associated with Silicon Valley has not always led to harmonious town and gown relations. The San Francisco Bay Area already had experienced the mixed blessings of prosperity and magnetism combined with escalating real estate prices and crowding. A question was whether the gains of having a new employer helped or harmed an established campus town. For example, when Google established a major outpost in the university town of Boulder, Colorado, it faced problems with local citizens. According to Conor Dougherty, reporter for the *New York Times*:

> The locals say they do not like the tech folks pouring into town to work at places like Google. They are insular. They are driving up housing prices. And the locals fear those newcomers are more like invaders than people trying to fit into their new community.[27]

Although a high-tech company such as Google may bring a substantial payroll and educated employees into a community, its large, lavish campus for 1,500 employees was feared by incumbents as the source of a dead zone for pedestrian and retail activity. To add to municipal problems of crowding and traffic, a concern was that Google had made provisions only for 600 parking spaces – far less than half its employees. According to one city council member, the newcomer company's claim that "Boulder was lucky to have Google" could be countered by the response that Google was "lucky to have Boulder."

One of the bold claims of the advocates of the "University City" category was that by definition it was characterized by relatively low crime rates. Perhaps so, but tragically and ironically in one "University City" this claim was tarnished a few weeks later when feature articles revealed that three university students had been charged in a robbery threat that led to a shooting death.[28] Indeed, the image of campuses and their neighborhoods as "safe havens" has come under increasing scrutiny, with justifiable questions about incongruities between campus crime report data and those of the surrounding municipality. Cities and communities often are at odds on provision of – and payment for – municipal services. One seemingly trivial example (which really is not trivial to a city) is the inordinate expenses caused by students sounding false alarms to local fire departments.[29]

CONNECTIONS AND QUESTIONS

How Is International Economic Development Connected with Higher Education?

Even though state university presidents along with governors and some politicians hail their nearby universities as "engines of innovation" and "a source of economic growth," research over time has suggested a different relationship: namely, investment in and funding of higher education usually follows a period of economic transformation and prosperity.[30] If one uses universities in late medieval Europe as the focus, one does find that they were indispensable for educating graduates who were highly competent for bringing order and coherence to the administration of a variety of institutions of government, church, empire, and commerce. Abilities such as drafting of regulations, legislation, and policies paved the way for prosperity and peace. True, universities then may provide an educated citizenry and workforce to fit into an increasingly complex national economy. And, educated alumni in a range of fields may provide technological and creative inventions that stimulate enterprise. But these usually are sequels or supplements to a fundamental economic boom, whether it is in overseas trade or domestic manufacturing. Historian Martha Howell of Columbia University, looking back at the rise of capitalism in various nations and regions worldwide since the 15th century, noted:

> New studies of the United States' emergence as a capitalist power, of European's moves into Asian markets, African lands, and South American mines during the Renaissance, or of South Asia's or China's entry into the global economy appear daily. The history of financial institutions is also receiving new attention from historians treating monetary policy, banking, and credit as central elements of the capitalist system that defines the West, not simply the subjects of technical studies.[31]

Yet the place of higher education remains at times uncertain and marginal in these epic economic developments. Invention – and adoption – of standard gauge railroad tracks across counties and states in the late-19th-century United States was more important to economic development than the founding of new universities of the same era. The "Knowledge Industry" that emerged after World War II was a successor to 19th-century industries of railroads, mining, and oil refining. It would stimulate new technologies and industries, but it would do so as a second act in national development. Even in business administration, M.B.A. programs have followed, not led, economic development and commercial organization models.[32]

University building was conspicuously absent from imperial expansion by England, France, Germany, Belgium, the Netherlands, Spain, Austria, Hungary, Sweden, Denmark, Italy, and Portugal in their respective colonies. These nations asserted their power by building castles, forts, railroads, churches, and cities as part of networks for extending commerce, religion, and politics. Compounds for living quarters to house civil servants, diplomats, and representatives of the Crown usually included schools that were typically restricted to their own children. And, families usually sent their sons back to the home country to go to universities such as Oxford, Cambridge, the Sorbonne, or Bologna. Only in the American colonies does one find initiatives for serious commitment to creating academic institutions that were chartered and funded.

Elsewhere, outside North America and Europe, the dynamic university is a paradox. It has been a relatively new institution in old cultures and political states. In India, China, Egypt, and numerous other countries one can find examples of libraries, museums, military academies, ecclesiastic seminaries, and other special purpose institutions. But universities whose purpose was to provide advanced learning accompanied by certification of academic degrees were rare.[33]

The newfound importance of university building in China, Japan, Latin America, and the expansion of integrated higher education partnerships of the OECD in Europe has been recent and reactive. They also have been unoriginal in that they have imitated Western models of institutional building, governance structures, data collection, and social organization for coordinated planning. They represented strategic responses to extend prosperity by refining initial economic growth into a later stage of diversification and educated innovation. Higher education was restrictive in two ways: first, it was confined to the education of a small percentage of the population, usually with the dual role of certifying experts and elites; second, it tended to concentrate the power of advanced education into an existing privileged elite, with some allowance for recruitment of new talent into its ranks. In a nation that experiences initial economic growth, governments and corporations tend to put into place formal institutions to provide the directing and tracking to shape how and where wealth – and education – will be distributed, usually characterized by institutionalizing and perhaps increasing inequities.

What Are the Prospects for and Trends in International Financing of Higher Education?

In contrast to the United States' reliance on a peculiar, hybrid model of financing colleges and universities, most nations elsewhere have had the benefit of direct support from a national ministry of education. An attractive consequence of this central governmental policy was that student tuition and fees traditionally were low and affordable. However, since about 2008 the nation-by-nation trend, whether in developed or developing nations, is that a downturn in the global economy, combined with initiatives to extend postsecondary education to a larger number and percentage of citizens, has changed the funding model. According to international research on higher education finances conducted by Bruce Johnstone and Pamela Marcucci of the State University of New York at Buffalo's International Comparative Higher Education Finance and Accessibility Project, there has been a widespread trend in which national governments and their universities have shifted an increasing percentage of higher education support to a cost-sharing model – with students and their families paying higher prices as part of overall institutional costs.[34] These trends, pronounced by 2016, represent a substantial change from a decade earlier in which higher education in the United States was singled out for its relatively high – and growing – tuition prices. The status as of 2016 is that universities in nations elsewhere have over time and perhaps belatedly drifted into a closer approximation of the U.S. funding model. In other words, low or no tuition for a higher education system committed to mass or universal access has been found to be untenable by most nations.

How Have Relations Between Traditional and For-Profit Colleges and Universities Fared?

Why was obtaining not-for-profit status important for a new institution – or for an established institution that wished to switch from its prior "FPCU" status? First, it meant that the university could qualify for tax exemptions on income and on real estate property taxes. Their faculty and staff probably would be eligible to apply for federal and foundation research grants. Donors would be allowed to claim philanthropic tax deductions. Second, in terms of institutional image and identity, the CEO of Grand Canyon University told reporters their desire was to "avoid the 'stigma' of being part of the sector, which has faced broad scrutiny and recent high-profile investigations and collapses." He said, "We have a lot more in common with traditional colleges that have a nonprofit status."[35]

One sign of competition between the FPCUs and traditional universities was within the state of Arizona. The President of Arizona State University, a highly praised advocate of higher education innovation, persuaded fellow presidents of universities in the Pac-12 intercollegiate athletic conference to resist overtures by the Phoenix-based FPCU Grand Canyon University to gain full participation as a member of the National Collegiate Athletic Association. This friction, however, also could be interpreted as a sign that some

FPCUs were now seen as an entity to be taken seriously by the established state universities.

In the first decade of the 21st century one could say accurately that the for-profit colleges and universities had changed the landscape of higher education.[36] In 2010 FPCUs reported robust enrollment growth, accounting for about 10 percent of students in degree programs nationwide. However, over the next five years FPCU enrollment declined by 26 percent, which according to Goldie Blumenstyk was a far greater dip than the 9 percent decline for all higher education in those years.[37] The University of Phoenix's enrollment went from 455,600 students in 2009 to about 216,000 in 2016. Between 2009 the FPCUs experienced a severe decline in their financial portfolios – with the ten largest publicly traded companies going from a collective worth of about $30 billion to about $1 billion. The Apollo Education Group, the parent corporation of the University of Phoenix, declined in stock market value from $10 billion in 2009 to less than $1 billion in 2016. By 2016 external problems for FPCUs had increased. The president and chief executive officer of the ACICS resigned. This came in the wake of Congressional hearings in which this accrediting agency was publicly criticized for having approved Corinthian Colleges, "right up until that company's collapse." In April 2016, 12 state attorneys general called on the U.S. Department of Education to deny federal recognition of ACICS, citing "extreme failures in the accreditor's evaluation of for-profit colleges, including Corinthian, Westwood College, the Education Management Company's Art Institutes and Brown Mackie College, ITT Tech, and Career Education Corporation's Sanford Brown campus."[38]

Yet many of the characteristics associated with the practices of for-profit colleges – sometimes critically – continue to surface at traditional colleges. This includes eliminating or at least reducing tenure track faculty positions; establishing satellite campuses without traditional campus landscaping and amenities; adding practical curricula; recruiting non-traditional student constituencies; and, at least partial reliance on online course enrollments.

How Has Distance Learning Fared at Traditional Colleges and Universities?

Illustrative of the adaptability and synthesis in American higher education is that numerous "traditional" universities have come to include and even celebrate their partnerships with distance learning. Consider the following mass e-mailing whose subject was "Earn Your Degree Online from ASU":

> Arizona State University is where innovation thrives. Click here for more info. Arizona State University is setting a new standard for online education. ASU offers over 50 of our undergraduate degrees online with the same curriculum and prestigious faculty as on campus, but with the added flexibility of learning on your own schedule. With nearly 90% of graduates receiving job offers within 90 days of graduation, it's time to see what being an ASU Sun Devil can do for you.

Among the attractions are "same courses as on campus," "Award-winning faculty," "100 plus degrees online," "Transfer credits accepted." The concluding note was that one can "Learn to Thrive at Arizona State University" – and, most important, "ASU was named the #1 university for innovation by U.S. News & World Report, ahead of both MIT and Stanford." Historians are expected to look at context and details. In this case the e-mail was dated "April 1, 2016." Evidently, however, it was no April Fool's joke from ASU.

So, one takes seriously the ventures and claims of established flagship state universities in extending their medium, message, and mission to embrace distance learning.[39]

If Arizona State University represents a traditional, nonprofit college or university that has adopted distance learning as a central feature, what is the box score or balance sheet for other colleges and universities? On balance, one finds that by 2016 there has been a remarkable synthesis in which most traditional institutions have come to accept and offer Internet courses and programs and distance learning at the very least as options within their respective arrays of curricular offerings. And, there is of course a wide range of incorporation and innovation. In April 2016 the editors of the *Chronicle of Higher Education* published a special report, *The Digital Campus: Tech Innovators 2016*:

> Meet this year's tech innovators – nine men, women, and projects using education technology boldly and broadly. This is the fourth time in recent years that *The Chronicle of Higher Education* has featured innovative uses of technology to solve problems – to develop more personalized instruction, preserve scientific integrity, help disabled vets get an education, and more. We were just as interested in projects with a shoestring budget as we were in bigger, more-ambitious projects. We considered leaders in various sectors, so you'll meet ed-tech entrepreneurs, student activists, a community college president, and a scholar who wants us to ask questions – many questions – about who benefits from technology.

CONNECTIONS WITH DIVERSITY AND SOCIAL JUSTICE

The kinds of innovations and expansions that are the focus of this chapter are for the most part incidental to colleges' and universities' commitments to diversity and social justice. More often than not, they have pulled a college toward goals and constituencies. Perhaps the major connection with diversity is that globalization means that a campus may draw students from nations and countries it previously had overlooked. However, this gain in international diversity was silent on increasing diversity among students in the United States.

The FPCUs suggest a potential link to diversity and social justice because they often have been established with an avowed commitment to serve non-traditional student constituencies that often were overlooked or deliberately neglected by traditional not-for-profit colleges and universities. In other words, for-profit colleges and universities enroll a large number and high percentage of students who fall into one or more of the following categories: non-traditional students – namely, adults who are working and prefer to pursue an academic degree via part-time study, often relying on evening classes and/or Internet instruction. Also, historically, FPCUs' enrollment has included a large number and percentage of students with marginal high school academic transcripts and who are from modest income families. However, the corollary and problematic side of this FPCU enrollment pattern is that these same recruited students have tended to experience high student loan indebtedness, a high dropout rate, and relatively low records of completing academic degrees. Also problematic has been the allegation that many FPCUs have not done well in fulfilling the explicit or implicit pledge of providing courses of study and certification that lead to jobs and job offers in appropriate professional positions related to the course of study.[40]

CONCLUSION

Although colleges and universities today still bear strong resemblance to their counterparts from 2000, both the large-scale innovations and incremental adaptations of the past 16 years represent a deceptively substantial amount of change in the structure and programs of American higher education. Academic institutions have in large measure been the crucible of inventors and innovators – namely, alumni who have gone on and gone out to create and then market new products and services associated with a digital age. And, Alma Mater, although not always in the vanguard of implementing such new systems and services, has slowly but surely embraced change as both necessary and exciting for an evolving, modern institution.

Innovation has followed a distinctive rhythm in which established colleges and universities are momentarily dazzled by new forms and financing elsewhere, such as those pioneered in the for-profit colleges and universities. Eventually, however, there is a synthesis in which traditional campuses make at least selective changes. One is hard pressed to name a college or university that does not make abundant use of the Internet, web pages, online instruction, and social media promotion, along with new partnerships with a variety of outside organizations and corporations. Every incumbent administrative office has moved into the digital era. It could be the development office's reliance on social network data systems to identify potential donors. The admissions office and its enrollment management also have moved into the 21st century with tracking and corresponding with potential applicants. The university library of the 21st century increasingly moves toward access to electronic databases and subscriptions, veering away from the traditional large building with book stacks.

Innovation within a campus probably is underestimated because of the decentralized character of a modern, complex college or university. For example, although a Vice President for Information Systems may have formal authority over Internet projects, most likely many faculty, staff, and students are working autonomously on their own innovations – with or without formal approval or funding from the top administration.

The degree of innovation in an established college or university is deceptive and, hence, under-acknowledged. The same understatement often holds true for the resilience of historical colleges and universities. Despite dire predictions around 2010, distance learning programs and Internet courses as emphasized by some for-profit institutions did not mean the demise of established colleges. Student demand for new modes of instruction and accessibility of services has coexisted with comparably strong insistence that colleges still provide facilities and services – upgraded, of course, with the latest wiring and technology. Interesting to note is that new FPCUs – and their advocates and architects – invoke the forms and symbols of the "traditional" campus. Internet bachelor's degree programs may not attract many physics majors nor demand construction of physics laboratories – but students and their families still insist on wearing academic gowns and having commencement ceremonies in the campus auditorium.

For all the soul-searching and worries of presidents, administrators, and trustees at traditional colleges in the United States, an irony is that American higher education persists in being both the standard and often the destination of students, scholars, faculty, and researchers from other nations. A price of this popularity in some cases will be disputes over admissions slots, especially if domestic taxpayers believe – accurately or not

– that *their* daughters and sons are being denied enrollment at their flagship state university in favor of international students who are willing and able to pay high out-of-state tuition prices.

This observation hardly gives license for American academic leaders to be complacent. At the same time it does provide a nod of affirmation that puts a curb on outlandish and desperate ventures. Perhaps the major temptation for concerned colleges and universities to avoid is that of mistaking *imitation* for genuine *innovation*. In 2009, for example, presidents and provosts returned from national conferences where invited speakers from expensive consulting firms relied on PowerPoint slides to "show" convincingly that for-profit institutions' record in enrolling students for Internet courses and degree programs were eroding the traditional campuses' base of students and tuition payments. So, perhaps one of the messages campus administrators carried home to their trustees, deans, and faculty was that Internet courses were the "wave of the future" and even the salvation for institutional problems. But were they? One mistake was to presume that new Internet courses and programs were inexpensive to establish and operate – and were going to be a convenient source of revenue.

Innovation is expensive and, done appropriately, is not a "quick fix" or panacea for a college or university that is floundering or stagnant. In fact, since the Internet course market was already saturated and sophisticated, a very bad decision would be to delve into the Internet enterprise without a lot of money or expertise. The initial investment in effective, attractive Internet courses is high – ranging from the technology of production to the payment for an accomplished, expert "instructor." Second, implementing an Internet program at a "traditional" campus did little to reduce dependence on familiar facilities – including libraries, laboratories, and dormitories. Third, the profitability of Internet and distance learning for the for-profit sector may have been exaggerated, perhaps illusory. The change in the financial profile and prospects of the for-profit institutions between 2010 and 2016 indicate a "boom and bust" pattern.

The same message holds for the confidence of the Bologna Process and the universities affiliated with the euro system from a decade ago – but which now has modest aspirations as the euro's value against the U.S. dollar gradually subsides.[41] As for the lure of a university in the United States establishing and then staffing a new campus overseas, this is a venture that perhaps a Yale University or a New York University can afford. But its aim ought to be educational rather than financial – as it will most certainly be expensive and time-consuming.

The danger zone for institutions within American higher education will be chronically underfunded public campuses in states where there is a decline in both the number of high school seniors and the percentage of those who opt to go to college. Small, independent church-affiliated colleges with modest endowments and located in isolated, underpopulated areas also are at risk. However, this latter group has an advantage in that they have long experience in facing adversity and operating on a lean budget. Differences within each group are substantial in the amount and appeal of their new programs and innovations.

Among student constituencies, the disappointing side to internationalization in American higher education is its relative lack of inclusion of modest income, first-generation college students. The trajectory of innovation and globalization has been to make American higher education more appealing and usually more expensive. This works well for education-minded, affluent constituencies. Unfortunately, it increases rather than lessens the gaps between social groups, promoting inequities and inequalities.

After having surveyed innovations involving campus and community, what stands out is the seemingly inexhaustible optimism associated with the topic. In addition to the "college town" or the "University City" or the contribution of Stanford to the flourishing of "Silicon Valley" in California, one finds yet another new stage for the higher education enterprise drama. Published in March 2016, a highly celebrated book, *The Smartest Places on Earth* by economist Antoine Van Agtmael and journalist Fred Bakker, advances the argument – and projection – that the "rust belt" cities of the upper Midwest and Northeast are poised to emerge as the "Brain Belt." Akron in Ohio and Albany in New York are illustrative of the cities, once associated with loss of jobs, that are now identified as the locus of educational, industrial, and entrepreneurial strengths which make them the "emerging hotspots of global innovation."[42] Whether as participant or observer – or both – we now are heirs to a new episode in higher education's exploration of innovation and internationalization. Along with the recurrent optimism of such academic ventures, we need to keep in mind that preoccupation with universities as "engines of innovation" and our American obsession with academic ratings also make our colleges and universities problematic with their complications and dysfunctions as "engines of anxiety."[43]

NOTES

1. Derek Bok, *Universities in the Marketplace: The Commercialization of Higher Education* (Princeton, NJ and Oxford: Princeton University Press, 2003); David L. Kirp, *Shakespeare, Einstein, and the Bottom Line: The Marketing of Higher Education* (Cambridge, MA and London: Harvard University Press, 2003).
2. Ben Wildavsky, *The Great Brain Race: How Global Universities Are Reshaping the World* (Princeton, NJ and Oxford: Princeton University Press, 2010).
3. Robert F. Arnove, Editor, *Philanthropy and Cultural Imperialism: The Foundations at Home and Abroad* (Boston: G.K. Hall, 1980).
4. Thomas Bartlett, "Phoenix Risen: How History Professor Became the Pioneer of the For-Profit Revolution," *Chronicle of Higher Education* (July 10, 2009) pp. A1–A13; John Sperling and Robert W. Tucker, *For-Profit Higher Education: Developing a World-Class Workforce* (New Brunswick, NJ: Transaction Press, 1997).
5. James Traub, "The Next University: Drive-Thru U: Higher Education for People Who Mean Business," *The New Yorker* (October 20 and 27, 1997) pp. 115–123.
6. A.J. Angulo, *Diploma Mill$: How For-Profit Colleges Stiffed Students, Taxpayers, and the American Dream* (Baltimore, MD: Johns Hopkins University Press, 2016).
7. Jennifer Gonzalez, "Advocate of For-Profit Colleges Mounts a Strong Defense Before Senate Hearing," *Chronicle of Higher Education* (June 23, 2010).
8. John R. Thelin, "Professors Shouldn't Be Afraid of Online Learning," *Inside Higher Ed* (July 10, 2012).
9. Blake Gumprecht, *The American College Town* (Amherst: University of Massachusetts Press, 2008).
10. Richard Perez-Pena, "How Cornell Is Creating a High-Tech Graduate School from Scratch (Very Seat of the Pants)," *New York Times* (April 14, 2013) p. ED14; Elizabeth A. Harris, "Bloomberg Philanthropies Gives $100 Million to Cornell Tech," *New York Times* (June 16, 2015) p. A21; Richard Perez-Pena, "Stanford Ends Effort to Build New York Arm," *New York Times* (December 17, 2011) p. A1.
11. Liz Robbins, "CUNY Schools to Lure Foreign Entrepreneurs to Campus with Visa Program," *New York Times* (February 18, 2016) p. A18.
12. Eric Weiner, *The Geography of Genius: A Search for the World's Most Creative Places from Ancient Athens to Silicon Valley* (New York: Simon & Schuster, 2016).
13. Tom Eblen, "As 'University City,' Lexington Can Leverage Unique Economy," *Lexington Herald-Leader* (October 19, 2015) pp. C1, C3; Jim Gray, "More Than a College Town … Lexington Is a University City," *Report from Office of the Mayor* (Lexington, KY: September 29, 2015); Tom Eblen, "University Town Economies Spurred by Collaboration," *Lexington Herald-Leader* (April 11, 2016) pp. 1C, 6C.

14. Tom Eblen, "Economic Development in University Cities Is All about Collaboration," *Lexington Herald-Leader* (April 10, 2016).
15. Keith Schneider, "Long a College Town, Worcester Now Looks the Part," *New York Times* (January 6, 2015) pp. B3–4.
16. Paul L. Gaston, *The Challenge of Bologna: What United States Higher Education Has to Learn from Europe, and Why It Matters That We Learn It* (Sterling, VA: Stylus Publishers, 2010).
17. Eric Kelderman, "Facing Pressure on Several Fronts, an Accreditor Promises Reform," *Chronicle of Higher Education* (April 29, 2018) p. A13.
18. Goldie Blumenstyk, "Hired Guns: 2014 Influence List of the Consultants," *Chronicle of Higher Education* (December 15, 2014).
19. Ellen Wexler, "University of Akron, a Struggling Regional, Hopes to Expand Worldwide," *Inside Higher Ed* (February 18, 2016).
20. Stephanie Saul, "Recruiting Students Overseas to Fill Seats, Not to Meet Standards," *New York Times* (April 20, 2016) pp. A1, A13.
21. John Hechinger, "Southern New Hampshire, a Little College That's a Giant Online: Southern New Hampshire University Profits from the Web," *Bloomberg* (May 9, 2013).
22. Ashley Smith, "University of Phoenix Lays off Nearly 500 Employees," *Inside Higher Ed* (April 7, 2016).
23. Tracy Urdan and Jeffrey Lee, "Postsecondary Education: Different Strokes," News Release from Credit Suisse (March 4, 2016); Tracy Urdan and Jeffrey Lee, "LOPE: GCU Terminates NFP Bid Following HLC Rejection," News Release from Credit Suisse (March 4, 2016).
24. Tracy Urdan of Credit Suisse as quoted in Paul Fain, "Stuck With Profit," *Inside Higher Ed* (March 7, 2016).
25. Beth Musgrave, "Councilman Wants Rupp Lease Talks Before UK Street Closings OK'd," *Lexington Herald-Leader* (April 7, 2006) pp. 3A, 6A.
26. "Initiative Formed to Promote Lexington," *Lexington Herald-Leader* (April 14, 2016) p. 7A. See also, *Lexington Together*, special insert magazine in *Lexington Herald-Leader* (April 16, 2016).
27. Conor Dougherty, "Gentrification Tension for Google in Colorado, Instead of San Francisco," *New York Times* (December 29, 2014) p. B4.
28. Michael McKay and Morgan Eads, "Three UK Students Charged in Robbery That Led to Death," *Lexington Herald-Leader* (April 13, 2016) pp. 3A, 6A.
29. Will Wright, "UK's False Alarms Rack up Real Costs," *Kentucky Kernel* (March 29, 2016) p. 1.
30. Holden Thorp and Buck Goldstein, *Engines of Innovation: The Entrepreneurial University in the Twenty-First Century* (Chapel Hill: University of North Carolina Press, 2010).
31. Martha Howell, "The Amazing Career of a Pioneer Capitalist," *New York Review of Books* (April 7, 2016) pp. 55–56. See also, Greg Steinmetz, *The Richest Man Who Ever Lived: The Life and Times of Jacob Fugger* (New York: Simon & Schuster, 2016).
32. Ivar Berg, *The Great Training Robbery: Education and Jobs* (New York: Basic Books, 1972).
33. Fernando Tejerina, Editor, *Universities: An Illustrated History* (Barcelona, Spain: Santander, 2011).
34. D. Bruce Johnstone and Pamela N. Marcucci, *Financing Higher Education Worldwide: Who Pays? Who Should Pay?* (Baltimore, MD: Johns Hopkins University Press, 2010). See also, Ian Buruma, "In the Capital of Europe: Brussels," *New York Review of Books* (April 7, 2006) pp. 36–39.
35. Paul Fain, "Accreditor Blocks Grand Canyon U's Attempt to Become a Nonprofit," *Inside Higher Ed* (March 7, 2016); Eric Kelderman, "For-Profit Education: Accreditor Rejects Grand Canyon U Bid to Turn Nonprofit," *Chronicle of Higher Education* (March 4, 2016).
36. Robin Wilson, "Profit Colleges Change Higher Education's Landscape," *Chronicle of Higher Education* (February 12, 2010) pp. A1, A16–A19.
37. Goldie Blumenstyk, "For-Profit Colleges May Be Down, But Don't Count Them Out," *Chronicle of Higher Education* (January 6, 2016).
38. Michael Stratford, "Head of Embattled For-Profit-College Accrediting Agency Resigns," *Inside Higher Ed* (April 19, 2016); "Under Scrutiny Itself, For-Profit Accreditor Gets Tough With ITT Tech," *Inside Higher Ed* (April 22, 2016); Andy Thomason, "President of Embattled Accreditor of For-Profit Colleges Resigns," *Chronicle of Higher Education* (April 18, 2016).
39. "Arizona State University Is Where Innovation Thrives," e-mail announcement on "Earn Your Degree Online from Arizona State University" (April 1, 2016). See also, Becky Supiano, "How a Huge University Promotes Its Small-College Appeal," *Chronicle of Higher Education* (April 8, 2016).
40. Marybeth Marklein, "For-Profit Colleges under Fire over Value, Accreditation," *USA Today* (September 29, 2010) p. A1.
41. Ian Buruma, "In the Capital of Europe: Brussels," *New York Review of Books* (April 7, 2016) pp. 36–39.

42. Antoine Van Agtmael and Fred Bakker, *The Smartest Places on Earth: Why Rustbelts are the Emerging Hotspots of Global Innovation* (New York: Public Affairs Press, 2016).
43. Wendy Nelson Espeland and Michael Sauder, *Engines of Anxiety: Academic Rankings, Reputation and Accountability* (New York: The Russell Sage Foundation, 2016).

Additional Readings

A.J. Angulo, *Diploma Mill$: How For-Profit Colleges Stiffed Students, Taxpayers, and the American Dream* (Baltimore, MD: Johns Hopkins University Press, 2016).

Robert F. Arnove, Editor, *Philanthropy and Cultural Imperialism: The Foundations at Home and Abroad* (Boston: G.K. Hall, 1980).

Ivar Berg, *The Great Training Robbery: Education and Jobs* (New York: Basic Books, 1972).

Derek Bok, *Universities in the Marketplace: The Commercialization of Higher Education* (Princeton, NJ and Oxford: Princeton University Press, 2003).

Ian Buruma, "In the Capital of Europe: Brussels," *New York Review of Books* (April 7, 2016) pp. 36–39.

Michael M. Crow and William B. Dabars, *Designing the New American University* (Baltimore, MD: Johns Hopkins University Press, 2015).

Paul L. Gaston, *The Challenge of Bologna: What United States Higher Education Has to Learn from Europe, and Why It Matters That We Learn It* (Sterling, VA: Stylus Publishers, 2010).

Blake Gumprecht, *The American College Town* (Amherst: University of Massachusetts Press, 2008).

Wendy Nelson Espeland and Michael Sauder, *Engines of Anxiety: Academic Rankings, Reputation and Accountability* (New York: The Russell Sage Foundation, 2016).

D. Bruce Johnstone and Pamela N. Marcucci, *Financing Higher Education Worldwide: Who Pays? Who Should Pay?* (Baltimore, MD: Johns Hopkins University Press, 2010).

David L. Kirp, *Shakespeare, Einstein, and the Bottom Line: The Marketing of Higher Education* (Cambridge, MA and London: Harvard University Press, 2003).

John Sperling and Robert W. Tucker, *For-Profit Higher Education: Developing a World-Class Workforce* (New Brunswick, NJ: Transaction Press, 1997).

Fernando Tejerina, Editor, *Universities: An Illustrated History* (Barcelona, Spain: Santander, 2011).

Holden Thorp and Buck Goldstein, *Engines of Innovation: The Entrepreneurial University in the Twenty-First Century* (Chapel Hill: University of North Carolina Press, 2010).

Gaye Tuchman, *Wannabe U: Inside the Corporate University* (Chicago and London: University of Chicago Press, 2009).

Antoine Van Agtmael and Fred Bakker, *The Smartest Places on Earth: Why Rustbelts are the Emerging Hotspots of Global Innovation* (New York: Public Affairs Press, 2016).

Ben Wildavsky, *The Great Brain Race: How Global Universities Are Reshaping the World* (Princeton, NJ and Oxford: Princeton University Press, 2010).

14

CONCLUSION

Beyond Business as Usual

SETTING AND OVERVIEW

This chapter brings together themes presented in the preceding chapters. It concludes with the proposition that the issues faced by colleges and universities today are fluid, persistent, and complex. They seldom have total or final solutions, and are not going to be easily addressed. So, these issues should not be ignored. Rather, they should be viewed as part of an extended ritual of actions and reactions, of accomplishments and unintended consequences. Their legacy is that conventional practices and policies at our colleges and universities warrant continual reconsideration. The message is that those who are active in higher education should avoid complacency and the stagnation associated with unexamined "business as usual."

The 30-year period 1985 through 2015 represents a distinct historical era. It has a start and an end, with its chronology framing distinguishing characteristics and kinds of events whose starting point was a year of economic recovery for the United States in general and higher education in particular. And by 2016 there were clear signs that American higher education was entering a new, challenging era. The practices and models that had been put into place and served colleges and universities well in surviving the serious disruptions prevalent in the early 1980s now were being exhausted – and becoming less effective. Some central strategies that had helped colleges and universities solve problems and maintain viability for the subsequent three decades were no longer going to be sufficient. To underscore how much the landscape of higher education has changed, it is crucial to note that by 2016 established, traditional colleges and universities would face both coexistence with and competition from a growing number of new kinds of institutions and groups, especially in the commercial and not-for-profit sectors. Such newcomers and mavericks once might have been dismissed by the traditional institutions and associations as a transient nuisance. The sobering reality, however, was that they were not going to go away or defer in the competition for resources and students.

To go beyond business as usual one needs a summit of representatives from various higher education constituencies. The *New York Times* seems to have had these good intentions with their full-page announcement on March 29, 2016, and then again on

June 8, 2016, for their "Higher Ed Leaders Forum" at The Times Center in New York City. The theme was "Face the Issues. Find the Solutions":

> This June, The New York Times will bring together influential leaders in higher education – presidents, provosts and chancellors of colleges and universities across the country – to address the urgent issues confronting them on campus today.
>
> In interviews with experts, Times journalists will seek solutions to challenges posed by race and free speech dilemmas, the STEM versus humanities debate, sexual assault on campus, the crisis in public funding and more. A unique feature of this event will be collaborative roundtables that allow participants to contribute ideas – namelessly if they wish – to conversations on some of the most controversial topics in education now. The Higher Ed Leaders Forum will be covered in a special section of The New York Times.

The forum's "presenting sponsor" was the Walton Family Foundation, joined by "associate sponsors" of New York University's School of Professional Studies, Oppenheimer Funds (identified by its motto, "The Right Way to Invest"), and, as a "supporting sponsor," the Carnegie Corporation of New York.[1]

Although the program was timely, it was limited due to its reliance on experts and officials. In urging readers to "Apply to Attend," the advertisement noted, "Participation is limited to senior leaders of accredited colleges and universities." No students and no student organizations were listed in the pre-conference program. The speaker roster were expert and insular since it was restricted to well-known representatives of the higher education establishment.

Elsewhere, other voices were taking stock of recent developments with an eye toward the future. The editors of the *Chronicle of Higher Education* published in June 2016 their report on trends in the decade ahead, pointing toward the year 2026, anticipating "seismic changes" in teaching, student values, and financing of higher education. Another example of this kind of thoughtful contribution came from William Bowen and Michael McPherson, in their 2016 book, *Lesson Plan*. Both are economists who had served as presidents of colleges and universities as well as presidents of major foundations. Their caution was that media coverage had brought inordinate attention and alarm to some higher education issues, while overlooking what they considered to be more serious concerns. They argue, for example, that focus on student loan debt, administrative bloat, the impropriety of large endowments, and the decline of tenured faculty should be shifted to increased concern about ways to improve student retention and graduation rates and for colleges and universities to devise new configurations to assure commitment to teaching by means of new definitions of faculty roles, asking hard questions about the over-proliferation of doctoral programs nationwide, and wrestling with the issue of the homogeneity in backgrounds and career paths of candidates for college and university presidents.[2]

These initiatives are good resources for analyzing the prospects for higher education. They are, however, a base that is no more than a prelude from which a new generation of students and future influential alumni should sort through the significant issues now facing colleges and universities – all the while adding their own nominations to the bill of particulars on problems and solutions.

ISSUES

The Worth of a College Education

Despite – or, perhaps, because of – all the arguments about higher education, a college degree was invaluable and appreciated by Americans. Even though large numbers of college graduates were under-employed, and even though many recent law school graduates often could not practice as lawyers, there was widespread agreement by Americans that a college degree still was necessary and worthwhile. Or, cast into defensive or negative terms, if one did not have a college degree, one was at a serious disadvantage in the job market – and, often stigmatized within the broader contours of American public life. Despite this overall favorable report, several corollaries suggested fundamental questions and problems for colleges and universities, which will be discussed in the later section on "Complexities and Conflicts: Implications for Decision-Making": namely, "Should everyone go to college?" It means probing to find out, "Who is *not* being well served by higher education?"[3] Second, what credentials and skills are necessary to enhance a "traditional" bachelor's degree transcript for students in the job market? And, third, given that college is worthwhile for many prospective students, how do we deal with issues of student debt and affordability?

Technology and Teaching

In 2010 there was widespread concern that innovations in Internet courses and teaching would compete with and undermine "traditional" classroom courses. The so-called MOOCs (massive open online courses), for example, were hailed as the new, accessible, and affordable medium for courses. In fact, one finds blending and coexistence of media and teaching modes. Mass online open enrollment courses that did not charge fees have not turned out to be integral to colleges and universities – and hardly have been a threat to traditional student campus enrollments. Internet courses have expanded both in their appeal and offerings. And this has taken place at all categories of institution, not just, for example, at for-profit online universities. The net result is that innovation in teaching, through Internet courses and programs, has been fused into the fabric of all higher education.

Uncertain Funding

By 2016 categories and institutional types within higher education seemed to be in a dubious competition: which group claimed the crown of being most at risk and most financially beleaguered and uncertain? Each category or type of institution seemed to have a tale of woe, making discussions appear to be a downward spiral of bragging rights for sorrow and pity. One emergent development was that old structures and expectations on revenue streams were incomplete, often in disrepair. Some analysts identified small, rural independent liberal arts colleges with small endowments as endangered.[4] At the same time, other feature articles argued that the regional public comprehensive universities, which did not have the benefit of selective admissions or high-powered research grants, were most vulnerable.[5] And this was most evident at campuses – both public and private – where geographic isolation led to declines in the number of applicants and enrolling students. The puzzle was that high enrollments elsewhere provided no protection from financial problems. The massive City University of New York dealt year after year with how to accommodate a growing number of students – combined with declining appropriations. A front-page headline story in the *New York Times* featured years of budget cuts at the City University of New York, noting that "Dreams stall as the city's engine of mobility sputters."[6] Leaky ceilings, electrical outages for computer systems, and cramped libraries were the dominant campus images.

Severe financial problems cut across institutions and were a commonality among prestigious and less well-known campuses. The world-famous University of California, Berkeley announced its new strategic plan that included reducing staff and streamlining educational operations.[7] Community college advocates pointed out that their institutions had suffered funding cuts and declining enrollments. Finally, several national reports showcased the problems facing public research universities as a paramount crisis in American higher education.[8]

Higher education's financial crisis can be a time when a president and board may invoke the academic equivalent of martial law. Within the institution a budget shortfall provides presidential license. Staff reductions (whether by retirement, attrition, or firing) require little explanation. At the same time, a president and board may then announce new spending initiatives or structural changes. The familiar explanation was because, after all, "to make money, you have to spend money…" Any action, whether spending or cutting, can be readily justified on the basis of the budgetary crisis. A new luxury dormitory is essential for being competitive in recruiting top students. An addition to the football stadium is important for keeping in touch with donors and alumni. Even though most of these announcements and decisions are untestable as to their effectiveness, a beleaguered campus is likely to acquiesce. Hence, adversity becomes a good stage from which a president can impose a particular plan with little, if any, obstructions.

Institutional Branding and Marketing

What are the expenses and benefits of large-scale public relations? To explore such college and university expenditures, it's useful to consider a few examples showcased by glossy brochures and other marketing items. One of many cases is the University of Massachusetts, Lowell – known as "UMass Lowell" – an institution that historically has not been a flagship campus or characterized by substantial revenues from endowment or research funding. On April 14, 2016, it took out a full-color, full-page advertisement in the first section (page A5) of the *New York Times*. Advertising rates suggest that this probably cost about $75,000. It proclaimed that "UMass Lowell" was "A National Leader Online & On Campus." Self-described as "One of the Fastest Rising Universities in the Nation," its accolades were listed as follows, with the source of the award listed at the end of the entry:

- 3rd Fastest Climb in the US News & World Report Rankings, 2011–2015
- Public Institution of the Year, by The Washington Center
- 10th Fastest Growing Public, Doctoral School in the Nation, The Chronicle of Higher Education
- $94,700 Average Mid-Career Salary of UMass Lowell Alumni with Bachelor's Degree, Payscale
- 4th Most Underrated University in America, Business Insider
- Designated a National Center of Academic Excellence in Cyber Defense Research by the Department of Homeland Security
- Over 25,000 Online Enrollments

- Blackboard Catalyst Award Winner for Exemplary Online Courses
- One of the Most Extensive Portfolios of Online Programs
- Winner of Six National Excellence Awards from the Online Learning Consortium
- 12th Best Computer Science School Online, Graduate Programs.com
- National and Regional Awards from the University Professional & Continuing Education Associations.

At about the same time UMass Lowell also published a 16-page full-color 8″ by 8″ special advertising supplement inserted into the *Chronicle of Higher Education*, with the title, "The Whole World in Their Hands (17,500 Students, Learning and Doing)," with the University's logo and the motto, "Learning with a Purpose." The introductory section noted, "Life is the only test." And, "That's why UMass Lowell creates so many opportunities for students to prepare themselves beyond the classroom, where reality puts a new lens on lectures and where learning can't help but become personal." The elaboration was, "It's hands on, and on and on. These experiences – added to tough academics taught by outstanding faculty – develop maturity, perspective, leadership, resilience and humility." And, "Every student is a story, and this brochure tells only a few. We are putting the whole world in their hands – because we know they will take good care of it."

The advertisements and brochures, along with the list of accomplishments, are attractive. What is less clear, especially to an outside reader, is precisely what the university officials posted as goals or benefits from such endeavors. What does the list of institutional accomplishments ultimately signal? What was the goal of the campaign? Was it to increase the number of applicants? Was it to attract more highly qualified students? Would such advertisements and brochures persuade donors to give to UMass Lowell? Or, perhaps, was the aim just to establish a general "image presence" and "branding" within the ranks of *New York Times* readers? UMass Lowell was not alone in staking out full-page color advertisements in the *New York Times*. The University of Connecticut's version, published on April 20, 2016, used New York City subway marker motifs with the message that its Storrs campus was so close to the city as to be equivalent to the "6th Borough" and that the university was able to span borders, "united by its commitment to excellence."

Clearly, marketing – and reliance on commercial marketing firms for planning and running campaigns – had become entrenched in college and university planning strategies. Less evident, however, was how each participating college determined the goals, let alone the cost–benefit of spending on such projects.

Admissions and the Prospective Student Pool

A small number of colleges and universities command disproportionate leverage in undergraduate admissions. Frank Bruni used satire to convey this message effectively in his 2016 column for the *New York Times* with the "shocking news" that Stanford University had suspended admitting students for a year. After all, according to his playful logic, if a college were so selective, how could any applicant qualify for admission?[9] One fictional disappointed Stanford reject was consoled with assurance that "she would be all right" and "would do well at Yale." The ironic fact which was not funny was that most colleges and universities in the United States were concerned about declining applications from high school seniors. Setting aside a small, albeit important, prestigious group of institutions, the dominant finding was that going to college was a buyer's market.

Media preoccupation with selective admissions was distracting and distorting because it obscured a widespread fundamental issue: what was the overall profile of prospective student applicants? And what were their realistic prospects? Winning the contest of selective admissions provided neither institutions nor individuals a guarantee of college fulfillment. Nathan Heller's 2016 profile of student subcultures at Oberlin College reported that there was what he called "The Big Uneasy" in which students at prestigious colleges struggled in balancing academic demands with individual commitments to social justice.[10]

Donations

Traditional generosity of alumni and other donors to colleges and universities is persisting – but it is uneven and uncertain. Good news was that on February 17, 2016 the venture capitalist Michael Moritz, the chairman of Sequoia Capital, and his wife gave $50 million to expand the University of Chicago's "initiatives catering to low-income students." Those included the Odyssey Scholarship Program for students enrolled at the University of Chicago, and the Collegiate Scholars Program, aimed at helping Chicago-area high school students apply to and prepare for entering college. Four years earlier, Moritz had donated $115 million to his alma mater, the University of Oxford, "to bolster the British university's financial assistance efforts." Earlier, he and his wife had given $30 million to the University of California, San Francisco "to bolster doctorate programs in the sciences."[11]

Moritz's donation to the University of Chicago was the "latest big ticket donation by Silicon Valley's top financiers to educational institutions." In 2015 Silicon Valley entrepreneurs had given $50 million to Rice University to "start a leadership program" and another $50 million to the University of Southern California (USC) for a brain research institute. USC also announced on April 18, 2016 that alumni Gayle and Edward Roski were donors of "A Visionary Gift" to name the Roski Eye Institute. It was the couple's latest in a series of generous donations to USC, including the USC Gayle Garner Roski School of Art and Design.

A good snapshot of major gifts and their distribution by kinds of institution and kinds of endeavor comes from July 1, 2016 in *The Chronicle of Philanthropy*.[12] These probably give the immediate impression that all is well in the support of college and university activities:

- $400 million to Ben-Gurion University (Israel) for Water Research
- $17.5 million to the University of Michigan to establish the Forbes Institute for Cancer Discovery within the university's Comprehensive Cancer Center
- $10 million to the University of Florida to endow the university's chemistry department and research, financial aid, and a new chemistry building that will be named for the donor
- $11 million to University of California, Los Angeles to create the Mani L. Bhaumik Institute for Theoretical Physics
- $7 million to the University of Oregon for renovation of a science building
- $5 million to San Francisco State University to establish and endow the Center for Iranian Diaspora Studies

- $5 million to the University of Delaware for the Donald Puglisi and Marichu C. Valencia Music Enrichment Fund.

An optical illusion with the dramatic press releases about major gifts was that the philanthropy was disconnected from the actual working life of a college or university. A $50 million gift for a science research center is substantial – and a cause for celebration. However, after the ribbon-cutting ceremonies, the sober and enduring fact of institutional life is that this gift probably generates about $2 million per year for the research center where expenses for equipment and professional personnel are high – and within a university whose total annual operating expenses are about $3 to $5 billion per year. Since most donors prefer to fund new initiatives rather than shore up existing budgets, a major gift simultaneously adds new revenue and also adds rather than reduces institutional spending. Placed in this context, $50 million is significant – but not sufficient to resolve the financial pressures facing all colleges and universities today.

Accommodating Athletics

Growth of intercollegiate athletics has pervaded all institutional categories. Justification is that such a commitment enhances institutional publicity, assists in the recruitment of students, increases the number of applicants, and appeals to the wishes and priorities of a large number and percentage of families who see participation in varsity sports as a magnet for their college-bound children. This requires a substantial financial investment for a college or university, whether it is in NCAA Division I, II, or III. Hence, there ultimately is a cost–benefit consideration. The Delta Cost Project study for the Knight Commission indicated that spending on intercollegiate athletics per student-athlete has escalated beyond what is spent on students.[13] Problems with inappropriate payments to student-athletes, long associated with big-time sports, in recent years has extended to some NCAA Division III programs where providing athletic payments to students is prohibited.[14]

The question for college and university presidents in addressing intercollegiate sports as part of institutional planning is to choose between reform and retreat.[15] Sad but true is that one way for presidents to deal with the serious problems of college sports is to run and hide. That was a message that came from Joe Nocera's 2013 op-ed column in the *New York Times* about the former chancellor of the University of North Carolina at Chapel Hill who left to become provost at Washington University in St. Louis, which belongs to the NCAA Division III.[16] A succession of academic scandals involving coaches and athletes took place on the chancellor's watch. NCAA Division III is hardly a "problem-free zone" or "safe place" for college sports. Academic leaders, whether at UNC Chapel Hill or Washington University in St. Louis, need to make sure that the varsity sports program is in tune with the respective institution's mission.

The Plight of Ph.D. Programs and Other Advanced Graduate Programs

Prestige and "mission creep" traditionally prompted institutions to add Ph.D. programs. By 2016, however, it became increasingly clear that there was an uneven and often depressed academic job market for tenure-eligible full-time faculty appointments. According to an article in the *New York Times* this situation, once associated with the humanities and social sciences, now extended into the STEM fields such as chemistry and physics, noting that there were "so many research scientists, so few professorships."[17]

This has confirmed that the academic job market is saturated. Institutional expenses in providing advanced degree programs has often relied on cross-subsidies from under-graduate tuition revenues. The further away an institution is situated from the most prestigious doctoral-granting institutions – such as the Association of American Universities – the more problematic the investment and maintenance of Ph.D. programs has become. All institutions need to review and reconsider their doctoral program offerings – and their motivations for doing so.

Doctoral programs are a long-time, obvious focus for cost overruns. But the problem extends to other graduate and professional programs, including law schools.[18] One estimate is that by 2016 about 80 percent of law schools were operating with an annual deficit and relied on some form of institutional subsidy. A persistent decline in law school applicants was consequential because law schools are dependent on tuition revenues, and do not have the ability to bring in external research grants as do the health sciences and physical sciences. Since law school deans are sensitive to national rankings, maintaining previous enrollment levels probably means absorbing a declining profile of LSAT scores and academic credentials of incoming students – a situation that probably would lower a law school's ranking. If a law school were to maintain its traditional academic selectivity it may have to do so by shrinking the size of its student body – a move that would reduce tuition revenues. How long and how much a provost would – or should – cross-subsidize a law school then becomes a source of university-wide concern. This is especially challenging because traditionally law schools were seen as a unit that often generated a revenue surplus. Adding to the complexity of planning is that forecasts for future employment of law school graduates are not expected to rebound or to regain their past profile.

The Uncertain Future of the Flagship State University

What should the modern American flagship state university be? If one relied on the dazzle of highly conspicuous university programs, one could be tempted to consider a ray of hope to restore prestige and morale to our beleaguered flagship state universities: namely, have "A&M" stand for "Athletics & Medicine."[19] It could be justified as a sorely needed marketing change from the archaic 19th-century definition, "Agricultural & Mechanical." This branding could provide state universities with both a jump-start and truth in advertising about their priorities. After more than a quarter-century of grumbling by presidents that they are losing resources and falling behind their elite private research university counterparts, public higher education has an opportunity to put new wine into the old A&M bottle. In 1981 the University of Maryland titled its long-range planning report, *The Post-Land Grant University.*[20] Perhaps it is time for a change because, after all, if one accepts the pronouncement of public relations consultants, aren't "Athletics & Medicine" the front doors and neon signs that now showcase an enterprising, dynamic state university?

Who will miss the old "A&M"? At most perhaps only a few curmudgeons, one might guess. The change could be seen as timely by a marketing director because at many land grant universities the traditional "A" already has tended to disappear. What about the "M"? Originally it meant "mechanics" – a 19th-century usage that approximates our notion of "engineering." But "mechanics" has little name recognition today and can be confusing because it is likely to bring to mind the vocational training programs in auto repair or air conditioning service provided by community colleges. In other words, the old "A&M" shell is vacant and ready to accommodate the new contenders, "Athletics & Medicine."

Both represent high-profile units of the university. Second, both are not only highly visible, they also are seen as indispensable and prestigious. Third, both are expensive – they bring in a lot of resources and also spend a lot. Fourth, both activities are integral to the local economy through services, construction, and employment. The new "A&M" also retains fidelity to the historic land grant service mission. Hospitals and clinics certainly represent health service to the public. And big-time athletics can even make a case for itself as a form of public entertainment and state pride. A few years ago a commissioner of a major athletics conference said in earnest that at the state universities in his conference, football ought to be regarded as a form of public service. True, this is not exactly the same as providing extension assistance on crop rotation – but who's to say that a state university team in the BCS championship or in the NCAA basketball Final Four has not reached out to the entire state's population?

Academic Medical Centers (AMCs) have represented a story of growth in the past decade. A College of Medicine and its affiliates can no longer be described as merely one of many academic units because it has achieved a size, prestige, and power that have transformed its presence. It's not unusual for a medical center and related health sciences nowadays to constitute more than half of a flagship university's faculty positions. Furthermore, for a university with an annual operating budget of about $2 billion, the AMC often accounts for 40 percent or more of the total university expenditures.

Athletics and Medicine provide an interesting symmetry in hiring, as both share the ability to compete for talent in a high-priced market. Hiring a new coach can, for example, be balanced by hiring a researcher with an M.D. and Ph.D. whose work deals with finding a cure for a serious disease. And, both new hires command a retinue of assistants, staff, and incentive bonuses to supplement base salaries. They are together the superstars of academia. A state university anchored on one end of the campus with the big "A" and anchored on the other end by the big "M" is formidable. Both units command expensive facilities – which quickly become obsolete. And the expanding, large facilities mean that the two units occupy a substantial percentage of campus real estate. There are trade-offs discussed later in the chapter that might temper enthusiasm for adopting higher education's "New A&M" image and model.

CHARACTERS AND CONSTITUENTS

External Start-up Companies, Consultants, and Institutes

The "higher education enterprise" refers to a network of numerous organizations and institutions not confined only to colleges and universities. Initiatives – and income – have come from enterprising groups outside the campus. Research institutes, consulting firms, foundations, think tanks, and other service organizations have changed the landscape and dynamics for all colleges and universities. Some are commercial in nature, others are not-for-profit. The thread that binds this disparate category is that innovative entrepreneurs have heeded the needs and demands of established colleges and universities. And, in turn, they have responded to provide, for a fee, services and expertise that colleges think they need. At some universities the board of trustees, for example, has paid more than $50,000 for an analysis of their president's salary and compensation package. The University of California, Berkeley in 2016 paid an external firm $200,000 for enhancing the chancellor's public image. Consultants advertise their services in enrollment management, budget plan implementation, hiring searches, providing academic curricula, and data analysis on degree programs and job markets. Some universities provide multi-year contracts along with a campus office to firms that provide expertise in strategic planning – even though those universities have a Vice President for Academic Affairs and large support staff. Outside firms promote privatization of academic services – ranging from boosting retention rates to offering specialized degree programs. A state university in 2016 paid a Washington, D.C. lobbying firm $15,000 per month to help the university secure more federal grants and research funding, as well as affect federal policy on higher education. The state university adds on this expense and expertise along with its own Director of Federal Relations, who receives a university salary.

Students as Consumers

The distinctive situation in American higher education is that applicants can be – and usually are – both consumers and students.[21] Each role tends to command a different treatment from college and university officials. Frank Bruni, columnist for the New York Times, wrote, "The turmoil on campus in recent years is only one reflection of a changed relationship between schools and the schooled, in which students often set the terms for a college's amenities, its atmosphere and the education it provides."[22] The historical fact, though, is that American colleges have long courted prospective students for the pragmatic reason that every college depended on tuition payments. The new chemistry, however, extends from admissions marketing to sustained investment in creature comforts and amenities that some college officials believe are essential for institutional survival. What is curious about this preoccupation is that a challenge for academic officials is tending to the learning and teaching of undergraduates, especially in light of concerns about rates of student retention and graduation.

Presidents

Have the crises and problems of higher education led to the changing role of the college and university president? Presidents – and the roles of campus presidents – are problematic. The dominant images are of having internal power yet being beleaguered in resolving unexpected problems. Boards of trustees increasingly characterize a college or university president as comparable to the CEO of a business corporation – as distinguished from, for example, a mayor of a large city, the governor of a state, or a general in the military. Bowen and McPherson, in their 2016 book, Lesson Plan, argue that gaining more diversity in applicants and selections for presidents persists as important – and also is difficult to achieve. One detriment to that, however, is an increasing reliance on search firms that tend to sand the sharp edges off applicants in the pool, tending to lead to safe, predictable résumés for candidates to be placed in the ranks of finalists. Giving priority, for example, to seeking a candidate who already is a "sitting president" narrows the pool and the vision of who might be a future college or university president.

Compensation for presidents is high – and rising. So much so that it has been called "platinum pay in the ivory tower."[23] It extends to generous retirement plans, financial incentives to continue to stay in office, or, in some cases, buy-outs and golden parachutes to incentivize leaving. The gap in compensation, including percentages of salary increases, between presidents and senior faculty is wide – and persistently getting wider. At a small, church-affiliated university in the mountains of Kentucky, a former president took the board of trustees to court, claiming that he deserved a lifetime annual compensation package of $390,000. In 2016 one state university board of trustees awarded the president a base salary raise of 17 percent and a total compensation package increase of 48 percent, totaling over $780,000, at a time when faculty and staff had a 2 percent merit increase salary pool. One peculiar characteristic of presidential compensation is that there seems to be no consistent relation with national ranking of institutions in terms of academic or research stature.

When a president does leave office, options usually are to become president of a foundation or to "return to the faculty." In the latter case, the president typically carries almost the full presidential salary. Some exiting presidents have negotiated faculty appointment clauses that explicitly state they are *not* required to teach. The net result is that the president-to-professor has raised all faculty salaries, at least statistically – and has lowered the average faculty teaching load. The irony is that some presidents when in office often share with legislators concerns about these very same trends in the faculty as a whole – allegations of high salaries and low teaching obligations.

How do some presidents fail? Why are they fired? One reason is that a president has done something that offends the board of trustees. The same closed circuit of boards and donors that provide a cushion for a president can, in some rare but high-profile cases, put a president's job at risk. Such is the case when a president is oblivious to long-simmering problems within the subcultures and groups within a campus, whether in the student body or in the ranks of faculty. According to a column in the *New York Times* on June 27, 2016, the primary explanation for the problems faced by the president of Baylor University was that amidst a long succession of incidents and allegations about misbehavior by student-athletes, there were charges of sexual harassment and lack of supervision of and by a high-profile head coach. The president was faulted because he "was not paying attention" to the life and workings of the campus and "did not know what was going on."[24] If so, this suggests that perhaps the insularity of a president in the orbits of trustees, donors, legislators, and alumni signals the serious danger of separation from students, faculty, and staff.

This book has contained numerous references to the rhetorical question, "Why can't a college be run more like a business?" One corollary of this mantra is that university presidents often are compared to the CEOs of major corporations. This base of administrative argument leads to an interesting question on reshaping the university presidency in the mold of a business executive.

What if colleges and universities were to embrace slogans about business practices and presidents of corporate CEOs? In fact, most college and university presidents have not had commercial business leadership experience – and, few really are in demand to be wooed from academia to the corporate boardroom, despite all the nervous claims from university trustees who invoke the specter of "market forces" in competition for presidents. Many college and university presidents serve on corporate boards – and are well compensated for that service. But often it is window dressing and a benign corporate concession to partnerships with higher education.

There are examples of college presidents who do combine academic institutions with the corporate model. One is Carl Barney, who in 2016 was 75 years old and represented a "rags to riches" biography. Barney came to the United States as an immigrant, unemployed from England after World War II. After working at such jobs as selling encyclopedias and real estate, Mr. Barney was pleasantly surprised to learn that in the United States one could literally "buy a college." He has done so, with numerous for-profit colleges, including the Center for Excellence in Higher Education along with the CollegeAmerica corporation.

Central to President Barney's academic leadership is applying Ayn Rand's ideas to education. As President of Stevens-Henager College, a for-profit institution, he "opposes government backed loans and grants on principle," even though he "has made his fortune in a business that is almost wholly dependent on them." According to a 2016 lengthy profile in the Business Section of the *New York Times*, Barney's students "borrow heavily to pay for their studies in hope of replicating Mr. Barney's up-by-the-bootstraps success, but often find themselves dropping out and burdened with loans."[25] Barney sees for-profit colleges as a good alternative to underfunded public institutions, especially community colleges. Carl Barney holds no academic degrees and has never been a faculty member or administrator at a nonprofit college or university. So, his case leaves higher education constituents with questions as to what should be the preparation and credentials of a college president. And, what is appropriate compensation? At established non-profit colleges and universities, both presidents and trustees would find Barney's résumé and leadership approach markedly different than their own. Yet he stands out as an interesting litmus because his extremes of applying enterprise to academia raise questions about the comparable statements trustees invoke in discussing presidents and higher education in terms of "market realities." It's doubtful that a Carl Barney would be a serious contender for a university presidency. Nor would he be accepted into the circle or club of incumbent university presidents. Academic legitimacy still matters – and for good reasons – despite a tendency for established boards and presidents to invoke the importance of business principles and market forces.

Trustees

Boards of trustees persist as a puzzling group that is both powerful and problematic. The external board structure has served American higher education since its origins. Less clear is whether it serves higher education well in the 21st century. There's little if any rationale or standards on qualifications to serve as an academic trustee. At state universities, many trustees are partisan appointees from a governor who is repaying a campaign debt with incidental attention to suitability for serving higher education. Perhaps the greatest insularity is the loop of a president and the board. Board members mimic the rhetoric of the corporate boardroom. This becomes evident in public relations announcements about presidential performance evaluations and related updates on salary, benefits, and compensation packages, as noted earlier.

The Faculty

A group that has experienced professional and institutional loss in recent years has been the faculty.[26] The prototype of the tenured – or, tenure track – professor who combines teaching, research, and service over a 30-year career represents a small and shrinking proportion of all college and university faculty. Faculty salaries have declined as a priority and as a percentage of salaries when compared to presidents, academic administrators, athletics officials, and coaches. The number of tenure-eligible faculty positions has tended to decline as they have been divided into such positions as lecturers and adjunct instructors. Faculty voice in shared governance has been muted. Within the faculty ranks, a relatively small number and percentage of "superstars" are able to command high salaries and research support – but these are unusual. College and university boards of trustees tend to underestimate the value of more and better full-time professors. According to a researcher at AAUP, "For every 10 percent increase in full-time faculty, you see a 2.2 increase in retention," which brings in more tuition dollars from students who stay in school. Furthermore, "Investing in faculty brings more innovation as well, in the classroom and in research," which tends to enhance both institutional reputation and revenues.[27]

State Governments

In 2016 feature articles about state government support of public higher education displayed common themes of long-term and widespread budget cuts. Headlines included "Illinois's Collapsing Colleges," with the elaboration that, "While politicians fight, the state's public higher education is dying."[28] For all state colleges and universities in Louisiana, the mood was one of "anxiety" over yet more state cuts.[29] The general trend nationwide was that "State spending on higher education has grown, but more slowly than before the recession" of 2008.[30]

Although state funding of higher education had started to rebound from the depths of the Great Recession, it was unlikely it would be robust – and, most certainly, would not fully recover per capita student state subsidy. Spending was unlikely to return to the levels of generous support of decades ago, and in the 21st century public higher education faced a new funding model. At times in some states there is hostility by a governor and/or a legislature toward public higher education. More often than not, however, increased demands for state funding from other organizations and constituencies combined with higher education's stature as a mature enterprise have squelched the enthusiasm of massive new funding in almost all states.

What one has is a situation where state university presidents and their staff publish both externally and within their own campus enthusiastic statements about how their university is the state's "indispensable institution." And, the sequel is that state legislators and governors each biennium provide a pool of money for public higher education that is shrinking either in annual rate of increase or in actual dollars. One vehicle for carrying out this strategy is to emphasize performance-based funding.[31] Using this category, the burden of proof has been on public colleges and universities to document that the institution is effective. A trend in recent years is for governors and state legislators to try to "rescue" public higher education with programs to jump-start the "economic engine." Gubernatorial appointments to higher education boards often are announced as deliberate moves to bring a business orientation to the trustees of state colleges.

Federal Government

The federal government, through both the legislative and executive branches, probably will deal with higher education issues with a focus on increased consumer protection and asserting a regulatory role along with continuing to serve as a provider of student financial aid and sponsored research grants. Federal agencies often now are expected to act as umpires and regulators on a variety of intramural campus disputes that have worked their way into external review, either by an agency itself or in a lawsuit.

Enforcement of Title VII and Title IX has surfaced with increasing frequency. Another area where the federal government has demonstrated increased scrutiny of colleges and universities has been in evaluating whether institutions have, indeed, complied with terms on selected federal student aid programs, especially those where job placement has been listed as a formal index of compliance. This has been most evident in scrutiny of for-profit colleges and universities – but not exclusively so, as a growing number of traditional nonprofit colleges and universities have been penalized and/or had funding withheld for failure to meet compliance targets.

One place where the federal government will be consequential is from time to time when the Supreme Court hears cases on college admissions criteria, especially as a matter of state policy for enrollment in public institutions. What is less certain is the directions in which Supreme Court rulings will head, as there have been high-profile decisions that have represented vacillations over time.

COMPLEXITIES AND CONFLICTS: IMPLICATIONS FOR DECISION-MAKING

Conflicts Between Past and Present

One surprising source of tension – and reconsideration – has dealt with the heritage of higher education. History mattered – and how a particular college or university reconciled its past and present became a source of critical observation from dissatisfied students. Monuments and memorials – who was honored – ceased to be acquiescent and benign. And, hence, in an increasing number of cases, they are less likely to be accepted by a new generation of students and alumni. Notable incidents included protests by some student groups at Yale University over a building named in honor of Yale alumnus John C. Calhoun, whose connections as an advocate for slavery and states' rights was deemed inappropriate for recognition.[32]

In addition to increased scrutiny of highly visible campus monuments, historical research has contributed to re-examinations of higher education's past. In 2016 researchers discovered in Georgetown University's archives substantial documentation of institutional involvement in owning slaves who worked on Maryland plantations owned and operated by the Catholic order. And, records were compelling in showing that the head of what would later be Georgetown College used profits from the sale of these slaves to provide funding to operate the academy and the college. The historical research meant that now Georgetown – and other colleges – had to confront their role in the nation's slave trade as part of their institutional histories. And, indeed, in summer 2016 the President of Georgetown did meet with descendants of those slaves in Louisiana and undertook a mission for the university to make amends.[33]

The Economy versus Education

The national economy faces a serious mismatch with higher education. It is a situation that is neither temporary nor transient. It is playing havoc with customary planning both by institutions and by students because students with completed degrees and earned credentials seeking suitable professional employment that would have been reasonable and realistic in the past have found that the number of positions have evaporated – and probably are not going to rebound. Student debt, for example, most likely would subside as a significant problem if college graduates were able to be hired for reasonable entry-level positions with commensurate salary and benefits. But positions are dwindling; and, in many cases, professional positions have been reconfigured in such learned professions as law, medicine, and faculty hiring.

In reviewing the debates associated with the topic of higher education and the economy, what seems to emerge is not the claim that a college education is unimportant or unnecessary. Rather, today having a college degree may be useful and necessary in landing a job, but it is often insufficient. The advice from employers seems to be that a student should acquire specific high demand skills along with completing a bachelor's degree. More prevalent is the pitch that a student with a bachelor's degree would do well to consider after graduation education and certification for "badges" or for "boot camps," which now are hailed by some as "the new master's degree."[34] A recurrent example is that a liberal arts major has advantages that are attractive to employers – namely, critical thinking, sophisticated literacy, and the ability to deal with complex literatures and information. And this would be enhanced (and employable) if the recent graduate also had certification for some specialized high-tech skill, such as (but hardly confined to) computer coding.[35] Yet even for recent college graduates who persevere through this labyrinth of credentials, internships, and badges, and succeed in landing a job in the new high-tech economy, there are some surprises that call for an adjustment in expectations. For example, one account of a competitive tech start-up company located in a renovated old factory building in Boston describes the entry-level jobs as paying reasonably well – but require the entry-level recruits to work exceptionally long hours per week, in cubicles, manning a telephone and a computer. The new work environment, for all its celebration and publicity, was actually a "digital workshop" in which "business opportunity representatives" worked a lot like what had been called "telemarketers." This new job environment has its own distinctive lexicon and protocols. Turnover among entry-level employees is high because there is a steep pyramid and long odds for promotion even among the graduates of elite colleges who have attractive credentials and experience.[36]

Recruitment versus Retention

Marketing campaigns that are expensive and integral to attracting applicants and, eventually, enrolling students tend to dominate college initiatives. One consequence is that American higher education is better at providing admissions and access to prospective students than it is to assuring educational achievement and advancement, including measures of retention and graduation. College and university officials have recognized that in pragmatic terms a student who drops out is an expensive matter – they represent lost revenue from tuition or forgone dollars from federal grant and loan programs. One response has been to create new administrative offices – often with a title such as "Associate Vice President for Student Success." What one finds is that recruiting students is easier than academic efforts for them to persist and maintain good academic achievement.[37]

Problems and Limits in Changing Philanthropy

Earlier in this chapter a profile of donors emphasized a roster of illustrative recent major gifts to universities for research centers, scholarship programs, and buildings. Those examples of "business as usual" in higher education giving are shifting toward other models. Direct giving with few conditions is a shrinking part of higher education philanthropy. Foundations and major donors often seek out new start-up groups or think tanks to carry out foundation projects rather than trying to enhance a particular campus – much to the consternation of college and university vice presidents for development. Some of this difference in focus between a campus and a foundation or donor is the latter's concern that a single campus alone is unlikely to be able to contribute a substantive solution to a major nationwide or international problem, such as lack of access or lack of affordability in going to college. One consequence is that colleges are less likely to receive unrestricted gifts from alumni, friends, and other individual donors than they were in previous eras.

The traditional major gifts coexist with other kinds of gifts along with a new legal, financial environment. Not the least of significant developments is the rise of what is called the DAF – a term that stands for Donor-Advised Funds. Foremost in this group are such financial firms as Fidelity Charitable, Schwab Charitable, and Vanguard Charitable. These charitable structures act as a holding pen between a donor and a recipient college. The donating individual or family who sets up a DAF essentially places monies in suspense, with no obligation to make a donation to a college or university for several years – even if the college is designated as the ultimate beneficiary or recipient. Also, from the perspective of foundation officers, colleges traditionally relied on "carrots" as gifts from individuals or foundations – attractive gifts anointed with encouragement to undertake a project. In the 21st century this has shifted to increasing reliance on offering colleges a "stick" – resources given but only with the commitment that the college would demonstrate it had delivered in effectively reaching some goal of achievement or performance.[38] Meanwhile, the donor receives numerous tax benefits and deferrals, and even is allowed to transfer the designated funds to heirs.[39]

Even major donors and well-endowed universities have problems with "business as usual" in their own decisions about philanthropy. The rise of financial management and hedge funds since 1990 has created new, great wealth for many college alumni and their families, giving them the opportunity to become major donors. Yet in a significant minority of cases, these new major donors have run into problems with tax fraud or investment schemes gone awry – episodes that literally leave colleges and universities holding the (empty) bag.[40] Although colleges and universities continue to attract donors, they will do so with increased, intense competition from other nonprofit organizations as well as from varied financial service institutions.

Competition and Imitation in Marketing and Branding

The conventional wisdom is that a college or university adopts a marketing plan, complete with logos and branding, which signals innovation and sets the institution apart from the pack. However, often what happens is almost the opposite because the branding and marketing new to one institution may resemble and even imitate initiatives elsewhere. In such cases, investment in changing the look and logo, along with the website and billboards, indicates that a college is spending in order to keep up or catch up. The pressure for conformity, often reminiscent of peer pressure within high schools, can also surface in college and university presidential offices and boardrooms. Furthermore, numerous colleges may rely on the services of a single marketing or public relations firm – which becomes the academic equivalent of "central casting."

In analyzing the question of why college brands look so similar, Ellen Wexler wrote:

In its brochures, a college is never *just* a college. A college is a gateway, or a launchpad, or a training ground.

Condensed into a few words, colleges' missions are similar, and the concrete elements of college life become less so: "Attending SF State is more than an education – it's an experience" … "Leadership isn't just an elective. It's a way of life," reads the University of Virginia's website.

But, it's that brevity – a tagline, a logo, a mission statement – that sells. Colleges want to stand out, but they also want to be pithy.

Start here. Go anywhere

Start here. Get there

Going anywhere starts here!

One book on this phenomenon cataloged college marketing clichés such as "Three and a Tree," also known as TAAT, heralding a website campus banner photograph of "three students of varying ethnicities and gender, dressed head to toe in college-branded merchandise."[41] It's important for college and university leaders to take seriously these problems of saturation and sameness. Investment in marketing campaigns is expensive; the State University of New York at Buffalo, for example, spent $314,000 on its website and marketing logo change.

Legal Conflicts Between Groups within a Campus

Historically, the legal problems facing colleges and universities often dealt with litigation and threats from hostile external groups. In contrast, by 2016 often the situation was that splits and tensions arose among groups *within* the campus. Typically, this has taken the form of dissident student groups versus faculty in questions of social justice pitted against academic freedom. This signals a gridlock in which consensus and even a forum of fair discussion is jeopardized. Furthermore, traditional means for resolving campus disputes have been rendered inadequate.[42] Internal bodies such as student conduct review boards staffed by student affairs deans, faculty, and students were frequently found wanting by one side or the other. Campus consensus had deteriorated – and in some cases had dissolved.

Convergence of Institutional Types

A great deal of news coverage in 2016 focused on convergence of public and private research universities. This seems misplaced because the fusion had been consummated long ago. When Clark Kerr described the ascent of the "federal grant university" in 1960, his new, super category included both public and private research universities. Second, it tends to overlook more exciting, innovative mergers and hybrids taking place in other sectors within American higher education. Even though there are taxonomies and classification systems that delineate an institution as, for example, a "private liberal arts college" or a "large state university," the trends in diversification and imitation have meant that institutions often "borrow" or "paste on" new kinds of units or programs historically not associated with their mission or heritage.

The Limits of the "New A&M" Model

The "modest proposal" for the "New A&M" demonstrates the dangers of usurping tradition to adopt dramatic changes that might enhance marketing and business model dimensions while neglecting the less spectacular but equally important fabric and substance of a university. One concern is that the "New A&M" casts athletics and medicine as silos often to the neglect of the essential, established academic programs between the A and the M. The proposal presented earlier in this chapter carries the baggage of a few liabilities in showcasing athletics and medicine as the new "A&M." Although both bring in a lot of money, whether in television revenues, ticket sales, major donations, Medicaid payments, federal grants, or fees from clinics, these fertile sources can be precarious. Even in the ranks of big-time college sports, most athletic departments lose money. Furthermore, both athletics and medicine tend to be removed from degree granting and course offerings. The department of intercollegiate athletics is an auxiliary enterprise, not an educational unit. As for medicine, even though an Academic Medical Center includes a large number of faculty, students, academic staff, and degree programs, its hospitals and clinics still lean toward delivery of health services and collection of fees, rather than teaching and instruction.

Furthermore, a medical center can be a risky foundation on which to build a more commercialized model for the operation of universities. Several years ago, for example, an article in the *Los Angeles Times* reported that UCLA's medical center "struggled for months with wobbly finances and internal dissension," characterized by a consulting firm's report as "problems ranging from inconsistent billing and plummeting revenues to a disorganized administration in which job duties overlapped." Perhaps the best example of the financial fragility of the expensive university medical centers came in 1996 at Georgetown University in Washington, D.C., where a shortfall in medical center income led the university president to try to impose an internal tax on the law school and business school as a convenient source of medical center fiscal fitness.

Today a university medical center typically faces three sources of financial risk: first, a downturn in number of patients; empty hospital beds run up expenses quickly. Second, any reduction in the federal Medicaid or Medicare reimbursement rate will require university medical centers to reduce drastically their income projections. Third, although many AMCs enjoy financial autonomy due to their own large endowments, these have quickly become undependable. It's not unprecedented, for example, that a university medical center endowment of $250 million in 2007 (most of which was earmarked to pay for an aggressive capital expansion and building program) by 2009 had shrunk about 40 percent down to $150 million – a one-year loss of $100 million due to unproductive investment choices. If and when these shortfalls do occur, most likely the state government and/or the university will bail out the medical center.

By 2016 some major universities were rethinking their configuration of AMCs. The serious question was, "Is it time for universities to get out of the hospital business?"[43] Vanderbilt University led by example in answering that a split was a hard but appropriate decision. The vacillations of health care insurance and federal medical repayment plans were problematic for the host university. Adding to the consternation of university presidents and provosts was that the complexities of hospital accounting were made more difficult by lack of transparency. Academic hospital administrators were hard pressed to explain their finances. It was clear that costs were rising, but not clear exactly how and why. Customary claims by medical center administrators that graduate medical education was expensive had become an inadequate explanation and frequently were not accompanied by persuasive details on where money was going.

Another complication was that many university-affiliated hospitals had established special foundations – perhaps called "University Medical Services Foundation," whose acronym was "UMSF." Even if created by a state university, it was not clear if the private foundation had public accountability. Even when a state attorney general ruled that the private foundation was subject to the Freedom of Information Act, university officials resisted releasing information to news reporters and other claimants.[44] The upshot was that a university hospital consumes a lot of the university president, provost, and board's time.

Comparable questions hold for flagship state universities with NCAA Division I intercollegiate athletics programs. A losing season in a revenue sport such as football or men's basketball quickly can bring a decline in ticket revenues and fewer invitations to be selected for nationally televised games. However, even if this were to happen, it's hard to imagine a state university abandoning football or basketball. The programs have become so important that their expenses must be covered, even if that were to mean transferring resources from other parts of the university.

What about the consequences for other academic units located on campus between the anchors of athletics and medicine? One possible concern is the endurance of the "A&S" acronym for "Arts & Sciences." Since this unit probably has increased difficulty in claiming primacy in the contemporary state university, a possible reform is to amend their branding to reflect a new, diminished status. "A&S" could be rebranded as "a & s" – with lower-case letters to connote shrinking budgets, deteriorating centrality, and reduced visibility. The glamour of marketing campaigns is a risky guide to sound educational planning. A president or board moving hastily to invoke "The New A&M" could abandon higher education's proud land grant heritage for two precarious silos. In sum, restraint in such changes might be a wise decision by the contemporary university.

CONNECTIONS WITH DIVERSITY AND SOCIAL JUSTICE

Both institutions and external groups in American higher education have since World War II placed emphasis upon access and admissions. They have done so with admirable commitment and reasonable, persistent gains over time. One shortfall has been that expanded access also often has been characterized by slotting and tracking – closely approximating family income and social class divides in American life. Diversity, although accommodated in the aggregate, is markedly uneven when broken down by institutional type. In this sense, as Suzanne Mettler has argued, colleges and universities have frequently behaved as sources of inequality, marked by calcifying disparities and segregation in American society into colleges and universities.[45] And, new and largely unexpected (by campus officials) by 2015 were schisms and tensions within student bodies. As a consequence of these disparities, an unexpected and unpleasant surprise for many universities was that student dissatisfaction with campus life was a paramount problem.

Yet there are interesting innovations and commitments at academically selective, well-endowed institutions. In recent years such colleges as Amherst and Vassar have demonstrated both commitment and results in boosting the number and percentage of modest income students attending those institutions. One indicator of this effective change is the increasing number and percentage of Pell Grant recipients as part of their respective student bodies. Furthermore, they have increased their enrollment of community college transfer students, first-generation college students, and military veterans.[46] Gains in diversity as signaled by admission and enrollment patterns are, however, only a first step. Where many of the academically selective colleges with generous financial aid now have serious questions and problems is in the culture – or, more accurately, the varied cultures – within their campuses. And here is where discontent by disenfranchised student groups has been illuminated by friction and tensions over campus symbols and monuments – episodes that are indicative of deep, unresolved questions.[47]

One source of commitment to social justice and diversity on the American campus has come from some major private foundations. Whereas donors to an institution put the institution first, several major foundations over the past 30 years have emphasized issues of nationwide access, affordability, and retention for underserved students. In recent years the Lumina Foundation and the Gates Foundation have been central both in public visibility and in dollars. And, important to note is the loss in 2016 of one of the pioneers, Alison Bernstein, who headed up some Ford Foundation initiatives between 1983 and 2010. According to her obituary in the *New York Times* on July 10, 2016:

> She worked on improving community colleges and increasing the transfer rate for students to four-year institutions; opening up higher education to more Native American students; and advancing women's and gender studies. She also helped start the foundation's International Fellowships Program which has a mandate of financing higher education for marginalized populations from developing countries.[48]

CONCLUSION

Image versus Reality in College Expectations

Our belief in individualism and opportunity is deeply ingrained in the American character. Anyone, according to the litany, has a chance to make a fortune, ascend the corporate ladder, gain election to public office, hit a home run, or earn a college degree, if only they will draw on a combination of talent and dedication.[49] However, the sobering rejoinder is that our life choices more often than not are in part mere probabilities shaped by collective forces outside our control. Historical timing, age, gender, religion, race, ethnicity, and family background are just a few variables that intervene with individual efforts, skill, and aspirations. Nowhere is this clash of democratic dreams and demographic realities more evident than in the American saga of higher education and social mobility, especially with the flourishing of state land grant campuses and, later, the availability of generous federal student financial aid – all intended to increase access and affordability.

On balance, today American higher education conveys simultaneously "Great Expectations" along with "Reasonable Doubts." The statistical profile of undergraduate enrollments over almost 400 years provides an alluring, albeit deceptively smooth pattern of growth. It is a numerical trajectory that suggests a national success story of expanding access. As sociologist Martin Trow wrote in *Daedalus* in 1970, within the 20th century "going to college" was transformed from an elite experience for less than 5 percent of late adolescent Americans and shifted to "mass higher education" in which about 30 to 40 percent of young Americans enrolled in college. And, the recent development around 1970 was an era in which the national commitment was to universal higher education.[50] In other words a diverse array of postsecondary institutions – including a relative new entity, the public community college – was able to accommodate about 70 percent of traditional high-school-age graduates. In the past quarter-century this typology has been dramatically altered by expansion of what are characterized as "non-traditional" students – students older than the conventional 18-to-21-year-old cohort that has proceeded directly from high school to college.

An unfortunate but undeniable situation today, however, is that we have what an editorial in the *New York Times* has called "a broken bargain with students."[51] American higher education is incredible in its accommodating and prompting those who are best positioned. But for a large percentage of college students, the experience and outcomes have been puzzling in their frustration and shortfalls. Interesting to note is that it's not merely a situation in which students are whining and complaining. Consider the observation by Professor Jeanne Theoharis at Brooklyn College of the City University of New York in a period of the university's financial malnourishment, including overcrowded classrooms and campus buildings in disrepair:

> The commitment of my Brooklyn College students to education can take my breath away. Over and over, they tell me how much the class means to them, how they share the readings with their parents and kids, friends and partners. Over and over, they face harrowing circumstances – homelessness, the death of loved ones, unsafe living situations – and they still show up with their readings done. Over and over, they work 30 or 40 or 50 hours outside of school and take care of families and make time for their homework in the early morning or late evening hours. Over and over, when I run into former students even after many years, they tell me they still cherish the coursepack of readings from our class and are still relating what we did in class to the world around them.
>
> Belying the stereotype that college students are jaded and only in it for the degree, my students palpably understand the power of the word. They regularly affirm the stakes of what is learned or not learned – what histories are told and which are not. They carefully make connections between what we are learning and its broader implications in the world, informing my scholarship in the process...
>
> My classes typically focus on racial politics and the history of race in the United States. These are difficult, at times painful and uncomfortable topics, and yet it is a rare day when a student interrupts another student, or when the difficult questions we explore become divisive. In this segregated country we live in, my classroom is a rainbow ... We confront America's past and present together.[52]

Professor Jeanne Theoharis's account is memorable; her experiences are exceptional but not isolated. At each and every campus in the United States teachers and students have their own versions of this story to tell. We should read and heed these stories in thinking about the present and future of higher education.

Innovation versus Saturation

If American higher education in the 21st century faces crises whose common thread is disappointment in having fallen short of our "great expectations," there has been no lack of efforts to resolve these dilemmas. What is hard to acknowledge is that many of the efforts have been both expensive and ineffective – and often counter-productive. Too often, measures such as new budgeting systems, a structural reform, or enhanced marketing and recruitment of prospective students which purportedly will set higher education aright are really wrong – or, at least, wrongheaded. In sum, many campus-based administrative strategies have proven to be indicators of rather predictable and unoriginal imitation, which, when diffused across many colleges and universities, leads American higher education into a situation of *saturation* rather than genuine, thoughtful *innovation*.

Consider a situation within a particular state where the number of high school graduates is static or declining. Five of the state's public universities invest in recruiters, college fairs, direct mailings, social media messages, campus visits, promises of research perks, special programs, and merit scholarships – all to catch the attention and application and, ultimately, the enrollment of a coveted student who has high grades, outstanding test scores, and a long list of extracurricular activities and awards. Might some of that time and money have been spent more imaginatively and effectively in providing for the college education of a student from an underserved constituency who would then add diversity and energy to the campus?

Another example of saturation has been the proliferation of law schools. As noted earlier in this chapter, numerous law schools – especially those that are relatively new and relatively low in academic selectivity – are at risk, as are their recent graduates. The reason for this bad situation is, once again, imitation and seeking some combination of quick tuition revenues and perhaps enhanced academic prestige led to over-building and over-enrollment. What was a sure thing and fast solution for one school becomes dysfunctional when extended over the entire nation.

The cumulative result is that colleges and universities are spending a great deal of time and money in a predictable manner. The strategies and methods are not original or innovative – rather, they signal a saturation of expenses and approaches that really are tired and dated – and neither efficient nor effective. The strategies face a diminishing return. One wonders if one of those recruiting colleges had considered seeking out non-traditional students such as military veterans or working single parents? Might not a college – and all of American higher education – make progress in both opportunities and achievements? What if some of the monies invested in recruitment of the high school valedictorian at a highly regarded suburban high school had been diverted to concern for retention? A good use of scarce scholarship resources might be to provide some modest amount such as $3,000 to shore up the financial aid package of a sophomore from a modest income family who may not be able to pay next semester's bills.

Another variation on the theme of dubious student recruitment has developed in the penchant of flagship state universities to seek applicants from out-of-state in large part because if these students enroll, they are charged tuition rates sometimes two to three times higher than those for applicants who are in-state residents. Presidents justify this approach on the grounds that declining state funding has forced them to seek fresh revenue sources. Whatever salvation it provides these campuses in the present, however, it tends to erode a compact with citizens and taxpayers in the state whose own children face a hard situation to gain admissions.[53]

One persistent tradition in higher education is that many college presidents and boards continue to be fixated on what has been called the "Edifice Complex." Choosing to construct new big buildings has been a familiar approach that now seems shopworn. Yet it persists. Ironically, around 2008 one of the promises of Internet courses and distance learning was that it was a means by which colleges could offer credit courses and instruction without investing in traditional campus buildings. In fact, the drift toward more campus construction has increased, not tapered. It is yet another sign of decisions that signal saturation rather than innovation – and expenses with little assurance of effectiveness in fulfilling educational goals.

Comparable patterns in which colleges and universities pursue imitation that then leads to widespread saturation rather than innovation are evident in major campus administrative units. Development officers tend to seek the same kinds of donor and make similar pitches. Establishing a new branch campus or a new program – such as yet another Executive M.B.A. program – to keep up with one's rival institutions is another example of actions that, although well-intentioned, are neither thoughtful nor original. These are the syndromes of "business as usual" against which I hope this book provides some alternative ways of thinking. Reflection, one hopes, will be based on sound values of social justice and educational equity, all of which help transform the study of higher education into insights and thoughtful ventures in what promises to be a challenging, exciting new era.

NOTES

1. "The New York Times Higher Ed Leaders Forum: June 20–21, 2016 at The Times Center," *New York Times* (March 29, 2016) p. A26 and (June 9, 2016) p. B16.
2. William G. Bowen and Michael McPherson, *Lesson Plan: An Agenda for Change in American Higher Education* (Princeton, NJ: Princeton University Press, 2016).
3. Scott Carlson, "Should Everyone Go to College?: For Poor Kids, 'College for All' Isn't the Mantra It Was Meant to Be," *Chronicle of Higher Education* (May 6, 2016) pp. A22–A25.
4. Lawrence Biemiller, "The Truth-Teller: Once a Small-College Champion, Now a Tough Critic," *Chronicle of Higher Education* (April 1, 2016); Anemona Hartocollis, "At Small Colleges, Harsh Lessons About Cash Flow," *Chronicle of Higher Education* (April 29, 2016).
5. Lee Gardner, "Where Does the Regional State University Go from Here?" *Chronicle of Higher Education* (May 27, 2016) pp. A22–24.
6. David W. Chen, "Dreams Stall as City's Engine of Mobility Sputters: New York Woes Mirror a Trend in Higher Education," *New York Times* (May 29, 2016) pp. 1, 17.
7. Colleen Flaherty, "Berkeley Announces Major Strategic Planning Process to Address Long-Term Budget Issues," *Inside Higher Ed* (February 11, 2016).
8. Ellen Wexler, "Lincoln Project Report Offers Suggestions for Public Research Universities' Financial Future," *Inside Higher Ed* (April 7, 2016); Ellen Wexler, "'Starving the Beast' Examines Ideological Shifts in Funding for Higher Education," *Inside Higher Ed* (March 22, 2016); Marilynne Robinson, "Save Our Public Universities: In Defense of America's Best Idea," *Harper's Magazine* (March 2016) pp. 29–37.
9. Frank Bruni, "College Admissions Shocker!," *New York Times* (March 30, 2016) p. A21.
10. Nathan Heller, "The Big Uneasy: What's Roiling the Liberal Arts Campus?" *The New Yorker* (May 30, 2016). See also, David Brooks, "Inside Student Radicalism," *New York Times* (May 27, 2016) p. A21.
11. Michael J. de la Merced, "Venture Capitalist's Latest Gift: $50 Million to the University of Chicago," *New York Times* (February 17, 2016) p. B6.
12. Maria Di Mento, "Gifts Roundup: Israel's Ben-Gurion University Lands $400 Million for Water Research," *Chronicle of Philanthropy* (June 27, 2016).

13. Donna M. Desrochers, *Academic Spending versus Athletics Spending: Who Wins?* (Washington, D.C.: The Delta Costs Project at the American Institutes for Research, 2013).

14. Jake New, "Baruch College Gave Players More than $250,000 in Impermissible Aid," *Inside Higher Ed* (July 1, 2016); Fernando Zamudio-Suarez, "NCAA Rules Baruch College Lacked Institutional Control," *Chronicle of Higher Education* (June 30, 2016).

15. John R. Thelin, "Reform or Retreat?" *Inside Higher Ed* (May 21, 2013).

16. Joe Nocera, "The Chancellor's Lament," *New York Times* (May 7, 2013) p. A25.

17. Gina Kolata, "So Many Research Scientists, So Few Professorships," *New York Times* (July 14, 2016) p. A3.

18. Noam Scheiber, "The Law School Bust," *New York Times* (June 19, 2016) pp. BU1, 6–7; Katherine Mangan, "Law Schools Cut Back to Counter Tough Financial Times," *Chronicle of Higher Education* (July 1, 2016); Elizabeth Olson, "Burdened With Debt, Law School Graduates Struggle in Job Market," *New York Times* (April 26, 2015).

19. John R. Thelin, "Higher Education's New 'A&M'," *Inside Higher Ed* (June 16, 2009).

20. Malcom Moos, Director, *The Post-Land Grant University: The University of Maryland Report* (Adelphi: University of Maryland, 1981).

21. Frank Bruni, "Student, or Customer?" "Collegiate Customers: Students Set the Terms," *New York Times* (June 23, 2016) pp. F1, F6.

22. Frank Bruni, "Student, or Customer?" "Collegiate Customers: Students Set the Terms," *New York Times* (June 23, 2016) pp. F1, F6.

23. Frank Bruni, "Platinum Pay in Ivory Towers," *New York Times* (May 20, 2015) p. A23.

24. Mimi Swartz, "Ken Starr's Sordid Second Act," *New York Times* (June 27, 2016) p. A27. See also, Marc Treat, "Baylor Demotes President Kenneth Starr over Handling of Sexual Assault Cases," *New York Times* (May 25, 2016) p. A1; Marc Treat, "Kenneth Starr to Resign as Chancellor at Baylor," *New York Times* (June 2, 2016) p. B12; "Sweeping Changes at Baylor," *Chronicle of Higher Education* (June 10, 2016) p. A6.

25. Patricia Cohen, "Selling the Self-Made Dream: For-Profit Colleges Made Carl Barney Millions, But He Says It's Ayn Rand's Vision of Unfettered Capitalism That Has Put Him on Top," *New York Times* (May 6, 2016) pp. BU1, 6–7.

26. Joseph C. Hermanowicz, Editor, *The American Academic Profession: Transformation in Contemporary Higher Education* (Baltimore, MD: Johns Hopkins University Press, 2011).

27. John Barshaw, Senior Researcher at the AAUP, as quoted in Linda Blackford, "At UK, Presidential Pay Heavily Outpacing Faculty Pay," *Lexington Herald-Leader* (July 3, 2016) pp. 1A, 5A.

28. Amy Hassinger, "Illinois's Collapsing Colleges," *New York Times* (June 4, 2016) p. A19.

29. Kaitlin Mulhere, "Anxiety over Massive Proposed Cuts to Louisiana's Colleges Felt Across the State," *Inside Higher Ed* (April 27, 2015).

30. Eric Kelderman, "State Spending on Higher Education Has Grown, But More Slowly Than Before the Recession," *Chronicle of Higher Education* (May 6, 2016) p. A15.

31. David A. Tandberg and Nicholas W. Hillman, "State Performance Funding for Higher Education: Silver Bullet or Red Herring?" *WISCAPE Policy Brief* (2014); Robert Kelchen, "(Still) Don't Dismiss Performance Funding Research," *Kelchen on Education* blog (April 18, 2016).

32. David Cole, "Race & Renaming: A Talk With Peter Salovey, President of Yale," *New York Review of Books* (June 9, 2016) pp. 42–44; James W. Loewen, "Ten Questions for Yale's President," *Chronicle Review* (June 10, 2016) pp. B11–B13.

33. Rachel L. Swarns, "Georgetown Confronts Its Role in Nation's Slave Trade," *New York Times* (April 17, 2016) pp. 1, 16. See also, Rachel L. Swarns and Sona Patel, "'My Heart just Broke': Surprising Clues to Past in Tale of Georgetown Slave Sale," *New York Times* (May 21, 2016) pp. A9. See also, Editorial, "Where Does Georgetown Start? By Listening," *New York Times* (June 3, 2016) p. A20; Rachel L. Swarns, "Intent on Reckoning With Georgetown's Slavery-Stained Past: School President Takes up Mission to Make Amends," *New York Times* (July 11, 2016) p. A11.

34. Rick O'Donnell (Founder and CEO Skills Fund), "Bootcamps Are the New Graduate School," paper presented at the American Enterprise Institute Higher Education Working Group (June 3, 2016), Washington, D.C.

35. Matt Sigelman (CEO Burning Glass Technologies), "A Hybrid Education for a Hybrid Job Market," paper presented at the American Enterprise Institute Higher Education Working Group (June 3, 2016), Washington, D.C.

36. Dan Lyons, "Congratulations! You've Been Fired," *New York Times* (April 10, 2016) p. A21.

37. William G. Bowen, Matthew M. Chingos, and Michael S. McPherson, *Crossing the Finish Line: Completing College at America's Public Universities* (Princeton, NJ: Princeton University Press, 2009).

38. Alison R. Bernstein, *Funding the Future: Philanthropy's Influence on American Higher Education* (Lanham, MD: Rowland & Littlefield Education, 2014).

39. Lewis Cullman and Ray Madoff, "The Undermining of American Charity," *New York Review of Books* (July 14, 2016) pp. 17–18.

40. Matthew Goldstein and Alexandra Stevenson, "A Family's Charmed Life Is Thrown into Turmoil," *New York Times* (April 6, 2016) pp. B1, B6.

41. Ellen Wexler, "Why Colleges' Brands Look So Similar," *Inside Higher Ed* (May 2, 2016).

42. Eric Kelderman, "Wave of Campus Activism Brings Fresh Challenges for College Lawyers," *Chronicle of Higher Education* (July 1, 2016). See also, Noah Remnick, "Concerns Linger after a Professor at Yale Is Cleared of Sexual Harassment," *New York Times* (July 9, 2016) p. A17.

43. Paul Voosen, "Is It Time for Universities to Get out of the Hospital Business?" *Chronicle of Higher Education* (June 10, 2016) p. A15.

44. Editorial: "Pattern of Silence at UK: Lots of Questions, Not Many Answers from UK HealthCare," *Lexington Herald-Leader* (June 12, 2016) p. 4C.

45. Suzanne Mettler, *Degrees of Inequality: How the Politics of Higher Education Sabotaged the American Dream* (New York: Basic Books, 2014).

46. Frank Bruni, "How and Why You Diversify Colleges," *New York Times* (May 15, 2016) p. B1. See also, Kerry Hannon, "A Focus on Diversity," *New York Times* (June 23, 2016) p. F7.

47. James W. Louen, "Ten Questions for Yale's President," *The Chronicle Review* (June 10, 2016) pp. B11–B1.3.

48. Daniel E. Slotnik, "Alison Bernstein, 69, Educator and Ford Foundation Official," *New York Times* (July 110, 2016) p. 20. See also, Alison R. Bernstein, *Funding the Future: Philanthropy's Influence on American Higher Education* (Lanham, MD: Rowland & Littlefield Education, 2014).

49. John R. Thelin, "Expectations and Reality in American Higher Education," in *Thought & Action* (Washington, D.C.: National Education Association, Fall 2007) pp. 59–70.

50. Martin Trow, "Reflections on the Transformation from Elite to Mass to Universal Higher Education," *Daedalus* (Winter 1970) vol. 99, pp. 1–42.

51. Editorial, "A Broken Bargain With College Graduates," *New York Times* (May 22, 2016) p. SR8.

52. Jeanne Theoharis, "The Travesty of Starving Public Universities," *Chronicle Review* (July 8, 2016) p. B20.

53. Stephanie Saul, "Colleges Chase Out-of-State Students, and Cash," *New York Times* (July 8, 2016) pp. A1, A17.

Additional Readings

Alison R. Bernstein, *Funding the Future: Philanthropy's Influence on American Higher Education* (Lanham, MD: Rowland & Littlefield Education, 2014).

Goldie Blumenstyk, *American Higher Education in Crisis?: What Everyone Needs to Know* (Oxford and New York: Oxford University Press, 2014).

Derek Bok, *Higher Education* (Princeton, NJ: Princeton University Press, 2014).

William G. Bowen and Michael McPherson, *Lesson Plan: An Agenda for Change in American Higher Education* (Princeton, NJ: Princeton University Press, 2016).

William G. Bowen and Eugene M. Tobin, *Locus of Authority: The Evolution of Faculty Roles in the Governance of Higher Education* (Princeton, NJ: Princeton University Press, 2015).

William G. Bowen, Matthew M. Chingos, and Michael S. McPherson, *Crossing the Finish Line: Completing College at America's Public Universities* (Princeton, NJ and Oxford: Princeton University Press, 2009).

Andrew Delbanco, *College: What It Was, Is, and Should Be* (Princeton, NJ: Princeton University Press, 2012).

W. Norton Grubb and Associates, *Honored But Invisible: An Inside Look at Teaching in Community Colleges* (New York: Routledge, 1999).

John Lombardi, *How Universities Work* (Baltimore, MD: Johns Hopkins University Press, 2013).

Suzanne Mettler, *Degrees of Inequality: How the Politics of Higher Education Sabotaged the American Dream* (New York: Basic Books, 2014).

Edward P. St. John, Nathan Daun-Barnett, and Karen M. Moronski-Chapman, *Public Policy and Higher Education: Reframing Strategies for preparation, Access, and Success* (New York: Routledge, 2012) (Core Concepts in Higher Education Series).

INDEX

Aaker, David 255
Abacus 292
Abrams, Frank 231
Academic Capitalism and the New Economy (Slaughter/Rhoades) 267
"academic freedom", the concept of 99–101
Academic Life: Small Worlds, Different Worlds, The (Clark) 29
Academic Marketplace, The (Caplow/McGee) 114
academic profession: accountability 105–6; compared and contrasted with other learned professions 113–14; connections between the academic labour market and University graduate schools 114–15; curricular policies, participation in 105; demographic perspective 117; depiction of professors 96; diversity and social justice perspectives 117–18; the hiring process 101–3; historical perspective 96; Hollywood's portrayal 96; legacy of World War II 96; place in the academic procession 95; preparation changes 116; profile 106–10; prospects for future profile and prestige 115–16; recruitment changes 116; social class and politics 118; socialisation changes 116; tenure, popular misunderstandings 97
Academic Revolution, The (Jencks/Riesman) 297
accountability: evaluation of teachers and teaching 61–3; faculty accountability for academics 105–6; faculty accountability for budgets and finances 157–8; increase in demands for 57; public policy on academic accountability 217
accreditation, regional vs specialised 59
Accrediting Council for Independent Colleges and Schools (ACICS) 311
Adelman, Clifford 80
admissions: marketing strategies, historical perspective 279–86; need-blind 289; and the prospective student pool 331–2; role of dean of admissions 291; role of vice president for enrolment management 292; selective 62, 113, 279, 289, 329, 332
advanced graduate programmes, the plight of 333–4
Agricultural and Mechanical College of Texas *see* Texas A&M University
aid, financial student aid *see* federal student aid; student financial aid
Alfred P. Sloan Foundation 233
alumni, governance and organisation role 137–8
A&M, the new model 344–5
American Association of University Professors (AAUP): declining faculty membership 135; role and responsibilities 110
American College: A Psychological and Social Interpretation of the Higher Learning, The (Sanford) 81
American Council on Education (ACE) 10, 216, 286
American Dream 297
American Higher Education in Crisis? (Blumenstyk) 7
American universities, stature 97
Angulo, A.J. 305
Animal House (1978) 90
annual college rankings, as source of consumer information 290
Arizona State University: distance learning publicity 320–1; *Ivory Tower* documentary 7; Ph.D.s completed in 2011–2012 261
Armstrong, Elizabeth A. 90
Armstrong, William 257
Arnove, Robert 303
Arum, Richard 90
Association of American Universities (AAU) 10, 111, 193, 216, 252, 308, 334
Astin, Alexander 62

Auburn University, college sports deficits 194

Babcock, Stephen 255
bachelor's degree, number of recipients 77
Baldwin, Roger 118
Barney, Carl 337–8
barter economy, of academic life 111–12
Basic Educational Opportunity Grant (BEOG) 143,
    284, 288; see also Pell Grant programme
Baumol, William 163–4
Bauries, Scott 99
Baxter, Frank 306
Baylor University 337
Beloit College, Mindset List 88
Ben-Gurion University, Israel, donation to for water
    research 332
Bentham, Jeremy 118
Berea College, Kentucky, tuition-free model 152
Bernstein, Alison 346
Bill and Melinda Gates foundation see Gates
    Foundation
Birnbaum, Robert 135, 138
Blackboard software 60
Bloomberg, Michael 30, 235
Blumenstyk, Goldie 7, 320
board of trustees see trustees
Bok, Derek 208, 250
books vs. ballgames debates 193
Bowen, Howard 115–16, 163
Bowen, William 64, 163–4, 178, 328
Bowman, John 24
Boys in White, The (Becker, Geer, Hughes and Strauss)
    82
branding and marketing: buildings as branding 20;
    competition and imitation 342–3; historical
    perspective of admissions and marketing 279–86;
    of institutions 330–1; marketing clichés 343;
    marketing revolution in academic enterprises
    and services 301; marketing strategies of colleges
    and universities 254–5; proactive dissemination
    of institutional branding 145
"Breaking Home Ties" (Rockwell) 76
Brown, John Nicholas 228
Brown, Nicholas, Jr. 254
Brown University: appointment of steering committee
    on slavery and justice 41; branding 254;
    discounting of tuition rates to attract students 50;
    endowment values 236; founding and
    background 228; nickname debate 24; University
    city 309; woman appointed as provost 145
Bruni, Frank 331, 336
Bryant, Bear 197
"Bucks for Brains" 31, 242
budgets and finances: compliance costs 162;
    components 151–2; cost vs price 155; cost-benefit
    analysis 156; cross-subsidies 153; diversity and
    social justice perspectives 169–70; efficiency vs
    effectiveness 155–6; endowment funds 160;
    enrolment, setting targets for 166, 168–9;

essential questions 158; and essential vs
    peripheral activities 155; faculty accountability
    157–8; federal compliance requirements 160–1;
    fictional comparisons 151; financial planning,
    private vs public institutions 166–7; fluidity and
    transparency of a campus budget 153; higher
    education costs, disease theory of 164; higher
    education costs, revenue theory of 163–4; higher
    education's bottom line 151–4; historical
    perspective 151; and inflation rates 161;
    intercollegiate athletics department 159–60;
    justification of expensive programmes 157;
    medical institutions on campus 159; merit vs
    worth 156–7; the mission statement 154–5;
    Oliver Twist analogy 151; paradox of the budget
    150; pay as you go approach 152; per capita
    student funding 167; president's role 158; primer
    and handbook provisions 153; and privatisation
    162–3; RCM budgeting model 164–6; reporting
    compliance requirements for receipt of federal
    funds 160–1; rising costs, reasons for 163; role of
    students' tuition payments 152–3; security and
    liability costs 162; student financial aid 168; and
    taxation 161–2; tenure, elimination of as solution
    to rising expenses 157–8; trustees, knowledge and
    responsibility 158; tuition charges, setting 166;
    university foundations 160; vice presidents,
    responsibilities 159; see also funding; fund-
    raising and philanthropy; land grant funding
    model
Burgan, Mary 95
Byer, Walter 182

Calhoun , John C. 40, 340
California: California Master Plan 205; "no tuition"
    policy 152, 296; tuition policies in public higher
    education, historical perspective 280; tuition
    subsidy provisions 167; unexpected consequence
    of tax reform 201
California Institute of Technology: collaboration with
    industry 253; University city 309
campus architecture: athletics facilities 23–4, 35–7;
    buildings as branding 20; campus relocation 37;
    changing configurations 22–3; "conspicuous
    construction" 30–1; contemporary construction
    and the creation of heritage 37–8; controversies
    over landmark buildings 24; demolition/
    renovation decisions 32–3; diversity and social
    justice connections 40–1; donor legacies 30; and
    enrolment leveraging strategies 18; faculty club,
    disappearance of as a traditional campus site
    26–7; fitness for purpose 18; funding
    construction and renovation 38–40; funding
    dilemmas 31; historical perspective 18, 20;
    historical revival architecture 24, 26, 229;
    influence on McDonald's 19; and institutional
    heritage 20–2, 37–8, 40; libraries 28; maintenance
    issues 33–4; mapping patterns of usage 22;
    Monopoly analogy 19; naming buildings 26, 33;

campus architecture *continued*
  navigation challenges 22; new construction, the
  appeal of 31–2; non-traditional students, growth
  of 38; official functions vs actual uses 24–6;
  residential status, the quest for 28–9; sacred
  ground narrative 19–20; social cohesion, bad
  architecture as perverse source of 21–2;
  "starchitecture" strategy 18; student facilities 28;
  and technological change 27–8, 35; thoughtful
  construction and priorities 32; transformation of
  the modern university campus 27–8; as a work in
  progress 17–18
campus disputes, resolving 343
campus life *see* student and campus life
campus misconduct, dealing with 86–7
campus security, evolution of 27
Canby, Henry Seidel 82, 307
Canvas software 60
Caplow, Theodore 114
Carnegie, Andrew 113, 230
Carnegie Classification 6–8, 262
Carnegie Foundation for the Advancement of
  Teaching (CFAT) 59, 203, 229–30, 241
Charles Koch Foundation 268
Charleston, South Carolina, church shootings 40
Chicago University: endowment values 236; *see also*
  University of Chicago
childcare/day-care 5, 26, 38, 86
Chingos, Matthew M. 64
choice of college, as a policy goal 287–8
Christensen, Clayton 140–1
Chronicle of Higher Education: almanac 88; coverage
  of women in academic positions 145; data
  provisions 10; drivers of news coverage 133;
  financial study 33; journalism provisions 216;
  mental health report 87; posting of faculty
  positions 102
Chronister, Jay 118
City University of New York, Ph.D.s completed in
  2011–2012 261
civic participation, influence of college on 91
Civil Rights Act 11
Civilisation (Clarke) 306
Clark, Burton 29–30, 81–2, 111
Clarke, Kenneth 306
classics departments, self-supporting potential 165
Clay, Henry 40
Clinton, Bill 200
Clotfelter, Charles 163
Coca-Cola 264
college basketball: average attendance of institutions
  playing in NCAA Division I 176; broadcasting of
  on television networks 176
college costs, national media coverage 293–4
college culture 73, 80–5; anthropological studies 84;
  "back to college" trends, decline in 89;
  domination by Greek letter fraternities and
  sororities 84; European perspective 81;
  Hollywood's portrayal 90; layers 82; recognition

of new constituencies 84–5; *see also* student and
  campus life
college education: affordability 287–8; the value of
  329; *see also* going to college
college football: Alabama Crimson Tide's performance
  192–3; broadcasting of on television networks
  176; coaches' compensation packages 183–4;
  football bowl revenues 177; viewing
  opportunities 176
College of William and Mary *see* William & Mary,
  College of
college sports: athletics directors 185; attendance and
  viewing statistics 175–7; broadcasting and
  pervasiveness of 176; business rationale 180–1;
  campus "front porch" narrative 175–6; coaches
  183–4; conferences 187, 189; Director's Cup 184;
  diversity and social justice perspective 196–7;
  educational benefits 177–80; faculty 187; financial
  impact 177; financial performance 194; fund-
  raising potential 194–5; historical root of college
  sports 177; inequity and its solutions 191–2;
  influence of non-academic groups 190–1;
  institutional stature and ranking enhancement
  potential 192, 194; legal status of student-athletes,
  the debate 182; NCAA Division II institutions
  and policies 192; premier governing body 189
  (*see also* National Collegiate Athletic Association
  (NCAA)); presidential control 195; presidents
  185–6; provosts and deans 187; scholarships,
  regulation of 181; stadiums and arenas 36; status
  195; student-athletes 181–2; symbols of campus
  loyalty 3; team mascots 182; Title IX Legislation
  196; trustees 186–7; women's participation 184;
  see also intercollegiate sports
college towns: Blake Gumprecht's model 307; *see also*
  university cities
colleges: historical perspective 2; mapping the growth
  of 2
colleges of medicine, campus growth 28
colonial colleges, obligations to international relations
  302
Columbia University: Eisenhower's tenure as
  president 129; endowment values 236; federal
  research expenditure 205; *Ivory Tower*
  documentary 7; Ph.D.s completed in 2011–2012
  261; sponsored research grants, value of 251;
  student enrolment figures 2
Coming of Age in New Jersey (Moffat) 22, 83
commercialisation, of colleges and universities 250–1
community colleges, as source of institutional
  founding 2
Commuters' Alma Mater, The (Mason) 38
competency-based education 47, 62
consultants and lobbying, examples and costs of 335–6
consumers, students and their families as: admissions
  and marketing, historical perspective 279–86;
  affordability of college expenses 287; changed
  relationship between schools and the schooled
  336; choice and accessibility 287; choosing a

college 287–8; COA vs POA 287; college costs, historical perspective 295; and the cost of a college education 286, 293–7; curricular innovation and consumer satisfaction 49–50; dean of admissions' role 291; demographic perspective 280; diversity and social justice perspectives 296; and family income 296; and the fashionability of college life 279; grants vs loans 293; guidance counsellors' role 291; IHEP's role 292; and institutional fit 280; and need-blind admissions 289; organised advocacy 291; and the price of going to college 286–7; pricing information provision, federal requirements 292; rankings as source of information 290; and the relationship between school and the schooled 336; and selective admissions 289; student aid and its sources 288–9; Student Loan Marketing Association 292–3; student retention rates, implications 290–1; tuition charges, historical perspective 278–9; vice president for enrolment management's role 292
Content, Robin 115
Coolidge, Calvin 250
Cooper Union, *Ivory Tower* documentary 7
Corinthian Colleges 216, 305, 320
Cornell, Ezra 45
Cornell University: campus location 28, 307–8; endowment values 236; namesake 45; Ph.D.s completed in 2011–2012 261; sponsored research grants, value of 251
Coursera 306
courses of study, variety of in US institutions 45
"Crisis of Big Science" (Weinberg) 273
Cuban, Larry 55, 267
cultural significance of going to college 11–12, 76–7, 277
"culture of mediocrity", persistence in some departments 111
curriculum change, criticisms 47
curriculum deliberations, power/prestige considerations 48–9
Curti, Merle 231–2

Daedalus (Trow) 346
Dartmouth College: "Indian School" 226; organised dissent 58
Dartmouth v. Woodward 234
Davis, Jefferson 40
Deep Springs College 7
degree-granting institutions: charters granted to 201; collaboration, example of 6; number of students enrolling annually 2; the route to degree-granting status 67
Degrees of Inequality (Mettler) 12
Delbanco, Andrew 7
Dickens, Charles 151
diploma mills 50, 203, 305
disabilities, students with 91
discrimination, and exclusion 40–1, 79, 84, 117, 162, 243, 271, 279

disease theory, of higher education costs (Baumol) 164
distance learning 46, 51, 60, 306, 320–1; and campus architecture 20; performance at traditional colleges and universities 320–1
distance learning/online instruction, impact 50–3
diversity: acceleration of in American higher education 11; of American higher education 5–6; on boards of trustees 125
diversity and social justice perspectives: on the academic profession 117–18; budgets and finances 169–70; campus architecture 40–1; college sports 196–7; consumerism in higher education 296; FPCUs 321; fund-raising and philanthropy 243–4; governance and organisation 145–6; innovations and internationalisation 321; post-war expansion of access 345–6; public policy 221–2; research and development 270–1; student and campus life 90–1; teaching and learning 67–8
Dober, Richard P. 33
donations: unevenness and uncertainty of 332–3; *see also* fund-raising and philanthropy
Dougherty, Conor 317
dropouts and transfers: financial impact 290; FPCUs 305; historical perspective 290, 295; reasons for 290–1, 295
Duke University: branding 254; campus architecture 18; campus construction 229; endowment values 236; federal research expenditure 205; Ph.D.s completed in 2011–2012 262; sponsored research grants, value of 251; Tom Wolfe's fictional portrayal 90
Dynarksi, Susan 290

economy, the vs higher education 340–1
"Edifice Complex" 30–1
education, competency-based model 46–7
Ehrenberg, Ronald 163–4
Eisenhower, Dwight D. 129
Eisenhower, Milton 27
Eliot, Charles 228, 230
Ely, Richard 52–3
Emory University: branding 254; campus construction 229; endowment values 236
endowments: "chair" endowment innovation 226; endowment rankings of universities and colleges 160, 236; function of endowment funds 160; IRS spending requirements 160; perpetual 238–9; Stanford's and Rice's reliance on 152
enrolment of students: in all colleges and universities in the US 45; annual figures 2, 73; and the "pay as you go" approach to college operation 152; prestigious institutions, applicants accepted by 277; Shady Grove (USG) 6; target setting process 166, 168–9; university with the highest enrolment figures in 1909 2
Envisioning Black Colleges (Gasman) 243
equality and excellence, as goal of higher education 219–20

Erasmus Plan 310
European Union 310
evaluation of student work, innovative solutions 67
Excellence (Gardner) 297

faculty: "academic freedom", the concept of 99–101;
    accountability for academics 105–6; adjunct
    faculty 108–9; administrative appointments
    97–8; assistant professors 107; associate
    professors 107; beyond business as usual 338–9;
    clinical professors 108; and college sports 187;
    concerns about the "invisible faculty" 118–19;
    "culture of mediocrity" 111; curricular policies,
    the academic profession's participation 105;
    departmental culture 111; departmental
    differences in customs and competition 112–13;
    elimination of tenure as solution to rising
    expenses 157–8; employment figures 106; faculty
    unions 110; full professors 107; hiring an
    academic professional 101–3; humorous
    depictions 96; instructors 108; lecturers 108;
    loyalty, prescription for increasing 139;
    membership association for professors 110;
    professional and institutional loss 338–9;
    professional misconduct, examples of 105;
    promotion and conferral of tenure 103–4;
    qualification and experience expectations of
    applicants 101–2; research professors 107–8;
    rewards system of colleges and universities
    111–12; roles and responsibilities 97–8; salary
    expenses 98; scholarly organisations and
    associations 109; scholarly publication
    obligations 110; teaching assistants 109; teaching
    vs research 110; tension between administrative
    leadership and 113; tenure, the concept of 98–9
faculty club, disappearance of as a traditional campus
    site 26–7
faculty of American colleges and universities,
    worldwide respect 97
federal agencies, role of in higher education 212–13,
    339–40
federal courts, role of in higher education 215–16
federal funds, reporting compliance requirements for
    receipt of 160–1
federal student aid: application tool 287; benefits of for
    proprietary colleges 304; and the COA 287;
    evolution 206–8; move from grant based to loan-
    based provision 293; reliance of FPCUs on 305;
    spending 213; student influence in drafting
    legislation 291; *see also* student financial aid
Feldstein, Martin 116
fifth estate 216
financial aid for students *see* federal student aid;
    student financial aid
financial crisis in higher education 330
Finnegan, Dorothy 115
flagship state universities, uncertain future 334–5
Flint, Michigan, faulty water system 271–2
Fluoristan 256–7

Football Bowl Series (FBS) 176–7; salaries of head
    coaches 183
Ford, Henry 229
Ford Foundation 229–31, 233, 303, 346
for-profit colleges and universities (FPCUs): business
    model operations 314; criticisms 305, 314–16;
    diversity and social justice perspective 321;
    enrolment patterns 320–1; for-profit vs not-for-
    profit models 218; innovations and
    internationalisation 304–5, 310; reliance on
    federal student aid 305
Foster, Norman 18
Foundation for Individual Rights in Education (FIRE)
    100
foundations: Alfred P. Sloan Foundation 233;
    budgetary considerations 160; Carnegie
    Foundation 59, 203, 229–30, 241; Charles Koch
    Foundation 268; criticisms 233; Ford Foundation
    229–31, 233, 303, 346; General Education Board
    (GEB) 203, 229, 233, 241; Hewlett Foundation
    230; increasing influence in higher education
    241; overview 236; primacy of in fund-raising
    and philanthropy 229–31; Rockefeller
    Foundation, 231, 302; Russell Sage Foundation
    203, 229
FPCUs *see* for-profit colleges and universities
fraternities and sororities, Hollywood's portrayal 90
"free" model of college provision, feasibility of 295
free speech, University of Chicago's statement 100
Freierman, Shelly 180
funding: concerns around the pursuit of 271;
    construction and renovation 38–40; dilemmas
    around maintenance and repairs 33–4; dilemmas
    around research funding 31; federal funding for
    university-based research 252; per capita student
    funding model 167; of research 204–5; state
    funding of higher education 339; uncertainty in
    329–30; *see also* land grant funding model
fund-raising and philanthropy: American culture,
    place of philanthropy in 225–6; "Bucks for
    Brains" 31, 242; "chair" endowment innovation
    226; changing philanthropy, problems and limits
    341–2; collaboration approach 242; and conflicts
    of interest 240; constitutionality of corporate gifts
    to private colleges 231; construction, legacies for
    30; corporate contributions, role of 231; and the
    creation of specialised professional service
    institutions 227–8; diversity and social justice
    perspective 243–4; donations, unevenness and
    uncertainty of 332–3; donor motivations 235;
    Donor-Advised Funds 342; donors 235; donors,
    influence on governance and organisation 138;
    eleemosynary institutions 234; endowment
    rankings of universities and colleges 160, 236;
    endowments, perpetual 238–9; family fortunes,
    impact on higher education 228; foundations
    236; foundations, criticisms 233; foundations,
    increasing influence in higher education 241;
    foundations, primacy of 229–31; friction,

potential for between donors and colleges and universities 240–1; gifts, destination of 234–5; gifts, sources of 234; higher education 242–3; historical perspectives 226–33; "Indian Schools" 226; inequity in distribution 239–40; major gifts and their distribution, a snapshot 332–3; "making the ask" 237; multiplier effects 242; national initiatives 233; non-profit sector 236–7; presidents' role 237; professionalisation of fund-raising 238; ranking of worthy causes 239; religion, connections between philanthropy and 234; scholarship funds, creation of 227; and slavery 228; status of donors, impact on 239; student-originated philanthropy 90; tax incentives for higher education 36, 242; terms and restrictions set by donors 238; vice president for development's role 237–8; *see also* endowments; foundations

Gardner, John 236, 297
Gasman, Marybeth 243
Gates, Bill and Melinda 235
Gates, Frederick 228–9
Gates Foundation 241, 243–4, 346
Gatorade 256, 267
Geiger, Roger 253, 273
General Education Board 203, 229, 233, 241
Georgetown University: basketball games, role of African Americans 197; historical involvement in the slave trade 340; shortfall in medical centre income 344
Georgia Institute of Technology: collaboration with industry 253; misconduct in research 264; Ph.D.s completed in 2011–2012 261; sponsored research grants, value of 251
GI Bill 50, 202–3, 205, 280, 304
Gilder, Richard 33
Gilman, Sidney 272–3
Godkin Lectures, Clarke Kerr's theme 2
going to college: choice of college 80, 278, 280–1, 283, 285, 287–8; COA vs POA 287; college costs, historical perspective 295; college culture 73, 80–5; the cost of 286, 293–7; cultural significance 11–12, 76–7, 277; defining *cost* and *price* 276–7; as an "engine of inequality" 296; expectations 346–7; Hollywood treatment 76; Norman Rockwell's depiction 76; the price of 286–7; the value of a college education 329; who goes where and why 77–80
Goitein, Lara 270
Goldin, Claudia 279
Google 88, 255, 317
Gothic Revival campus architecture 24, 26
governance and organisation: the academic college 124; academic deans 132–3; administration staff 133–6; administrative expansion 145; board composition, demographic changes 125; Board of Trustees 124; boards and their members 124–5; bureaucratic characterisation of the campus 141–2; business-campus transplants 138–9; comparison with business model 123; and the creative disruption theory of business success and failure 140–1; Dean of the Law School 124; Director of Athletics 124; diversity and social justice perspective 145–6; donors' influence 138; dysfunctional and disorganised characterisation of the campus 142; faculty loyalty, prescription for increasing 139; foundations and associations 136–7; innovation, testing 139; legacy of early colonial colleges 122–3; meetings, scheduling 139–40; presidents 123–4, 126–30; presidents vs deans 140; the professionalisation of administration 142–3; provosts 130–1; role of alumni 137–8; self-perpetuating boards 126; "shared governance" model 123; staff senate 136; students' role 137; transparency, public relations and 143–5; trustees 125; vice presidents 124, 131–2
Grand Canyon University 315–16, 319
Great Depression 279
"Greek life", influence on campus life 84
Guaranteed Student Loan (GSL) 207, 288, 293
guidance counsellors, role of 291
Gumprecht, Blake 307

Hale, William Harlan 24
Hall, Mark 197
Hamilton, Laura T. 90
Harvard Medical School, location 28
Harvard University: campus architecture 18; campus construction 229; computer centre 27; endowment values 160, 236; fiduciary responsibility motto 164; financial position 159; founding 2; fundraising, administrative approach 230; "Indian School" 226; marketing strategy 279; MOOCs 53; Ph.D.s completed in 2011–2012 261; presidential firing 136; sabbatical leave policy 98; women students invited to be members of historically all-male clubs 84
Hastert, Dennis 26
head coaches, salaries 183
Hearst, William Randolph 240
Heller, Nathan 332
Henry VIII 48
heritage: campus architecture and institutional heritage 20–2, 37–8, 40; creation of in new buildings 37–8
heritage of higher education, as source of tension 340
Hermanowicz, Joseph 111, 115–16
Hewlett, William 235, 257
higher education: American attitudes towards 2; fit with the ethos of philanthropy 242–3; historical conflicts 340; innovation vs saturation 348–9; the national economy's mismatch with 340–1; symbolic importance 11–12 (*see also* cultural significance of going to college)
Higher Education Act 11
higher education costs: disease theory of 164; revenue theory of 163–4

Higher Education General Information Survey (HEGIS) 10, 161
higher education institutions: issues facing 4–5; profile 2–4; ranking culture 8–10
Higher Education Learning Commission (HLC) 310, 315
Higher Education Price Index (HEPI) 161, 286
Higher Education: Tuition Increasing Faster than Household Income and Public Colleges' Costs (GAO) 161
Hofstadter, Richard 96
Horowitz, Helen Lefkowitz 82
How College Affects Students: A Third Generation of Research (Pascarella/Terenzini) 81
How Colleges Work (Birnbaum) 138
How Scholars Trumped Teachers (Cuban) 55
Howell, Martha 318

I Am Charlotte Simmons (Wolfe) 90
Images of Organisations (Morgan) 6
"Indian Schools" 226
Indiana University: Ph.D.s completed in 2011–2012 261; student enrolment figures 2; university enterprise model 257
Indianapolis Pump and Tube Company 232
inequality, functioning of American higher education as engine of 296, 345
innovations and internationalisation: ACICS 311; the Bologna Process 310; community initiatives 306–7; community-based organisations 312; Confucius Institute 311; connecting international economic development with higher education 317–19; consulting firms 312; Cornell University's story 307–8; criticism of internationalisation as a student recruitment strategy 313; criticism of university expansion within a community 313; criticisms of academic imperialism 312–13; criticisms of FPCUs 314–16; distance learning 306; distance learning, performance at traditional colleges and universities 320–1; diversity and social justice perspectives 321; financing prospects and trends for higher education 319; for-profit colleges and universities 304–5, 310; historical perspective 302; HLC 310–11; international relations 302–4; local innovation and expansion 307–10; OECD 310; and relations between traditional and for-profit colleges and universities 319–20; "study abroad" programmes 303–4; town vs gown 316–17; United States Department of Education 311; the "University City" 308, 310
innovative solutions to evaluation of student work 67
Inside Higher Ed 10, 50, 102, 216
Institute for Higher Education Policy (IHEP) 10, 292
institutional types, convergence of 343
Integrated Postsecondary Education Data System (IPEDS) 10, 150, 161
intercollegiate sports: alumni 190; and donations to colleges and universities 239–40, 243; financial

perspective 159–60; reform and retreat, the choice between 333; scandals 194; status of in the US 177; see also college sports
Invisible Tapestry, The (Kuh/Whitt) 81
Islam, philanthropic perspective 234
Ivory Tower (documentary) 7
Ivy League institutions, anti-trust lawsuit against 166

Javon Marshall, et al. v. ESPN, Inc. et al. 180
Jeanne Clery Disclosure of Campus Security Policy and Campus Crime Statistics Act 86–7
Jefferson, Thomas 18
Jencks, Christopher 114, 297
John C. Calhoun 340
Johns Hopkins University: administrative tensions 259; donor legacies to campus architecture 30; faculty club debate 26–7; federal research expenditure 205; financial decline in the 19th-century 152; Michael Bloomberg's philanthropic contributions 235; Ph.D.s completed in 2011–2012 261; research abuse of human subjects 265; sponsored research grants, value of 251
Johnson, Owen 90
Johnstone, Bruce 319
Journal of Higher Education 10, 280
journalism, benefits for higher education 10

Kahn, Louis 18
Kastor, John A. 259
Katz, Lawrence 279
Kennedy, Donald 113
Kerr, Clark 2–3, 35, 48, 57, 75, 130, 166, 204, 250
Kinkead, Katherine 282
Kirwan, Brit 195
Kissinger, Henry 47, 134
"Knowledge Factory" 3, 109, 142, 250
Knowledge and Money (Geiger) 273
knowledge-based economy, research and development and the 267
Kolowich, Steve 50
Krugman, Paul 52
Kuh, George 81

LaGuardia Community College, Queens, New York 5–6
land grant funding model: and affordability of advanced practical education 281; desegregation and eligibility 79; disuse and rediscovery 154; future prospects 334, 345; historical perspective 202; lobbying power 202; and patterns of college building 2; and research capabilities 250
language and culture promotion organisations 311
Lapham, Lewis 237
Law and Order 97
Le Corbusier 18
lecture format, decline and resurrection 47
legal conflicts, beyond business as usual 343
Lehigh University 86
Lepore, Jill 141

Lesson Plan (Bowen/McPherson) 328, 336
Let Me Heal: The Opportunity to Preserve Excellence in American Medicine (Ludmerer) 269–70
letter grades, alternative evaluation method 67
Levin, Sarah 178
Lewis, Jerry 96
Liberty University 5–6
libraries, value of to students 30
life on campus *see* student and campus life
lobbying: examples and costs of consultants and 335–6; lobbying power of land grant funding model 202
local government, role of in higher education 214
Louisiana Purchase 302
Louisiana State University: college sports deficits 194; home attendance for football games 176
Lowe, Rob 76
Lowen, Rebecca 48
Ludmerer, Kenneth M. 269
Lumina Foundation 241, 346

McCormick, Alexander 8
McDonald's, "Hamburger University" 19
McGee, Reese 114
McPherson, Michael 64, 328
maintenance and repairs, funding dilemmas 33–4
Management Fads in Higher Education (Birnbaum) 138
Manhattan Project 96
Marcucci, Pamela 319
marketing *see* branding and marketing
Mason, Tisa Ann 38
Massachusetts Institute of Technology *see* MIT
Massing, Michael 245
massive open online courses (MOOCs): and campus architecture 20; coexistence with traditional forms of instruction 53; impact 329; *see also* distance learning
medical institutions on campus, financial perspective 159
Mettler, Suzanne 12, 345
Miami University, campus architecture 24–5
Michener, James 197
Michigan State University, Ph.D.s completed in 2011–2012 261
Michigan, University of: endowment values 236; *see also* University of Michigan
Middaugh, Michael 157
Middle Income Student Assistance Act 293
Mindset List, Beloit College 88
misconduct on campus, dealing with 86–7
MIT: anti-trust lawsuit against 166; collaboration with industry 253; endowment values 236; "hidden curriculum" 65; MOOCs 53; Ph.D.s completed in 2011–2012 261; price-fixing accusation 286; sponsored research grants, value of 251; university enterprise model 257
modern American flagship state university, the: uncertain future 334–5

Moffat, Michael 22, 83
Moll, Richard 282
Morgan, Agnes Fay 41
Morgan, Gareth 6
Moritz, Michael 332
Morrill Act (1862) 2, 50, 79, 154, 201–2; *see also* land grant funding model
murder, Lehigh University 86
Murphy, Eddie 96
Mysteries of the Universe Explained 1

Nader, Laura 117
naming of buildings, symbolism 26, 33
Napolitano, Janet 3
Nash, Roderick 231–2
Nation at Risk, A 11
National Association of Intercollegiate Athletics (NAIA) 176
National Collegiate Athletic Association (NCAA): Division I category membership 176; Division II Institutions and Policies 192; dormitory regulations 181; Ed O'Bannon's compensation petition against 182; headquarters 189; Prop 48 standards 197; revenue generated 189; scholarship regulation 181; statistics 175–6; status and responsibilities 189–90; use of COA 287; women's sports, position on 196
National Endowment for Humanities 161, 165
National Endowment for the Arts 161
National Institutes of Health (NIH) 109, 156, 160, 204, 208, 241, 253, 268
National Science Foundation (NSF) 109, 160–1, 165, 204, 208, 222, 241, 251, 253
Native Americans, colonial education programmes 226
Nerad, Maresi 67
New York Times, weekend courses offered by 219–20
Newcomb, Sophie 244
Nidiffer, Jana 85
No Child Left Behind 11
Nocera, Joe 193
non-traditional students, as the tradition at USG 6
North Carolina State University, Ph.D.s completed in 2011–2012 261
Northwestern University, endowment values 236
Notre Dame, endowment values 236
Novartis 33, 267

Obama, Barack 77, 294
Obama, Malia 77
O'Bannon, Ed 182
O'Donnell, Richard 157
Ohio State University: home attendance for football games 176; impact of segregation 40; Ph.D.s completed in 2011–2012 261; sponsored research grants, value of 251
Olivas, Michael 100
online courses, Liberty University's programme 5
online education, implications for higher education 53

outsourcing 39, 162–3, 209, 312, 315–16
overseas campus expansion 312
Owens, Jesse 40
Oxford University, abolition of canon law as a field of
    study 48

Packard, David 257
Papa John's Pizza corporation 268
parking: as problem for universities 35; reserved
    spaces, status and 35
Pascarella, Ernest 81
Paterno, Joe 26
Paying for the Party: How College Maintains Inequality
    (Armstrong/Hamilton) 84, 90
peer influence, role of in shaping information and
    values extraction 46
Pell Grant programme: creation of 143; effectiveness
    207; as indicator of income and need 11, 80;
    influence in shaping college choice 284; launch
    and growth 283, 293; maximum award in
    2014–2015 207; portability 218; the programme
    288; qualification criteria 293; value of the grant
    169
Pennsylvania State University: campus architecture
    26; home attendance for football games 176;
    Ph.D.s completed in 2011–2012 261; sexual abuse
    case 194; sponsored research grants, value of 251
Pepperdine University, relocation 37
per capita student funding, the model 167
Perkins Loans 288
philanthropy: definition 225, 233–4; *see also* fund-
    raising and philanthropy
philosophy, as familiar target of funding cuts 155
physics departments, expenses 165
Pitzer, Kenneth 270
Politics of the Budgetary Process, The (Wildavsky) 154
Pomona College, California, presidential portraiture
    tradition and omissions 25–6
Post, Robert 100
postsecondary education coordinating councils 57
presidents: budgeting role 158; CEO comparison 336;
    changing role 336, 336–8; and college sports
    185–6; compensation packages 336–7;
    governance and organisation role 126–30;
    options after leaving office 337; role in fund-
    raising and philanthropy 237; welcoming parents
    and students, typical behaviour 74
pricing information, federal requirements 292
Princeton, appointment of woman as provost 145
Princeton University: campus construction 229; donor
    families' discontent 240; endowment values 160,
    236; football stadium 36; Ph.D.s completed in
    2011–2012 262; student thesis custom 66–7
Pritchett, Henry 230
private vs public institutions: financial planning
    166–7; public policy 217–18; student aid 166;
    tuition charges, historical perspective 279–80
privatisation, and its impact 208–12
Procter & Gamble 257

professional associations 10
professors: areas of responsibility 97; assistant 107;
    associates 107; clinical 108; constitutional
    protections 99; ethnic minority applications for
    professorships 118; full 107; mean age of full
    professors 107; membership association 110;
    research professors 107–8; tenure and terms of
    employment 98–9
profile of higher education in the US 2–4
Prop 48 standards 197
proprietary schools and colleges 218, 304–5
Protestantism, philanthropic perspective 234
public institutions, percentage of students enrolled in
    78
Public Interest, The (Bok) 208
public policy: academic accountability 217; choice vs
    affordability debate 217; diversity and social
    justice perspectives 221–2; elementary/secondary
    education vs postsecondary education 218–19;
    equality and excellence, as goal of higher
    education 219–20; federal courts, role of in
    higher education 215–16; federal government,
    role of in higher education 212–13; federal
    regulation 208; for-profit vs not-for-profit
    models 218; higher education associations
    216–17; historical perspectives 201–6, 216; local
    government, role of in higher education 214; per
    capita student funding model 167; private vs
    public institutions 217–18; privatisation and its
    impact 208–12; research funding 204–5; research
    sponsorship 208; state legislatures, role of in
    higher education 213–14; state postsecondary
    education councils 214; state vs federal
    government 219; student aid, loans vs grants
    debate 217; student financial aid 206–8; "town
    and gown" issues 214–15; vice president for
    government relations 212
public relations: dominant themes 74; expenses and
    benefits 330; and transparency 143–5
Purdue University, Ph.D.s completed in 2011–2012
    261

racial desegregation, federal enforcement 221
Raise.me, micro-financing tool 296
ranking of higher education institutions 8–10
Reagan, Ronald 75
Real Estate Investment Trusts 39
regional accreditation 59
rejection letters, family anxiety about 12
religious perspectives: connections between
    philanthropy and religion 234; Liberty University
    5
research: and decisions about institutional priorities
    34; federal sponsorship 208–12; funding
    dilemmas 31; professors' responsibilities 97;
    relationships between teaching and 55–7; and the
    transformation of campus architecture 27–8
research and development: branding 254–5; business
    schools 260; collaboration with industry 253; and

the commercial focus of colleges and universities 250–1; concerns around the pursuit of funding 271; conflicts of interest, corporate sponsorship and 264; corporations vs campus debate 263; diversity and social justice perspectives 270–1; enterprise, encouraging creativity and 267–8; ethical abuse 265–6; federal expenditure 204–5; federal funding for university-based research 252; federal role 208; financial abuse in applied research 264–5; foundations, role of 230; fraudulent research 263–4; and the knowledge-based economy 267; law schools 259–60; list of sponsored research grants 251–2; master's degree programmes 260; medical doctors, rethinking education and professionalisation 269–70; medical institutions 258–9; monetisation 253; off-campus research parks, investment in 257–8; Ph.D. programmes 260–3; post-doctoral fellowships 262; research professors 107–8; sponsored research, rethinking the model 268–9; teaching hospitals, administrative tensions 259; Tuskegee study on penicillin and syphilis 265; universities reporting more than $1 billion each on federal research expenditures 205; university enterprise model 255–7; university hospitals, commercial character 266

research institutes 10, 163, 241, 258, 335

research parks, as new addition to campus architecture 22

residential status, the quest for 28–9

Responsibility Centred Management (RCM), budgeting model 164–6

retention, recruitment vs 341

revenue theory, of higher education costs 163–4

Rhodes, Cecil 302

Rice, William Marsh 254

Rice University: branding 254; endowment values 236; Silicon Valley entrepreneurs' donation 332

Riesman, David 114, 297

Rockefeller, John D. 229, 235, 239

Rockefeller Foundation 231, 302

Rockwell, Norman 76

Roksa, Josipa 90

Roosevelt Island 307–8

Rosenthal, Alan 206

Rosenwald Fund 229

Roski, Gayle and Edward 332

Roski Eye Institute 332

Rosovsky, Henry 56

Rossi, Andrew 7

Rudolph, Frederick 58, 76, 96

Russell Sage Foundation 203, 229

Rutgers University: college sports deficits 194; membership of Big Ten conference 193; Michael Moffat's study of freshmen 22, 83–4; sponsored research grants, value of 252

Saban, Nick 192

sabbatical leave, tenure and eligibility for 98

sacred ground narrative: McDonald's appropriation 19; pervasion of in American campuses 19–20

Sallie Mae (Student Loan Marketing Association) 292–3

San Francisco State University, donation towards Iranian diaspora studies centre 332

San Jose State University, *Ivory Tower* documentary 7

Sanford, Nevitt 81, 114

Saval, Nikil 17–18

Scarborough, Scott 313

scholarly organisations and associations 109

scholarships: benefits of for student-athletes 178–9; commercial influence 251; corporate contributions 231; created by religious denominations 227; designation of funds 168; Eric Suder's "First Scholars" initiative 240; for foreign scholars 303; GI Bill 203, 205; graduate students 261; historical perspective on the creation of scholarship funds 227; Ivy Group prohibition on merit scholarships 288–9; merit scholarships, attractiveness of 168; misleading use of by coaches in recruitment of outstanding African-American athletes 197; need-based vs merit-based 168, 170, 293; and the philanthropy of women 244; as recruitment ploy 197; as redistribution strategy 283; regulation of athletic scholarships 181, 190; Rhodes Scholarships 302; for students pledging to be teachers 151; terminology 281

Schumpeter, Joseph 141

Schuster, Jack 95, 115–16

Schwartz, Robert 85

Scott, Robert 142

Scripps, Ellen Browning 244

segregation, building names and the legacy of 40

selective admissions 62, 113, 279, 289, 329, 332

service, professors' responsibilities 97

service learning 58, 234

sexist jokes 271

sexual assault 89, 328

sexual harassment 86–7, 337

Shady Grove, Universities at (USG), enrolment of students 6

shared governance: the concept of 123; disagreements around 135; faculty's role 339; inclusion of campus staff 136; as key value of UC 4

Shulman, James 178

Silicon Valley 317

Simmons, Ruth 41

slavery, and heritage conflicts 340

Smelser, Neil 115

Smith, Sophia 244

social class and politics, in the academic profession 118

social cohesion: adversity and 25; bad architecture as perverse source of 21–2; and campus athletics facilities 23

social justice: status of as a higher education issue 11–12; *see also* diversity and social justice perspectives

sororities, social trends 90
Soros Foundation 244
South, the: Confederate campus monuments debate 40; resurgence of higher education, as source of pride 20
Southern New Hampshire University 314
Sparks, Frank 232
Spelman College 7
Sperling, John 304
Spitzer, Eliot 294
Sports in America (Michener) 197
St. John, Edward 288
Stagg, Amos Alonzo 23
Standard Oil 231–2
Stanford: anti-trust lawsuit against 166; endowment values 236; Jane 235, 244; percentage of full-time professors with tenure 107
Stanford University: applicants accepted ratio 277; collaboration with industry 253; commercialisation 267; endowment values 236; federal research expenditure 205; funding experiment 152; Larry Cuban's study 55; MOOCs 53; Ph.D.s completed in 2011–2012 261; research scholarship, status of 55; sponsored research grants, acquisition strategy 252–3; sponsored research grants, value of 251; University city 309
state funding of higher education 339
State Higher Education Executive Officers (SHEEO) 214
state legislatures, role of in higher education 213–14
Steenbock, Harry 256
Stetson University, branding 254
Stover at Yale (Johnson) 90
student activism, Clark Kerr's comments 75
student and campus life: in American literature 89–90; "coddling" concerns 88; coeducational dormitories 84; data, sources of 88–90; dealing with student misconduct 86–7; Dean of Women 85; disabilities, students with 91; diversity and social justice perspective 90–1; freshmen, life experience survey 88–9; "Greek life" 84; handling misconduct 86–7; Hollywood portrayal 90; influence of graduating high school seniors 89; and the maintenance of family ties 84; mental health service provisions 87–8; patterns of 73, 80–5; philanthropic activities 90; positive imagery 88; problems and frustrations, examples of 89; Rockwell's illustration of going to college 76; safety and welfare concerns 86; social class and family income differences 90–1; support services 85–6; *see also* college culture
student enrolment *see* enrolment of students
student financial aid 168; creation of federal programmes 143; as diversity and social justice issue 170; evolution of federal programs 206–8; federal spending 213; historical perspective 281; loans vs grants debate 217, 293; merit-based 288–9; microfinancing online service 296; need-based 288; prestigious private colleges, two-step

procedure 281; private and public institutions' practices 166; sources of 288–9; state government spending 213; *see also* federal student aid
student learning process, evaluation 64–5
student loans: banks' attitudes 293; cost of student loan debt 7; indebtedness levels 284, 293, 294, 305; loans vs grants debate 217, 293; Sallie Mae (Student Loan Marketing Association) 292–3
student misbehaviour, guidance counsellors, role of in dealing with 291
student retention rates, implications 290–1
students: governance and organisation role 137; non-traditional 6, 38, 62, 80, 85, 314, 321, 347; unrest, legacy of 137
"study abroad" programmes 303–4
Suder, Eric 240
Suggs, Welch 196
Suing Alma Mater (Olivas) 100
Super Bowl, advertising spending 180
Supplementary Educational Opportunity Grant (SEOG) 143, 288; *see also* Pell Grant programme
symbols of campus loyalty and college sports 3
Syracuse University, attendance at basketball games 176

taxation: colleges and universities' status 161–2; tax incentives for donors 36, 235, 242; unexpected consequence of tax reform in California 201
Teach for America 90
teaching and learning: accountability, evaluation of teachers and teaching 61–3; campus ethos 3–4; college curriculum as forum for polemics and politics 53–5; competency-based education model 46–7; consumer satisfaction and the curriculum 49–50; consumerism and 57–8; the contest between students and faculty 58; curriculum change, forgotten sources 48; curriculum change, the process 58; curriculum deliberations, power/prestige considerations 48–9; curriculum reform 47; distance learning, origins of innovation 60; distance learning/online instruction, impact 50–3; diversity and social justice perspective 67–8; effectiveness and efficiency 63–4; evaluation of student work, innovative solutions 67; external bodies 59; grass-roots character of curricular planning 57; the hidden curriculum 65–6; institutional realities, academic ideals and 66–7; lecture format, decline and resurrection 47; legacy of lethargy concerns 46–7; online education, implications for higher education 53; professors' teaching responsibilities 97; questions about the college curriculum 46; regional accreditation, vs specialised accreditation 59; student learning process, evaluation 64–5; teaching and research, relationships between 55–7; technological change and 59–60; technology and teaching 329
technology: campus architecture and technological change 27–8, 35; and teaching 329

Temple University, Philadelphia, football stadium 37
tenure: the concept of 98–9; and eligibility for sabbatical leave 98; elimination of as solution to rising expenses 157–8; popular misunderstandings 97; promotion and conferral of 103–4
Terenzini, Patrick 81
Texas A&M University: donations for intercollegiate sports 243; endowment values 236; home attendance for football games 176; performance data-collection system 157; Ph.D.s completed in 2011–2012 261; sponsored research grants, value of 251
Theoharis, Jeanne 347
Title IX Legislation 11, 102, 162, 170, 196, 213, 222, 340
"town and gown", public policy issues 214–15
town vs gown: contemporary perspective 215; historical perspective 81, 214–15, 307; innovations and internationalisation 316–17
transparency: laws and sausages adage 206; public relations and 143–5
Transylvania University 40
trigger warnings 100
Trow, Martin 82, 346
trustees: burdens of responsibility 125; and college sports 186–7; demographic perspective 125; expected contribution 125; financial knowledge and responsibility 158; governance and organisation role 125; potential perks 125; responsibilities 123; rewards 125
tuition charges: college costs, historical perspective 295; "free" model of college provision, feasibility of 295; historical perspective 278–9; increase in 163; influencing factors 286–7; institutions' reliance on students' tuition payments 152–3; national media coverage 293–4; public-private differential, historical perspective 279–80; reasons for rising costs 294; setting 166
Tuition Rising (Ehrenberg) 163–4

UC Berkeley: branding 255; building names and the legacy of exclusion/discrimination 41; campus layout 19; campus parking 35; cohesive influence of bad architecture 21–2; college culture 81–2; college sports deficits 194; costs of enhancing the chancellor's public image 336; hiring process study 115; Ph.D.s completed in 2011–2012 261; "sacred ground" 19; sponsored research grants, value of 251; staff reductions 330; staffing cuts 315; university enterprise model 257; women, enrolment in the sciences 271
UC Davis: Ph.D.s completed in 2011–2012 261; sponsored research grants, value of 251
UC Irvine, Ph.D.s completed in 2011–2012 261
UC Los Angeles: sponsored research grants, value of 251; *see also* UCLA
UC Merced, Janet Napolitano's observations 3–4
UC San Diego: federal research expenditure 205; Ph.D.s completed in 2011–2012 261; sponsored research grants, value of 251

UC San Francisco: federal research expenditure 205; Michael Moritz's donation 332; sponsored research grants, value of 251
UC Santa Cruz, campus architecture 29
UCLA: campus architecture 37; campus parking 35; and competition for funding 212; federal research expenditure 205; medical centre, financial position 344; Ph.D.s completed in 2011–2012 261; role of the presidential spouse 126; sacred ground 20
United Negro College Fund (UNCF) 243
universities: status of in the community 2; university with the highest enrolment in 1909 2
Universities at Shady Grove (USG) 5–6
university building, international perspective 318–19
university cities: advantages 308–9; Blake Gumprecht's "college town" model 307; candidates for designation 309; civic advancement 316; crime rates 317
University of Akron 312–13
University of Alabama: equal opportunity policy 197; federal enforcement of racial desegregation 221; football programme 192–3; home attendance for football games 176; sued by Eric Suder 240–1
University of Arizona, Ph.D.s completed in 2011–2012 261
University of California: California Master Plan 205; College of Natural Resources 267; complexity 3; endowment values 236; federal research funding 252; the Hearst family's discontent 240; learning ethos 3–4; mission reach 4; multi-campus system 2–3; percentage of undergraduates qualifying for Pell Grants 11; structure and governance 124–5
University of Chicago: campus architecture 24; football stadium 23; free speech policy statement 100; Michael Moritz's donation 332; Ph.D.s completed in 2011–2012 261; public relations understanding 143–4; resistance to presidential initiatives 137; scientific influence 23–4; undergraduate resistance to presidential initiative 137
University of Cincinnati: campus expansion plans 17–18; debts 18; "starchitecture" 18
University of Colorado, Ph.D.s completed in 2011–2012 262
University of Delaware: donation towards music enrichment fund 333; selection of trustees 126
University of Florida: donation towards a new chemistry building 332; Ph.D.s completed in 2011–2012 261; sponsored research grants, value of 251
University of Florida College of medicine 256
University of Georgia: lobbying efforts of the president for funds 204; Ph.D.s completed in 2011–2012 261; "sacred ground" 19; symposium 115; University Athletic Association 191; University foundation 137

University of Illinois: Ph.D.s completed in 2011–2012 261; rescinding of faculty appointment letter 104; "sacred ground" 19; sponsored research grants, value of 252

University of Kentucky: attendance at basketball games 176; University Athletic Association 191

University of Louisville, attendance at basketball games 176

University of Maryland: building names and the legacy of segregation 41; building repairs, estimated cost 34; college sports deficits 194; Ph.D.s completed in 2011–2012 261; *The Post-Land Grant University* report 334

University of Massachusetts 310, 330

University of Michigan: appointment of woman as provost 145; donation towards new research facilities 332; federal research expenditure 205; football stadium 36; home attendance for football games 176; Ph.D.s completed in 2011–2012 261; sponsored research grants, value of 251

University of Minnesota: athletic abuse 197; Ph.D.s completed in 2011–2012 261; sponsored research grants, value of 251

University of Mississippi, federal enforcement of racial desegregation 221

University of Missouri: resignations 128, 137, 146; student demonstrations 128, 137

University of North Carolina, Chapel Hill: attendance at basketball games 176; Ph.D.s completed in 2011–2012 261; sponsored research grants, value of 251

University of Oregon: academic reputation 194; branding 255; donations for intercollegiate sports 243; football game against Ohio State University 176; sports programme operating figures 185; "University of Nike" identity 193–4

University of Pennsylvania: administrative tensions 259; endowment values 236; football stadium 37; Ph.D.s completed in 2011–2012 261; research institutes 10; restrictions to growth 20; sponsored research grants, value of 251

University of Phoenix: annual student enrolments 80; campus architecture 20; "Drive Thru U" nickname 304; enrolment growth 320; founding 304; as model for SNHU's transformation 314; online courses 52; purpose 304; staff reductions 315; stock market value 320; workforce reduction 315

University of Pittsburgh: campus architecture 24; campus construction 229; challenge to the medical centre's tax-exempt status 266; improvements to athletic facilities 32; sponsored research grants, value of 251

University of Southern California: Ph.D.s completed in 2011–2012 261; Silicon Valley entrepreneurs' donations 332; sponsored research grants, value of 251

University of Tennessee, football stadium 36

University of Texas: endowment values 236; performance data-collection system 157; Ph.D.s completed in 2011–2012 261; sponsored research grants, value of 251

University of Virginia: endowment values 236; Ph.D.s completed in 2011–2012 262; presidential firing 136

University of Washington: federal research expenditure 205; Ph.D.s completed in 2011–2012 261

University of Wisconsin: attendance at basketball games 176; economics department 52; federal research expenditure 205; and the "land grant legacy" 202; Ph.D.s completed in 2011–2012 261; sponsored research grants, value of 251; university enterprise model 255–6

University: An Owner's Manual, The (Rosovsky) 56

university presidents, portraiture traditions 25

Uses of the University, The (Kerr) 35, 57

USG *see* Shady Grove

Vanderbilt University, sponsored research grants, value of 251

varsity basketball, coaching compensation packages 183

Veblen, Thorstein 263

vice presidencies: examples of 123; financial responsibilities 159; government relations 212; role in enrolment management 292

Virginia Commonwealth University, campus architecture 37–8

Virginia Tech University, Ph.D.s completed in 2011–2012 261

voting behaviour, influence of college on 91

Wabash College, Indiana 232

Walker, Darren 244

Washington University in St Louis: endowment values 236; sponsored research grants, value of 251

Weinberg, Steven 273

Westerberg, Charles 89

Wexler, Ellen 313, 343

Wheaton College, Illinois, campus architecture 26

Whitt, Elizabeth 81

Wildavsky, Aaron 154, 163

Wildavsky, Ben 302

William & Mary, College of, Virginia: "Indian School" 226; solution to financial insolvency 151

Wisconsin Alumni Research Foundation (WARF) 256

Wolberger, Ofer 17

Wolfe, Tom 90

women: athletics directors 185; coverage of barriers to 117; Dean of 85; enrolment in the sciences at UC Berkeley 271; female students invited to be members of historically all-male clubs at Harvard University 84; number of colleges exclusively for 244; percentage of college students 78; presence of in intercollegiate athletics 196; presidents of Ivy League institutions 146; provost appointments 145; representation amongst

medical and law school students 222; representation in professorships 117; STEM subjects, enrolment in 271
Woodrow Wilson School of Public and International Affairs 240
Wren, Christopher 18

Yale University: campus architecture 18, 24; campus construction 229; endowment values 236; fraternity membership, rejection of 84; Henry Seidel Canby's memoir 82; Ph.D.s completed in 2011–2012 262; renovation work 33; sponsored research grants, value of 251

Zimbalist, Andrew 182
Zuckerberg, Mark 245